Regular Army O!

Original song sheet for "The Regular Army, O!" published by William A. Pond Co., 1874, and performed by the duo Harrington & Hart. (Courtesy Paul L. Hedren)

Regular Army O!

Soldiering on the
Western Frontier, 1865–1891

Douglas C. McChristian

Foreword by Robert M. Utley

University of Oklahoma Press : Norman

This book is published with the generous assistance of the
McCasland Foundation, Duncan, Oklahoma.

Library of Congress Cataloging-in-Publication Data
Names: McChristian, Douglas C., author.
Title: Regular Army O! : soldiering on the Western frontier, 1865–1891 /
　Douglas C. McChristian ; foreword by Robert M. Utley.
Description: Norman, OK : University of Oklahoma Press, [2017] | Includes
　bibliographical references and index.
Identifiers: LCCN 2016039781 | ISBN 978-0-8061-5695-8 (cloth) |
　ISBN 978-0-8061-6455-7 (paper)
Subjects: LCSH: West (U.S.)—History, Military—19th century. | United
　States. Army—Military life—History—19th century. | Soldiers—West
　(U.S.)—Social conditions—19th century. | Frontier and pioneer life—West
　(U.S.) | Soldiers' writings, American.
Classification: LCC F594 .M118 2017 | DDC 355.10978/09034—dc23
LC record available at https://lccn.loc.gov/2016039781

The paper in this book meets the guidelines for permanence and durability of the Committee on Production Guidelines for Book Longevity of the Council on Library Resources, Inc. ∞

Copyright © 2017 by the University of Oklahoma Press, Norman, Publishing Division of the University. Paperback publised 2019. Manufactured in the U.S.A.

All rights reserved. No part of this publication may be reproduced, stored in a retrieval system, or transmitted, in any form or by any means, electronic, mechanical, photocopying, recording, or otherwise—except as permitted under Section 107 or 108 of the United States Copyright Act—without the prior written permission of the University of Oklahoma Press. To request permission to reproduce selections from this book, write to Permissions, University of Oklahoma Press, 2800 Venture Drive, Norman OK 73069, or email rights.oupress@ou.edu.

To Jose, Kim, Daniel, and Alexa

I could never begrudge a soldier a bit of cheer after the hard marches in Arizona, through miles of dust and burning heat, their canteens long emptied and their lips parched and dry. I watched them often as they marched along with their blanket-rolls, their haversacks, and their rifles, and I used to wonder that they did not complain.

> Martha Summerhayes, wife of 2nd Lieutenant
> John W. Summerhayes, Eighth Infantry

Contents

List of Illustrations	xi
Foreword, by Robert M. Utley	xiii
Preface	xv
Introduction	3
1. "Taking to Soldiering": Enlistment	13
2. "We Are Kept Pretty Busy": Life at the Recruiting Depot	44
3. "Don't Grieve after Me": The Journey West	79
4. "Deployed as Skirmishers": Regiments and Companies in the West	98
5. Brain, Bone, and Sinew: Officers and Noncoms	131
6. "It Is Just Dragging Out a Miserable Existence": Forts and Garrison Routine	171
7. "The Bed Bugs Are Too Numerous for Me to Sleep": Some Material Aspects of Army Life	212
8. "Offensive in Every Particular": Medicine, Hygiene, and Sanitation	251
9. "It Is So Lonesome Out Here": The Domestic Side of Enlisted Life	294
10. "We Have Our Little Amusements": Recreation and Pastimes	323
11. "The Moral Condition Is Very Poor": The Seamy Side of Enlisted Life	360

12. "There Are a Great Many Deserting from Our Regiment":
 The Problem of Desertion ... 399
13. "I Will See Some Real Wild-West Life": Preparing for
 Field Service ... 430
14. "More Than I Ever Thought I Could Bear": Life in
 the Field ... 450
15. "Our Orders Were to Go after Them": Regulars and
 Red Men ... 493
16. "The Government Pays You to Get Shot At": Combat ... 529
17. "Thank God I Am Done Soldiering": Enlistment's End ... 572

Appendixes
 A. 1872 Army Pay Table ... 599
 B. Glossary of Army Slang ... 601
 C. Selected Regular Army Ballads ... 609
 D. Enlisted Soldiers Whose Personal Accounts of
  Service Were Consulted for This Book ... 615
Abbreviations ... 625
Notes ... 627
Bibliography ... 707
Index ... 729

Illustrations

Original song sheet for "The Regular Army, O!"	*Frontispiece*
Steel engraving: "Will He Enlist?"	279
Tenth Cavalry sergeant at Fort Sill, Indian Territory, ca. 1872	280
Sergeant James S. Hamilton and fellow noncommissioned officers of Company K, First Infantry	280
Second Cavalryman Adelbert Butler	281
An unidentified soldier with his wife	282
Sunday inspection of a battalion of the Eleventh and Seventeenth Infantry at Fort Abraham Lincoln, Dakota Territory	283
William E. Matthews, who served with the Eighth Cavalry in Arizona and New Mexico and subsequently in Texas	284
Thirteenth Infantry noncoms during the 1886 Geronimo Campaign	285
Sergeant Perley S. Eaton of Troop K, Third Cavalry	285
Camp Grant, Arizona Territory, in 1870	286
Private William B. Jett, Fourth Cavalry	286
Signal Corpsman Will C. Barnes	287
A group of Sixth Cavalrymen at Camp Grant, Arizona Territory, early 1880s	287
Squad room at Fort Robinson, Nebraska, ca. 1890	288
Recruiting depot, Davids Island, New York	288

Sergeant John Ryan	289
One of Brigadier General George Crook's bivouacs during the Starvation March	289
Sergeant Major Alvarado M. Fuller, Second Cavalry	290
Charles A. Windolph	290
Private Thomas N. Way	291
Quartermaster Sergeant Richard P. Hanley	291
Private William Earl Smith, Fourth Cavalry	292
Ex-sergeant Charles A. Windolph in 1938	292
Recruit wearing an ill-fitting as-issued uniform	293
1872 army pay table	599

Foreword

Robert M. Utley

No one is more qualified to write this book than Doug McChristian. Indeed, he began living the life of the frontier soldiers forty years ago and has never ended his quest for knowledge about them. As an assistant director of the National Park Service, with a special interest in the West, I toured many of our historical areas. In the early 1970s I came across a trio of young interpreters clad in the blue uniforms of the frontier soldier. At Forts Laramie, Larned, Davis, Union, and other western parks, Doug McChristian and his cohorts demonstrated for park visitors every aspect of the life of these soldiers: how they were clad, how they were armed, how they lived in barracks and camp, what they ate. In short, they lived the life of the frontier soldier. To do that, they had to know all that there was to know about these men.

In *Regular Army O!* McChristian vividly demonstrates that much more has become known about these men in the decades since those reenactments at the western historic sites. And it has become known largely through the untiring efforts of Doug McChristian. He has not only continued his wide-ranging research on the lives of army enlisted men in the West but has unearthed scores of firsthand letters and reminiscences that personalize the findings of his research. He has combined his research with the words of these writers to present seventeen chapters that lead the soldier chronologically from enlistment to discharge. At each stage of the term of service, we are introduced to an all-encompassing view of what soldiering was really like at that time. Four informative appendixes enlarge the knowledge set forth.

McChristian builds on a popular earlier work, *Forty Miles a Day on Beans and Hay: The Enlisted Soldier Fighting the Indian Wars* by Don Rickey Jr. (University of Oklahoma Press, 1963). In this book McChristian takes the story far higher: it will likely stand as the definitive treatment of the subject.

Preface

Don Rickey Jr. was clearly the pioneer historian regarding this subject; he blazed the trail for all the rest of us. Upon reading his classic *Forty Miles a Day on Beans and Hay* for the first time during college days, I was drawn into what would become a lifelong area of interest. It has now been well over half a century since Rickey began his research. At that time, in 1952, he found that 316 surviving Indian Wars veterans were still alive. Two years later, there were only 240. Obviously, he knew that he could not afford to tarry. Relying on the records of the Veterans Administration and the still-active United Indian Wars Veterans Association, Rickey tracked down many former regulars, contacting them by mail and coaxing them into completing his questionnaire and in a few instances interviewing them personally. His foresight resulted in an invaluable contribution to history. By the time his landmark study first saw print in 1963, those veterans were nearly all gone; hardly a dozen were still living. Two years later, in a most selfless gesture, Rickey convinced a concerned congressman to rectify an injustice by presenting an Indian Wars campaign medal to Simpson Mann, the last qualified black veteran, aged 103 years, who had never received one in recognition of his service. Soon all of those self-proclaimed "Winners of the West" were gone. Rickey's enduring legacy is that he was our last living link with those soldiers of the western frontier era.

The publication of *Forty Miles* had a far-reaching effect, inspiring other western historians to recognize the significance of soldier diaries, journals, letter collections, and personal reminisces of frontier army service. Among descendants of veterans the book also created a better appreciation for the historical value of the letters and diaries that families had tucked away and given only scant attention. Dozens of these accounts have since found their way into public archives or in other ways have come to the attention of interested historians, who in many instances have edited and published them. Although too numerous to acknowledge individually, their names are found in my bibliography. I owe them, one and all, a great debt of gratitude for their contributions in bringing to light those personal narratives of frontier army life. I have shamelessly borrowed from those and many other sources, not the least of which are Rickey's original data collections.

I have had the advantages, therefore, of perspective and being able to draw upon a broader sample of accounts than were available to Rickey when he did his work. Thus it is no mere coincidence that the title of this volume follows his title as the next line in the classic 1874 Harrington & Hart ballad. Drawing from more than 350 accounts by soldiers who served during the period, I have attempted to relate this story, to every extent possible, through their own words and observations and those of their contemporaries. I have consciously strived to avoid imposing myself or modern societal norms on the treatment of these men. To judge them by any measure other than the conditions and standards of their own time would be an injustice. It is, after all, *their* story. Those soldiers were not the stuff of dusty records, legend, or distorted portrayals on the silver screen. They were real people possessing all of the emotions, strengths, and frailties of human kind. I found above all that many had a keen sense of humor in regard to their circumstances, even during great hardship. My challenge has been to present these soldiers within the historical context of the times and the army in which they served and in so doing to represent their lives and experiences as authentically as possible.

The inspiration for his volume initially came from my friend and former National Park Service colleague Jerome A. Greene, who quite a number of years ago urged me to undertake this project of building on the solid foundation laid by Rickey, utilizing the rich resources that have since become available. Friend and National Park Service colleague Paul L. Hedren, with whom I worked at Fort Laramie National Historic Site in our younger glory days, has also encouraged and gently prodded me to bring this study to fruition. Over many years, both men have generously shared documents, articles, and tidbits that they thought might be useful to me in the course of this study. Through their many publications, Jerry and Paul are widely recognized as advanced scholars in the field of frontier military history, particularly of the Great Sioux War, and thus were uniquely qualified to serve as the publisher's peer reviewers of the draft manuscript. I am deeply indebted to both for their thoughtful insights and constructive suggestions for improving my work. Charles E. Rankin, editor-in-chief for the University of Oklahoma Press, who enthusiastically embraced the concept of this study from the outset, has my profound gratitude for his unfailing encouragement and patience to see it through to publication.

I would be terribly remiss if I failed to acknowledge my long-time friend and fellow frontier army historian John D. McDermott. In a conversation several years ago, while attending a Fort Robinson History Conference, Jack and I discovered that we both had ambitions for revisiting the social history of the enlisted soldier. Jack, a prolific writer who never seems to be at a loss for topics, graciously offered to step aside and relinquish the project to me. Moreover, he later gave me access to his voluminous files to continue my research. Thank you, Jack: I hope that I have done justice to the subject.

A project of this scope always requires a great deal of assistance from many individuals and institutions. All of the following have my sincere thanks for either hosting me personally or responding to my requests remotely: the Arizona Historical Society Library staff; Sandy Barnard; Anne W. Bond; the late Tom Buecker, much missed friend and fellow student of the Indian Wars; Bill Chachula; Jennifer R. Clark, archivist, and Thomas Dewey, librarian, both of whom generously assisted me with access to the Indian Wars Widows Project files at Jefferson National Expansion Memorial, St. Louis, Missouri; my respected friend William A. Dobak, for sharing his copies of Inspector General (IG) reports, General Court Martial Orders (GCMOs), and other records; John A. Doerner, former colleague and historian at Little Bighorn Battlefield National Monument; Gerald H. Groenewold and Connie Triplett, for providing copies of Private Adelbert Butler's letters; librarian Dennis Hagen, who has always been so helpful and responsive to my needs while working in the Western History Collections, Denver Public Library; the Reverend Vincent A.

Heier; Linda Hein, reference assistant, Nebraska Historical Society; long-time comrade-in-blue B. William Henry Jr.; Tamsen E. Hert and the American Heritage Center staff, University of Wyoming; the Huntington Library staff, San Marino, California; Dr. Stan Larson, Manuscripts Division, J. Willard Marriott Library, University of Utah; Thomas A. Lindmier, my bunkie of more than four decades, for generously lending copies of the Richey diary and the Fort Fetterman records; Sandy Lowry, librarian at Fort Laramie National Historic Site, for her long-suffering assistance to me with unfailing cheer; Professor Kerby Miller, University of Missouri–Columbia for his gracious permission to quote extensively from the Maurice Wolfe letters; Laura Mooney, Nebraska Historical Society; Lorrie Morrow, Montana Historical Society; Brigadier General Steven R. Mount, Wyoming Army National Guard; James Mountain, who generously allowed me to use the Hubman letters; my friend independent historian Mark J. Nelson, for sharing his considerable knowledge of Plains Indian culture; the Oklahoma Historical Society library staff; James E. Potter, Nebraska Historical Society; Bob Rea, manager and historian at Fort Sill State Historic Site, for providing copies of little-known reminiscences; Bob Reece with the Friends of Little Bighorn Battlefield; Nan V. Rickey, for encouraging me to undertake this project; Mary Robinson, archivist, Buffalo Bill Historical Center; Superintendent Marie Sauter, Fort Union National Monument; Douglas L. Schlepp, Billings, Montana; Ryan R. Schumacher, Texas State Historical Association, Austin; Kim Allen Scott, archivist, Montana State University Library, for sharing copies of the Doane letters; Dr. Sherry L. Smith, Southern Methodist University; the Special Collections staff at the University of Arizona Main Library; the Special Collections staff at Norlin Library, University of Colorado–Boulder; Jack Spencer, for kindly permitting me to draw from the John O. Stotts journal; Robert L. Spude, former Southwest Region historian, National Park Service; Patricia Y. Stallard, recognized authority on army dependents; reference historian Zoe Ann Stoltz, Montana Historical Society; my friend Glen Swanson for sharing Seventh Cavalry images from his collection; Baird Todd, curator, Fort Laramie National Historic Site; the staff of the U.S. Army Heritage and Education Center, Carlisle, Pennsylvania, particularly Steve Bye, Terry Foster, Rodney Foytik, and Jessica J. Sheets, for their cordial assistance during my work there; historian Robert M. Utley for generously sharing the John Vance Lauderdale material, with special thanks for graciously consenting to write the foreword for this volume; former Wyoming assistant state archeologist Danny Walker; the staff at the Wyoming State Archives, Cheyenne; and Samuel R. Young, U.S. Cavalry Association.

Finally, I owe my heartfelt thanks to my wife, Frances, not only for her steady patience and understanding throughout the many months I spent with "the Boys" but for her constant support throughout the process.

Douglas C. McChristian
Tucson, Arizona

Regular Army O!

Introduction

On a quiet summer evening in the mountains of central Idaho a few dozen bearded, disheveled, blue-clad soldiers solemnly assembled around a shallow open grave. On a blood-soaked blanket beside the hastily dug pit lay the body of Private Harry Egan, victim of an Indian bullet that had torn through both thighs during a skirmish earlier that day. A comrade wrote of Egan: "He leaves a wife and daughter. We rolled his body in blankets and buried him. No shot was fired and no word spoken, but he was left to rest as peacefully as if there had been pomp and ceremony. No more, old comrade, will you be called to fat bacon and bean soup, to climb mountains nor damned by civilians for a lazy lout." That somber epitaph aptly epitomized the service of the Indian Wars regulars.[1]

Egan, a thirty-two-year-old private midway through his second enlistment in the army, was one of approximately 875 United States regulars killed in action with Indians on the western frontier during the period 1866 to 1891. During that time the army experienced more than one thousand engagements with Indians, most of those being minor skirmishes involving only detachments or companies. As conflicts go, the casualty figure was hardly significant—unless one happened to be the likes of Harry Egan or Private Martin Davis, a young black Tenth Cavalryman killed at an all-but-forgotten place called Rocky Ridge in the Trans-Pecos region of Texas. Despite the low combat losses, frontier soldiering was always a dangerous occupation, and many more men died of disease, accident, or the effects of the natural environment.[2]

During the period between the war with Mexico and the Civil War, the United States Army was occupied primarily with guarding the seacoasts and protecting the major overland routes of travel from "the States" to the Southwest and to California and the territories of the Pacific Northwest. The small available force did well to hold its own in manning a network of far-flung outposts along these lines of communication and, in a few instances, conducting small-scale offensive operations against bands or tribes of troublesome Indians.

At the outset of the Civil War, the army embraced ten regiments of infantry totaling 5,240 men, but in 1861 those ten-company units were augmented by nine larger regiments, each composed of three eight-company battalions. Within a few months after the South's secession from the Union, most of the regiments of the regular army were withdrawn from the western frontier and concentrated in the East. The infantry was organized in what became known as the Regular Army Division, commanded by Major General George Sykes. The regular cavalry, after being parceled out to various divisions and corps for a time, was eventually organized into all-mounted divisions, comprising two cavalry corps, one belonging to the Army of the Potomac, the other to the Military Division of the Mississippi. For the duration of the war, federalized volunteer regiments raised in the various western states and territories back-filled the void left by the exodus of the regulars. These troops, often poorly trained and disciplined and led in many instances by indifferent politically appointed officers, did more to inflame the Indian situation than to maintain peace.[3]

Enlistments in the regulars, meanwhile, stagnated in the face of competition stemming from state loyalties, aggressive local recruitment efforts, and the proffering of monetary bounties. Compounding the situation, attrition resulting from discharge, battle casualties, and disease drained the strengths of all the regular regiments to critically low levels. Those losses effectively became permanent because the available manpower was attracted, either voluntarily or by draft, to state units while enlistments in the regulars dwindled to a mere trickle. Most of the federal regiments were forced to consolidate companies, often several times, until by late in the war many could muster just three or four companies useful only for provost, guard, or escort duties. The adjutant general reported at the end of May 1865 that even though the regular army was authorized a total of 448 companies, 153 of those existed only on paper.[4]

The months immediately after the Confederate capitulation at Appomattox marked a period of transition as the million-man volunteer force was rapidly dismantled and mustered out of service. The actual strength of the regular army stood at only 22,310 officers and men, a figure far below its congressional authorization of more than 39,000. Clearly, the army had to be rebuilt—and quickly—to carry out increased responsibilities for policing the reconstruction of the South and meeting the demands of a restless citizenry ever-bent on migrating westward. To those ends, the Recruiting Service renewed efforts to restore the army to its prewar numbers, supported by a congressional act in July 1866 increasing the legal strength to slightly more than 54,000 men. Those infantry regiments (Eleventh through Nineteenth) formerly composed of three battalions were abolished, with each of the battalions forming the nucleus of a new regiment of ten companies.[5]

The resulting organization consisted of forty-five regiments of infantry, ten regiments of cavalry, and five of artillery. Four of the infantry regiments, the Forty-Second through the Forty-Fifth, composed the Veteran Reserve Corps, a body of seasoned men who had served faithfully during the war and had received wounds that, while not crippling, were serious enough to prevent them from performing full duty in line units. Significantly, the new organization reflected a successful wartime experiment with enlisting black men in segregated regiments led by white officers. More than 169,000 former slaves and northern free black men had answered the call to serve the Union cause. The United States Colored Troops, as they were designated, had served as faithfully as any other soldiers and compiled creditable combat records, suffering a loss of 1,514 men killed in action and nearly 32,000 deaths from other causes. Accordingly, six of the new regular regiments, four infantry and two cavalry, were set aside exclusively for black enlisted men. Unlike the black regiments authorized during the war, however, these new units no longer carried the stigma "colored" in their official titles. They were simply U.S. regulars, uniformed, armed, and equipped like their white counterparts.[6]

Subsequent years witnessed further modifications to the army's structure, the most significant occurring in 1869 when Congress cut the size of the army to a total of 37,313 officers and men. To achieve such a severe contraction, the act mandated: "There shall be no new commissions, no promotions, and no enlistments in any infantry regiment until the total number of infantry regiments is reduced to twenty-five." Congress thus relied primarily on attrition to accomplish much of the reduction in force affecting the rank and file, though all four regiments of the Veteran Reserve Corps were dissolved immediately and the members mustered out of service. Downsizing the army line, however, proved more challenging. The reduction in the number of infantry regiments left the army with some nine hundred officers in excess of its needs. Retirement boards worked overtime to usher out those who chose voluntarily to return to civilian pursuits. Others were subjected to "Benzine Boards" convened to cleanse the army of substandard officers with poor performance records or, not infrequently, histories of alcoholism and other personal deficiencies. Working to the army's advantage was the reality that the numbers of enlisted men actually carried on unit rolls still were well below authorized strength, a factor readily permitting soldiers to be consolidated in companies of the same or different regiments while adhering to overall maximum legal limits. For example, the black Thirty-Eighth and Forty-First Infantry were consolidated in a new Twenty-Fourth Regiment, while all of the companies of the Thirty-Ninth and Fortieth were combined to form the Twenty-Fifth Infantry. The rest of the higher numbered regiments (above twenty-five) likewise were eliminated and their personnel melded into other units, bringing them up to or near full-strength. The respective compositions of the cavalry and artillery remained constant.[7]

Still, the parsimonious Congress considered the military establishment too large and, more to the point, too costly for a nation ostensibly at peace and trying to overcome a staggering war debt. Little more than a year after the purge of 1869, it enacted legislation further slashing the number of enlisted men from 35,000 to 30,000 and again in 1874 to only 25,000. The officer corps numbered only slightly more than 2,000. Thus Congress had halved the regular army in just five years. The reorganization of 1874 was to cast the army in its basic form until the outbreak of the Spanish-American War. In the opinion of the chairman of the subcommittee responsible for this gutting, "the Army has very little active service to perform outside of the neighborhood of mischievous and unfriendly Indians." What the congressman failed to recognize, however, was that those "mischievous" Indians numbered in the thousands and came from various tribes and cultures and that their "neighborhood" extended over thousands of square miles beyond the Mississippi River.[8]

For a dozen years following the Civil War, the army was charged with dual missions: on the one hand, facilitating the nation's obsession with fleshing itself out to the Pacific; and on the other, executing President Andrew Johnson's directives for restoring the vanquished South. Heading the list was the reestablishment of state governments loyal to the Union by citizens who swore allegiance to the United States. Johnson extended a liberal amnesty policy to include all former Confederates who owned property valued at less than $20,000, granting amnesty to nearly all of those in the exempted class who applied for it. Amid the turmoil and shambles characterizing local government in the South, however, lawlessness became rampant, as recently freed former slaves sought to make a living for themselves and ex-Confederate soldiers returned to a ravished economy. "Those who were not in the South at this time can form little idea of the conditions," wrote a former regular who had served there. "The whole country was overrun with a lawless element, many of whom were returned soldiers who had lost their all by the war." The regulars were tasked with maintaining order and enforcing federal laws until effective civilian authority could be restored. Meanwhile, the army hunted down illegal distillers, combated the Ku Klux Klan, contended with northern carpetbaggers, upheld new election laws, and enforced court orders. Southern whites, understandably, resented the very presence of federal troops in their midst; conversely, most regulars considered Reconstruction duty to be an onerous, thankless assignment. Nevertheless, until Reconstruction formally ended in 1877, the army necessarily committed a significant portion of its small force to that mission. Approximately 40 percent of the troops were so occupied in the years immediately following the war, a figure that declined steadily to about 15 percent by the mid-1870s.[9]

The more familiar role of the post–Civil War regulars was as the vanguard of western settlement and development, the so-called Indian fighting army of the frontier. The army was under no illusions concerning the challenges of its frontier mission, as reflected in an observation by General of the Army Ulysses S. Grant in 1866: "With a frontier constantly extending and encroaching upon the hunting-grounds of the Indian, hostilities, opposition at least, frequently occur. To meet this, and to protect the emigrant on his way to the mountain territories, troops have been distributed to give the best protection with the means at hand. Few places are occupied by more than two, and many by but a single company. These troops are generally badly sheltered, and are supplied at great cost." Uncertain as to just how the demands of Reconstruction might affect the army's ability to meet requirements in the West, military leaders initially adopted a defensive posture aimed at protecting several principal travel and communication arteries to the extent possible.[10]

In the north, the upper Missouri River traversed Dakota Territory and provided a viable avenue for steamboats all the way to Fort Benton in western Montana. The Platte River route across southern Nebraska had long been the main emigrant thoroughfare leading from the States and branching to California, Oregon, and Utah. During the war a major gold strike in western Montana Territory gave rise to a new road departing from the North Platte River west of Fort Laramie and passing northward along the eastern base of the Bighorn Mountains then turning west along the Yellowstone River to the Beaverhead River country.

Congress had chartered the first transcontinental railroad in 1862 along what was known as the Central Route, connecting Omaha with Sacramento via Salt Lake City. After delays resulting from inadequate funding and the prosecution of the war, the Central Pacific and Union Pacific Railroads commenced work from west and east, respectively, with the goal of meeting somewhere between and finally linking the nation. A bit farther south, tracing the course of the Smoky Hill River, was a corridor that had initially served Colorado-bound miners and mail coaches. After the war, however, it became the obvious path for a rail line connecting Kansas City with the burgeoning gold-rich city of Denver. Also traversing the level plains of Kansas was the Arkansas River route (the Santa Fe Trail), which for decades had been the principal commercial outlet for the United States to the greater Southwest and Mexico. Competing with the Central Route were roads originating at Fort Smith, Arkansas, and the Gulf Coast to merge in

Texas before crossing the desert to southern California. This southern overland route eventually would support another of the planned transcontinental railroads. Protecting all of these avenues with the available cavalry and infantry was a nearly incalculable task.

In an effort to oversee military operations throughout such an enormous area, the army divided the Trans-Mississippi into two great geographical military divisions. The Division of the Missouri, headquartered in Chicago and first commanded by Lieutenant General William T. Sherman, encompassed the Indian Territory, Kansas, Nebraska, Dakota (including what would become Wyoming), Montana, Colorado, Utah, and New Mexico, in addition to four midwestern states. Attempting to bring perspective to the complexity of his responsibility, Sherman wrote: "I must state . . . that this military division embraces the vast region from the Mississippi river to the Rocky mountains, of an average breadth (east and west) of one thousand three hundred and fifty miles, and length (north and south) of over one thousand miles, viz: from the south border of New Mexico to the British line." Within his huge jurisdiction were at least eight Indian nations that Sherman considered to be hostile at the time—Sioux, Cheyenne, Arapaho, Kiowa, Comanche, Ute, Apache, and Navajo—in addition to a dozen or so peaceful ones.[11]

The states and territories of the Far West (California, Arizona, Nevada, Oregon, Washington, and Idaho) were assigned to the Military Division of the Pacific, with headquarters in San Francisco. Major General Henry W. Halleck cited the Bannack, Paiute, and Snake people as the principal sources of trouble in the northwest, though the Modocs, too, would give the army fits within a few years. More rancorous than these, however, were the Apaches residing in Arizona and southern New Mexico Territories. "The Apache," Halleck noted, "is a bitter enemy to all white settlers, having been at war with them for the last half century." He might also have included the Apaches' unremitting resistance to Spanish and later Mexican interlopers for the previous two centuries.[12]

No one quite knew what to do with Texas. Because it had allied with the Confederate states, the army initially assigned it to the Division of the Gulf for the purposes of Reconstruction. Of more pressing concern, though, were the Indians in the far western and northern parts of the state. Comanches, Kiowas, and Plains Apaches roamed the regions of the Panhandle and the Red River, while Lipan and Mescalero Apaches raided throughout the Trans-Pecos during their migrations back and forth across the international border with Mexico. By 1871 army headquarters had concluded that operations aimed at contending with these tribes could be better coordinated by attaching Texas to Sherman's Division of the Missouri, thus extending his authority over the entire central portion of the nation from the Canadian border south to the Rio Grande and from the Mississippi to the Rocky Mountains.

That portion of the army, mainly cavalry and infantry, assigned to the western frontier was distributed among approximately a hundred forts and semipermanent camps at any given time during the quarter-century following the Civil War. Circumstances in the West demanded that the limited number of troops be parceled out where they might be most effective in carrying out the army's frontier mission at any given time. Garrisons ranged in size from one to several companies, three or four being most common, and were often composed of both infantry and cavalry. The result was that regiments were fragmented within geographical departments, with headquarters and a few companies at one post, while the rest were distributed among other forts and cantonments across a wide region.

Beginning in 1868 the army shifted from a defensive posture to an offensive strategy aimed at defeating those tribes considered to be hostile and refusing to submit to living on reservations. On both the northern and southern plains Sherman and Sheridan employed a strategy of multiple columns of troops converging on areas inhabited by these tribes in efforts to corral the Indians and bring them to bay. Hounded relentlessly in both summer and winter, the Indians eventually were defeated and removed to reservations. After 1880 active campaigning largely ceased everywhere except in New Mexico and Arizona, where small bands of Apaches continued raiding on both sides of the international border.

In accordance with a plan devised by General Sherman, the army began consolidating the troops into a considerably smaller number of forts with larger garrisons beginning in the early 1880s. By that time the Indians had been confined, or at least assigned, to prescribed reservations. Sherman's idea was to concentrate some of his troops at posts in the vicinities of the reservations to mitigate potential problems by their very presence and to be at hand in the event that they were needed to quell any trouble. Most of the rest of the army in frontier regions was posted to existing or new forts served by the expanding rail system in the West. Railroads had supplanted the long overland routes of travel and commerce. With the Indians mostly contained, there was no longer a need for numerous small garrisons scattered along those routes for protection. Railroads made it possible for troops to be rapidly dispatched from consolidated garrisons to wherever they might be needed. The last of military field operations against free-roaming Indians concluded with the surrender of the Chiricahua Apache Geronimo in 1886. However, the wisdom of Sherman's consolidation strategy was borne out with the Lakota Sioux uprising on the Pine Ridge Reservation in 1890. Troops were immediately ordered out from the nearest posts ringing Sioux country, while an overwhelming additional force was marshaled by rail from stations as far away as Kansas, Utah, California, and elsewhere. While it is recognized that Indian trouble did not absolutely cease after the Wounded Knee Massacre, most historians consider that signal event as the close of the Indian Wars.[13]

Commenting in 1890, General George Crook characterized Indian warfare as "the most dangerous, the most trying and the most thankless. Not recognized by the high authority of the United States Senate as war, it still possesses for you the disadvantages of civilized warfare, with all the horrible accompaniments that barbarians can invent and savages can execute."[14] That the thinly spread force of regulars eventually prevailed over the Indians testifies in part to the ability of some key commanders, notably Colonel Ranald S. Mackenzie, Lieutenant Colonel George Armstrong Custer, Brigadier General George Crook, and Colonel Nelson A. Miles, to adapt to the unorthodox conditions that they encountered on the frontier. They and others demonstrated that "Indian thinking" as well as experience and dogged determination were crucial to success. In the final analysis, however, the army owed much of its success to the discipline, courage, and endurance of the rank-and-file soldiers, who shouldered the day-to-day burden of implementing the government's will. Something less than a quarter of a million enlisted soldiers entered the army during the entire twenty-five-year period following the Civil War, and only a portion of those saw frontier service. Since then the frontier regulars have been variously hailed or vilified according to the times and societal perspectives. The truth lies somewhere between. This study examines who they were and what their lives were like within the context of the army of their day and the Indian wars in the West.[15]

CHAPTER 1

"Taking to Soldiering"

Enlistment

Summer 1865: four years of bloody war had finally ended. The Union was intact, though tattered, and now faced new challenges. Of nearly 3 million soldiers who had served in the Union army during the course of the conflict, approximately half still were in the process of being mustered out: thousands every day. The once vibrant industrial complex so vital to the North's victory was receding as government demand for arms and military supplies of every sort evaporated overnight. The huge influx of returning veterans imposed on a declining labor market suppressed wages for already scarce jobs. An unforeseen effect of the economic situation was an abundant supply of army recruits, many of them experienced, at a time when logic would have predicted the number of enlistments to be low in the comparatively small regular army. "There was many a returned soldier out of employment, and the slogan was give the ex-soldier employment first, but times were dull," reflected a veteran who lived through it. "Many a young man, dissatisfied with his environment in the East, made every effort to go West . . . and the cheapest way to go West in 1865 was to enlist in the Army."[1]

There was only one way to get in the regulars: by voluntary enlistment. Unlike the state forces during the war, the regulars had no three-month or one-year terms, no draftees, no paid substitutes or promises that a soldier's service would terminate with the end of the conflict. Enlistments had been reduced temporarily to three years as a wartime concession to attract recruits, but the lack of a sufficient pool of men to fill the ranks was no longer a problem. Congress soon restored the standard term to five years. Even so, men of all backgrounds and nationalities turned to the army not only to make a living but for an endless array of other reasons: a few well-considered, many on a whim, some in desperation. In one way or another, the West beckoned.

"One day I was sitting there feeling pretty blue," recounted a veteran in later years. "All of a sudden it seemed to me that somebody said to me, 'Why don't you enlist. . . .' The recruiting office was about two squares from the hotel . . . I went in and said, 'If I enlist now when can I go away?' The officer said, 'If you enlist now, you go tonight.' . . . I said, 'Take my measure!'" His story was typical of many men who enlisted in the regulars during the Indian Wars. If they shared a common trait, it might be impetuosity. An officer of many years' experience observed: "He may be a mechanic tired of routine life, a farmer with a taste for life on the frontier, a student tired of his books, a young business man who has not made a success of his first venture, an emigrant who cannot find work, or possibly owing to the simple reason that he wishes to become a soldier, or for any one of a hundred and one reasons." Whatever their individual motives, they were restless young men in a young America on the move.[2]

In early spring 1866 eighteen-year-old James D. Lockwood was dejectedly walking the streets of his hometown Troy, New York, when he happened upon a recruiting office. Having little money in his pockets and no prospects for a job, Lockwood, who had previously served three years as a drummer with a volunteer infantry regiment, "resolved once more to offer himself for the service of his country, knowing quite well that he could fight if he had the chance; and as the Indians were on the warpath throughout the great west, he did not doubt having the chance." Now of legal age to be a full-fledged soldier, he enlisted and was later assigned to the Eighteenth Infantry, a regiment soon to garrison new posts along the dangerous Bozeman Trail traversing far-off Dakota and Montana Territories.[3]

Some individuals discovered that readjusting to civilian life was not as easy as they had expected. Commenting on some of those veteran volunteers who frequented recruiting offices in the immediate wake of the war, First Sergeant Henry H. McConnell observed: "At the close of the war some uneasy spirits who had learned to like the lazy, irresponsible, reckless life of the camp, and found the restraints of civil life insupportable, sought the regular army." But men of that ilk were quickly disabused of the notion that life in the regulars would be like the volunteers. Robert Greenhalgh, who had served in the First Dragoons before and early in the war, reenlisted in 1865 when he was unable to find work. Looking askance at the demeanor of his new comrades, Greenhalgh perceptively observed: "We have received over five hundred recruits. . . . They have most all been in the volunteers before, spent all their money, then enlisted again. Of course there are some hard cases among them. . . . They think they can carry on about the same as they did in the volunteers . . . but they will find out that is played out now." Indeed the regulars were professional soldiers, owing allegiance only to the United States and their oath to follow lawful orders. "From the moment . . . an enlisted man enters his regiment he is taught two things by both precept and example," an officer wrote. "They are the honour of the service and the necessity of always and under all circumstances doing his duty." Thus the tone was established for all that would follow.[4]

The excitement of wartime service stood in sharp contrast to what many now saw as a drab existence back on the family farm, clerking in a store, or performing manual labor for meager wages. Soldiers became accustomed to the routine of military life and the camaraderie of other men. Then too, combat, for all its horrors, was an adrenalin-charged experience that had no comparison in civil life. Veterans not infrequently felt adrift in that vacuum, trying one job and then another in searching to satisfy a psychological need. As an infantryman in a Massachusetts regiment, John Ryan had fought in nine battles, including Antietam, Fredericksburg, Chancellorsville, and Gettysburg, suffering three wounds. "After remaining home a short time while getting rested, not having a trade, I went to work at the Aetna Mills in Watertown. After a while, I left there and secured a position with . . . the Newton Oil Company . . . [and after a stint as a coachman] I went to work . . . carpentering . . . and finally the army fever struck me. I met two friends of mine, and we made it up to enlist in the United States Army."[5]

Another segment of ex-soldiers had not worn Union blue at all but had served in the Confederate States Army or Navy. Southern veterans commonly returned home to find only ruined or long-neglected farms and a devastated economy. The war had destroyed much of the South's previously limited manufacturing capability. With nothing more to lose, many Confederate veterans joined the westward migration, especially to Texas, in search of better opportunities. Yet a few had developed a genuine attraction to military life. Some of the former combatants acknowledged almost immediately a mutual, if grudging, brotherhood as soldiers—American soldiers all. One U.S. regular present at Lee's surrender spoke with a North Carolinian: "When we were giving them [Confederates] our rations after the surrender at Appomattox, a tall lanky tarheel said to me, 'You all and we'uns can lick all hell.'"[6] In that vein, some Confederate veterans overcame their aversion to Union blue and later joined the regulars, though their exact numbers will never be known, because there was no requirement for them to divulge that information to recruiters. The general amnesty granted to all former Confederates stipulated that they take a new oath of loyalty to the United States, so nothing barred them from serving in the ranks of the army. Seventh Cavalryman John Ryan attested that Confederate veterans were often found in the ranks during the late 1860s. "We had one hundred and one men assigned to our company," he commented. "A great many of those men had seen service in the Union army during the Civil War and quite a number of them, about seventeen, had served in the confederate service . . . some had been commissioned in the confederate service." A few, like Virginia farmer John W. Jenkins, even became career soldiers. Formerly a cavalryman in General Jubal Early's corps, Jenkins joined the army in 1869, eventually serving three enlistments.[7]

Compounding the labor situation, especially in the Northeast, was a continuing influx of immigrants from abroad. Alone in a foreign land and willing to work at almost anything to survive, the recent arrivals posed a threat to other workers by competing for already scarce jobs. While native-born Americans representing every state in the Union consistently accounted for more than 50 percent of enlistees during the era of the Indian Wars, the Irish and Germans represented the next largest segments, 20 and 12 percent, respectively, between the years 1866 and 1874. The predominance of those two nationalities rightly contributed to enduring stereotypes of frontier soldiers. "The Irishman," McConnell observed, "is by far the best soldier in our army.

Oppressed and robbed at home, virtually without a country of his own to fight for, he had been at the front, and in the fiercest of the fight, on every battlefield from Fontenoy to Appomattox, and he has always held his own with honor to the flag under which he fought." In contrast, probably because of his own ethnicity, McConnell denigrated the Germans as "good army laborers and first-class dog robbers." As time passed, however, the percentage of Germans joining the American army increased, with many of them becoming career soldiers.[8]

The composition of the army reflected the international complexity of America's population as a whole. From the late 1860s to the mid-1870s army recruits represented an average of some forty foreign nations. Ranking in order after Ireland and Germany, England, Canada, Scotland, France, and Switzerland accounted for the largest numbers of enlistees, while Denmark, Sweden, Norway, Holland, and Belgium also contributed significantly to the rank and file. Not to be overlooked, however, were such diverse origins as Arabia, China, Egypt, Turkey, the West Indies, Mexico, and several South American countries. The idea of America as a "melting pot" of nationalities is not just a cliché, and nowhere was that more evident than in the army of the post–Civil War era. By 1880, however, foreign nativities of new enlistees represented just seventeen countries, accounting for only 31 percent of the men joining the army. Captain George F. Price, a Fifth Cavalry officer detailed on recruiting duty in 1884, told the *New York Tribune*: "Contrary to the general impression a large percentage of the enlistments in the Army is of men of American birth. The percentage of foreigners is small, and of these the German come first, the Irish and English next. There are few Frenchmen and Scotchmen. We accept about one man in ten of those examined." Even though the variety of national origins represented declined during the latter part of the era, the proportion of foreign-born soldiers remained constant at over 30 percent.[9]

Those immigrants hailing from non-English-speaking countries were immediately disadvantaged by an inability to communicate meaningfully in American society. Thus it was not unusual for those men to seek out the nearest recruiting station as a means of acculturating themselves. "I was twenty-one years of age at that time and unable to speak the English language at all," recounted Max Littman, a former cigar-maker from Germany who landed at New York City in 1866. "I was desirous of seeing something of the country to the west before making any attempt to establish myself in business." He and a countryman, Frederick Claus, who emigrated and enlisted a few months later because "times were hard," were to experience more than they ever imagined as participants in the desperate Wagon Box Fight against Sioux and Northern Cheyenne warriors.[10] Danish-born Christian Madsen said: "As soon as I entered the army my main goal was to get to know the language and the country during the 5 years of my life as a soldier." The constancy of foreigners turning to army life as a means of establishing themselves in the United States is found in the experience of Norwegian immigrant Robert C. O. Norman, who expressed similar reasons for his decision to enlist near the end of the era.[11]

Other foreign-born men cited a combination of reasons for entering the army. In many European countries military service was compulsory, causing some young men to leave their homelands and migrate to the United States. Bergen shoemaker Charles Windolph, for example, related his experience:

> I was eighteen in the spring of 1870, and by June it looked pretty certain that Prussia was going to fight Napoleon the Third of France. I was booked to be drafted in the Dragoons but a few days before I was to report for duty I skipped out for Sweden . . . then I got a boat for America. I was about the greenest thing that ever hit New York. I couldn't talk more than a dozen words of English and I had exactly $2.50 in money . . . I got a job as a boot maker in Hoboken. But the methods were all different from the way I had been taught. Finally an old man who was working next to me, and who talked German, told me to join the army and learn English so that I could amount to something.

The irony of his situation was not lost on Windolph. "Funny, here we'd run away from Germany to escape military service, and now, because most of us couldn't get a job anywhere else, we were forced to go into the army here."[12]

Poking fun at the Germans, First Cavalryman James O. Purvis claimed that they enlisted for another reason: "In the German army a soldier is obliged to write home to his wife once a month. This explains why so many Germans come to this country to escape military duty."[13]

Quartermaster Sergeant Maurice H. Wolfe, an Irish immigrant himself, cited a more sinister motive for the large influx of Irishmen into the rank and file during the late 1860s. "There is scarcely a soldier in this camp that is not a Fenian. It's just the same all over the U.S. Army. There are a great many men in the Army who enlisted expressly for the sake of learning the art of war." Founded in Ireland early in the nineteenth century to resist British domination, the Fenian Brotherhood extended its movement to America for the purpose of invading and wresting Canada from the British in order to hold it in exchange for Irish independence. Wolfe would have been privy to barracks conversations among secret members of the society who had joined the army to become trained soldiers and, potentially, leaders in that effort.[14]

"There came to the United States during the latter part of the war, when bounties were high," a veteran recalled, "men who had served in about all the armies of Europe. Some were men of superior education. . . . When the war ended many of this class joined the Regular Army." Among these were immigrants like Hans Spring and several friends, who set out from Switzerland in 1864 on a grand mission to serve the Union cause in America. Upon his arrival in the States, Spring made good on his pledge by enlisting in a New York regiment and was subsequently wounded in action just prior to the war's end. By July 1865 he had recovered sufficiently to be discharged from the volunteers. But rather than pursuing a civilian livelihood he immediately attempted to enter the regular service. His recent wound had not healed sufficiently, however, and the recruiting officer rejected him. Undeterred, Spring worked at odd jobs for a few weeks before again trying to enlist, this time successfully.[15]

The Civil War made a deep impression on many young men thirsting to experience what they considered to be a great adventure. In some instances underage boys with a desire to taste military life had accompanied their soldier-fathers in the field during the war, a practice that appears to have been overlooked by some commanding officers.

First Cavalryman John H. Cady, for example, had been among the camp followers with the Fifth New York Volunteer Infantry prior to his joining the navy. Another underage boy, who later became a member of the Eighth Cavalry, had assisted his father, a quartermaster serving with a Maryland regiment. Moreover, thousands of boys who had remained at home were influenced by the war tales of their fathers, uncles, and older brothers. John O. Stotts recalled:

> Nearly all my relatives had been soldiers, and like many other boys who had been raised in war times, my mind was on the life of a soldier instead of being on my books. I finally went home [from college] and told my Father that I would never be satisfied until I had tried soldier life. He finally consented. . . . but he told me plainly that I would find out in time that a soldier's life was a hard one and that I would many times wish that I could sit down at Mother's table. . . . He finally said that he had one request to ask of me, and that was that I would faithfully serve my time and come home with an honorable discharge in my pocket.[16]

Recruiting for the black regiments differed in some respects from that for white regiments. General of the Army Ulysses S. Grant needed troops in the West as quickly as possible to replace the demobilizing volunteer organizations. With some 12,500 soldiers of the U.S. Colored Troops still in service in late 1866, and with plans already laid to abolish those organizations, Secretary of War Edwin M. Stanton directed that the new regular regiments be filled so far as possible with men transferred from the volunteers. The black volunteers had the advantage of being trained soldiers—often combat veterans—and therefore were capable of taking station on the frontier without delay. To facilitate the process, their officers served collaterally as recruiters to attract as many men as possible to the ranks of the regular army. That effort proved highly successful, and the preponderance of the men initially filling the six black regiments came directly from the volunteer organizations.[17]

Recently discharged soldiers augmented active-duty men. Even more than their white counterparts, black veterans had difficulty finding employment, a situation exacerbated by the paucity of industry in the South, a primarily agrarian economy struggling to recover from the war, and racial prejudice. Perhaps the most fortunate blacks were those who found employment through labor contracts with white landowners or were able to gain some degree of self-determination by negotiating sharecropping arrangements. Regimental recruiting officers took advantage of these conditions by forming recruiting parties consisting of both veterans and recent enlistees moving from town to town every few days. Texas and Louisiana proved to be especially fertile recruiting grounds for black men immediately after the war, but states in the upper South, as well as the District of Columbia, later provided perhaps the majority of the army's black recruits. In 1870, for example, the adjutant general directed the colonels of each of the segregated regiments to detail an officer to recruit for their respective organizations at Memphis and Nashville, Tennessee, and Paducah, Kentucky.[18] Well-fed black regulars, nattily dressed in army blue adorned with gleaming brasses, were powerful inducements for others to join. As one officer who served more than a decade with the Ninth Cavalry attested: "When a Negro gets on a uniform . . . he is in his glory. It elevates him. He regards enlistment in the Army as something to be proud of . . . as a soldier . . . he is as good as any other man that I have ever served with."[19]

Many black recruits, however, were not veterans; former slave Reuben Waller had become attracted to military life merely by circumstances of association. "My master was a general in the Rebel army," Waller stated. "He took me along as his body servant and I was with him all through the war, was with him in 29 battles. While being with Stonewall Jackson's cavalry, I engendered a great liking for the cavalry soldiers, and on July 16th, 1867, I went to Fort Leavenworth, Kansas . . . and I enlisted [in Tenth Cavalry] . . . for the Indian war that was then raging in Kansas and Colorado."[20]

The Civil War, coupled with hard-fought legislation culminating in the Thirteenth Amendment to the Constitution, had secured the abolition of slavery in America; subsequent action additionally granted to all citizens the right to vote, regardless of race or color. As a result of these measures, concludes one historian, "Black Unionists had at least as strong a relationship with the government as northern whites for its boon to them and their sacrifice for it were both enormous. . . . Black Americans were not passive recipients of this government concern.

Their sacrifices for the nation were those of people determined to earn their right to the nation's gratitude."[21]

The army, while not the most tolerant institution in the country, was in some respects more progressive than contemporary American society on the whole. The army was one of the few environments in which black men could elevate themselves under the same conditions afforded whites. For many black civilians, particularly ex-slaves, the army presented a better quality of life than they had ever known was possible. As a Twenty-Fifth Infantryman put it, "I'd ruthuh be in de army den a plantation slave." Being well clothed, housed, fed three meals daily, given medical care, and paid a salary on par with that of their white comrades-in-arms were benefits almost beyond comprehension. Not to be overlooked were the psychological benefits that blacks derived from military service. Their loyalty and contributions during the war had proven what many whites had questioned—that blacks could and would bear arms faithfully and courageously in defense of the Union. They had amply proven their worth as soldiers on many fronts. Even more than a source of unspoken pride, wearing their nation's uniform was for many black soldiers a symbol of manhood, a badge of equality. "The ambition to be all that soldiers should be is not confined to a few of these sons of an unfortunate race," wrote Chaplain George G. Mullins, Twenty-Fifth Infantry. "They are possessed of the notion that the colored people of the whole country are more or less affected by their conduct in the Army."[22] Mullins's statement suggests that black soldiers often felt a particular obligation to acquit themselves well as a positive reflection on their race as a whole.

Throughout the late nineteenth century a vacillating economy and occasional labor strikes continued to keep unemployment at or near the top of the list of motives for men joining the army. Nineteen-year-old William E. Matthews, who had traveled to Cincinnati on a lark with two friends in 1869, was literally down to his last penny and unable to find work of any kind to support himself. "As a last resort [I] went down to the Recruiting Office for the purpose of enlisting . . . there is not much chance for anything else here." He kept that penny as a souvenir to remind himself of hard times. A Fourth Infantryman at Fort Bridger, Wyoming Territory, writing to a cousin in Ireland on the eve of the Panic of 1873, complained: "There is no money afloat. Manufactories are all stopped and so are the majority of the Government works throwing thousands of men and women out [of] employment. A great many men are taking to soldiering for a change." One of those men was James S. Hamilton, who enlisted in 1876 "after the panic of '73 . . . work was hard to find and so the army seemed a good opportunity . . . to acquire more education and learn some trade."[23]

The army of that day sometimes provided willing soldiers the rudiments of an education, a factor motivating a few men to enlist, yet the service offered no formal training in the skilled trades. "A good mechanic who can earn $18 or $20 a week is not going to enter the service for $13 a month without he has some stronger reason than money-getting," wrote the editor of the *Army & Navy Journal* in 1873. The army nevertheless afforded a measure of economic security for men who were willing to sacrifice self-determination and submit to rigid discipline for several years. An 1882 article compared the benefits of soldiering with an average laborer making less than forty dollars per month:

> Out of this he has to support himself and family, and in case of sickness, to pay for medicines and a doctor. His room is generally squalid. He is untidily dressed, and seldom looks bright or cheerful, and has all the cares that a man can manage. Now take the soldier. At the end of every month he gets his $13 sure, but besides that he gets good, substantial rations, is comfortably and warmly housed and clothed, in case of sickness has medical attendance and hospital accommodations free, and is not obliged to work.[24]

Despite the inaccuracy of the last phrase, particularly as it applied to western frontier service, army life had some advantages over that of the common laborer across nineteenth-century America. Twenty-four-year-old Washington McCardle signed on "because I was tired of working 16 hours a day for 50 cents a day [in an iron foundry]." Another young man, William Hunteole, likewise decided that army pay would be better than the $2.00 a week he earned as a grocery store clerk.[25]

Of 5,006 recruits of all races accepted by the army in 1880, for example, 1,405 (28 percent) previously had been common laborers, followed by 564 (11 percent) who were reenlisted soldiers. Bryan McDonald, a twenty-two-year-old Irish immigrant, was among 2 percent of enlistees who served as sailors prior to joining the army.[26] Other occupations were representative of the nation's working classes on the whole, with a breakdown of almost 10 percent farmers, 5 percent clerks, and 5 percent teamsters and hostlers. Men skilled in various trades such as carpentry, painting, blacksmithing, baking, harness-making, and printing were also represented in significant numbers, while a considerably smaller percentage of professionals, including architects, schoolteachers, and machinists, resorted to military service when thrown out of work during times of economic hardship or when they had succumbed to liquor.[27]

Perhaps the most unreliable men were those enlistees known as "floaters . . . men who have no settled homes or places of abode, and who 'take on' because they have nothing better to do at the time . . . the loose class who would want some place for winter." The ebb and flow of seasonal jobs, such as those related to farming, canals, and rivers, often threw laborers out of work, making it difficult, if not impossible, to find employment during winter to tide them over. Others of this class resorted to the army for no other reason than to obtain transportation to the West, and perhaps better opportunities, at government expense.[28]

Even though uncertain economic times continued to account for the majority of enlistments throughout the late nineteenth century, the passage of time and receding memory of the Civil War gave rise to a younger generation of men with no personal involvement with or recollection of the conflict. Through newspapers, pulp magazines, and dime novels, the youths of that generation became fascinated by the lure of the American West. The prospect of adventure, seeing real Indians, as opposed to those in dime novels, and the opportunity to travel to exotic places at government expense were temptations that many young men could not deny in an age when few citizens ventured more than a hundred miles from home. John E. Cox, an Indiana farm boy, yearned to "see the world" before settling down to some type of work acceptable to his parents. Sitting atop a barnyard gate one morning, Cox pondered: "How can I travel? . . . I have no money. I never was away from home, and don't know how to get away." About that time a like-minded neighborhood friend rode up and proposed that they enlist in the army. But, as Cox related, "I was so 'green' that I didn't even know that there was such a person in existence as a U.S. Soldier! . . . a trip to California! . . . My mind was made up in ten seconds." Knowing full well that his parents would not consent to the idea, Cox simply informed his father that he would not be home that night and left.[29]

A natural thirst for adventure, common to most teenaged boys regardless of the time, spurred many to embark on such quests. Fred Munn was reared on a farm in New York and "lived the life usual to a boy of that time." At age eighteen he and two chums left home bound for New York City with the intention of going to sea. By the fourth day, and nearly broke, they came across a recruiting office. The sergeant in charge made a profound impression "with his large yellow chevrons and the wide stripe down his pants leg . . . he painted the life on the plains with a rosy hue, convincing us the way to see the West was to join the Army and chase Indians." Munn was hooked. A young German, Armand Unger, confided that "when a teenager I always was dreaming of our great West. I had a growing desire to see some of it. I especially wanted to acquire an intimate knowledge of the life and habits of Indian tribes." After seeing a recruitment ad in the newspaper, a Baltimore youth decided "what a fine thing it would be to go west at Uncle Sam's expense and have a good horse to ride . . . so off I went as fast as I could to the point specified." In the spring of 1884 Charles Ashdown happened by a cigar store in Rochester, New York, where he saw a display of relics allegedly from the Little Bighorn Battlefield. "It was really that exhibit . . . that aroused my interest in the west." The exhibit was attributed to frontiersman and showman extraordinaire William F. Cody, who likely was using the artifacts to promote one of his acclaimed Wild West performances.[30]

Some adventuresome spirits traveled to the beckoning frontier only to be disillusioned at finding that even there opportunities were limited. Grandison Mayo, later a member of the Twenty-Fifth Infantry, wound up "stranded in St. Louis without money and no job." Similarly, two former clothing clerks, Ernest Selander and his friend Wyman, left Omaha in the spring of 1881, intending to work their way west as railroad laborers. Their prospects for a bright future lost their luster, however, before they reached the opposite end of the state. Selander recalled: "When the train arrived at Sidney, Nebraska, we left it and in skirmishing around we observed the U.S. flag waving at

Fort Sidney . . . as we were about broke, Wyman suggested that we enlist." They did. Wallace Bingham also saw the army as an easier way to make a living than either ranch work or stonecutting, both of which he had tried for a time in southeastern Kansas. Encountering a unit of the Fifth Cavalry camped at Caldwell for the purpose of preventing "boomers" from invading the Cherokee Strip, Bingham quickly concluded "that was the life—Uncle Sam feed and clothe you and all that had to be done was to lay on your bunk and wait for the war. But I soon found out differently."[31]

By the 1880s young black men had increasingly become aware of military service as a means for advancing themselves in life. One of these was Horace Bivens, a native Virginian born free in 1863. By the time he was twenty-four, Bivens had attended Hampton Normal and Agricultural Institute as well as Wayland Seminary. Seeing a notice that the army was "recruiting colored men of education who could fill positions as non-commissioned officers," he immediately enlisted in the Tenth Cavalry and made a career of the army.[32]

Englishman Reginald Bradley was an atypical enlistee. Leaving the comforts and security of a well-to-do family in 1889 and purchasing what he was told was a proper outfit for western America, he sought his fortune in far-off New Mexico Territory. "I wanted adventure, so I picked the place on the map that had the least names on it," he said. Within a few months he was a self-made cowpuncher riding for a ranch near old Fort Cummings. But when the gentleman-turned-cowboy found himself out of work and down on his luck following the fall roundup, he decided to enlist. By that time he was nearly destitute, having sold what was left of his equipment, retaining only a photo of his fiancé. A restaurant waiter paid $15.00 for his dress suit and "was mighty glad to get it." Following the railroad west from Deming, mostly afoot, Bradley wound up at Fort Bowie, Arizona Territory, where he enlisted in the Fourth Cavalry.[33]

A factor common among many enlistees throughout the period of the Indian Wars was simply an attraction to military life—the "honor of the cloth"—either by personal inclination or to continue family tradition. "[I] was raised on a farm until I was 18 years of age," Lawrence J. Henry recalled. "I always had the Army fever and wanted to go when I was 16 . . . but they would not take me without my parents' consent which was not given. I tried to enlist again at 19, but with the same luck . . . I succeeded in enlisting the 27 of August 1876." A young black man, Alexander Hatcher, presented himself for enlistment "because I thought I would like it." Having a sense of obligation to uphold family tradition, William G. Bowen, whose father soldiered in the Civil War, claimed to be "decended [sic] from a family of soldiers who served under England's Kings . . . at the Palace of the Guards." Another man enlisted because he had relatives on both sides of his family who had fought in all American conflicts since the Revolutionary War. Occasionally the army would be gifted with a prize recruit like John Bangerd, who had served four years in the German army "and liked soldiers [sic] life." William G. Wilkinson spoke for 85 percent of the enlistees of the mid-1880s when he candidly admitted: "I had no particular reason, other than I wanted to be a soldier."[34]

The desire of these individuals to serve in peacetime, however, should not be confused with flag-waving patriotism, which was rarely a consideration. A Maryland recruit wrote: "As to my patriotic feelings, I can candidly say, I have none. I have never been blessed with the inspiration." The relatively few men who expressed a view of the matter defined it more in terms of a sense of obligation to the nation. George Neihaus, an Indianapolis, Indiana, native, demonstrated an uncommonly mature attitude when he expressed his motive for enlisting as "my desire to serve my country . . . many of my crowd of young men were getting into trouble, I wanted to avoid that." So did Sam Evans, a twenty-three-year old shoemaker from Philadelphia, who related: "I thought I should put some time in the service of my country, at the same time I needed the discipline." In an age when the majority of immigrants came to the United States not only to better their condition but to prove themselves worthy, contributing citizens, one German said: "I came over from Germany as a boy, and as I did not wish to be in the German Army. I nevertheless wanted a Military career and felt that since I came to make the United States my future home, I wished to serve her."[35]

At the bottom rung of the ladder was a class of men who joined for less noble reasons. One man candidly admitted: "every time I got spiflicated [drunk] I wanted to enlist." A black farmer from Monroe County, West Virginia, enlisted at age twenty-seven after "doin' wrong" drinking moonshine whiskey supplied by his neighbors. After his mother "whomped me twice," he followed the C & O Canal to

Cincinnati, where he joined the army. Druggist Joe Byers and his friend Murray, the son of a preacher, went on a drinking spree in Kansas City and, remorseful for their debauchery, joined the army. The conditions and hardships that they encountered in military life often caused them to regret their impetuous decision.[36]

Others resorted to the army after running afoul of the fairer sex. Frederick Wyllyams, another educated Englishman with a respectable background, had come to grief when he formed "a fatal alliance . . . while sewing his wild oats" in London, for which his family disowned him. Wyllyams came to America and immediately enlisted in the army. A chagrined Henry Hubman also resorted to the army rather than face his family after an extortion attempt by a promiscuous girl in Keokuk, Iowa. "I am not the first one that she has got into trouble," wrote Hubman. "She has not the least claim on me for money. . . . I will get even with her and her Brother if I have to serve in the Iowa Prison." In the wake of the affair, Hubman turned to alcohol in an effort to drown his misery, lamenting that "from the time I left Keokuk till I enlisted I did not draw one sober breath and fearfully I had to pay for it." In 1873 Irish-born Thomas P. Downing fled from home at age sixteen to hide in the army after impregnating a girl. Had he stayed home to face the consequences, he would have fared better than ending up in an unmarked grave along the Little Bighorn River in far-off Montana Territory.[37]

For some young men the army presented an alternative to a troubled home life. New York farm boy George H. Cranston may have overreacted after he and his father engaged in a heated altercation over milking the family cows. Cranston left home in a huff and enlisted, afterward informing his sister that "the wages of a common soldier are $100 for clothes a year and $18 a month. Now Gertrude do you blaim [sic] me for what I have done?" Another boy simply felt pushed out of the nest by a guardian who was anxious to see him leave. Other men found themselves in more serious circumstances with the law. In one instance, a judge in Syracuse, New York, gave a man accused of attempting to murder his wife the choice of going to the penitentiary or enlisting in the army. An outraged local newspaper labeled the bargain "a disgrace which should not be allowed is heaped upon the soldier's life." No less a figure than Elizabeth Custer recognized that soldiers joined the army to evade the law. "It often happened that the soldiers changed their names in enlisting, and sunk their identity in the ranks of our army; but sometimes even there an irate wife, who had been deserted in the States, found out her culprit husband, and compelled him to send her money out of his pay for her support." Evidently the practice happened frequently enough that she recalled hearing a marching cadence that went: "Left—left—left my wife and seven small children behind me."[38]

A survey of 415 prisoners admitted to the U.S. Military Prison at Fort Leavenworth in 1884–85 reported that 352 said they enlisted simply because they wanted to be soldiers, 32 as a consequence of drinking, 21 because they had been out of work, 6 as a result of family trouble, 1 to go west, 1 to work as a mechanic, and 1 to study as well as 1 who was "forced" to enlist, presumably by a judge.[39]

Army recruitment was conducted under the auspices of the Recruiting Service, a small bureau within the Adjutant General's Department. Headquartered in the Army Building at the corner of Houston and Greene Streets in New York City, it was commanded by a lieutenant colonel and organized into several geographical districts, each headed by a staff officer of the line functioning as superintendent over a general depot (training facility) within his assigned area. These officers, usually majors, were on temporary detached service from their regiments, during which they were under the direct command of the adjutant general.[40]

Depending on the type of station, whether it was operated by the General Recruiting Service or Mounted Recruiting Service, and current demand for replacements, officers were authorized to enlist men for only one branch or the other (general or mounted). By the 1870s, to effect greater efficiency and to attract more black men by making enlistment more convenient, segregated stations were discontinued in favor of universal recruitment to include the four segregated regiments. General Service recruiting stations usually operated full-time, because foot organizations were more numerous and hence had a greater demand for replacements. Recruiting was suspended periodically for the mounted service, however, and at times only for the black cavalry regiments, when additional men were not needed.

The Recruiting Service established stations, frequently referred to as "rendezvous" because they served as gathering points for recruits, in northern and midwestern population centers to take advantage of the greatest concentrations of potential enlistees. A typical example was the year 1875, when stations were found in Baltimore, Chicago, Cleveland, Indianapolis Jersey City, and St. Louis, along with five more in the state of New York at Albany, Brooklyn, Buffalo, and two in New York City. Seldom were rendezvous located in the states of the Deep South because of lingering antipathy. Consequently the majority of desirable black recruits during the 1870s and 1880s hailed from northern and former border states, particularly Maryland, the District of Columbia, Kentucky, and Tennessee.[41] A recruiting sergeant in Washington, D.C., attested to this when interviewed by a newspaper reporter in 1887. "We enlist quite a number of colored men," he said. "They make good soldiers too, and very seldom desert . . . we are glad to enlist them."[42] The locations of recruiting stations were not permanent, however, being shuffled about from time to time according to need and statistical results. For example, the army opened a short-lived station in San Antonio, Texas, in 1877 exclusively to provide men for the regiments within that military department. Left unsaid was that the Tenth Cavalry and both black infantry regiments were posted within the state, so the effort was undoubtedly aimed specifically at the local black population to maintain those units at full strength.[43]

Recruiting in the Division of the Pacific differed in some respects from the rest of the country. Because of the region's great distance from all the depots and the headquarters of the Recruiting Service itself, the adjutant general delegated authority to the division commander to conduct recruiting directly for the regiments stationed within his jurisdiction.[44] Rendezvous operated in five cities along the Pacific Coast in 1869, but within a few years that number fell to only two, San Francisco and Benicia, and remained so thereafter. The number of recruits enlisted in California and the Pacific Northwest remained relatively small throughout the era as a result of competition from a high demand for labor in the civilian market, particularly in the mining, farming, and timbering regions. As a result, supplemental drafts of recruits were routinely dispatched by rail from the depots in the States to San Francisco for distribution to the regiments.[45]

During the mid- to late 1880s, the Recruiting Service experienced moderate success with establishing offices in small cities, such as Detroit; Milwaukee; Davenport, Iowa; and Kansas City, Missouri. The opening of a rendezvous in Denver, Colorado, in 1884 was a sure indication that a discernible frontier had virtually disappeared. Augmenting those central rendezvous, recruiting parties circulated throughout the surrounding rural areas, sometimes operating temporary branch rendezvous in smaller towns on the theory that a better class of men might be obtained from those now more densely populated sections of the country. The effort was rewarded with only mixed results, however. Although the numbers of recruits proved disappointingly low, the adjutant general happily announced in 1890 that the quality of the men was "considerably above the general average" found in older metropolitan areas.[46]

The government rented buildings for use as recruiting stations and staffed them with a commissioned officer, one noncommissioned officer (usually a sergeant), and a couple of privates to drum up recruits and carry out basic functions at the station. Recruiting officers, either lieutenants or captains, were drawn from regiments and placed on detached service for two years as a reward for faithful service or meritorious conduct. Officers posted in the West welcomed these plum assignments as a departure from the isolation of frontier life, especially when the assignment was in proximity to relatives. The enlisted men at the stations belonged to either the General Service or the General Mounted Service, rather than line units, and were detailed from the nearest depot garrison. The men making up the detachments were chosen for their soldierly bearing, reliability, and general good conduct. Not infrequently, they were experienced soldiers with one or more prior enlistments.[47]

A New York newspaper reporter described a typical urban recruiting station:

> The outward insignia of such a station are not marked. Generally there is a small flag, the staff of which protrudes from a window. There may be a sign on the street. . . . On the side of the house may be tacked a printed handbill stating in a brief business-like way exactly what is wanted. Sometimes a soldier, perfect in tenue, with folded arms, may stand near the door as a kind of living sample of what is a well-to-do, comfortable, and contented man-at-arms.[48]

A typical recruiting station consisted of two or three small offices (one each for the officer, the sergeant, and perhaps a separate one for the use of the doctor), a bathroom, a sleeping room with a few bunks for the enlisted detachment and recruits, a storeroom, a kitchen, and a dining room.

For impressionable young men, the allure was difficult to resist. "I walked back and forth past that fluttering insignia," said one. "To me it was a symbol of Abraham Lincoln, whom I had been taught to consider as a god among men. I decided to inquire about this army business."[49] Twenty-year-old Ohioan William C. Slaper was out of work in September 1875, "and while walking along the street . . . I observed the sign 'Men Wanted,' in front of the United States Army Recruiting Station. Although I had passed that sign numberless times before, it never held any attraction for me until that morning. I stopped and read it. Then I wondered if they would take me as a soldier." A Baltimore youth had similar doubts when he saw an ad in the newspaper that read "'Wanted, 100 Men for U.S. Cavalry service out on the plains, . . . ,' so off I went as fast as I could to the point specified, very much afraid the 100 men would be procured before I could apply . . . I afterward found they were taking all that applied."[50]

Perley S. Eaton vividly remembered his initial greeting: "I went in and there sat at this desk was the recruiting Sargeant [sic]. And he says, well young man what can I do for you? I told him I wanted to enlist in the Cavalry. He looked at me a minute and said, what do you want join the army for? . . . That is about the toughest place in the U.S." But other recruiters were not so discouraging: just the opposite, as a recent immigrant from Ireland recalled: "The new arrivals were not attracted by the prospect of spending any great portion of their military terms in the dull routine duties . . . when enlisting, they had been told of many opportunities for active service 'out west.'" John Cox recounted that a glib sergeant assured him in glowing terms that "they would be sent right over to California after they enlisted."[51]

Once the prospective recruit confirmed his determination to enlist, either the sergeant or the officer questioned him more closely as to his age, place of residence, occupation, and habits, especially his propensity for drinking alcohol. "The inebriate presenting himself to a recruiting officer," wrote the editor of the *Army & Navy Journal*, "will admit that he drinks, but avers that he never does it to excess, that he has never had the delirium tremens. Knowing that in our country there are but comparatively few men who never drink, the recruiting officer after satisfying himself of the unimpaired physical condition of the applicant, enlists him." Joining the army in 1882, William B. Jett "later discovered that while this stock question must be answered in the negative, that after enlistment the soldier could drink all he wanted to just so he was not drunk when called to duty." One youth played the fool by accepting a dare proposed by a shady stranger with whom he had been drinking at a saloon in St. Louis, Missouri. Seeking out a recruiting office he said: "I hardly knowing what I was doing told him I would do it . . . and while they were examining me, he stepped out and that is the last I seen of him, but I was in for it and have to make the best of what I can."[52]

In addition to sobriety, regulations traditionally stipulated that any man applying for the first time be free, white, single, and between the ages of twenty-one and thirty-five years, though an exception was made for the acceptance of married men during time of war. In the wake of the 1863 Emancipation Proclamation, at a time when demand for manpower peaked in the North, the army had somewhat relaxed its rules, eliminating the race restriction and lowering the minimum legal age for enlistment without parental consent to eighteen. Minors younger than age eighteen were required to present written consent by a parent or guardian, a rule frequently ignored.[53] But the army appropriation act of March 3, 1869, mandating the consolidation into twenty-five regiments, changed the minimum age without consent back to twenty-one. Thus for the remainder of the era the majority of first-time enlistees were in their early to mid-twenties. Whereas boys as young as twelve (some were actually younger) could and did serve as musicians during the war, the army revised the minimum age, with consent, for drummers and buglers to sixteen in 1864. In ensuing years some officers argued in favor of once again lowering the minimum age for musicians, claiming that to be successful at the art required instruction at an earlier age, but it remained sixteen through the era of the Indian Wars.[54]

The physical standards for recruits varied from time to time during the period, in compliance with general orders, and seem to have been rather inconsistently applied by recruiting officers. In fact, prior to 1871 the only requirement was that applicants be at least five feet three inches tall, except musicians, who for many years could be enlisted at virtually any age below eighteen regardless of stature. For a period of about three years, 1871–74, the minimum height was increased to five feet six inches as one means of meeting a congressional mandate to reduce the overall strength of the army to thirty thousand men and at the same time improve the physical quality of soldiers. But in December 1874, when the demand for recruits was greater, the rules were again modified to stipulate a minimum height of only five feet four inches and for the first time established weight parameters between one hundred and twenty and one hundred and eighty pounds for infantry and artillery soldiers. Cavalry recruits were to stand between five feet five and five feet ten inches and weigh no more than one hundred and fifty-five pounds.[55]

Beginning in the late 1860s and continuing thereafter, the adjutant general, in cooperation with the superintendent of the Recruiting Service, made increasingly concerted efforts to tighten the controls governing the acceptance of army recruits. Their aim was to improve the initial screening out of undesirables in order to reduce both the illegal enlistment of minors and the number of early desertions. The adjutant general announced in 1876 that these measures "have secured for the Army a superior class of men." When William Slaper presented himself for enlistment that year, he was impressed that his "examination was a very rigid one, because out of ten applicants that morning, but two were accepted, I being one of them." These measures (some of which are detailed later) eventually had a beneficial effect: official statistics showed that the army rejected more than 73 percent of the 309,060 men who applied for enlistment between 1880 and 1891.[56]

Some abuses of the system nevertheless continued. Even though regulations enjoined recruiting officers to make every effort to ascertain an applicant's true age, in practice that factor may not have been critical, depending on the current need for recruits and the earnestness of the applicant's desire to serve. As late as 1880 the editor of the *Army & Navy Journal* pointed out:

> The officers at the recruiting stations do not feel sufficient interest in obtaining good men . . . they wish naturally to make the best show they can in numbers, and a great many are taken who are entirely unfit for the service. . . . Recruits are

frequently sent from the recruiting station . . . a thousand miles to Columbus or New York and from there to San Francisco, only to be discharged as minors. This is a useless waste of public money.[57]

While undergoing questioning by the recruiting sergeant, one man admitted he was a month short of being twenty-one, "but the sergeant insisted that I surely looked older than the necessary legal demand. He summoned a lieutenant, and this man likewise expressed confidence in my full attainment of manhood . . . I suddenly grew a year older." A young Danish immigrant related that a private of the recruiting detachment "talked me into joining the Army notwithstanding the fact that I was only 17 years old . . . I was supposed to be 21, but he told me that didn't matter just tell the Officer you are 21. . . . I looked to be all of that." However, the army alone was not to blame for illegal enlistments. In many instances, underage boys such as Francis Johnson Kennedy arrived at the rendezvous with the intention of deceiving the recruiter. Kennedy later confessed: "I did not give my full name, I was too young and I went by the name of Francis Johnson." A young black man, Barney McKay, enlisted illegally under the surname "McDougal" in 1881 but looked back upon it years later as "merely a boyish prank."[58]

Official birth records were practically nonexistent during the latter part of the nineteenth century. Only a few states and cities had established any sort of systematic recordation, and even those were imperfect and not readily accessible by modern standards. Some families followed the practice of recording births and marriages in family Bibles, while others provided the information to churches through baptismal records. Half a century after his stint in the army, Bernard S. Bivenour, formerly of the First Cavalry, confessed: "I enlisted under alias of Henry Wilson to hide from the law for thumping a fellow on account of a young lady." Verifying the actual identity and age of an individual was difficult at best and relied heavily on his physical appearance and the officer's judgment. Adjutant General Edward D. Townsend grumbled with frustration in 1877: "It is hardly possible, in many cases, to discover the exact age of a man near his majority, and with the utmost vigilance, officers may be easily deceived by such men. . . . it is an easy matter for a soldier to procure affidavits and testimony utterly unreliable, yet bearing the appearance of truth, as to their age, parentage, &c." A survey of the rolls for the Seventh Cavalry in 1876, for example, revealed that at least eighty-six men serving in the ranks at that time had enlisted under assumed names. Regardless of the reasons for adopting an alias, concealing one's true identity could result in tragic consequences. Veteran James B. Kincaid spoke to the possible consequences of adopting a false identity: "Many a young man enlisted in the army under an assumed name, thinking he could keep it from his family, little thinking what he would have to face on the western frontier, and many of them left their bones to bleach on the plains or sleep in a nameless grave and their whereabouts will forever remain a mystery to their parents."[59]

Soldiers later discovered to have enlisted fraudulently by being underage or for some other reason were discharged from the army by special order, thus sacrificing all pay and allowances due at that time. The money normally paid honorably discharged soldiers for return travel and food to reach their place of enlistment also was withheld, forcing the men to be responsible for their own expenses.[60]

The term of enlistment had traditionally been five years, although that had been reduced to three for infantry in 1863 in an attempt to attract more men during the darkest days of the war. When Congress directed that the army be reorganized and consolidated in 1869, however, the required term was restored to five years for all branches. That seemed a long time to a young man like Eddie Matthews, who was surprised to learn that the regulations had changed only a few months earlier: "I . . . went down to the Recruiting Office for the purpose of enlisting in the regular Cavalry for 3 years, but found out that they were only taking men for 5 years." After reconsidering a few more days, and having no prospects for a job, he felt compelled to sign on anyway.[61]

Having determined that a man was suitable, the recruiting sergeant or officer invited the applicant to return to the office at a specified time to undergo a physical examination: "In the meantime the sergeant is speculating upon the amount to be realized from the sale of the citizen's clothes now on the young man's back." Commissioned army surgeons performed such examinations when circumstances permitted, though in many instances local civilian doctors were contracted to perform that service. Hygiene being what it was in the nineteenth century, with bathing weekly or less frequently among the working classes, the applicant for enlistment was directed to fill a tub in the bathroom at the rendezvous and bathe. Afterward, standing completely nude in the presence of both the doctor and the recruiting officer,

> he is weighed and measured and his body is carefully inspected. If he is flat-footed, and therefore a poor walker, if he has ingrowing nails, if he is troubled with varicose veins, if one of his joints is stiff, if hernia has claimed him for a victim, if his lungs are weak . . . he is sent away as unfit . . . and these are only a few of the causes which may lead to such a result. That upon which most men fail to come up to the required standard is the power of vision, which is rigidly tested.[62]

One man remembered that the doctor then asked him to "walk around on my heels and toes" and perform a series of physical maneuvers resembling "the freaks of a half-grown monkey after which he is bid to put on his clothes, and [having passed the examination] is told to hold up his right hand. He is then sworn in, without even understanding either the nature or words of the oath he had just taken." Nevertheless, one German-speaking recruit was impressed with the presence of the recruiting officer as "about the finest looking soldier I had ever seen."[63]

Once he was verbally sworn and had signed the Oath of Enlistment (or had his mark witnessed), the recruit was officially a soldier, whereupon he was "issued one uniform and one set of underclothing," according to Charles Maurer. A soldier writing to the *Army & Navy Journal* complained that recruiting sergeants were largely unconcerned with the fit of the garments. Taking the neophyte to the storeroom, the sergeant began grabbing items from the various stacks, at the same time instructing him: "Put this on, and this and this; poor devil, only five feet six, pants three sizes too large for him, blouse ___, and boots, great God! What boots, number 10s; shirt and cap to correspond . . . he naturally looks around for a looking glass. What does he see? The reflection of a half-grown boy in clothes large enough for the Cardiff Giant."[64]

In most instances soldiers were not permitted to retain any civilian clothing. Immediately outfitting enlistees in uniform was an initial step in the psychological process of equalizing the status of men from varied backgrounds and instilling a degree of cohesion among them. They were no longer civilians; they now belonged to the army. On a more practical level, the uniform visually distinguished soldiers from civilians, a factor calculated to discourage early desertion from the recruiting station by making it difficult for deserters readily to blend into the general populace. Then there was the question of how to dispose of the personal clothing. James B. Frew chose to pack up his things and mail them home to his father. However, in another instance when a recruit timidly asked the sergeant if he might send his clothing to a friend, the sergeant tersely responded: "'No, . . . roll up them togs, and hand them to me. Go and get your dinner.' Meantime the South street Jew comes, the clothes are held up for his inspection, the bargain made, the money pocketed, and the sergeant sits himself down to wait patiently for the next victim." Taking advantage of "fresh fish," as recruits were known, in this manner was a widespread practice. Enlisting at Louisville, Kentucky in 1870, recruit George S. Raper was handed a uniform twice his size, "and the sergeant, being a good-natured sort of a cuss hating to put any unnecessary work on us, gathered up all of our citizen clothes and took them away and sold them. I have often wondered if it was just absent mindedness [sic] that prevented him from 'whacking up' [settling] with us."[65]

Newly recruited men remained at the station for a period of a few days up to a couple of weeks until enough men, usually five to ten or more, accumulated to justify their transfer to the appropriate recruiting depot. A few like Daniel Haley, who joined at Buffalo, New York, in 1878, immediately had misgivings—he deserted from the rendezvous only five days after enlisting. William B. Jett, son of a devout Episcopalian father, was not favorably impressed with "two tousled headed, dirty looking Germans, who gave me my first distaste for the service. When shown up the stairs where the rest of the recruits were, they hailed me with 'Hello Pard, let's sell your citizen's clothes and we will all go around and get a drink on the money.' I told them I did not treat people who asked me to." Jett also secretly wished he were a civilian again, yet he stayed. As the recruits awaited transfer, members of the station detachment introduced those having no prior experience to the basics of military discipline and courtesy. Living conditions at the station, meanwhile, were Spartan. At those times when the number of recruits exceeded the accommodations at the station, the anxious recruits were put up in a cheap local hotel.[66]

In addition to designated recruiting rendezvous in cities, every military post also served in that capacity, though to a lesser degree. Each post commander was required to assign an officer, usually the adjutant, for collateral duty as recruiting officer for the purpose of reenlisting soldiers of the garrison as well as taking outside enlistments. Although soldiers reenlisting from the local garrison posed no problem, post recruiting officers nevertheless had to be discriminating when considering civilians who presented themselves. Previously discharged soldiers were expected to have their certificates in hand as evidence of prior faithful service and acceptable character. Yet some civilians joined the service simply to obtain free transportation to the West and subsequently deserted for the goldfields or other more profitable ventures. A Seventh Cavalryman claimed that "a number of men after the war, especially in the cavalry, enlisted for gain and a great many of them . . . to get a couple of good horses and light out with them. . . . Captain Frederick W. Benteen . . . lost no less than seven private horses during his service. . . . the officers got so as they had to chain them to the post in camp in order to save them."[67]

In an effort "to prevent deserters at large and men who have been discharged with bad character from imposing themselves again upon the service," the army implemented a measure in 1874 denying officers at the company and post levels the authority to execute original enlistments without special authority from the Adjutant General's Office. Such a request prompted the adjutant general to direct his headquarters clerks to review the enlistment registers and unit muster rolls to ascertain whether or not the applicant had any prior service and, if so, the nature of his character as recorded by his former company commander. The delay, meanwhile, afforded the recruiting officer several days during which he could observe the applicant's conduct and demeanor. Still, the order had virtually no effect on first-time applications at regular recruiting stations. Despite the reforms, the problem with enlisting or reenlisting undesirables persisted throughout the period because inadequate records systems, both military and civilian, made identifying individuals and checking their backgrounds problematical at best.[68]

Men enlisting for the first time at a post or directly in a regiment had a somewhat different experience from those joining at a regular recruiting station. One youth, John Stotts, left home a year after the Civil War and journeyed to St. Louis, where he learned that the Third Infantry had arrived en route to stations in Kansas and the Indian Territory. The strength of the regiment had declined to barely more than two hundred officers and men by the close of the war. Accordingly several of its companies had to be completely reconstituted by the enlistment of new men. Stotts encountered a seventeen-year-old member of the regiment on the street, who encouraged him to enlist in his company. "I found their quarters there," Stotts related, "and wanting recruits they were sadly in need of men to fill up the Regiment. . . . I went to the adjutant's office and was accepted and was wearing the Blue in one hour after enlisting." Just a few days later the Third marched through St. Louis to take a steamer up the Missouri River bound for Fort Leavenworth, Kansas. Unlike most new recruits, Stotts instantly experienced the thrill of belonging to a unit: "That day when the whole Regiment fell into line and they marched through the City . . . was the first time I had saw all my Regiment together, with the Regimental Band of 46 pieces, Drum Major leading them in full regalia, colors flying we made a big sensation for the onlookers as we wended our way to the wharf."[69]

Fourteen-year-old Louis E. Hills, unemployed and trying to make his way back home to Wisconsin, happened on the Seventh Cavalry's camp at Memphis, Tennessee, shortly before the regiment's transfer to Dakota Territory. Some officers coaxed him into enlisting, even though he was underage, recording him as a musician and falsifying his age as sixteen. After a physical examination by the surgeon, "I was given a blue suit of clothes, very much too large for me," the five-feet-four-inch Hills said, "and a white cow pony named Frank . . . also a bugle and a large revolver." With that he was suddenly a cavalryman.[70]

German-born Emil A. Bode was adrift and hungry on the streets of New Orleans in 1877 when just before noon he came upon a huge granite-walled edifice occupied by the Sixteenth Infantry. Entering through the front gate, he proceeded to a barracks within and was directed upstairs to see the first sergeant. The sergeant critically eyed Bode head to foot, inquired as to whether he had eaten, then invited him to dine in the mess hall. Bode was only too happy to oblige and was afterward taken to see the captain for oral examination, which he passed. Bode recounted: "I and another forlorn individual were taken to a small room where the doctor, a clerk, and the hospital steward were waiting. We were now ordered to dress a la Adam and Eve and put through different maneuvers. The body and mouth were examined, the breast sounded, and the eyes—taking squints with first one then the other eye at charts with different colors and letters. I was declared passed, the other [recruit] rejected." In compliance with the 1874 order cited previously, Bode's "descriptive list and surgeon's certificate was sent to Washington, D. C. for approval before the oath to the flag could be administered." He was sworn in by his captain five days later and "clothed from Uncle Sam's clothing store. I was now a soldier."[71]

Those enlisting at posts, however, were not necessarily destined to serve in a unit stationed at that particular location. Depending on whether one of the resident companies had a vacancy, and upon whether the recruit appeared to be good soldier material, the adjutant might be inclined to retain the man. Other times companies of the same regiment posted elsewhere might have a greater need for replacements, or men sometimes requested that they be assigned to a particular unit as a condition of enlistment. The adjutant would honor such requests when the particular company's aggregate strength was below the legal maximum. An example was Joseph Lehman, who enlisted at Fort D. A. Russell, Wyoming Territory, in 1882 and was granted permission to serve in Company C, Fourth Infantry, then in garrison at Fort Fred Steele, farther west along the Union Pacific Railroad. Just what his motive may have been for requesting the assignment is not known. Sometimes members of nearby garrisons struck up friendships among local townsmen and encouraged them to enlist in the company, or the unit may have had a reputation for being a "good feeder" and generally treating the men well. Receiving regular—if meager—pay, decent food, and having a roof over their head, in addition to sharing life among congenial comrades, could be strong inducements for young men in frontier regions to enlist.

Ami F. Mulford's experience at Fort Leavenworth was similar to Bode's. Because he arrived late in the day, however, the adjutant summoned a sergeant to take the prospective recruit to his company's quarters for the night, where he was allowed to wash up and was fed a supper of mush and molasses, his least favorite dish. When Mulford hesitatingly asked whether mush was served often in the army, the sergeant saw an opportunity to have some fun at the green kid's expense. The sergeant enthusiastically replied that during all of his twenty-one years in the service, he had eaten mush once a day on average. Recoiling at that unpleasant prospect, Mulford further quizzed the sergeant if it was served to units on the frontier, to which the sergeant responded emphatically: "No! I heard that they once issued an order to that effect, but the men threatened to mutiny, and since that time they have not dared to mention the subject west of the Missouri River." Still uneasy, Mulford then hesitatingly inquired as to which regiment he might join on the frontier where he would not be subjected to mush. "The Seventh Cavalry!" boomed the sergeant. "The crack Cavalry regiment of the whole army! . . . They are equal to ten thousand cow-boys! They are terrors!" Mulford, now assured of a future in the army without mush, confidently responded: "Sargent [sic], if I enlist I am going to the Seventh Cavalry, I want no mush on my plate!" After his first night sleeping in a barracks, young Mulford was conducted back to the adjutant, who examined, passed, and signed him up for the Seventh Cavalry. "Now," he declared, "I am a soldier, and at once draw a uniform and a sutler's check!" Obtaining a pass to go into Leavenworth City, he "paid [a visit] to our Uncle, the pawn broker and dealer in worn clothing etc., and a new suit of clothes is soon exchanged for a very small sum of cash."[72]

Meanwhile, back at the rendezvous, after a few days of anxious anticipation, the recruits were told that the time for transfer to a recruiting depot had arrived. One man's experience on the day of departure was undoubtedly typical:

> He gets a knapsack, haversack, and canteen, and is told to pack his traps and get himself ready to go to the general recruiting depot. He looks first at the knapsack, then at the haversack wishing that the latter was a little larger, so that he could stuff his overcoat and blanket into it, but finding that impossible he tumbles them altogether in the knapsack, and supposes himself ready to travel. The sergeant comes along . . . asks him what he means, and orders him to repack it, and according to regulations, and, of course, without an explanation by the sergeant . . . the sergeant becomes furious, and commences to use lan-

guage such as the man probably never heard before . . . he is made to pack, unpack, and pack until he is almost crazy, and is finally made to throw it across his shoulders, fall in, and march for the railroad depot.[73]

The former soldiers among the party knew what was coming, but the greenhorns were decidedly apprehensive about the future as a short-tempered noncom, in an exercise akin to herding cats, accompanied them to the railroad station for the trip to the depot. No matter who they were, or what they had been, their lives were about to become radically different.

CHAPTER 2

"We Are Kept Pretty Busy"

Life at the Recruiting Depot

Green recruits typically anticipated that they would be going immediately to the Great West beyond the Mississippi, finding there excitement in plenty—perhaps fighting Indians—certainly adventure enough in some form to satisfy a young man's thirst for experiencing the world beyond his current horizon. If nothing else, army life would provide the security of a steady income and a roof over one's head until something better came along. Before any of that happened, however, most rookies were surprised to learn that the army had a detour planned for them—to the recruiting depot. Later generations of Americans would refer to such places as "basic training centers" or "boot camps"; but no matter what they were called, their purpose was the same: to transform civilians into soldiers.

At the end of the Civil War the regular army maintained only two principal recruiting depots, one for the mounted service, including light artillery, at Carlisle Barracks, Pennsylvania, and a general depot for all other branches at Fort Columbus on Governors Island in New York Harbor. The superintendent of the General Recruiting Service, at General Sherman's direction, subsequently established two additional depots, one for foot troops at Newport Barracks, Kentucky, to be in closer proximity to populations potentially yielding a high number of black recruits, and a western depot at Fort Leavenworth, Kansas, serving the needs of all three combat arms, particularly the cavalry and light artillery batteries.[1]

When the old facilities at Carlisle Barracks proved to be inadequate for the task posed by ten regiments of cavalry, the army relocated the Cavalry Depot to St. Louis Barracks early in 1871. The decision to abandon Carlisle depot was all the more logical because virtually all cavalrymen were destined for assignment west of the Mississippi. At the same stroke, the Recruiting Service closed Newport Barracks, along with the short-lived depot at Fort Leavenworth, to consolidate the instruction of mounted service recruits at St. Louis. With Newport being phased out, some infantry recruits were redirected for a time to St. Louis, in addition to those for cavalry. Nevertheless, it soon became obvious that the city's railroad network and burgeoning industrial district surrounding the depot constricted the amount of open space necessary for conducting mounted drill. Therefore in 1878 the Mounted Recruiting Service moved its depot to Jefferson Barracks, a venerable antebellum post a few miles south of the city, where it remained until well into the next century.[2]

In fall 1875 the adjutant general named Columbus Barracks in Ohio as a depot for the General Recruiting Service, at the same time ordering training at the temporary Newport subdepot to be discontinued effective April 17, 1876. Like Jefferson Barracks, Columbus would continue to operate as a primary recruit rendezvous and training facility well beyond 1890.[3]

The last of the original depots to be axed was the ancient Fort Columbus, where "an immense amount of military material is stored . . . dilapidated trains of battery wagons, artillery in various forms, and acres of shells . . . erected in uniform and numberless pyramids . . . [and] muskets were stacked from the floors to the ceilings." In 1878 the recruiting depot was moved to Davids Island, situated in Long Island Sound about a mile and a half from New Rochelle, New York. Like Columbus Barracks, which served the more westerly regions, Davids Island was designated as a general service depot to collect recruits for all the dismounted branches of service from rendezvous in the northeastern states. Governors Island thereafter served as headquarters for the Military Division of the Atlantic and was home to only a small artillery garrison.[4]

The small numbers of men enlisting specifically for the Signal Corps were an exception to normal practice. These men, usually possessing a higher level of education than the norm, underwent written examination unique to that branch of service. If recruits passed both that and the usual physical examination, they were sent directly to the Signal School at Fort Myer, Virginia, for basic and specialized training.[5]

The depots were arranged much like other eastern military posts of the time. One young cavalry recruit arriving at Carlisle Barracks in spring 1866 described it as "beautifully laid out on an elevated level, the buildings are of stone, one story high and are so built as to form a square parade, with flag-staff in the centre guarded by a parked battery of artillery." New York's Governors Island encompassed about sixty-five acres and was situated in the East River off the tip of lower Manhattan. "Castle William, at the western end of the Island," observed a recruit, "is a circular structure, pierced with three tiers of embrasures. . . . Fort Columbus . . . was on the westerly side of the Island on raised ground, a square-built, old-style fortress . . . through the deep sally port one entered the interior . . . having a sodded parade ground, with quarters surrounding its four sides." Newport Barracks, situated along the banks of the Ohio River, "with its high stone fence, and big sombre buildings [three-story barracks], had a prison-like appearance," according to recruit John Cox, who arrived there in 1872.[6]

Although the physical appearances of the depots may have outwardly resembled other forts, the garrisons were not composed of line units. Instead the troops belonged to the General Service or, in the case of the Cavalry Depot, the General Mounted Service. A field-grade officer temporarily drawn from the line commanded each depot and was assisted by a small staff composed of a lieutenant serving as adjutant, another who functioned as the acting quartermaster and commissary officer, one or two medical officers, a hospital steward, and an ordnance sergeant. One or two officers, either captains or lieutenants detached from line units, commanded each recruit company.[7]

One company at each depot was termed the "permanent party," described by one officer as "a picked body of men comprising old soldiers or young ones of exceptionally fine physique and intelligence." The noncommissioned officers served as drill instructors and were detailed periodically to supervise recruiting parties at the designated stations.[8] Representative of the veteran depot men was William Kane, a prewar dragoon who continued in service as a sergeant in the regular cavalry during the Civil War. Upon entering his fourth enlistment in

1867, Kane was assigned to the permanent party at Carlisle and later transferred to St. Louis when the Cavalry Depot was relocated in that city. He spent his fifth term as a member of the Seventh Cavalry, surviving the Battle of the Little Bighorn only because he was left behind sick at the base camp on the Yellowstone River. His sixth and last enlistment, at age forty-three, found him once again a private in the permanent party at the Cavalry Depot. With five service chevrons on the sleeves of his dress coat, Private Kane must have indeed seemed a demigod to the fresh recruits twenty years or more his junior.[9]

The men belonging to permanent cadres fully appreciated their status and went out of their way to present an exceptionally natty appearance by having their uniforms either tailored to a form-fit or completely custom-made. That the garrison soldiers created the desired impression was not lost on the recruits. Writing from Carlisle to his parents, one explained: "You can't get in the permanent Troop here without you have been in the Army before. I would not go in it if I could. It would almost take your wages to keep clean and dress like some of them do."[10]

Apart from maintaining the spit-and-polish appearance and soldierly deportment expected of members of the permanent party, the duty was comparatively soft in contrast to that in line units, particularly those posted on the frontier. While small detachments were assigned on rotation to staff the various recruiting stations, the rest of the members served at the depot, where they ostensibly were responsible for assisting with training recruits and carrying out the routine garrison duties. In practice, however, that happened infrequently because the recruits provided an almost constant source of manpower for the necessary guard and fatigue details, cook's police, and other tasks. "They are having nice times now," a recruit at Carlisle observed, "but soon as the recruits leave here they will have hard work. Will have to clean all the horses and stables as well as make all the garden in the summer time." General Service noncoms not infrequently made a career of the duty by requesting the assignment upon reenlistment or simply reenlisting time and again in the same company at the depot.[11]

Arriving by train "about five in the afternoon we reached Carlisle and marched out to the barracks, situated about a mile from the station," a recruit recalled of his introduction to the depot. "As we entered the garrison and marched past the guard-house we were greeted with cries of 'fresh fish,' 'greenies.'" The noncommissioned officer in charge of a "batch" of recruits, as they were commonly known, reported his party to the post adjutant, one of whom, recalled Frank E. Woodward, kept the "recruits waiting for some time while he continued his inspection of a game of lawn tennis." After turning over the recruits' enlistment papers and descriptive rolls, his job now finished, the noncom returned to his station. The new men were then marched, or what passed as marching, to one of the company barracks for their first night at the depot.[12]

Upon entering the squad room, one recruit was somewhat surprised to find "the sergeant in charge of Company B's quarters was asleep . . . he appeared to feel a trifle ugly on account of being disturbed from his nap and eyed us with little favor. On account of the construction of his eyes he was able to look the three of us in the face at the same time." After visually sizing them up with a disdainful glare, the sergeant impressed upon the recruits that strict obedience was to be the inviolate rule from that moment forward. Approaching to within a few inches of one intimidated soul's nose, the sergeant blurted: "'You hear me!' . . . I said that I did. 'Shut up!' he yelled frantically. 'Don't speak until you are told to.'" Thus the regulars' hallmark reputation for discipline became stark reality.[13]

Formed in some semblance of ranks for their initial roll call, a batch of raw recruits presented a sorry appearance, according to an observer at Davids Island. "Some of the men are in uniforms that have not been fitted by the post tailor; some are in ragged citizens clothes, the coats with frayed edges, the trousers sprung at the knee, wrinkled at the heel, and not long enough by several inches, the hats greasy and worn at the edges, the shoes broken at the toes, while a few are so sleek and well clad as to suggest that poverty is not always the author of soldiers."[14]

After a generally rude introduction set the tone of discipline, the recruits were told to select unoccupied bunks for themselves in the dormitory. "This room [at Newport Barracks]," reported the post surgeon, "has bunks for the accommodation of 120 men. It now contains about 100 men, who are, seemingly, comfortable. It is only when more than 200 men are packed into this room . . . covering the floor like red-herrings in a box, that discontent becomes irrepressible."[15]

The primitive wooden bunks, wide enough for two men to lie down side by side, stood two or even three tiers high and were arranged in rows down either side of the long room. Surgeon J. H. Brill admitted that he did not bother to inspect the recruit quarters at Governors Island because one might "as well make an examination of a pig-sty. They disregard every modern notion of hygiene; they are dark, damp, windy and cold." One of Surgeon Brill's colleagues lamented that "it is sad to contemplate the feelings of a young recruit . . . fresh from feather beds, butter, eggs, and pumpkin-pies . . . assigned to little else than standing room in a dormitory." Recruit Eddie Matthews, a nineteen-year-old from Westminster, Maryland, confessed that he "sat down in the room and read awhile and cried awhile. I could not help it although there were about half a dozen soldiers in the room. Of course, some laughed and said I was homesick which is true." Conversely, young men who had not previously had life so easy, like German immigrant Michael Vetter, reacted differently. "I am very well and satisfied," he wrote to his brother, "and everything makes me lots of fun."[16]

Settling into quarters, each man drew a bed sack of cotton drilling nearly seven feet long. Recruit Charles Kolarik recalled that his party at Jefferson Barracks "was marched to the stable with a bed sack to fill with hay and carry back to quarters on our backs, no sheets or pillows, four . . . three-quarter by 3 inch slats for springs is what our beds consisted of." The men then were marched to the quartermaster storeroom to receive a blanket each and an initial or supplemental issue of clothing, depending upon whether they had been outfitted at the recruiting station. "A cross old sergeant . . . pitched the clothes to us . . . without regard to the size of clothes or men," recalled a recruit at Newport Barracks. An 1876 enlistee, Fred Munn, scoffed that "my uniform would have fitted a 200 pound man. The cap, called a 'nosebag' was the same style used in the Civil War." According to another recruit, his "pants would have made the fortune of a comedian. They were about three inches too short . . . when I coaxed them down towards my shoes there was another difficulty. There was absolutely no waist to them. So I had to compromise by leaving them in a neutral position." Besides the poor fit of the outer garments, one man complained, the coarse army-issue underclothing "including socks, were of the roughest material and 'stickers' abounded in their warp and woof . . . and the brogan shoes were of the stiffest leather." Because the army did not provide pillows to troops until the mid-1880s, recruits often were advised to draw an overcoat, even during warm seasons, to be rolled up and used for that purpose.[17]

The final insult of the day came before supper when the sergeants informed the recruits that the depot issued neither eating utensils nor the material necessary for maintaining a strictly enforced neat appearance. Until late in the era each man was obligated to buy the required articles, and the price was deducted from his first pay. Accordingly, wrote one recruit, "each man had to draw [$]3.00 worth of Settler [sutler] checks to buy the little necessaries to keep clean and neat. You have to get a quart cup, tin plate, knife and fork, and spoon, blacking brush, p[ai]r of white gloves, towel and soap, plate powder to clean your [belt] plate and buttons, a little thread . . . for . . . [$]2.30." Neglecting to buy a brush with which to clean his brass uniform buttons, recruit Matthews elected instead to put his own toothbrush to double duty. With their first day in the service almost at an end, the recruits, shiny new utensils in hand, were hurried to the mess hall for a meager supper, as one man recalled, consisting of "about a quart of an infusion, called tea, and a slice of bread."[18]

Once quartered, the new recruits became acquainted with the individuals with whom they would share the next several weeks, if not months. According to one man, his fellow recruits included "men without the least knowledge of the English language . . . another had to leave on account of a girl . . . men of intellect and stupidity, sons of congressmen and sons of farmers, rich and poor, men who are willing to work and can't find it . . . men who are looking for work and hope that they never find any; gamblers, thieves, cutthroats, drunkards, men who were formerly commissioned officers." Another wrote of a new comrade: "My bunk or bed fellow is 37 years old . . . and from his appearance I judged he had seen better days, he seemed to be a gentleman, more so than any of the rest." Henry Hubman may have been more fortunate than most when he made friends with "a very nice young man from Kentucky having a first class education being a teacher in a High School before he had to enlist. He . . . got into a row about a girl, knocked a fellow down and being half drunk almost killed him. He would have got the Penitentiary, but got away and enlisted before they could arrest him." Nevertheless, each man in this conglomerate of humanity, thrown together for the first time, began adjusting to barracks life. According to an experienced officer, "the fact that practically he is never alone is soon borne in upon him and it is one of the actual hardships of an enlisted man which it is most difficult for him to finally accept and eventually become accustomed to." Recruit Charles White vividly remembered the scene: "Our barrack building was resounding constantly with profanity and obscenity. Noise, roughhouse, brawling, actual fighting, was the usual condition. To me this was not exactly congenial, but it was new and interesting."[19]

During their first morning at the depot, recruits were placed temporarily in the lowliest of the companies, one composed of the unexamined men, and those previously rejected and awaiting discharge. Within the following two days the new arrivals were subjected to another "minute and critical" physical examination by depot doctors for the purpose of further screening out enlistees deemed to be physically or otherwise unsuitable. Even so, some recruits who should have been disqualified prior to being sworn slipped through the screening to enter the ranks.[20]

Just how thorough the medical officers may have been in making these subsequent examinations, at least early on, is questionable. In 1871 the post surgeon at Fort Laramie, Wyoming Territory, complained that "a considerable number of the recruits recently sent here are unfit for service, many of them being affected with incurable organic diseases for which some of them (under other names) have been already discharged." When two men deserted from nearby Fort Fetterman two years later, one was described as being "rather stupid looking," while the other was "cross-eyed and right eyelid hanging down." Certainly the degree of competence and conscientiousness varied from one doctor to another; but once a recruit fell into the army's clutches, it was reluctant to release him. As time passed, the army came to realize that it was doing itself no favors by retaining defective men. Early desertions, discipline problems, unreliability, and guardhouses filled to overflowing gradually caused the service to be more discerning in its selection of men. That the effort bore favorable results was expressed by the adjutant general in 1878: "The great care with which the inspection of recruits is made, and the practice of discharging at the depot men who develop disease or vicious character, instead of sending them to regiments, continues to result in keeping up a high standard in the ranks."[21]

Depot garrisons were organized into several provisional "companies of instruction," with aspiring musicians, styled "music boys," grouped apart for special training. The permanent party usually was designated

Company A (or had no letter), although sometimes depots had two such units lettered differently. A veteran said that "there were about one hundred recruits in the mob to which I was attached, it being designated 'C' troop, and formed one of the three troops or companies into which the whole number of recruits was divided, the other troops being 'A' and 'B,' respectively. The garrison at Carlisle consisted of one full company of cavalry, known as the 'permanent troop,' filled up from time to time with men selected from among the recruits at the garrison."[22]

During the late 1860s, when a great many enlistees had prior volunteer experience during the Civil War, such men (then termed "select recruits") underwent only refresher training to bring them up to regular army standards of deportment and drill before being sent to regiments. Experienced men credited with one or more prior enlistments in the regulars later were immediately segregated into a special company of "disposable recruits," where they would remain for a short time performing guard and other routine duties until transferred to permanent units. It was not uncommon for ad hoc instructors to be drawn not only from the permanent party but also from these transient veterans while at the depots. New men initially learned the basics of the school of the soldier in so-called awkward squads of only four, necessitating large numbers of experienced soldiers to teach the scores of recruits arriving almost constantly. Such duty was not looked upon with much favor by old soldiers, who simply wanted to get back to line outfits as soon as possible. One of those snared for the duty was second-term Private Green Settle, a twenty-nine-year-old Kentuckian who reenlisted at Jefferson Barracks in 1888 and was immediately "put to drilling recruits which tries the souls of men." A former Third Infantryman, Lafayette Schall, traveled to Ohio to visit his parents following his discharge at Fort Custer, Montana Territory. When he reenlisted at Columbus Barracks shortly thereafter, Schall, a former corporal standing nearly six feet tall, was spotted as an ideal candidate for depot recruiting duty and was quickly assigned to the General Service Infantry.[23]

Only after parties arrived from various points were black recruits formally segregated from other recruits and placed in separate companies designated "colored infantry" or "colored cavalry." These men may have received less favorable treatment, as suggested in a comment by an 1869 white enlistee at Carlisle Barracks who mentioned that "the barracks are full . . . no place to put any men unless in huts. The Colored Troops are in tents now."[24] The available evidence leaves it unclear whether black or white noncoms trained black recruits because army records for the most part make no racial distinction. Monthly returns for the various recruiting depots are more confusing than helpful in that regard. Because none indicate a segregated detachment of permanent party noncoms, it can be surmised that white noncoms trained the black recruits most of the time, especially in the early years before enough experienced black noncoms were available to form such a cadre.[25]

By the 1880s, however, Jefferson Barracks listed a "colored detachment," in addition to a company of instruction, both commanded by an officer of the Tenth Cavalry, suggesting that at least by that time black noncommissioned officers were training black recruits for the Mounted Service.[26] Some companies of instruction at the general depots were desegregated, at least late in the era, as reflected in an 1890 newspaper article stating that "the colored recruits are mixed in with the whites indiscriminately. In the army the two races are regimented by themselves, but at the recruiting depot blacks and whites occupy the same dormitories, march and drill together, and mess together. An officer who has been on duty at Davids Island for a year recalls but one difficulty in that time on the race question." That statement suggests that far more societal experimentation took place in the military at that time than in much of the populace as a whole.[27]

The bulk of the new men were carried on the returns as "unassigned recruits" and until the early 1880s were subdivided into two or three companies, with the squads of each geared to ascending levels of training and proficiency. Each morning the sergeants conducted what was known as setting-up drill, a series of calisthenics consisting of four prescribed arm and body-bending motions designed to develop physical strength and stamina. Recruit Mulford described it as "very trying to one not accustomed to it. . . . The recruits are formed in line, or as near in a line as they can be got, with head up, eyes fifteen paces to the front; then they are ordered to place their palms together, to step forward, bend over and touch the floor with the tips of the fingers, without bending their knees or in any way spoiling the rigidity of their positions." The drill instructors also took advantage of such exercises to instill discipline in the new men. Arthur S. Wallace remembered "the sergeant holding a confab with another sergeant, and you, waving your arms in the air about ready to drop, and at last the welcome order 'as you were!'"[28]

Instruction in the basics of the "school of the soldier" began immediately. Under the tutelage of the noncoms and experienced privates of the permanent party, recruits learned the intricacies of military courtesy, such as saluting all commissioned officers but not noncommissioned officers and then only when outdoors except when on fatigue under the supervision of a noncom or when indoors under arms. It was a lot to learn and remember in a very short time, and there was no room for error. On one occasion music boy Alson B. Ostrander failed to salute an officer but received only a mild reprimand after he innocently explained that he had not yet received instruction in military protocol. A member of the permanent party who had observed the exchange later told him: "You got off mighty lucky, sonny. That is Captain Wilkins of the Third Infantry. . . . If any one of us had passed him without saluting, it would have meant thirty days in the guardhouse on bread and water." Recruits soon learned how to stand at attention, render a proper salute, and execute the facing movements and other elementary motions.[29]

Included in the daily routine were three roll calls: at reveille, retreat parade, and tattoo. The sergeants insisted that recruits respond properly "and if you don't answer to your name away to the guardhouse you go," a recruit informed his parents. Discipline in the regulars was strict, and dissension was not tolerated. "My three months at Jefferson Barracks was, perhaps, the most disagreeable of my entire life," one veteran recalled. "The weather was sultry hot, and many men fell standing at attention on the parade ground. The mosquitoes were awful in the day time and at guard mount or on inspection [we] were not allowed to brush them from our noses." An officer of many years' experience wrote: "If a country lad or a mechanic, he has probably been accustomed to debating and even arguing as to the good sense of the instructions. His first remark in this direction after enlisting in the army is curtly cut short by the corporal or sergeant over him, and he is sharply told to 'obey, not argue.' It is really difficult for an American recruit to accept the fact that he is only a cog in a vast machine." It was enough to make some recruits want to desert, and some did. A twenty-three-year old former cook, Charles O. Woods, had his fill of the army after only a few days and made good his escape from Newport Barracks.[30]

A measure designed to impress upon recruits their place and obligations within that machine was the reading of the Articles of War. Found at the back of the army's "blue book" of regulations, the articles codified 101 ordinances governing the personnel of the army. It must have seemed to recruits that their every act, word, and movement was controlled by a bewildering array of rules, coupled with prescribed punishments to be exacted for transgressions. A soldier had to toe a razor-thin line to avoid violating one or more of the articles. Even if he managed to escape all the provisions of the first ninety-eight, there was the catch-all Article 99 covering everything construed to be "to the prejudice to the good order and military discipline, though not mentioned in the foregoing articles." To ensure that recruits were thoroughly indoctrinated, regulations required that the entire Articles of War be read to them monthly and that those portions relating to the duties of noncommissioned officers and privates be rendered weekly.[31]

The routine of garrison life set in quickly. "We are kept pretty busy," wrote a cavalry recruit. "First thing in the morning at daybreak a cannon is fired to arouse all up to roll call, then we eat our breakfast." Afterward the men washed up at tubs provided for the purpose "like cats," he thought, and "eat first and then wash." When Recruit Henry McConnell, also at Carlisle, started to leave the squad room following roll call his first morning, the corporal immediately spotted him and ordered him to return to his bunk. "I was then and there initiated into the mysteries of folding my blankets according to 'regulations,' and rolling my overcoat according to the method of a cavalryman."[32]

After placing their bunks and possessions in order, policing the barracks, and brushing their uniforms, recruits reported for dismounted drill first by squads and later in company formation, which occupied the rest of the morning. Drill, which quickly advanced to marching in formation, continued for another hour or two in the afternoon, followed by retreat parade, including a second roll call and an inspection. "We had drills, parades, and inspections every day until my brain was almost paralyzed by the heavy load of 'Upton' which it was trying to digest," John Cox recalled. Then came supper and another roll call before bedtime. Even those routine assemblies could be a test of endurance. A civilian observer at Columbus Barracks in December 1880 noted that each roll call for the 250 recruits required "a quarter of an hour, and is an interesting pastime with the thermometer about 10 deg. below zero." During those periods when recruits were not occupied at drill they were put to work in the vegetable garden or at some other menial task such as sawing firewood, sweeping snow from the walks, or policing trash from the grounds.[33]

Recruits quickly learned that their daily lives were regimented by periodic drumbeats or bugle calls signifying the commencement or termination of various activities. "Although he has been a soldier for only two days," said one man, "he knows what it means; and he has also learned two other calls he can whistle without a break . . . *Recall from Fatigue*, and the other is *Mess Call*!" Recruits readily identified the sound of mess call by its timeless improvised lyrics:

Soupy, soupy, soupy, not a single bean;
Coffee, coffee, coffee, not a bit of cream;
Porky, porky, porky not a streak of lean.[34]

Even though recruits initially welcomed the call to meals, their enthusiasm quickly shriveled when they found that these lyrics were distressingly descriptive of depot food. Breakfast at the Cavalry Depot, according to recruit Matthews, was "composed of a little colored water without any sugar called coffee and a slice of bread. Sometimes we have a little fat meat." After his first exposure to a similarly wretched breakfast at Newport Barracks, an infantry recruit recalled with considerable indignation the recruiting sergeant's glowing descriptions of the excellence and variety of the food that he could expect at the depot. Other meals were hardly better. One man at Governors Island complained that dinner, the main meal of the day, "consisted of a small piece of boiled beef, and a piece of bread . . . this was varied two or three times a week; then we would get bean soup with boiled salt pork or bacon and sometimes one or two boiled potatoes." Of mess hall food at Columbus Barracks, Recruit Henry Hubman grumbled: "Here our food is dished out to us and I have not seen one yet that got enough to eat." A black cavalry recruit lamented that he and his comrades were served only three prunes and a piece of bread for supper. Even as late as 1889, a recruit at Jefferson Barracks condemned the food as being so bad that "I have a number of times taken my ration of meat from my plate and given it to a dog that hung around the company's quarters, but he would chew a little and then decline to eat it. . . . This may sound like an exaggeration, but it is not." Cavalryman William B. Jett complained with dripping sarcasm that the "tea or coffee made out of muddy Mississippi water was only different from the plain water in that it was warmer."[35]

Although the younger men coming to the depots usually were in good health, that Mississippi water, if not the food, probably accounted for widespread dysentery that soon ravaged Jett and his comrades. "The week I spent in the uncouth hospital with untrained soldiers as nurses was tormenting," he recalled. A man passing through Newport Barracks explained that the recruits were marched to the hospital each morning at sick call and were given a drink of whiskey and quinine to ward off whatever might ail them, which could include a variety of venereal diseases, according to Jett. "Many of the men had the most unclean diseases, and with these you had to eat and drink and occupy the same quarters, where the vilest conversation and profanity prevailed."[36]

The problems prevalent with the quality and insufficiency of depot food did not go unrecognized by higher authority, yet they persisted. Career army surgeon John S. Billings, who had served five years at Newport Barracks, confirmed that complaints voiced by recruits were so bitter that "on several occasions the men were ready to break into open mutiny." Certainly part of the problem, particularly for those men who had come from a normal home life, was a perception that army cooking was "not at all like home cooking, and they didn't satisfy the appetite of a growing boy." One recruit, probably speaking for many others, groused that he simply could not become accustomed to the food. "I have never yet eated [sic] all they gave me, but then it does me no good. I am just as hungrey [sic] when I get up from breakfast and supper as [I] was when sit down. The dinner [I] feel a little better on, but not very much." Conversely, for those who had come from the lower rungs of society or had been down on their luck and out of work, the army diet may not have seemed so bad. Simply having the assurance of three meals a day, whatever the quality, was an improvement.[37]

The standard army ration, computed on a daily allowance per man or per hundred men, was consistent regardless of where troops might be located. Staples of pork and beef, in various forms, were augmented by white or corn bread, dry beans and peas, rice, sugar, coffee, and tea. Vinegar provided resistance to scurvy. The regulation quantities of these commodities were ample, yet the depots had a perennial reputation for being poor feeders. Charles Kolarik, who passed through Jefferson Barracks in the 1880s, faulted the system of rationing companies every ten days. "If we had sixty men in the Company on ration day," Kolarik explained, "and two or three days later twenty new recruits came to the Company they had to subsist on the same rations till next ration day."[38]

A portion of the fault also was attributable to a lack of oversight and concern for the welfare of recruits by both officers and surgeons posted at the depots. Both were responsible for periodically inspecting the kitchens and the quality of the food being served, yet the pervasive complaints suggest that those were not as thorough as they might have been. Such negligence created an atmosphere fostering corruption, an accusation that recruits readily believed. "I do not wish to state that the government intended to starve its soldiers," Peter Thompson attested, "but the provisions passed through the hands of such dishonest men from the Commissary Sargeant [sic] to the cook, that it is no wonder that the rations were short to those who were bound to take what they could get." The recruiting depots being located in cities would have made it convenient and relatively easy for unscrupulous commissary officers, noncoms, and cooks to cooperate in black market schemes to sell or barter rations for personal gain, yet no documented scandal of that sort came to my attention during this study. Whatever the reasons, many recruits experienced real hunger and had little alternative for acquiring additional food. At one time in 1869 famished rookies at Carlisle resorted to purchasing slices of ginger bread from a local boy who brought it to the depot and sold it for his mother. A recruit at Jefferson Barracks said that he became so hungry he "went to the dining room to steal a piece of bread and was caught. I was lucky not being sent to the guard house."[39]

By the late 1880s, however, the army was transitioning to a system of general mess halls at large posts, including the recruiting depots. All the companies ate simultaneously, or in shifts, at the same facility, depending on its capacity. Rather than trusting to mostly ill-trained General Service cooks and recruit-assistants, the army began experimenting with permanently assigned chief cooks, whose kitchens were closely supervised by officers detailed for the duty. At Davids Island, and presumably at the other depots, three recruits from each company of instruction were detailed as trainees under the chief cook. Once they became qualified, these men were eligible for assignment as cooks in line companies upon special requisition. The officer of the day was charged with inspecting and reporting to the commander on the bill of fare for each meal as a quality control. The beneficial effect of these reform measures was reflected in an 1890 article: "An average dinner at the Davids Island mess hall consists of a soup, roast or boiled meat, a vegetable, a pudding, a pie. Sometimes there is a stew, in which case there is no soup, and then the men have coffee at the three meals of the day. Ordinarily they have it twice a day. They have meat three times a day."[40]

For those men lacking prior military experience, learning the ropes of army life was a constant and often humbling ordeal. As a veteran sergeant put it: "The Army is good enough for a man that has served one term in it and understands the discipline, but a Recruit suffers untold miseries when he first enlists." The first time John Nixon saw his name on the duty roster for kitchen police, he assumed that it was a high honor and spent all evening polishing his buttons and shoes. However, upon reporting to the cook early the next morning, Nixon "was introduced to a big heap of spuds [to be peeled] and a lot of greasy pots and pans." Another greenie naively thought the detail was a position of authority to enforce proper deportment of the men while in the mess hall, but the cook peremptorily disabused him of that notion by telling him: "Here kid, get after those tin plates and dishes and wash 'em."[41]

One unsuspecting rookie learned a hard lesson by neglecting to put his name or other identification mark on items drawn against his clothing account. A fellow recruit stole William White's unmarked blanket and sold it to a civilian, in the meantime substituting his own blanket on White's bunk. When the thief subsequently reported to the sergeant that his blanket, bearing his name, had been stolen, it was of course found in White's possession and no declaration of innocence would do. Thus the thief recovered his own blanket and the victimized recruit suffered both the punishment and loss of his blanket. Recourse was out of the question, as recruit William B. Jett explained: "The officers were entirely unsympathetic and wholly autocratic and discipline was over enforced in an unfriendly way."[42]

Many noncommissioned officers were no better, perhaps worse. Recruit Hubman characterized them as "very mean swearing at you and kicking you around as if you were a dog in fact we are not treated as good as some people treat their dogs." Another rookie was astonished that "some of the non-commissioned officers are not murdered for their brutal treatment to the recruits, but the men are so thoroughly cowed by threats and even acts of violence, that they dare not take any steps to redress their wrongs."[43]

Some old depot sergeants were legendary. Most of the recruits passing through Governors Island during the late 1860s, particularly those selected as musicians, distinctly remembered long-time comrades Sergeants Michael Moore and Charles Henke. Moore, a native New Yorker and drum instructor for the depot, had served in the army continuously since enlisting at age eleven during the War of 1812. Stationed at the depot since 1841, he enjoyed a reputation for being an excellent noncom, seldom missing a practice session and always on hand "showing the boys how to hold their sticks, and teaching them the mysteries and intricacies of 'Mammy Daddy.' He used to make the boys laugh and wonder when he would display his great feat with the sticks by whirling them in the air and catching them again without losing time on the drum." Even though Moore was a rigid disciplinarian and harsh taskmaster known for rapping the boys on the knuckles for not beating properly, he nevertheless became playful and talkative with his impressionable charges after duty hours, often regaling them with stories of his many army experiences.[44]

Henke had emigrated from Denmark, enlisted in the U.S. Army at age thirty in 1829, and served his first three enlistments as a musician alongside Moore in the Second Infantry, participating in both the Creek and Seminole Wars. In the early 1840s Henke also found a home at Fort Columbus, where he spent the remainder of his career as drum major of the General Service Band and overseer of the music boys. When Alson Ostrander came to Governors Island as a music boy in 1867, he immediately encountered Henke, whom he rated as "the most feared man . . . at the same time, the best liked by the boys . . . because they found he was fair and impartial, tempering justice with mercy." Another former recruit was less kind when he referred to Henke as "our great flogger . . . whom we always held in awe and the greatest respect . . . was a good old man . . . notwithstanding he was a little severe on the boys." As fife instructor, Henke awed the boys with his demonstrations of the proper playing of the service calls and quicksteps. "It was a caution and a treat to see and hear old Henke blow on the fife," one veteran remembered. "When he and the second instructor [Moore] would get together and play some favorite quick-step it was a great treat indeed for the boys and of course they thought, as the drummers thought of Moore, that he was the greatest fifer in the world."[45]

Even though depot noncoms could be uniformly characterized as stern disciplinarians, some even as petty tyrants, occasionally one revealed a degree of paternalism for the well-being of his recruits by helping them to learn the ropes of army life. In one instance, a sergeant at the Cavalry Depot advised the new men to place their shoes and other personal items under their pillows at night "for if left on the floor they might not be there in the morning." The sergeant was keenly aware that watchful thieves in the company would readily take advantage of unworldly youngsters accustomed to trusting those around them.[46]

Once the recruits were competent at performing the school of the soldier and the various evolutions of marching in formation, they graduated to the most advanced company, where they drew arms (either rifles or carbines and sabers, depending on whether they belonged to the dismounted or mounted service), along with a basic set accouterments. At Fort Myer recruits of the Signal Corps, which was classed as a mounted organization, also were issued carbines. At this stage recruits were schooled in the manual of arms under the watchful eyes of their noncoms and subsequently learned to execute the various motions while marching. A German-born recruit admitted that he initially experienced some difficulties as a result of the language barrier, but "I'd had some drilling in the Manual of Arms in Germany and I caught on to the American Manual quick enough."[47]

After being at the depot a few weeks, when time permitted, recruits in the senior company began participating in the daily guard mounting ceremony, a time-honored tradition that would be an integral part of the regimen throughout their time in the service. Private Eddie Matthews proudly informed his parents: "I have been promoted from D Troop to A. I don't have any fatigue duty to do. Do guard duty instead." Those selected for daily guard duty underwent a meticulous inspection, first in front of the company quarters when the selected detail formed. "When the bugle blew for guard mount," Matthews explained, "we fall in to ranks all looking as clean as possible, boots blacked, white gloves on and buttons shining . . . the Sergt. inspects your carbines he examines your cloth[e]s . . . every man tries to be the cleanest and have his arms . . . the cleanest." As an incentive, the best-appearing man in every detail was excused from all duty until dress parade the following afternoon.[48]

A company sergeant then marched the detail to the main parade ground, where he turned it over to the adjutant, who again minutely inspected the assembled detachment. When the ceremony concluded, the officer of the day, assisted by the sergeant of the guard selected from the permanent party, took charge of the new guard for the next twenty-four hours. William B. Jett recalled: "Sometimes we had a negro Sergeant of the Guard. This, as a rule, was very pleasing to the whites on guard, as the negro sergeant was more lenient than the white sergeants were and made the negro guards do more duty than the whites."[49]

The officers and noncoms of the guard spared no effort to impress recruits with the gravity of their responsibility, upon which the security of garrisons and troops in the field ultimately depended. Every sentinel had to memorize and be able to repeat upon demand a dozen general orders, plus any special orders issued for a particular beat. Reminiscing about his first time on guard, a veteran asked if others remembered when, as intimidated rookies, they "started to speak but something came up in your throat and you could not say a word?" But learn they did, often as a result of corporal punishment aimed at instilling in recruits that guard duty was not to be taken lightly. On one occasion at the Cavalry Depot, the officer of the day showed up at the guardhouse shortly after midnight while making his required rounds. Regulations stipulated that those members of the guard not walking post were promptly to turn out armed and equipped. In his rush to fall in the formation, one half-awake recruit neglected to take his belt and cartridge box, for which the officer had him confined behind bars for two days.[50]

In addition to watching over storehouses and other government property, sentinels were responsible for securing prisoners at the guardhouse and while on work details. Writing from Columbus Barracks in 1881, a recruit described the prisoners as "deserters . . . [and] men that have fallen asleep on Post, fighters, men that have disobeyed orders or have committed some offense against the U.S. Government. They have a very hard time of it, have to work from half past seven till twelve and from one till five, when they are not at work, they are locked in a cell four by eight with a little square hole to let air and light in, are not allowed to talk or write and all the bedding they have is a blanket spread on the floor." Recruits appreciated that they themselves were only an infraction away from being in the same situation. Yet the potential consequences of following orders to the letter presented a serious moral conflict for some men with beliefs founded on religious principles. "Doing guard duty over recalcitrant soldiers with command not to allow them to escape and yet with the dread of having to shoot to stop them and being subject to court martial if you did shoot one . . . was one of my most dreaded ordeals," one man confided. Indeed it was serious business. Henry Schuldt cited an incident at Jefferson Barracks when some forty-five prisoners broke out of the guard house; three were shot dead and six more were wounded.[51]

Musicians, meanwhile, followed a somewhat different daily regimen than other recruits. With the sounding of the call for guard mounting at eight o'clock in the morning, the drummers, fifers, and buglers fell in for inspection by their officer, the adjutant, in front of their quarters. Their sergeants then marched them to the main parade ground to witness the daily ceremony. Formed to one side, the trainee musicians thus were habituated to the orders, tactical movements, timing, and music of the ceremony. Whereas other soldiers spent much of the rest of the day drilling, the music boys attended class and practiced with their respective instruments during the remainder of the morning and for an additional two hours in the afternoon. "The buglers went up into the deep moat which surrounded Fort Columbus, where they could 'blow their heads off' without disturbing anyone," said drummer Ostrander. "The drummers went outside, under the east wall of the South Battery, and made racket great enough to be heard over in Brooklyn on the other side of the Buttermilk Channel." At Jefferson Barracks Karl Tetzel, who had been a musician prior to enlisting, applied to become a trumpeter part way through his recruit training. "I received a trumpet and a book of the calls . . . I went and practiced for 4 days and learned all the 87 calls in the woods back of the barracks." Late in the afternoon, following music practice, the sergeants instructed the musicians singly, by squads, and by company in the school of the soldier, always without arms. Because their hands were occupied with instruments, musicians were not authorized to have weapons, except for a light straight sword issued to dismounted men and a regulation saber for cavalry trumpeters.[52]

Signalmen at Fort Myer, Virginia, many of whom were destined for western service, had experiences similar to those of recruits at the general depots, although conditions were better and more like belonging to a line unit because the corps itself was comparatively small. Nevertheless, when an already homesick Harry B. Boyer reported to the Signal Service Training School, soldiers at the barracks immediately surrounded him, laughing and howling "Fresh fish! Fresh fish!" But the hazing was all meant in good fun, and his new comrades showed him where to find "Top Sergeant Mahaney, a product of the old military school of noncoms, to whom I reported." On his first evening at Fort Myer, Stephen R. Richey and his fellow recruits immediately underwent setting-up drill, after which they dined, not surprisingly, on a supper of bread and coffee.[53]

The training schedule at the Signal School was more accelerated and complex than the schedule for other common recruits. Company noncoms drilled the recruits, usually numbering from one to only a few men, in the school of the soldier with and without arms. After being in the army only three days, Richey had already drawn a full dress uniform and participated in Sunday inspection. Recruits were rapidly melded into their assigned signal companies for drills, inspections, and retreat parades within only a few days. Between times recruits were placed under the supervision of a stable sergeant for instruction in saddling, riding, and horse care. Concurrent with basic tactical instruction, Signal Corps recruits maintained a rigorous schedule learning the technical skills peculiar to their branch of service, including telegraphy and its mechanics; constructing and repairing transmission lines; signaling with flags, torches, and the heliograph; and recording meteorological observations. Like other recruits, signalmen served on guard duty, though their experience quickly elevated them to acting as corporal and later sergeant of the guard. One noted that he was assigned to drilling new recruits after being in the service only two months himself.

Enlisted Signal Corpsmen had to pass a rigid final examination prior to assignment. Their technical competency was especially important because their service at Fort Myer would likely be the only time they served with their respective companies. Most would be detailed singly to frontier posts where they would maintain weather records, conduct training in field signaling, and perform telegraphy and repairs at those posts served by the U.S. Military Telegraph System.

Signal sergeants were not immune from exercising their own brand of sarcasm in an effort to bring recruits up to the expected level of proficiency. After missing the final examination with his class, Boyer was sent to the Signal Office in nearby Washington, D.C., where a sergeant set up test keys on a local system within the building. With Boyer theoretically in Baltimore receiving at one key, the sergeant began transmitting text from a newspaper, gradually increasing his speed. When the number of words per minute reached about twenty-five, a frustrated Boyer jumped up from his chair, shouting: "'Sergeant, slow down; you're going too fast for me.' Dropping the key and whirling around, Robinson gave me a long, steady look and grunted, 'When did you arrive? Darned fast trip that! . . . You were supposed to be in Baltimore weren't you? . . . Fine operators they're turning out up at Fort Myer!'" Boyer got the sergeant's message and humbly returned to his table to complete the test.[54]

Those men who had enlisted for the cavalry soon learned that there was much more to being a trooper than simply being transported on horseback. The Cavalry Depot maintained a complement of horses for training recruits, with an animal assigned to each man. If these animals were not ornery by nature, they surely became so after being handled by so many inexperienced and often indifferent men. A particularly vicious horse at Carlisle was known as "The Bounty Jumper." Immediately after breakfast recruits marched to the stables to spend a full hour grooming their mounts, "and should one of the horses kick you or bite, you must not hit him for it," wrote one man. The stable sergeant impressed upon recruits from the outset that mistreating a government horse was a punishable offense. William C. Slaper vividly remembered: "We were taught how to groom a horse in regulation style by a crusty old sergeant named 'Bully' Welch [sic]" at Jefferson Barracks in 1875.⁵⁵

Sergeant Robert Walsh certainly made an indelible impression on virtually thousands of cavalrymen during the Indian Wars. A native of Cork, Ireland, and former laborer, the five-foot five-inch Walsh joined the U.S. Army in 1847 and saw combat with the Fourth Artillery in several engagements during the Mexican-American War. The stubby Irishman subsequently enlisted in the dragoons, serving on the New Mexico frontier until 1860 when he transferred to the General Mounted Service. Walsh became an institution at the Cavalry Depot for the next three decades. By the time he finished his fifth enlistment in 1864, he had risen to the rank of sergeant in the depot's permanent party. When the Cavalry Depot moved to St. Louis in 1871, Walsh went with it to continue training recruits. Finally, at age fifty-one, with nine enlistments to his credit, the old sergeant retired on a disability pension in 1881. Former cavalryman Henry McConnell said that Walsh, "whose brilliant row of enlistment and service stripes was the envy and admiration, as well as the terror, of all us recruits, was an odd character, and his extreme pride in his position and the dignity attached to it, brought down his truculent wrath on the offending recruit who addressed him without proper respect."⁵⁶

After about ten days—perhaps even less—of drilling on foot, most cavalrymen were introduced to mounted drill. The neophyte troopers became well acquainted with the "bullring," a large corral at the Cavalry Depot where recruits rode at prescribed gaits around the perimeter, while a sergeant stood in the center shouting orders and pointing out mistakes. Riding was done first with the horses bareback, or with only a blanket, to teach the men balance and coordination with the motion of the animals. After a couple of hours of this each day, recruits were "too sore to sit down and too tired to stand up." It was even worse for some men like Clarence Allen, who remarked: "I got fearfully galled riding bareback, so much so that the blood would come through my pants and when I would get back to the barracks, I would go to the kitchen and get a handful of salt and hold it on to the chafed parts, which was tough."⁵⁷

The next stage of instruction involved proper saddling and mounting according to the manual. Regardless of living during the horse-drawn age, many men were not at all familiar with horses and had little or no previous riding experience. The patience of the drill sergeants often was tried to extremes when teaching the basics of horsemanship to raw recruits. Sergeant Marshall Crocker, a former Second Cavalryman and member of the permanent party at Jefferson Barracks in the 1880s, demonstrated a memorable technique for teaching rookies how to mount a horse. When one recruit complained that he was unable to mount his tall steed, Crocker ordered: "'Give me your foot.' The man gave him his foot and he said, 'Mount!' . . . Crocker gave him a heave and he went completely over the horse, head first on the ground on the other side, getting a bad shaking up." The recruit undoubtedly learned that mounting a horse according to the manual was less painful than Sergeant Crocker's method.[58]

The rookies may have thought that graduating to the use of saddles would make riding a great deal easier, but in this they were sorely disappointed. Even though they saddled their mounts, the men were not permitted to use stirrups, again for the purpose of teaching them balance and coordination with the movement of the horse, beginning at a walk and progressing to a trot and canter. To ensure that the men used only their knees and poise to secure a seat, the stirrup straps were crossed over the saddle behind the pommel. The agony of such drill, remembered Arthur S. Wallace, was "how your seat hurt and you grabbed the horse's mane to keep from breaking apart." Sergeant Crocker may have been the same noncom that another veteran remembered as "that cock-eyed drill sergeant . . . who used not very polite language whenever one of us accidentally fell off the horse." Cavalrymen never forgot the bullring.[59]

Mounted training continued for one or two hours each afternoon, five days a week, yet it was never enough to make proficient cavalrymen of former pedestrians off the street. "Heretofore all mounted service recruits have been sent to Carlisle Barracks," one cavalry officer observed. "Some of them receive but very little instruction in riding, on account of being forwarded to their regiment soon after arrival at the depot." That was exactly the crux of the problem—not enough time. When allowed to remain at the depot several weeks, which was rarely possible until the late 1880s, the men steadily gained confidence in their abilities until riding became second nature. In those rare instances, the instructors could advance to teaching saber drill and tactical evolutions appropriate to conventional warfare.[60]

Not all men, however, were so inexperienced. Those reared on farms, or at least in rural areas, often knew the basics of horseback riding and had only to learn the army way. One trooper said that he "had good training of riding before and Sergeant Luders saw at once I was a good horseman." The sergeant, mistaking him for a reenlisted soldier, took him aside and inquired in which regiment he had served. The recruit had to confess that he had not served previously: he had learned to ride at school.[61]

Gradually, according to their length of time at the depot, the recruits became novice horsemen according to the book and many, perhaps most, began to take pride in their newly acquired skills. Before long those in the more advanced squads or companies could look upon the newer men with a sense of superiority. "The one pleasure in the midst of all the unhappy conditions was had when we were summoned to drill on horseback," one soldier declared. "It was very amusing to see some of the men who had never been on a horse before . . . the officer, with a whip in his hand, had us going around in a circle on the walk, trot, gallop, and run, a recruit fell from his horse to the ground, rolled right in the path of the running horses, and was trampled on by several steeds before he could crawl to one side. 'Get up,' said the officer, 'you will never make a good soldier till you get killed two or three times.'" Following drill came another hour at the stables grooming and feeding the horses, and after that supper and retreat parade.[62]

Infantry recruits at Davids Island underwent a similar grind, except for mounted drill and caring for horses. A local reporter wrote: "He is up early in the morning; he is almost constantly under orders during the day; he drills three hours . . . and is so far advanced as to be drilling in the manual of arms, he must be at dress parade in the afternoon. . . . To the average American citizen the soldier's life is full of terrible and depressing monotony." Some depot commanders invited local civilians to witness the regular Sunday dress parades while enjoying the band music. Parades were an opportunity to show off the garrison and, incidentally, to attract potential recruits through an impressive display of drill by soldiers brilliantly uniformed in army blue with gleaming brass buttons and insignia. The ploy was effective, according to a recruit at Columbus Barracks, who "got to talking with a farmer's boy and he said he wished he was [a] soldier, it was so nice. I told him he had better stay out if he knew what was best for him. . . . That is the way they catch young men."63

"So passed one day much like another," said McConnell, "without any variation, except on Saturday, when in lieu of drill, a thorough cleaning, technically called 'policing,' was given the parade grounds, quarters and stables, If 'cleanliness is next to godliness'—cleanliness in everything: cooking, bedding, in person, clothing—is the one feature of army life that can lay claim to even remotely approaching any sort or kind of 'godliness.'" Saturday afternoon also marked compulsory bath day for the men, some of whom had never been exposed to regular personal hygiene prior to joining the army. By this time many recruits, now feeling like soldiers and taking a degree of pride in their appearance, had post tailors alter their issue uniforms or drew unassembled blouses and trousers at reduced cost to secure a custom fit.64

During their time at the depot, recruits were either dead broke or had what little money they had possessed at the time they enlisted. Although their uniforms and other clothing were charged against a fixed annual allowance, the cost of alterations and minor necessities not provided by the army (such as combs, toothbrushes, mess utensils, leather blacking, and button polish) either required cash payment or was credited against their first pay. Recruits were supposed to be paid bimonthly, as were other soldiers, yet they were allowed to receive only one-half the amount due while at the depots. Even so, most would not see a payday until after joining their permanent units simply because depot commanders appreciated that recruits with the means might well desert. One man wrote to his brother asking "if you could send me 1 or 2 or 3 dollar [sic], then I would have a couple of cents in my pocket. We may not get any pay maybe for 2 or 3 months." Some impoverished recruits resorted to black market schemes by drawing army clothing then selling the items for cash, either to neighborhood civilians or to other recruits better off financially than themselves. Recruit Greenhalgh wrote to his mother that he would be sending home a new overcoat, valued by the army at $15.00, that he had purchased from another recruit for only $3.00. "Some of them will sell their shirt off their back for whiskey," he declared. "One of our men was telling me . . . that he sent home about five blankets and the same number of overcoats, blouses and boots that he bought for a trifle." Meanwhile more honest recruits were compelled to get by with what they had or survive on a meager $3.00 credit advanced by the depot's civilian merchant.[65]

Recruits had little time they could call their own, Saturday and Sunday afternoons being the only exceptions, unless they were on guard duty. Musician Ostrander said that the music boys at Governors Island were obligated to attend guard mounting, even on Sundays, after which they were marched in a body to the chapel where they were compelled to attend services. The depots often had a chaplain in residence, who may have insisted that the more impressionable underage youths attend church. Older recruits were allowed to follow their own inclinations, but the evidence suggests that few felt the calling.[66]

Not optional was a routine Sunday morning inspection of the men and their quarters by company commanders. After that the recruits were at liberty to do as they pleased, so long as they stayed at the depot. Most took advantage of the respite to catch up on their sleep, read, write letters, and simply loaf with their comrades. Those possessing some degree of education may have gone to the post library to keep up on events by perusing the available newspapers. Some of the more energetic souls at Carlisle in 1869 formed a baseball team to play against civilian teams from the local community. The games had to take place on the post, however, because it was nearly impossible for a recruit to secure a pass, at least during his first few months in the army. Depot commanders probably theorized that recruits, being in such close proximity to urban populations, could not be trusted to return. Some men did go off post, either with or without permission, as indicated by a cavalryman at Jefferson Barracks who attested that a small rowdy element in his company frequented bawdy houses near the depot, while a recruit bound for the Ninth Cavalry said that Sundays afforded less amorous recruits an opportunity to visit neighborhood farms, where they filled up on beer and the luxury of home-cooked food. Recruits at the Signal School enjoyed somewhat greater latitude through the granting of weekend passes to those not assigned to guard and who consistently passed the rigid head-to-foot inspections.[67]

After spending a few weeks at the depot, under constant scrutiny by hard-nosed officers and noncoms, not a few recruits regretted their decision to enlist. Reality having set in, a despondent Henry Hubman expressed the feelings of many of his contemporaries when he lamented "how I wish now that I had staid [sic] at home and made a farmer of myself . . . most all of the boys drink like everything so as to keep from thinking for it is not very pleasant to think that you have got to make a mark out of yourself for some outlaw or Indian to shoot at . . . nobody knows better than myself how deep I have fallen and how dear I have to pay for it." When a cavalry recruit at Carlisle encountered a close civilian friend from his nearby hometown, "he took one step backward and asked if he was dreaming . . . after I explained why I was here he said I was a fool and I suppose he is right."[68]

A great majority of the civilian populace shared a less than favorable view of the army, as expressed by a contributor to the *Army & Navy Journal* in 1882: "The people at large seem to think the Army composed of fugitives from justice, and whenever they hear that a neighbor's son has enlisted, break out into ejaculations of pious horror. The name 'soldier,' as they use it, seems to be a synonym for all that is degrading and low." The disrespect conveyed by civilians for the regular army during peacetime was not lost on those wearing army blue. An army veteran confided: "At that time, any young man wearing the uniform of a United States soldier was looked upon as an idler—too lazy to work." Fearing he would embarrass his family, one recruit sent home a photograph of himself, but intentionally "left off gun and belt and uniform as much as [I could] so that if anyone should get a hold of it, it would not give me away." Another decided against having his picture taken at all because he had been issued only a common fatigue blouse and was ashamed to have his family see him in it. Still, the heady effect of army blue and brass buttons was difficult to deny, and most newly minted soldiers could not resist pausing to view themselves in the reflection of nearly every window.[69]

The length of time that recruits spent at the depots varied according to the pool of available men and the urgency for replacements at any particular time. A constant demand for cavalry in the West, particularly during the late 1870s, resulted in recruits designated for the mounted service usually spending less time in training than their infantry counterparts, even though they had considerably more to learn. Cavalry recruits at Carlisle Barracks and Jefferson Barracks routinely spent about a month at the depot prior to being transferred to their permanent units, though even that length of time was not always possible under the exigencies imposed by active Indian campaigning. At no time was this more evident that during the Sioux War of 1876. Enlisting on May 25 that year, twenty-year-old James B. Frew wrote home less than a month later that he was already at Fort Leavenworth en route to join his company. Frew had expected to be at Jefferson Barracks for three or four months, but after being called out for the Fifth Cavalry his departure from St. Louis "was very sudden and unexpected."[70]

In the wake of the decisive Sioux and Cheyenne victory over the Seventh Cavalry at the Battle of the Little Bighorn, and in consideration of the other casualties suffered in several actions on the northern plains that spring and summer, Congress temporarily supplemented the cavalry arm with 2,500 men over its authorized strength. These reinforcements, dubbed "Custer Avengers," necessitated reducing somewhat the standards for mounted recruits and suspending some of the restrictions on recruitment imposed two years earlier, at least in the Division of the Missouri.[71]

This resulted in enrolling less qualified men, who frequently proved to be less capable or dedicated soldiers, often deserting shortly thereafter. These recruits, moreover, were rushed to "the front" with little or no training of any sort to be integrated into units already in the field. Typical of the Avengers was Peter Allen, a September 1876 enlistee who said that he and his fellow recruits were shipped to St. Louis, "where we remained in the barracks for three weeks. . . . We were then transferred [to] . . . Bismarck, Dakota Territory, where we were assigned to the 7th U.S. Cavalry." In the fall of that eventful year a downcast Adjutant General E. D. Townsend reported: "The hope entertained in a previous report, that the service might be so conducted as to permit of the detention of raw recruits at depots for three or four weeks with a view to instruction in the first principles of drill and subordination . . . has, owing to the demands of the service, only been partially realized." The injection of woefully ill-trained men into the ranks of the army, when they stayed at all, had the effect of reducing the combat effectiveness of line units even more than it had been previously. In short, units already engaged in active campaigning, particularly cavalry, were made worse off by the infusion of burdensome raw recruits than they would have been without them.[72]

These conditions persisted, even worsened, as the Sioux War continued and a new conflict flamed with the Nez Perce tribe in Idaho and Montana. "The organizations are so small," Townsend lamented in late 1877, "that they must be maintained . . . by drafting recruits as fast as they are enlisted . . . often joining their companies while on active duty in the field. There is not time to instruct them; they are therefore always awkward soldiers . . . because they are called on to do what they have not been taught how to do." Recurring demands of Indian campaigning during the remainder of the decade ensured that the army could not realize for some time its best intentions to provide longer, more thorough training at the depots. Even three years after Little Bighorn, the adjutant general reported that a chronic shortage of horses at the depots, coupled with unremitting demands for recruits to maintain companies at effective strengths, "prevents the detention of recruits long enough in depot to give them even the rudiments of drill . . . men thus initiated, if not totally worthless from their ignorance of the care and management of horses, can rarely make really good soldiers." As late as 1880, the editor of the *Army & Navy Journal* charged: "It frequently happens that of 100 recruits forwarded from the General Rendezvous to a regiment, not one-tenth of them have been for two weeks in service or seen a single drill." While his claim may have been exaggerated, it nevertheless served to call attention to what had become a serious problem for the army.[73]

Beginning in the early 1880s, as active Indian campaigning subsided everywhere except in the Southwest, the Cavalry Depot generally was able to retain recruits an average of six weeks. Private Lawrence Lea, for example, commented that he enlisted in Chicago on May 11, 1881, just a few weeks after emigrating from Norway, arrived at Jefferson Barracks two days later, and underwent training until he was sent to the Second Cavalry in mid-July. Still, the time devoted to training was inadequate, considering that green recruits right off the streets and farms had to learn both dismounted and mounted tactics; the manual for at least two, if not three, different weapons; horsemanship and care of horses; and, of course, the intricacies of guard duty. In view of their short tenure at the depots, recruits dispatched to cavalry units were hopelessly disadvantaged as effective members of their units. Only near the end of 1886, after active campaigning in the West had virtually ended, was Adjutant General Richard C. Drum able to boast that all newly enlisted recruits were being given at least three months' training before being assigned.[74]

Infantry regiments, although more numerous, with few exceptions saw less extensive field service and suffered fewer casualties, so overall turnover in personnel was slower. A further advantage was that the two depots for foot troops had access to a larger pool of recruits than did the mounted service, and infantry training was less complex than cavalry training. Combined with a lower demand for replacements, these factors enabled the general depots to provide training for a somewhat longer period in most instances. During the same peak of Indian activity on the frontier, infantrymen routinely spent four to six weeks at the depots.

During the 1880s that period lengthened, with infantry recruits at Columbus Barracks and Davids Island undergoing three to four months of training. A former Third Infantryman, Lafayette Schall, attested that after he enlisted in mid-November 1882 he was sent to Columbus Barracks for "the usual three months training" before joining his company at Fort Ellis, Montana Territory. Occasionally recruits stayed even longer. An unusual case was that of Phillip Schreiber, who had been a barber prior to joining the army in 1884, which did not escape notice by the first sergeant of his company of instruction. Always on the lookout for men with useful skills, the sergeant asked Schreiber to set up a barbershop, then arranged with the chief bugler to enroll him as a trainee musician to ensure that the company would retain its new barber for a year.[75]

An important step taken to improve recruit training was the abolition of permanent parties in favor of a modified organization of so-called depot detachments. The decision resulted in the transfer of most of the 1,710 enlisted men from the depots to line units, while complying with the overall limitation on the size of the army imposed by Congress. The measure also helped to avoid stagnation among permanently assigned drill instructors. While training continued to be conducted primarily by permanent depot noncoms, they were now supplemented by deserving sergeants of the line, six infantry and two cavalry, serving on rotational details of one year. These sergeants, selected by their respective regimental commanders as a reward for ability and faithful service, added fresh dimensions to recruit training—current field experience coupled with a sense of the practical skills essential for new soldiers to function effectively.[76]

The order also reorganized each depot garrison into four companies of instruction composed of at least eighty men each, plus six drill sergeants. Rather than grading the respective companies on an ascending scale of proficiency and passing the recruits upward, company to company, the new companies were subdivided into four squads of about twenty men each, with the members classified according to their time in service. The squads were graduated from fourth class (one month or less of service) to first class, respectively, with new arrivals assigned and advanced accordingly within the same company. (Reenlisted soldiers were automatically considered first class men.) Only first class men having at least four months experience were considered "disposable," that is, available for transfer to regiments.[77]

The rest of the depot detachment was composed of the necessary clerks, cooks, extra-duty men, and bandsmen, all supervised by the post adjutant. The *Army & Navy Journal* summed up the effect: "The new organization adopted is simply putting all the recruiting parties, odds and ends, necessary for running the recruiting service and depot into one company called the Depot Detachment."[78]

Recruits were introduced to the manual of firing (without ammunition) to acquaint them with the functioning of their carbines or rifles, though target practice was not conducted at the depots prior to the 1880s. The deficiency in basic training became so acute in the 1870s that it prompted the inspector general of the army to report: "Urgent calls for recruits to fill vacancies in the different regiments upon the frontier have generally prevented them being kept at the depots more than a week or two, and they frequently join their companies knowing nothing of the use of arms, or even the position of a soldier." Only after recruits were retained longer at the depots, and the army began emphasizing a formal course of target practice, did some recruit companies receive any instruction in shooting. An infantry recruit who had been at Columbus Barracks for over three months in 1881 bragged in a letter to his brother: "We have to practice shooting every day that we are not on guard. Firing at 200, 500, and 1200 yards. Standing up, lying down, with our feet and then our heads towards the mark. . . . We are armed with breech loading Springfield rifles . . . do not think that you can beat me at shooting at a mark the way you used to." However, this seems to have been an atypical experience, as most soldiers did their first live firing only after joining their companies.[79]

Regimental commanders periodically submitted to the adjutant general consolidated requests for the numbers of replacements needed to bring their companies to full strength or at least to augment them. From time to time, company commanders also made additional special requisitions for skilled men, such as blacksmiths, carpenters, field musicians, tailors, and saddlers, needed in their units. Depot commanders reported periodically, through the superintendent of the Recruiting Service, the numbers of disposable recruits available at their respective posts. The Adjutant General's Office thus served as the clearing house where these reports converged, resulting in certain numbers of recruits being sent by special order to designated regiments.[80]

Headquarters clerks at the depots ensured that news of an impending call for recruits did not remain confidential for long. "So many rumors are flying around that you can't believe anything," remarked a recruit at Carlisle Barracks. A sure indication that something was about to break was a sudden influx of raw recruits from the stations, causing overcrowding in the barracks. At Governors Island in 1867, when the mounted service was suffering a shortage of men, Frank Lowell recounted that "a call for volunteers for the Fifth Cavalry was received. No one wanted to go, but the rations were so scanty at the barracks where the commissary department was getting rich on the men, that I and several others decided to go." Nevertheless, a few men got cold feet at the prospect of being sent to the Indian country. "There were several names that failed to respond when called," Henry McConnell confided, "the owner's having 'skipped out' on the eve of departure," rather than take their chances.[81]

With that much-anticipated day of deliverance finally at hand, the sergeants passed the word for the recruits to "pack your traps," recruit John Cox recalled, and the mood of the men changed immediately. "The last two days of our stay, we were kept shut up in our 'quarters' . . . [to prevent desertion]. The spirit of mischief and riot reigned supreme. There was no attempt at discipline and we became a mob. . . . There was singing, large talk, wrangling over cards, quarrels over cards, quarrels over politics and numerous 'scraps.'" In other instances, the noncoms eased up on disposable recruits by extending small liberties. Sergeants at Carlisle in 1869, for example, granted Sunday passes to trustworthy recruits to enjoy a day in town before leaving.[82]

Shortly before their departure from the depot, excited recruits fell in line at the storehouses to turn in arms and accouterments, in exchange for canteens and haversacks, if they had not arrived from the rendezvous with them, and sometimes rations enough for at least part of the coming journey. Those needing replacement or additional clothing also drew that from depot supplies, but no arms were sent with recruits. Most, like William B. Jett, "had very little packing to do; so I just washed up my one change of underclothes, shaved, blacked my brogans and got my mess kit, consisting of a tin cup, knife, fork, spoon and a folding tin platter in order, [and] fell in line at the call of the bugle." Few recruits had any fond memories of their days at the depot; they just wanted to leave. Private Clarence Gould attested: "Of my three months experience [at Jefferson Barracks] . . . they had the toughest non-coms and the roughest horses of the service, so it is not surprising that when volunteers were called for . . . in the Indian country, I was one of the first to have my name placed on the list."[83]

Recruit Matthews described the scene at Carlisle Barracks when the garrison formed on the parade for the reading of transfer orders: "Monday morning about nine o'clock we were drawn up in line to hear what Regiment we were assigned to. It took about one and a half hours to call three hundred and forty names, had to stand in line all that time with knapsack and accouterments on." Matthews happily learned that he was assigned to the Eighth Cavalry and therefore would be going to what many recruits considered the best of all places—California. The hundred or so black recruits who had left a few days earlier were less fortunate in their assignment. They would join the Ninth and Tenth Cavalry, then stationed on the plains of Indian Territory and the desolate regions of western Texas.[84]

Batches of assigned recruits numbered from about a hundred to three or four hundred, depending on need, destinations, and the number of disposable men available at the time. Smaller detachments often went to a single regiment, whereas larger drafts were divided into temporary companies for convenience in transportation and messing. Even so, more than one of these groups might be dispatched to fill a single regiment, when the need was urgent, such as before a coming campaign or after a unit had suffered serious combat losses. Although recruits usually had no choice of assignment, depot officers sometimes made exceptions. Recruit John G. Brown (alias George Campbell) related that a recruit "could remain at a Depot & choose the Regt. he wanted to go to." Perhaps because he had functioned as company clerk of the Music Boys at Davids Island, Brown was retained at the depot an unusually long time from July 1879 until March 1880, when he was allowed to select the Thirteenth Infantry, then stationed in the Department of the South, because he preferred to live in a warm climate. It was not uncommon for black recruits, being fewer in number, to be sent en masse from one of the depots to bolster the ranks of a single regiment. At other times, the temporary companies, regardless of race, might separate en route when bound for different units.[85]

"After being worked hard, fed poorly, drilled a little, and abused much," the troops stepped off smartly in columns of fours while the depot band played them out to the stirring strains of "The Girl I Left behind Me," a popular Civil War tune adopted by the regulars and played almost universally whenever troops left a post for campaign or transfer. "Few tears are shed by the recruit as he leaves Carlisle behind him, for the recollections of his first experiences of regular army life are generally the reverse of agreeable," declared a Fourth Cavalryman. The ordeal of surviving that rite of passage had ended, but another phase of the recruit experience was about to begin: the high adventure of going to the western frontier.[86]

CHAPTER 3

"Don't Grieve after Me"

The Journey West

Most new recruits bound for regiments on the frontier eagerly anticipated the coming journey to join their units. Getting there promised the thrill of new sights and exotic places for young men who, with few exceptions, had not experienced the vastness and grandeur of the American West. The trip virtually always began with a train ride—the first for many youths—of shorter or longer duration. Before the advent of the transcontinental railroad, some went only as far as the nearest seaport, where they embarked on a ship bound for the Gulf or the Pacific Coast. Later drafts of recruits would be exposed to the novelty of a train trip entirely across the North American continent. Most recent enlistees, in fact, went west by rail as the most expeditious and economical means for the government to transport large numbers of men from the recruiting depots to their permanent units or at least somewhere in proximity to their units. However, those men destined for posts dotting the interior of the western territories discovered that the railroad network beyond the Missouri River remained quite limited well into the 1880s. For them, the journey frequently became an agonizing trek on foot over dry, treeless plains or across inhospitable, cactus-studded deserts. Nevertheless, getting to the regiment—finding their new homes—was all part of the adventure. One recruit, inspired with a sense of awe undoubtedly felt by many of his comrades as the journey unfolded, wrote: "Through Kansas City, on over the great western plains and into Colorado we went until the giant Rockies loomed into view and I began to think more and more of what a great country we lived in."¹

William H. White, a former Indiana farm boy, was among a draft of recruits bound for the Second Cavalry then stationed at posts in Wyoming and Montana territories. Having a sense of liberation from the depot at last, he and his comrades, secure in the knowledge that the miseries of the past few weeks were behind them, vented pent-up opinions of officers and noncoms under whose iron-fisted control they had been for weeks. He recounted with some amusement: "As we were about to board the train somebody called out: 'Three cheers for Sergeant ———,' naming the superior non-commissioned officer at our St. Louis barracks, who was well liked. . . . Then came 'Three groans for that ——— ——— ——— Captain.' Everybody knew which Captain was meant. There was a big chorus of triple groans. The officers present merely smiled."²

Prior to departure, the senior officer present briefed the men, outlining the itinerary, the procedures for meals, and the behavior expected of them, with a firm admonishment about the possible consequences of improper conduct during the trip. It usually had little effect. Members of the depot permanent party often accompanied the recruits for at least part of the way as a degree of security against desertion. "About 11 o'clock we left Carlisle under an escort of 20 men who were stationed at every door with orders to let no man pass out of the cars, not even from one car to the other," recruit Eddie Matthews wrote. Once entrained aboard day coaches (they would sleep sitting up) the various batches of recruits traveling to the western frontier began the first leg of what was to be a long and often arduous journey. Provided that they served out their enlistments, the men would not be seeing their families or friends, or the States for that matter, for the next five years at least. Some who took to the army would not return for many more years, some not at all. "Don't grieve after me," Matthews beseeched his parents. "I will try to be a good soldier."³

As batches of recruits left the depot, one or more commissioned officers accompanied each party destined for a particular regiment. The adjutant general of the army coordinated such assignments by detailing officers, often members of the regiments receiving the new replacements, who were scheduled to return to their stations following leaves of absence or some detached service. Lieutenant George M. Templeton, formerly an enlisted man during the war and freshly commissioned in the Eighteenth Infantry in 1866, recorded in his diary that he was "ordered to report at once at Fort Columbus, New York Harbor. The Regt is at Fort Leavenworth, Kansas, and are ordered to the plains. I presume I am to assist in conducting recruits to the Regt." Templeton rendezvoused with a colonel and five other officers at Governors Island to conduct ninety recruits to their new posting.[4]

Temporary noncommissioned officers, termed "lance sergeants," selected from among the recruits, assisted the officers in supervising the groups en route to their regiments. These acting noncoms frequently were reliable reenlisted soldiers or, less often, promising recruits who had shown particular aptitude during training. Although their fellow recruits had recently been their peers, regulations required that recruits exhibit the same respect and obedience accorded to regularly appointed noncommissioned officers. "I was appointed a sergeant of one of the troops, and soon learned that a little authority involved a heap of trouble," remarked Private Henry McConnell, a former Pennsylvania infantryman with three years' wartime experience.[5]

Despite the measures taken to control recruits leaving the depot, keeping recently confined and closely disciplined young men in check during a cross-country train ride was all but impossible. The editor of the *Army & Navy Journal* wrote:

> There is no necessity for the disgraceful scenes that occur every month in the year, when a large detachment of recruits is sent from New York to some distant station under command perhaps of a young lieutenant just appointed, and without a sufficient number of old soldiers to act as guard. Such detachments have frequently taken possession of the trains of cars, and small western villages have been devastated by them. Drunken recruits have been scattered along the road from Chicago to Cheyenne and the Army has been brought into disrepute by this pernicious method of trying to get recruits to their regiments.[6]

This statement was hardly an exaggeration. "It was a hilarious crowd of young men as we rolled along over the iron tracks singing as we went, 'Going to fight the Modocs, never to return,' and other songs which I never heard before," one man remembered. Idle minds ever being the devil's workshop, recruits invented countless schemes for combating boredom along the way, often at the expense of local civilians. At those times when the train stopped in some town or city,

> one recruit would dangle the end of an army blanket out the coach window and offer to sell it to a passerby. If he appeared interested, another recruit in the adjacent window would do the same with another prospective buyer. Each was induced to pay a dollar for a blanket and to take hold of the dangling end, but with the understanding that he must not draw it into his possession until the train started, so that the illegal sale could be kept secret. When the train pulled out, the purchasers found they had opposite ends of the same blanket and were compelled to let loose as the train picked up speed.

Such stunts were guaranteed to keep the boys in blue in stitches for miles thereafter.[7]

The steady attrition of recruits that had begun at the rendezvous and later at the depots continued as the detachments proceeded toward the frontier. As a carload of recruits was passing through Pennsylvania on its way from Davids Island to San Antonio, one of the men jumped headfirst from a window while the train was clipping along at thirty-five miles an hour. Whether the man was attempting to desert or was drunk was not recorded, though miraculously he sustained only "slight injuries and was able to accompany his detachment." Fourth Cavalryman Henry McConnell remarked on this point: "Each night some of our party would desert, so that by the time we arrived at Austin, for final assignment to the regiment, our number had been materially reduced." A Second Cavalryman also confirmed that "a few had deserted along the way, had failed to return to the train at some one or another station where we had stopped. Desertions greatly increased in number after we reached Fort Sanders [where they paused en route to Montana]. By the time we had become well settled in our military post there were only about fifty of us left." While awaiting a connecting train at an un-named town in Arizona in 1889, "the men were allowed to walk about to get a little air and exercise. When the train moved on, five recruits were missing. Upon investigation it was found that one had missed the train through carelessness, two had been arrested by the civil authorities and the other two had gone into a saloon to take a drink and had been drugged and robbed and thrown into an alley." Other than the financial investment wasted on such recruits, the army did not greatly mourn their loss. Rather, commanders of line units were inwardly glad not to have to deal with men who in all likelihood would have been troublesome or would have deserted later anyway.[8]

Human nature being what it is, one class, no matter how oppressed, always seems to find some degree of self-elevation by discriminating against another. Private William H. White related that unruly recruits riding the Union Pacific across Nebraska targeted Chinese section hands "as being the recipients of any kind of indignity that might be put upon them. Our amateur militants exercised themselves at the expense of the mild-mannered yellow workers. Chunks of coal were hurled from windows and platforms. We spent all of one frosty night . . . without any fire in the cars. All of the coal in the bins had been used up during the day throwing at the Chinamen."[9]

When the rowdies lacked other victims, they sometimes picked on their own. "One certain soldier among us was especially soft . . . possibly foolish," a veteran recollected. "He was easily imposed upon . . . some of the boys told him, 'You have been promoted to the Marines,' and they congratulated him upon the wonderful forward step he had taken so quickly." The pranksters convinced the young man that upon their arrival at Salt Lake City he should apply to the quartermaster for transportation to his new assignment. The officer, of course, unceremoniously informed the recruit of his error and promptly remanded him to the train.[10]

A group of 150 recruits on their way from Newport Barracks arrived at the hub city of St. Louis, where they had to be transported from one rail line in East St. Louis to connect with another on the west bank of the Mississippi. A member of the party later described the scene: "Imagine, if you can, 15 or 20 buses loaded inside and on top, with young recruits for uncle Sam's Army, going thru the principal streets of St. Louis."[11] Little did he know that most of the citizens of St. Louis were inured to the antics of the batches of recruits frequently passing through their city.

Private Frank G. Prescott described the mayhem created by a raucous draft of infantry recruits bound for Dakota Territory:

> The six Commissioned Officers in charge together with Squad Sergeants and Corporals appointed temporarily or until we reached the regiment to which we were assigned had little if any control over them while en route from Governors Island to Jefferson Barracks, Mo. All along the route they took anything and everything they could lay their hands on. There were but few whole windows in the coaches that made up the special train—run from Jersey to St. Louis. In St. Louis tradesmen on the streets . . . took inside everything and closed their doors. Those who failed to do so had nothing to take in after this . . . gang passed.[12]

During a layover at Fargo, Dakota Territory, recruits spotted a special car occupied by commercial hunters. When the hunters complained to the officer in charge that two dozen ducks hanging on the outside of their car had suddenly gone missing, the lieutenant allowed the civilians to search the government coach. "But not the least sign of a duck was to be found!" one of the perpetrators exclaimed. "Then the callers looked under every seat, in the racks at the sides of the car, and in fact they looked in every place big enough to hold a duck, except the coal box [for the stove]." With the ruse successfully executed, the boys later obtained a boiler at Bismarck, dressed the ducks, and cooked them with stolen "salt, onions, pepper . . . or anything else that lay loose" about the town. No doubt their officer caught the scent of boiled duck wafting from the car, but stayed at a distance and said nothing.[13]

Private William C. Slaper attested that even the acting noncoms were not above instigating such plots, probably based on past experience. "An Irish sergeant in charge of our car—seemingly an old veteran—instructed a bunch of recruits to go to a certain saloon not far from the station, take their canteens and guns, and . . . trade them for liquor. On their return with the whiskey, he then took a squad of recruits, armed them as guards, and marched them over to the saloon. He threatened the proprietor for buying government arms and immediately confiscated the pawned weapons!" The longer Eighth Cavalryman Eddie Matthews was forced to be in close quarters with some of his companions during the trip west, the more he more regretted his decision "to associate myself with the scrapings of . . . penitentiaries, jails, and everything else combined to make an army suitable for this government. . . . The officers steal from the men and men steal from each other. . . . Well, I have only 58 months to serve yet."[14]

Even though drafts of recruits traveled to their destinations predominantly by rail, the army used other forms of transportation as necessary to get them there. The most expeditious way to get to Texas, for example, was by sea. McConnell's group, consisting of nearly five hundred men organized in three companies, went by rail only as far as Baltimore, where they boarded a transport bound for the Gulf port of Indianola in Texas. McConnell and his bunkmate, a likable though inexperienced Dublin professor's son, managed to avoid the stifling, malodorous quarters below decks by bedding down beneath their shared blankets and overcoats on the main deck. Throughout the nine-day voyage, the cooks in the galley invariably served only two meals a day—hardtack and coffee for breakfast; soup or boiled potatoes and pork for dinner. There was no evening meal, and on those occasions when rough weather and a rolling ship made cooking impossible, the men received no food whatsoever. From the Texas seacoast the recruits rode a primitive short-line railroad for about thirty miles then walked the rest of the way to Austin, headquarters of the Fourth Cavalry.[15]

Prior to railroads accessing the interior regions of the frontier, troops could ride trains only as far as construction had been completed; beyond that point it was not uncommon for recruits to march overland. Private James D. Lockwood, one of the Eighteenth Infantry replacements with Lieutenant Templeton, recounted that they took the cars to St. Louis and were then transported by steamboat up the Missouri. "After some five or six days of this most tedious of voyages, the steamer came to a standstill at Fort Leavenworth . . . where the troops were ordered to disembark and proceed overland to join their regiment, which was then under marching orders at Fort Kearney [Nebraska Territory]." In describing their equipment, one of Lockwood's comrades revealed that the new men were not yet looked upon as soldiers. "We were issued nothing at Governors Island but clothing and Camp & Garrison Equipage," he recorded. "No arms until we were assigned to our respective Companies at regimental headquarters at Ft. Kearney, Neb."[16]

From that point the entire regiment continued up the Oregon–California Road, eventually occupying the new posts along the Bozeman Trail in the territories of northern Wyoming and southern Montana. By September 1867 construction crews had laid track just beyond the Missouri, but no bridge yet spanned the river. Replacements for the Thirtieth Infantry crossed by ferry to Omaha, where they were armed and equipped, and again rode a train for the last forty miles to end-of-track. Private Lauren W. Aldrich said that his party detrained in the middle of the barren prairie and "started at once on foot on a forced march from dawn to nearly dark every day [averaging twenty-five miles] over what seemed an endless desert, in the face of hot winds and blistering hot sun, suffering daily for the lack of water" until they ultimately reached their destination near present-day Rawlins, Wyoming.[17]

Others were no less fortunate. Private William F. Hynes (alias William Jones) groused that his party of dismounted cavalry recruits marching along the Smoky Hill Trail west of Fort Riley, Kansas, was supplied with only one blanket apiece—usually rain-soaked—and had

> no arms, except the Major's pistols, the Winchester of the ambulance driver, and the few heavy 45's [sic] carried by the muleteers [civilian drivers], but the one hundred recruits had none. . . . Our absurd equipment, or rather want of equipment, was often made the source of amusement by the wits and wags of the Company. Bill Baker, the jolly philosopher from the City of Brotherly Love, asked one evening . . . "Which is the most to be admired for the terror it creates in the hearts of the enemy, a soldier without a gun or a cavalryman without a horse?"

Baker's black humor was not lost on his comrades, who were keenly aware that Cheyenne warriors actively roamed the area. Another man in the same detachment confided: "We were disappointed in not getting horses, but some 40 of us were ordered to Co. M then in camp at Pond Creek Station. . . . At last we reached the company, tired and footsore, and many of us barefoot, having worn our shoes out on the march."[18]

The situation improved for a brief time in the latter part of the decade when Fort Leavenworth, a major supply post strategically located on the Missouri River near the origins of both the Oregon and Santa Fe Trails, served as a mounted recruiting depot. Officers in the field frequently complained about the superficial nature of training, especially horsemanship, conducted at the St. Louis Cavalry Depot. First Lieutenant William R. Parnell of the First Cavalry contended that most cavalry recruits "receive but very little instruction in riding, on account of being forwarded to their regiment soon after arrival at the depot; in many cases their instructors (acting non-commissioned officers) having but little knowledge of the method by which a cavalry soldier should be taught to ride, or the art of imparting that knowledge to others." It was not uncommon, consequently, for cavalry recruits who had previously been at other depots to be given supplemental instruction at Fort Leavenworth en route to their regiments. Seventh Cavalryman David W. Luce explained: "Carlisle Barracks was the recruiting camp. . . . It did not take long to make a raw recruit a full-fledged soldier on foot, but when he reached Fort Leavenworth, Kans., he was taught to be a good mounted trooper." Private Frederick Platten was also among those fortunate enough to receive additional mounted training. After a stint at Carlisle, he and the other men bound for the cavalry arm "went to Leavenworth, Kansas at the edge of the Indian country. We were given a three months course of military training at Leavenworth, after which we were assigned to 'H' Troop, Sixth Cavalry." For a few years Fort Leavenworth, with its attendant arsenal, functioned as a critical funnel for training and equipping both cavalry and infantry recruits designated for assignment to units posted in the Department of the Missouri. When three hundred recruits bound for the Third Cavalry passed through Fort Leavenworth on their way to New Mexico, a neophyte trooper recorded that they paused for a few weeks at the post, where "we were equipped with arms and mounted. We started on the march over the plains over the Santa Fe Trail, some 800 miles." What these troopers had failed to learn about being horsemen at the depots, they certainly learned by the time they reached Fort Union, New Mexico.[19]

Getting troops to the Division of the Pacific in the early days posed even greater challenges. Most replacements destined for the Far West took trains from the eastern depots to the nearest Atlantic seaport, from which they sailed to Panama. Crossing the isthmus by rail, the troops were met on the western shore by a ship that would convey them on to San Francisco. All was not drudgery, however. One young soldier fondly remembered Panama as an educational high point of the trip: "We observed with some astonishment the scarcity of clothing indulged in by the natives, full-grown young and very pretty girls included."[20]

When the Fourteenth Infantry, bolstered with many new recruits, was sent to Arizona Territory to relieve volunteer forces in spring 1866, it traced the same convoluted route to the Presidio of California, whereupon the battalion to which Private John Spring belonged was dispatched by steamer to Drum Barracks, south of Los Angeles. From that point the companies marched overland to Yuma and continued across the desert to their assigned stations in the southern region of the territory. The last segment of the extensive journey required nearly two months to complete. In a near-epic trip to join their regiment in the fall of 1869, a batch of recruits destined for the Eighth Cavalry, also posted in Arizona Territory, enjoyed the luxury of the recently completed transcontinental railroad. The passage from Baltimore to San Francisco, miraculously, took only eleven days—a far cry from the time, much less the effort, previously required for traversing the nation. After reaching California, however, it was still a long, circuitous trip to reach northern Arizona. To get there, these recruits took a steamer down the Pacific Coast and rounded the Baja to sail up the Gulf of California to the mouth of the Colorado River, where one proclaimed in a letter written at Fort Yuma "I am now seven thousand miles from home and not done going yet." That was an understatement. Boarding a riverboat, he and his comrades still faced a two-week journey up the Colorado to Fort Mojave, where they would disembark for a 175-mile trek on foot to their final destination at Fort Whipple.[21]

As late as 1873, with the railroad only partially completed, a recruit detachment bound for Camp Lowell, a few miles east of Tucson, still had to cross more than 300 miles of inhospitable desert on foot, no horses being available to them until they reached the post. "I shall never forget that march," Fifth Cavalryman Frank Lowell said. New Yorker George Cranston also found the desert to be a harsh, foreign environment. "The brush, cactus, . . . even the toads and frogs on the banks of the Colorado and Gila river are honestly covered with prongs . . . there is snakes from Yuma to Tucson, . . . from 5 to 30 [killed] a day. . . . There is one pest greater than the snake, that is the scorpion. . . . [I] waked up many mornings and found a scorpion in bed with me." The experience was not without benefit, however. The experience of marching for hundreds of miles across the unforgiving western landscape introduced the men to conditions that were to become an accepted part of military life. Describing the appearance of his fellow recruits upon finally reaching their destination, an infantryman stated grimly: "We were a tough looking bunch and as hard as nails." Not until 1879 did rails finally bridge the expanse between the Pacific Coast and southern Arizona Territory.[22]

Whereas in 1865 only about 3,200 miles of track existed in the West, by 1890 railroad companies had constructed a network between the Mississippi and the Pacific Coast totaling some 70,000 miles of rail. During the 1870s, and even more during the building boom of the 1880s, an expanding railroad system facilitated the transportation of recruits directly to their destinations or at least much nearer than had previously been possible. Rapid development of railroads in the primary corridor across the central plains immediately benefited military access to posts along the Union Pacific from Omaha to Salt Lake City and beyond. Also of immediate advantage were the Kansas Pacific, linking Kansas City with Denver, and the Atchison, Topeka and Santa Fe, extending from eastern Kansas to Pueblo, Colorado.

Lagging behind, however, was a transcontinental rail line servicing the Dakotas and Montana and a southern route from Texas to California. During favorable seasons, many forts in the Dakotas could be readily accessed by steamboats owing to their placement along the upper Missouri River and by roads connecting the riverfront posts with those more removed. However, travel was complicated when the river froze in winter. In one instance, a party of First Infantry recruits aboard a steamer got as far as Fort Randall in September 1876, but the boat could go no farther. The recruits had to remain at that post until the following April before they could reach their assigned companies upstream. Fort Benton, in western Montana Territory, lay at the terminus of the navigable waters of the Missouri, yet troops had to march overland from there to reach other stations along the northern Rocky Mountains. Not until the early 1880s did the Northern Pacific provide rail service to that region. In the absence of a railroad across western Texas and the Southwest, replacements going to forts in those regions were compelled to march overland until the early 1880s, when the Southern Pacific was finally completed.[23]

While railroad development increasingly facilitated troop movements, numerous forts still lay at considerable distances from the tracks, so getting to them imposed further hardships for the new men reporting to their units. The lucky recruits were those whose companies happened to be garrisoned at the headquarters post. Once there, they were home. Only in rare instances, however, were more than three or four companies of a regiment present with the headquarters staff, the others being distributed to other forts in the region. "On reaching Fort Union in New Mexico [in 1867]," according to Private John F. Farley, "we were assigned to our various troops in our regiment. With some 20 other recruits, I was assigned to Troop K, located at Fort Selden, some 400 miles from Fort Union, where we arrived a month later." With no rail connection yet available through the territory (and not available for more than another decade), these cavalrymen had no alternative but to walk the remaining distance.[24]

Within a few short years, however, the Kansas Pacific Railroad had extended track into eastern Colorado Territory, which facilitated military traffic bound for the Southwest. A group of recruits assigned to the Eighth Cavalry and the Fifteenth Infantry rode day coaches as far as the railhead at Kit Carson, disembarking there for a march afoot to their posts in New Mexico. Many years later a member of that party observed that "anyone passing over the Atchison, Topeka, and the Santa Fe Railroad [today] . . . probably would not appreciate what a God-forsaken country that hike took us through back in the fall of 1870."[25]

Conveyed over the Kansas Pacific in 1873, because the Santa Fe line had progressed only as far as the great bend of the Arkansas River, Private Herman Harbers and his party of Third Infantrymen "arrived at Hayes [sic] City on the 12th of September, and marched 125 recruits to Fort Hayes [sic]. I drew Company D, and left on foot to Camp Supply, Indian Territory by way of Fort Dodge, Kansas. As there were no bridges over the Arkansas River, we all had to cross overhand by a rope which had been stretched across the river. . . . Marched an average of 15 mi. a day after that." Harbers added that no one in the party was armed, except the officer in charge, who used his Springfield rifle to provide the men fresh meat along the way then lent the rifle to the night sentries over the camp. Rapid development of transportation in the West was readily apparent only a decade later, however, when William Jett and his comrades rode the Santa Fe railway all the way to Pueblo, Colorado, where they transferred to the Denver and Rio Grande for the remainder of the trip to Fort Garland.[26]

In 1876 replacements destined for the Fourth Cavalry at Fort Sill, Indian Territory, rode the Missouri, Kansas and Texas Railway from St. Louis as far as Caddo, where they joined a detachment taking delivery of horses for their regiment. For the recruits, forced to ride the new horses bareback 150 miles, it was a long trip to Fort Sill. Even so, suffering painful crotches and bowed legs was marginally better than walking that distance. By that time on the northern plains the tracks of the Northern Pacific extended only as far west as the Missouri River in Dakota Territory. After training at Jefferson Barracks for a mere three weeks immediately after the Battle of the Little Bighorn, Seventh Cavalry replacement Peter Allen traced the roundabout route that his party had to take "from St. Louis via Chicago, Ill. and St. Paul, Minn. to Bismarck D[akota] T[erritory] and thence across the Missouri River to Fort A. Lincoln."[27]

Second Cavalry recruits found getting to western Montana Territory even more challenging. After spending less than two weeks at the Cavalry Depot in fall 1872, William H. White and some 130 other recruits transferred by rail, via Omaha and Cheyenne, to the regiment's headquarters at Fort Sanders, Wyoming Territory. The trouble was that many of the new men were assigned to companies of the Second's "Montana Battalion," headquartered at distant Fort Ellis in southern Montana Territory. Perhaps because of the lateness of the season, and in view of the superficial training they had received at Jefferson Barracks, the recruits were retained at Fort Sanders until the following spring, when they finally boarded another train that would carry them farther west to the junction with the miners' road leading to Virginia City and Fort Ellis. "After a day and a half of preparation in Corinne [Utah] we set off for the long journey northward," White commented. "These Cavalrymen had not yet been given horses to ride, so they had to walk. We had no warfare accouterments—no guns, no sabers, nothing except uniforms and blankets." That last leg of the trek took about three weeks to complete. Another Second Cavalryman, Fred Munn, who enlisted four years later, related a similar experience when his party followed the identical route to Fort Ellis. They also paused at Fort Sanders, but only for two weeks, during which they too received additional training.[28]

When construction on the Northern Pacific Railroad stalled at the banks of the Missouri for more than a decade, steamboats remained the primary means for traveling from Bismarck to the northerly regions of Montana. Private Henry Hubman was among a draft of Eighteenth Infantry recruits trying to reach Fort Assiniboine in 1881. "We have been traveling 24 days today. We went by rail from Columbus [Barracks] to Bismarck . . . and there we took the Steamer . . . Dakota I do not like at all. . . . What they claim is the best part of it is all a level prairie as far as the eye can reach. There is not a tree in sight. You do not know how to appreciate a tree till you get where there is none." Nearly two weeks later the boat tied up at Coal Banks Landing. From there the troops walked nearly fifty miles to their destination.[29]

As rail lines became more extensive in later years, and the numbers of men making up drafts generally were smaller, recruits not uncommonly enjoyed the relative convenience of wagon transportation from the railhead most convenient to their stations. A group of new Fifth Cavalrymen going to Fort Washakie, Wyoming Territory, in 1884 detrained at Laramie City, where an armed sergeant met them with a six-mule wagon to take them on to the post, some 150 miles away. The sergeant, the only armed man, shot deer and antelope for the evening meals, quite a novelty for recruits fresh from the East. In the peaceful days after the cessation of Apache trouble in Arizona Territory, the commanding officer at Fort Grant sent a noncom with a wagon to Willcox to pick up recruits arriving there by train.

The ranking officer accompanying recruits was responsible for seeing that the men were fed en route to their stations. In some instances commissary officers at the recruiting depots issued a few days' rations to begin the journey, particularly when recruits would be going by rail to a port then boarding a ship for an ocean voyage. For overland travel in the States, the army Subsistence Department negotiated contracts in advance with restaurants located in towns and cities along the commonly used rail routes. In those instances the officer had only to telegraph ahead to notify the contracted vendor that a certain number of men would be arriving on a scheduled train in order that a meal could be prepared and ready. Ami F. Mulford, the man who hated mush, upon reaching Fargo, Dakota Territory, was content when a restaurant delivered to the train a plain supper of coffee, boiled potatoes, soft bread, and butter. Taking no chances with his unruly charges, the lieutenant placed two guards over the doors at either end of the car to prevent the men from going into the town after eating. "But notwithstanding this precaution," Mulford boasted, "every member of our party, except the guards, did go out and view the town that night. But not one of the bunch passed through a door-way of the car."[30]

Recruits detraining for a rest at Omaha, Nebraska, saw an opportunity to engage in a time-honored soldier tradition: foraging. Spotting boxed fruit on the platform, they waited for the right moment. Just as the train began pulling out, they pushed over some of the stacks, stuffed as much fruit as possible inside their blouses, and jumped back aboard the moving car.[31] In the 1880s the army began stocking canned baked beans, which proved to be a convenient travel ration, in addition to precooked bacon and hardtack. Samuel D. Gilpin remarked: "The recruits wanted second helpings so often . . . I fed them beans three times daily throughout the five days on the train. We had an old soldier with us, a friendly German, who emphasized the novelty of canned baked beans. . . . He had eaten them before from a Dutch oven in the field."[32]

When recruits left the train or steamer to walk the final distance to their posts, they discovered the purpose of those haversacks issued to them at the depots. From that point they had to subsist almost exclusively on the regulation field ration. William Hynes vividly remembered his introduction to that sparse fare. "Our diet consisted of pork of a very poor kind, hardtack, not of the best—far from it—and coffee that could not be made much worse." Hynes and his fellow Second Cavalry recruits had plenty of time to get used to it, perhaps even like it: after marching from Fort Leavenworth to regimental headquarters at Fort Harker, Kansas, they were informed that the companies to which they were assigned were posted at Fort Laramie, Dakota Territory, several hundred miles farther away.[33]

Members of the elite Signal Corps were spared the depot experience and when sent to western posts enjoyed somewhat better travel arrangements after graduating school at Fort Myer, Virginia. Already fully equipped and armed, "a soldier transferred to a new station by himself," Will C. Barnes explained. "A Transportation Request . . . secured for him only the right to ride in a day coach. Soldiers didn't use Pullmans then. They were offered their choice of what was known as 'cooked travel rations'—corned beef, crackers, cheese, etc.—or the huge sum of seventy-five cents a day in cash." In any event, the lengthy train trip was infinitely more pleasant than that endured by recruits destined for line units.[34]

The men who had been snared by regimental recruiters in the frontier regions and in California had a distinctly different experience than those who passed through the conventional recruiting depots. "After enlistment [at San Francisco] I was sent . . . to Angel Island located in San Francisco Bay for a few days' drilling," recalled Emanuel Roque, a former laundryman born in the Azores. "There were only recruits at this place and I was the only one of the 12th Infantry." However, already being in the far West during the late 1870s did not necessarily mean that joining one's regiment was any less complicated. Roque's party of a dozen recruits was ordered to rendezvous with the Second Infantry, only recently arrived from the Department of the South, en route to new stations in the Pacific Northwest. The men of the Second, with the recruits in tow, left Oakland by steamer to Fort Vancouver, Washington, headquarters of the Department of Columbia. From that point the troops continued on a lengthy trip eastward via riverboats, rail freight cars, and steamers again to eventually reach Camp Lapwai on Idaho's Snake River.[35]

Recall that Mulford had enlisted at Fort Leavenworth. While he and a few others waited for the accumulation of enough recruits to warrant drill, the Fifth Infantrymen of the garrison took full advantage of these would-be cavaliers. The rookies quickly discovered that "the recruit is expected at all times to do the little jobs and the dirty work ripe old soldiers know so well how to avoid. The recruit is the one that has an extra amount of dishes to wash, of wood to cut, water to carry, potatoes to peel, slops to empty, floors to scrub, knives and forks to scour, and is very often jollied into heel-balling belts and burnishing equipment—in fact impelled to do the very work that the noncoms . . . should do themselves." After about a dozen fresh fish had assembled, an infantry lance sergeant gave them basic instruction in the school of the soldier during the month prior to their assignment to the Seventh Cavalry in Dakota Territory. This bevy of recruits apparently saw more fatigue than drill: when an officer "marched" them to the railroad depot, Mulford later admitted "now that I know what the word march, keep step, dress to the right and the numerous other orders . . . mean, I must own up that we walked or straggled!" One of the party, John Goll, had already had enough; he abandoned his army career after only nineteen days.[36]

"There is not a bit of regret expressed by the beginners at the order to move, as they are so sure of being on an equal footing with the rest of their regiment and free from the petty persecutions of the old coffee-cooling Infantrymen at the Fort," said Mulford. But he was overly optimistic. Going by rail to Fort Snelling, Minnesota, whence the cavalry recruits would travel to Fort Abraham Lincoln, Dakota Territory, the party encountered a delay of about ten days to await the arrival additional recruits. Hosted by a company of the Twentieth Infantry for rationing purposes, Mulford and his pals were put to work by the doughboys "digging cellars, drawing dirt, grading, setting out trees, sawing wood, etc." When a noncom overheard one of the recruits complaining that he had not enlisted to use a pick and a shovel, he provided the man a knapsack filled with fifty pounds of bricks "which he had to carry on parade for three days, when he was glad to . . . resume farm work." Mulford ever after remembered C Company as "the meanest lot of Regulars it was ever my lot to come in contact with in any manner." But in time this latest indignity, too, ended and the recruits once again continued on their way.[37]

Upon his arrival at some forlorn, sun-baked railhead, a recruit's first impressions of frontier society likely contrasted sharply from his previous civilian surroundings, though conditions may have realistically reflected the popular dime novels of the day. The train carrying R. Eugene Pelham and a batch of Sixth Infantry replacements rolled up to the station at the center of Hays City, Kansas, on what should have been a quiet Sunday afternoon. "We were very abruptly introduced to what was certainly the 'wild and wooly' West," Pelham declared. "The smoke of battle had scarcely cleared away from the little pleasantry that had taken place between two cavalrymen and two citizens. Casualties, one dead soldier, and one shot in three places; one dead citizen and one shot up pretty well. . . . I told the boys if that was soldiering I wanted to go home, but I soon learned that I had hardly got started into the primary class as far as the lessons of frontier life were concerned."³⁸

At length the bedraggled recruits got to the post serving as their regimental headquarters. For members of frontier garrisons starved for any break in the usual monotony, the arrival of a new batch of rookies was always a special treat. "In the heat of the day the detachment arrives at its destination, footsore, hungry and tired. They are marched to the adjutant's office, and drawn up in line for the inspection of the officers and the idle gaze of the whole garrison. This and that man's appearance is remarked upon, and without the least desire or inclination on their part to keep from hurting their feelings." A recruit confessed his embarrassment when "all the members of the 7th Cavalry not on duty gathered as near us as they dared to. . . . They laughed heartily at our very best attempts to stand at 'attention.'" Upon seeing a batch of fresh fish at Fort Sill, Indian Territory, an infantryman declared: "Oh what a variety of humanity from a very intelligent society man to Darwin's missing link of some backwoods—just fresh from the farm. . . . Another was from the Puritan City in the Bay State. He read too many dime novels . . . and wanted to go west to kill Injuns. . . . There stood a young man, apparently from a better class and more intelligent than the general run . . . apparently dreaming of the nice home he had so recklessly thrown away." Nevertheless, picking out the ex-soldiers among them "was a matter of no difficulty," wrote Fifth Cavalry Adjutant Charles King. "They were already acting as noncommissioned officers of the recruit companies."³⁹

Standing before the formation, such as it was, the adjutant called the roll in the order of company assignments, "and for the first time, [I] become a high private in Company 'M,' 7th U.S. Regular Cavalry," Mulford announced. After that the first sergeants took charge of their new arrivals and conducted them to the barracks. Those men belonging to companies posted elsewhere, however, continued on until they too found homes. "I was sent to the Fifth U.S. Cavalry [and] was at Fort Russell [Wyoming Territory] but two or three days until I was assigned to Company M of that regiment," Private John J. Suttles said of his 1876 experience. "I was then sent to my company . . . stationed at Fort McPherson, Nebraska," which the train had passed by a few days earlier. Sending all of the regiment's recruits to its headquarters was necessary, however, for an initial muster at which they were officially added by name to the unit returns.[40]

For Signal Corpsman William W. Neifert, traveling with another new signalman to their assigned station at Fort Bowie, Arizona Territory, in 1886, the experience was somewhat different, though it still had its embarrassing moments. By that time rails even reached into previously isolated southern Arizona, enabling the two recruits to ride trains all the way from Virginia to Bowie Station, where they caught a stagecoach for the last thirteen miles to the post. The driver, finding that he had two tenderfeet as a captive audience, did his best to scare the daylights out of them with hair-raising tales about the Apaches. Apparently the two had not been instructed to report to the post adjutant upon arrival at the post. They therefore proceeded directly to the imposing commanding officer's quarters, dumped their gear on his front porch, and tried to raise the major by knocking at the door. When a resident signalman happened to see them, he sprinted over and reproved them, saying: "Do you want to disgrace the service? That's where you belong, over in those tents." Fortunately for the two rookies, the CO was not home at the time.[41]

For the enlistees it had been an eventful several weeks from the day they entered the recruiting station to their eventual arrival at their permanent posts. Now, at long last, they would belong to a unit where they would be accepted as equals by the members of their companies and to begin "real" soldiering—or so they thought.

CHAPTER 4

"Deployed as Skirmishers"

Regiments and Companies in the West

After much anticipation about joining their regiments, recruits were in most instances disillusioned to discover that they did so in name only. During the rebellion, states conducted their own recruiting efforts, with regiments being raised within particular counties or local regions. As a result, volunteers had identified primarily with their regiments, which usually remained cohesive units in camp and field, thus reinforcing the bonds among the members. But the situation on the western frontier was entirely different. The multifaceted nature of the army's duties in the Trans-Mississippi, coupled with the enormous geographical area, resulted in troops being scattered across the landscape by companies at forts and temporary cantonments. A Seventh Cavalry officer likened the situation to being "deployed as skirmishers—one company or squadron here, and another there." Regiments were assigned to the army's various geographical departments with regimental headquarters and a few companies at one post. The remaining companies were distributed among several others, often with only one or two companies serving together at any one station. An anonymous soldier writing to the editor of the *Army & Navy Journal* in 1876 complained that he had "served with an infantry regiment almost continuously during ten years, without once seeing it together or witnessing a battalion drill."[1]

When eleven troops of the Tenth Cavalry assembled at Fort Davis, Texas, in 1885 in preparation for transferring to Arizona, it was the first occasion when so many of the regiment's components had been together at the same place since its organization nineteen years earlier. "The effect of this scattering process," according to an Eighth Cavalry officer, "was not beneficial to the discipline and morale of either officers or men. Serving at widely different posts, under different post commanders, who sometimes had widely divergent views as to discipline, drill, equipment, care of the men and of horses . . . made more or less friction." Whereas garrisons composed only of infantry, or infantry and cavalry, were the norm, only more rarely did they include companies from different regiments of the same branch of service.[2]

As a consequence of this necessary dispersal of companies, one officer claimed, "regimental pride did not exist."[3] Although the degree of regimental esprit de corps experienced during the war may not have prevailed on the frontier, it was nonetheless evident, perhaps to a somewhat greater degree among the rank and file than among officers, who were required by regulations to transfer from one to another to gain promotion above company grade. In the wake of the Battle of the Little Bighorn, a Second Cavalry private, Edward Williams, thought his regiment was doing more than its share of field service, while "that godforsaken mob of the 7th Cav. is laying [*sic*] and cooling coffee."[4] When a civilian gambler at Walla Walla, Washington, derisively referred to all First Cavalrymen as sons of bitches, Fourth Cavalryman Emil Miller, who had previously served in the First, overheard the remark and took offense. Turning to the gambler, Miller said calmly: "I was a 1st Cavalryman; I am one of them." The gambler cursed the soldier as he drew a pistol from beneath his coat and shot Miller in the chest, mortally wounding him. On another occasion, a Sixth Cavalry farrier at Fort Niobrara, Nebraska, made a derogatory remark about the Seventh Cavalry within earshot of one of his corporals, who happened to be a former member of that regiment. The corporal "politely walked up to Mr. Bailey and pasted him in the face and of course a fight followed. Bailey got whipped." Even though a regiment's companies may have been widely separated, the members nonetheless shared a common loyalty to the number worn on their caps.[5]

Following a wartime experiment with three-battalion infantry regiments, the army reverted to the traditional composition of ten companies, lettered A through K, while those of cavalry were organized in twelve companies (or troops), designated A through M. In the United States Army the letter "J" was traditionally excluded from the series: in an age when all orders, correspondence, and other records were handwritten, its similarity with the letter "I" would have resulted in errors and misunderstandings, quite possibly critical ones affecting field operations. (The tradition prevails to the present day.) Officially, these subdivisions of regiments were known as companies, although the term "squadron" was applied to cavalry units at least as early as 1841 and continued in official parlance with the adoption of Colonel Philip St. George Cooke's *Cavalry Tactics* in 1861.[6]

The term "trooper," denoting a horse-mounted dragoon or cavalryman, also appeared throughout both the 1841 and 1861 tactics manuals, although the authors of those official publications refrained from applying "troop" to the company unit. Nevertheless, "troop" seems to have appealed to the cavalryman's ear and became so common that its use was widespread by the end of the Civil War. Viewing their branch to be the elite of the army line, cavalry officers and enlisted men alike used both terms universally and interchangeably. Irascible General of the Army William T. Sherman, however, took umbrage at the use of the word "troop," for whatever reason, which resulted in the promulgation of an official edict in 1873 stipulating that "in all orders and communications the word 'company' will be used to describe that unit of organization in all arms of the service—artillery, cavalry, and infantry." Accordingly, "troop" was expunged from the new *Cavalry Tactics* published the following year, although "trooper" was not. Despite Sherman's order, the term "troop" was already so firmly rooted in army tradition and in the vernacular it defied suppression, except in official records.[7]

Only in 1881, just two years before his retirement, did Sherman finally concede to the obvious. "After many years of diversity of nomenclature," announced the editor of the *Army & Navy Journal*, "the General of the Army has decided that the designation 'Troop' instead of 'Company' has been adopted . . . and should be used in all cavalry organizations." Taking advantage of the uncontested ground of his annual report, however, Sherman was unable to resist firing a final round of sour grapes by pointing out "the absurdity of styling companies of foot artillery, armed with muskets and without guns, 'batteries.' They are not batteries in any intelligent sense. The same as to 'troop' for cavalry. All should be styled what they are in fact, 'companies.'" But company, battery, and troop were cemented in the army's culture, and there they would remain despite a disgruntled Sherman's personal objections.[8]

Informally, infantrymen were commonly referred to as "doughboys" (sometimes appearing in contemporary accounts as two words, "dough boys"). Most Americans associate the term with the U.S. soldier during the First World War, but its use dated at least as early as the Mexican-American War, quite possibly even earlier. The origin of the nickname is even less certain. According to an officer whose service predated the Civil War, "the term . . . is a relic of the times of white belts and pipe clay. The effect of soaking rain on a well-pipe-clayed belt, as well as on the clothing of the wearer, made the term sufficiently appropriate for army use." The infantry used belts made of white buff leather for cartridge boxes, swords, and waist belts until about 1850, when black leather was substituted for these articles. Indeed, according to some sources, "doughboy" may well have stemmed from the white trim adorning infantry uniforms as far back as the birth of the regular army itself in the 1780s. Another officer commented: "The somewhat pasty effect of white . . . as appearing upon the blue of a former day . . . elicited from the irreverent of other arms the epithet 'Doughboy,' in designation of the soldier of infantry." The nickname may have derived from either of these, or both, yet a veteran of the 1876 Sioux Campaign offered an even more practical and convincing reason for the moniker: "Infantrymen are called 'dough boys' because they tramp through the mud," as if kneading dough. Whatever its origin, the sobriquet stuck and was certainly a fixture in army parlance during the Indian Wars. In fact, infantrymen themselves embraced the term and wore it proudly.[9]

A less common, yet unambiguous, nickname given to the infantry—"walk-a-heaps"—was peculiar to the era of the Indian campaigns. John F. Finerty, a Chicago newspaperman who accompanied the Big Horn and Yellowstone Expedition in 1876, credited this colorful epithet to the Indians of the northern Great Plains.[10]

Attached to each regimental headquarters, and invariably accompanying it, was a band composed of sixteen privates overseen by the adjutant. Bandsmen, according to law, were drawn from the companies according to an assessment determined by the commanding officer. The men were thus dropped from the company rolls and taken up on a separate return for the band, which mustered with the regiment's noncommissioned staff. Sometimes band musicians were soldiers who happened to possess musical talent and volunteered (or were assigned) for the band; at other times they were specially requested through the system discussed earlier. As a correspondent writing to the *Army & Navy Journal* observed, "Occasionally, a wandering musician, out of work, runs across a regimental headquarters and enlists, but when . . . he contemplates his pay and allowances, finds them by no means encouraging, and most likely disappears. Then bandsmen are often sent to regiments from the recruiting depots, whose knowledge of music is so limited that it may be months or years before they are able to take their proper places."[11]

Some regiments undertook special efforts to recruit bandsmen. The Eighth Infantry, for example, "loved good music, and had imported its musicians direct from Italy," according to an army wife. In the late 1860s the Fifth Infantry band was composed largely of Frenchmen. After the end of the Civil War, when the U.S. government reaffirmed its long-standing Monroe Doctrine with regard to the French occupation of Mexico, a veteran recalled: "Many of the French soldiers from Maximilian's army had deserted and come to the United States. Some of them had joined our army . . . The leader of the band was one, and he could not speak English, but he could speak Spanish and taught the band in that language as about all the members of the 5th could speak Spanish." Bandsmen nevertheless were to be trained as soldiers and were subject to being recalled to their respective companies as necessary.[12]

Regimental bands, many of which included a string ensemble or orchestra of a half-dozen musicians to play for dances, were a source of unit pride and a popular source of amusement with the men. "We have music by the band at guard mount and some times in the evening it seems like home to hear the band playing old familiar pieces," wrote an Eighteenth Infantryman at Fort Phil Kearny, Dakota Territory. A Thirteenth Infantry officer at Fort Stevenson recounted: "The military band . . . has a most happy effect on morale, and I should almost say on the physical condition of the men, who their day's work done, like to listen to the music, resting in a group in front of company quarters." Although bandsmen seldom participated in field operations, the Seventh Cavalry was a notable exception, the band being the pet of its commander, Lieutenant Colonel George A. Custer. Former sergeant Charles Windolph fondly remembered the regiment's band mounted on white horses. They'd never fail to play the regiment's own song "Garry Owen." . . . I faintly remember some of the other tunes they used to play on that trip [Black Hills Expedition] . . . [like] "The Mocking Bird" and "The Blue Danube." . . . On nights when the moon was out and the stars cracking in the sky, and the air was crisp and cool, it was something to stretch out before a big open fire and listen to the music. Soldiering wasn't half bad those times.[13]

However pleasant their music, army bandsmen seem to have had a propensity for disciplinary problems. Seventh Cavalryman John Ryan recalled the time musicians rebelled against playing on extremely cold mornings during the 1868 Washita Campaign:

Some of the bandsmen had an idea if there was anything amiss with their instruments they would not have to play. There was a number of their instruments defective, and I believe some of them punched holes in them on purpose. . . . Custer got on to the racket and ordered the men that had anything the matter with their instruments to walk and do the usual fatigue duty while on the trip. . . . After a few days the biggest part of those instruments were brought into service.

After the Sixth Cavalry band gave a July Fourth performance in Tucson, Arizona Territory, Adjutant John B. Kerr ordered the musicians to assemble at their wagon immediately following the fireworks display for transport back to nearby Fort Lowell. At the appointed time, however, many of the members went missing. When the lieutenant finally rounded them up, he was dumbfounded to discover that several of his inebriated bandsmen had traded their instruments to civilians for booze. A comment by Fifth Cavalry Adjutant Eben Swift suggests that such behavior was characteristic. Upon arriving at Fort D. A. Russell, Wyoming Territory, in 1876 Colonel Wesley Merritt directed Swift to "come and straighten out the band which had been left behind and was in a bad condition of discipline and otherwise."[14]

There was little fraternization between the men of different companies and still less between those of different branches. "Two regiments in the same command are often comparative strangers to each other," wrote an officer of long experience. "The cavalry going its way, the infantry its way. Not because there are unkindly feelings between them, but because each is sufficient to itself." A degree of rivalry nevertheless existed among the service branches, particularly between the cavalry and infantry serving in close association with each other on the frontier. Reynolds J. Burt, who spent much of his youth at frontier posts as the son of an infantry officer, confirmed: "There was little mingling between Cavalry troops and Infantry men. The former 'backed' by their mounts tried to look down in a wise-cracking way on their 'brothers' the infantrymen. The latter from their bunks at early dawn, would mentally chuckle, 'There go the sore-asses to "chambermaid" their horses.'"[15]

In the field cavalry units often reached camp before the doughboys, yet when the latter arrived they were at liberty to eat and relax almost immediately, while enjoying the satisfaction of watching the troopers feed and groom their horses before being allowed their own supper. During General George Crook's "Starvation March" in 1876, with rations exhausted and starving horses dying by the score, doughboys grimly joked that "if we only marched far enough, they would eat all the cavalry horses." Conversely, cavalrymen countered with jabs of their own. Writing candidly to his mother in 1877, a Seventh Cavalry officer smugly confided: "They used to have a saying during the war in the Infantry, 'who ever saw a dead cavalryman' but out here you would have to look some distance before you would see a dead Infantryman, or an Infantryman who has seen a dead Indian." No love was lost between the two branches, as is apparent in the comment made by a Seventh Cavalry recruit aboard the steamer *Carroll* traveling up the Yellowstone River in July 1876. When Sioux warriors attacked a camp of the Twenty-Second Infantry just after the boat passed by, the trooper was prompted to write: "I have one consolation in knowing I am not now under the command of such a man as the 'doughboy' colonel of the 22nd."[16]

Sometimes little provocation was required to spark open conflict between soldiers of the two branches. At Fort Robinson, Nebraska, animosities peaked as Ninth Cavalrymen observed some men belonging to the Eighth Infantry abusing a dog. When the infantrymen hit the dog, the black troopers promptly intervened to protect the animal, thus precipitating a fistfight. "Infantry and Cavalry didn't get along well," acknowledged former Ninth Cavalryman Simpson Mann. Nevertheless, there were exceptions. For example, an infantry soldier who had been in close association with a company of the Seventh Cavalry for three years on the plains offered the contrasting opinion about "being with them on many scouts and sharing with them all kinds of hardships. I will say here there never was a finer or braver company of men gathered together." The circumstances in which soldiers of different branches found themselves at a particular time undoubtedly influenced their views. The mutual confinement and boredom of garrison life tended to heightened tensions, while sharing the dangers of a campaign and combat promoted mutual respect and more amiable relations between branches. The greater the danger, the less conflict between the two.[17]

The successive acts of Congress steadily diminishing the size of the army unavoidably translated into smaller units among the three combat arms. The act of July 28, 1866, established the strength of cavalry companies at ninety-nine enlisted men and sixty-nine for infantry companies. The infantry maintained that level into the following decade. When Congress further slashed the army appropriation in 1874, however, foot companies were allowed only forty-eight men and the strength of cavalry companies fell to eighty. Indeed the actual numbers were usually less than the paper authorization owing to delays in reporting the loss of men by discharge, desertion, and death; slow communication; and the time required for the Recruiting Service to process the requests and transport replacements to the frontier. Even after their arrival, the steady attrition of veterans continued, with the result that line units were virtually never at full strength. The constant turnover resulted in an average of about 10 percent of the men being classed as "green" recruits.[18]

Once at their assigned stations, recruits were apt to be disillusioned with the stark reality of the first place that they could call home. This was especially so immediately after the Civil War when many forts in the West, particularly those located along the expanding lines of communication, had been established only recently, while those active before or during the war had generally fallen into disrepair for want of adequate funds to maintain them. When a party of Second Cavalry recruits hiked into venerable Fort Laramie, Dakota Territory, in December 1866, a dismayed Private Robert Greenhalgh declared: "We arrived here after a journey of about six weeks from Fort Ellsworth [Kansas], and a miserable hole it is. We are stuck in quarters you would not put your cousin in. In fact they are but little better than outdoors." The facilities at permanent posts usually improved over time as a result of new construction, but even so a recruit walking into Fort Ellis, Montana Territory, in the mid-1870s was surprised to find "the buildings grouped around the rectangle were mostly of pine and fir logs. There was no stockade nor fence enclosing the area. Double-story block houses stood at two diagonally opposed corners of the structural array."[19]

Recruits quickly learned that the depot experience, regardless of the discipline imposed there, was merely a prelude to serving in the line. Briefly addressing a recently arrived batch of Sixth Cavalry recruits at Fort Hays, Kansas, Colonel James Oakes left no doubt in their minds about his expectations: "Young men you have turned your backs on civilian life, and have sworn your allegiance to the United States of America, to serve in her Army for five years. . . . There are three elements that are absolutely essential to make a good soldier. The first one is obedience—obey all orders, rules and regulations, and keep neat and clean. The second essential is obedience, and the THIRD ONE IS OBEDIENCE."[20] His welcoming speech, probably resembling those voiced by other commanders, made a lasting impression on the new men.

Regulations required that recruits be subjected to yet another medical examination upon reaching their respective stations. Although some post surgeons, particularly contract surgeons, may have occasionally ignored this rule, evidence suggests that recruits were routinely inspected soon after joining their regiments. Assistant Surgeon Robert M. O'Reilly, a regular army doctor at Fort Laramie, complained that "the recruits lately assigned to the 14th Infantry are in many cases men who should not have been enlisted. Certificates have been furnished . . . to two men . . . in whom the disability undoubtedly originated prior to entrance into the service. In the case of Pvt. Cahill, who is disqualified . . . by reason of flat feet, the most cursory examination should have shown his unfitness for military duty." Men with serious physical defects were summarily discharged and sent back to their place of enlistment. But those were not the only problems with recruits. At Fort Sidney, Nebraska, in 1882 Assistant Surgeon James P.

Kimball found that "not one of the detachments of recruits received from Jefferson Barracks, Mo. . . . but has contained a number of men, either suffering at the time of arrival or taken down soon after with fevers—typhoid, remittent, and intermittent—contracted . . . at Jefferson Barracks." Doctor Kimball attributed their condition to exposure to such diseases while at the depot and urged that the matter be investigated to avoid long-term deleterious effect on the cavalry.[21]

Upon joining their companies, recruits found their reception a familiar one. "We went through the same experience as at Jefferson Barracks —filling bed sacks and rookie initiations in drill and duties," a cavalry trooper recalled.[22] Private Fred Munn, among a batch of replacements recently arrived at Fort Ellis, Montana Territory, described a similar welcome: "We were issued clothing, mattresses, guns and side arms by big Jim. . . . He was First Sergeant of L Company, Second Cavalry and I remember him taking us down to the stables and saying, 'Come on boys, fill your bed ticks.'"[23] Immediately thereafter the new men were parceled out among the squads and directed to select bunks from those currently unoccupied.

Each soldier was assigned a unique number of one or two digits, without particular regard to the alphabetical order of his name on the roster, for purposes of marking laundry and for equipment accountability. If that number, perhaps vacated by a former member of the company, was not already on the gear issued to him, it was applied to the items; if previously issued equipment already bore different numbers, those were either obliterated or left unaltered and entered beside his name. Regardless, each soldier was held personally and financially responsible for the property.[24]

The first sergeants immediately had the new arrivals armed and equipped and drew the full regulation allowance of clothing for each man. Some of the men's garments were already showing wear after being worn at the depot for a few weeks then subjected to the trip west. "At the recruiting station each man had been issued one uniform and one set of underclothing and our 160 miles march [on remount horses] with a blanket for saddle had put our clothing in the worst possible condition," said a Fourth Cavalry trooper of his 1875 trek. Upon reporting at Fort Sill, Indian Territory, he continued: "Each man was issued a saddle, bridle, saddle blanket, saddle bags, and side lines . . . a lariat, picket pin, a curry comb and brush, and a canteen. For arms we were issued a .45 carbine, a .45 pistol, a saber, and some ammunition. We were proud indeed of our new possessions."[25]

The company clerk, copying data from the enlistment record that had accompanied each recruit to his destination, entered new arrivals in the Company Descriptive Book, a ledger listing the soldier's name, date and term of enlistment, previous occupation, physical description, date and reason for discharge, character, and when appropriate the date of death, desertion, or transfer. This information would prove useful in several ways. Were he to desert, the unit would be able to provide his physical description to a pursuing detachment not of his own company and if necessary to promulgate that information among law enforcement officers.[26]

The first sergeant, always mindful of any special skills possessed by members of his company, noted particularly the new men's prior occupations. Tradesmen—carpenters, bricklayers, plasterers, and the like—were always in demand for details in the Quartermaster Department to construct and repair buildings. Former blacksmiths, harness-makers, and hostlers were especially valuable commodities in cavalry troops. Likewise, men possessing musical talent might be detailed to the band and former clerks, teachers, and others possessing formal education would be singled out for duty as clerks or to oversee the post school. Sometimes the need for various skills was given higher priority than the soldier's fundamental training. "A recruit has been assigned to a company," complained a correspondent to the *Army & Navy Journal*. "Within a week, perhaps, it is discovered he is a carpenter, and without any training as a soldier, he is, by post order, detailed on 'extra duty' as a carpenter. Then . . . that individual is pursuing his jack-plane existence, patching up the post hen coops, free from drills, parades, stable calls, etc."[27]

What became immediately apparent to most recruits was the different atmosphere encountered in a line unit compared with the atmosphere of the recruiting depot. This at last was real soldiering, and recruits could not help being impressed with the businesslike tone of the company, where a "man's full duty as a soldier is expected of him, and nothing else will be tolerated."[28] "At reveille the next day I had a good look at the officers, non-commissioned officers and men of my company," said a cavalry trooper, "and was well pleased with their general appearance." A First Infantryman remarked that, unlike those at the recruiting depots, "our officers took an interest in us, the sergeants and corporals were not petty tyrants, 'quarters' were roomy and . . . 'grub' was abundant." Private Eddie Matthews, who had expressed a decidedly dim view of the recruits traveling with him to the frontier in 1869, was pleasantly surprised when he first entered his troop quarters at Fort Whipple, Arizona Territory. "When we arrived yesterday evening we were welcomed heartily by our Company. Men came and shook hands and welcomed us the same as though they had known us for a number of years. . . . I feel much better. All are young men, and seem to be gentlemen in every respect. I don't think I ever saw finer looking men in my life. . . . [They] are as different from the recruits that came with me as day light is to darkness."[29]

Perhaps a more common reception was comparative silence as the old-timers of the company scrutinized the new men without being too obvious. They did, however, look to the recruits for recent news from the States, as the established portion of the country was known. "The soldiers were not slow in coming to see the recruits," wrote Private Mulford. "The vets all wanted to know what was going on in the outside world." Sharing news of current events was a comfortable means for the rookies to open a dialogue with their new comrades and begin integration into the company. One recruit who wished to notify his family that he had arrived safely at his post, finding he had neither postage stamp nor money, cautiously approached a veteran trumpeter to ask if he might borrow a stamp. After sizing up the young man, the older soldier handed him enough change to purchase several stamps. The two thereafter became good friends.[30]

Nevertheless, a recruit's adaptation to new circumstances and routine was not without its trying, sometimes comical, moments. The first morning following the arrival of a batch of recruits at Fort Assinniboine, Montana Territory, one of the new men arose at dawn, strolled outside the barracks, and sighted a range of hills, or so he thought, a short distance from the post. Inspired to climb to the top for a quick look around the countryside before breakfast, the youth began walking, without realizing that in the clear western atmosphere features appeared much nearer than they actually were. The "hills" he saw actually were the Sweet Grass Mountains, some seventy-five miles away. Two days later a mounted detachment caught up with the recruit, brought him back to the post, and confined him to the guardhouse. "I have often thought what a good infantryman the service lost by permitting him to enlist for the cavalry," chuckled a First Cavalry comrade.[31]

Thus began the process of assimilation into the society of men with whom the recruit would be in close association for the next several years. Acknowledging the presence of "blackguards and criminals of various degrees" in his troop of the Sixth Cavalry in 1866, Civil War veteran Henry McConnell noted that there were "some honorable exceptions—the veterans of ten and fifteen years of service . . . who have made the army the business of their lives." He initially considered himself fortunate to be placed in a squad that included three old regulars who had served continuously since before the war. Yet he was chagrined when they "looked with contempt on the fellow whose experience only dated from the volunteer service . . . the profound contempt felt by the regular soldier for everything and everybody connected with or pertaining to the volunteer soldiery would be very funny if it wasn't about correct." Those case-hardened antebellum regulars provided valuable continuity for service traditions and institutional memory in the ranks for many years. An example of one of those old soldiers was Private Daniel E. Munger, who first enlisted as an artilleryman in 1858, served through the end of the war, then joined the infantry. After spending two enlistments on the western frontier, he signed on with the Second Cavalry, fought at the Battle of the Rosebud, and continued soldiering with the same company until he died of heart failure in the field during the Geronimo Campaign in 1886. This informal, yet venerated, hierarchy changed somewhat over the years as veterans of the prewar "Old Army" dwindled in numbers and their legacy gradually passed to the ex-volunteers still in service.[32]

Although a man's wartime service in the volunteers was not recorded on his enlistment form (and did not count for regular army purposes), the company noncoms were usually able to pick them out simply by their demeanor and familiarity with military life. Not all men, however, wanted to be identified as ex-volunteers, as James D. Lockwood explained: "There was but one man who knew of his [Lockwood's] former services, and he, being an old member of the Fourth New York heavy artillery, recognized the former drummer boy, but was prevailed upon by him to keep it a secret, as he did not wish to give cause for jealousy among his new comrades." A soldier's previous service usually became known throughout the company, but in this instance Lockwood may have feared that he would be detailed to the comparatively soft life of a musician, rather than doing regular duty.[33]

Former Union state volunteers nevertheless brought to the rank-and-file of the regular army a strong element of seasoning. Describing an infusion of recruits to the westward bound Thirteenth Infantry shortly after the war, Musician James C. Bothwell wrote: "On arriving at Fort Leavenworth we went into camp and was there joined by a Squad of recruits from Governors Island, N.Y.[,] which added about two hundred men to the strength of the Batt[alio]n, and as most of these men had seen service in the civil war . . . and some were old Regulars, we had no trouble assimilating them and the command took on the airs of old." An 1866 visit by Major General William T. Sherman, commanding the Division of the Missouri, to Fort Kearny, Nebraska, happened to coincide with the Eighteenth Infantry's arrival there on its march across the plains to occupy posts in Dakota Territory. Some fifty to sixty of its members, veterans of the Atlanta Campaign, paid a soldiers' tribute to their old commander with a special formation to render military honors. Sergeant Lauren W. Aldrich estimated that of the eight hundred recruits in his batch bound for the Thirtieth Infantry in Wyoming Territory in 1867 "about 75% . . . had served in the Civil War and knew something of discipline." Even in the early 1870s, Private Charles Windolph, Seventh Cavalry, estimated that "about half of the 150 new men we had were men who either had Civil War service or had already served a five-year hitch in the army."[34]

Nonetheless, these veterans, most of whom had endured the hardships of field service and had survived combat, tended to be a rough crowd. "If a like number of dare-devils were ever together before we never heard of them," Private James W. Foley said of his Fourth Cavalry comrades in 1865. "Some of them were desperados . . . perhaps not by nature but the war had made them such." A soldier posted at Camp Crittenden, Arizona Territory, was critical of the majority of the men in his company for being "Democrats . . . [who] fought during the war more for the object of gain, being bounty jumpers, and was [sic] driven into the service this time because they are to[o] shiftless to work."[35]

A man writing to the *Army & Navy Journal* commented: "When a detachment of recruits is assigned to a company . . . the recruits, like boys entering boarding school or freshmen at college, or 'tenderfeet' everywhere, must bear some chaffing and practical jokes from the older men." While reenlisted veterans were spared the indignities of practical jokes (nor would they have tolerated them), old soldiers invariably took advantage of the impressionable neophytes by feeding the rookies hair-raising tales about Indians. "They wanted to know all about Indians and the dangers of prairie life," Sixteenth Infantryman Emil Bode recounted. "A couple of our best yarn-spinners made the poor fellows think that their hair wasn't their own when outside of camp." The ruse was so prevalent that it came to the attention of Colonel Philippe Régis De Trobriand, commanding Fort Stevenson, Dakota Territory. Concerned with its effects on morale, he wrote: "Many of our recruits have let themselves become frightened by the absurd stories and ridiculous reports about the Indians, until they have become accustomed to think of them as such dangerous enemies that they are rather to be avoided than attacked." A Seventh Cavalry sergeant related that raw recruits coming to the regiment in the early 1870s frequently inquired about the famous 1868 Battle of the Washita. Taking full advantage of a virgin audience, an old trooper or noncom would meet the challenge with the somber introduction: "You wish to hear about the battle of the Washita, do you? Well, sir, it was 4 o'clock in the morning and the band played 'Garry Owen,' and the whole circle of old vets would begin to laugh." Only later would the puzzled recruits appreciate the humor. Custer had taken the band into the field then ordered it to play at the opening of a fight, which struck the men as being so theatrical that it was "ever a subject of standing ridicule in the regiment."[36]

Some of the company pranksters became adept at devising ways to embarrass recruits, without themselves being exposed as the instigators. After their arrival at Fort Grant, Arizona Territory, "One rookie asked about butter and was told to go ask the first sergeant for 'butter money' and as it was only the 8th of the month there would be about $1.50 coming. . . . Well, after we had our slum and coffee . . . we had our leader go for his butter money. . . . And the way he came out! . . . The first sergeant wanted to know who sent him in. All soldiers look alike to a rookie, so it was never known who sent him in." The very next day First Cavalryman John T. Stokes, a recruit in the same party, recalled: "I was on stable police. One man told me to ask [the first sergeant] for a star and a club. I saw a lot of stars when I asked and got the club or something bigger!" Going to even greater lengths to intimidate some new arrivals, he said: "Hal Winslow of K Troop took his big U.S. belt buckle, daubed it with red ink and branded a big U.S. on his [own] hip and then told the rookies that they were to be branded with a hot iron. He slipped his trousers down and showed them his brand. Two of that bunch of rookies were never seen after than evening."[37]

"A troop is a family of big boys. Some of them big bad boys, and an odd thing about it is that these are not always the unpopular ones," noted a Fifth Cavalry trooper. Units nearly always included a few toughs and bullies in their ranks. A recent arrival at Fort Kearny in 1867 recalled that his recruit detachment was allowed to rest for a few days, "and it was during this resting spell that the old soldiers vigorously put in practice an established custom of hazing and even slugging the most likely recruits. No serious harm [was] intended of course but only for the sole purpose of entertainment." Entertainment may have been only part of the motive. Often the individuals who had established themselves as bullies at the recruiting depots suddenly were themselves subjected to intimidation when they joined their permanent companies. Old soldiers in the company, even though only privates themselves, took pride in their status and were not loath to impress upon the new men that they were not yet in the same class. When a newly arrived Tenth Cavalry recruit accused Private Willis McReynold (a three-year veteran) of pilfering his haversack, McReynold lectured the neophyte: "Do you know who you're talking to? Do you know that I's an old soldier? You wait till you're an old soldier before you try to dominize over me. You ain't nothing but a recruit, that's all you is. Instead of dominizin' over old soldiers you ought to salute every time you see 'em, that's what you ought to do. You try dominizin' over me, I knock your head off." Although individuals in some companies likely intended their rough treatment of new men to establish a pecking order, such behavior served a broader purpose. "There was no coddling of weaklings," a former first sergeant stated. "If you couldn't take it you found life in the Cavalry very unpleasant."[38]

In any event, according to Sergeant Armand Unger, the noncommissioned officers and older privates kept things from getting out of hand by making the troublemakers "straighten up and act decently" toward the new men. The hazing and practical jokes subsided after a few days because the veterans of the company appreciated that "we had to make the best of it, since we were together most of the time."

In instances when a unit had suffered significant combat losses, such as after the Battle of the Little Bighorn, company members were solemn and lay aside pranks and hazing of the replacements. Assigned to Company C at Fort Abraham Lincoln, Dakota Territory, in the fall of 1876, Seventh Cavalryman Lawrence J. Harvey found the mood somber because "the company had only 16 men left, 47 being killed in the Massacre." Taking soldiering seriously and pulling one's own weight were paramount to earning acceptance in the brotherhood, as recruits quickly "realized what it is in part to be a full-fledged Regular."[39]

According to the very nature and variety of its members, each unit tended to acquire a unique personality. Attempting to describe his company of the Second Cavalry in 1866, one man wrote:

> The men of E Troop were young men, none exceeding thirty years, some were not twenty. They represented nearly every state in the Union, and almost every country in Europe . . . Baker the philosopher, . . . rollicking Burke, . . . Sullivan, the quaint, . . . Dolpher the Prussian disciplinarian, . . . Von Hammerstein, the Austrian scholar, . . . Jones, the son of an English minister, . . . Chevaunce, the Gascon and mathematician, . . . Jones of Michigan, a sharpshooter during 1861–65 . . . and others—God knows where they came from, with a fair average of riff-raff, but all were fearless in a fight, a motley gathering that would be hard to duplicate with a like number.[40]

By the time a recruit reached his company, it was already well established that he would be serving with recent immigrants from the world over, many of whom had been attracted by monetary bounties to join state regiments. "When the war ended many of this class joined the Regular Army," wrote a former cavalryman. "It was nothing in those days to have men in the ranks who could speak and write two or three languages, and many of them were well grounded in Latin and Greek. With these men were civil engineers, architects, artists, navigators, and some of the best musicians." One such soldier was Private John Spring, a Swiss immigrant and former New York volunteer serving in the Fourteenth Infantry in Arizona Territory. In addition to his native language (Italian), Spring was fluent in German, French, and Latin. "They represented all sorts and conditions of men—character studies of every nationality," a native-born American said of his Twenty-Seventh Infantry comrades. "Many spoke but little English. A rougher and more lawless set I had never before come in contact with."[41]

European immigrants sometimes brought with them old national animosities, allowing current politics and conflicts on the Continent to color relationships with their new comrades. According to the composition of any particular garrison, such events may have created conflicts. During the Franco-Prussian War of 1870–71, for instance, Quartermaster Sergeant Maurice Wolfe observed: "The Irish are all French sympathizers. Last payday here and for two days after, a patrol had to be kept around this camp to keep the Irish and Dutch from licking each other. The Irish would go for them every chance they got." Conversely, an Eighth Cavalry trooper commented that at Fort Union, New Mexico Territory: "Sympathy for either side *viz* France or Prussha [*sic*] . . . among soldiers is not very great. All say it is no money in their pockets or will they lose any relations on either side."[42]

Foreign immigrants not infrequently discovered fellow countrymen, sometimes even former neighbors, serving in the American army. An Irish infantryman at Camp Brown, Wyoming Territory, for example, happily announced to a family member: "I have seen several young men from home in the Army here. There is a young man in Co. B, 5 Cavalry who served his apprenticeship at James Stacks in Listowell. . . . His name is Michael Fitzgerald. There is a man named Dennis Moore who lived near old Darcey's place on the road from Ardagh to Newcastle. . . . He is a smart young man." Such relationships founded on common culture and experience undoubtedly aided in immigrants' adjustment to a foreign land and army life.[43]

If former volunteers added seasoning to the army, those of foreign birth provided spice. According to experienced officers, the men of various nationalities seem to have possessed about equal capacities for soldiering. Still, certain traits often emerged among the recent immigrants. "The Englishman is most likely to be insubordinate. He has the habit of pretending to have fallen from a superior situation. If he is a deserter from the British army, he is still worse. The Irishman must be closely watched. He is one of the best soldiers when he is good, and one of the worst when he is bad. The Germans and Scandinavians are very trustworthy." Other contemporary opinions echoed praise for the Germans. "None are more trustworthy and efficient, or show more cheerful obedience to discipline." Of the men he served with in the Sixth Cavalry, Private George Whittaker said: "I thought the Germans made very good soldiers. They all had military in Germany." And while the Irish may have been prone to falling from grace, an officer related that they "were the first to hurray at the chance of a fight . . . and no matter how gloomy or dismal the campaign, if there is any fun to be extracted from its incidents, he is the man to find it."[44]

While ex-Confederates were not common in the postwar regular army, some were nonetheless present in the ranks. A Seventh Cavalryman recorded that among the men in his company during that regiment's formation in 1866, "three had served in the Confederate service. One of them had served in Harry Gilmore's guerillas . . . one in a North Carolina regiment, and one in the Texas Rangers." Lawrence Dugan, a member of the Fourth Infantry during the late 1870s, was a veteran of three years' service in the Confederate army as well having been a soldier of fortune in Central and South America. Because comparatively few southerners joined the regulars in the immediate post–Civil War years, the available evidence suggests that conflicts with northerners in the ranks seldom arose. A possible exception involved Privates Ransom Davis and William Darnel, young South Carolinians who enlisted in April 1867 and were assigned to Company H, Sixth Infantry. Davis deserted three months later, but Darnel stayed on until only a month before he would have been discharged. Whether either of these men was a victim of hazing because of regional nativity can only be speculated.[45]

In any event, most regulars seem to have been able to put their differences aside, and domestic sectional rivalries were of little or no consequence to the foreigners. Sergeant James S. Hamilton, who served in the First Infantry, 1876–81, allowed that by that time the "feeling was not too strong because few men from the South enlisted, had they been there ill feeling would of prevailed." Of course, the strict discipline imposed in the regular army undoubtedly had a quelling effect on any outward displays of sectional bitterness. Any residual animosities that may have existed initially diminished with the years as subsequent generations of young Americans entered the ranks. William G. Wilkinson attested that he never heard the subject mentioned in his troop of the Eighth Cavalry in the late 1880s, while a former Second Cavalryman spoke for the overwhelming majority of regulars: "A soldier was a soldier. If he was good, he was judged by his own merits."[46]

No company would have been complete without a couple of "beats and Jonahs."[47] The "beat" (slang for deadbeat) was a chronic shirker who managed by any creative means to avoid doing his share of fatigue or company duty, whether in garrison or in the field. The Jonah, in contrast, no matter how well-intentioned, was both careless and accident-prone. He was the one who put on his waist belt upside down, managed to strike his cap visor when bringing his piece to the position of "inspection arms," kicked over another man's coffee, or collapsed a shelter tent by tripping over a guy rope. Such a character, the constant vexation of the first sergeant, was described as "splay-footed, knock-kneed, pumpkin-bellied, round-shouldered . . . beyond all possibility of being drilled . . . a physical aberration, the type of which is well-known in the service; too lazy to desert and too good natured to be punished, and thus finally permitted in despair to subside into the company kitchen among pots and kettles, or put permanently at whitewashing the woodshed."[48]

Like all families, companies had to accept the bad along with the good. An anonymous correspondent to the *Army & Navy Journal* in 1868 admitted that "every company in the service has a few worthless men—men who are unfitted for the service, but who enlisted from ignorance, or were discharged from jail or penitentiary, and unable to obtain work for want of character . . . and enlisted to be transported at Government expense to a new field for thriving operations. These men . . . desert from one post, and when hard up enlist at another—desert and enlist, and so on." An infantryman reinforced this statement by confirming that "a great number of men had simply enlisted for the purpose of obtaining a free passage to California . . . with the intention of deserting their colors as soon as possible after their arrival."[49]

If men were not already hardened to life when they enlisted, those who made the grade and served out their terms certainly became so. Young men from good backgrounds soon learned that they had to stand up for themselves. While they were seated at the mess table, a soldier adjacent to Private William Jett reached over and took Jett's eating utensils because none had been placed at his own plate. Jett immediately grabbed the man's hands and wrenched the utensils away from him. When the other soldier offered to fight it out, Jett coolly replied that he had gotten what he wanted and returned to eating his meal. Seventh Cavalryman Clarence Allen remembered: "There was a fellow by the name of Kearn, who was a fairly good boxer. We were out back of the barracks and something came up where we squared off." After Allen bested the man, "that element never, from that time on . . . tried to crowd me." In other instances, interpersonal conflicts were not settled so easily. Private Louis Zinser related that during the Sioux Campaign of 1876 two Third Cavalrymen had a dispute that led to blows, "whereupon the saddler took his revolver and shot at the private . . . the ball striking about three feet from his mark. He was put under arrest. I didn't quite know whether it was for shooting, or whether it was for being a poor marksman." An altercation at Fort Davis, Texas, in 1878 ended more tragically. After Twenty-Fifth Infantrymen Sergeant Moses Marshall and Corporal Richard Robinson engaged in a heated verbal exchange in their barracks, Marshall returned a short time later with his rifle and deliberately shot the corporal through the head as he lay asleep on his bunk. Attesting to the regular army's well-deserved reputation, one soldier aptly characterized it as "a tough bunch."[50]

A soldier's principal identity and loyalty lay with his company, and he usually remained in the same one for the duration of his enlistment. It was not unusual for men to reenlist in the same company, sometimes repeatedly. "Troop K was the best troop," one former First Cavalry sergeant boasted of his old outfit, noting that both of its officers were veterans of the Civil War and the Indian campaigns. Most men, in fact, considered their own companies to be the best. The company, commented Sergeant Theodore E. Guy, "was like one big family." Many veterans expressed a similar feeling of camaraderie and unit pride. Writing in the field during the 1876 Sioux Campaign, a Second Cavalryman noted in his journal: "My company is living well, better than I expected, and not like F & L Co. Them is mobs, they live well in the Garrison, but out in the field, where it is needed, they starve." And not unlike families, the men may have had some differences among themselves, but they closed ranks against any outside threats. Private Hartford G. Clark, serving with G Troop, Sixth Cavalry at Fort Niobrara, Nebraska, recorded such an incident in his diary: "There was a big fight last night in front of our quarters. K & A troop fellows were against G, lots of excitement. Consequently there are many black eyes to be seen in those troops today." Such occurrences were not out of the ordinary, as suggested in the droll comment made by a Ninth Cavalry trooper: "Cavalry got along pretty well. . . . Sometimes fought—[but] hardly ever killed one another."[51]

Although noncommissioned officers were invariably addressed by rank and surname, privates were universally referred to by last name alone. Bearing this out, Seventh Cavalryman Theodore W. Goldin claimed that during his time in the army he learned the first name of only one soldier in his troop. When more than one man in a company shared the same surname, the individuals were numbered according to the alphabetical order of their first names: for example, Michael Murphy and Thomas Murphy became "Murphy 1" and "Murphy 2" for purposes of roll call. It was not unusual for men having common names, Brown for instance, to be "Brown 4" or an even higher number. Those designations not infrequently extended to everyday use in the company, and the individuals often were known by no other name.[52]

Beyond numbering, men in the company frequently gave their comrades nicknames based on some personality trait, characteristic, or incident. First Sergeant John Ryan recorded that "Telegraph" Smith got his sobriquet by being a gossip and the "biggest liar in the company." It was not unusual for the youngest, or the most youthful appearing, man in the company to be known as "Kid," and men of foreign birth were routinely accorded names like "Dutchy" or "Sauerkraut" for Germans and invariably "Frenchy" for Frenchmen. It may have been that Sergeant "Give-a-Damn" Smith of Company D, Sixth Cavalry commonly used that phrase. Prior to joining the army, "Tinker Bill" Myers had worked as a tinner's apprentice. The cook of Company G, Twenty-First Infantry was called "Smokey Jack" for obvious reasons. As a former Third Cavalry sergeant, Perley S. Eaton, recalled: "There were some nicknames, such as Brute, and Nigger, and Josh—some Shorty, some lengthy. One fellow, they called him Guts. His name was Guttier. Another they called him Brigham Young. His name was Young." Once applied, a nickname usually clung to a soldier for as long as he remained in the company.[53]

Within a day or two after reporting to their stations, raw recruits were segregated from those having prior service and formed into separate squads for drill. Former regulars needed only a short period of refresher training, perhaps a day or less, before being turned to duty with the company. Those who had served with volunteer organizations during the war required additional training for a few days under the tutelage of a noncommissioned officer well posted in tactics. Although the cavalry arm continued to use Cooke's manual until 1874, the infantry had adopted a new system developed by Lieutenant Colonel Emory Upton shortly after the war. Accordingly, those volunteers who had been in the cavalry had considerably less to learn than did those previously in the infantry or artillery. The small arms of both dismounted and mounted branches had likewise changed after the war with the advent of breech-loading rifles and carbines using metallic cartridges. Here again ex-cavalrymen required less training: by the end of the conflict virtually all Union cavalry regiments were armed with either Sharps percussion or Spencer repeating carbines, and the army continued to use those basic designs for a number of years after the war. The infantry, however, witnessed a radical and rapid advancement from muzzle-loading rifle muskets to Springfield single-shot breech loaders during the late 1860s. Those replacements who had previously served as foot soldiers during the war thus were challenged by both new tactics and new-pattern rifles.[54]

William F. Hynes (alias William Jones), who had spent only three days at Carlisle Barracks before being sent to his unit, recalled that his initiation to horsemanship was abrupt. "A few days after the horses were first assigned [at Fort Laramie] . . . I had not yet received any drill or instructions whatever on horse or equipment, or even how to mount or dismount. About twenty of us were called one evening near sundown to saddle up. . . . I had never saddled a horse . . . nor had I ever ridden one. . . . However, I was quickly shown, and in ten minutes . . . we were on our way to disturb a band of hostiles who had run off a herd of stock." After the establishment of the Cavalry Depot at Jefferson Barracks, Sixth Cavalryman William W. Fitzgerald and his comrades experienced somewhat better initial training prior to being sent to Fort Hays, Kansas, where they began the process of becoming genuine troopers. "Then the fun commenced," he recalled. "This was December 1873. It was drill, drill, drill, in the snow, in the rain, on frozen ground, in the mud, on horseback, jump ditches, mount, dismount, drill on foot, drill with arms, sidearms, drill putting up tents, taking down tents." Private Ami F. Mulford, who had enlisted directly in the Seventh Cavalry and therefore had not passed through the depot, recorded that he experienced his first mounted drill after joining his company at Fort Abraham Lincoln:

> I excelled as a rider of horses . . . but somehow this was different! First you are given a horse to ride bareback . . . next you are given a horse with an army saddle on . . . the stirrup straps are crossed in the saddle . . . then the recruits were made to ride with their feet in the crossed stirrups . . . my knees up to my chin . . . took several falls, but survived. The next day all recruits were drilled with their Company, each recruit fully armed and equipped.[55]

At Fort Totten, Dakota Territory, in 1880, Seventh Cavalry replacements were drilled in the school of the soldier twice daily, except Sundays, the commanding officer stipulating that recruits were not to be placed on any other duty that might interfere with their training. If weather prohibited outdoor drills, they were to be conducted in a vacant cavalry stable. However, those recruits who may have thought—probably prayed—that they had seen the last of the hated bullring at the recruiting depot were often disappointed. As John Stokes, who reported to Fort Grant, Arizona Territory, lamented: "Then came the bull ring drill, riding a horse with a blanket. We rode the horse from one end to the other. After a few days [of] bull ring drill, we had no use for a chair."[56]

When a company of the Fourteenth Infantry received an infusion of about forty recruits in 1867, they were subjected to only two hours of drill daily: tactics in the morning and, oddly enough, bayonet exercise in the afternoon. As the bayonet was virtually never used for Indian fighting, it is puzzling why the commander considered this element of tactics to be a priority. By contrast, some years later Fourth Infantry recruits at Fort Omaha, Nebraska, received four hours of instruction in setting up exercises and the school of the soldier five days each week. The Fourth's more enlightened colonel prescribed a progressive curriculum, not unlike depot training, advancing recruits by stages to the manual of arms and basic movements by squads, after which the most proficient men graduated to a select squad in which they would be honed to perfection by a commissioned officer.[57]

Noncommissioned officers from the respective companies conducted the recruit drills, under the general supervision of one of the company officers. An effort was made to select noncoms who were not only skilled in all aspects of the school of the soldier but also possessed the temperament to make effective instructors. It was not an enviable job, according to Private Emil Bode, who recognized that the noncoms "had not an easy task . . . to make soldiers of them. It required more than a public school teacher's patience to do this." Sometimes even experienced privates were pressed into that role, though Seventeenth Infantry Private John C. Ford swore that he wanted no part of it: "I refused to drill recruits . . . I reloaded shells." Even years later, however, some former regulars had favorable memories of the veterans who had treated them decently and painstakingly molded them into soldiers. One of those was Eighth Cavalryman George S. Raper, who recalled: "We had a splendid drill master in Sergeant Patrick Golden, an old soldier of several years' service."[58]

And learn they did. After the rough was taken off and the new men began to settle in, they were rapidly integrated into the company. "Recruits learned from older soldiers," said one Second Cavalryman: "Advice [was] given and received gladly" to help the new men learn the ropes of army life and the little tricks of the trade that went to make up professional soldiers. "Aspinwall took me in hand after I 'jined,' and instilled into my mind the two prime requisites for a soldier," wrote Private Theodore Goldin. "1. Do whatever you are told to do and violate no regulations so that an officer or non-commissioned officer gets a hold on you. 2. When thrown in contact with officers keep your place, never presume, and above all, don't tell in the quarters what you may have learned on 'officers row.'" The editor of the *Army & Navy Journal* added: "Those of the recruits who are decent, well-intentioned young men settle down in a few days and are treated as equals by the old soldiers." Within a few days or weeks, most rookies formed friendships among the other new men in the company and more gradually with the older ones.[59]

A soldier's closest associate was his "bunkie," a term that stemmed from earlier times when the army used double-wide wooden bunks and men slept side by side, sharing the bunk and their blankets in winter. Many years after his army service, former private William A. Murphy still remembered his bunkmate at Fort Phil Kearny, Private John

Donovan, who was "a good man and was a Civil War veteran." Such relationships were founded not only on mutual compatibility but on confidence and trust between friends. A Fourth Cavalryman recalled that once in the dark he had given his bunkie a five dollar gold piece, thinking it was a nickel. "I did not discover this until he brought the gold piece back to me next morning." Even though the soldier could have easily taken advantage of the mistake, a man did not go back on his bunkie.[60]

Some old-timers, as a matter of company honor, also felt an obligation to try to keep the new men out of trouble. When Private William B. Jett inadvertently missed a roll call that he thought he had been excused from attending, his first sergeant promptly remanded him to the guardhouse. "Nihause [Henry Neihause], an old soldier of nearly thirty years standing . . . was my friend," Jett related. "Without permission of either First Sergeant or Captain, and thus at the risk of his own freedom, he went to Colonel Royall . . . and stated the case to him. Colonel Royall had me released immediately." Saddler Neihause demonstrated his loyalty to Jett by placing himself in serious jeopardy by violating protocol. It was probably only his credibility and long standing in the troop that prevented his superiors from retaliating against him.[61]

Even after the adoption of single iron beds in the early 1870s, bunkies often arranged their beds adjacent to each other, particularly when they were both in the same squad. "I sleep next to Sergeant Strupp," wrote a fresh member of the Sixth Cavalry. "He has been in the cavalry very near 29 years in this country and ten years in the cavalry in the old country (Germany) and he has been telling me a great many interesting stories about what he has been through. He was an officer . . . in Germany and is a very smart and witty old man. . . . He calls me his bunky." Speaking of the men in his company, Sergeant Grandison Mayo, Twenty-Fifth Infantry, attested that he "considered them as brothers." Such relationships tended to form lasting personal bonds among the men that sometimes paid large dividends when the going got tough in the field and in combat.[62]

Trumpeter Karl Tetzel, Third Cavalry, described the thrill that he experienced with the unique circumstances of his acceptance: "I came to the Post as the best Trumpeter they ever had. The 5th day after my arrival I was put on Guard. I was watched all day by Officers and men . . . I had a B [flat] trumpet and I used it for Taps. My Troop first of all congratulated me, every man of it." Private Jacob Horner, who had joined his regiment in the field, noted that drilling in earnest began upon the troop's return to post and that the veterans "began polishing him and other recruits in to shape." The men of C Troop, Second Cavalry, realized that they had a prize recruit in Reginald Bradley, the man who had walked into Fort Bowie, Arizona Territory, to enlist. When he began responding to drill commands as he learned them at an English military school, his comrades joshed him about being a deserter from the British army. It was incumbent upon every man, as a matter of unit pride, to do his utmost for the company's general efficiency and make a smart military appearance on parade. That period of adjustment usually took about a month. "Indeed, it was not long then, before the batch of recruits of which I was one . . . had been hammered into a pretty fair semblance of Cavalrymen, and we had taken our places in the troop along with the old-timers," a veteran remarked.[63]

Having survived his rite of passage into the troop, First Cavalryman Ben Goodin proudly noted in his diary: "Am through drilling and turned for regular duty and am glad of it." By this time, new men had adjusted fairly well to army life and were ready to get on with soldiering, though Goodin may not have realized the truthfulness of his statement regarding drill. An *Army & Navy Journal* correspondent wrote that "after the month drill terminates, the recruit is then considered ready to perform duty as a private. He is now subject to calls of duty of any kind. . . . Often such men have never had one day's drill with their company, and when company drill does take place—which on frontier posts, it does not always—the officer under whose immediate charge men are employed on extra or daily duty will at once request to have said men excused from drill." Consequently, the men who most needed company drill often did not receive it with any sense of urgency or with regularity. In those instances, they simply had to be carried along in the formations until they acquired the basic movements.[64]

Just as advanced recruits had learned at the depots, guard duty was of paramount importance and was considered the pinnacle of military achievement, as Private Emil Bode explained: "I was considered an accomplished warrior after receiving thorough instruction in drill and the manual of arms. Our Jewish drill sergeant . . . seriously contemplated putting me on guard duty, which in a recruit's eyes is the highest accomplishment, a knight's last stakes to a soldier."[65] Yet the majority of recruits passing through the depots prior to the 1880s had practically no exposure to it. Their initial experiences in an actual garrison therefore could be intimidating, if not downright dangerous. After being posted as a sentry, Bode confessed: "A string of orders was turned over to me, but the only thing I recollected was how many prisoners I had to watch . . . in five minutes, I did not know how many I ought to have." He was not alone. When detailed for his initial guard tour, a First Cavalry trooper admitted: "I surely had one grand time trying to make believe I knew the general orders."[66] Inspecting a detail in 1879, a Ninth Cavalry lieutenant remarked that when addressed the new men "get so nervous and scared they can hardly tell their own names." Upon discovering dust in the bore of one recruit's carbine, the lieutenant commented: "I could hardly keep from laughing in his face and hadn't the heart to punish him for it, he looked so pitiful."[67]

Placing men on duty before they were fully trained sometimes had serious consequences. For example, a recruit standing guard at Fort Laramie accidentally shot himself, not fatally though seriously enough to justify a medical discharge from the service. Upon investigation of the incident, it was revealed that the soldier "had never received any drill or instruction to fit him . . . to handle a loaded carbine, except two drills in the kitchen of Co. K, 4th Infantry." No explanation was offered as to why this cavalryman was being drilled in an infantry barracks kitchen in the first place. This was not an isolated incident, however, as reflected in another event related by an Eleventh Infantryman at Cheyenne Agency, Dakota Territory, in 1877: "I have observed . . . men placed on guard to protect (?) a place, and actually these men would be afraid to fire off their pieces should there be a necessity for so doing. There was one instance . . . a sentinel letting his piece fall out of his hands from fright when the officer of the day came on his rounds one night." Such occurrences suggest that some officers placed greater importance on the ceremonial aspects of guard duty than on basic training in firearms familiarity and safety.[68]

Some rookies were placed at a further disadvantage by not joining their companies at a western fort. Circumstances not infrequently required recruit detachments to report to their units when troops were about to take the field or were actually in the field, at times even during active Indian campaigning. Such instances placed the new men at a distinct disadvantage and imposed a hardship on the company at a critical time by burdening it with ill-trained, inexperienced men. A practice march undertaken soon after joining the regiment enlightened raw Tenth Cavalry recruits that being a real cavalryman was unlike anything they had experienced at the depot. One of those "young soldiers," as recruits were dubbed in black regiments, was Eugene Frierson, who vividly recalled: "The first day out from the fort found a great many of our 'recruit aspirants' wishing that they were at home by their mother's side, or at least in post, for their seating capacity was very much worn from fare [sic] wear and tear, occasioned by their inability to maintain a firm seat in the saddle during several miles of the regulation gait of eight miles an hour." Another Tenth Cavalry recruit, Perry A. Hayman, was better prepared than many of his contemporaries, having spent six weeks at Jefferson Barracks in early 1874 before being assigned to M Company. Once with his troop, Hayman and other recruits were given an additional two weeks of intensive instruction prior to leaving Fort Sill, Indian Territory, on summer field service.[69]

During periods of active campaigning, however, recruits were transferred directly from the depots, sometimes even from recruiting stations, to wherever their regiments happened to be located at that time. During the late 1860s, the higher percentage of reenlisted volunteers and regulars temporarily masked a problem that was to become acute within few more years. Lieutenant Edward S. Godfrey noted, with no apparent concern, that the Seventh Cavalry, encamped south of Fort Dodge, Kansas, received about five hundred recruits to fill its ranks while staging for the 1868 expedition against the Cheyennes. When his company was allotted some of these new men, Farrier Winfield S. Harvey commented: "We had thirteen new recruits came this morning and some very good men with them." Considering this occurred in 1868, he probably referred to veterans of prior volunteer service; but undoubtedly a large number of the recruits were green, which did not bode well. The command took up the march south into Indian Territory just three days later and would engage Black Kettle's Cheyennes in the Battle of the Washita in less than three weeks.[70]

As time passed and the infusion of nonveterans into the ranks increased, the effect became more evident. The experienced adjutant of the Fifth Infantry, First Lieutenant Edmund Rice, addressed this situation, criticizing particularly the quirk in the recruiting system that disallowed the enlistment of mounted and general service recruits at the same rendezvous. When the army had attained the required number of men for one branch or the other, recruiting was interrupted for that branch, sometimes for a period of several months. Suddenly, on the eve of a campaign, the regiments involved submitted requisitions for the numbers of recruits needed to bring their units to full strength, thus triggering the reactivation of enlistments. "The officers . . . who have the assignment of these recruits," Rice observed, "wait for an emergency and then send from one hundred and fifty to two hundred of them, undrilled, incompletely clothed and outfitted, to a regiment, which they generally reach while it is on the march through Indian country, or on some such active duty where the services of drilled and disciplined men are needed at once." The consequences were predictable. Colonel Wesley Merritt, Fifth Cavalry, complained that, "from the nature of cavalry service, it is safe to say that an enlisted man who is not instructed before he joins his regiment stands a good chance of never receiving a proper ground-work of military education. If he joins just before a campaign, or while the command to which he is assigned is in the field, as is too often the case, he is given the little hurried instruction that may fit him to equip his horse for the march, and he manages to mount and blunder along with the command." Faced with this dilemma, some commanders, unsurprisingly, preferred to screen out green recruits, taking to the field only men having some degree of prior experience, thereby avoiding the encumbrance of rookies. Inexperienced recruits were left behind either at home posts or at field depots to manage and guard supplies.[71]

The Sioux Campaign of 1876 imposed extremely heavy demands on the army's manpower resources. Numerous regiments, both infantry and cavalry, took the field that spring in three strike columns under Brigadier General Alfred Terry, Brigadier General George Crook, and Colonel John Gibbon. During the months leading up to the campaign, all of those units were bolstered to some extent with recruits. The need for replacements became more acute in the aftermath of several subsequent engagements, notably the Battles of the Rosebud and Little Bighorn, just as more regiments were summoned to the northern Great Plains in a concerted effort to defeat the Sioux and Northern Cheyennes. Custer's defeat, particularly, spurred a knee-jerk reaction by Congress to enact emergency legislation temporarily increasing the strength of all cavalry companies to one hundred men each. These factors combined to create urgent demands for replacements, and the news about Little Bighorn motivated many civilians dubbed "Custer Avengers" to enlist. Congress failed to take into account, however, the time and training required to produce an effective horse soldier. Pressured to take decisive action against the Indians, the army nevertheless began prematurely dispatching drafts of recruits to the theater of operations in late summer and fall to join units already in the field.[72]

Navigable rivers, chiefly the Missouri and the Yellowstone in the north, made reaching "the front" considerably easier than it might have been in other regions of the West. Private Samuel Meddaugh, for example, noted in his diary that recruits joined his company of the Sixth Infantry at the mouth of Powder River on the Yellowstone in early August 1876. Others bound for the Second Cavalry and Seventh Infantry with Gibbon's column simultaneously traveled downstream by wagon from Fort Ellis.[73]

Recruits bound for the Fifth Cavalry, recently transferred from Kansas in response to the crisis, found reaching their regiment even less convenient. Sent by rail to Cheyenne, Wyoming Territory, some four hundred cavalry recruits, in addition to others assigned to the Fourth, Ninth, and Fourteenth Infantry, were fully armed and outfitted at Fort D. A. Russell before marching overland northward toward the Black Hills. At Fort Laramie "the [cavalry]men were divided into four troops," Lieutenant Eben Swift recorded, "mounted on new and untrained horses and each man was leading a horse. . . . It is a commentary on the military service of that day to tell of green recruits on green horses, rushing forth to field duty." He was not alone in his criticism of the quality of the recruits so hurriedly assembled and dispatched to the front. Lieutenant King concluded from his own observation of the new men that "the recruiting officers were less particular in their selections than would otherwise have been the case, and from the purlieus of Philadelphia, Baltimore, and New York the scum of the country was eagerly grasping this method of getting to the Black Hills at Uncle Sam's expense."[74]

The influx of such recruits continued into fall, filling the ranks with men unprepared and often personally ill suited for active military service. A Seventh Cavalryman at Fort Abraham Lincoln, Dakota Territory, reacted in much the same way when a train load of some five hundred recruits arrived to fill our sadly depleted ranks, and a cosmopolitan bunch they were, English, Irish, Scotch, Italians, French with a goodly share of Americans. All ages from sixteen to forty and from all parts of the country, from farms, mines, cities, and towns, not one with the slightest idea of army life. There they were dumped down out there on the frontier at the beginning of a hard winter. . . . They were at once assigned to the various Troops and officers, non-commissioned officers and the rest of the older well drilled men, we started the task of making soldiers of them . . . right there the fun began, breaking those horses and trying to teach the poor homesick recruits to ride them gave us both plenty of work and amusement.[75]

There can be no doubt that the large numbers of ill-prepared recruits, many of whom were poor- to mediocre-quality men anyway, that came into the army during the months after Little Big Horn detracted from the army's efficiency as a fighting force in the field. Former trooper Theodore W. Goldin disgustedly recalled how the old soldiers, most of whom were combat veterans by then, reacted to the infusion of these men into their once-proud regiment: "We of the rank and file didn't have much to be proud of when we gazed upon the 'field' of the old Seventh in '77. There wasn't a genuine soldier in the lot. Simply a prize aggregation of 'coffee coolers.'" Many of the Custer Avengers, whom King sarcastically referred to as "heroes," promptly deserted. Several years would be required for the army to either mold these men into useful soldiers or rid itself of the chaff. The editor of the *Army & Navy Journal* reported in 1880 that "within the last eighteen months a steady weeding out of bad characters from the rank and file of the Army has been going on, and that the Secretary of War has discharged in the neighborhood of one thousand of these impedimenta. Much more pains than formerly are now taken in the acceptance of recruits."[76]

Despite the newness of it all, the hazing, stern discipline, and the hardships, by far the majority of soldiers stuck it out, remaining loyal to their oaths, come what may. One man who had made the adjustment was Private Adelbert Butler, who had joined the army about six months prior to writing to his sister: "I feel quite at home; soldiering suits me to perfection." In a letter to his sweetheart in 1876, Ninth Infantry private George McAnulty probably expressed the feelings of many of his comrades: "I am resigned to it now but do not like it & never intend to soldier any more if I live to serve this term out. . . . I do not know what possessed me to enlist."[77]

CHAPTER 5

Brain, Bone, and Sinew

Officers and Noncoms

The essence of the regular army was duty, discipline, and unquestioning adherence to orders. Recruits coming directly from civil life soon learned those rules. Even men who had served in the Civil War found that, despite similarities with their previous military experience, this was a different organization, a different world than they had known. As a veteran of the volunteers who afterward served in the army on the frontier observed, "A volunteer soldier, even after three years active campaigning, finds himself a novice in all things pertaining to real army life when he joins the regulars, and 'gets onto' the devices of 'sure enough' soldiers in time of peace." Making certain they were indeed "sure enough" soldiers in deportment, appearance, obedience, and every other respect were the officers and noncommissioned officers.[1]

The army's line unit command structure relied on a framework of both, ranging from corporals at the lowest rung to colonels commanding regiments. Reflecting on his twenty-three years of army experience in 1885, First Lieutenant Henry Romeyn metaphorically described their relationship: "If the commissioned portion is called the brain of the army, then the non-commissioned part may be likened to the skeleton, and it must be well formed and developed from good material, or the whole physique be of little utility."[2]

Although the focus of this study is on the enlisted men of the army during the Indian Wars, it is essential to address the officer corps as an integral part of the line organization and to define those interrelationships. Most of the rank-and-file, unless they were part of a regimental headquarters staff, had relatively little contact with officers beyond those of their own companies. The hierarchy of a regiment, known officially as the "field and staff," was a small entity so far removed from the common soldier as to be nearly foreign to him. In fact a recruit's arrival at regimental headquarters for his initial assignment might very well be one of the few times, if not the only time, when he had any personal contact with the staff. Typifying the view from the ranks, Sergeant Perley S. Eaton confessed: "I can't tell you very much about Col. Brackett [Third Cavalry], for we seldom ever saw him."[3]

The field staff included a colonel, lieutenant colonel, and three majors for cavalry regiments, but only one major for infantry regiments, plus company lieutenants detailed as adjutant and quartermaster/commissary. Rarely if ever were all of the field-grade officers present at the designated headquarters post during the Indian Wars. Some in fact made careers of securing assignments as far as possible from the frontier. Although the colonel, as regimental commander, would be at his headquarters under normal circumstances, it was not unusual for him to be detailed to some other duty or to be absent on leave for extended periods. A typical example was the Seventh Cavalry, whose first two colonels, Andrew J. Smith succeeded by Samuel D. Sturgis, virtually abdicated their unit responsibilities, leaving Lieutenant Colonel George A. Custer the de facto commander from the regiment's organization in 1866 until his untimely death a decade later. Such absences were even more common among the lieutenant colonels and majors, who actually had no particular roles to fill when not commanding battalions in the field.[4] When these officers were present, and senior to their counterparts of other regiments in the same geographic department, a lieutenant colonel or major might be assigned to command another post at which a portion of his regiment was garrisoned. In other instances an excess field officer might be delegated responsibility for instructing target practice or conducting training in signaling. He was also the logical choice for detail to myriad other chores attendant on routine post operations, such as chairing courts-martial, boards of survey, and councils of administration. Perhaps it was not surprising that field officers frequently managed to be away from their regiments commanding one of the recruiting depots, sitting on some special board convened in the East, securing a plum assignment observing foreign military activities, or simply taking lengthy leaves of absence.

The interdependence between men of the rank and file and commissioned officers was predicated upon a rigid caste system as old as the army itself. A deep gulf existed between the two classes, officially and socially. "Officers were very strict to their command and we had no social contacts of any kind," remarked Sergeant James K. Hamilton, First Infantry. A former Fifth Cavalryman employed an apt metaphor to describe the relationship: "Earth is considerably remote from the stars. This distance is not greater, however, than the distinction socially between an enlisted man and a commissioned officer of a troop." Beyond routine contact incident to official duty, their orbits rarely overlapped.[5]

The majority of officers above the rank of lieutenant, and many lieutenants, too, had seen service during the Civil War and understandably considered it the height of their military careers, if not their lives. Former Eighteenth Infantryman Phillip Schreiber, looking back on his army service, commented: "I came in contact with veterans of the Civil War, where nearly all the sergeants and officers from captains up and a good many first lieutenants were Civil War veterans. I had great respect for them and was always ready to take their advice." In fact a great many of those holding field or higher grades were graduates of the United States Military Academy, having served during the Mexican-American War of 1846–48 or against Indians in the Far West during the antebellum years or both. A great many officers had secured commissions in the volunteer forces during the war. Not a few of those had begun the conflict as enlisted men, either regulars or volunteers, gained commissions on the basis of their ability and experience, and rose through the ranks. An old army saying held that officers promoted from the ranks had "found their commissions in their knapsacks." Some of those, like First Lieutenant Gustavus C. Doane, Second Cavalry, learned well the profession of arms yet did not forget their days in the ranks. Doane, having served as both an enlisted man and a line officer of cavalry throughout most of the war, earned the respect of his men, according to one of his sergeants, for "his ample stock of native common sense and his utterly brave heart. . . . He always shared with his men every hardship, never claimed any special provision for his personal comfort, mingled with and conversed with his followers . . . yet no enlisted man ever forgot that Doane was boss."[6]

However common it may have been for enlisted men to gain commissions during the war, making that transition in the postwar era was infinitely more difficult. Regulations prescribed that all vacancies at the rank of second lieutenant were to be filled first by graduates of the U.S. Military Academy. When openings were insufficient to accommodate the available graduates, they were to be attached to line companies as temporary (brevet) additional lieutenants. Only as attrition created vacancies at the higher ranks did all those below move upward, thus providing the brevet lieutenants permanent rank. The only avenue open for an enlisted man in those days was for his commanding officer to certify that a corporal or sergeant was deserving of meritorious status so that he might appear before an examining board of officers. Just what questions those officers asked is not clear, but they probably had more to do with academic subjects than with practical military knowledge. First Sergeant Frederick Stortz, K Company, Seventh Infantry, revealed in a letter to his father the challenges that he encountered in that process: "I was probably a little to[o] ambitious in aspiring to a higher position than the one I now occupy which fact demonstrated itself . . . in nearly a complete failure on my part yet I scarcely had time to prepair [sic] myself for any elobriate [sic: elaborate] examination and hope has not left me yet for I intend to try again if I survive the coming Campaign." Stortz's ambitions were cut short a few months later when he was killed at the Battle of the Big Hole.[7]

For many years determining an officer's true rank by the appearance of his insignia alone could be challenging because of the system of brevet rank. In the absence of decorations, the army had adopted the brevet system during the War of 1812 as a means for recognizing deeds of heroism or other exemplary service performed by commissioned officers. Brevet rank was merely honorary, however, and did not confer right of command and pay at the higher rank unless specially authorized by the president. It was not uncommon for veterans of the Mexican and Civil Wars to hold several brevets, and it was customary as a matter of military courtesy for those individuals to be addressed by their highest brevet rank.[8]

The burden of responsibility for being aware of an officer's current brevet lay with his subordinates. A former Seventh Cavalry sergeant,

Charles Windolph, said of his captain: "We usually called him 'Colonel.' . . . That was the usual custom in those days. . . . It was a little confusing though." The confusion was compounded when an officer insisted upon wearing the insignia of his brevet, even though the regulations were vague on that point. Only in 1870 did the army clarify the matter through a new law stipulating that brevetted officers were not to wear *on duty* any uniform (or insignia) other than that prescribed for their actual rank or to be addressed officially by their honorary rank. A soldier at Fort Laramie, Wyoming Territory, commented on the effect: "Nearly all of our officers having gracefully dropped their brevet rank . . . and, in consequence, instead of 'General,' 'Colonels,' or 'Majors,' we have plain 'Captain' and 'Lieutenant.' O! what a fall was there!" The order, however, did not apply to social interactions outside of duty hours, thus muddying the waters more than they had been previously. But the commanding officer at Fort Clark, Texas expressed it succinctly in an edict that all could understand: "If any officer or soldier of this garrison addresses me *officially* by my brevet title, I will court-martial him; but if any officer or soldier *privately or off duty* fails to address me by my brevet title, I will mash his —— head!"[9]

The post commander's principal administrative assistant was the adjutant, usually a lieutenant detailed from one of the companies. When a station also happened to be the regimental headquarters, the lieutenant functioned in a dual role as regimental adjutant. His was the most harried existence on post: translating the commander's orders into written directives, drafting correspondence, consolidating figures from the morning reports into monthly returns, supervising the daily guard mounting and parade ceremonies, overseeing the headquarters staff, supervising the band, and generally ensuring that the headquarters operated efficiently. Captain Charles King, Fifth Cavalry, who had performed the job numerous times, described the experience:

> We all know what the adjutant should be,—a soldier in everything, in carriage, form, voice, and manner, the soul of parade and guard-mounting, the reliable authority on tactics and regulations, the patient student of general orders, the ridged scrutinizer of returns and rolls, the scholarly man of the subalterns, the faithful adherent and executive in spirit and in letter of the commanding officer. We all know how easy it is to formulate

rules and regulations for his guidance on all matters of duty and routine in garrison,—we all know just what day the regimental returns should reach Washington, the post return department head-quarters, the company papers the adjutant's office, but until we have tried to "run" the head-quarters of a frontier post and of a cavalry regiment in the heart of the Indian country . . . we have not . . . the faintest conception of the trials of staff-officers as exemplified in the case of the adjutant.[10]

While this key position required a capable, well-organized officer, the assignment deprived the company of his services. Additionally, another lieutenant was siphoned off company duty to act as quartermaster and commissary, while still another might be appointed ordnance and range officer when an excess field officer was unavailable to perform those duties.

Enlisted men came into contact most frequently with the officers of their own companies, yet "the relationship . . . was strictly business," remembered Twenty-Fourth Infantry musician Alexander Hatcher. A captain commanded the company, assisted, ostensibly, by a first and a second lieutenant, though it was not unusual for one of the lieutenants to be detailed for some other duty, as previously outlined. After about 1870 second lieutenants, more often than not, were recent West Point graduates, commonly dubbed "shavetails." The metaphor derived from inexperienced army mules, identified by trimming the hair from the upper portion of their tails. In the absence of the captain, company command fell to the senior lieutenant present for duty. Sometimes all three officers would be unavailable for one reason or another, in which case a lieutenant from another company would be temporarily assigned to head the orphan unit.[11]

Personal qualities and leadership abilities of officers, as perceived by the rank and file, varied from one individual to another and from one unit to another and were unavoidably influenced by a soldier's personal experience. "Some of the officers were gentlemen to us, others were rough and hard on the men," attested Sergeant Reinhold R. Geist, Eighth Cavalry. During the years immediately after the Civil War, the officer corps was glutted with an overabundance of ex-volunteer officers who had managed to gain regular commissions based on popularity, wartime records, or political influence. Not a few had joined state regiments as enlisted soldiers and subsequently achieved commissioned rank during the war, which was not especially difficult in view of the heavy casualties incurred by line units. Many of these officers nevertheless remained conscious of their own humble backgrounds and developed into competent leaders who, as one soldier recognized, "had learned their trade in a hard school."[12]

All too often, however, former volunteer officers proved to be of marginal quality by abusing their authority and displaying tyrannical behavior over subordinates. At Camp Grant, Arizona Territory, the post surgeon recorded that Lieutenant Frederick E. Camp, commanding the post, dictated that all soldiers in the garrison except patients in the hospital should attend roll calls under arms. When two men confined to quarters failed to comply—one having his arm in a sling and the other so bandaged with a broken rib that he was unable to carry a rifle—Camp ordered them jailed in the guardhouse. Captain Jacob Lee Humfreville, Ninth Cavalry, cruelly abused several members of his company during a 450-mile march across Texas. As punishment for a perceived offense, the captain handcuffed the men in a gang and tethered them with a rope to the rear of a supply wagon for a number of days. Humfreville further made each man, after marching in this fashion an average of twenty-five miles daily, carry a twenty-five pound log and walk a ring under guard until midnight. For these and other offenses, the captain was eventually court-martialed and cashiered from the service. Another ex-volunteer, First Lieutenant James Collins, was tried and dismissed from the army in 1871 for having ordered soldiers at target practice to commence firing just after he had been alerted that a man down-range was dangerously exposed. In response to the warning Collins had casually replied: "He will get out of the way soon enough when you fire."[13]

Some officers exhibited exceedingly poor personal conduct, which on rare occasions prompted some enlisted men to take direct action against them. Second Lieutenant Theodore Decker, for example, visited the house of a Mexican prostitute at Eagle Pass, Texas, where he got into a shooting affray with one of his own Twenty-Fourth Infantrymen who claimed the woman as his personal mistress. When the smoke cleared, Decker had suffered two wounds and the prostitute was dead. At Fort Bridger, Wyoming Territory, in 1874 Captain Charles G. Bartlett, who had served through the war both as an enlisted man and as an officer, openly insinuated at the sutler's store that one of his sergeants, standing within earshot, was a "dirty catholic Irishman" for having anonymously penned a letter critical of his officers to a St. Louis newspaper. "The expression was scarcely uttered when he measured his length on the floor," the offended sergeant later boasted. "I then tossed him out of doors. There were two other officers there, but I had too many backers . . . that would not wish for better sport than to give them officers a beating." Even though the sergeant lost his stripes, he escaped being court-martialed, probably because the captain wanted to avoid further exposure of the incident.[14]

It was not unusual for officers on the frontier to become lax in their duties and sometimes to turn to drink as a result of boredom induced by long periods of garrison doldrums. While the adjutant may have had too much to do, other officers had too little. Serving as commissary at Fort Buford, Dakota Territory, in 1872, Second Lieutenant David L. Craft described his typical day:

> I get up in the morning . . . about 8 o'clock, breakfast, go to my office . . . remain till noon—then go to the club room, take a drink, . . . play a game of billiards and then go to lunch, from there to the office, where I stay till three, and my days work is over. From this time till dinner (5 o'clock) either a ride, then pins or billiards take up the time . . . it is awfully monotonous to be sure.

A former Third Cavalry sergeant claimed that his lieutenants, even when not detailed elsewhere, seldom visited the company in garrison because there was nothing for them to do.[15]

That monotony sometimes drove men, particularly those without wives present, to unseemly conduct if not outright debauchery. "The Officers out here are all confirmed drunkards," opined a soldier at Fort Whipple, Arizona Territory, in 1870. Bolstering the truthfulness of that statement, at least as it applied to some officers, an Eighteenth Infantry lieutenant stationed at Fort Leavenworth, Kansas, went on a drinking binge in the nearby town, where he remained drunk for a month. Unbecoming behavior undermined morale and the respect that soldiers were required to accord their leaders. Sixteenth Infantryman Emil Bode, for example, indicated that it was common knowledge that the post commander, Lieutenant Colonel John W. Davidson, was "an opium and morphine eater . . . seen by the guards . . . in unworthy and ridiculous places for a commanding officer." An officer's antics became all the more scandalous when it involved fraternization with enlisted men, such as a public display at Fort Davis, Texas, when a Tenth Cavalry captain, serving as officer of the day, drank and hobnobbed with one of his soldiers, "going over to the Guard House with his arm around him."[16]

Nevertheless, enlisted soldiers sometimes showed forbearance and loyalty to otherwise good officers when they temporarily fell from grace. When one of their officers was arrested and jailed for being drunk in town, some Seventh Cavalrymen collectively paid the fine to secure his release. In a field camp in Colorado a soldier assisted Lieutenant Alexander Rodgers, Fourth Cavalry, back to his tent after he found the lieutenant lying on the ground in a drunken stupor. Upon learning of this act of kindness, a less generous member of the troop grumbled: "I wish I had found him. I would have placed my foot on this face and ground it into the earth." Even so, Rodgers later vindicated himself in the eyes of many of his men through an act of personal kindness to the very soldier who had made the disparaging remark. Upon learning that the trooper was ill and suffering with chills during a subsequent rain-drenched march, the lieutenant passed his own raincoat down the column to provide the man some comfort.[17]

Unseemly conduct certainly besmirched the reputation of the officer corps; but the army showed only limited tolerance for disreputable individuals. Members of the Inspector General's Department, during their periodic visits to posts, were enjoined to be watchful for and report any officers displaying intemperate habits or other unprofessional conduct. Any officer found guilty by a military court of the catchall charge "conduct unbecoming an officer and gentleman," and specific violations of regulations, could be sentenced to suspension of command without pay for a specified period or in more serious cases be dismissed from the service. In so doing, the army managed over time to rid itself of many of the disreputable officers it had inherited from the war.

The most significant purging resulted from the army appropriation act of 1869, which effected a consolidation of the forty-five infantry regiments into only twenty-five. That, along with subsequent reductions of the army budget in 1870 and 1874, left numerous officers unassigned and in a state of both career and financial uncertainty. Attrition alone would have taken far too long to eliminate some nine hundred officers made surplus by the various congressional measures. Many, when faced with this prospect, particularly those having seriously blemished records, quietly resigned their commissions to return to civil life. For those who did not leave of their own volition, the army convened review boards, so-called Benzine Boards, at various levels of command to cleanse the corps by subjecting all officers to a thorough evaluation of their records. Individuals found professionally deficient, or simply of undesirable character, were given a year's pay and peremptorily cut loose. Although the process sometimes worked a real hardship on the individuals forced out, the great exodus benefited the army immeasurably. While the resulting officer corps was not perfect, the overall quality of the remaining officers was appreciably enhanced, most being regulars of good character and highly qualified former volunteers. In the years to come, even though a few officers would be commissioned from civil life, the majority by far would be West Point graduates, a trend that would mirror the army's gradual professionalization during the era.

"Soldiers had an irreverent way of nicknaming every officer who had any salient point about him," wrote Sergeant Henry McConnell. He recalled that some of those in the Sixth Cavalry were known as "Old Paddy," "Jack-of-Clubs," "California Jack," and "Johnny-Come-Lately." Perhaps the most famous moniker of the era was applied to Brigadier General George "Rosebud George" Crook immediately following the Battle of the Rosebud in June 1876. A participant in the fight, Sergeant George S. Howard, Second Cavalry, explained: "The fighting was so poorly conducted that the enemy came in our rear and stole everything left back where we were when the fight commenced. The soldiers have lost all confidence in General Crook." A Fourteenth Infantry veteran remembered that Major Alexander Chambers earned the name "Route Step" for his habitual use of that command when starting a column in motion in the field. Seventh Cavalrymen dubbed Lieutenant Colonel Elmer Otis, Custer's replacement, "Bulldozer" after he made the men stand in line waiting to mount while he bade his family goodbye "for about the dozenth time." Second Lieutenant Lovell H. Jerome, Second Cavalry, was descriptively and not so kindly referred to as "Bullheaded Jerome." Some of the officers in the Eighth Cavalry, as recounted by Sergeant Charles Johnson, were Captain "Vinegar Jack" Hennissee, Captain "Bully" Ellis, Major "Mickey" Wells, and Lieutenant Colonel "Bigfoot" Sumner. Second Cavalry Major James S. Brisbin, known variously as "Old Sticks" or "Grasshopper Jim," earned his sobriquets from his avid interest in promoting western agriculture. Under no circumstances, however, did an enlisted man risk using an officer's nickname, favorable or not, in his presence, though officers usually became aware of them. "And so it goes," wrote one soldier, "the men have a nickname for each officer—some complimentary, some otherwise."[18]

Prevailing opinion among enlisted men was that most of their company officers were competent, particularly those who had seen combat during the war or in prior service against Indians. Captain Frank West, Sixth Cavalry, exemplified that class of officers. Graduating from the U.S. Military Academy in 1868, West received a brevet for gallantry in action during the 1874 Red River War and the Medal of Honor for his actions against Apaches at the Battle of Big Dry Wash in Arizona Territory. One of his troopers characterized West as quick tempered and tough yet expressed confidence in his captain: "G Troop is a pretty hard troop or at least there are a good number of . . . what one may call bullies but Capt. West will make a good troop out if it if anybody can." A Second Cavalry trooper, William F. Hynes (alias William Jones), described his company commander, Captain Elijah R. Wells, as a "humane officer, yet as brave a man as ever entered a fight; he had ability and was endowed with exceedingly good judgment. . . . He was held in high esteem by all the men in the Company, except the drones and slackers." Wells, incidentally, had served as an enlisted man in the Second Dragoons (later designated Second Cavalry) before the Civil War, rising from private to first sergeant, and was commissioned a second lieutenant in 1862. He received three brevets (to major) during the conflict and was promoted to captain in 1867. Tenth Infantryman George Neihaus spoke of First Lieutenant Robert C. Van Vliet, as "a wonderful man & all the men looked up to him as a friend." Representing the majority of enlisted men, Sergeant James S. Hamilton wrote: "For the most part we had good commanding officers. The unqualified were in the minority. We preferred West Point officers because they were better qualified." However, another veteran added the caveat that "a couple of green Lieutenants needed training," though he probably meant experience.[19]

Enlisted men tended to overlook minor character flaws and weaknesses evident in some officers who nonetheless enforced discipline fairly, if firmly, and knew their profession when it mattered. Evaluating Colonel Ranald S. Mackenzie, known to his men as "Three Finger Jack," one soldier considered him to be "one of the ablest fighters in the West. . . . He was strict, but well-liked by all his subordinates, his strong hands kept order." Sixth Cavalryman Louis Ebert considered his officers "very good if you obayed [sic] orders and done your duty." The officers were "never intimate, but always kind, commanding respect & obedience without question," according to a former Third Cavalry sergeant. "Most of the officers were West Pointers. Our captain was not, but a soldier through & through." Reginald Bradley, a member of the Second Cavalry, echoed the view that his officers were "strictly apart and I believe this is as it should be." Bradley, like most soldiers, appreciated the adage controlling officer-enlisted relationships, "familiarity breeds contempt."[20]

Still, there were rare cases of informality. While serving as orderly to Colonel Mackenzie at the Battle on Red Fork of Powder River in 1876, Private William Earl Smith must have felt as though the heavens had parted and the Almighty himself had descended when Mackenzie found Smith alone at the headquarters campfire the morning after the fight. When the colonel inquired as to whether he had been ill during the night, Smith recorded in his diary: "I node by this that he had not slept a toll during the night. I asked him if he would have a coop of coffe and he sed he would. While he was drinking he talked to me a good deal about the fite a[nd] seemed to feel bad about the boys that had been hirt and ciled [killed]" (all odd spellings in the original). Mackenzie was undoubtedly feeling the weight of command and had a very human need to commune with someone, even if only a private. First Lieutenant John Bigelow, Tenth Cavalry, recorded a minor instance when he overlooked a breach of formality by one of his sergeants. After being absent for some time, Bigelow arrived in camp and "Sergt. Young swaggered up to me in a broad grin and said 'I am glad to see you back Lieut. I hope you are well, Sir.' He held out his hand for me to shake; it went against my military instinct . . . but my natural instinct forced me to do so." Bigelow let it pass because the sergeant's concern was obviously sincere and intended as a gesture of respect. Class distinction was nonetheless vital, because officers were charged not only with enforcing discipline among a complex amalgamation of men but also with making life and death decisions in combat. Their word invariably had to be law, with unquestioning obedience by soldiers under their command.[21]

Despite the sharp distinction drawn between officers and enlisted men, good officers appreciated the value of occasionally extending small indulgences and favors to deserving men. After Private Lawrence Murphy, Seventh Cavalry, was found guilty of allowing three prisoners to escape while he conducted them to the latrine, First Lieutenant John F. Weston went to his defense because the prisoners had overpowered Murphy. Weston, who had emerged from the war a major of volunteers, successfully petitioned higher authority for the remission of Murphy's sentence in view of "his previous model conduct together with his long services in the Army during & since the rebellion." Private Wilmot P. Sanford's respect rose for Second Lieutenant Thomas G. Townsend when the lieutenant retained Sanford on light duty the day after he came off sick report. In return for Sanford's help in cleaning up his quarters following a party the previous night, Townsend presented the private with a welcome gift of some cigars and leftover whiskey. The captain of G Troop, Sixth Cavalry, bolstered the esteem of his men when he put up his own money to purchase a billiard table for the barracks, for which he charged a nominal sum per game until the cost was repaid. Such acts of paternalism contributed in no small measure to a company's morale and cohesion. "The captain of a troop was looked up to, much as a family looks up to a father," according to an Eighth Cavalryman. "He was always spoken of as the 'old man.'"[22]

Indeed some company officers took a personal interest in members of their units, particularly if the man were young and appeared to have future promise. In one instance, a nineteen-year-old First Cavalryman credited his captain, Camillo C. C. Carr, with encouraging him to use his spare time studying to improve himself, and to avoid mixing with the hard drinkers in the troop. Another youthful soldier, perhaps attempting to allay the fears of his parents, wrote to them saying: "Lieutenant [Edmund] Luff has always taken a greater interest in me than any officer I ever met. And I know he will do what is right." Since the lad had joined the army without their knowledge, his parents probably found some comfort in knowing that an officer was looking out for his best interests.²³

Soldiers were often fiercely loyal to those officers who commanded their respect. "We bragged about our officers," said one former sergeant. Such sentiments were a matter of company pride. Trooper Ami F. Mulford boasted that his captain, Thomas H. French, was "a great hunter and a splendid shot—I think the best in the whole regiment, either with rifle or revolver." Among the members of Company G, Third Infantry, their courageous lieutenant, Edward A. Belger, was affectionately known as "Old Granny," because "he was the best man in the regiment and there was not a man in his company that would not have risked his life for [him] . . . he stood by us through thick and thin, always doing something for us. . . . He was our commander for three long years and we wanted no other." That unit loyalty extended to officers' families as well. "A feeling of regimental prestige held officers and men together," wrote the wife of an Eighth Infantry lieutenant. "I knew the names of the men in the company, and not one but was ready to do a service for the 'Lieutenant's wife.'" When some infantrymen were drinking and carousing in an Arizona field camp, frightening the wife and children of an absent Tenth Cavalry officer, his daughter later recalled: "The loud voices awoke my mother, who then discovered that George Clark [a private of A Troop] was sitting just in front of the tent door . . . and his carbine was lying across his knees while he watched the white men." As two of the drunks approached the officer's tent, Clark warned them that he would shoot to kill, whereupon the intruders retreated.²⁴

Now and then a soldier formed a rather personal attachment with one of his company officers, and at the same time might supplement his own income, by hiring on as a "dog robber" to do menial work at his quarters. The practice was supposedly outlawed in 1870, yet it persisted throughout the era, because civilian domestics were often in short supply on the frontier.²⁵ Second Lieutenant Micah J. Jenkins, stationed at Fort Garland, Colorado, in 1879, said that he paid five dollars a month for a man "to make up my bed, sweep out, clean my shoes, bring water, carry my clothes to and from the laundry, take care of my horse . . . clean my saber, pistol, and little things of this kind that no officer to my knowledge does." The moniker, according to an officer's daughter, derived from "intimating that the family dog was deprived of tidbits by the presence of the striker." The latter term, also widely used during the period, had its origin in soldiers taking down, or "striking" in military parlance, the officers' tents upon breaking camp.²⁶

Although a striker was supposed to be subject to company duty, the officer usually made certain that he was needed at his quarters, which created ill feeling among the other men. Private John O. Stotts, who joined the Third Infantry in 1866, explained why other company members resented these men: "One of about the first things I learned and had impressed on me was to hate a dog robber . . . a man that will wait on an officer, do all the dirty work for him, in fact be his servant. By doing this he had no guard duties to perform and go to bed and sleep at night while some other poor boy is standing guard probably where he should and would be if he was with his company and checked for duty." When asked by his first sergeant if he would strike for the captain, Eighth Cavalry trooper Eddie Matthews rejected the proposition because "I did not enlist for a waiter . . . we are too much of a slave for them now, without going into their houses." Some dog robbers nevertheless moved their bunks and belongings to the officer's quarters, if a servant's room was available, and were excused from virtually all military duties, even roll calls. Family-oriented strikers sometimes became quite attached to officers' families. In at least one instance an old soldier in the Eighth Infantry "seemed to consider himself a sort of protector to the officers of Company K, and now, as well, to the woman who had joined the company . . . he was allowed more latitude than most soldiers." Others, like Private Simpson Mann, cooked and carried out associated chores, availing himself of better food than he might have gotten otherwise, but slept in his troop barracks. Despite the negative connotation, a First Cavalryman confided, the "dog robber . . . is always liberally paid and well treated, so that he can apply a very healing salve to his feelings if they become hurt perchance by . . . comrades who would, in most cases, be only too glad to change places with him if they had the chance."²⁷

For most of a quarter-century after the Civil War promotions stagnated within the officer corps because of the army's lineal system of promotion. Officers were ranked and promoted according to seniority according to date of commission, rather than experience and proven ability. As a result, company-grade officers, lieutenants and captains, frequently remained with their regiments for many years before gaining higher grade, if ever, though they sometimes moved from one company to another within that regiment according to their numerical standing, of which every officer was keenly aware. (Military academy graduates always began their careers at the grade of either a brevet [extra] or second lieutenant.) Field officers of the line, because of the smaller number of positions available, transferred from one regiment to another within the same branch. Making light of the irony of his promotions, which happened to be among regiments in numerically inverse order, Lieutenant Colonel Andrew S. Burt quipped: "Captain in the 9th; major in the 8th; lieut. colonel in the 7th; Heaven help the 6th!"[28]

The transfer of a popular officer sometimes prompted members of the garrison to show their respect through the presentation of a gift by which he might remember them. In 1869 officers and enlisted men of the Thirtieth Infantry, about to be disbanded at Fort Fred Steele, Wyoming Territory, as a result of the army's reduction, recognized Colonel John D. Stevenson with an engraved gold watch and chain reportedly costing $400–500. Nor was it unusual for the death of a favorite officer to elicit expressions of esteem and comradery from the veterans of his unit. The men of Company E, Seventh Infantry, posted at Fort Bridger in 1883, met to formalize several resolutions honoring the memory of Captain Walter Clifford, who had recently died of heart failure. Having joined the regular army as a private in 1860, Clifford held a particular affinity with his soldiers. Serving through the Civil War and later the Sioux Campaign of 1876, Clifford distinguished himself as not only a brave and faithful officer, but "a kind friend . . . whose whole mind was centered in the men of his company and whose aim and object was their welfare." As a tribute to their old commander, the soldiers contributed money to purchase a marble headstone "to mark his final resting place, the last act we can do for our noble departed Captain."[29]

A Fifth Infantry officer testifying before a congressional committee in 1878 expressed his view that the noncommissioned officers of the army were "the bone and sinew of a regiment." Like most officers, he recognized that reliable noncoms were absolutely essential to the functioning of the military machine, shouldering many of the day-to-day activities in garrison, instilling unit cohesion, and providing first line discipline and steady leadership in combat.[30]

Noncommissioned officers (all enlisted men) were of three distinct classes: company, regimental, and general staff. Until 1870 each line company embraced a first sergeant, a quartermaster sergeant, four sergeants, and eight corporals. In that year, however, a second congressionally mandated contraction in the size of the army compelled the elimination of half the corporals in all line branches in order to maintain the other grades at their current numbers. "Sergeants and corporals had mostly been in the Army a long time," a former Ninth Cavalry trooper said. For many years after the Civil War, sergeants typically were veterans of either the regulars or the volunteers. A few, like German-born Sergeant Herbert Von Hammerstein, had even held commissioned rank. A nephew of the commander-in-chief of the Austrian army during the Crimean War, Von Hammerstein had become acquainted with General George B. McClellan prior to the Civil War then came to America to offer his services and was made the general's aide-de-camp. Before the war ended, he had risen to colonel of a New York infantry regiment. "On the termination of the Civil War he discovered he was utterly incapable of earning a living outside of the army. When this latter fact had impressed itself upon his conviction . . . he entered the regular service, where I found him," a former Second Cavalry comrade remembered. On the frontier the ex-colonel served as a sergeant of E Company. "He was prematurely old . . . but the one outstanding feature of his personality . . . was his attractive gracious manner, which was impossible to resist." Regardless of his other attributes, Von Hammerstein had developed an addiction to alcohol, which finally compelled him to take a disability discharge at Fort Laramie in 1867.[31]

By the late 1880s and early 1890s most regiments could claim generally high-quality noncoms of long experience. Private Hartford Clark attested in 1891 that the first sergeant of his troop of the Sixth Cavalry had served for seventeen years; two sergeants were veterans of twenty-eight and fifteen years, respectively, while the other three each had ten years' service to their credit. The three corporals present at that time had served ten, nine, and five years, respectively. An ex-Eighth Cavalryman noted that during his time of service in the early 1890s two of his sergeants had been in grade for twenty-two years each. Reginald Bradley commented: "Our troop had a German captain, naturally pretty near all the C Troop [Fourth Cavalry] non-commissioned were German when I joined—not Sgt. Kerr, he was Irish—but born in this country."[32]

The rank of corporal was the first step on the noncommissioned ladder, yet it was an important introductory level position for both the individual and the company. Even when no positions were vacant, or when a permanent corporal might be absent for some time, company commanders, usually with the advice of their first sergeants, would appoint promising men as "lance" (temporary) corporals to evaluate their potential as noncoms. Such appointments were announced in orders to ensure that the privates knew who the acting corporals were and treated them with the respect demanded for all other noncoms, even though the rank carried no insignia. Sometimes officers merely directed a private to execute a more responsible task as a demonstration of his ability. A heady Eighth Cavalryman writing in 1870 remarked: "On two occasions lately when we drill the Captain has taken me out of the squad I was drilling in and gave me a squad to drill myself. It is no trouble for me to drill either with Carbine or Saber. And I explain the drill to the men better than the majority of our Non Commissioned Officers." Such assignments often were the first step toward permanent promotion.[33]

Company commanders selected corporals from among the privates of their units and recommended them to the colonel of the regiment for approval. Captains and first sergeants were always watchful for potential candidates who demonstrated a particularly soldierly appearance and conduct. No minimum tenure was required for advancement, though a soldier usually served for several months to more than a year before being considered for promotion. "I had been in the army just three months when I was made a corporal," recounted Sergeant Perry A. Hayman, Tenth Cavalry. A Third Cavalryman, Private James S. McClellan, said that he had served just over nine months when his captain promoted him, but Corporal Emil Bode, Sixteenth Infantry, remained a private for a year and a half before receiving chevrons.[34]

Most soldiers seem not to have actively sought advancement, but a few did. One of those was Private Eddie Matthews, who informed his parents: "The day will come when I will get two stripes on my coat sleeves, if not three." A short time later, when two corporals deserted from his company, he wrote: "Well I can't say [I] am not sorry they have gone. So much the better chance for promotion. There is five noncommissioned officers short in the Company and I think . . . W. E. Matthews will be found among the five . . . but I aught [sic] not to be so certain for I have not been in the Company very long, and it is not so easy to get stripes in the Regulars." Other men viewed promotion as an unwelcome burden. A bugler in the Eighteenth Infantry lamented: "It seemed that my captain had a grudge against me for he took the bugle away from me and decorated me with corporal stripes." A few individuals, like Private William B. Jett, absolutely rejected the prospect of promotion, and the responsibility that came with it. He told his first sergeant: "I did not want to be a Non-Commissioned officer as this was a stepping stone to a commission, but if I did not want it I need not be made a corporal." Nonetheless, he was later promoted over his objections. Corporal Emil Bode, whose superiors had forgotten to inform him of the action, first learned of it when he heard his name read out in an order detailing him on detached service. "There was surely a mistake somewhere," he thought, "as a man when promoted or reduced to ranks is published to the company or regiment when drawn up in a line so as to acquaint the command with the fact, which in this case had been neglected."[35]

Upon approval of his appointment by the regimental commander, each NCO was presented an impressive vellum document called a warrant, attesting to his grade, unit, and the effective date. Noncoms wore the chevrons of their rank on both sleeves of the dress coat and blouse and cloth stripes down the outer seams of the trouser legs. The Quartermaster Department issued these insignia, but their cost was charged against the man's clothing allowance. Thus a corporal's increased pay of two dollars a month (to fifteen dollars) might have been of only marginal benefit initially, as newly promoted Corporal Charles N. Hayden explained: "I drew two sets of Corp. stripes and Shivrens [sic] costing 84 c[en]ts. I had our Troop tailor sew them on . . . bought [another] Pr. Stripes and Shivrens of Seeberger [a fellow soldier] . . . paid Tailor $1.00 for sewing on stripes and shivrens." Regardless of how soldiers may have viewed their elevation to noncommissioned rank, their first appearance in public as a noncom could be intoxicating. "I was given the corporal's chevrons and was so proud I nearly became cross-eyed trying to gaze upon all my 'stripes' at once," First Infantryman John Cox admitted.[36]

As assistants to the sergeants, corporals drew assignments of limited responsibility, such as drilling recruits, serving as the charge-of-quarters, and supervising fatigue parties. Although it was not common, in some instances a corporal was detailed as company clerk and in at least some cavalry organizations one of the corporals had the honor of carrying the troop guidon in mounted formations. Perhaps the greatest advantage to promotion, in addition to the extra pay, was the exemption from all physical labor; corporals and sergeants functioned only as overseers of work details. Unquestionably, a corporal's most important duty was taking his turn as corporal of the guard, during which he had to be familiar with all of the guard beats as well as general and special orders and be able to post reliefs in the prescribed manner.

It was incumbent upon corporals consistently to present a smart military appearance, carry out their orders promptly and efficiently, and maintain proper distance from the privates who were so recently their peers. Suddenly being in a position of authority over former comrades could be challenging, but demanding obedience in an equitable manner from privates, even friends, was expected of noncoms. Sometimes, of course, a noncom took advantage of his newfound power to exact revenge on an old enemy, though he had to do it discreetly, lest he be brought up on charges. "Now I was corporal," one man gloated, "the leaf had turned and I was given the first chance at a man who was hated by everyone in the company. It was a pleasure to order him at the heaviest and dirtiest work."[37]

Some men, however, decided early on that being a noncommissioned officer did not agree with them, because they disliked the additional responsibilities or felt inadequate to perform the duties. Because he was a veteran of a prior enlistment as an infantry musician, a Sixth Cavalry private was promoted to corporal only a week after joining his new troop. "But at my own request," he confided, "I was reduced to the ranks, as I did not care to serve as a non-commissioned officer until I was more proficient [at cavalry tactics]." The same Corporal Jett, who had been promoted despite his objections, arranged his own demotion a short time later by intentionally ignoring an order to drill a new batch of recruits. Purposefully failing to do one's duty was a not uncommon way to get removed from the job. Farrier Winfield Harvey, Seventh Cavalry, cited another instance when "we had two corporals broke today . . . they would not come out to roll call today."[38]

The rank of corporal usually but not always was a stepping stone for becoming a sergeant, often informally referred to as a duty sergeant to distinguish him from the first sergeant. A soldier who accepted responsibility and proved himself an able noncom usually progressed steadily from one grade to another, depending on how long he stayed in that company. Yet in exceptional cases men were jumped directly from private to sergeant, without ever being corporals. German immigrant Max Littman, who enlisted at age twenty, related: "In seven months after I enlisted I was made sergeant of my company, although I had not by any means mastered the language. All my orders . . . were written down for me in English, which I memorized word for word." Sergeant Fred Platten's experience was more typical: "I served eight months as a private and was then elevated to corporal; 12 months later I was promoted to sergeant, a position I held throughout the remainder of my service with the Sixth Cavalry."[39]

The army relied heavily on sergeants for the everyday functioning of the organization. Cavalry companies and batteries of light artillery were authorized five sergeants, while infantry companies, being smaller, had only four. Regardless of branch, however, sergeants functioned as chiefs of squads. Accordingly, the company was divided into squads of approximately equal proportions. Their duties were many and varied, depending on whether in garrison or the field, though in noncombat situations they did not differ greatly from those of a corporal, except for the level of responsibility and the numbers of men supervised. Like corporals, sergeants were responsible for the cleanliness and neatness of the men, their arms and accouterments, and their bunk areas. On post, the sergeants took charge of larger fatigue or other details and took their turns at being the NCO in charge of quarters and sergeant of the guard. Sergeants were absent from their stations on detached service in command of wood-cutting details, guard detachments at stage or telegraph stations, small scouting parties, and escorts for various purposes, such as paymasters, supply trains, and mail parties. At times experienced and trustworthy sergeants led detachments of a few mounted men in pursuit of deserters. In formations sergeants were relied upon for their steadiness as file closers, marching in the rear or to one side of the company to maintain the ranks or column and to prevent straggling on marches. Their role in combat was to post themselves a short distance behind a company deployed on the firing line to help preserve order and maintain fire discipline and to prevent any men from breaking ranks or running away, even shooting them if necessary.

Sergeants had to possess two traits: they had to be tough in order to maintain control over the rough elements that were a portion of every company and they had to be reliable. Old sergeants, ever loyal to their profession and to the army, were intolerant of behavior that they considered insubordinate. Attesting to this, a Ninth Cavalry officer happened to overhear one of his sergeants gruffly dressing down some young troopers complaining about field rations: "He yelled out, 'you shut up, there. There ain't one of you ever had a square meal in your life before you came into the army, an' you know it.'" That upbraiding undoubtedly caused the men to reflect on their previous quality of life, and grousing ceased. The sergeant also had to be able to back up his rank with his fists when necessary. In one instance, new arrival Lauren Aldrich, Thirtieth Infantry, immediately found himself in a bare-knuckles fight to the finish against "their authorized company slugger." After the young recruit broke the bully's jaw, his captain thought Aldrich had met the requirement and had him promoted.[40]

Sergeants were expected to be steadfast in stressful situations. Illustrating this, a mixed detail composed of Fifth Infantryman and Seventh Cavalrymen from Fort Hays, Kansas, was dispatched to adjacent Hays City to break up a crowd of white civilians who had rioted against some black residents, looting their homes and throwing their belongings into the streets. "There was one man in particular who was mounted on a dry goods bar inciting the people," recalled a trooper present at the time. "There was one sergeant in one of the infantry companies who was very anxious to drop the speech maker. He drew a bead on him with his rifle and he passed the remark to the lieutenant in charge, 'Lieutenant, I have him covered, give the word and I will drop him.' This sergeant . . . would have carried his words into effect but the lieutenant . . . advised him not to do it." The timely arrival and unflinching demeanor of the regulars caused the crowd to quickly disperse.[41]

Having one friend promoted over another in the same company could be awkward, though most soldiers accepted it in good humor as a natural part of army life. When Second Cavalryman Tom Sullivan received his promotion to sergeant, his bunkie and fellow Irishman, Jack O'Halloran, approached him, snapped to attention, and executed a pretentious salute, saying with emphasis, "*Sergeant*, I report for duty." Caught off guard at first, Sullivan stared momentarily at his friend then replied in a tone of disgust: "Oh, go to hell!" O'Halloran, affecting tearful rejection, turned to a group of onlookers and complained that the first order given him by his old friend was to go to hell.[42]

Duty sergeants were numbered in descending order of seniority, the number dictating their respective positions in the company formation. The second sergeant, nominally termed "first duty sergeant" in some outfits, carried somewhat more prestige than the others because he presumably would be the next man promoted to first sergeant of the company. That was not always the case, however, because the second sergeant might not have wanted the job, preferring to remain where he was, or the captain might have had reasons for promoting another man. In any event, according to tactics, the first sergeant had charge of the first platoon (half a company) and the second sergeant, positioned on the left flank of the company, supervised the second platoon.[43]

Until 1873 every line company included in its organization a quartermaster sergeant with responsibility for the "garrison and camp equipage," as well as the forage, fuel, and food for his unit. His was the next most responsible position under the first sergeant, and he wore a distinctive chevron denoting his rank. Although the quartermaster sergeant needed to be familiar with tactics, he usually functioned in a support role in the field, having charge of the company wagon, supplies, and equipment allotted to the company. He also oversaw the alignment and erection of tents, acquisition of firewood, ration issues, preparation of latrines, and, in cavalry troops, putting up the picket line. In garrison he had a soft job, as Quartermaster Sergeant Maurice Wolfe, Company B, Fourth Infantry explained in a letter to his cousin:

> I never had such good times in my life. I have only about a day's writing to do in the month. The rest of the time I loaf. I need not go to bed or get up until I think of it. I have no Guards or any other of the exercises of the Company imposed upon me. My only work is to keep the books and papers of the company, also draw clothing and rations for the men, and take charge of the company property, which I consider no trouble whatever.[44]

A parsimonious Congress, however, became equally aware that the company quartermaster sergeant was a plum position that might just as well be eliminated. Quartermaster Sergeant Eddie Matthews, Eighth Cavalry, tendered his resignation after learning that recent legislation authorizing longevity pay for duty sergeants simultaneously deprived quartermaster sergeants of that benefit because the rank was to be abolished. Matthews expressed his displeasure with the new law: "It is not the rank that I am after, but the dollars and cents that is what I want." Matthews's captain explained to him that by taking a voluntary reduction in grade to sergeant his net pay would actually increase over time, but the captain likewise recognized what Congress did not—that the function was indispensable. As Matthews accurately perceived the situation, "I suppose there will always be a Sergeant acting in the capacity of a Q.M.S. . . . Since there is to be no more Q.M. Sergeants, the 1st Sergt. will be supposed to perform those duties in addition to those at present . . . as our 1st Sergt. has more to do now than he is capable of doing, I don't see how he is going to get along." He soon learned that his assessment was correct when the captain asked him "to continue in the office just the same as before," but as a duty sergeant. Thus throughout the remainder of the period one of the sergeants functioned as the company quartermaster for no additional pay, and wore no special insignia, though in practice he was relieved of some of the customary duties of other noncoms. In some units the second sergeant continued to carry the informal title of "acting quartermaster sergeant" to distinguish him from other duty sergeants.[45]

"The first sergeant had everything to do with running the troop—officers didn't do anything much like that," contended a Fourth Cavalryman. That truism was further borne out in the admission of Second Lieutenant Eben Swift, who shortly after his graduation from West Point in 1876 accompanied a batch of four hundred recruits from Fort Laramie to join his regiment in the Black Hills: "My First Sergeant was George K. Kitchen, an old Fifth Cavalryman, a soldier of the highest type so I had little trouble and learned much from him by letting him run things. Not for a moment did he disclose the fact that he knew I was as green a recruit as any of the rest of the men." Kitchen, who was actually only twenty-seven years old at that time and in his second enlistment, obviously made a deep impression on the young lieutenant.[46]

The first sergeant could be likened to the foreman of a company; according to an army manual of the period, "whilst he does not receive as much pay, his position is one of the most responsible and most honorable that non-commissioned officers can occupy." Through him passed all communication to and from the company commander. A long-standing custom of service required any member of the company who desired to speak to the captain first to report to the first sergeant, stating his business and obtaining the sergeant's permission. The first sergeant was responsible for screening out inappropriate and frivolous matters and, when he did grant permission, making certain that the soldier knew the proper protocol for reporting to the captain. This reflected directly on the professionalism of the first sergeant.[47]

In order to preserve strict discipline and the ability to correct his own noncoms, the first sergeant could afford no close friends in the company. This could mean a rather lonely existence, with off-duty associations confined to other first sergeants or staff noncoms and to a lesser degree, and even then guardedly, with the sergeants of his own company.

The top sergeant was selected by the captain from among the other sergeants, often but not always the most senior man, depending on the captain's opinion as to which one might best perform the job. Some old duty sergeants were content with their stations in life and did not mind being passed over. A junior sergeant, Henry McConnell, recounted that his captain unexpectedly "informed me that he had concluded to promote me to be First Sergeant of my company, which position I hesitated to accept, as most of the other non-commissioned officers were old and experienced men, but he insisted on it . . . I consider this the most satisfactory and respectable position an enlisted man can aspire to in the army." It was not unusual, in fact, for company commanders to go out of their way to select men in whom they had developed particular confidence and trust. The captain of G Company, Fourth Infantry, even reached down to a veteran private whom he considered to be a superior soldier by promoting Private Conrad Bahr to sergeant just prior to the discharge of his first sergeant. Bahr, then in his fifth enlistment, had been a member of the regiment since 1859 and had previously been a noncom. When the company's first sergeant left two days later, the captain immediately promoted Sergeant Bahr to the position. A few men, like Corporal John F. Casey, H Troop, Tenth Cavalry, were promoted over their peers in recognition of distinguished service.

Casey was made first sergeant for his role in the pursuit and capture of Apache leader Mangas and his band in 1886.[48]

The duties of company noncommissioned officers were demanding and unremitting, especially those of the first sergeant, sometimes becoming so irksome that incumbents elected to forfeit their stripes. Although regulations prohibited noncoms from resigning their warrants of their own accord, they could request to be reduced; failing that, they could intentionally commit some minor violation that would get them busted. That happened in the case of First Sergeant John Ryan, M Company, Seventh Cavalry, who related:

> I had a quartermaster sergeant, . . . also a clerk. . . . They were both pretty smart, but they both liked their drop of the juice that cheers, and just at the time when I would need them most, they were liable to be on a racket [drunk]. . . . I finally got disgusted with it and made request to Lieutenant [Thomas] Custer to be restored to my former position as 1st duty sergeant of the company. He would not agree to that . . . so one day I left the company and went down to Leavenworth City and remained there a couple of days. . . . After reporting back to my company my request was granted and I was made 1st duty sergeant, . . . but I also got a severe reprimand. . . . I did not better myself any, as I was still acting 1st sergeant of the company.[49]

In this instance Lieutenant Custer had followed regulations by recommending Ryan's removal as first sergeant to the regimental commander. Noncoms could be reduced by only one other method: the verdict of a general court-martial. The charges had to be serious and sustainable, however, because the captain usually backed the actions of his noncoms. When Sergeant Emanuel Stance, Ninth Cavalry, engaged in a fistfight with his troop saddler over a misplaced curry comb, Stance's captain sustained his actions. But Stance was not so fortunate a few years later when he got into a fight with First Sergeant Henry Green, biting off part of Green's lip. For that, Stance lost his stripes and was confined in the guardhouse for six months. A man who served with Stance characterized him as "dirty mean." Even though Stance, a recipient of the Medal of Honor for gallantry in action, was an outstanding combat soldier, he could not effectively channel those abilities to managing a troop in garrison.[50]

Finding well-qualified men to fill positions as noncoms could be problematical, because those having strengths in one area might not have other requisite qualities. Those best able to enforce discipline, with their fists when necessary, might not possess the personal integrity or education necessary to carry out the other duties required of noncommissioned officers responsibly, and vice versa. A Fourth Cavalry recruit learned early on that not all noncoms were trustworthy. "We were truly glad when this two-hundred mile march [from Fort Garland to Ouray, Colorado] was ended," he wrote, "especially as the sergeant in charge had 'shoved up' [sold] part of our provisions to get money for his own private use and we had not enough to eat during the whole trip." This soldier would discover that the misappropriating of rations was all too common. A frequent complaint was that company commanders delegated too much authority and autonomy to their first sergeants. A private who had previously been a quartermaster sergeant at Fort Union, New Mexico Territory, complained to his captain that the members of his company were being deprived of their full ration because "when the meat was brought to the Company Kitchen the Non-Commissioned Officers in charge had the choice part of it cut off and . . . put on the Non Com's table." At Fort Stanton, New Mexico Territory, an especially underhanded sergeant and an accomplice worked a scheme to pocket money donated by their comrades for the purchase of beef then stole a steer from a local rancher to provide the promised meat for the company mess. When the sheriff came to the post in search of the thieves, they hid in an abandoned bakery until the officer left. But food was not the only commodity that prompted some noncoms to abuse their positions. A company quartermaster sergeant of the Ninth Cavalry at Fort Bayard, New Mexico Territory, was reported by a private for having illegally sold government forage to a civilian, for which the sergeant was arrested and court-martialed.[51]

In other instances some noncoms failed to fulfill their basic responsibilities. On one occasion a corporal in charge of a detachment guarding a stage station in Kansas allowed the men to go fishing in the Smoky Hill River some distance from the house. Making matters worse, the irresponsible corporal even permitted the men to leave their rifles behind for the use of the civilian teamsters in the unlikely event of an Indian attack. Soon afterward Sioux warriors raided the station, but the soldiers were able to return quickly enough to repulse the attack. The corporal later reported only that a skirmish had taken place but mentioned nothing of the fishing expedition, thus narrowly escaping a trial.[52]

Dereliction of duty, intentional or otherwise, was a sure way for a noncom to lose his stripes. Corporal John J. Mitchell, Company L, Eighth Cavalry, succumbed to his desire for drink and feminine companionship by abandoning his post as NCO in charge of the herd guard at Fort Union. Mitchell rode to Loma Parda, a vile little village a few miles away, and remained there until late that night. Even though it was his second such offense, Mitchell must have had other redeeming qualities, because he not only recovered his rank but finished his enlistment as a sergeant. A former Second Cavalryman related an occurrence when the officer of the day caught Corporal of the Guard Leonard Lambert soundly napping in a chair in the guard room. "He called him by name, but he [Lambert] didn't notice, then he walked right in and touched him on the shoulder . . . that was the end of him as a corporal." For allowing a prisoner to escape at Fort D. A. Russell, Wyoming Territory, in 1873, the sergeant of the guard was reduced in rank after being found guilty of neglecting his duty. In what must be a near-record, three Seventh Cavalry sergeants and a corporal were busted to private simultaneously after attempting to desert from a camp near Stark's Ranch, Dakota Territory, also in 1873. In other instances, the reasons for a noncom's reduction were more subtle. For example, Corporal Garner O. Ault, Fourth Infantry, lost his stripes when his captain became aware of his "grumbling about the food fournished [sic] the Company, thereby creating dissatisfaction among some of the Privates . . . and for making use of expressions tending toward the disparagement of his Commanding Officer." Regardless of their personal opinions, noncommissioned officers were expected to uphold the command structure and integrity of the company.[53]

Unlike privates, noncoms placed under arrest were spared the indignity of being confined to the guardhouse, unless aggravating circumstances suggested that they might desert. Accused of aiding in the escape of a prisoner and influencing other men to desert, one Seventh Cavalry sergeant was restricted to the stable, under guard, until his trial. Under normal circumstances noncommissioned officers remained on duty on their own recognizance until charges were either preferred or dropped. Only after a court-martial found an individual guilty, sentenced him to be demoted, and confined him when warranted was he jailed. Captain Albert Barnitz, Seventh Cavalry, recorded one such instance: "My 1st Sergeant Francis S. [*sic*: L.] Gordon, was reduced to the ranks for absence without leave, and drunkenness . . . and confined to the guard house. Since then the company has been somewhat demoralized, as they sympathize with Gordon, who was quite a favorite." Even though some otherwise capable noncoms committed indiscretions for which they were reduced, company commanders were inclined to forgive past missteps by later reinstating those individuals who were adept at managing the men and had proven themselves reliable field soldiers. In Gordon's case, he deserted immediately after his release, but was apprehended about a year and half later. Captain Barnitz apparently arranged for him to return to the company and he was later discharged as a corporal. It was not unusual for some old sergeants to have been demoted more than once, only to be restored through the influence of a captain who had confidence in them. As one veteran put it, "I have heard more than one old army officer remark that 'a man was never fit to be a non-commissioned officer until he had been a few times in the guard house or before a courtmartial.'"[54]

In contrast to promotion, the reduction of a noncom presented the possibility of an unpleasant reversal of roles. Not only could a soldier promoted in his stead now make life uncomfortable but he would be back on the same level with his former subordinates, men that he might have alienated. Private Frederick Stossmeister, recently demoted to the ranks after serving as a noncommissioned officer for three years in I Troop, First Cavalry, apparently found the readjustment troubling, because he applied for appointment as a telegraph operator "at some government station at as early a date as practicable. . . . I have chosen this method of being removed from the Troop in preference to a transfer."[55]

Demotion was effected through a special regimental order published at a company or garrison assembly. However, according to First Sergeant John Ryan, Seventh Cavalry, "There have been cases known where a non-commissioned officer whose sentence was to be read out and to be reduced to the ranks of a private soldier had the stripes cut off of his clothes in the presence of the command."[56] Some officers apparently chose this exceptional and humiliating method for the purpose of making an example of a noncom gone wrong and as a warning to others.

Company noncoms had to be of a no-nonsense nature to maintain discipline with a firm hand, yet the best ones tempered their treatment of the men with commonsense discretion. Upon learning that his brother back in Ireland was considering coming to America and joining the army, Corporal Maurice Wolfe attempted to dissuade him by advising a family member: "If he does enlist, he will curse the hour he was born. I can get along well enough in the Army, but I don't believe he could, as his stubborn disposition would not do for him here . . . soldiers are knocked about here." A former Ninth Cavalryman offered a contrasting view, asserting: "Some of the Sergeants were pretty friendly with soldiers . . . all were about the same." Harvey J. Ciscel, who had been a private in the Eighth Cavalry, similarly contended that his sergeants maintained their distance but "didn't bull-doze [haze] us much" once men were integrated into the company.[57]

Those men who did their duty, abided discipline, and conducted themselves responsibly got along all right. Privates quickly learned, however, that forbearance by noncoms was not to be confused with familiarity, at least on duty. Sergeant James Fegan, Second Cavalry and a regular since 1851, indelibly impressed this on a recently arrived recruit serving on guard duty. When the greenhorn made the mistake of addressing Sergeant of the Guard Fegan as "Jim," "Whack! and the neophyte was sprawling, while seventy-five inches of irate Hibernian . . . roared out, '*Jim*, is it?' Whin I'm on duty it's 'Sergeant Faygen' y'ell call me. Whin I'm off duty, thin, and not *till* thin, I'm *Jim*! D'ye mind it! D'ye mind it! And he again flourished a fist as big as a Missouri ham in the face of the terrified recruit" (all odd spellings in the original).[58]

Sergeant Grandison Mayo of the Twenty-Fifth Infantry confirmed that noncoms were strict and tolerated no foolishness on duty, even ordering men who dared to laugh in ranks to fall out and double-time at port arms around the parade ground for fifteen minutes. Fourth Cavalryman William B. Jett remarked that on one occasion, as a member of the old guard, he thought that he was excused from attending retreat roll call. "That night the First Sergeant came up into the quarters and said to me, 'Get your blankets,' and had me marched off to the Guard House."[59]

There were also those who carried their authority to extremes. First Sergeant Max Lipowitz, Fourteenth Infantry, was "a perfect martinet, who was of a very trying temper at times and at all times over-strict to men, a goodly number of whom were used to the less rigid discipline of the volunteer service," according to a Swiss quartermaster sergeant, John Spring, who served with him. Spring conceded, however, that the first sergeant looked after his men (some of them anyway), citing an occasion in 1866 when the company was encamped just outside Tucson, Arizona Territory. A German private rushed up to the headquarters tent excitedly to inform Lipowitz that he had discovered a brewery in town—music to his countryman's ears. As it was the day before payday, all three were broke, so the first sergeant improvised. Plucking from an open case ten packages of .58-caliber musket ammunition, soon to be replaced by metallic cartridges anyway, he directed the quartermaster sergeant to go barter for beer, an errand that might have fallen within his duties if broadly interpreted. The mission proved successful. The three were soon sharing six quarts of admittedly mediocre beer, but nevertheless beer.[60]

Some noncoms took special pride in their positions, sometimes developing near-paternalistic bonds with their men. Private James C. Bothwell, a company musician in the Thirteenth Infantry, praised one of his sergeants for his exceptional stamina and concern for the men during long marches. "During the day while some of the men would be almost exhausted," Bothwell recalled, "he would go to them and take their guns and carry them for the men, until some times he would have three or four guns." In another instance, two Seventh Cavalry recruits, George Denny and William Morris, decided to go hunting for prairie chickens without first receiving permission from their first sergeant. During the ensuing hunt, Morris accidentally shot Denny through both knees, crippling him permanently. Although the company commander was determined to court-martial Morris for taking his carbine from the barracks in disobedience of orders, First Sergeant John Ryan prevailed upon him to show leniency, "explaining that these men were only new recruits, and that Morris probably did not intend to do it." The captain finally relented and dropped the matter. Ryan subsequently "went around the company and took a subscription among the enlisted men, and also among the men of the other companies and the commissioned officers also took a hand and raised quite a large sum of money. . . . This was turned over to the pay master to be given to Denny at a future time. . . . It was fixed up in such a way that Denny received a pension." The compassion shown by the first sergeant and the other men indicated that, despite being a recruit, Denny exhibited the traits of a promising soldier and accordingly was treated as one of their own. Acts such as these contributed significantly to morale and esprit de corps. Writing to his brother in 1881, Private Henry Hubman said of his first sergeant: "He is very good to me and I like him first rate. He has been in the U.S. A[rmy] 35 years." He then added a postscript that might have characterized a great many noncoms of that day: "The only fault is that he swears like a pirate and drinks 'Rot' like a fish."[61]

Although most white noncoms possessed a modicum of education, the same was not true of the corporals and sergeants in the black regiments, particularly in the immediate postwar years. "The amount of writing devolving upon officers during the earlier years of the regiment [Ninth Cavalry] is not to be passed over lightly. . . . The enlisted men were totally uneducated . . . but one man in the entire regiment was found able to write sufficiently well to act as sergeant-major. . . . It was not an uncommon thing for a captain to assist his first sergeant in calling the roll . . . and every record . . . was prepared by an officer." The establishment of post schools that could be attended by soldiers after duty hours contributed significantly over time to improving the general educational level of enlisted men and increased the pool of potential candidates for noncommissioned rank.[62]

Privates usually viewed noncoms as having a softer life than their own and generally assumed that attaining rank was little more than gaining authority over others. A soldier elevated to noncommissioned rank suddenly realized that there was more to it, however, and that he now belonged to a special cadre within the company and regiment. As recruits and privates they had learned to execute the tactical movements of the school of the company, but as noncoms they were required to be instructors and not only had to be thoroughly familiar with their own tactical positions but had to be able to assume those of their superiors if necessary. As a foundation for this, post commanders often required all noncommissioned officers, except those sick and on guard, to attend two weekly recitations in tactics during evenings conducted variously by the post adjutant, officer of the day, or company commanders. Assignments for each session were outlined in advance as specific sections of Upton's *Tactics* manual and could be demanding. Corporal Charles Hayden, recently promoted, recorded in his diary: "I have not been on any duty today. Have been studying Tactics most all day." At some posts classroom instruction was followed by special drills only for noncoms. The post commander at Fort Laramie, for example, issued orders that the noncommissioned officers of companies were to be "formed on their respective company ground by the first sergeants . . . and marched to the battalion parade ground where they will be united into a body and drilled as a company by the Adjutant."[63]

Noncoms were often accorded minor privileges in deference to their rank. Many first sergeants seated all of the sergeants together at a separate table in the mess hall, assigning a corporal to supervise each of the other tables. At Fort Davis First Lieutenant John Bigelow, Tenth Cavalry, worked diligently to improve his noncoms as drillmasters and rewarded them for their efforts. "It is picking up," he noted in his journal. "The great difficulty in commanding colored troops is to get good N.C. officers, hence my desire to afford mine a room of their own." Bigelow's intention was to set aside and furnish a small barracks storeroom with its own outside entrance as a sort of club room where the noncoms could associate apart from the privates when not on duty. Extremely close bonds, the result of almost daily contact as well as shared hardship and danger, sometimes developed between company commanders and their first sergeants. As a veteran of the Fourth Cavalry explained: "Oftentimes an Officer, in recognition of well-performed service by his First Sergeant, would on parting for change of assignment, present to the Sergeant, a top-flight railroad conductor's lantern. The First Sergeants always prized the lanterns and the tribute that was implied."[64]

Particularly ambitious company noncoms, usually career men, sometimes graduated to one of several enlisted positions (all senior sergeants having special roles) on the regimental headquarters staff. The highest ranking of those was the sergeant major (more an administrative than a command position), closely assisting the adjutant in his varied responsibilities by supervising the headquarters clerks to see that all records, returns, orders, and correspondence were copied correctly (by hand) in duplicate. He maintained the regiment's NCO roster, clocked the timeliness of daily bugle calls regulating all post activities, and, in the absence of the adjutant, supervised the band. Perhaps his most visual role was participating in guard mounting by verifying the company details and reporting the results to the adjutant. He also interacted on a daily basis with the first sergeants by reviewing and consolidating their morning reports and disseminating instructions to each for guard, fatigue, and special details. A former sergeant major wrote to the *Army & Navy Journal*:

> General Kautz, in his book . . . says . . . that the duties of the sergeant-major are, "to watch the clock, and see that the bugler sounds the calls at the proper hours, make the details," etc. My three years' experience . . . taught me that General Kautz is egregiously mistaken. . . . I found out that the sergeant-major must be au fait in all the duties pertaining to a commissioned officer, non-commissioned officer, and private; must be able to drill from a squad of recruits to a regiment, must be able to write letters for the commanding officer and his adjutant on all subjects, must be able to make out proceedings of all sorts of boards, court-martials, councils, etc; must almost know the regulations by heart; must know how to make out returns and reports of every description . . . [and] must be a gentleman and a man of education and refinement.[65]

At those stations not designated as regimental headquarters, the local commander invariably appointed for this essential job an acting (sometimes called post) sergeant major as a functionary for which no additional pay was authorized. "The last year that I was at Fort Rice," recalled Fist Sergeant John Ryan, "there was no regular sergeant major at the post. Each one of the 1st sergeants of the companies stationed there had to take his turn as acting sergeant major." Perhaps the most common way to fill the job was to detail a well-versed and literate duty sergeant, or even a corporal, to the position.[66]

A regimental quartermaster sergeant assisted the officer delegated responsibility for the unit's (and usually the post's) supplies, property, buildings, and vehicles, and as such he had to be both literate and adept at figures, as well as a man of high integrity. The temptation would have been great to misappropriate government material for his personal benefit. In addition to maintaining proper accountability and protection of the property in his charge, the quartermaster sergeant served as foreman for all daily fatigue and extra duty details working for the quartermaster as well as the assigned teamsters. He received his direction from the post quartermaster (titled acting assistant quartermaster) and then conveyed those to the company noncoms in charge of the various labor details. Like the sergeant major, a quartermaster sergeant was vital to post operations; so when the regularly appointed incumbent was unavailable, the post commander named a temporary substitute. Such duty was not necessarily a hardship, particularly at a post experiencing little construction and repair activity, as related by a Fourth Cavalry sergeant who "was relieved of company duty and appointed Quartermaster Sergeant of the post, the duties of which position were far pleasanter, as my time was my own. I had a comfortable office and two clerks."[67]

With the act of 1866 each regiment was augmented by a commissary sergeant to handle the requisition, issue, and accountability of food stuffs and other material provided by the Subsistence Department. The grade was short-lived, however, because it soon proved to be impractical for conditions on the frontier, where regiments never served as cohesive units in garrison and only rarely during field operations. Consequently, the commissary sergeant could serve only those companies that happened to be at the headquarters station; those elsewhere were dependent on the respective post commissary officers for their food supplies. The army abolished regimental commissary sergeants in 1870 in favor of delegating those duties to quartermaster sergeants. But even that arrangement was unsatisfactory for the same reason that acting quartermaster sergeants had to be appointed at those forts not occupied by the regimental field and staff. The situation persisted until 1873, when the army created the coveted rank of post commissary sergeant, a member of the general noncommissioned staff attached to the station, rather than to a line unit, and under the direct supervision of the post commander. These individuals transferred from one fort to another infrequently and only by order of the adjutant general of the army.

Peculiar to the noncommissioned staff of a cavalry regiment were two additional enlisted positions: a chief trumpeter and a saddler sergeant. The former was a highly skilled musician responsible for instructing the field musicians or company trumpeters in the proper sounding of calls, for maintaining rosters for them, and for assigning musicians to guard duty, fatigue, and service as orderlies when required, usually in the field. Similarly, the saddler sergeant, usually an experienced harness-maker, trained and oversaw the work of the troop saddlers, at least those of the units present, and devised methods for repairing and modifying equipment.

The army table of organization authorized only three positions for infantry bands: a chief musician, sometimes termed the band leader or drum major, and two principal musicians. The leaders were in many instances accomplished musicians specially recruited from civil life, while the other two were senior musicians who functioned as duty sergeants of the band. Cavalry bands, however, were authorized only a chief musician. Regardless of service branch, a correspondent wrote to the editor of the *Army & Navy Journal*, "all the bandmaster can do, or should be expected to do, is to train his band to play together and keep them well in hand." Chief musicians not only directed and trained the band but selected the pieces to be played at ceremonies and concerts and sometimes applied themselves to composing their own arrangements and original scores.[68]

The grade of color sergeant (one per regiment) had been a custom of long standing in the army, even though it was not recognized officially until 1883. The position was one of great honor and distinction, as the sergeant was selected from those of the line companies for his record of "gallantry and military bearing." He carried the regimental colors on all occasions, including parades, musters, inspections, and in battle. He was entrusted with caring for and protecting the colors whenever they were in his possession. The rank was not listed in the table of organization; nor did the soldier cease to be a member of his company, but the color sergeant was accorded a special chevron readily identifying him to all.[69]

The most coveted noncommissioned officer grades were those specialized positions on the general staff of the army. These senior sergeants, mostly career soldiers, were a venerated class unto themselves who exemplified the finest of the enlisted regulars. They were attached, one each, to posts rather than regiments, to carry out property management functions for ordnance, subsistence, and quartermaster materiel. With the elements of regiments scattered widely and the line officers charged with those collateral responsibilities subject to transfer or replacement at any time, these staff sergeants provided needed operational continuity in the respective departments.

The rank of ordnance sergeant (not to be confused with a sergeant of ordnance) was the oldest of the three, having been authorized in 1832. The other two, commissary sergeant created in 1873 followed by post quartermaster sergeant in 1884, were a direct result of the army's frontier mission. The basic qualification for ordnance and commissary sergeants required applicants to have served faithfully for eight and five years, respectively, meaning they had to have had at least one prior enlistment. Additionally, they had to have been noncoms of the line for at least four and three years, respectively. The standards for post quartermaster sergeant were somewhat lower, probably because (as discussed above) some company sergeants performed similar duties and the property involved was less sensitive than either ordnance or subsistence. Those individuals seeking promotion were required to have a minimum of only four years' service to their credit and had to possess character and education fitting them "to take charge of public property and to act as clerks." An applicant's captain attested in writing as to his qualifications, experience, and general fitness for the position, yet army regulations outlined another overarching motive for the selection of these sergeants: "While the law contemplates in these appointments the better preservation of public property at the several posts, there is also a further consideration—that of offering a reward to faithful and well-tried Sergeants, and thus giving encouragement to deserving soldiers to hope for substantial promotion." Indicating the stature of these positions, all appointments had to be approved by the secretary of war.[70]

Many if not most of the men promoted to staff noncommissioned rank were exceptional, both as soldiers and as individuals. Post Quartermaster Sergeant Gustave W. Fahlbush represented that class of foreign-born regulars who became professional soldiers in their adopted country. A twenty-two-year-old optician by trade, Fahlbush emigrated from his native Germany to the United States, enlisting in 1870. Serving in D Troop, Eighth Cavalry, he completed his first enlistment at the rank of first sergeant. Fahlbush remained the top soldier in his troop for more than ten years, quite an accomplishment in itself, before being elevated to post quartermaster sergeant in 1885. With thirty years' service to his credit in 1900, Fahlbush retired during his seventh enlistment while posted in Cuba following the Spanish-American War.⁷¹

Ordnance sergeants, among the army's most highly paid enlisted men, like other noncoms attached to posts, were liable to be stationed anywhere in the nation, although they could apply for a particular fort or depot where a vacancy existed. A few, like William Delany, elected to remain on the western frontier throughout their careers. Delany joined the army in 1866 at age eighteen and followed the fortunes of the Twenty-Ninth and Eleventh Infantry for twenty-two years from Texas to Dakota Territory, including the Red River War, until he was appointed ordnance sergeant. Thereafter he was posted at Fort Huachuca, Arizona Territory, and eventually retired at Benicia Barracks, California in 1897.⁷²

Commissary Sergeant James W. Foley served through the war in both the Ninety-Seventh and Twenty-Eighth Pennsylvania Volunteer Infantry Regiments. Within a month after his honorable discharge in May 1865, he enlisted in the regulars and remained a member of the Fourth Cavalry until he was chosen as one of the first men promoted to the newly created rank of commissary sergeant in 1873. Another Fourth Cavalryman, Thomas H. Forsyth, another Pennsylvania infantry veteran, also joined the regulars immediately after the war and went west with the Second Cavalry, serving on the Bozeman Trail until his discharge three years later. Reenlisting in 1869, Forsyth was identified as an experienced veteran and assigned to the Mounted Recruiting Service as a drill sergeant in the cadre at Fort Leavenworth Depot until the station was disbanded the following year. He subsequently transferred to the Fourth Cavalry, where he quickly rose from private to first sergeant of Company M. During Mackenzie's fight with the Northern Cheyennes on the Red Fork of Powder River in November 1876, First Sergeant Forsyth distinguished himself by rallying men under fire to protect the body of his fallen lieutenant. For that he was promoted to sergeant-major a few months later and was afterward awarded the Medal of Honor. In recommending him for the medal, Captain Joseph H. Dorst expressed a view that might have applied to many staff noncoms: "I know Sergt. Forsyth well having had him as Sergt. Major for three years while I was regimental adjutant and I know that he is honest, brave, modest, sensitive, and conscientious in every respect. I have as high a degree of respect for him as I have for any man."[73]

The creation of additional positions in the general staff grades not only filled a practical need but provided an avenue toward further promotion for highly capable, ambitious sergeants of the line. Still, some career-minded individuals aspired to commissioned rank. The single, and largely subjective, means for an enlisted man to achieve a commission was by being recommended by his superior officer as deserving of "meritorious" status, so it is hardly surprising that few realized that goal. Officers had little or no incentive to help elevate soldiers above the ranks. Even when some took that step, the applicant was made to face that examination by an army board to determine his qualifications. During the 1870s complaints increased that it was nearly impossible for enlisted men to break through that ceiling.

The situation improved somewhat in 1878 when the army began offering greater incentive for enlisted men to improve themselves, strive for promotion, and perhaps make a career of the service. Even though West Point graduates continued to be accorded priority placement in all vacant positions at the rank of second lieutenant, a general order gave the next highest priority to worthy unmarried noncommissioned men between the ages of twenty-one and thirty. The commissioning of civilians was relegated to third priority, and only when more vacancies existed than could be filled by West Point graduates and noncoms qualified as officer candidates.

More important, company commanders were now obligated to take a pro-active role by reporting annually such noncoms "as, in their opinion, by education, conduct, and services, seem to merit advancement, and who have served not less than two years in the Army." Captains' recommendations were forwarded through the regimental commander, who added any candidates belonging to the regimental noncommissioned staff, whereupon the compiled endorsements were routed to department headquarters. A board of five officers evaluated the applications, and those successfully passing the board's scrutiny were endorsed by the department commander and forwarded to the secretary of war by June 1. Even though the examination had been made somewhat less subjective in nature, evidence suggests that the subjects still were biased against individuals without the benefit of higher education of the West

Point variety. A soldier writing to the *Army & Navy Journal* took issue with the method of testing applicants:

> There are very few of the civilian or volunteer appointments now officers in the Regular Army who could pass the examination as laid down in G.O. no. 62, if ordered before a board to-day. . . . It does not require a knowledge of mathematics to enable a man to lead a skirmish line, and the elements of surveying are not a necessity to make a man a brave and efficient officer. If a 1st sergeant of a company can keep all the books, drill the company, take care of the property, preserve the necessary discipline and perform his duties to the satisfaction of his superiors, there is nothing to prevent him . . . from performing the duties of a 2d lieutenant.[74]

Those candidates who successfully passed the exam were certified as officer candidates, a status that they retained for a full year after they were approved. During that period every effort was made to place them in vacancies in their own regiments, once they were officially commissioned. It was possible for an enlisted man to achieve commissioned rank through this process, as was demonstrated by Alvarado M. Fuller, an 1870 enlistee who rose through the ranks to sergeant major of the Second Cavalry by 1879 and was promoted to second lieutenant that same year under the new system. During the Spanish-American War, Fuller rose to the rank of captain in the Ninth Cavalry.[75]

The commissioned and noncommissioned officers were indeed the brains, bone, and sinew of the regular army, while it might be said that the privates formed the muscle. Even though the officers may have served as the brains, the noncoms formed the vital sinew linking the bones and muscle. Class distinctions would always exist and be observed, but the dawning glimmer of reform, however slight, illuminated a tenuous bridge over the chasm separating the worlds of the rank and file and the officer corps.

CHAPTER 6

"It Is Just Dragging Out a Miserable Existence"

Forts and Garrison Routine

Soldiers sent to the western frontier were dispersed among approximately two hundred military stations, variously called forts, subposts, camps, or cantonments, depending on their purpose and how permanent the army envisioned their occupancy to be. In reality, some camps were active longer than some forts; conversely, some forts were redesignated as camps but later renamed forts. Even some cantonments and subposts, considered to be the most temporary of the four classifications, developed into permanent garrisons termed "forts" as the role of the places changed. No matter what the designation, western stations shared one trait in common: monotony. Describing Fort Wallace, Kansas, in 1868, a visiting newspaper correspondent likened this small post on the high plains to "a ship at sea; isolation within and desolation without." It was an apt metaphor appropriate to most frontier posts regardless of name or function.[1]

Virtually all western posts were established to satisfy some particular immediate need. With few exceptions they were perceived to be temporary installations, a factor reflected in the materials and quality of the structures. Some, in fact, were short-lived and were abandoned after only a few years when the need for their establishment passed and the maintenance of garrisons at those locations could no longer be justified. Others lasted for a decade or two, each passing year anticipated to be their last, while the inhabitants existed in patched up "temporary" buildings. Some forts nevertheless continued to sprawl, with additional buildings and facilities presenting the illusion of greater permanency. A few remained active for many years after outliving their military usefulness, as buildings were replaced or added, so that the complex sometimes represented a jumble of architectural styles and materials—adobe, log, stone, frame, and even concrete.

The general location of a military post was based on strategic considerations within the scope of the army's frontier mission: to protect lines of travel and communication; to control water sources, critical mountain passes, and geographical regions traversed by troublesome Indian tribes; to serve as bases of operations against Indians considered hostile; and, as the frontier diminished, to serve as guardians of settled regions and Indian reservations. The actual placement of a frontier post invariably relied on the availability of three natural resources in sustainable quantities: water, timber, and grass. Nevertheless, as a wag at Fort Maginnis in central Montana Territory sarcastically noted, sometimes even those elements were not in evidence. Nor in fact was the value of the post readily apparent to the troops residing there:

> It is to the unenlightened eye unaccountable why a military post should have been established in such a location; it has not one redeeming feature about it . . . no water, no grazing . . . very little wood, but it was established right on the Indian trail leading into British Columbia. Yes, the Indian going north, must go right through Fort Maginnis. . . . Not much he musn't; he can select his own trail east or west from the Dakota to the Idaho boundary line. . . . There are no Indians within two hundred miles of the post! And we are glad of it. . . . Yet Maginnis has its advantages . . . ice all year round and snowstorms in August.[2]

Only rarely were forts the target of Indian attacks. The warriors wisely preferred to avoid army strongholds in favor of conditions that favored the finely honed guerrilla-style tactics of the hunter-warrior culture. Nevertheless, some forts, particularly those established during the 1860s and situated in close proximity to strong Indian forces perceived as hostile, were constructed within classic log stockades reminiscent of those used in forested regions of the early American frontier east of the Mississippi. Describing the appearance of Camp Cooke,

Montana Territory, in 1866, Musician James C. Bothwell related that it "was built in a hollow square, something over 400 feet on each side, each company with a building 20 × 100 feet, a frame of timber weather-boarded like any frame house, and filled in between the studding with adoba [sic] brick, and a dirt roof. . . . A stockade of heavy plank was erected about thirty feet outside the quarters, which was about ten feet high and three or four inches thick."[3]

Perhaps the best known of the stockaded forts were the principal posts situated along the Bozeman Trail across northern Wyoming Territory to the Montana goldfields: Forts Reno, Phil Kearny, and C. F. Smith. Private William A. Murphy, who helped build Fort Phil Kearny, described the massive undertaking: "We started building the . . . stockade which was six hundred feet by eight hundred feet. The logs were set three feet in the ground, projected eight feet and were hewed on two sides to a touching surface. We built quarters for the officers, ware-rooms, settler's [sic: sutler's] store, guard house, stockade for the mules and quarters for the men. . . . There were all kinds of mechanics in the army." By mid-decade even venerable Fort Laramie, situated two hundred miles southeast at the confluence of the Laramie and North Platte Rivers, could boast physical defenses in the form of an extensive earthwork surrounding the north perimeter of the post, plus a large quartermaster corral constructed of adobe brick designed with loop-holed bastions on two corners. Lacking enough troops for properly manning those works had it been necessary, the army allowed the field fortification to deteriorate, while the corral bastions housed civilian teamsters.[4]

Farther south on the nearly treeless central plains finding enough usable timber for building purposes posed a continuing challenge for the army. A Second Cavalry trooper arriving at Fort Ellsworth, Kansas, in 1866 related that he was a member of a detachment sent up the Smoky Hill River to abandoned Fort Fletcher "to pull down four log shanties to put up here for our quarters. . . . You may be sure timber is scarce when they sent us 60 miles for log shanties." Troops at Fort Larned, farther south on the Santa Fe Trail, were somewhat more fortunate in that a source of brown sandstone lay nearby and prairie sod was abundantly available. When Captain Albert Barnitz arrived there with his company of the Seventh Cavalry in spring 1867, he commented that the post "consists of a couple of stone buildings, one of which is the Suttler's [sic], and the other the Commissary building—a few low uncouth looking adobe structures, occupied by two companies of the 3d Infantry . . . a few stables dug out of the river bank, and covered with poles, straw and mud, and some houses dug out in the same manner!" An Indian outbreak in the region three years earlier had prompted the army to construct a separate stone blockhouse (which Barnitz failed to mention), set a few yards off one corner of the parade ground, and to install rifle embrasures in the outer walls of the commissary and quartermaster storehouses built shortly afterward.[5]

Posts in the Southwest tended to be even more primitive, if that were indeed possible. Private Henry I. Yohn, First Cavalry, recorded that "Troop G was sent to Tucson and established Camp Lowell. . . . Our quarters were tents—we had nothing else to live in. We cut the timber out in the Catalina Mountains—cottonwood, I suppose . . . cut them with forks and set them in the ground, then covered them with green brush for shade." Adobe was the predominant material used in constructing permanent buildings by both Hispanics and Anglo-Americans throughout the entire region, a practice the army adopted early on. Adobe was economical, requiring only labor to produce limitless numbers of bricks using local gravely soils, hay for binding, and abundant sunshine for curing them. As a result, military posts, though more orderly in their arrangement, presented an appearance little different from that of local settlements. While many forts in the Southwest embraced walled corrals that conceivably could have been used as defensive positions had the need arisen, Fort Cummings, New Mexico Territory, presented a rare exception to the general rule. An army surgeon who visited this extremely isolated one-company post guarding vital Cooke's Springs on the Mesilla-Tucson road was astonished when he found a fort that would not have been out of place in the deserts of North Africa:

> Here was a veritable walled garrison. A somewhat pretentious front of "doby" (adobe) wall, with archway on either side of which were guard rooms, gave the fort an ancient look, which made the American flag floating from the tall flagstaff in the center of the parade ground look almost out of place. These walls, about 15 feet in height, extended around the garrison buildings, forming a square, with only one opening, the door

in the rear [*sic*: front] where a sentry always walked his beat day and night.⁶

The great majority of frontier "forts," in contradiction to the term, were not defensive works at all, simply because there was no justification for physical barriers. Even before the advent of motion pictures, which have indoctrinated the public with a false notion that walled forts were universal on the western frontier, earlier generations equally unfamiliar with western Indians were similarly misinformed. Regular soldiers of the era, primarily natives of the eastern United States and Europe, were as unprepared as any other tenderfeet upon encountering a post in the West. One young recruit hiking into Fort Sanders, Wyoming Territory, for the first time found part of it "enclosed by four low, adobe walls that one, taking a good run, could vault. Its largest and heaviest gun was a rifle. . . . Those frontier so-called forts did not convey to the mind anything like what that term would imply, and least of all Fort Sanders." An experienced officer commented that the newcomer to the West

> who for the first time visits a frontier fort is usually surprised at what he sees and apt to be somewhat disappointed in his expectations. Instead of bastioned walls, deep ditches, and grassy ramparts, from which frown deep-throated cannon, he sees before him . . . what at first sight appears to be a small village set well out in the plain or possibly at its edge near an outlying mountain generally embowered in shade trees with a tall flagstaff in its centre, from which floats the flag of his country.⁷

He might have added that forts shared another trait in common: a foul stench. Approaching from down-wind, one could smell a fort before actually seeing it. This repulsive olfactory insult was a combination of rotting garbage, outdoor toilets, manure, animal urine, offal, and open dumping of all manner of refuse near the post.

By the late 1860s Indians were being crowded farther into the recesses of their homelands, away from forts and traveled routes, and the army realized that actual fortifications were all but unnecessary. So it transitioned from defensive to offensive planning. The older forts that remained active into the following decade, and nearly all of those established after about 1870, conformed to the essential "village" plan, making for a largely self-sufficient community.⁸ The core of all posts consisted of a parade ground of varying size, depending on garrison size and suitable terrain; officers' quarters arranged in a row along one side, barracks along the opposing side, and an adjutant's office (headquarters) and guardhouse occupying the others. Outside this nucleus were a hospital, often at some distance behind officers' row; quartermaster and commissary store houses, a bakery, workshops for the butcher, carpenters, blacksmiths, and saddlers; cavalry and quartermaster corrals to the rear of the men's quarters; and a post trader's store. Some posts, especially in later years, were fortunate enough to offer a multipurpose building used as chapel, school, and theater. Arrayed haphazardly at the outer perimeter of the enlisted side of the post were quarters—often mere shacks—for noncommissioned staff officers, laundresses, and civilian employees. A Third Cavalryman arriving at Fort Verde, Arizona Territory, in 1881 called it "one of the most dreary and desolate places I ever saw." This was a typical reaction of newcomers to the frontier.⁹

The enlisted man's home was the barracks, and the heart of the barracks was the dormitory, usually referred to as a squad room. It was the center of the soldier's universe. As one officer put it, "The 'youngster' learns many things in and about a barrack room which are not in the drill book or the regulations." Most barracks incorporated two such rooms, with a platoon (half a company) quartered in each, while band barracks normally contained only one because of the smaller number of men. A Seventh Cavalryman described the appearance of a typical squad room:

> In the quarters . . . were little iron beds with single mattresses filled with straw from the Quartermaster's Department, and if straw could not be obtained hay was used. . . . These iron bunks had four wooden slats in them running lengthwise from head to the foot. We also had at the foot of every bunk a little wooden box about a foot high, a foot wide and about three feet [*sic*: two feet] long known as a locker, where the men kept their dress uniforms.¹⁰

The orderly room, usually partitioned off one end of a squad room, or extending to the front with a private doorway at one end of the porch, served as company headquarters. Some barracks afforded first sergeants the luxury of a separate bedroom, sometimes shared with his company clerk, connecting with the orderly room, but in most instances his bunk and locker occupied one corner of the orderly room itself.[11]

The company clerk and the acting quartermaster sergeant, in addition to the first sergeant, worked in the orderly room on a daily basis. The clerk, charged with doing all the company writing, including the morning reports and bimonthly muster rolls, maintaining the company descriptive and sick books, and writing orders and correspondence for the company commander's signature, received no additional pay but was excused from other duty. Noncommissioned officers were not supposed to be assigned as company clerks, but sometimes were, according to George Brown, a Thirteenth Infantry corporal who doubled as clerk. Some imaginative first sergeants found ways to induce men to take the job, even though it may not have been according to the letter of army regulations. After seeing a letter Private John Spring had penned in his native German, the first sergeant arranged to make him company clerk with the rank and pay of lance corporal.[12]

It was tedious, exacting work nonetheless. Serving as clerk of Company L, Eighth Cavalry, in 1873, Private Eddie Mathews, formerly a sergeant, grumbled: "Have been scratching away day after day until the sight of pen and paper has almost become distasteful to me. Every return and letter has to be written twice, three and sometimes four times. . . . I get so tired of doing it at times that I leave the Office in disgust and almost wish I was doing duty in the Company, but I soon get over this kind of feeling and go back to my work." An ex-first sergeant of the Fourth Cavalry characterized the clerk as "usually . . . a fellow addicted to the flowing bowl, not ambitious for military duty nor for promotion; frequently had been a non-commissioned officer who had been reduced to the ranks and not fit for much else." Underscoring his opinion, the veteran related an incident in which an Irish clerk was arrested for drunkenness. Asked by an officer why it seemed to be that worthwhile clerks always seemed to be drunkards, the man had a ready answer: "Sir, if it wasn't for whiskey, there wouldn't be any clerks in the army."[13]

All scheduled activities at military posts were regulated by a series of daily service calls sounded by bugle or trumpet. "Bugle calls measured the hour of officers, soldiers, women, and children in garrison life," remarked the daughter of a Tenth Cavalry officer. At garrisons composed only of infantry, some signals were sounded by drum and fife. The times for the daily calls, always dictated by order of the post commander, usually varied somewhat from one post to another according to the season and the CO's discretion.[14]

The orderly trumpeter, a field musician detailed in rotation from one of the companies, went on with the daily guard and remained at the guardhouse to sound the calls at the appropriate hours throughout each twenty-four-hour period. Every company and troop had two field musicians drawn from the depot pool. These individuals, paid as privates, were members of the company, not the band, though not particularly popular ones. First Sergeant Henry McConnell, who served with the Sixth Cavalry in the late 1860s, declared: "If there is any one class or individual whom the old soldier looks upon as his natural enemy it is the bugler. Not subject to any duty but the one pertaining to his specialty—sounding calls—being a boy and full of mischief, he usually spends his ample leisure in indulging in pranks distasteful to the veterans." He related that on one occasion the trumpeter of his troop played a particularly vexing prank on an old soldier, who went to the company commander "to get permission to kill the boy in order to save the boy from being hung at no distant period . . . since the good regulation of whipping them had been abolished." The captain denied the request, of course, even though he may have been inclined to agree with the old soldier.[15]

Other than the post guard detail, the cooks were the first men up every day, most rising a couple of hours before reveille to begin preparing breakfast. The cook's first duty was to awaken his assistant, designated second cook, sleeping in the squad room. This man assisted the chief (or first) cook with food preparation and progressed to the head position for the following ten-day period, unless the first cook chose to remain in that role. Another man, sometimes two, the kitchen or cook's police, reported immediately after reveille roll call to begin "assisting the cooks, washing the dishes and pots, scrubbing the tables and floors, chopping wood for the kitchen, also for the dining room in winter, in general the roustabout in the kitchen. . . . There was continual work, with a few hours rest in the afternoon, from morning until seven or eight at night," a soldier wrote. It was expected that the kitchen police would acquire some practical experience that would benefit him when he took his turn as cook. "Of all the jobs on earth I believe I had rather have any of them [than?] the one that I had today being kitchen police," groused Private Hartford G. Clark. This soldier's lamentation was heard throughout the ages, yet everyone appreciated that the distasteful elements were mitigated by a few unwritten compensations.[16]

An infantryman noted in his journal that every kitchen was supervised by "a corporal [or] sergeant who had to draw the rations every ten days for all the men in the company and supervised their proper cooking and division among the men." He was also there to back up any instructions the cook gave the kitchen police. Speaking to the importance of the responsibility, First Sergeant John Ryan, Seventh Cavalry, added that this noncom "was detailed from each of the companies every day and he was obliged to inspect the dining room and kitchen every day, and if any fault was found by his superior officers . . . he was hauled over the coals." One of the company officers personally inspected the kitchen daily, usually in mid-morning.[17]

Contrary to popular belief, soldiers did not awaken to the strains of "Reveille." Rather, the garrison was jolted from its slumbers by the shrill notes of "First Call," the familiar call heard today at horse races, which notified soldiers to prepare for certain activities. (It was heard throughout the day prior to guard mounting, drill, fatigue, and so forth.) "At the first streak of daylight in the morning First Call for Reveille would be sounded by the Trumpeter of the Guard, and ten minutes later Assembly," recounted Trumpeter Ami F. Mulford. The troops hurriedly arose and dressed—cavalry troopers in white stable frocks and overalls. "Then all would fall in on the company parades and stand at parade rest while Assembly was sounded by all the trumpeters [grouped at the flag staff]." Immediately thereafter the assembled field musicians sounded "Reveille."[18]

A recently married army wife new to the routine was shocked by the cacophony when "three or four bugles played a little air, which it was impossible to hear because of the horrible howling and crying of dogs," which was further intensified by the loud boom of a single shot from the salute gun, Sundays excepted, parked near the flag staff. At the same instant, the first sergeants all along the line simultaneously brought their companies to attention as the sergeant of the guard, assisted by two men, flung the national colors to the breeze and raised them to the top of the flag staff. All along the line, the first sergeants rapidly called the rolls, with each man present loudly answering "Here!" as his name was called. The respective duty sergeants answered for those of their squads on guard, kitchen police, or some other assigned duty. The names of any others unaccounted for were taken down as absent without leave. The first sergeants then reported the results to the officer of the day standing on the parade ground, after which the companies were dismissed.[19]

Infantry soldiers then had about half an hour to wash up, at tubs behind the barracks or, if they were fortunate enough to have a modern barracks, in a dedicated bathroom, after which they made their bunks and swept out the quarters prior to eating breakfast. Cavalrymen, however, did not have that small luxury. Immediately following roll call, "Water and Stable Calls would summons [sic] every man not on other duty, to the stables. Each man wore a white frock and overalls [to protect his blue woolen uniform] and they were a prim-looking lot as they marched to the stables. The horses would be led to the river for water, then returned to the stables and groomed for a whole hour under the immediate direction of the First Sergeant, and woe to the man who did not give his horse strict attention and a thorough going over with currycomb and brush." Meanwhile, two men excused from stables remained at the quarters to sweep the floors and, in suitable weather, open windows to air out the squad room. Upon the return of the company, troopers made use of the intervening time before breakfast to perform their morning ablutions and immediately after eating squared away their bunks and surrounding areas as prescribed by the company commander. The arrangement, however, was near-universal. "First thing after coming from stables in the morning," wrote Private Eddie Matthews, "you roll your bed sack up, place it at the head of your bed, fold your blanket up nicely, and lay them on the bed sack. All the bunks look the same."[20]

One of the noncommissioned officers, either a sergeant or corporal, was assigned daily as charge-of-quarters. He, along with the chiefs of squads, made certain that every man's bunk area was neat and made up correctly with the mattress "folded up into three thicknesses and set up against the head of the bunk. The woolen blankets would be folded the width of the bed ticks . . . [and] laid out smooth on top of the bed ticks." Extra pairs of boots and shoes were placed under the bunks, either along one side or the other or at the foot just behind the locker. The charge-of-quarters supervised a man detailed as "room orderly," who was responsible for the general cleanliness of the squad room, security, wood boxes being filled during winter, ashes being removed from the stoves, spittoons being emptied, and water being replenished in fire barrels. The room orderly, remaining at the barracks all day, "holds his job as long as he wishes, and when holding that job he is excused from drill, roll call, guard mount, and other duties, with the exception of taking care of his horse," Seventh Cavalryman John Ryan recorded. It was not unusual for the first sergeant to favor the oldest man or two in his company, when they were not physically able to do full duty, with near-permanent details as room orderly.[21]

Even though meal times were regulated at specified hours of the day, not all cooks could be expected to serve at the same moment. Depending on the particular fort, a general mess call may have been sounded by the trumpeter of the guard, but only when the cook said it was time to eat did one of the kitchen police summon the men of his company to the mess hall using a small brass bell, an iron triangle, or a gong made of a piece of flat iron. Corporal Emil A. Bode recorded that Company D, Sixteenth Infantry, employed a common cowbell for this purpose. Still, this informal system could create a certain amount of confusion, as evidenced in an order promulgated at Fort Totten, Dakota Territory, in 1878: "The practice of the Companies ringing triangles or gongs for supper before the retreat roll call is over will be discontinued, fully five (5) minutes will intervene between the breaking of ranks and the sounding of such instruments."[22]

Seventh Cavalryman Mulford described a typical mess hall as "a long room, no chairs, bare wooden tables, wooden benches to sit on; a tin plate, with a knife and fork beside each, arranged in order, are all we see on the tables." Food was delivered to the tables in large bowls and platters by the cook's police and served family style. In many companies, a noncom—usually a corporal—presided over each table to maintain order and ensure that every man received equitable portions.[23]

As a cook at Fort Union, New Mexico Territory, confided, "The 1st Sergt., Quarter Master Sergt., & three Cooks mess by ourselves. We always have something extra. Such as Eggs, Milk, Butter, Bread Pudding, Doughnuts, & etc." It was not uncommon, in fact, for the sergeants to sit at a table apart from the rest of the men as distinction of rank. In some companies the sergeants and cooks even ate after the others, knowing that special foodstuffs would be resented by other company members not so privileged. On one occasion a soldier overheard the company quartermaster sergeant direct the cook to draw fewer rations of fresh beef than there were men in the company. With the first sergeant's permission, he reported the incident to the captain, who made an immediate investigation, discovering that the noncoms were indeed high-grading the best cut of meat for their own table, at the same time shorting the rest of the men. The captain promptly set the matter straight by ordering the sergeant to draw the full ration and to see that the men received all of it. After the introduction of consolidated mess halls at some large posts, noncoms were accorded separate messes as a morale factor. Private Andrew M. Flynn, serving with the Seventh Cavalry at Fort Riley, Kansas, in 1888, said of the arrangement: "The non-coms there had their own mess hall and, boy, didn't they live high."[24]

After breakfast, soldiers who were ill reported their symptoms to the first sergeant, who made an initial judgment as to the veracity of their claims. He then directed the company clerk to enter their names in the company "sick book," which First Sergeant Henry McConnell termed an "institution," because "on it are entered the names of all those who wish to attend 'surgeon's call' . . . also [there] are the chronic 'dead beats' and by a perusal of its pages a fair history of each man can be in a manner traced." At the sounding of "Sick Call" (or "Surgeon's Call"), usually at about seven o'clock, "the sick, lame and lazy," according to one trooper, assembled to be conducted to the hospital by the first sergeant, or one of the duty sergeants, for examination by the surgeon:

> If the symptoms are serious, the men are placed in the hospital; if otherwise, they are given medicine, sent back to their quarters, and excused from guard duty, or if there is only a very slight trouble that will easily yield to treatment they are given the necessary medicine and ordered to report to the first sergeant for light duty. Of course now and then some inefficient soldier is a malingerer, but the army surgeons soon detect such cases, and an unusually bitter dose of medicine, taken on the

spot . . . together with a sharp order to report at once for duty, usually prevents a recurrence . . . by the outwitted shirk."[25]

Shortly after breakfast, commensurate with "Sick Call," came the least popular signal of the day, "Fatigue," summoning all the men detailed from the companies for various work projects at and in the vicinity of the post. "It does them good to make them work at least part of the day," one officer divulged. "Haven't so much time to growl, loaf and get into mischief, don't you know." General laborers performed an almost infinite variety of tasks necessary for the operation and maintenance of a fort. "As ex-clothing clerks our first experience was rather strenuous," remembered Private Ernest A. Selander, Fifth Cavalry. "As rookies we were put to digging trenches for water pipes . . . and shoveling coal . . . for our quarters, and hauling sand to fill in ground for new stables and the like, until our hands were blistered." Some jobs were universal, regardless of location. All posts required drinking water, usually obtained from a nearby stream (occasionally from wells) by bucketing it into barrels on a wagon or filling a tank wagon then hauling the water to the post and siphoning it into covered barrels situated behind or inside the various inhabited buildings. In winter at northern posts fatigue details shoveled snow from walkways and sometimes even roads, while others harvested ice, using special vertical hand saws, then hauled it by sled or wagon to a subsurface ice house where it was stored for hospital and summer use. Compensating somewhat for the hard labor in cold weather, an infantryman at Fort Sill, Indian Territory, wrote that "there was plenty of whiskey and hot coffee to keep us warm." In an age of wood-burning stoves for cooking and heating, there was a constant need for fuel. It had to be hauled from long stacks of cordwood in the quartermaster area of the post and delivered periodically to all occupied buildings, where it was later sawed into usable lengths.[26]

Beyond these jobs, there was always general policing to be done (cleaning up trash from the parade ground, roads, sidewalks, and around the buildings; collecting and hauling refuse to the post dump), all under the supervision of the police sergeant. Grousing bitterly about one unavoidable recurring chore attendant to large numbers of horses and mules, a Sixth Cavalry private noted in his diary that he was "on general fatigue shoveling manure this forenoon and it just made me sick."[27]

Some of the men were continually detailed for various periods to work for one of the supply entities at the post: quartermaster, subsistence, or ordnance. Apart from lesser tasks (such as digging drainage ditches and hauling sawdust to the stables), new construction, building repair, and painting invariably dominated the activities of fatigue parties sent to the Quartermaster Department. Men possessing some degree of education served comparatively soft duty as clerks in the office. Only rarely in frontier regions were civilian tradesmen available to perform skilled work; besides, utilizing soldiers was more economical. Private Albin H. Drown, Second Cavalry, recalled that in 1866, while encamped at Pond Creek Station on the Smoky Hill Trail in Kansas, "an order came to establish a post to be named Fort Wallace. The company . . . broke ground and worked on the foundations. The stone was quarried a few miles distant by our boys and carted to us . . . we would saw the stone [limestone] . . . into square blocks." During the construction of barracks at Fort Reno, Indian Territory, ex-Sergeant Christian F. Sommer, Twenty-Third Infantry, explained that "the best mechanics were picked out from the enlisted men and put to work building quarters for the officers." The principal reason for determining a recruit's previous occupation at enlistment, of course, was to provide a record of skills possessed by its members. "I was assigned to Co. H, 11th U.S. Infantry and was one of the many soldiers who helped build [Fort Custer, Montana Territory]," said Private Rolando B. Moffett. "I drove a mule to grind the clay to make the bricks . . . I enlisted as a potter. I knew clay thoroughly, and was the soldier who selected the clay out of which to make the bricks." Construction projects required the skills of numerous ex-tradesmen, including carpenters, masons, bricklayers, and plasterers, plus a bevy of laborers. One Fourth Cavalryman in the Southwest recalled: "There was some hard work . . . I have not forgotten carrying the hod of mortar on my bony shoulder many a day up to the men who were laying the sun-dried adobe bricks in the erection of the barracks." Skilled and/or educated men frequently wound up with near-steady jobs in either the Quartermaster or Subsistence Departments.[28]

Other details worked at the warehouses, unloading and storing supplies as they arrived by wagon or steamboat. Worn-out equipment, once declared surplus or condemned, was then either boxed and shipped to a central depot or taken to the post dump and destroyed. Subsistence stores in particular were inspected periodically and rotated. The ordnance sergeant required less manual labor on a regular basis, yet artillery pieces and limbers exposed to the elements had to have the wheels rotated and be repainted now and then; ammunition shipments had to be off-loaded and stacked in the magazine. "I worked harder to-day than I ever did in one day since I enlisted," wrote one private at Fort Niobrara, Nebraska. "I was moving ammunition in boxes that weighed 150 pounds." All of this was accomplished by the labor of the troops.[29]

At varying distances from forts were timber and haying operations suited to soldiers who had been farmers, lumbermen, and common laborers. For instance, the garrison at Fort Laramie, Wyoming Territory, manned a sawmill operation in the mountains some fifty miles from the post to produce dimensioned lumber for building construction. The workforce averaged a dozen or more men, up to an entire company, detailed to the camp for a month at a time. Such assignments, although isolated, were viewed by many men as a welcome respite from the grind of garrison life and being constantly under unrelenting discipline. "There was always plenty to do, but none of it hard enough to hurt a man," admitted Trumpeter Ami Mulford.[30]

Some men resigned themselves to physical labor as a necessary part of military life and made the best of it, perhaps even acquiring useful skills through the experience. One of those was Regimental Quartermaster Sergeant Maurice Wolfe, Fourth Infantry, who informed his uncle in Ireland: "A man [in the?] United States Army can learn a good deal . . . and will see all sorts of work done (more especially in the western country). He must be a carpenter, mason, [illegible], painter, clerk, and glazier and a good soldier to boot, all of which he will be made acquainted with in the Army." Other enlisted men, in contrast, expressed considerable discontent with the amount of work imposed on soldiers. Ex-Fourth Cavalryman William B. Jett explained how they subtly manifested their displeasure: "It usually took four or five soldiers to do what one good citizen would have done. They worked as slowly as possible. I suppose this attribute of soldiers while at work gave origin to the expression, 'Soldiering on the job.'" Among the civilian populace, regulars had a reputation (not altogether undeserved) for being indolent when it came to labor. Writing to the editor of a local newspaper in 1886, Private James O. Purvis, First Cavalry, attempted to bring perspective to the soldier's apparent lack of motivation: "The objection to labor . . . is not on account of laziness or a dislike of work, but simply because it is not his profession." That they had enlisted to do military duty, not common labor, was a complaint voiced widely by the rank-and-file of the army.[31]

Unlike modern forces, the army of the late nineteenth century had few designated specialists at the company level. While other soldiers were employed on fatigue details about the garrison, these men applied themselves to their particular jobs. Companies of infantry included only two, an artificer and a wagoner. The artificer, always a manually skilled individual by previous occupation, acted in the capacity of the unit's handyman to execute simple repairs to rifles and any other equipment belonging to the company, sometimes modifying equipment or fabricating nonissue items, and, if capable, repairing shoes.[32]

By their very nature, cavalry companies required more men possessing special talents. Although cavalry companies had no designated artificer, the troop saddler functioned in a similar role: repairing horse equipment and modifying or making leather and canvas equipment of various kinds. A blacksmith spent his days trimming hooves and shoeing the troop horses, a constant and physically demanding task. Assigned as the blacksmith's assistant, Seventh Cavalryman William H. White admitted that he "knew only the rudiments of the work, but I was anxious to learn, and it was not long before I could shoe mules and horses about as well as any expert . . . [but] the physical strain incident to struggling with the animals . . . put me into ill health, so I had to relinquish the place after eight months." The farrier was concerned with the health and well-being of the troop horses, though he frequently assisted the blacksmith. He had to be an experienced, observant horseman, "whose business was to look after the welfare of the horses in so far as treatment, food and medicine were concerned." In short, according to Private David Lynch, "the farrier is the veterinary of the co[mpany]." Additionally, every company and troop had one man designated as wagoner, the nineteenth-century equivalent of truck driver, who was charged with care and maintenance of the vehicle, its four-mule team, and the harness. Whenever the wagon was needed, either around the garrison or in the field, he was the teamster.[33]

Meanwhile, as the rest of the company went about its regimen, first sergeants returned to their offices to coordinate the preparation of the daily morning reports with their respective clerks. This vital report, rendered by all companies and the band, accounted for every enlisted soldier and his whereabouts, whether away from the post on detached service, assigned to an extra or daily duty detail, ill in the hospital, confined, or occupied elsewhere. The most important figure was the current effective strength of the company. After all other men were deducted from the total strength of the company, it was not unusual that less than a dozen to perhaps twenty soldiers remained available as "duty men," meaning the legitimate duties of a soldier such as drill and guard. The company commander came to the orderly room to review and sign the report as well as to communicate with his first sergeant about company matters. With that done, the first sergeant delivered the report to the post adjutant's office no later than eight o'clock.[34]

The highlight of the military day—guard mounting—happened at about 8:30 or 9:00 every morning, day-in and day-out, regardless of weather. In combined commands, cavalry and infantry were to share the duty equally, but in practice guard duty often fell more heavily on the infantry at posts where cavalry had a great deal of scouting and other field service to perform. At most posts a soldier could expect to draw a "trick" at guard one night out of four, perhaps one of three at some posts. While rookies recognized the familiar routine, the solemnity of the event at a post impressed them as being different. It became quickly obvious that guard duty was assigned a great deal more importance than at the recruiting depot. New soldiers sensed instinctively that they had entered the big league.[35]

In generally fair weather seasons, summer and fall, guards donned full dress uniforms, with buttons and brasses glittering, accented with white cotton gloves. Soldiers, expected to present an immaculate appearance, devoted considerable time and effort to preparing for the ceremony. A trooper wrote: "It is very hard to work up a belt and cartridge box and gun and gun stock and shin[e] up the cartridges so you can see your face in them. Also have your boots blacked in such a way that no fault whatever can be found with them and have a clean shave, clean clothes, and clean gloves and then put on the best soldierly appearance." More than being a matter of simply passing inspection, an immaculate appearance was important to unit pride; being replaced by a supernumerary (substitute) was to embarrass the company. In less favorable seasons soldiers attended guard mounting in fatigue uniform—blouse, trousers, and forage cap, but with the traditional white gloves marking them as sentinels. The more comfortable blouses facilitated the addition of overcoats as conditions dictated. Pulling guard during winter on the northern Great Plains was still another matter. "In Dakota's severe cold it looked like a parade of animals at the Zoo!" witnessed Mrs. Elizabeth Custer. "All were compelled to wear buffalo overcoats and shoes, fur caps, and [fur] gloves." As might be expected, inspections under such conditions were somewhat less stringent.[36]

Competition among companies for the neatest soldiers having the most military demeanor was razor edged because the man selected became orderly for the post commander, an honor for both the individual and his company. (At some posts, the runner-up became orderly for the officer of the day.) Akin to the fastest runner or best marksman in the company, the "orderly bucker" was the pride of his comrades. Buckers, one or two in every company, were fiercely competitive not only as a matter of unit honor but for the personal benefits derived. The orderly's duty was easy, having only to be available at the commander's quarters or headquarters to carry any messages or instructions he might have for members of the garrison. In fair weather the orderly hovered around the front porch, but in inclement weather he was permitted to sit just inside the door. According to one Seventh Cavalry trooper, "an orderly did not have to stand guard or do much of anything but buzz the hired girl in the kitchen and eat up all the cold victuals he could find." He was also allowed to return early to his company's mess hall to "obtain the first hot food servings at meal time" in order to be absent from his post only a short time. Perhaps the most coveted reward came when the commanding officer dismissed him at the end of the day, after which the orderly was free to do as he pleased, and he was allowed to sleep in his own bunk, rather than at the guardhouse. As a further incentive to competition, some commanders authorized the orderly a pass to be off-post with no duty the following day.[37]

As First Sergeant Ryan asserted: "There is hardly a post or a camp where United States troops are stationed but there are some men who make a practice of running for orderlies at guard mount and it would surprise an outsider so see how some of these men clean up and fix their arms and equipment for this purpose." Orderly bucking became a finely honed art for those individuals—some even bathed for the occasion. The bucker meticulously polished every button and other piece of brass about his uniform and accouterments to bring them to a brilliant shine. Friends sometimes combined efforts to assist the recognized company champion in his preparations for the contest. One former Fourth Cavalry trooper remarked that he kept aside a special saber belt and cartridge box used only for orderly bucking and he treated those "with Dadiac polish to shine like patent leather." Likewise, it was not uncommon for buckers to draw or purchase additional uniform items, often tailor-made, that were reserved specifically for guard mounting. Arms came under especially close scrutiny: "it was important that the stocks of their rifles or carbines shone like satin; that the 'blueing' [sic] on metal parts was unscratched; that screw heads were unmarred. . . . [and] that all rifle or carbine barrels within should be without a speck of dust or undamaged by cleaning rods." A former Thirteenth Infantryman attested that he kept three polished rifle cartridges especially for inspection purposes. Once ready, the candidate was closely examined by a comrade or two, who ensured that nothing had been overlooked and gave his uniform a final brushing to remove any vestige of dust or lint.[38]

First Sergeant Ryan wrote: "At the first call for guard mount . . . the detail from each company [two or three usually] immediately proceeded to the street in front of their quarters and fell into line, where they would be inspected by the 1st sergeant of their company to see that they were neat and clean. Then at assembly call they are marched [by the first sergeant] to the parade ground and fall in line with the balance of the guards from the other companies and are reported to the sergeant major." One or two men from each company were designated as supernumeraries in the event one of the others became ill or failed to pass inspection. These men prepared for guard just like the primary selectees and attended the ceremony; but if not needed they were subsequently dismissed, only to be the first named for the duty the following day.[39]

The ceremony was invariably accompanied by music, performed by the band at a regimental headquarters, otherwise by the assembled field musicians playing a selection of quicksteps. Where drummers and fifers were present, they too would participate in the performance. Observing such a ceremony at Fort Hays, Kansas, in 1867, Captain Albert

Barnitz admiringly commented that "the music of our eight buglers, or 'trumpeters' rather, is really very fine. They are improving daily."[40]

Those persons in the garrison not otherwise occupied, including army families and other civilians, became critical spectators at guard mounting, eyeing every detail of the proceedings for correctness. "What it is that makes guard mount so absolutely fascinating to both the oldest officer and soldier as well as to the raw recruit of soldierly instincts it is hard to say, but that it is so, the frequent attendance of both . . . fully confirms." With new and old guard detachments (minus any sentries walking beats) formed on the parade, the post adjutant proceeded to inspect the members of the relieving detail. An officer described it: "The exquisite appearance and soldierly bearing of these privates is something astonishing. The perfect fit of their clothing, the absolute cleanliness of the their clothing and person, their neatly brushed shoes, clean shaven faces, closely cut hair, polished buckles and belt plates, and perfectly immaculate arms and equipments make them living models for the new recruits." The adjutant passed down the rank carefully surveying each man—up, down, and behind—then ordered inspection of arms. "The adjutant inspecting the barrels had a jaunty way of swinging the butt up to the sky to throw light into the barrel, and then dip it down with a continuation of the jaunty swing," Reynolds Burt remembered of one officer. "Sometimes it is next to impossible to determine who should be selected," noted Captain Albert Barnitz. "Even the heads of the screws in their carbines are closely scrutinized, . . . even to the bottom of the little notch intended for the point of the screw-driver."[41]

At times the adjutant had difficulty making a choice between two men. In those instances, he would march them to the guardhouse, where he had them perform the manual of arms, watching for the slightest imperfection in its execution. That would often decide the issue. But if not, explained one veteran, "I have known men to be taken to the guard house or the adjutant's quarters and part of their clothes removed to tell which was the cleanest man." In so doing, the keen-eyed adjutant also brought into play another deciding factor, noting any nonissue clothing items such as shirts and socks. Some officers preferred to reverse the order of the final elements of the inspection. Private Hartford G. Clark explained that when the adjutant could not make up his mind, he had those tied "fall out . . . and the one that drills the best, stays the longest without making a mistake, catches the orderly." In some outfits the honor was known as "taking the cup," in jocular comparison with horse races and other sporting events. The other men watching from the barracks porches or perimeter of the parade ground waited anxiously for the adjutant to finally give an approving nod to his selection. "There was no open applause, but 'soldier' congratulations when the winner reached his quarters to put away his arms, and then leave for the C.O.'s office." A cavalryman selected as orderly retained only his saber, an infantryman only his bayonet.[42]

With the old guard replaced, the officer of the day immediately marched the new detail to the guardhouse, where the first relief fell in under the corporal of the guard and made the rounds to relieve the old sentries over prisoner details.[43] The members of the former detail then assembled for what was known as "old guard fatigue" under command of their sergeant, who transitioned to the role of police sergeant. Having been awake and on their feet all the previous day and much of the night, privates of the old guard pulled light duty for the remainder of the day. That took a variety of forms, such as policing up garrison streets, pulling weeds at the post cemetery, some light drill, or target practice. Whatever the assignment, no one expected it to be carried out with much energy. "We looked forward with delight to the afternoon that we were the old guard," related former Eighth Cavalryman George S. Raper. "As we then had the splendid duty of herding the horses for grazing. It certainly was fun to get the horses all excited in the corral (when there were no officers around), and then turn them loose and run them until they got their play out." Some post commanders even left policing and other odd jobs to the prisoners or the regular fatigue details. At Fort Buford, Dakota Territory, for example, Private Wilmot P. Sanford recorded in his diary that he "came off guard in the morning and [went] down and got my washing. Sleeping and reading the rest of the day."[44]

Guard duty itself was anticipated with little enthusiasm by most soldiers, and for good reason—it was usually boring and always tiring. The duty lasted twenty-four hours, weather notwithstanding. During that time the members of the guard were not permitted to remove any of their clothing (except gloves while in the guardhouse) or accouterments, except to attend to calls of nature, so as constantly to be ready to respond to any emergency. The details were divided into three reliefs, the number in each corresponding to the number of guard posts or beats established at the particular garrison. Each post was numbered. Sentinels walked their beats for two hours until relieved, when they returned to the guardhouse for four hours. While one relief walked assigned beats, the other two remained at the guardhouse and were designated as the reserve guard. Post Number One was always immediately in front of the guardhouse, with four to six others designated about the fort at storehouses, at the quartermaster stables, behind the officers' quarters, and perhaps at the magazine or near haystacks. Under normal circumstances only Number One, the most demanding post, walked his beat during daylight hours, the reliefs for the others being activated at dusk for a period of ten or twelve hours.[45]

During the day members of the reserve guard provided security over prisoners engaged in work details, which was known as "chasing prisoners." For about four hours in the morning and four or five in the afternoon, the inmates carried out the most unpleasant jobs, such as collecting offal from the butcher shop and garbage from behind the kitchens, liming pit privies, dumping ashes, and emptying and cleaning dry-vault privies. Other times they performed the general policing of the post and cleaned up the officers' yards. Those men sentenced to hard labor worked under close guard, sawing wood for the entire garrison or breaking rocks with a sledge hammer. From a cache at the guardhouse, the noncoms of the guard issued whatever hand tools the prisoners might require for their work and, as a security measure, accounted for those when the detail returned. A provost sergeant, appointed for varying periods from among the duty sergeants of the command, supervised the prisoners and the guards placed over them. At the end of the day he returned the prisoners to the guardhouse.

Formal guard mounting was dispensed with at some small posts garrisoned by only one company where there was no perceived danger. Under those circumstances the informal "detachment guard mounting" was substituted merely as a formality to satisfy the regulation requiring every station to post a guard. In this abbreviated ceremony the members of the guard appeared in fatigue uniform. A trooper stationed at Fort Bowie, Arizona Territory, in 1890 explained that "only a corporal or a sergeant and 3 privates at a time formed the guard, as only the non-commissioned officer of the guard and one private [post no. 1] were on duty at a time. When the officer came near the guard house, the guard would talk loudly or make some noise, so the non-com would be sure and wake up, if asleep." He added that they did not take the prisoners, even if there were any, out to work during the day.[46]

Conditions within the guardhouse were austere. The building usually contained three rooms: a small office for the officer of the day and sergeant of the guard, another larger space accommodating the reserve guard, and a general confinement room. Two or three solitary confinement cells occupied one end of the prison room or were partitioned in a separate section.

The office was furnished only with a table or desk, a couple of chairs, and a clock. The clock was vital, because it was supposed to keep the official time at the post, regulating the daily service calls sounded by the orderly bugler. But, as the post surgeon's wife at Fort Washakie, Wyoming Territory, complained: "The clocks are always being put either ahead or back—to suit the convenience of the trumpeters." She happily announced that a sundial had been erected on the parade to ensure the exact time. Moreover, after sunset each sentinel, starting with Number One, was obligated to begin challenging and marking the time by calling out in turn his post number and the hour, followed by "all's well." In the event a sentry failed to sound off, Number One alerted an NCO of the guard, who immediately turned out the reserve guard and rushed to that position to investigate.[47]

During winter a tour of guard at northern stations could be absolutely brutal. As a civilian overnighting at Fort Laramie in December 1877 recalled: "It was very cold that night—about eighteen below with the thermometer going down rapidly. It seemed . . . that we had just fallen asleep in our tent, when [we] were awakened by the sentry, a gruff old German, calling the time. 'Eleven o'clock and all is well,' he chanted. Then, sotto voice, 'and cold as hell.'" When blizzards raged and temperatures plummeted to twenty-five to fifty degrees below zero, outlying sentries might be retracted, but Post Number One was always manned. Even with soldiers encased in buffalo overcoats and other winter gear, reliefs had to be changed every fifteen to thirty minutes to prevent severe frostbite in the potentially deadly conditions.[48]

A typical guardroom contained "a table and a chair or two and a couple of bunks, with springs only, for the guard to rest on when not on duty," recalled a Fourth Cavalryman. As a substitute for bare bunks, some guardrooms featured only a simple board dais upon which a few men at a time could recline, wearing their uniforms and belts. A few blankets were provided in winter. The unloaded arms were placed in a rack if available; otherwise rifles and carbines were kept in possession of the soldier. At Fort Sill, Indian Territory, a recently relieved guard related that he experienced a close call because the room had no rack. "No sooner asleep when there came an order [to] turn out the guard for the officer of the day. Everybody seized his gun and ran outside, I, half-asleep, could not find my gun and grasped a broom standing in the corner, appearing with it in the line of the guard. The officer passed down the line in front of the guard and prisoners . . . I was passed without being detected." Had the unarmed soldier been noticed, he would have been arrested and jailed.[49]

Incarceration in a guardhouse could be little short of torture, especially at posts experiencing harsh winters. The general confinement room had no furniture; prisoners were expected to bring their blankets with them at the time they were arrested and to sleep on the floor. Not even a heating stove was provided because of the potential for prisoners to use kindling as clubs or to create a diversion with fire. The kitchen police of the prisoners' respective companies brought meals consisting of the regular ration to the guardhouse and later collected the plates and utensils. Guards delivered the food to the prison room and were supposed to make certain that all utensils were accounted for afterward. Even so, some prisoners were always watching for sentries to become lax in their duties. At Fort Union, New Mexico Territory, a particularly bold prisoner "took up a lot of pans and walked out of the Guard House, past the Sentry on duty and has got away. The Sentry thought he was one of the cooks, and let him pass."[50]

Dangerous prisoners were shackled with leg irons and sometimes handcuffed as well. In some instances, with the post commander's approval, cavalrymen serving sentences were permitted (under guard of course) to attend stable call to relieve other troop members from having to groom the horses belonging to prisoners. The reserve guards were responsible for conducting prisoners to the guardhouse privy as needed, but having prisoners unconfined was always problematical. When Private Charles Morgan, Fourth Infantry, allowed his prisoner to escape while walking to the sink at Fort Bridger, Wyoming Territory, Morgan was sentenced to three months' confinement and a $30.00 fine. The transformation from guard to prisoner, in fact, could be swift. In this regard, Private Charles N. Hayden, Seventh Cavalry, noted in his diary that "Pvt. Tully was on guard and while out with Prisoners he got drunk and was run in the guard house." At Fort Omaha, Nebraska, the commanding officer became aware that some of the prisoners in the guard house had become too drunk to work. Just how they got access to alcohol was unclear, but it may have been placed in the adjacent privy by some of their friends. In any event, the officer declared that if any further infractions occurred the sergeant of the guard would be confined and charges would be preferred against him.[51]

The corporal (sometimes two) and sergeant of the guard usually shared the duty of posting reliefs throughout the night. The noncom, lantern in hand, assembled the relief in front of the guardhouse, verified it, and directed the guards to load their weapons. At forts threatened by Indians, soldiers had no compunctions about shooting at intruders, but they often hesitated to fire on other soldiers, even when they were prisoners. "They are called upon to guard their friend and to oversee him while engaged in labor," read a soldier's letter to the *Army & Navy Journal*. "A certain degree of sympathy for him arises in the breasts of his comrades, commensurate with his former popularity in his company, and . . . by the reflection that they too may be so unfortunate as to occupy a similar position in the future." A Third Infantry sentinel charged with guarding a deserter left him for a few moments before others spotted the prisoner running away. A witness recounted that the officer of the day threatened the sentry that "'if that man escapes I will tie you up where he was.' . . . The guard dropping to his knee quickly aimed and fired. . . . Going to him we found him dead. . . . The OD later tried to fault the guard for killing the man, but . . . his company commander came to his defense saying that the OD was responsible because he ordered the man to prevent the prisoner from escaping, and the men of G Co. were trained to obey orders."[52]

Indeed army regulations were mute on the matter. If such orders were expressed at all, they "are only verbal, and in most cases given by a non-commissioned officer," one man claimed. Most soldiers assumed, naturally enough, that being armed and charged with preventing the escape of prisoners implied that they should fire on them when they could not be stopped otherwise. But, as a concerned soldier at Fort Selden, New Mexico Territory, pointed out: "In case a sentry discharges his carbine . . . should the prisoner actually make good his escape, that sentry is placed in confinement . . . perhaps for months . . . and it is well known that if a sentry shoots a prisoner he will undoubtedly be tried by the civil authorities for murder." One soldier recounted that when new to the service he was assigned to guard prisoners chopping wood some distance from the post. When the officer of day instructed him to shoot any prisoner who attempted a getaway and failed to halt when ordered to do so, he explained: "I most respectfully asked the officer to deliver the order . . . to me in writing and signed. Then . . . I will either bring all my prisoners in, or will furnish jobs for the Surgeon and Undertaker. The officer declined to do this." Although this posed a serious dilemma in the minds of enlisted men, the judge advocate in the Division of the Pacific claimed: "I was not aware that such a view had ever been questioned." He "supposed" the law held that guards should not use more force than might be necessary to prevent the prisoner's escape and could "maim or even kill him" if the man failed to comply with an order to halt. It would seem that the safest choice for a sentry in that situation was to err on the side of performing his duty by "attempting" to stop the escapee, yet intentionally aiming so as not to hit him.[53]

Acting Assistant Surgeon Thomas G. Maghee recorded that when Private James Jones, a captive deserter, made good his escape from Camp Brown, Wyoming Territory, in 1876, he was "fired at by Pvt. Parks who was on post at the time and . . . is known as a personal friend of Jones." Even the lowliest private understood that only he could know for certain whether he had missed his mark by error or deliberately. In 1883 Brigadier General Christopher C. Augur undermined the basic premise of army custom by overturning the findings of a court-martial in which Private James Manning, Eighth Cavalry, was found guilty of allowing a prisoner to escape. In rendering his decision, Augur dismissed the court's finding because "it is not an offence on the part of a sentinel to permit the escape of a prisoner placed under his charge." Simply put, there could be no violation of a nonexistent law.[54]

About half an hour before noon fatigue details were recalled from their work to give the men, other than cavalry, time to clean up before eating dinner. "Water Call" sounded immediately after recall to direct cavalrymen not on other duty to the stables. "Each man in each company would stand by his horse at the picket rope with a saddle blanket on him and a water[ing] bridle . . . they would immediately mount and form into line and move out from camp, one company following another to water," an ex-first sergeant remembered.[55] A few minutes later, "First Sergeants Call" summoned all top sergeants to post headquarters, at which time the sergeant major returned their morning report books and distributed any new written orders. At this time he also announced each company's quota of men required for guard and other activities for the following day. Minor operational matters were conveyed verbally and noted by the other sergeants, who then returned to their barracks. The first sergeant and the clerk devoted the time immediately after dinner to making up and posting the detail assignments for the next day.

The call to dinner, the most substantial meal of the day, sounded at noon, followed by the bells, gongs, or triangles employed by individual companies to summon their men to the mess halls. This was a somewhat less hurried meal, because no further activities were scheduled for a couple of hours thereafter. After dinner soldiers not on kitchen police were at liberty to lounge about the barracks—on porches or out back during fair weather—or maybe visit the post trader's store, until the bugle signaled a resumption of fatigue and perhaps drill.

Even though drill may have been something of a priority for rookies, mainly to prepare them to participate in guard duty, it was less so for the company as a whole. The type and frequency of drills were directly affected by the size of the garrison and the additional demands placed on it, such as escorts, scouting, and other forms of detached service. "Drills are almost unknown here, for the reason that after the details for laborers are made for the day, there are no men left," Major William B. Royall wrote from Camp Lowell, Arizona Territory, in 1875. He added that some of his Fifth Cavalrymen claimed they had not been drilled in three years. Appearing before a congressional committee three years later, First Lieutenant Edmund Rice testified that companies of the Fifth Infantry could turn out only about sixteen men for drill on any particular day, the rest being occupied elsewhere. A soldier writing to the *Army & Navy Journal* complained about the effect of such haphazard training:

> At the sound of drill call a company, whose strength present at post averages 45 men, will very seldom turn out more than

about 20 men for drill, including non-commissioned officers. These 20 men are nearly all "duty men" who go on guard once or twice every week, and thus learn a soldier's duty; whereas those men who are excused for service in the various departments in which they are employed are the very ones who need to be drilled. . . . Then when it happens that the whole of the company has to turn out . . . it is wondered at "why the company does not drill better." The reason for this is obvious enough, men who have never drilled are mixed pell-mell with those who have drilled, and the appearance of the whole company is spoiled.[56]

When drills were conducted, they routinely consisted of refresher training in the manual of arms but placed greater emphasis (depending on the number of men available) on company evolutions by sets of fours. Some sessions were hardly more than squad drills. Only rarely were battalion drills scheduled before the late 1880s. If other demands were not enough to limit training, weather and climate also constrained such efforts. In northern regions during summer troops had little time to drill because they not only were kept busy with construction and maintenance of their posts but were in the field for a variety of reasons. This was especially true of the cavalry. However, winter precluded many of these activities, at the same time limiting opportunities for drill during the season when soldiers had the most time on their hands. A Sixth Infantryman at Fort Buford, Dakota Territory, made numerous entries in his diary to the effect that he and his comrades were limited to practicing bayonet exercise in their squad room for an hour and a half every afternoon, weekends excepted. Although it might seem peculiar for soldiers on the frontier to engage in bayonet drill, that and the manual of arms were about the only exercises that could be conducted indoors.

Moreover, greater emphasis on drill came only on the eve of a campaign, that being too little, too late to have any appreciable effect on a unit's combat readiness. Some officers failed personally to place any great importance on drill, especially the tactical movements necessary to prepare men for combat. Captain Guy V. Henry, a West Point graduate who served through the war and for many years afterward in the West, opined that some of his fellow officers considered training a waste of time: "Drilling in some regiments of cavalry . . . is considered highly improper. On scouts you don't drill, therefore it is unnecessary. On the same principle you might as well give your men a general furlough, to be called together only for a fight."[57]

The army's overarching deficiency was the lack of standards for scheduling or conducting training, those decisions resting with individual regimental, and even company, commanders. While a few officers largely ignored the issue, others took pains to see that their men received as much instruction as possible under the circumstances. The emphasis on training often bore a direct correlation to a unit's proximity to hostile Indians or the likelihood of active campaigning. One of those concerned with his regiment's preparedness was Lieutenant Colonel George A. Custer, who assembled the newly organized Seventh Cavalry at Fort Riley, Kansas, just prior to taking station on the plains. One of his men recalled that during "the winter of '66 and the spring of '67 we put in a great deal of time at squad drill, setting up drill, dismounted drill, saddling and unsaddling the horses, preparing to mount and all the tactics pertaining to a mounted trooper." Colonel Franklin F. Flint was another. Soon after assuming command of the Fourth Infantry in 1868, he ordered that all noncoms at Fort Laramie assemble in an ad hoc company to be honed in various aspects of tactics by the adjutant for an hour every morning, except weekends. The companies as a whole then drilled for an hour during the afternoons. Sergeant John Spring's company of the Thirty-Second Infantry at Camp Wallen, Arizona Territory, located in the heart of Apache country, commenced drilling two hours every day, but only after it had completed the construction of adobe barracks and received an influx of forty recruits. In 1876, in the wake of the Sioux victory at the Battle of the Little Bighorn, Colonel Nelson A. Miles directed his Fifth Infantrymen at Cantonment on Tongue River, Montana Territory, to practice skirmish drill for three hours daily.[58]

Officers who considered drill vital sometimes circumvented competing demands during the duty day by conducting sessions in early morning or in the evenings after supper. Nevertheless, in the time available to them, the regulars learned, and learned well, under strict discipline. It was a matter of company esprit de corps. Evaluating his Company G, a Sixth Infantryman asserted that "all in all, I think they would compare favorably with the best of Uncle Sam's soldier boys.

It was considered the best drilled company in the regiment." During drills officers and noncoms paid meticulous attention to every motion, the placement of every hand, every finger, the stride and military bearing of every man. Viewing them, one would never mistake a unit of regulars for anything else. With obvious pride, one infantryman wrote that his company "went through the motions in drilling like a machine."[59]

For more than a decade after the Civil War, no particular attention was given to target practice in the army. In fact, the service had no formal system of marksmanship training until the adoption of its first manual on the subject, authored by Captain Henry Heth in 1858. Even though the rifle musket in use by infantry during and for a couple of years after the war was considerably more accurate than the old smooth-bore musket, the target employed consisted simply of a board six feet tall by twenty-two inches wide (or a multiple thereof, depending on the range), with a wide black cross painted on the surface as an aiming mark. The best marksman was the man who placed his shots nearest to the center of the intersecting stripes, determined by a string tacked to the center point. This program continued in use sporadically through the war. The customary method of practice was to have the members of the old guard fire at a target, thereby unloading their muskets at the same time.[60]

Afterward, amid the chaotic atmosphere of disbanding the volunteers, reorganizing the regulars, and garrisoning the frontier, the army was slow to resume marksmanship training. Lacking central direction, many units conducted little or no target practice, yet there were notable exceptions among those regiments posted to Indian country, where hostilities were likely. In 1866, for example, a battalion of the Eighteenth Infantry held special practice soon after arriving at the site of what would become Fort C. F. Smith on the Bighorn River in southeastern Montana Territory. Having no formal awards available, a lieutenant reported that makeshift prizes for the best shots consisted of hats, shirts, and a pair of fine gloves. Despite that encouraging start, such training was soon overshadowed by the need to shelter the troops before the onset of winter and to build defenses in anticipation of a Sioux attack. A veteran of the same regiment, who served at nearby Fort Phil Kearny, recorded that it was customary "to have the guards have target practice when they came off guard, but our guns were loaded when we got into the Indian country and were kept so. We had no target practice of any kind."[61]

The great number of wartime veterans in the ranks in the late 1860s gave some officers the impression that no special training was needed, and to some extent that was a valid opinion. Arriving at Fort Kearny, Nebraska, near the end of 1867, Thirtieth Infantryman Lauren Aldrich reminisced about his company's first exposure to target practice:

> All the officers . . . were present and expected to see wild shooting by the Recruits, S[c]hober was first to receive instructions and after the Officer had fully explained what the sights on the gun were intended for etc., S[c]hober hastily . . . fired off hand at the target and the . . . attendant signaled bull's eye . . . he repeated five times making a perfect score. There were about twenty-five of the forty-six recruits who made perfect scores . . . [the officers] had not taken into consideration the fact that nearly all of these men were from . . . the southern states and that their most treasured companion . . . had been the gun. Added to this was much service during the Civil War and still added was their almost daily practice [during the march to Utah and back] with the new Springfield breech loading needle gun.[62]

Company commander Captain William H. Powell, Fourth Infantry, was exceptional for his interest in marksmanship training. He issued orders at Fort Sanders, Wyoming Territory, in 1873 advising his men that anyone "missing the target at any regular practice will be turned out the following day to drill for one hour from 7 A.M. to 8 A.M." A battalion of the Seventh Cavalry posted at Fort Abraham Lincoln, Dakota Territory, conducted practice by having each member of the old guard fire three rounds for score with his carbine after being relieved and offering a generous incentive to the soldier having the best score by excusing him from his next trick and granting him a day's pass.[63]

In perhaps the majority of regiments, however, marksmanship was practiced only irregularly at the unit level, when it was done at all. While a regimental commander exercised direct control over those companies at his own post, he had little or nothing to say about those stationed elsewhere, particularly when those posts were commanded by officers belonging to other regiments. The situation was aggravated by the passage of time as the number of Civil War combat veterans in the ranks steadily dwindled and with them the troops' overall shooting proficiency. A cavalryman at Fort Lyon, Colorado Territory, complained to the *Army & Navy Journal* in 1872: "Target practice in the Regular Army is nothing more than a humbug. We are marched to the practice ground . . . where each man fires three rounds . . . at the target, regardless of whether he hits the object aimed at or not." Writing at Fort Whipple, Arizona Territory, an Eighth Cavalryman amplified his own frustration with ineffective training: "Went out on Target Practice . . . this morning and missed the target at twenty-five yards, shot once at it . . . and missed it. Threw down my carbine, picked up a stone and hit it the first time." Beyond the lack of systematic instruction in the principles of rifle marksmanship, it is hardly surprising that men unaccustomed to shooting failed to become proficient marksmen, considering that the allotment of practice ammunition at that time was limited to ten rounds per man per month, weather permitting. When even that meager allowance went unused, it was forfeited.[64]

The campaigns against the Sioux, Northern Cheyennes, and Nez Perces during 1876 and 1877, including several sound defeats for the army, pointed up significant deficiencies in its training, not the least of which was target practice. Captain Otho E. Michaelis, chief ordnance officer for the Department of Dakota, summed up his observations:

> The disjointed system we call "target practice" . . . does very little good in improving our men. I know of one regiment of cavalry where no so-called "target practice" has taken place for a year past. I do not mean to be understood that this was owing to any neglect; it was probably due to the varied duties the men were called upon to perform. Still, the fact remains that while the companies were in garrison nothing was done to improve individual marksmanship.[65]

Although Colonel George W. Wingate, inspector of rifle practice for the New York National Guard, published a more detailed manual on the subject in 1872, his system was not embraced officially by the regular army, though some officers elected on their own to purchase and use the manual to train their companies. Not until 1879 did the regulars adopt a more thorough system of instruction developed by Colonel Theodore T. S. Laidley. His curriculum, backed by General of the Army William T. Sherman and coupled with the doubling of the ammunition allowance for practice in the wake of Little Bighorn, had a beneficial effect almost immediately. The army's interest in target practice and competitive shooting increased with each passing year thereafter, with matches being held at department, division, and army levels. The Seventh Cavalry, for instance, having learned hard lessons in combat, began conducting target practice twice weekly in 1881. Within only a few years, marksmanship training became as much a passion as it had been ignored previously. In 1886 Private James Purvis, First Cavalry, proudly reported:

> The American army has followed no old world fashions in respect to rifle practice, but [has] adopted a genuine Yankee style of its own which has made nearly every soldier of two years' service an expert. . . . Five years ago only a few men in each company could make a respectable score at a greater distance than 100 or 200 yards . . . the allowance of ammunition for target practice has been increased to such an extent and so much time given to practice, that the result . . . has been most wonderful.[66]

One trooper who disagreed with that assessment was Private Hartford G. Clark, Sixth Cavalry. After firing forty rounds with his .45-caliber Springfield carbine in a single afternoon, Clark complained that "my shoulder is black and blue from firing so much laying [sic] down."[67]

Perhaps the most practical and popular form of marksmanship training during the 1880s was skirmish practice, whereby the men advanced by squads or platoons in extended formation against iron-framed canvas silhouette targets, firing upon command at unknown distances. The prizes offered in the Seventh Cavalry—two kegs of beer to the highest scoring troop—were a great incentive and morale factor for every man to do his best. "Every man would take pride in drill so long as it was useful skirmish drill accompanied by the manual of arms," commented one doughboy. "But when it came to the bayonet or saber exercise—the infantry not using the bayonet and the cavalry [not using] the saber in the field—then a man [would] lose interest."[68]

Target practice, however, involved more than shooting. Soldiers also took turns as markers in the pits below the targets down-range. One groused that he had been "down in the target pit all day from 6.30 this morning. I don't want any more of it. I think it is the worst fatigue I ever was on, say nothing of the danger. The bullets would whistle about a foot over your head in fine style . . . several struck the wood work of the target and glanced down. . . . I got struck on the shoulder with one but it had not enough force to do any harm." He added, however, that he was glad the bullet had missed his head. An Eighth Infantryman, Private Charles Hemstreet, was not so fortunate. While serving as a target marker on the range at Fort McDermitt, Nevada Territory, in 1883, he took shelter behind the supposed safety of a mantlet enclosed with two-inch planks and packed with soil more than two and a half feet thick. Nonetheless, a rifle bullet passed entirely through the protective barrier, instantly killing Hemstreet. The division commander subsequently recognized the power of the .45/70 cartridge by ordering all target range mantlets to be filled with sand rather than earth.[69]

The soldier's day began to wind down by the latter part of the afternoon. Drill usually lasted only until three or three-thirty in the afternoon, "Recall from Fatigue" sounding about an hour and a half later. An infantryman enjoyed some free time until supper, but not so the cavalry trooper. The horses, having been out grazing a few hours under supervision of the herd guard, had been driven back to the post and required further tending. The troopers who had been working at various tasks had about ten minutes after recall to return to their quarters and don their white canvas stable outfits to turn out for afternoon "Water and Stable Call . . . when the 'Government ghosts' would again march to the stables and water and groom their horses." Soldiers devoted whatever spare time remained to preparing for evening parade.[70]

After supper "Assembly" usually sounded a half-hour before sunset to signal retreat, a daily occurrence often preceded by a dress parade. (Weather conditions might dictate that undress parade be held in fatigue uniform without arms or canceled altogether, sometimes for the entire winter season.) Retreat was an important tradition, whether or not it was accompanied by dress parade. The companies formed in ranks on the streets in front of their barracks and the first sergeants again took roll call, reporting the result to the company commander standing nearby. Also at this time the first sergeants announced any company orders and read off the next day's details for guard and other assignments. When a parade was scheduled, the captains then conducted their respective units to the parade ground, where they formed in battalion. Corporal Emil A. Bode described such a ceremony at Fort Sill, Indian Territory, in 1878:

> There were a lot of fun in them for the soldiers dressed in their glittering uniforms, marching up to the parade ground for inspection with their gallant officers in front and rear. [With] the troops all in line the band played a lively tune while marching and counter-marching in front of the line. . . . The troops were marched in review and brought back into line, with a couple of repetitions of the same . . . we had to keep our eight-pound [sic: nine-pound] guns at a "carry" that is, the hammer resting over the middle finger, for at least fifteen or twenty minutes, causing something like a cramp to the muscles of that finger.[71]

After the band (or assembled field musicians) had performed, and the adjutant reported the parade formed, the post commander usually ordered the command to execute a portion of the manual of arms. Then, at the direction of the adjutant, the first sergeants reported their companies "present or accounted for," after which the adjutant read aloud any new general or post orders for the information of the garrison. The assembled buglers (or drummers) then sounded "Retreat," as members of the guard slowly lowered the colors. At the last note two other guards fired a blank cartridge from the evening gun.

Even among the regulars, boyish pranks sometimes overcame common sense, not to mention discipline, such as when a gun crew at Fort Sill, Indian Territory, decided to produce a louder report by ramming down a wet gunnysack and a rock atop the usual powder charge fired in the cannon. Just as retreat was sounding, with the gun pointed toward the nearby creek and the gunner poised with lanyard taut, the gunner "saw the major of our fort on his evening drive coming up the road which passed between me and my target. My blood changed from hot to cold to hot again as I pictured to myself the punishment in store for me. . . . To my relief he was passed and over the hill by the time of firing . . . the stone rattling in the trees as it left my cannon and went straight to its mark, striking the hill on the other side."[72]

Immediately following retreat at cavalry posts, and without any formality, a corporal from each troop conducted three privates to their respective corrals as "stable guard," where they would remain until the next morning. The details at most stations occupied a small unheated room in their stables or a wall tent erected nearby, though a few posts offered a designated "guard shack" housing the combined stable guards. Unlike the regular post guards, these men were unarmed and simply walked through the stable to prevent the horses from escaping or becoming tangled in their tethers and to maintain security over horse equipment and forage. They also enforced any special orders relating to the care of the animals or facilities. The corporal kept the time, with each private patrolling his assigned area for two hours, resting for four, until the duty ended at "Stable Call" the next morning. At the sounding of "Reveille" (except in foul weather) the stable guards led the horses from the barns and tied them to either side of the picket line (a thick rope perhaps a hundred feet long suspended head-high between several upright posts). While the stalls were thus empty, the guards placed a feed ration in each box as a man designated as "stable police" cleaned out the stalls. After attending to their own mounts, the guard detail fell in with the rest of the company to return to the quarters for breakfast.[73]

From retreat to tattoo, those men who were not on duty or had a pass to be elsewhere had the liberty of the post. This was a rather short period during long summer days, and longer during winter when retreat occurred with early sunsets. It made little difference, because there was not much to do. At 8:25 or 8:55 P.M., according to the commanding officer's preference, the orderly bugler sounded "Assembly," signaling all enlisted men to fall in on their company parades. Five minutes later, with the troops standing at parade rest, the rather doleful notes of "Tattoo," played by the assembled buglers, wafted across the post. The first sergeants then called the rolls for the third and last time of the day. "Tattoo" may have notified the men to secure to quarters and prepare for bed, but that did not always happen. At Fort Omaha, Nebraska, the commanding officer noted: "It appears to be the practice of some enlisted men to attend 'Tattoo' roll call, and afterwards, instead of retiring to their own quarters, to visit Officers Kitchens. . . . Company Commanders . . . will take such steps as are necessary to compel these men to retire to their own quarters after 'Tattoo' roll call." The boys were only too aware that practically the only non-Indian single women of their social class on post were officers' cooks and housekeepers. "Taps" sounded half an hour afterward, directing that all lights in the barracks be extinguished and that silence be observed, neither of which would have interfered with those nocturnal rendezvous at the officers' kitchens. After that, according to a Seventh Cavalryman, "all would then be still except the click of billiard balls in the Officers' Club room at the Sutlers." The sentinels would call out the hours throughout the night, every hour on the hour, until "First Call" for reveille split the air the next morning, and the routine began all over again.[74]

Weekends were only slightly less demanding, but some activities—roll calls, guard mounting, kitchen police, stable call, stable guard—continued without interruption. One activity dominated the weekend: Sunday morning inspection. This was an old tradition that gave the captain the opportunity to examine the condition of his men, their arms and equipment, and their quarters, including mess halls and kitchens. "Every man has to be as clean as a new pin, with Arms Shinning [sic], brasses so bright that you could almost see yourself," remarked an Eighth Cavalryman. The editor of the *Army & Navy Journal* commented:

> The preparations for this duty are made on Saturday, which, as a rule, is observed as cleaning day at every Army station in the country. . . . It is the day when bedding and clothing are aired (weather permitting), the floors and tables scrubbed, stoves polished, clothing mended, and all arms and accoutrements cleaned and put in order. In large commands this occupies about half a day, but small garrisons, where but few men are available, the entire day is sometimes occupied in putting things in proper order.[75]

First Sergeant John Ryan explained how his company cleaned the squad room at Fort Rice, Dakota Territory:

> There would be no drills on Saturday . . . after stable calls the men would wash up the floors, that was done by taking a little

ashes and scattering it over the floors, taking some buckets of water and throwing the water on the floor and then scrubbing the floor thoroughly with corn brooms and then it would be rinsed off with clean water. . . . Sometimes we used what they called "Holy Stones." . . . They would get a lime stone about a foot and a half square and flat on one side, attach a rope to the sides of it, throw sand on the floor and a couple of men would get hold of this stone and pull it backwards and forwards over the floor, That would whiten the floors, and . . . the sand would be swept up. The bunks would be taken out into the yard [behind the barracks] and scrubbed with sand and water to make them clean.[76]

On those occasions when the cavalry stables also were to be inspected, troopers had the additional burden of thoroughly policing the buildings and corrals and cleaning their horse equipment, at the same time making certain that everything was displayed in the prescribed manner.

The men spent the remainder of the day bathing, getting shaved and perhaps having their hair cut, and cleaning their own uniforms, equipment, and arms. Location made no difference; it was the same wherever troops might be posted. Writing to his sister from isolated Camp Stambaugh, Wyoming Territory, Private Adelbert Butler declared: "We had inspection in full dress this morning; we have to keep very neat and clean here." Private Emil A. Bode was deeply impressed the first time he viewed his company's well-disposed squad room ready for inspection,

> with iron bunks around the wall, bed sacks folded up and nicely deposited at head of the bunks on which were blankets and clothes displayed for inspection. The bed slats were scoured white—on which were the haversacks and knapsacks, the latter filled with rolled up trousers, drawers, socks, and towels. The harness [infantry equipment brace], canteen, and polished tin cup, blackened belts, and cartridge boxes ready for inspection. At the foot of each bunk stood a small box in which was kept the cleaning kit and rest of the clothes. Back on the walls were shelves and racks in which covered and uncovered guns stood ready for use.[77]

The troops might stand Sunday inspection in full dress, or more commonly in fatigue uniform, at the discretion of the post commander. Some COs delegated the choice of uniform to the company commanders, particularly during cold weather. The men would be permitted to wear overcoats during those seasons, or the entire inspection would be held indoors.

> The ceremony of company inspection is very simple and occupies about one hour; usually from 8 to 9 o'clock in summer, and from 9 to 10 o'clock in winter. When the weather is fine the companies are formed in front of, or near, the respective barracks, every officer and soldier being clothed, armed and equipped as the captain may direct, and prepared to undergo his critical inspection. This ended, the enlisted men repair to the barracks and stand at their bunks, when the captain, accompanied by his lieutenants, makes his rounds, during which he examines the lockers, bed clothing and such other personal effects as have to be examined in ranks. He notes the condition of everything, including floors, bath tubs, lavatories, mess-hall, kitchen, rations and sinks, giving such instruction in each case as may be necessary.[78]

Sixth Cavalryman Henry McConnell recalled a memorable time when an Irishman in his troop narrowly escaped being gigged for an infraction "as the officers passed slowly along the rear of the line, Banes' spurs were noticed to be very rusty behind, while his accoutrements otherwise were unexceptional. The officer called attention to it, but never moving a muscle, Banes replied, 'A good soldier, sir, never looks behind him.' The reviewing party passed on, with a grin, and said nothing further, for Banes was a good soldier."[79] His experience, however, was the exception. Another soldier related in his diary that four of his comrades were given company punishment, each carrying a log on his shoulder, for appearing dirty on inspection.

When inspection included the stables, cavalry troopers proceeded there immediately after the captain completed his tour of the squad room, each man standing at attention at the rear and to one side of his horse. Sometimes in fair weather a post commander would order a battalion dress inspection on the parade ground with the cavalry mounted and saddles packed in either light or heavy marching order.

Tradition aside, Sunday inspections were not popular among the rank and file, or among many officers for that matter. Trumpeter Edward Convers, Fourth Cavalry opined: "The Sunday question is to my mind purely and simply as to whether soldiers—in common with other men—enjoy one day of rest out of seven. . . . The answer I think should be most emphatically 'Yes.'" A soldier at Fort Robinson writing to the *Army & Navy Journal* under the pseudonym "War-Hat" advocated ceasing fatigue and other nonessential duties at noon on Saturday "and give the afternoon to the men to clean up, and at retreat roll call have an inspection of troops, barracks, etc." Concurrent with other army reforms during the mid-late 1880s, the preponderance of sentiment in the army favored setting aside Sunday as a day of rest and relaxation, as it was in civil life. Even so, the prospect of scrapping such a hallowed custom approached sacrilege in the minds of some prominent older officers, led by retired general Sherman, who vigorously protested the suggestion. Despite such weighty opposition, both the secretary of war and General John M. Schofield, the army's current commander, supported the measure. Accordingly, the president implemented the reform by executive order in 1889, declaring that weekly inspections thereafter be conducted on Saturday morning and that no work other than the normal guard and police duty be performed on Sunday.[80]

By the mid-1880s it was obvious to most observers that the Indian campaigns were all but over. Shortly before his retirement in 1883, Sherman had laid out a new policy of consolidating troops in larger, more permanent posts located at burgeoning cities along rail lines where it would be easier and more economical to supply and maintain the forts. There entire regiments could finally serve and train together. Not to be overlooked from the enlisted men's perspective was the advantage of distributing guard and fatigue among a greater number of men, thus lessening the burden on individuals. The only outliers were those forts left to watch over Indian reservations. The rapidly developing network of railroads and telegraph lines across the western United States had made it possible to immediately dispatch additional troops wherever they might be needed.

In reducing the number of posts, the army allowed many of the less useful stations, particularly those lacking political protection, simply to die on the vine. Typical of those was Fort Stockton, Texas. With the Comanches long gone and the post situated far from either of the two railroads traversing the region, a Sixteenth Infantry officer lamented in 1884: "All is crumbling, from the effect of rain, heat and wind. Rain pours through the broken roofs and washes the plaster down. The parade is two acres in area, a few dry and dusty weeds make a struggle to grow upon it . . . the dazzling glare of the sun on the post at midday is painful to the eyes, and the general appearance is like that of a deserted brickyard."[81]

Aside from dress parades, garrison duty at western posts was anything but glamorous and could be characterized as simply marking time. As Private R. Eugene Pelham summed it up: "The life of a soldier on the frontier is monotonous, to say the least, the isolation, the long weary waits between mail days, and all things considered, made the time pass slowly. . . . We had our little recreation . . . but the daily grind was about the same day after day, with but little variations." That relentless routine differed little from one fort to another, week in, week out, month after month. "Of all the dull and unendurable lives the one of a soldier on the plains is the worst," moaned a soldier at Fort Laramie. "It is just dragging out a miserable existence."[82]

CHAPTER 7

"The Bed Bugs Are Too Numerous for Me to Sleep"

Some Material Aspects of Army Life

The era following the Civil War has sometimes been perceived as a period of stagnation for the army, a view presumably stemming from congressional reductions in the army's size, as well as its budget, primitive frontier living conditions, and an absence of technological advancement. To perpetuate that belief, however, would distort the evidence. In reality the Indian Wars marked the beginning of a pivotal half-century period of reformation as the army steadily, at times haltingly, progressed toward eventual emergence as a modern force on the world stage in the twentieth century.

Climatic conditions, varying greatly from one region of the West to another, coupled with the availability of natural resources, largely dictated the quality of life for the inhabitants of frontier army posts. This was reflected in a soldier's letter from Camp Stambaugh in central Wyoming Territory in which he commented: "Our winter up here has been, as usual, severe, fully twelve feet of snow now lying on the parade, and the customary tunneling process had been resorted to in order to enable us to make graceful entrances and exits . . . from the several buildings comprising this post." At the opposite end of the spectrum were places like Camp Grant, Arizona Territory, where Private George Cranston grumbled: "I have been in this Territory for three months and have not see[n] [a] drop of rain yet. The ground is as hard as stone. Everything seems like [an] oven." Despite such conditions, the soldiers managed to adapt to the circumstances they encountered in the West.[1]

Frontier army posts represented self-contained, highly organized communities where each building had its specific function supporting the overall operation. Most important to the enlisted men were the barracks; they were as near being a home as soldiers would have during their time in the service. Some barracks constructed during or just after the Civil War represented a design long used by the army wherein squads were quartered separately either in small rooms—hence the term "squad room"—within a larger building or in individual huts, each accommodating two or three squads. The building materials available in any particular locale on the frontier usually dictated the design and construction of barracks. "We are quartered in log houses," wrote an Eighth Cavalryman at Fort Whipple, located in northern Arizona Territory's Bradshaw Mountains in 1869. "Our company have [sic] three large Houses, besides a large building for the cook house. Each building has only one large room . . . each room contains six double Bunks . . . one above the other, four men to each bunk." A former Third Infantry private, Herman Harbers, remembered that the barracks at Camp Supply, Indian Territory, in 1873 "were of stockade construction, dirt floors, heated by wood stoves. In winter, snow would pile up in quarters, which were made U-shape."[2]

More commonly, however, the men were consolidated in larger barracks of frame, adobe, or occasionally stone construction with shingle roofs or sometimes a combination of materials, such as when adobe bricks were used to insulate board-and-batten walls.[3] The Quartermaster Department, with input from army doctors, made a study of barracks requirements in the early 1870s, resulting in the adoption of standards for their design and construction. Thereafter, barracks incorporated uniform basic features—one or two spacious squad rooms accommodating a company of men, an orderly room, storeroom, mess hall, and kitchen—although floor plans sometimes varied somewhat from one post to another and materials were dictated by location and availability. Some barracks adhering to the standard plans also included a day room, washroom, library, and a small workshop used by the artificer or saddler. Even so, the new design had its critics. "The old practice of . . . dividing barracks into squad rooms," an anonymous correspondent wrote to the editor of the *Army & Navy Journal*, "was much better than the present system of living in one large room. Many men are forced out of the service . . . from sheer inability to stand the manner of their fellows."[4]

Particularly faulted were the archaic wood-constructed double bunks, two tiers high, accommodating four men. "Now I must not be accused of prudery or squeamishness, when I say that this style of packing the men is decidedly an improper one," wrote one man. "The system of making men sleep together . . . ought . . . to be avoided. . . . It is not always possible for a soldier to have his own choice of a bedfellow . . . and nothing is so repulsive and disagreeable as to be brought into such close contact with a person of totally different habits and disposition with ourself." Noting in an 1870 report that wooden bunks were still in use at over one-half the posts in the nation, Assistant Surgeon John S. Billings labeled them "an evil which should be put an end to with the least possible delay. . . . No one acquainted with the first principles of sanitary science will approve of their use." Billings won his point: during the following year the army began purchasing single bunks consisting of two iron trestles connected by four wood slats, usually of ash or oak. In a follow-up report in 1875, he stated: "I am glad to say that the double and two-story wooden bunks are now very nearly abolished, and that the iron bunks now furnished . . . are very satisfactory."[5]

Nevertheless, throughout most of the era a soldier's bedding consisted only of a so-called bed sack (mattress) about seven feet long made of cotton drilling. Those intended for use on the double bunks were four feet wide; those for single bunks measured about thirty inches wide. Along the center seam of the sack was a slit, closed with cloth ties, for filling it with hay or straw. "No sheets or pillows are furnished . . . ," noted Surgeon Billings, "the men come into direct contact with the blankets, and use their greatcoats for pillows." A cavalryman at Fort Whipple, Arizona Territory, recorded that "for a pillow we roll up our pants and blouse, which make a very nice pillow. I sometimes spread my handkerchief over my blouse, so as to make it have the appearance of a white pillow. We [he and his bunkie] have four blankets and two Great Coats over us, sleep very warm." Even after the adoption of individual bunks, soldiers stationed in cold climates commonly "drew their beds together and 'doubled up' to keep warm" by combining their blankets and body heat. During winter in extreme northern climates like Montana and Dakota Territories, it was not unusual for the men to acquire a number of blankets (Ninth Cavalryman Simpson Mann claimed to have had seven), sometimes augmented by a buffalo robe.[6]

Bunks were aligned in two rows, one along either side of a central aisle, with heads to the walls, and when necessary one or two bunks at the ends of the room. During the 1860s recruits were issued knapsacks to transport their belongings to their stations, after which the packs served as receptacles for storing spare clothing (such as overcoats) in the barracks. Strapped to the ends of the bunks, the knapsacks were hardly large enough to accommodate shirts, trousers, underwear, and dirty clothes, much less the dress uniform coat or cavalry jacket. Addressing the subject of the hated wooden bunks, an experienced officer recommended not only that they be replaced with bunks made of iron but that "each bunk be supplied with a neat drawer or locker, and thus do away with the necessity of the knapsack in barracks." Some practical-minded captains permitted their men to acquire wooden chests in which to keep their extra clothing. Soldiers commonly paid carpenters at the post or a nearby community to build such chests for them. In 1870 an Eighth Cavalry trooper wrote that he "bought a box from a Corporal of our Company to put my cloths [sic] in for one dollar." By mid-decade the argument for lockers was so compelling that the army finally began providing plain wooden chests that, like bunks, became permanent barracks fixtures. The standard lockers were dimensioned to fit conveniently between the legs of the foot trestle of the iron bunk, although some soldiers preferred to purchase their own lockers, which were often somewhat larger and featured a removable tray. Some soldiers acquired an extra locker and placed it beneath the bunk for additional storage.[7]

Of necessity, each man provided himself with a "clothes bag" with a drawstring to hold his dirty laundry. The bags, an out-of-pocket expense for the soldier unless he could procure a stout seamless flour sack, usually were suspended from the hook strip above the bunks. Only in 1884 would the army finally begin issuing a brown canvas barrack bag to each soldier.[8]

In the central aisle separating the bunks was a large cast-iron box stove; a couple of sand-filled spittoons, usually simple wood boxes fabricated locally; and frequently a small table and chairs for reading, writing, and card games or checkers.[9] A simple shelf with a hook strip below extending along the walls above the bunks held dress head gear, spare clothing, and accouterments. Soldiers often tacked a cloth curtain to the front edge of the shelf to prevent dust from accumulating on the garments and equipment hanging below. Prior to 1880 arms were stored in vertical racks, affixed either to the walls between bunks or to foot-ends of the two-tier wooden bunks. Some barracks, like those at Fort Union, New Mexico, had "seven upright posts, and places around each post for eight Carbines and Sabers, also a place to hang belts on," according to a cavalryman stationed there. Revolvers were usually kept in their fitted shipping crates and stored either in the orderly room or locked in the company store room until needed. Because of the difficulty experienced in securing firearms from theft or misuse, the army adopted free-standing circular floor racks holding twenty rifles or carbines and with locking mechanisms to prevent the removal of arms except when authorized. A former Ninth Cavalry soldier remembered that in his troop it was customary for the second duty sergeant to be the keeper of the keys. Regardless of unit, each man was responsible for knowing the serial number of his weapon so that he always used the same one and was responsible for it.[10]

Lighting in barracks was traditionally provided by candles, both for economy and for safety. Only in 1881 did the army adopt standard patterns of brass hanging and bracket lamps fueled by mineral oil for barracks and other structures. Depending on the length of the squad room, most were provided with two or more double-burner lamps suspended along the midline of the squad room. To maximize illumination, barracks interiors usually were whitewashed, with woodwork painted a hue of blue or dark red.[11]

Squad room walls usually were unadorned, except for a small pendulum clock and a bulletin board affixed to a wall outside the orderly room for posting recent orders and the daily duty rosters. In rare instances a company might display a trophy captured in battle. A member of F Troop, Ninth Cavalry, said that only one picture hung in his barracks: a portrait of Abraham Lincoln.[12]

Fireplaces and wood-burning stoves, not to mention cooking ranges and oil lamps, posed a constant fire danger to western posts. Post commanders invariably ensured that barracks contained water barrels and fire buckets as a first line of defense. A man who had soldiered at Fort

Rice, Dakota Territory, recalled that each squad room was provided with "little platforms about a foot from the floor built on each end of this room and on them were iron hoop pork barrels. There were some water buckets hanging over these on hooks. These barrels were always kept filled with water." The commanding officer at Fort Laramie similarly ordered that three filled barrels and a dozen buckets be kept in each company kitchen for purposes of firefighting. Patented fire extinguishers such as the Babcock were prevalent by the early 1870s, and the army purchased large quantities of them to augment traditional bucket lines. Photographic evidence suggests that these extinguishers sometimes occupied a prominent place on stands in the squad rooms.[13]

Companies were organized as a fire brigade. The various units were assigned responsibility for fire extinguishers, the water wagon, and one or more bucket brigades, and usually one served as a hook-and-ladder company. A few stations boasted hand-pumps and hose carts to draw water from cisterns, at least in warm weather. Many garrisons periodically conducted fire drills so that everyone knew his duty. Upon the outbreak of fire, the orderly trumpeter sounded "Fire Call," which was immediately taken up by all the other trumpeters and buglers on the post. At Fort Custer, "a fire broke out in the quarters of one of the officers," a soldier's son recalled. "The men lined up and passed buckets from various faucet taps to the fire center, and it soon was extinguished." The garrison at Fort Sully, Dakota Territory, was not so successful during the winter of 1884. When fire broke out in a barracks, it could not be brought under control before the three barracks, the band quarters, and the guardhouse were reduced to smoldering ruins.[14]

In accordance with army tradition, the men thoroughly policed their quarters every Saturday. Following a division of labor, the sergeants supervised their squads to clean windows, black the stoves, shine lamps, and carry out ashes in winter. If a barracks had dirt floors, soldiers first swept out loose material before sprinkling water over small areas at a time and rubbed them smooth on hands and knees using river stones or bare hands. Regulations called for wood floors to be "dry rubbed," meaning swept with brooms and clean sand. In practice, however, the soldiers often took shortcuts. Third Cavalryman James S. McClellan, for example, noted in his diary that during warm weather at Fort D. A. Russell, Wyoming Territory, he and his comrades "washed the Quarters out. Got the Hoes [sic: hose] and don[e] it in a short time." There were good reasons why the army frowned on wet-mopping the floors. Objecting to the practice at Fort Laramie, the post surgeon cautioned that "the floors of some of the dormitories . . . are defective being full of large cracks and holes thus permitting dirt and filth to accumulate beneath them and allowing the water used from scrubbing . . . to run through and saturate the soil and dirt below." Exposed to a soaking every week, wood floors rotted within a few years and eventually had to be replaced if the post was occupied long enough.[15]

Bedding ideally was to be aired and bed sacks refreshed on a weekly basis, but that seldom happened in practice. Frederick Kurtz, who had served in the Eighth Cavalry at Fort Clark, Texas, recounted that their bed sacks "had to be washed and scrubbed every four weeks for monthly inspection, and we usually filled it once a month at the quartermaster's corral. Before filling our bed sack, we usually took a pitchfork and shook the snakes and cactus out of the hay, for the Mexicans who supplied us with the hay were not any too particular what it contained, so long as the weight was in it." George Neihaus stated that his company of the Tenth Infantry refilled their ticks twice monthly. Other company commanders were not so particular, however, and the sanitary condition left much to be desired. "There is no order about refilling the bed sacks and airing the bedding," grumbled a post surgeon in March 1877. "And in many cases the sacks have not been refilled, and the bedding not aired since October or November last." He called upon the post commander to direct that the bed sacks be washed and the hay replenished at least every six weeks and that all blankets be exposed to fresh air every two weeks. It was a problem that nevertheless went unresolved, prompting a cavalryman at Fort Niobrara as late as 1891 to resort to sleeping on the barracks porch because "the bed bugs are to[o] numerous for me to sleep in the quarters until cold weather."[16]

Facilities for eating—"messing" in army parlance—varied little from one post to another. Mess halls and kitchens, especially during the mid-1860s, sometimes were constructed as separate buildings directly behind each company quarters, though the usual custom was to integrate them into the barracks building as a rear wing.

Throughout the frontier era, the army had no specially trained cooks, with generally predictable results. "No man in his sound senses would voluntarily turn over his provision to a person who positively declares that he never cooked so much as a potato all his life," groused one soldier. According to regulations, each private took his turn in rotation for ten consecutive days, with another man assigned as second cook to assist with food preparation as well as clean-up. At the end of that period the second cook, now supposed to be proficient at the craft, advanced to the first or chief cook and so forth. Addressing this ubiquitous problem, a soldier signing himself "Reformer" wrote to the *Army & Navy Journal* in 1869: "Ignorance of . . . cooking is the rule . . . and it cannot be otherwise from the manner in which cooks are detailed every ten days until it runs through the roster . . . each man detailed thinking of nothing but how to get through his dirty job—preparing each meal as fast as he can, not carring [sic] one cent whether the food is palatable or not." Another man attempted to bring perspective to the issue by factitiously raising the question, "Why should not everybody take a turn at being captain for the same reason?"[17]

Even though the army had an official cookbook that presumably was available at the company level, instruction in cooking was mostly handed down through the various details and by trial and error. Some companies with a reputation for being "bad feeders" received only basic dishes: the unskilled cooks playing it safe. "We boiled everything," remarked a former Eighteenth Infantryman. "I believe the bacon [rancid with age] would have killed men if it had not been thoroly [sic] boiled." A young Eighth Cavalry trooper, who clearly resented being detailed as cook, nevertheless admitted: "It does not require a Pastry or French cook for a lot of soldiers. . . . All that is necessary for a company cook is to know how to make a Kettle of Coffee, make a hash in the morning and a few other little things like that." It was a fortunate company indeed that included a man with any prior experience at restaurant or boardinghouse cooking, even more so when he volunteered to remain as first cook for a longer period, sometimes permanently. Assistant Surgeon Billings recognized that "this regulation is practically disregarded, as regards the chief cook, at the majority of posts. Were it literally enforced, the results would be very bad." Providing three meals a day on a rigid schedule for several dozen men nonetheless could be real drudgery. As one soldier observed of cooks, "after ten days' services . . . their clothing has become greasy, dilapidated, and unserviceable." Still, there were benefits. Cooks were exempt from roll calls and other duty, and the first cook slept in the kitchen or in an adjacent private room. He was at liberty to retire when he pleased, usually earlier than most of the other men, and ate better than most of them.[18]

Because the army issued no mess hall tableware until the late 1880s, companies were expected to acquire their own from commercial sources. Plain metal items were preferred because they were both inexpensive and durable. First Sergeant Ryan said that "the mess kit of the company . . . consisted of quart tin cups, tin plates, iron handled knives and forks, and common malleable iron table spoons." Even so, when pieces were pilfered, the captain of Company G, Fourth Infantry, found it necessary to remind his men that "the cups, plates, knifes [sic], and forks in the Mess Room belong to the Company and not to any individual man and the men are forbidden to take them from the mess room." It was not uncommon for some companies, especially when it became faddish in the 1880s, to purchase unit-monogrammed white ironstone china and commercial flatware, also unit-marked, as a matter of company pride.[19]

Under normal circumstances, companies were rationed for ten-day periods. The company commander submitted a ration return listing the number of men and authorized laundresses present with the unit at that time and detailing the types and quantities of foodstuffs requested. After approval by the commanding officer, the return then became an authorization for the commissary officer to issue the supplies when called for by a company noncom and his detail. The army ration, meaning the type and amount of food allowed each man, had not changed materially since 1861:

Pork or bacon	12 oz.; or
Salt or fresh beef	1 lb. 4 oz.
Soft bread, or flour	1 lb. 6 oz.
Hard bread	1 lb.
Corn meal	1 lb. 4 oz.
To Every Hundred Rations:	
Beans or peas	15 lbs.
Rice or hominy	10 lbs.
Green coffee	10 lbs., or
Roasted & ground coffee	8 lbs.
Tea	1 lb. 8 oz.

Sugar	15 lbs.
Vinegar	4 lbs.
Potatoes, (when practicable)	30 lbs.
Molasses	1 qt

In addition, the Subsistence Department furnished the men with salt, pepper, soap, and candles.[20]

Bread was the basic element in the army diet. Every post had its bakery, usually containing two ovens, where bread was made fresh daily and issued to the companies pro rata according to the number of men present. Loaves in excess of that issued, termed "baker's bread," could be sold to anyone on post. Flour, as reflected in the ration table, was sent directly to the bakery, where it was converted into bread for the companies. Because producing an eighteen-ounce loaf of bread required approximately one-third less than its weight in flour, a surplus automatically accrued. Although post commanders retained the authority to issue that surplus flour to the respective companies, it was normally sold to civilians and officers.

An 1873 article in the *Army & Navy Journal* explained the use of the funds derived:

> Regulations have long required that after the expenses of the bakery are deducted from the saving on the flour ration the remainder shall be equally divided between the post and regimental funds. The post fund is chiefly devoted, especially at smaller posts, to the purchase of reading matter; the regimental fund to the support of a regimental band and library. These last may be very worthy objects to those who receive benefit from them, but to the companies that are permanently detached from headquarters . . . they have not the most remote interest.

The final comment refers to the share devoted to regimental funds being prorated according to the number of companies of each regiment in mixed garrisons. Accordingly, the money was transferred to the regimental headquarters. Those companies not posted with the field and staff therefore gained no benefit from either the regiment's band or the regimental library, though the portion supporting a post library was of benefit.[21]

For years after the Civil War the army continued to be plagued with large quantities of foodstuffs procured through wartime contracts. Private William Murphy, a member of the Eighteenth Infantry on its march up the Bozeman Trail in 1866, commented on the condition of some of the supplies with which they were provided: "We loaded up some sacks of bacon [at Fort Reno]. I do not know how old it was, but the fat had commenced to sluff [sic] off from the lean and it was from three to five inches thick. There was a lot of flour in the store rooms and the mice had tunneled through it and the bacon for some time." Another infantryman posted at isolated Fort Phil Kearny complained that "we had no fresh meat, no vegetables. We did get one small loaf of bread issued to us daily . . . after that was gone we had to fall back on musty hardtack, salt pork, and black coffee. Occasionally we had bean soup."[22]

Conditions improved somewhat as years passed, yet the everyday fare was always plain, not unlike the fare of the average working-class household of the day. One man serving in 1877 related: "We had potatoes, soft bread, bacon, bean soup, baked beans, and beef stews for changes, and taken as a whole, we lived pretty well." Meats consisted almost exclusively of pork and beef, supplemented at times with wild game bagged by members of the company. Bacon, not surprisingly, was far more popular with the troops than was salt pork, both as field and garrison fare. The slabs were bagged in cloth sacks, one hundred pounds each, while salt pork was barreled in brine and had to be thoroughly boiled before it was edible. Even then it contained little lean. Salt beef, similarly preserved, was even less favored by soldiers.[23]

Fresh beef, not surprisingly, was far more appealing to the men. "We have beef seven days out of ten when we are in Camp," wrote a soldier at Fort Whipple. "The three days you have pork. For breakfast we have coffee, bread, and boiled beef, dinner roast beef, sometimes bean soup, or boiled potatoes with their jackets on, as some of the boys say, supper bread and coffee." A surgeon noted that "the beef is usually baked, or, as the diet table phrases it, roasted, and is generally overcooked as few soldiers will eat rare beef." Contracts for beef were let either by the department subsistence office or, if cattle were available locally, by the commissary officer at a post. A butcher shop was operated either by a civilian quartermaster employee or soldiers, who processed the meat and, having no refrigeration, issued it to the companies every morning. Nothing went to waste, however. A favorite breakfast dish served with some regularity was hash, made from "roast beef left from dinner, cut up and mixed with water, flour, potatoes, onions and seasoned," remembered Fourth Cavalryman Reginald Bradley.[24]

Beans, always an army staple, provided another ready source of protein, especially when there was a shortage of beef. Dried beans, put up in barrels containing three hundred pounds each, were durable and were easily prepared by inexperienced cooks. White beans were the army standard, although troops stationed in the Southwest were known to trade with local Hispanics for locally grown pinto beans. No matter what the variety, beans were always prepared by baking or boiling, seasoned generously with salt and pork or bacon. They appeared on the menu so routinely that one trooper was prompted to exclaim that "we have had bean soup for dinner, and baked beans for supper every day for the past month . . . and I like them . . . still when one has beans for about a thousand meals in succession the thing becomes monotonous." But even beans were not always done to perfection, as attested by Captain Guy V. Henry, Third Cavalry, who overhead his first sergeant ask the cook if his beans were boiled soft. The cook replied: "No sir. If they don't rattle, the boys swear they don't get any."[25]

Coffee, which the soldiers considered the most vital component of the army ration, was the Rio variety imported from Central and South America. Issued green in hundred-pound sacks, the beans first had to be roasted then ground, usually on a daily basis by the kitchen police. The men demanded that coffee be made strong, and it was normally not diluted with milk or sugar. Corporal Emil Bode declared that when old-timers in his company found the coffee too weak for their taste, they swore it "was made by boiling the shadow of a coffee bean suspended above the pot." Every man consumed a pint or more with each of his three daily meals.[26]

Several factors affected the quantity and quality of the food that actually reached the mess tables. Troops in garrison were by no means restricted to the basic staples, although some companies gained reputations for being poor feeders when inexperienced cooks exhibited little imagination, much less skill, beyond attempting to make the regular ration edible. "Men would come in exhausted and hungry, look at the grub set before them, and then fall to crying from sheer rage, cursing the day they were born," said Private Axel Dahlgren, Company K,

Thirteenth Infantry. Perley S. Eaton, who served in the Third Cavalry in the 1880s, remembered that his troop did not fare much better: "For breakfast we had beef hash, dry sliced bread, no butter & coffee, no milk; for dinner sliced beef, dry bread & coffee, no milk; for supper coffee straight just dry bread and coffee." At the same time, others managed to live exceedingly well through judicious management, close oversight by responsible noncoms, and capable cooks.[27]

A vital element in the soldiers' quality of life was the company fund, derived from the sale of rations (except flour) drawn in excess of the unit's needs. The ration, according to one man, "is enough, and more than a man can eat; yet one third of it sold and strictly accounted for, will furnish a company with all necessary articles needed on the table." Some items, such as tea and rice, were not particularly popular but were drawn for the specific purpose of sale or barter with local civilians. Company Quartermaster Sergeant Eddie Matthews, Eighth Cavalry, explained how he took advantage of local supply and demand in the vicinity of Fort Bascom, New Mexico Territory, where cattle were plentiful but pigs were not: "Here we are issued a full ration of bacon, and can sell it for 15 cents per lb. and can buy beef for 5 cents. . . . About a week or two ago I sent off to be sold over five hundred pounds bacon, two hundred pounds Sugar, one barrel of Vinegar, one hundred pounds Rice, one hundred pounds Hominy, and one box Soap, savings of rations, but I tell you it keeps me busy to watch that nothing is wasted." In other areas of the West, however, the troops were not so fortunate, as illustrated by a soldier writing from Fort Stevenson, Dakota Territory: "Now, after saving these rations, we have no one to sell them to except hostile Indians, and so we have to turn them in to the commissary at their own price; and then we have a Company Fund." Even in those circumstances, the army was under no obligation to refund the cost of the rations, if in the opinion of the commissary of subsistence a loss might accrue to the government. In some companies the men elected to contribute a portion of their pay to a mess fund in order to obtain nonration commodities.[28]

The fund, administered by the captain in consultation with a committee of soldiers, was used to purchase a wide array of items to benefit his men. A list of acquisitions by one company stationed in the Department of the Platte in 1869 serves as a fair illustration of the types and variety of items:

7,768 lbs. potatoes, 1,300 lbs. onions, 200 lbs. beets, 400 lbs. turnips, 100 lbs. beans, 655 lbs. flour (for duff), 145 lbs. dried apples, 100 lbs. corn meal, 420 lbs codfish, 6 cans oysters, 158 lbs. turkey (Christmas dinner), 29 lbs. cabbage, 24 cans tomatoes, 12 gallons pickeled [sic] onion, 15 lbs. tea, 20 lbs. peas. Some three hundred dollars were expended for mess furniture, lamps, and oil for barracks, soda, yeast powders, footballs, checker boards, white gloves, emery, rotten stone, etc.[29]

With regard to foodstuffs, companies were at liberty to purchase from the post trader, local civilians, and the commissary storehouse (on designated days, usually two per month) and by special order. First Cavalryman Henry Yohn, posted in southern Arizona Territory in 1866, noted that his company procured "watermelons . . . pomegranates, and limes from the south [Mexico] . . . potatoes that were a greenish color inside at forty cents a pound . . . frijoles, tortillas . . . we had no bacon—only salt meat from the East." He added that he never saw an egg in two years. Dakota garrisons situated along the Missouri River were advantaged by having ready access to commerce from cities below. "When the spring opened the river up, the boats would come up . . . and the first loads they would bring up would consist of eggs, butter, cheese . . . I recollect on several occasions buying several hundred dozen eggs for the company . . . at the rate of twenty-five cents a dozen." A Sixth Infantry doughboy at Fort Buford related how his company in true entrepreneurial spirit purchased an entire barrel of eggs off the last boat passing downriver in the fall of 1872. "But they were kept on the quiet until Christmas when they were sold for $2.50 per dozen—the most of them being used for eggnog. If there had been ten barrels they would have been consumed."[30]

Although canned evaporated milk was readily available, some companies elected to purchase a cow as a source of fresh milk and butter, the expenses for its upkeep also being a legitimate use of the company fund. At Fort Stanton, New Mexico Territory, civilians were permitted to operate a dairy on the military reservation on condition that they supply the garrison with those luxuries.[31]

The Subsistence Department included potatoes on its inventory, but transporting them by wagon to distant frontier forts was impractical because they would spoil by the time they reached their destination.

Providing fresh vegetables from central sources of supply was also virtually impossible. During the 1850s the army had begun purchasing a novel product known as desiccated mixed vegetables, which was quickly corrupted by soldiers to the more descriptive term, "desecrated" vegetables. It was nevertheless a useful ration, consisting of a combination of chopped cabbage leaves and turnip tops, sliced carrots, parsnips, turnips, potatoes, and other vegetables, all bound together by some substance that "defied the powers of the analyst to give it a name." After being thoroughly mixed, the concoction was mechanically compressed into "tablets" to remove the juices then dehydrated in ovens until rock-hard prior to packaging. According to Musician Alson B. Ostrander, the cakes were "approximately nine inches long by three inches wide by almost an inch thick. Packed in air-tight [tin] caddies. When opened they look just like a big plug of tobacco, but when placed in boiling water, how they do swell!" Each man was allowed an ounce of the condensed vegetables. When boiled with pieces of cooked salt or fresh beef, and hunks of bone and seasoning for flavor, desiccated vegetables produced a passable soup to feed a company economically and at the same time forestall scurvy.[32]

A diet lacking in citrus fruits and vegetables created an ever-present threat of scurvy. The cause of scurvy, a deficiency of vitamin C, had been long understood by the medical profession, so vinegar was included in the army ration table. Although some recipes called for small amounts of vinegar to be added to soups and beans, it was often not enough to prevent the disease. Some conscientious army doctors, supported by post commanders, ensured that the men consumed adequate quantities of cider vinegar, which was perfectly drinkable. "We had to drink vinegar to combat scurvy, because we got no fruit or vegetables for over two years," stated a Twenty-Second Infantryman. Desiccated vegetables proved effective in combating the disease, yet it was not preferred when there was any possibility of obtaining the fresh article.[33]

At the urging of post surgeons, many western garrisons established vegetable gardens to provide that vital and welcome supplement to the plain army diet. One or two men, usually experienced farmers, were regularly detailed as gardeners for a month or longer. The fields often were located some distance from a post, wherever fertile ground and perhaps a water source could be found, so a wall tent or rude shack was provided as sleeping quarters. Such duty was popular with most men because it exempted them from all other duties and roll calls. "One summer I worked there with another one [soldier] . . . cultivating five acres in a field of twenty-five where the other companies had also their garden sections," related a Sixteenth Infantryman. "The water was brought the same as to the company quarters, by water wagon." The post chaplain, provided there was one, often supervised the garden operation; but in the absence of a "Holy Joe," the job fell to the commissary officer or the post adjutant. Of course, having unsupervised men camped some distance from the post also had drawbacks. Reporting from Fort Custer, Montana Territory, Private James O. Purvis wrote:

> The gardens . . . here are situated on the banks of the Little Big Horn River, about two miles from the post. Yesterday some of the gardeners made the raise of a small barrel of whisky, wherewith to drink prosperity to the crops of '86. After liberal "irrigation" in honor of their new "spuds" etc., they started in to drink success to agriculture generally throughout the territory. The sentiment was good enough but the whisky was of that quality which usually incites its patrons to become sluggers. . . . One of the party was badly hurt and the others not improved any. The greater portion of the liquor was seized by the guard last night.[34]

Irrigating crops in the generally arid West sometimes posed a challenge, though most commands were able to utilize the nearest stream, provided suitable bottomland was available. In extreme circumstances, such as at Fort Bowie, Arizona Territory, located high in the Chiricahua Mountains, the post commander was compelled to establish a garden some sixty miles away on the San Pedro River. After that proved impractical, probably because of the Apache threat to the isolated camp, the post began purchasing large quantities of onions, turnips, and beets from farmers at Silver City, New Mexico Territory. A correspondent at Fort Laramie in 1869 informed the editor of the *Army & Navy Journal*: "Owing to the lack of rain, there is . . . scarcely any vegetable growth here, except where some means of irrigation are adopted." An innovative solution to the problem, he said, was the construction of a waterwheel to lift water from the stream and deposit it in an elevated lateral trough that conducted it to the garden.[35]

"There was a spirit of friendly rivalry among the soldiers of the different companies as to which garden produced the finest fruits or vegetables," wrote Surgeon Bernard J. Byrne. "If Company B had a finer display of potatoes than Company H, there would be a celebration by Company B. If Company H had a better showing of cabbages than Company C, then Company H would give a dance in honor of its success." Under favorable conditions and adept farmers, some companies experienced phenomenal success with their crops. Serving at Fort Ellis, Montana Territory, Private William F. Zimmer, Second Cavalry, bragged: "Our gardener raised 1500 bushels of potatoes & about the same number of cabbage heads, besides carrots, onions, and rutabagas by the hundreds of bushels & they are all nicely stored away in 2 underground cellars . . . we can live like kings while we are in the fort." Many companies made use of the vinegar ration to pickle cucumbers and to make sauerkraut. "I put up, from cabbage in the garden," Corporal William B. Jett remembered, "ten or twelve barrels of sauerkraut, which was much enjoyed during the winter months by the men; though Jantzen, a young Dutchman, said it would not be good till it got worms in it, just as limburger cheese was not."[36]

Company gardening nevertheless had an unavoidable downside—what became of the garden, particularly during the growing season, when units transferred? The only option, besides outright abandonment, was to sell the crop, along with any produce that could not be transported to another station, to one of the companies left behind. This, of course, created a buyer's market, resulting in considerable financial and crop loss to the departing company.[37]

By the mid-nineteenth century commercial canning was a well-established industry in America. Such products as tomatoes, fruit of various varieties, a wide range of vegetables, sauces, soups, meats, and even seafood were readily available. The development of improved canning techniques and materials led to a plethora of products on the market by the end of the Civil War. Although canned goods were initially expensive, thus limiting their use to the more affluent, competition and more efficient manufacturing lowered costs, inducing the army to begin purchasing greater quantities of such goods for the small postwar army. This was reflected in an 1868 general order allowing companies to purchase certain canned items for their kitchens, including lima beans, green corn, peaches, and jelly.[38] This trend continued through the 1870s and 1880s with the ever-expanding availability of vacuum-packed foods. Nevertheless, the standard ration remained virtually unchanged until 1879, when dried or pickled fish and fresh mutton could be substituted for the usual meat components and canned molasses could be used in lieu of raw sugar. Two years later the issue of canned fresh and corned beef, along with ready-made canned baked beans, proved to be a highly popular innovation among the rank and file. Thirteenth Infantryman Samuel D. Gilpin recalled: "Canned baked beans were new to us recruits from David's [sic] Island in 1885. I recalled more vividly the baked beans in cans than any other incident of that 5-day trip [to join their regiment]. The recruits wanted second helpings so often! I fed them beans three times daily."[39]

The widespread use of tobacco, smoked or chewed, was an accepted fact of life at the time. "Most every soldier uses it," an Eighth Cavalryman claimed. "It is one of the greatest comforts we enjoy, thus we nearly all smoke and have to buy pipes. Cigars are too expensive. . . . When on guard duty . . . if you have a bit of the weed you can chew away to your hearts [sic] content and be happy." He confided that he had been using tobacco since the age of eight, and as a result of chewing he had "every reason to believe it has preserved what few teeth I have left." Second Cavalryman William White stated: "A pound of plug tobacco was issued monthly to each man. There was but one kind, 'Army and Navy Plug,' being the brand imprinted on it. . . . I did not chew. . . . I used a jack-plane for shaving off slices to dry for smoking." Simpson Mann remembered that among his Ninth Cavalry comrades "more chewed than smoked."[40]

Heavy users were permitted to purchase additional quantities, when authorized by their captains, though company commanders had to be discriminating in signing such requisitions because some speculators acquired extra tobacco purely for resale. Nonusers often drew their tobacco ration, only to sell it to others addicted to smoking or chewing. By waiting until the end of the month, when others were running short, recalled Tenth Cavalry trooper Perry Hayman, "I sold my tobacco at auction. I cut the plug in half, receiving $4.50 for one piece and $4.00 for the other piece." Other more generous souls gave it away to their bunkies and other friends in the company. By 1878 the

Subsistence Department was also providing two brands of smoking tobacco, "Lone Jack" and "Old Seal," in addition to the traditional plug. Even then some army doctors suspected that smoking might be an unhealthy habit, though few men took heed. Not to be denied his pleasure, a hospital steward at Fort Union, New Mexico Territory, complained in a letter to his niece: "The old man [surgeon] . . . has made me quit smoking my pipe so I haft [sic] to steal a march on him after I go to bed."[41]

An alternative source of goods not provided by the army was the civilian sutler or post trader as he was later known. Before the Civil War, one such civilian was authorized to operate a general store at every military post, but regimental sutlers predominated during the conflict, with most of the state troops mobile in the field. The 1866 statute reorganizing the army abolished sutlers altogether, a decision based largely on General William T. Sherman's opinion that the traders were a nuisance whose function could be better performed by the Subsistence Department. Many in the army were of the opinion that sutlers took undue advantage of soldiers by charging exorbitant prices and supplying liquor to the troops, whereas the army would sell goods at cost.[42]

The effective date of the law was postponed until July 1, 1867, to give the Subsistence Department time to acquire the necessary stock of supplies and for the sutlers to close out their businesses. Meanwhile, unforeseen problems arose that threatened to scuttle the concept. A primary purpose of the sutler on the frontier was to make basic necessities available to civilian emigrants, travelers, and local residents that otherwise would have been prohibited for sale at military posts. Abolition of those stores thus would deprive citizens on the frontier of those sources of supply. Making matters worse, the conservative postwar Congress declined to authorize the estimated 3 million dollars required to purchase the inventory necessary for the commissaries to assume the function. For a time it appeared that frontier forts would be left empty handed. Subsequent emergency legislation passed on March 30, 1867, granted a reprieve to so-called post traders in the West by allowing them to remain in business wherever the army considered them necessary, despite having no legal standing, and at the same stroke prohibited the Subsistence Department from selling to enlisted men. This stopgap situation continued until mid-1870, when a new act modified the earlier decision to eliminate sutlers and to permit the secretary of war to authorize trading establishments at frontier posts "not in the vicinity of any city or town when he believes such an establishment is needed for the accommodation of emigrants, freighters, and other citizens."[43]

Even though the law provided that more than one trader could be appointed at a fort, thereby keeping prices competitive, the secretary of war refused to do so. Consequently, the intended checks on abuse were negated. At some forts officers willingly took full advantage of buying at wholesale prices, while enlisted men were gouged for the same articles. A resentful soldier remarked: "The post trader is an indispensable evil of the forts. There everything from a collar button to a saddle, and all kinds of hardware and grocery goods could be obtained [by] paying exorbitant prices. Drinks were furnished direct over the bar or through an order signed by an officer . . . at the rate of twenty-five cents for one glass of beer and $2.00 a quart for 'rot-gut' stuff called whiskey."[44] Some unscrupulous traders curried political favor to secure their monopolies, while others gave kickbacks to politicians and post commanders to protect their interests. Still others franchised their businesses among several posts, thereby reaping a share of the profits from all. Many, in contrast, were honest merchants working to make only a reasonable profit. One of those was William H. Quinette, who arrived at Camp Supply, Indian Territory, in 1878. He was employed initially as a clerk and subsequently occupied a respected place in the garrison as post trader for well over a decade.[45]

Officers were accorded the privilege of charging their purchases at the trader's store, sometimes to his detriment when units were transferred and officers departed without settling their accounts. The rank and file, however, did business under a different system: cash or tokens made of brass or copper. First Sergeant John Ryan explained the process:

> If a man did not have ready cash . . . he could obtain what was called a sutler's check. He would go into . . . the 1st sergeant [who] would give him a check out of a checkbook for any amount he desired up to $5., but not over. The man would then sign the check and the 1st sergeant would take it with the company morning report to the company commander for his approval . . . then give it to the man . . . who would take it to the post traders where it would be cashed. He would receive in

return for the check one dollar checks [tokens], and fifty and twenty-five cent checks, as it was almost impossible . . . for the men to buy anything for less than twenty-five cents.⁴⁶

This credit system freed the trader from having to maintain separate ledger accounts for each man to be presented in vouchers against his pay. The paper check signed by the soldier would be held until the next payday and presented to the paymaster, who conveyed the appropriate deduction directly to the trader. The trader's tokens, once purchased, could be sold or bartered among members of the garrison because they were as negotiable as cash at that licensee's store, but nowhere else. Should a soldier's unit be transferred, the tokens were useless unless redeemed before he left that fort. Soldiers also resented the tokens because even when they paid with cash, clerks often made change with tokens, claiming they were short of specie, thus ensuring retention of the full amount.

In the wake of the elimination of sutlers and the regulations controlling their activities, graft, corruption, and influence peddling were rife throughout the post trader system. The situation came to a head during the Grant administration and the trial of Secretary of War William W. Belknap. Those events caused a renewal of the head-tax on post traders, in exchange for the exclusive privilege of conducting business on military reservations. In addition, the enlisted men were provided a measure of protection by the reinstitution of reviews every six months by a committee of officers, known as the post council of administration, to examine invoices and to "establish . . . the rates and prices at which the goods shall be sold." That list, after being approved by the post commander, was posted prominently in the store.⁴⁷

Prior to 1861 troops had been paid in gold and silver, but that practice changed with the outbreak of the Civil War and the sudden expansion of the army. Thereafter the troops were paid in currency and specie, but soldiers discovered that frontier merchants routinely discounted the face value of greenbacks by as much as 30 percent compared to silver and gold. "I don't think that is right," complained a newly joined cavalry trooper. "If they discount paper money, the Gov't. ought to pay the men off with money that is at par." But that was not the only disappointment in store for recruits on their first payday after joining their units. They suddenly learned that several recurring deductions would be taken from their gross pay, including twenty-five cents to support the Soldiers' Home. A malcontent writing under the pseudonym "Climax" declared that "pay-day is a delusion and a mockery devoid of any real advantages to him [the recruit], for when his name is called . . . it is only to be told there is nothing due him, that his clothing account, tailor's bill, debt due the laundress and for tobacco have not only absorbed all of his first allowance of pay but have eaten largely into all he can earn in the next two, perhaps four, months."[48]

The pay for a first enlistment private, thirteen dollars a month (forty-three cents a day), may have sounded niggardly compared with the pay of a civilian laborer, averaging one dollar to a dollar and fifty cents a day, yet the disparity was not so great, taking into consideration that the army provided a soldier's shelter, food, medical care, and clothing. (The monthly pay of corporals was fifteen dollars, sergeants seventeen dollars, and first sergeants twenty-two dollars.) Beginning in 1872, as a measure to reduce desertion, the monthly base pay of a private was increased to fourteen dollars in his third year, and a dollar more was added in each of the last two years of his enlistment, for a total of sixteen dollars during the fifth year. The bonus pay was retained to his credit and paid to him in a lump sum at the time of his discharge, providing the veteran with finances for some enterprise if he chose to return to civil life. However, his retained pay could be forfeited if he deserted, was convicted of a crime by a civil court, or was guilty of repeated misconduct while in the service. Soldiers who reenlisted within thirty days after receiving an honorable discharge were granted two monetary incentives: the rate of pay that they had been receiving in the fifth year of their previous term plus two dollars per month longevity pay (one dollar of which was retained) during the second enlistment. Each subsequent enlistment added another dollar to a soldier's monthly pay, so reliable career soldiers, particularly noncoms, could earn a substantial income and afford to lay aside a considerable nest egg.[49] (See appendix A for a complete enlisted pay table.)

Men assigned to so-called extra duty, defined as "employment as artificers or laborers . . . or other constant labor of not less than ten days duration," received additional pay. Laborers and teamsters, when such work could not be performed by the regular fatigue details, earned twenty-five cents a day if stationed east of the Rocky Mountains and thirty-five cents a day west of the Rockies. Qualified clerks and mechanics, including post bakers, were paid fifteen cents more per day. Noncommissioned officers also qualified for extra duty pay when they were detailed to oversee work performed by parties of not more than twenty men each. A regimental quartermaster sergeant, for example, might have been assigned to supervise a construction or building repair project, or a duty sergeant might have overseen a crew digging post holes for a telegraph line.[50]

A high degree of uncertainty invariably overshadowed an anticipated visit by the paymaster. According to regulations, troops were to be paid on the last day of each even-numbered month of the year. Whereas western garrisons located along the rail lines and other major travel routes could be fairly confident that the paymaster would maintain a reasonable schedule, weather conditions and the great distances to be traveled caused many delays at more remote posts. Paymasters, obliged to travel from the department headquarters to every station within that geographical area, most frequently traveled overland in light wagons or army ambulances, though they were conveyed by steamboat where navigable water routes were available, notably to the posts along the Upper Missouri River. Winter on the northern plains and in the Rocky Mountains often precluded the paymaster's visits altogether for a number of months. "I do not know when we will be payed [sic] as the pay master does not come here more than twice[e] or three times a year," lamented a soldier at Fort Fetterman, Wyoming Territory. This was a familiar complaint. Paymasters were invariably accompanied by armed escorts coordinated in relays from one post to another. The strength and composition of each escort was determined by the respective post commanders, who were best positioned to know the country, conditions, and potential dangers of the region to be traversed on the paymaster's route.[51]

Paydays witnessed a muster of the entire garrison, except the sick and a few men excused for specific reasons. Conduct of the inspection varied according to the discretion of the post commander. During winter troops often assembled on the parade ground under arms and wearing overcoats or in full dress uniform in their squad rooms. In fair weather, however, a battalion parade was conducted more formally. Most commanders directed the troops to appear in dress uniform, with the cavalry either mounted or dismounted. Some commanders insisted that the companies turn out in "heavy marching order" (with the cavalry mounted) to ensure that every man possessed a complete issue of field equipment, flawlessly packed in the prescribed manner. Private Hartford G. Clark, Sixth Cavalry, described such a ceremony at Fort Niobrara, Nebraska, in August 1891:

> This morning we mustered for inspection etc. Cavalry mounted in heavy marching order and infantry dismounted, of course, in heavy marching order. The commanding officer inspected us out on the prairie. We stayed out there three hours in the sun. It was terrible hot. After the inspection of troops, the quarters were inspected, delaying our dinner until 1.35 making a cold dinner today.[52]

As a First Cavalryman related, the preparation for standing inspection and the discomfort could be tempered by the timely arrival of the paymaster. "He is always the most welcome visitor we have," declared Private James O. Purvis. The afternoon was devoted to paying the troops. In some commands the men were required to wear dress uniforms to the pay table, but in most instances they changed to undress before reassembling for pay. A teenaged Reynolds Burt, son of Lieutenant Colonel Andrew S. Burt, Seventh Infantry, vividly remembered the procedure:

> All troops were prepared to "form" in spruced up uniforms not full dress, but wearing white gloves, a long established custom. The Paymaster had proceeded to the Commanding Officer's desk, where the funds were stacked for distribution. The various payrolls were presented, and the leading company (with 1st Sergeant leading) approached the desk. The men had formed in single file beginning at the office doorway; and as each man's name was called by the clerk from the payroll list he answered "Here" and stepped to the desk, saluted, removed his right hand glove, and received in <u>loose silver</u> the amount called out by the Clerk. This was the high-light of the excitement! After receiving the silver the man "about-faced" (most militarily) and marched out. There was no return barracks formation. I never saw anyone count his pay in front of the paymaster but outside there were various countings. Younger men (from

inward excitement) often tossed coins in the air and juggled with it like children.[53]

Once paid, those men not on guard or other assigned duty enjoyed something of a holiday, being at liberty to pursue whatever forms of recreation might be available. The first order of business, however, was to settle one's outstanding debts. Private Charles Hayden's diary entry showed how complex accounting might be after a lapse of several months: "I received $27.75, two months pay. I paid Jordan $2.00, Library .50, Bangs .75, Laundry .50, Barber .25, [post] Canteen .30, Fleming Pd. me $4.00, Scott payed [sic] me $6.00, Bangs $2.40, McGuire $2.00, Nilson $2.00, Morris .25, Graham .25, Shriver $1.50, Loaned Corp. Morris $4.00; Bought one suit unmade clothes of Renaud $2.50."[54] Hayden's record suggests that he may have been a payday lender, described as "thorns in the unit commander's sides . . . close-fisted ones who always had a 'bit of change.' When the 'spenders' simply had to have a dollar or two, the lenders would hand out the requested amounts to be paid back on payday, 'two for one.'" A soldier also may have been indebted to the company tailor, if he had had uniforms made or fitted, or chevrons and stripes applied.[55]

Only rarely did a soldier try to save part of his pay or send some money home to his family, if he had one. Musician Robert Greenhalgh explained to his parents: "We were paid again today. . . . Enclosed is the amount [$20.00], I could send more but this thing of depriving myself of little extras for the sake of a few dollars I never will do, but I am determined to spend no money foolishly." Those little extras often consumed a considerable share of a soldier's pay. Even though he intended to send money regularly to his parents, Private Eddie Matthews enumerated some of the out-of-pocket expenses he had to bear: "Nearly every soldier wears paper collars in Camp 40¢ a box . . . then comes combs, hair and tooth brushes, a little hair oil . . . The Gov't. does not provide you with towels and one cannot always use his shirt tail."[56]

Ranking next to diet in a soldier's creature comforts was his clothing. Most of it was made of wool or flannel. The army's reasoning was twofold: these fabrics were durable and soldiering was essentially an outdoors occupation requiring men to be subjected to the full range of climatic conditions. Although such garments could be excruciatingly uncomfortable during daytime in southern and desert regions, temperatures often dropped significantly at night. Army surgeons generally took the stance that soldiers on guard and in the field were better off being too warm at times than too cold.

Army clothing remained fairly basic for a number of years after the Civil War. The army, satisfied that the wartime uniform had proved adequate, saw no compelling need for revisions, especially when warehouses bulged with stocks of clothing purchased during the conflict. For daily wear an infantryman was issued a dark blue forage cap with a tall, floppy crown; a loose dark blue woolen sack coat or blouse; sky blue woolen trousers; and shoes, often termed bootees or brogans. For dress occasions, he had a broad-brimmed black felt hat and a tight-fitting coat with sky blue piping, which had skirts extending to mid-thigh. In cold weather a sky-blue woolen overcoat with elbow-length cape augmented the other clothing. Beneath his outer clothing, he wore a pull-over flannel shirt (gray or white), canton flannel drawers, and stockings.

The outfit for cavalry was the same with respect to undergarments. The standard uniform was a short dark blue jacket trimmed with yellow worsted braid, though most officers in the West allowed their men to substitute the more comfortable sack coat for everyday wear, reserving the jacket for dress occasions. The cap and dress hat were of the same basic patterns provided to other branches of service, while the mounted-style overcoat was double-breasted with a cape extending to the wrists. Troopers drew both shoes and boots (the latter usually reserved for mounted duty). The only specialized garments consisted of an almost knee-length white cotton frock and overalls worn over the woolen uniform for stable duty.

The supply of surplus clothing was adequate until the early 1870s, when it became depleted by the consumption of average sizes, coupled with poor storage conditions at many of the eastern supply depots. In 1872 a reluctant Quartermaster General Montgomery C. Meigs, a staunch defender of the Civil War uniform, conceded to pressure for new clothing. A board of officers convened that year compiled recommendations for distinctively different styles of both dress and fatigue uniforms, based on trends of major European armies, except for retaining the traditional army blue color. The cut and adornment of the new dress coats for all branches reflected British and German influence, the plumed cavalry dress helmet likewise being distinctively British. The infantry dress cap and the universal forage cap, now with low crown, were of French origin, while the initial pattern of pleated blouse was a Swiss contribution. With the exception of the odd-looking fatigue blouse, which was resoundingly rejected by the rank and file and replaced by a plain pattern not too different from the old sack coat, this uniform remained in use with only minor modifications for the remainder of the era.[57]

Perhaps the most important concession to the army's frontier mission was the adoption of a broad-brimmed campaign hat for use on fatigue and in the field. A style long favored by rural folk, such hats had been procured by soldiers on the frontier prior to the war and had been worn widely by the state volunteers during the conflict. Regulars in the West not infrequently improvised by drawing extra dress (sometimes called "Hardee") hats and using them without the brass trimmings in the field. The campaign hat underwent a design change and improvement in quality in 1876 and seven years later assumed its final appearance when the color was changed from black to drab to reduce heat absorption.

The soldier was given a clothing allowance, an account against which the government charged the various items. The allowance was based on a calculation of the quantity of each item that might be reasonably needed during each year of his enlistment, every item being priced according to a standard table that was periodically revised. A veteran noncom of the Seventh Cavalry in the 1870s remembered well how the system worked:

> When a man enlisted in those days, he was given a new suit of clothes and a complete outfit. That would consist of a forage cap, an overcoat, a blouse, a pair of pants, a pair of cavalry boots, two flannel shirts, two pairs of flannel drawers, two pairs of socks, one pair of mittens, and one woolen blanket. . . . When he arrived at the company to which he was assigned, he would receive a uniform, dress coat, helmet, and a couple of pairs of white Berlin gloves. . . . There is a set price on each article . . . and each man is allowed so many articles every year until they mount up to a specified amount. The clothing account was generally settled up about every three months, or

quarterly. If a man was indebted to the government for clothing it would be deducted from his pay on the first pay day after the quarterly account was made up, and if the government was indebted to him, i.e., if he did not draw the amount of clothing which was regularly allowed him it would be credited to him on his clothing account, and when his term of service expired, all the money . . . would be given to him.[58]

Regulations notwithstanding, not all line officers agreed with the quarterly settlements. First Lieutenant John Bigelow Jr., Tenth Cavalry, adopted a more realistic approach, noting in his journal: "That seems to me too long a time ahead to require the men to provide themselves for. I have determined to have issues twice quarterly or every six weeks." Sixteenth Infantryman Emil Bode recorded that soldiers sometimes resorted to another expedient to acquire what they needed. "The captain kept enough clothes on hand to meet the immediate wants of the company and would issue every month or fourteen days to every man who was in need, charging it to his clothing allowance. . . . If our gallant soldier should not be successful in the above, he would wait until dusk, hook a pair of shoes or blanket unobserved, and throw it out of the window where a pal would catch it on the fly." Bode's experience with pilfering the storeroom was reason enough for most company commanders not to keep a supply on hand but instead to fill out a clothing roll based on individual needs and submit that to the post quartermaster.[59]

The table of allowances, of course, represented the optimal life expectancy of clothing, but in reality that varied according to the conditions in which the various articles were used. Rough labor and field service might well wear out certain items more rapidly than foreseen. The established allotment did not necessarily restrict a man only to those specific articles; but if he drew additional clothing or blankets, the cost was charged against him and reconciled at the pay table. Most men took advantage of the widespread practice of buying unwanted clothing and blankets from discharged soldiers before they left the post. That was advantageous for both parties in that the ex-soldier was relieved of the extra baggage and his former comrades could wear the used items for fatigue, thereby preserving their own uniforms and allowing the money allowance to accumulate in savings.

Some entrepreneurs took advantage of the system to raise cash by drawing clothing on their allowances then selling it for cash to willing comrades who were only too happy to acquire garments and blankets at a considerable discount. Another way to obtain a needed item sooner than authorized, without being charged, was to ask a friend to draw it on his allowance on the promise to repay the item in kind when the borrower's account permitted. Some men (such is human nature) took advantage of their more trusting fellows, as reported in the *Army & Navy Journal*:

> Our attention is again called to the subject by a recent court-martial in Texas, where a soldier was tried for "Buying an overcoat from Private Nickerson, with the understanding that he would draw one for him at the next issue, but did fail to do so and did sell said coat. Buying from Saddler Patterson a blanket, saying he would draw one for him at the next issue, did fail to do so and did sell said blanket. Buying a blanket from Private McCaffrey, with the understanding that he would get one for him at the next issue, did fail to do so and did sell said blanket." Although punishment overtook that clothes dealer, yet we infer that under a different system he could not have secured an opportunity either to buy or to sell.[60]

For several years after adoption of the new uniform, the Quartermaster Department was burdened with great quantities of war surplus clothing that Congress mandated must be issued to the army, rather than sold on the open market. The only way to induce soldiers to draw it, however, was drastically to reduce the prices below those for the current uniform. Moreover, by that time only the very large and very small sizes were available, which forced most soldiers to draw oversize garments that could be altered to fit, leaving most of the smallest sizes eventually to be sold on the civilian market. After purchasing an old-style dress coat at Fort Buford, Dakota Territory, in 1874, Private Wilmot Sanford, Sixth Infantry, wrote that he was using his spare time "macking [sic] a blouse out of a dress coat." Cutting off the long skirt of the 1857-pattern frock and replacing the standing collar with a rollover style was a common practice among both infantry and cavalry soldiers. The obsolete items often were relegated to fatigue and field purposes though they did not entirely disappear from the ranks until the end of the decade.[61]

By the mid-1870s conditions encountered on the northern Great Plains influenced the army to adopt special winter clothing, including buffalo overcoats, muskrat fur caps, fur gauntlets, and rubber overshoes. Because these special items were required only in certain climates, they did not form a part of the uniform allowance but were issued to a soldier for his use, as were arms and equipment, and were deducted from his pay if lost or damaged through his negligence.

Regulations prohibited enlisted soldiers from possessing any clothing other than the government-issue, yet officers generally overlooked civilian under garments such as shirts, vests, and underwear, so long as they remained concealed under the uniform during duty hours. During hot weather soldiers often substituted cotton or linen shirts purchased from the trader. "White shirts is another virtue to the majority of the boys," Private Eddie Matthews informed his parents. "Although we are so far from civilization and have no pretty girls . . . to rumple our slick fronts we still like to look clean and feel comfortable." Supplementing one's outfit could be expensive, however. Private Henry Hubman wrote from Fort Assinniboine, Montana Territory, to one of his brothers asking if he would "put some of the under shirts, shirts, drawers, [and] shawl in a paper box and send them to me . . . [here] under shirts cost $2.00, shirts $3.50, and a shawl $5.00."[62]

Every company included among its members at least one tailor who made and altered uniforms. Army clothing, particularly clothing dating from the Civil War, was notoriously ill-fitting. The company tailor, formerly a tradesman in civil life, was "an institution . . . absolutely indispensable, as none of the clothing issued was fit to wear until it had been altered from top to bottom . . . he frequently made them into very respectably fitting uniforms," according to First Sergeant Henry McConnell. A regular in California groused that troops were being victimized by the system because "we are charged by the Government nine dollars and twenty-five cents for a cavalry jacket, five dollars and ninety cents for a pair of pants. . . . Now, as our company commanders will not allow us to appear on inspection without having our clothing altered to fit, we must go [to] the tailor who charges ten dollars . . . in legal tender for a jacket and trowsers, making twenty-nine dollars and forty cents in all for two garments that could be bought in New York

City, made to order, for fifteen dollars." His ability to add may have been faulty, but the soldier's message was clear enough. Soldiers felt, justifiably, that by making clothes in only four sizes (and rather crudely at that) the Quartermaster Department compelled them to make up for the disparity from their own pockets. As a matter of personal choice, however, some regulars, particularly noncommissioned officers, willingly paid company tailors or local women to construct their uniforms from finer commercially produced cloth for a custom fit.[63]

Although it was not an official position, no company would be without a tailor for very long. If none of the members possessed that talent, the captain would specially requisition a tailor through the recruiting system. The job was a lucrative one, because the man not only altered and mended uniforms but usually sewed on chevrons and trouser stripes for all the noncoms. The company commander excused the tailor from all company duty and established the tariff of prices that he could charge for his work. In a typical example from 1878, company tailors at Fort Sanders, Wyoming Territory, charged $2.00 for fitting a dress coat and 25 cents for adding service chevrons to the sleeves, $1.75 for trousers, $2.50 for tailoring a blouse, $2.50 for altering an overcoat, and 75 cents and 50 cents, respectively, for applying chevrons and trouser stripes for noncommissioned officers. "There is a great demand for tailors in the army," Sergeant F. Z. Aber declared in 1881. "It is safe to say that any tailor who enlists now is sure of $100 a month besides his regular pay."[64]

As in the case of clothing, the quarter-century embracing the Indian Wars was a period of almost continual evolution in arms and personal equipment. During the first two years after the Civil War the regulars continued to be armed and equipped as they had been during the last year of the conflict, but that soon changed. The infantry posted west of the Mississippi, with the exception of only one regiment, was universally armed with the Springfield .58-caliber rifle-musket. Even prior to the end of the war, however, the Ordnance Department had been experimenting with converting the rifle-musket to a breech-loader capable of firing a self-contained metallic cartridge. That effort eventually resulted in a design designated as the Model 1866, a rifle differing little in outward appearance from the musket but chambered for a new .50/70 cartridge. By mid-1867 most of the infantry units on the frontier were armed with the new rifle. Upon the arrival of a supply train at beleaguered Fort Phil Kearny, Dakota Territory, a former sergeant recalled: "We were mighty pleased to see them, but what tickled us most was the seven hundred new breech-loading Springfield rifles of fifty-caliber, with one hundred thousand rounds of ammunition, which they brought to supersede the old muzzle-loaders with which we had been previously armed." The .50-caliber Springfield breech loader, subsequently modified and improved, continued to be the standard infantry rifle until the middle of the following decade.[65]

Meanwhile, the infantryman's personal equipment, like his clothing, were drawn from surplus stores left from the war. The accouterments, made of black leather, were the same for garrison and field: a waist belt with brass U.S. plate, a bayonet and scabbard, and a large, heavy cartridge box, either slung over the shoulder or worn on the waist belt. As a badge of rank in garrison, sergeants carried a light straight sword, remembered by one veteran as "a useless weapon which the cavalry irreverently designated as a 'cheese-knife,' or 'toad sticker.'" For field service, doughboys added a cloth haversack and a knapsack, though most soldiers adopted the more comfortable blanket roll worn horseshoe-fashion across the body.[66]

The Ordnance Department experimented with and issued various styles of load-bearing equipment during the 1870s with the objective of finding a better means for the soldier to transport his kit. Although soldiers wore such equipment in garrison, when ordered to do so for inspections, they persisted in rejecting such devices in favor of the time-honored blanket roll when actually in the field. While the designs of the equipment were found to be impractical by the troops, their failure cannot be attributed to any lack of interest on the part of ordnance officers to seek improvements. That the basic principle had merit is borne out in equipment designs used by U.S. soldiers beginning in 1910 and continuing in various forms to the present day.

Perhaps the most significant piece of personal equipment to come out of the Indian campaigns was the cartridge belt, an item initially fabricated at the field level as a practical and comfortable means for the soldier to carry metallic ammunition so that it would be readily available in combat. After several years of resisting the idea, the army finally manufactured official patterns. In various forms the looped cartridge belt became a universally popular accouterment for the rest of the century and in pocket-form continued in use until the late 1950s.

Cavalrymen, too, used virtually the same equipment that had been issued late in the war. Seventh Cavalry First Sergeant John Ryan described their weapons: "The revolvers that we used at that time were the Colt, six shot, .44 caliber. The carbines . . . consisted of the Spencer eight shot, a very good weapon. We also had a saber. Sabers . . . were about as much good as a broom stick fighting Indians." The Spencer carbine had a seven-shot magazine and fired a rim fire metallic cartridge. The army issued both Colt and Remington .44-caliber percussion revolvers, the best designs to survive the war, for nearly a decade afterward. The leather accouterments—saber belt, holster, cartridge box, and carbine sling—were the same patterns that had been in use since 1861.[67]

The Sharps .52-caliber percussion-primed carbine had been a reliable, effective weapon also favored by the Union cavalry during the war. Being a single-shot breech loader, it readily lent itself to being converted to fire metallic cartridges. In the late 1860s the Ordnance Department contracted with the Sharps Rifle Company to modify thousands of the surplus arms already stored in government arsenals. The conversion of Sharps carbines to .50/70 at once resulted in a considerably more powerful cavalry arm and lent itself to the army's effort to simplify logistics by using the same ammunition in both carbines and rifles. However, sacrificing fire power in favor of range was not immediately appreciated by many cavalry troopers. When the Eighth Cavalry exchanged its Spencers for Sharps in the spring of 1870, one trooper opined: "Don't like them half so well as the seven shooters." The Sharps conversion carbine nevertheless proved to be a rugged arm having considerably longer range and therefore was generally better adapted to plains warfare than the rather anemic Spencer.[68]

The early 1870s saw the army experimenting with a variety of improved firearms designs in an effort to find a replacement for the Springfield and Sharps conversions. The Springfield system, designed at the National Armory, won out over the other types, some of which were as good as if not better in some respects than the Springfield. In 1873 the army abandoned the .50 caliber in favor of a more refined pattern of Springfield chambered for a cartridge having better ballistic qualities: "This was a 45-caliber single-shot gun," a former Second Cavalryman explained. "The cavalry and infantry were using the same model of Springfield, except the infantry gun barrel was longer and this weapon's cartridges contained seventy grains of powder, while the shorter cavalry rifle, known as the 'carbine,' used cartridges containing only fifty-five grains of powder." Rather than drawing the less powerful carbine ammunition for their men, some experienced cavalry company commanders requisitioned infantry loads, which were advantageous at longer ranges even in carbines. First Sergeant Ryan personally preferred using rifle ammunition, attesting that "I traded some of my . . . fifty-five grain cartridges for some of the . . . seventy grain cartridges when I wished to do any long range shooting." The Model 1873 Springfield was extremely well made and was as accurate as any military-grade rifle of its day. While critics have faulted the Ordnance Department for being wedded to an outmoded design, it should be remembered that virtually all of the recognized military powers of the world at that time, including Great Britain, France, and Germany, also were armed with comparable single-shot arms.[69]

Some infantrymen complained that the Springfield rifle—nicknamed the "long Tom"—was "very cumbersome and heavy," even though it weighed only nine pounds. "We could have been better armed," said former sergeant James S. Hamilton, First Infantry. Another soldier considered the rifles "good killers—[but] hard on your shoulder when firing." Recoil was especially evident after the Ordnance Department began issuing rifle ammunition loaded with five hundred grain bullets. As a prank, cavalry troopers enjoyed slipping a rifle cartridge into a comrade's belt on the firing range just to see him wince when it was fired.[70]

Soldiers were strictly accountable for their weapons and equipment, each item bearing an inflated price to be charged against the man's pay if it were lost or damaged through his own negligence. Prior to 1868 Springfield Armory did not apply serial numbers to weapons at the time of manufacture, so it was possible for a soldier to cover a loss by obtaining a substitute rifle. In one such instance Third Infantryman John Stotts accidentally clogged and split the barrel of his new Model 1866 rifle while hunting along the Arkansas River. The unharmed Stotts panicked and threw the rifle in the river to hide the evidence. The trouble was, he then had no rifle. His bunkie came to his rescue by sneaking into the nearby camp of a unit on the march to New Mexico and stole one of their rifles of the same pattern. "Some poor fellow of the 38th Col[ored] Infantry had a gun to pay for instead of me,"

Stotts proudly announced. As a measure of control some units marked weapons with unique numbers, sometimes adding the company letter and number of the regiment. The loss of a weapon could be a serious matter. "If a soldier loses his carbine, he is charged one hundred dollars and fifty dollars for a pistol, while they cost the government eighteen dollars for a pistol and twenty-four dollars for a carbine," First Sergeant Ryan attested. After the advent of serial numbers on Springfield rifles and carbines, company quartermaster sergeants recorded the numbers of the weapons and the names of the men to whom they were issued. Thus fixing responsibility for lost, sold, or damaged weapons was relatively easy. Even though these measures and increased physical security made theft more difficult, desertions continued to result in the loss of arms because they could be readily sold to civilians.[71]

American soldiers have had a long tradition of possessing personal weapons, in addition to their issue arms, and those serving during the Indian campaigns were no different. Acquiring commercial guns, especially pistols, and knives seems to have been a fairly common practice. Some company commanders insisted that personal arms be turned over to the first sergeant, both for safekeeping and to prevent misuse. In other instances the men took their revolvers to local towns or whiskey ranches for personal protection. Less frequently, soldiers purchased their own long arms, and a few even found their way into combat. An Eighteenth Infantry corporal serving at Fort C. F. Smith in 1866, for example, acquired his own Henry .44 repeating rifle. Another well-known example was First Sergeant John Ryan, Seventh Cavalry, who purchased a .45/70 Sharps hunting rifle, with telescope, and took it on the 1876 Sioux Expedition. Will Barnes, a Signal Corpsman at Fort Apache, Arizona Territory, in the 1880s provided himself with a Marlin repeater, also chambered for the .45 government cartridge.[72]

The retirement of career staff officers in the early 1880s and their replacement by more enlightened bureau chiefs, the likes of Quartermaster General Samuel B. Holabird, accelerated reforms that heralded better conditions for enlisted men. General living conditions improved in seemingly minor ways that were nonetheless important to soldiers by making army life more bearable. In 1885 his department began substituting "woven wire bunk bottoms" in lieu of the unforgiving wood slats used with both the double-decker and iron bunks. Cotton-filled mattresses supplanted the archaic concept of hay-filled ticks, and for the first time American soldiers were provided pillows, sheets, and pillow cases. Upon the receipt of these items at Fort Custer, a grateful First Cavalryman exclaimed: "Who would have very well believed four years ago that we would have spring mattresses, linen [*sic*: muslin] sheets, and feather pillows today? . . . We are all the better for them in mind, body and allegiance to the giver of all these good things—our Uncle Sam."[73]

By about 1890 all but the most remote surviving frontier posts boasted piped water systems, ice-making machines, and street lamps. Steam pumps and hydrants greatly enhanced safety by increasing the ability of garrisons to combat fire.

The army had at least recognized the inconsistencies in food preparation, as reflected in the publication of its first official cookbook in 1879, with an expanded edition released four years later. Still, relying on the availability of a cookbook assumed that all men were literate in the English language, which many were not, and that all would study it assiduously, which many did not. The quality of the food turned out by unmotivated men with little or no experience with cooking continued to be the subject of bitter complaint. As Adjutant General Richard C. Drum noted: "The accidental presence of a good cook in one company is productive of great discontent among the men of the other companies at the same post, who contrast . . . the positive distress in their own, resulting from ill-prepared and ill-cooked food." Nevertheless, Drum's plea for regularly enlisted cooks went unheeded and the army offered no formal training for cooks and bakers until after the end of the Indian campaigns.[74]

Late in the era, however, the concept of the consolidated mess was introduced at some large posts in an effort to improve the quality and uniformity of food and more efficiently use the men as cooks and kitchen police in the hope of reducing desertions. The idea was to have willing men permanently assigned as cooks on extra pay, with the mess hall and its operation supervised by a commissioned officer. This system, which became more prevalent during the 1890s, went a long way toward improving mess hall food, but it would not be until the Spanish-American War that the army finally included company cooks in the official table of organization.[75]

So common were canned goods in the army by the early 1880s that the Subsistence Department began stocking patented can openers. In

1884 Major John P. Hawkins announced: "There is hardly a military station in the land where officers and soldiers and their families do not habitually use canned foods, and as a class Army people are without doubt the largest consumer of canned articles in proportion to their number of any other in the country . . . [and] army surgeons . . . tell they have no knowledge of any cases of poisoning from canned goods." The army contracted directly with commercial canneries for meats, fish, fruit, vegetables, and preserves of all kinds. At the end of the decade, in an attempt to expand the products available to soldiers, the Subsistence Department even purchased a nondairy butter substitute, which the surgeon at Fort Bliss, Texas, rated as "pretty poor stuff," suggesting that it more nearly resembled wax.[76]

In a further move to enhance the soldier's environment, and at the same time relieve the company fund of its obligation to purchase kitchen and mess hall furnishings, the Quartermaster Department started contracting in 1889 for standardized ironstone tableware, eating utensils, and kitchen tools, including coffee mills. Companies therefore had more money available to purchase nonissue foods and other items.[77]

During the 1880s, as the once-great buffalo herds were decimated by commercial hunters, the bulky army overcoats made of their hides gave way to trimmer blanket-lined canvas coats and special canvas winter headgear for troops in northern latitudes. Troops in the Southwest were cheered by the availability of white cotton summer uniforms and cork summer helmets. Also issued were brown canvas fatigue outfits to satisfy the often-voiced complaint that soldiers were compelled to work in their more expensive and uncomfortable woolen garments. A blue woolen overshirt, along with a cotton undershirt, replaced the universal gray wool shirt that had been worn next to the skin, which had been making soldiers miserable for the previous two decades. As another concession to comfort, the Quartermaster Department went to the extent of providing lightweight barrack shoes made of canvas and leather as an alternative to wearing their heavy leather shoes and boots while off duty.

Among the sweeping changes to the soldier's wardrobe implemented during the 1880s were the issue of heavy and lightweight blue woolen fatigue uniforms better suited to varying climates than the single weight previously imposed on the men regardless of where they might be stationed. At the same time, the number of sizes of blouses and pants was increased and the depot patterns were refined so that most soldiers were able to get a reasonably close fit with garments off the shelf, though tailoring garrison uniforms to affect a rakish appearance reached faddish proportions. As a concession to this practice, the Quartermaster Department made available "unmade" blouses and trousers. These were shipped from the manufacturing depots precut but unassembled, giving the soldier the option to draw a uniform at less cost and then have his company tailor custom-make it. The decade also gave rise to the Quartermaster Department's purchasing of higher-quality fabrics and employing improved dying techniques, so that American soldiers were as well dressed as any army in the world.

Meanwhile, the Ordnance Department had continued a quest, albeit half-hearted, for a magazine repeater to replace the single-shot Springfield. Objections were loudest following the disastrous defeat of the Seventh Cavalry at the Battle of the Little Bighorn in 1876, prompting questions about the suitability of the Springfield and why it had not been supplanted by the Winchester .44 repeating rifle used by many Indian warriors. What many of the Springfield's critics failed to understand was the relationship between the .45 Government cartridge, which had the power and range needed for military purposes, and the state of arms technology at the time. The design of the Winchester, while perfectly adequate for its far less powerful cartridge, had a comparatively fragile action that could not be adapted to handle the considerably larger government round, which the army was not about to sacrifice. Therein lay the paradox.

Sometimes ignored is that on two separate occasions, once in the late 1870s and again the early 1880s, the Ordnance Department invited submission of magazine repeaters chambered for the government cartridge for testing. Although most of these arms incorporated the bolt action design, all thirty failed to meet the army's expectations for durability, reliability, and accuracy. When the results of the second field trial were tabulated in 1885, the troops overwhelmingly still favored the single-shot Springfield. Consequently, the chief of ordnance opted to postpone replacement of the venerable Springfield to "wait a reasonable time for further developments of magazine arms."[78]

Events in Europe left no doubt that repeating rifles were the way of the future and that weapons using small-caliber smokeless powder ammunition had relegated to obsolescence the .45-caliber Springfield.

The handwriting was on the wall—if the United States should find itself in a conventional war with a foreign power, its soldiers would be hopelessly disadvantaged. The army finally retired its beloved "trapdoor" Springfield in 1892 in favor of a weapon of Norwegian design, the Krag-Jorgensen, a .30-caliber rifle with a five-shot magazine. The Krag soon earned a reputation for fine quality and extreme accuracy, though the design was already outclassed by clip-charged German Mausers in the hands of several European nations, including, significantly, Spain. Taking lessons from the Spanish-American War, the U.S. Army also adopted a rifle mirroring the Mauser in 1903, a design that would carry it to the eve of the Second World War.

By the early part of twentieth century, other seeds of reform planted during the Indian Wars would come to fruition in the form of commodious, steam-heated brick barracks, trained cooks serving wholesome food in consolidated messes, and further modernization of clothing and equipment. Soldiers in the new age of olive drab could thank their predecessors of the Indian Wars for many of the comparative luxuries from which they now benefited.

CHAPTER 8

"Offensive in Every Particular"

Medicine, Hygiene, and Sanitation

Military posts had a commonality with frontier towns—if approached from downwind, they could be smelled before they were seen. The offensive stench that wafted from a fort was a combination of odors emanating from dozens of outdoor privies—"sinks" in army parlance—garbage, offal rotting in open barrels or on the ground, stagnant water, pig pens, animal manure and urine, all of that seasoned by wood smoke. Commanding officers often gave scant attention to matters of sanitation and hygiene despite the best efforts of army doctors, who themselves possessed only limited knowledge of disease prevention. Not until 1874 did regulations require post surgeons to prepare monthly reports concerning the sanitary conditions of posts (addressing cooking, water quality, drainage, and hygiene) and to make recommendations for correcting the deficiencies discovered. Nonetheless, post commanders, many of whom considered the doctors a nuisance that had to be tolerated, often ignored their reports or found excuses not to take corrective action. Shortly after his arrival at Fort Laramie, Wyoming Territory, in 1874, Acting Assistant Surgeon George W. Towar found the post

> badly dilapidated & out of repair. The sinks in rear of the men's quarters being especially bad & in some instances constituted a nuisance. . . . The general police of the Laramie river in the

immediate vicinity of the post is bad. And the peaks of manure from the cavalry stables and the filth & rubbish from the post, all of which has accumulated & been deposited for many years on the north side of and immediately contiguous to the post, is offensive in every particular.[1]

The daily fatigue parties, along with prisoners, made an effort to police the post, but even so sanitation was limited. Garbage and other refuse were transported in carts or wagons to the place designated for a dumping ground, usually a nearby ravine or stream, or simply deposited on the open prairie some distance away. They were not often burned, unless an officer directed that certain surveyed property, particularly discarded ordnance items, actually be destroyed to prevent further use. Otherwise the waste lay in heaps to disintegrate over time, thus attracting scavenging animals and swarms of flies that made their way back and forth to the kitchens and mess tables.[2]

Sinks were a universal fixture behind every officer's quarters, barracks, laundress quarters, quartermaster corral, and other inhabited buildings, although guardhouses commonly furnished only buckets or tubs for toilet purposes in the prison rooms, which were emptied by the inmates during morning police.[3] Most privies were of the common pit variety. Fatigue details covered the accumulated excrement with dry earth and sometimes quicklime to create a caustic reaction. When the vault filled to capacity, it was covered and the enclosure was relocated over a new one. The houses themselves received little attention, though some post surgeons pleaded that they be cleaned with carbolic acid or at least soap and water. That seldom happened, as reflected in one surgeon's repeated appeal to his commander, calling attention to "the very offensive condition of the Company Sinks[, which] besides being liable to produce disease are disgusting to all who are brought into near proximity to the same."[4]

By the late 1880s some progressive-minded post commanders adopted consolidated sinks flushed with running water. Such a facility at Fort Bidwell, California, was located "at the edge of a deep pit, through which ran a small stream and which in winter months was dry . . . [inside] was a rail some 20 feet long . . . upon which a man sat his posterior hanging over the pit . . . at one end of the building was a wooden trough lined with tin [urinal] which emptied into the pit. The pit was well limed." A similar privy constructed of concrete at Fort Laramie in 1886 was flushed by means of a water pipe directly into the adjacent river.[5]

Nineteenth-century working-class men normally bathed and shaved once a week, and the army was no different. The Saturday (or Sunday) night bath was a tradition in American culture, and thus the army's ritual of devoting that day to cleaning. The army expected soldiers to be clean, yet so completely ignored the means by which they were to bathe that the Quartermaster Department did not even stock galvanized tubs. Reporting on the hygienic condition of the army in 1875, Assistant Surgeon John S. Billings bitterly observed: "The providing of conveniences for bathing . . . is too much neglected, and were it not for the fact that the officers and the men . . . provide themselves with such makeshifts for bathing . . . as can be obtained, the results would probably be serious." The same year a First Cavalry officer attested: "I have served for the period of twenty-one years in the Cavalry . . . and have never been stationed at one post during that time where a bathhouse had been provided for the enlisted men, except one that I myself built for the company." He added that even after a concerned merchant donated the lumber, the post commander had threatened the quartermaster with arrest for loaning a team to haul it to the post. At Fort Phil Kearny, Dakota Territory, Sergeant Samuel Gibson and his comrades of the Twenty-Seventh Infantry "had no place in barracks to wash, and after the creeks were frozen over we could not take a bath until they thawed out the following spring." Bathing in nearby creeks during warm weather was the expected norm at nearly all frontier posts, but winter imposed an inconvenience on those men accustomed to a weekly bath.[6]

Private Eddie Matthews said that it reminded him of bathing at home on Saturday night with his little brothers. "We borrow a tub from one of the Laundresses, put on a large pot of water . . . jump in . . . wash yourself as you can in front, then get one of the boys to wash your back." A company occasionally included a man or two who had not been reared to appreciate regular bathing. In those instances his comrades "sometimes take the affair into their own hands, and, finding from their captain that they will not be interfered with, the untidy one is taken on a compulsory journey to the creek and 'ducked' until the soldiers consider him endurable."[7]

Soldiers sometimes shaved themselves, but the more common practice was to be shaved weekly by the company barber using a straight-razor. His was not an official position; as in the case of the tailor, at least one man in every company served informally in that capacity. According to regulations, the hair was "to be short; the beard to be worn at the pleasure of the individual, but, when worn, to be kept short and neatly trimmed." Maintaining reasonably short hair was more than just a military requirement; it was often a practical necessity, according to Private Henry Hubman. Writing from Fort Assinniboine, Montana Territory, to his brother in 1882, Hubman explained: "We have to keep our hair cut short so that we can catch the lice." While full beards had been common during the war, especially among the volunteers, they were far less prevalent among regulars on the frontier. Sergeant Samuel Gibson related: "All of our men were smooth shaved . . . most of the grown men wore mustaches, but no beards." Photographs taken during the era indicate that among soldiers mustaches were by far the most common form of facial hair, varied now and then by a Van Dyke, but beards were a comparative rarity. According to a man serving in the Seventh Cavalry in 1891, the company barber's price for a haircut and shave was twenty-five cents.[8]

In the field of medicine, the Civil War had been a great proving ground for the treatment of projectile wounds and executing amputations as expeditiously as possible but had resulted in few advances in the areas of disease prevention and general health improvement. Drawing a medical analogy, one army surgeon wrote of the state of army medicine in the immediate postwar years: "It is not unfair to say that hygiene . . . was yet unborn. . . . Medicine was in labor with the twins bacteriology and hygiene. . . . the puerperal state was to be long and hectic, but mother and children were to survive." In the meantime, however, many soldiers would not survive.[9]

Through the years the field of medicine had produced a few signal accomplishments—an immunization for smallpox, for example. An effective vaccination against this highly contagious disease that had once ravaged populations in both Europe and America had been discovered near the end of the eighteenth century and was in widespread use by the middle of the nineteenth. Assistant Surgeon Washington Matthews, stationed at Fort Rice, Dakota Territory, in 1869, made the effort to obtain vaccine for his garrison but regretted that after treating the children and only twenty-two high-risk soldiers "there is but a limited amount of virus, we cannot vaccinate all."[10] Yet the causes of many other maladies that claimed human life were not well understood, if at all. The source of cholera, an extreme and deadly form of dysentery, had been correctly linked to contaminated water, though the real cause (bacteria) was not known. Most physicians at that time believed that the source of infectious diseases was miasmas, toxic vapors borne in the air. Consequently, army doctors viewed abundant hospital ventilation, and the removal of garbage and other sources of foul odors, as of the utmost importance, while they ignored cleansing their hands, instruments, and surroundings before performing surgery. Being fast was considered paramount, both to reduce exposure to those air-borne contaminants and to minimize the patient's liability to going into shock. Pain-killing drugs such as chloroform and laudanum (a solution of opium and alcohol) made such procedures bearable for the patient.

Even though isolated outbreaks of cholera occurred in frontier garrisons, they were not common and simply had to run their course once the source—often human waste leaching into wells—was identified. Former Tenth Cavalryman James Tucker recalled: "In 1867 my company lay out on Wilson's [Creek, Kansas], which was a stage stand. There we buried 13 men with cholera. . . . We just dug holes and buried them as we didn't have any coffins and no doctors."[11] Typhoid fever and other forms of acute dysentery, usually stemming from polluted water, contaminated food, or rotting carcasses and other matter, frequently claimed soldiers' lives through the effects of septicemia, diarrhea, extreme dehydration, and blood loss.

In the late 1860s outbreaks of scurvy ravaged many western garrisons. Surgeons reported 132 cases in 1868, followed by 198 the next year. The cause, a severe deficiency of nutrients found in certain foods not included in the army ration, particularly citrus fruits and fresh vegetables, had been known for decades, yet the ration table included only one reliable antiscorbutic, vinegar. It was assumed that companies would procure potatoes, onions, or other sources of essential vitamin C, but that was not always possible. Regular units were only then occupying, or reoccupying, forts in the West. Many did not maintain gardens when faced with the higher priorities of building those forts, guarding travel routes, and participating in active field operations. An

Eighteenth Infantry soldier who had been at Fort Phil Kearny in 1867 described the effects: "All the men that were at the fort at the time it was established got the scurvy. Some lost teeth and some the use of their legs. In the spring when the grass came up there were lots of wild onions and the scurvy gang was ordered out to eat them." Farther south at Fort Caspar, Dakota Territory, Second Cavalry trooper William F. Hynes contended that he and his comrades were so desperate for "vegetables of any kind . . . we gathered in early spring the weed called 'lamb's quarters.' . . . It proved a good dish and was said to prevent scurvy." The appearance of scurvy steadily declined in the ranks after 1870 and eventually nearly disappeared, presumably because more posts had gardens and greater access to canned fruits and vegetables, particularly tomatoes.[12]

Other afflictions most often cited by post surgeons included malaria and other fevers, diarrhea, rheumatism, venereal disease, and catarrh (sinus infection). Tuberculosis—consumption as it was then known—was less prevalent, though highly contagious and often fatal. The warmer southern regions of the West, notably Arizona and Texas, experienced higher rates of illness and death than did colder areas in the north. This apparent contradiction was reflected in a letter from Private George Cranston, serving at Tubac, Arizona Territory, advising his family: "As for the health of the Company, it is very poor. We muster about 70 men and have only about 15 for duty, but the weather is getting cooler and more healthy." Surgeon John Vance Lauderdale reinforced Cranston's comment with a broader perspective: "There is no part of the country that is so severe on the health of our soldiers, as the territory of Arizona." The Southwest afforded considerably longer periods of hot dusty weather, which were both debilitating to the men and conducive to the proliferation of bacteria. In the Department of Dakota the temperate season was short, the winters long but comparatively healthy. "I have not been on the sick list but once since I joined the Army," an Irish soldier wrote from Fort Fred Steele, Wyoming Territory. "Soldiering is a healthy profession in this country. . . . I think this is the most healthy spot in the world. We have pure mountain air." Regardless of unsanitary conditions, the majority of soldiers, like this man, seldom contracted anything more serious than the common cold.[13]

Soldiers generally had little experience with either doctors or hospitals prior to entering the service. In the nineteenth century most ailments were treated at home with home remedies, and a hospital was considered a place where one went to die. The post hospital "is so inhospitable as to present few attractions, and all keep away from it as long as possible," claimed a soldier stationed in Texas. Private Herman S. Searl, an Eighteenth Infantryman serving as a hospital attendant at Fort Fetterman, Wyoming Territory, in 1868, described the recently completed facility in a letter to his parents. "They have pretended to finish the Hospital . . . it is a shame to place pacients [sic] in such a place as this. It is a log building chinked and muded [sic] in the cracks between the logs. The floor is not fit for a barn floor. The roof is no beter [sic] and the wind has a fine chance to circulate freely through them both." A sympathetic army wife mourned: "The Post Hospital seemed to me a lonesome place to die in, although the surgeon and soldier attendants were kind to the sick men." Bed rest, special diet, and some kindness were often the best treatment that could be offered.[14]

Before the late 1880s post hospitals were primitive by almost any standard. Assistant Surgeon William H. Arthur vividly recalled the facility that greeted him upon his arrival at Fort Washakie, Wyoming Territory:

> The hospital was a log building chinked with mortar . . . "built by the labor of the troops." It was typical of the frontier post hospital . . . [,] a long parallelogram of five rooms, a ward of twelve beds, an office, dispensary, kitchen and store-room, heated by wood burning stoves, lighted by candles and ventilated by leaks in the chinking, all around the windows. The water supply consisted of two or more pork barrels outside the kitchen. In winter . . . the water supply was simply ice or snow melted on the kitchen stove.[15]

According to the size of the garrison, hospitals usually embraced one or two wards containing a dozen beds each. A notable exception to the norm was Fort Union, New Mexico Territory, which boasted a large hospital with six wards and a total capacity of one hundred patients. Approaching the concept of a medical center, it provided care for the garrison of several companies and a higher level of "referral" treatment for patients transferred from other posts in the territory. In addition, it also served the needs of several hundred civilian employees at the extensive Fort Union Quartermaster Depot. Post hospitals, besides having a storeroom or separate storehouse for medical supplies, almost always had a small "dead house" situated in the backyard where corpses were laid out, sponged clean, and dressed prior to burial.

Army doctors were of two classes: regular army medical officers with the title "surgeon" or "assistant surgeon" and civilian physicians contracted by the army as "acting assistant surgeons." Assistant surgeons held the rank and pay of cavalry lieutenants for three years, after which they were eligible for promotion to captain. Surgeons ranked as majors or colonels. The position of acting assistant surgeon had been created during the Civil War to meet the demand for doctors and was retained during the Indian campaigns because the army was fragmented at so many far-flung stations. With the Medical Department numbering less than two hundred officers, there simply were not enough to go around. Contract doctors frequently served independently as post surgeons for small garrisons, and at larger forts they assisted the regular army physician. Still, the army had to be extremely cautious and discriminating in its selection of contract surgeons.

By the mid-nineteenth century the title "doctor" had become a status symbol in American society and the profession was rife with imposters practicing outright quackery. In that day three avenues existed for becoming a physician: graduate from a medical school, apprentice under an experienced doctor, or simply purchase a diploma from any number of fraudulent sources and then open a practice. Well aware of the situation, the Medical Department did its best to weed out unqualified men by requiring civilian applicants to undergo a rigid examination, lasting up to a week, covering all aspects of the profession, including anatomy, diagnosis, treatment, diet, surgery, and pharmacy. A high percentage of applicants failed to pass, but during the Indian Wars the rules were sometimes bent in an effort to acquire enough physicians to meet current needs. Regular assistant surgeons also had to submit to a demanding professional as well as personal examination initially and again five years after first being appointed. Testing extended to knowledge of foreign languages, mathematics, and geography. Depending on the outcome, they were either promoted to captain or dismissed from the service. The majority of post surgeons, particularly the regular army doctors, proved to be as competent as the state of the profession admitted, many also being accomplished naturalists who studied and recorded the flora and fauna of the West.[16]

Army physicians frequently treated civilians in addition to their military patients simply because they were often the only doctors available within great distances on the frontier. Army regulations were silent on the matter of treating civilians, though post records indicate that it was often done because physicians were unable ethically to turn away the sick or injured. Those patients who were able to pay were charged a daily fee to reimburse the hospital for the costs of their care. One surgeon related that he treated "all the cowboys, miners, and odds and ends of civilians . . . who came in for a radius of 150 miles, and this was all charity practice, for the people were very poor."[17]

Until the late 1880s, the only enlisted man permanently attached to the hospital was the steward who, like an ordnance sergeant, was a member of the noncommissioned staff of the army. In practice, he was the sergeant in charge of the hospital operation on a daily basis and was responsible not only for compounding medications but for supervising the soldiers detailed as cooks and nurses as well as the hospital laundress. Beyond that, he computed and drew the rations, maintained property and supply inventories, and saw to the cleanliness of the entire building. A hospital steward serving in 1874 outlined his harried existence:

> As to his "regulation" duties, first he must be an efficient and correct druggist; second a fair clerk; and third, he must be a sober man by day and by night, as well as honest, reliable and intelligent. . . . But he has besides them other numerous and never ending tasks to perform, if he can, to the satisfaction of his post surgeon, . . . even if his post surgeon be a citizen contract doctor. Unless it be a four or six company post, where a steward may possibly manage to have an assistant in his dispensary, he must be his own druggist, shopboy, clerk, grocer, and servant, and in addition thereto, the moment the doctor goes outside the post for a walk or necessary recreation, he must be able to meet any emergency as a kind of acting post surgeon.[18]

Although being a steward was supposedly a nonmedical position, a steward of five years' experience contradicted that impression, stating that it was "an almost daily necessity either by the request, consent, or absence of the Post Surgeon, to look after nearly the whole of the hospital and outside sick myself. I have been on the scout [in the field] for months at a time without any doctor, and had as a mere matter of course to treat, prescribe for, and nurse, both sick officers and sick men myself." The steward's quarters were invariably located adjacent to the hospital, whereas the post surgeon resided on officers' row, thus placing the steward in a position where he would be available to handle matters that might arise during the night and at other times when the surgeon was absent.[19]

That was not the only inequity perceived by the stewards; another concerned their linear rank and command status as noncombatants. "A steward ranks next above the first sergeant of a company," grumbled one steward. "And yet, although he belongs to the non-commissioned staff of the Army, he is out-ranked at any post by the regimental sergeant-major and quartermaster sergeant, and further at most posts, there being only an acting sergeant major of post, who may even be a private, the steward is obliged in certain respects to accept directions, instructions or orders from him." With regiments so widely dispersed across the frontier regions, the practice of delegating acting post sergeant-majors to handle the necessary administrative duties could not be avoided, so the situation had no immediate resolution.[20]

In the absence of any army dentists, that responsibility often fell on the shoulders of the stewards. In 1873 a doctor outlined the situation to the editor of the *Army & Navy Journal*:

> The teeth seem particularly prone to undergo decay at remote stations . . . where a dentist is never seen, and [it] is especially desirable that such stations should be furnished with at least a sufficiency of instruments to meet the immediate demands of those who find their teeth going, and to hold the process of decay in check till the services of a practical dentist are available. . . . Medical officers could attend to the requisite cleaning and filling, which really requires the exercise of but ordinary care and mechanical skill.[21]

However desirable regular dental treatment might have been, the basic instrument kit issued to army doctors included only tools needed for tooth extractions, not the mechanical drills and other instruments necessary for decay removal and filling cavities. Thus, even though properly equipped surgeons undoubtedly could have saved the teeth of many soldiers, extraction became the only remedy for toothache. "I had to suffer for several days with a tooth while at Cimmerrone [sic] before a [civilian] Doctor could be found to draw it out," an Eighth Cavalryman wrote from New Mexico Territory. "When I did have it drawn the Dr. was drunk, and had to make two or three pulls at it. Hurt a great deal but felt all right after [he] got it out." Now and then a lucky patient encountered a dentist advanced enough to employ nitrous oxide as an anesthetic, but on the frontier whiskey was more common, though not very effective.[22]

Itinerant civilian dentists occasionally visited military posts for a few days to address the dental needs of the garrison. In one such instance, Denver dentist B. H. Rogers responded to an officer's request by traveling some two hundred miles to attend the personnel at Fort Laramie. The post surgeon extended Rogers professional courtesies, making office space and a sleeping room available in the hospital for the duration of his stay. The trouble was, trained dentists were seldom present when emergencies arose. More often than not, the hospital steward substituted in his "nonmedical" capacity. The person afflicted with toothache usually endured the pain for as long as possible before finally submitting to the steward's unskilled hand to remove it. Private Emil Bode, Sixteenth Infantry, left a vivid description of his experience:

> I was soon resting my head upon the back of a chair while this worthy man of quinine pills and medicine stood over me with a pair of tongs, having hold on my sick molar. Our combined efforts could only bring [it] halfway out and I was dismissed, unable to speak or close my jaws. A little shake and pressure brought the tooth back to its place, permitted to reoccupy its former position, which it held without giving further annoyance.[23]

Experiencing dental problems while in garrison could be bad enough, but in the field they could be positively excruciating. Private Edgar Hoffner, a First Cavalry trooper, related the degree of desperation that he reached during the Sheepeater Campaign in 1879: "I was troubled with an aching tooth during the night, and having no dentist, I sat astride a log and pried out the offender with my pocket knife." A relieved Hoffner continued the march without any apparent ill-effects.[24]

It is necessary to view oral care in the frontier army, however, within the larger context of the general populace at that time. Regular periodic dental examinations were not habitual among nineteenth-century Americans, with the possible exception of those affluent enough to afford such services. The great majority of people went to a dentist only when they experienced pain, if then. A scientific study of oral health among Seventh Cavalrymen killed at the Battle of the Little Bighorn concluded that 27 percent of the teeth examined exhibited decay and that "antemortem tooth loss most likely resulted from caries, abscess, and periodontal disease, and it indicates the result of a lifetime of dental disease rather than simply the active state of oral ill health at the time of death."[25]

Teeth that became troublesome usually were extracted, until the individual lost so many teeth that he was compelled either to adopt a diet of soft foods or to resort to dentures. Nearing the end of his enlistment in 1874, Private Eddie Matthews admitted that he had lost several teeth during his five years in the army. When his sister suggested that he could buy better teeth rather than trying to save his own, Matthews responded: "Perhaps I can, but this also will cost both pain and inconvenience. . . . Although what teeth I have left are not very good, I hate to think of parting with them." Looking back on his army service, another man commented: "My teeth were good when I enlisted, but no provision looking to the welfare of soldiers' teeth was made by the Government, and I only saw one dentist while in was in the army. I had him do some work for me at my own expense. When I left the army my teeth were getting in bad shape."[26]

Being responsible for funds and a post's supply of medicinal alcohol sometimes proved too tempting for hospital stewards, some being found guilty of misappropriation and embezzlement. Soon after a new post commander arrived at Fort Davis, Texas, he reviewed the steward's books and found great discrepancies between the amount of liquor requisitioned and that dispensed to patients, compared with the quantity on hand. At Fort Yuma, Arizona Territory, the surgeon discovered that his new steward was a drunkard and filed charges against the man. "And how rare to find a Hospital Steward, of any character that is, thoroughly good," he despaired. "The one that just left me had been in the service since Forty-eight. . . . He was about the best I have seen, but he too had a fall from the strict path of temperance once this summer." The amount of liquor in the inventory at Fort Laramie provides an insight to why stewards were sometimes tempted to imbibe: 282 quarts and two barrels (77 gallons) of whiskey, 72 quarts brandy, 231 bottles of sherry, 27 quarts port.[27]

Nursing at frontier army hospitals was strictly a male occupation and by regulation nurses were soldiers detailed from the companies. A correspondent to the *Army & Navy Journal* in 1873 contended that "intelligence and sobriety should be the qualifications . . . [but] under the present plan it is hard to find men suitable for the responsible position of a hospital attendant. Should good men be found (which is not always the case), company commanders generally object . . . to having their best men detailed away from their companies." First sergeants, as might be expected, usually detailed the most expendable men, yet "no one wanted the job," according to Private Herman Harbers, Third Infantry. "The pay was extra duty pay, but the duties that the men had to perform did not suit them, so it was hard to get a man to stick to that job." Most soldiers did not relish their assigned tasks of monitoring patients, often overnight, changing bedding, assisting patients with eating and drinking, and helping those that needed it either to reach the latrine or use a bedpan. One of the nurses tended the hospital garden, cared for the livestock, and delivered rations from the storehouse. In a December 1876 letter to his girlfriend, Private George W. McAnulty, Ninth Infantry, confided: "Doubtless you will think I am a rather awkward Nurse. . . . I do not like it at all to[o] much confinement & sitting up at night. Does not agree with me. Am trying to get relieved every day but cannot succeed."[28]

A few men nevertheless preferred nursing to daily duty with the company. Even though nurses may have found some of the ward work disagreeable, for the most part it was not physically demanding. Besides, they got to sleep away from the squad room; were excused from roll calls, guard, and inspections; and usually enjoyed better meals that they would have gotten at the mess hall. "I have been detailed for duty in the Hospital, which I am inclined to think this is a good place," a soldier commented. "Eny [sic] way I shall try to keep it." Of course, the stewards valued such men and did their best to retain them. When elements of the Fourth Cavalry were ordered out on campaign in 1876, Hospital Steward Seymour Kitching at Camp Supply, Indian Territory, lamented: "Some of the best of the nurses and attendants will leave with their troops so I will be inconvenienced getting new ones to take their place." The quality of inexperienced nurses was always problematical, and in any event the steward was responsible for training them.[29]

"Hospital cooks with a knowledge of small order cooking and of special diet dishes were hard to find," one man remembered. Nevertheless surgeons appealed to company commanders to cooperate to every extent possible, reminding them that their own ill men would be among the recipients of the food. Even when a surgeon was fortunate enough to get a competent cook assigned, he had to train him in the nuances of preparing broths and other special dishes suiting the dietary needs of the patients. Whenever conditions permitted, they maintained a garden nearby to provide fresh vegetables for both patients and staff. It was not unusual, moreover, for the hospital to keep a cow for fresh milk and butter. In 1868 the post surgeon at Fort Laramie, Henry S. Schell, inventoried not only a cow but seven pigs and a flock of seventy chickens. Since most hospitals had no dedicated dining room, the cook and attendants ate in the kitchen.[30]

A female matron was employed intermittently at the hospital (occasionally two), charged with doing the laundry as well as general housekeeping and assisting the surgeon with childbirths. The job was an enviable one, because she was the only women officially recognized by the army with both regular pay (ten dollars per month) and a daily ration. A married steward usually arranged for his wife to occupy the position, an advantage to the operation because she resided at or near the hospital and to the steward because of her income and ration. When the steward was unmarried, the wife of another soldier eagerly applied for the vacancy.[31]

By modern standards, military medicine in the late nineteenth century was primitive but comparable to the medicine generally available, particularly in isolated conditions on the western frontier. Doctors, civilian as well as military, were only beginning to understand the relationship between germs and the transmission of disease, though all doctors current in the profession knew the value of disinfectants, along with soap and water, for preventing infection. Having no diagnostic tools beyond an oral thermometer, a stethoscope, and a blood pressure meter, army physicians became adept at making diagnoses mostly by evaluating external symptoms based on training, experience, common sense, and remaining current through constant reading of medical journals and texts. Even so, army doctors were largely helpless to aid victims of such maladies as pneumonia, meningitis, Bright's disease, consumption, and various forms of cancer—all common causes of death among postwar regulars.

One ex-soldier recalled that prevalent medicines included alcohol, iodine, quinine, castor oil, morphine sulfate, and blue mass pills, a pain-killer containing large amounts of mercury. When Private Reginald Bradley, Fourth Cavalry, was sent to the hospital with a cold, he "thought the treatment was good, because I got a little whiskey." The dispensing of medicinal whiskey and brandy being common knowledge, some soldiers used any excuse to report for sick call in hopes of receiving a liberal dose. Ginger, in solution with medicinal brandy, was commonly administered as a treatment for a variety of digestive system ailments, including stomachache, cramps, diarrhea and dysentery, and even cholera. Both liquor and quinine, sometimes in combination, were used extensively as medicine, along with the frequently prescribed "CC pill" (compound cathartic), for whatever might ail a person. "Scarcely any other medicine is use in the Army," insisted one soldier. "If you have a sore back, three pills are prescribed for you, if a bad cold, three pills, and for anything more a dose or two of quinine is considered just the thing."[32]

Men simply trying to shirk duty attempted to feign sickness in hopes of being excused and confined to quarters. Some contract surgeons unfamiliar with army ways may have fallen for the ruse until they gained more experience. But as a former first sergeant asserted: "The fellow who imagined he could fool an old army surgeon was speedily undeceived, for the army surgeon becomes wiser than any one [sic], owing to the kind of material with which he had to contend." The doctor would "cure" them by administering "the most nauseous medicines" and marked them for duty anyway. Private Axel Dahlgren, a

Swedish immigrant, considered some of the doctors overly calloused, because they "diagnosed anything that didn't call for the knife or saw as malingering."[33]

According to one veteran frontier army doctor, surgery was limited to amputations for frostbite, gunshot wounds, fractures, and dislocations. While treatment of superficial wounds, splinting broken bones, and amputations were well within the capabilities of army doctors, surgery involving opening the body cavity was still considered highly dangerous because of the risk of infection, often resulting in the death of the patient for lack of means to combat it. The onset of gangrene usually resulted in amputation of a limb or death when the unchecked infection spread to vital internal organs. Deprived of dedicated operating rooms, army surgeons improvised as best they could. After a cavalryman had been accidentally shot through the thigh, the surgeon determined that gangrene was inevitable and that the only alternative was to amputate the leg at the hip. Surgery was performed in the ward at night by candlelight on a table borrowed from a company mess hall. The hospital cook was pressed into service to administer the anesthetic. After the steward fainted and "was shoved under a bed and left to come to in his own good time," another patient crawled out of bed and volunteered to assist with the operation. Unsurprisingly, the patient died a few hours later. Although shock was an identifiable symptom, doctors lacked a full understanding of its prevention or its potentially deadly effects on the body. Following the amputation of a leg, Third Cavalryman Bernard Kelley's symptoms appeared to be improving until about two hours after the operation, when "he suddenly raised his head and shoulders . . . and looked down where this leg had been, then instantly fell back the eyes rolled up . . . and he was dead inside of three minutes."[34]

At stations on the northern Great Plains, frostbite was an ever-present danger during winter. Mild to moderate cases were usually treatable by gentle restoration of circulation, but severe cases were another matter. Writing from Fort Benton, Montana Territory, a soldier lamented: "Today the Surgeons are going to cut off both feet for a man named Steward from 'K' company who froze them last Monday while out on Escort Duty." He explained that after Steward had become so drunk that he could not walk, his comrades placed him in one of the wagons "and the first thing they knew he was froze." The patient apparently survived, a tribute to the surgeon's skill and luck, but others were not so fortunate. Sergeant James S. Hamilton, First Infantry, remembered a man who had suffered such extreme exposure that some of his internal organs were frozen. Unable to do anything for the soldier, the surgeon administered "a merciful drug to give him his last sleep. Treatment was not available to help. . . . The doctors were wonderful men and well trained but they were hampered by lack of equipment and drugs."[35]

Chloroform was widely used as an anesthetic, and liberal dosages of morphine were given to dull pain. While army physicians provided all the medical treatment afforded by the knowledge of the day, as well as psychological support and nourishing diet, they had to rely heavily upon the human body's natural resiliency and ability to heal itself. Bullet wounds were often treated only with the repeated application of wet dressings, particularly when the projectile did not lodge in the body. When the bullet remained in the body or limb, and could be located by probing with finger or instrument, surgeons usually attempted to extract it unless the surgery posed obvious danger to other organs or vessels. Otherwise it was left alone. When Sergeant John F. Farley and a small detail of Third Cavalrymen were ambushed by Apaches a few miles from Fort Bowie, Arizona Territory, in 1871, Farley received a bullet in the hip. The next day he and his men were rescued and taken back to the fort where Farley was placed under the care of the surgeon. "For the first two weeks while I was in the hospital," Farley remarked, "I suffered intense pain from my wound before it commenced to heal. The only medical attention that could be applied to the wound was a wet cloth laid over it to keep down the inflammation."[36] Farley survived, nevertheless, after a stay of five months in the hospital.

Even though Indians were armed largely with firearms by the late 1860s, arrow wounds among soldiers remained common enough during the Indian campaigns that they became a special field of study and treatment. Army surgeons found that the first reaction of many men when struck by an arrow, or their comrades trying to be helpful, was immediately to pull it out, which usually caused additional tissue laceration and blood loss, often with fatal results. When the arrow lodged in soft tissue, surgeons were advised simply to push it through intact, rather than further endangering the patient by attempting to draw it out backward. An alternative recommendation was to leave the arrow in place, with the shaft serving as a guide for the doctor to locate the projectile point, which might otherwise be problematical. The longer the arrow remained in the body, however, the more blood-soaked the sinew fastening the head to the shaft became, causing it to soften and stretch. Attempting to remove the arrow at that stage more often than not resulted in the shaft pulling free from the head, leaving it in the wound. Surgeons dealing with arrow wounds improvised various instruments for extracting them, one of the most effective being a length of annealed iron wire looped and passed down the shaft and over the projectile point then twisted tight, carefully withdrawing the entire arrow.

Arrows were particularly deadly when fired at close range and could embed themselves deeply in bone, from which they were practically impossible to extract, even if the patient survived long enough to be treated by a doctor. In those instances, the accepted method called for the surgeon gently to wiggle the arrow to loosen the head from the bone then to complete the extraction by using the wire snare. On the plains, instances were known of arrows passing entirely through a buffalo or horse when the missile failed to strike bone. By comparison, the human body offered considerably less resistance.[37]

Statistics indicated that soldiers tended to receive the majority of such wounds in the upper torso (the logical aiming point) and the arms, when the soldier involuntarily raised an arm to ward off the projectile. Despite one surgeon's encouraging report that arrow wounds of the chest and lung were not necessarily mortal, at the same time he had to admit that 72 percent of those victims died. That high mortality rate resulted in part from men being wounded in the field, where medical assistance was seldom available. Some soldiers were fortunate enough to incur wounds in close proximity to a fort, where they received medical attention within a reasonable time after the incident. In one such instance, Fourteenth Infantryman William Drum suffered two arrow wounds during an encounter with Apaches near Fort Whipple, Arizona Territory, in 1867. "One arrow struck him on the left side of the face and passed along the bone beneath his eye to within half an inch of his nose," Dr. Passmore Middleton recorded. "Another entered his right side, penetrating 2½ inches toward his spine," yet the man lived to reach the hospital. Middleton, a regular army surgeon, successfully removed both arrows and provided follow-up treatment, pronouncing Drum fit for duty about three weeks later.[38]

MEDICINE, HYGIENE, AND SANITATION 269

Aside from being wounded or killed in combat, soldiering on the frontier could be a dangerous occupation in other ways. Soldiers were at great risk of being killed in almost every way imaginable, with accidental drowning heading the list. Unbridled and unbridged western rivers, often laced with quicksand, made fording and ferry operations ever-treacherous. While attempting to traverse the swollen South Platte River at Julesburg, Colorado Territory, in 1866, an Eighteenth Infantry battalion fabricated a raft to ferry men and supplies to the opposite bank. Private William Murphy remembered the ordeal: "On trying out the scow we found it would not work owing to the quick-sands and shallows. In places the water would be only two or three inches deep while a few feet away there would be seven or eight feet of water. Two of our men got caught in the quick-sands and were drowned." It was a common occurrence everywhere in the West. Even normally dry streambeds in the Southwest could suddenly become deadly torrents during summer rains, as evidenced when Tenth Cavalryman Joseph H. Titus drowned while attempting to ford the Pecos River in Texas in 1876.[39]

Bathing in streams was the leading cause of accidental drowning among soldiers posted on the western frontier. The lack of regular bathing facilities directly contributed to the risk, especially for those men unable to swim, when soldiers were compelled to enter potentially hazardous streams at their own peril. The North Platte claimed the life of Private James W. Sullivan at Fort Fetterman in 1871. Two years later Private James Kearney, a member of H Company, First Cavalry, was swept under while bathing in the Rio Grande near Fort McRae, New Mexico Territory. The bodies of many drowning victims were never recovered. Even when they were, multiple victims could not always be recognized in those days prior to the army's adoption of metal identification tags. When three men drowned in the Yellowstone River near Fort Custer, Montana Territory, Private James Purvis reported that "one body has been recovered in an unrecognizable and greatly swollen condition. Boots and spurs, and cavalry trousers worn by the deceased led to almost certain identification. . . . The other men belong to Infantry companies and have not been heard of."[40]

Soldiering in the West was fraught with occupational hazards that claimed men's lives. The risk of being kicked by a mean-tempered or startled horse was an ever-present danger to unwary cavalry troopers, like Canadian-born Joseph O'Brien, a private in the Second Cavalry, who took a shod hind hoof squarely in his groin at Fort Walla Walla, Washington Territory. Suffering a ruptured scrotum and bladder, O'Brien agonized for sixteen days before finally succumbing to his injuries. Nor was it uncommon for soldiers to be run over and killed by heavily laden army wagons or to die by accidental falls from horses —or by horses falling on them. Sawmill operations, too, always posed a particular danger by their very nature, such as at Fort Totten, Dakota Territory, where a Twentieth Infantry soldier, William Jewitt, was killed when he fell onto the large circular blade "while in motion."[41]

Natural hazards likewise accounted for many soldiers' deaths, particularly exposure to subzero temperatures during winter. Despite the preponderance of deaths by freezing or as the result of extreme frostbite in northern latitudes, it was not unknown even in the Southwest. Private Frank Smith, Fifth Cavalry, expired at Camp Apache, Arizona Territory, after having both feet severely frostbitten. And at Fort Mojave, on the Colorado River west of there, three Twelfth Infantrymen were crushed to death when their barracks collapsed on them during a tornado. Not surprisingly, walking exposed guard beats during thunder storms resulted in numerous men being killed by lightning strike. A carbine or bayonetted rifle held by a sentry at the required right shoulder or carry positions made for a natural lightning rod. One such victim was twenty-one-year-old Edward Diffley, a private in the Fourth Infantry, who was struck and killed while walking his beat at Fort Laramie in May 1881.[42]

Army tactics manuals devoted scant attention to firearms safety, though some measures were built into the instructions for firing weapons. Depot drill instructors and line company noncoms presumably imparted the basics of safely handling the principal tool of the trade, based on experience and common sense, though this study found little evidence supporting that supposition. The many occurrences of accidental gunshot wounds suggest that few soldiers, other than former veterans, initially had much experience with using firearms.

Many accidental shootings resulted merely from soldiers carelessly pointing loaded arms, such as when Private Moses Hunter, Thirty-Eighth Infantry, accidentally fired his Springfield rifle in the company quarters at Monument Station, Kansas. The heavy .50-caliber bullet struck Private James Smith in the back and exited through his mouth. Two of the most common firearms accidents occurred as soldiers carelessly drew rifles or carbines with exposed hammers from vehicles. After cautioning the members of a paymaster's escort about that very hazard, Sergeant David Gordon, Seventh Cavalry, pulled his Sharps carbine from a wagon, the hammer somehow snagged, allowing it to fall and discharge. The bullet shattered his knee. He died a few days later after having his lower leg amputated in the hospital at Fort Larned, Kansas. In a similar incident at Fort Laramie in 1877, a Fifth Cavalryman was removing his carbine from a wagon when the piece discharged, killing company clerk Charles Stimson, seated at his desk in a nearby tent. Another soldier accidentally shot and killed one of his comrades in their quarters at Fort Canby, Washington Territory, when he forcibly closed the breechblock of his rifle on an improperly reloaded cartridge.[43]

Mishandling of revolvers accounted for numerous accidents among cavalrymen. The cause was usually simple carelessness, resulting in men shooting themselves or others. But in at least one case horseplay was responsible for the death of a Ninth Cavalryman. Two troopers at Fort Niobrara, Nebraska, "by way of innocent diversion on guard . . . were snapping empty pistols at each other" when one of the presumably "empty" pistols fired, killing Private Samuel Devine.[44]

It is interesting, though perhaps not unexpected, that accidental deaths connected with target practice increased markedly during the 1880s, commensurate with the army's emphasis on marksmanship training. Nearly all of the associated deaths were among soldiers who needlessly exposed themselves while serving as markers in the target pits. One of those was Musician James Holmes, First Infantry, who was shot through the head at Fort Davis when he raised it above the pit just as a man on the line fired.[45]

Noncombat deaths by gunshot sometimes were inflicted by guards attempting to stop escaping prisoners or deserters, but more often than not homicides were related to alcohol and spontaneous fits of rage. When a cavalry detachment from Fort Union stopped at a road ranch where whiskey was available, some of the men became inebriated and quarrelsome, leading to a fight. "In the melee one of the party, a young man named McCaffery, was shot in the head and instantly killed," wrote Private Eddie Matthews. "It is too bad that a young man should be killed in that manner, but nearly all the deaths among soldiers on the frontier occur in that manner. Very few die from sickness or at the hands of Indians." Although Matthews's opinion was a misimpression, a significant number of regulars stationed in the West were victims of homicide, often murdered by their own comrades or killed by civilians. A particularly tragic instance of the former occurred in December 1877 when Company A, Third Cavalry, was scouting near Spearfish, Dakota Territory. Private John M. Kennedy became involved in an altercation with First Sergeant John Van Moll, whereupon Kennedy shot and killed the popular sergeant. Kennedy was arrested and confined but was found the next morning hanging from the ridge pole of the guard tent. Even though Kennedy's death was recorded as a homicide, it went uninvestigated and the case was closed. Sometimes soldiers were killed by law enforcement officers when they got out of hand in neighboring towns; at other times they engaged in shooting affrays with tough frontier types. One of those was Eighth Infantryman Daniel Guiltnane, who got into an argument and was shot by a cowboy in a saloon near Fort Halleck, Nevada.[46]

Nearly as many soldiers took their own lives as were killed as a result of homicide. The circumstances driving men to suicide usually were known only to the victims, though depression, melancholia as it was then known, induced by isolation, boredom, and excessive use of alcohol seems to have accounted for the majority of suicides. Private Elwood Russell, Seventeenth Infantry, was diagnosed with melancholia when he entered the hospital at Fort Yates, Dakota Territory, in January 1886. The treatment provided obviously was ineffective, because he hanged himself in the hospital water closet about a month later. Private John Hallauer's suicide by shooting at Fort Laramie was attributed to stress over gambling debts he had incurred.[47]

Writing in his journal at Fort Davis on December 6, 1884, First Lieutenant John Bigelow lamented: "Another funeral this afternoon. The corpse was an infantry soldier, a victim of drink. He graduated in Medicine at the Glasgow University and entered the army no doubt from inability to conduct himself soberly outside. This is the 4th funeral since our arrival here [three weeks earlier]."[48] While regulars may have displayed considerable irreverence at other times, the burial of a fellow soldier occasioned genuine solemnity and respect for the honor of the cloth. Military funerals were a recurring event at frontier forts and were invariably conducted with the prescribed protocol and formality.

Trumpeter Ami F. Mulford left a graphic account of the ceremony held for the late Private Henry Baker, D Company, Seventh Cavalry, who died of heart disease at Fort Rice in 1877:

> The body was dressed in full uniform and placed in a neat coffin, and resting in a ward at the hospital, was viewed by all the men at the Post. After all take [a] final look upon the silent face . . . the Companies were formed in line in front of the hospital, and as the body was carried out, they presented arms, the trumpets were played and the coffin was placed on the two gun caissons which had been joined, were trimmed with black, and draped with the garrison flag—the flag that Baker had helped to unfurl so many times. Hitched to the caissons were six horses, each with a large black plume on its head, and each led by a dismounted trooper. Then came the horse that Baker had ridden. It was saddled, bridled, equipped as for a march, and his boots were tied in the stirrups with the heels to the front. The horse was led by two troopers. Then followed the four companies of the 7th Cavalry . . . with carbines reversed and on foot. The line led by eight trumpeters, playing the funeral march, slowly crossed the parade, pas[s]ed the guard-house; where the guard stood with arms at a present, then to the cemetery . . . [where] the troops were formed on three sides of the grave. The burial service was then read by the Post Adjutant. Then the firing party fired three rounds over the open grave. Then Taps were sounded by one of the trumpeters, and we marched back to the Fort.[49]

The solemn mood lasted only briefly, however. As soon as the musicians passed out of the cemetery, they struck up "a lively march, and the men marched off back to the fort—the man just buried a thing of the past," a soldier wrote. The band's object, of course, was to dispel the gloominess and restore morale, a process that likely continued afterward at the soldiers' bar.[50]

Deceased soldiers frequently became a thing of the past not only in immediate memory but also officially. Post surgeons were supposed to record the pertinent information for each and officers serving as quartermasters were charged with the marking of graves and maintenance of cemeteries. Problems arose, however, as a result of lack of coordination between the two departments, coupled with more pressing obligations on both officers. Although the post quartermaster always erected a headboard—painted or plain—over the grave, the gravesite itself often was not recorded, even when the cemetery was laid out with a regular order of numbered rows and plots, which was not always the case. Making matters worse, the collateral duty quartermaster, harried by a plethora of other demands, often had little time to devote to the cemetery. Consequently both post cemeteries and burial records were neglected and over time the wooden headboards weathered, the inscriptions often becoming unreadable. The markers themselves sometimes were knocked down by animals or became so rotted at the base that they fell over, then were disarranged or removed entirely. These factors combined in the complete loss of identity for many graves, as reflected in the frustration of one post quartermaster describing a cemetery in 1879: "The spot within garrison lines—abandoned and neglected—the graves only noted by the indentations and stone mounds—no head boards, and the last trace will ere long be obliterated—no records of the number of the graves to be found here."[51]

That same year the Quartermaster Department, responding to public pressure to properly mark the graves of soldiers who had died during the Civil War, adopted marble headstones for all military burials. However commendable that effort may have been, quartermasters at frontier posts often failed to apply for the stones, and even when they did the identity of many graves had already been lost. As late as 1891 Private Hartford G. Clark commented in his diary on the condition of the Fort Niobrara cemetery:

> I was old guard fatigue today . . . I with others cleaned out the cemetery. It was a very poor apoligy [sic] for a soldiers['] cemetery. There is one stone gravestone and the rest are boards stuck up with a number on it marked carelessly with a lead pencil. The government allows a stone gravestone for every deceased soldier but some quartermaster has put up boards instead of

tombstones for those that have served their country faithfully and are now dead.[52]

Soon after the funeral, the company commander searched the effects of the deceased soldier to see if he might have left a last will and testament, which was rarely found. In the absence of a will, the officer inventoried the man's personal property, turning over to his quartermaster sergeant the arms, accouterments, and any other property belonging to the government. When that had been done, and in the absence of a claim by the next of kin, he requested the post council of administration to convene for the purpose of formally disposing of the man's effects. Using the inventory, the council conducted a public cash auction, wherein company members and other soldiers purchased the material. Provided the interested parties were approximately the same size as the deceased, they were able to acquire uniforms and other clothing at prices significantly lower than those charged by the Quartermaster Department, thus realizing a savings on their accounts. Miscellaneous items such as pipes, watches, writing materials, and pocket knives also were auctioned to the highest bidders, though purely personal items such as photographs or letters were returned to the next of kin, if any were known. The proceeds of the sale, along with any money discovered in the man's effects, were recorded, certified, and deposited with an officer or sometimes the post surgeon to be held until the next visit by the paymaster. At the same time, the company commander submitted to the paymaster a Final Statement for the deceased, which was an accounting of the pay, savings, and unused clothing allowance due the man at the time of his death. The paymaster subsequently credited the total amount to the man's name, depositing it with the U.S. Treasury until claimed by the legal representative, usually the nearest living relative.[53]

Army medical care began improving, if slowly, during the late 1880s as knowledge in the field of medicine advanced. Research by French physician Louis Pasteur significantly advanced the theory that germs were not the result of "spontaneous generation," as had long been accepted, but rather that the fermentation and growth of microorganisms were actually responsible for disease. Once that was understood, Pasteur proved they could be controlled and even destroyed.

That signal discovery opened the way to further advances by other physicians, including the English physician Joseph Lister, who developed ground-breaking antiseptic techniques for both surgery and the treatment of gangrene. Lister found that spraying surgical instruments, incisions, and dressings with a solution of carbolic acid greatly reduced the risk of infection. Likewise, swabbing major wounds as soon as possible with the same solution made the onset of gangrene far less likely. The first army surgeon to fully appreciate and become an advocate for the use of antiseptic surgery was Swiss-born Captain Alfred C. Girard, who was exposed to Lister's method during a trip to Europe in 1877. Girard shared his findings in a detailed report to the surgeon general so that the methods and results of the technique might be disseminated throughout the Medical Department. Although Lister's method continued to be ridiculed by many in the medical community, some army surgeons began using it by the 1880s as the more progressive minds studied bacteriology, antisepsis, and modern hygienic techniques. Many army doctors were staying abreast of such advances and putting them into practice, as reflected in the use of the antiseptic method in 5 of 179 operations during 1884 and in 42 of 170 surgeries the following year.[54]

Post commanders had long been notorious for paying scant attention to (or ignoring entirely) the reports and corrective recommendations made by surgeons regarding sanitary conditions at forts. Of special importance was their concern for protecting potable water sources from pollution and the realization that fecal and water-borne germs were the probable causes of typhoid fever. At Fort Laramie in 1887, for example, Post Surgeon Arthur W. Taylor urged that "a new well be dug further from the post and at such a point that it can not be fouled by the filtration from old sinks, barns, corrals, and the filth that must necessarily collect about a house." A change in regulations two years earlier required post commanders to review and personally endorse the monthly sanitary reports then forward them to department headquarters, rather than simply file them away. While the intent was to impose greater pressure on commanders to respond to surgeons' recommendations, and that did spur improvements overall, some unenlightened line officers still avoided taking decisive action. Responding to Taylor's concern, Colonel Henry C. Merriam pointed out that the cost of construction of a new well along with a new pipeline, while it might be beneficial, would be considerable. Besides, in his considered opinion, there was still "reasonable doubt" about the validity of the surgeon's contention. When department commanders elected to take no further action, the matter ended. Nevertheless, by the end of the era typhoid cases in the army decreased markedly as a result of improved sanitation and preventative inoculation.[55]

Post hospitals, too, improved over time as some forts achieved a degree of permanency and the consolidation of posts initiated by Sherman continued to eliminate numerous smaller forts that no longer had a purpose beyond housing troops or were not strategically located near rail connections. In stark contrast to the criticisms voiced two decades earlier, a trooper of the First Cavalry at Fort Custer confidently boasted: "Our post hospital is a model institution, a credit to the medical department of the U.S. Army, and a godsend to many of its soldiers who have found there the oasis in the desert of their affliction and disease." Despite such impressions, frontier army hospitals were still a far cry from what they would become in the following century. Recalling years later his days as post surgeon at Fort Douglas, Utah, during the 1880s, Colonel William H. Arthur described his state-of-the-art facility as "a forty-bed stone hospital with some modern improvements, but even here the building was very primitive. There was no laboratory or operating room, no running water except from a hydrant outside of the kitchen, no water closets. . . . We were allowed coal oil lamps instead of candles . . . and the building was heated by a central hot-air heating plant. It was considered the finest military hospital in the Department of the Platte, if not in all the west."[56]

Medical care for soldiers took another stride forward with the authorization of a separate Hospital Corps, with its own distinctive uniform, on March 1, 1887. Attached organizationally to the Medical Department, its personnel—141 stewards, 50 acting stewards, and 588 privates—were not included in the total number of enlisted men authorized by Congress and therefore did not detract from the strength of the combat arms. Qualified soldiers serving in line units were permitted to transfer voluntarily to the Hospital Corps, however, while others were screened and regularly enlisted for the duty. Within a year this decision effectively disposed of the old system of detailing line soldiers away from their units—usually against their will—as reluctant nurses and indifferent cooks, which was a happy outcome for all concerned.

Even more important, it created a body of trained medics dedicated to caring for the sick and injured in the field as well as in garrison.[57]

Interest in sanitation grew as line officers gradually accepted the concept that relatively simple, low-cost measures would ensure that fewer of their soldiers would be on the sick list and thus would be available for duty. A few even went so far as to erect bath houses out of consideration for the general well-being, health, and morale of their men, if not their military appearance. By the late 1880s the annual non-combat death rates for enlisted men fell to the lowest levels ever experienced by the army. The average death rate from disease among both white and black enlisted soldiers in 1871 had been 11.5 per 1,000 men. That number declined to 8.8 per 1,000 men in 1885, and by 1891 the figure had fallen by more than half to a mere 5.03.[58] Soldiering would continue to be a hazardous occupation with regard to the wide array of accidents that might befall men, but the physicians of the army's Medical Department had accomplished much to help them survive disease, injuries, and wounds received in combat and to improve the army's sanitation and hygiene in general.

Steel engraving: "Will He Enlist?" from *Harper's Weekly*, May 26, 1888 (Author's collection)

This dapper Tenth Cavalry sergeant exudes the regulars' hallmark discipline and confidence. He was photographed at Fort Sill, Indian Territory, ca. 1872. (U.S. Army Military History Institute)

(*Below*) Sergeant James S. Hamilton (*far left*) poses with his fellow noncommissioned officers of Company K, First Infantry. (U.S. Army Military History Institute)

Second Cavalryman Adelbert Butler intermittently wrote letters home from Camp Stambaugh, Wyoming Territory, and Fort Custer, Montana Territory. Commenting on the dearth of single white women at the latter post, Butler said that the situation was offset by an abundance of Crow Indian women, "dusky maidens but they are girls all the same." (Courtesy Groenewold-Triplett collection)

An unidentified soldier poses with his wife. The army made no allowance for wives of enlisted men, unless they were fortunate enough to be appointed as company laundresses. (Author's collection)

Sunday inspection of a battalion of the Eleventh and Seventeenth Infantry at Fort Abraham Lincoln, Dakota Territory. (Author's collection)

Down on his luck and unable to find work, native Marylander William "Eddie" Matthews resorted to joining the army in 1869. He served with the Eighth Cavalry in Arizona and New Mexico and subsequently in Texas during his second enlistment. Matthews's letters to his family form an unparalleled contemporary account of army life. (Courtesy National Park Service, Fort Union National Monument)

Photographed during the 1886 Geronimo Campaign, these Thirteenth Infantry noncoms reflect the practical garb often worn in the field. Corporal Clarence Chrisman (*kneeling center*) maintained a diary of his experiences. (Arizona Historical Society, Gatewood Collection, No. 19607)

Sergeant Perley S. Eaton, interviewed by Don Rickey in the 1950s, offered many insights into soldier life during his time in Troop K, Third Cavalry. (Courtesy Don G. Rickey estate)

Some posts, like Camp Grant, Arizona Territory, shown here in 1870, were bleak, primitive, and isolated. These factors made for a monotonous existence, resulting in disciplinary problems and overindulgence in alcohol. (National Archives)

Private William B. Jett, Fourth Cavalry, was a member of a detail ambushed by Apaches at Guadaloupe Canyon, Sonora, Mexico. Jett survived his five-year enlistment to become a rancher and later graduated from a theological seminary. He left a superb chronicle of frontier army life. (Arizona Historical Society, Fort Huachuca collection, No. 73355)

Signal Corpsman Will C. Barnes earned the Medal of Honor for his actions in an engagement at Fort Apache, Arizona Territory, in 1881. Following his discharge from the army, Barnes remained in Arizona, where he engaged in ranching and later worked as a range inspector for the U.S. Forest Service. (Arizona Historical Society, Barnes collection, No. 242323)

A group of Sixth Cavalrymen at Camp Grant, Arizona Territory, in the early 1880s. (Arizona Historical Society, Fort Grant collection, No. 1225)

The squad room was the soldier's home. This one at Fort Robinson, Nebraska, ca. 1890, is typical of the improved barracks constructed during the 1870s and 1880s. (National Archives)

Davids Island, New York, became one of three principal recruiting depots in 1878. (National Archives)

Sergeant John Ryan served in the volunteers during the Civil War plus ten years in the Seventh Cavalry afterward. He saw action at the Battle of the Washita in 1868, on the Yellowstone Expedition of 1873, and at the Battle of the Little Bighorn. Following his discharge as a first sergeant, he spent the rest of his life employed as a police officer in Massachusetts. His detailed reminiscence of army life in the West stands as one of the finest. (Courtesy Sandy Barnard)

Photograph taken by Stanley J. Morrow in 1876 showing one of Brigadier General George Crook's bivouacs during the infamous Starvation (or Horse Meat) March. Note the Indian-style shelters fabricated by covering frameworks of branches with army blankets. (Courtesy Paul L. Hedren)

Sergeant Major Alvarado M. Fuller, Second Cavalry, took advantage of an 1878 army reform allowing enlisted soldiers to compete for promotion to commissioned status. Fuller passed all of the required examinations to be promoted to the rank of second lieutenant in 1879. He completed his career after the turn of the twentieth century. (Courtesy Paul L. Hedren)

A shoemaker by trade, Charles A. Windolph emigrated from Germany to the United States to avoid compulsory military service. Finding acculturation difficult in his adopted nation, he joined the Seventh Cavalry in 1871, was wounded in action at the Battle of the Little Bighorn, where he earned the Medal of Honor, and was discharged as a sergeant in 1883. His no-nonsense company commander, Captain Frederick W. Benteen, once synthesized the lot of the regular soldier: "The government pays you to get shot at." (Courtesy Glen Swanson)

In 1873 Private Thomas N. Way penned a moving description of the field burial of one of his comrades. Just three years later, Way was killed in action and interred in an unmarked grave on the Little Bighorn River in Montana Territory. (Courtesy Glen Swanson)

During the Battle of the Little Bighorn, Company Quartermaster Sergeant Richard P. Hanley risked his life by turning back under fire a stubborn ammunition-laden mule headed for the Indian lines. Awarded the Medal of Honor for bravery, Hanley later admitted that his principal motive at the time was fear of being held financially responsible for the loss of the mule. (Courtesy Glen Swanson)

After returning from the field, Private William Earl Smith, Fourth Cavalry, represents the appearance typical of regulars following a hard campaign. At the 1876 fight on Red Fork of the Powder River, Smith spared an elderly Northern Cheyenne woman, only to return to her lodge later to find that she had been murdered. (Courtesy Sherry L. Smith)

Regular army discipline left an indelible mark on veterans. When photographed in 1938, ex-sergeant Charles A. Windolph unconsciously placed his feet in the position of "Parade Rest," as prescribed by tactics. (Courtesy Glen Swanson)

This recruit, probably photographed at Columbus Barracks, Ohio, wears an ill-fitting as-issued uniform and has yet to acquire the hallmark demeanor of a regular. (Courtesy Bill Chachula)

CHAPTER 9

"It Is So Lonesome Out Here"

The Domestic Side of Enlisted Life

"As for females we don't see one here except for a few soldiers' wives, which are a very poor consolation," groaned a soldier at Fort Sedgwick, Colorado Territory, in 1867. Indeed the fairer sex was scarcely evident on the enlisted side of frontier army garrisons of that time. The primary reason, of course, was that regulations restricted peacetime enlistments to unmarried, childless males, at least initially, without special permission from the adjutant general of the army. In the army's view, wives made for unnecessary encumbrances on both soldiers and the service, and married men, generally speaking, made for more cautious warriors because of concerns beyond their own safety.[1]

Throughout most of the era, laundresses, their teenaged daughters, officers' domestics, and occasionally a precious few others provided the only consolation for soldiers starved for feminine companionship, and vice versa, at isolated garrisons. "The laundresses and women servants were the honoured guests at the dances, theatricals and other entertainments given by the men," an officer related, "and the former responded with merrymaking in their own quarters, where the space was small but the enjoyment huge . . . for let it be known that no woman, old or young, beautiful or homely, has ever yet entered a garrison without having a wooer at her feet." One of those eager suitors was Sergeant John Cox, First Infantry, who confided that he "was considerably 'sweet' on the pretty seamstress at the post trader's" at Fort Randall, Dakota Territory, but that in order to visit her at night he "had to dodge the cross old sentry at the [corral] shack . . . and be [back] in quarters before the Officer of the Day came around on his 'nosing' expedition." That single women were in great demand was an inescapable reality of garrison life, and they did not remain single for long. "The frontier is the best place in the world for Old Maids to migrate," quipped a young Eighth Cavalryman. "They can always get a husband, and will always be admired by the rough frontiersman and boys belonging to Uncle Sam's outfit, whether they are pretty or not." Well aware of this, some enlisted men's wives played cupid by inviting their unwed sisters to join them at frontier posts, confident that willing suitors would readily flock to them.[2]

Despite official deterrents, soldiers were permitted to marry while in the service, with their company commander's permission, and could subsequently reenlist so long as the captain raised no objection. Company commanders, ever mindful of the potential distraction from duty posed by a wife, did their utmost to discourage their men, particularly young soldiers, from marrying—and for practical reasons. A soldier's pay was hardly adequate to support a wife, much less the children that were sure to follow. Then, too, there was the practical consideration of where the wife would be quartered. Barracks, of course, were for soldiers only, so a married man would be faced with having to find or improvise some other residence on the post and have permission to reside there with his wife. For that reason, a captain's decision usually hinged on his company's current need for a laundress and the availability of quarters.[3]

The most promising source of single women was the cooks and housekeepers working for officers, much to the distress of officers and their wives, who frequently imported domestics from the East at considerable trouble and expense, only to lose them when they married soldiers to take up residence on Soapsuds Row. When no laundress position was available in the company, of course, the new bride wisely remained in the officer's employ so that she might be quartered and contribute to the family income. In one such instance a trooper belonging to the garrison at Fort Union, New Mexico Territory, was on detached service for several months but somehow learned during his absence that one of his lieutenants had returned from the East with a new servant. The lieutenant's wife, dismayed at the man's presumptuousness, recalled that the soldier "engaged a carriage at Las Vegas

[30 miles away] for the wedding trip before ever seeing her. His pluck must have pleased her, for three days after his return, she accompanied him to Las Vegas, where they were united for life." A soldier at Fort Custer, Montana Territory, noted that social interaction between soldiers and household servants became so prevalent that

> a sentry has been posted in the rear of our officers' quarters, much to the terror and discomfort of the garrison dudes who pay attention to the kitchen belles "along the line," because they have had to resort to all kinds of strategy in order to see the girls without being caught. Recently however, this unpleasant barrier was removed and the dudes are again happy in the performance of nightly back-gate osculatory exercises.[4]

Like their counterparts of any era, some soldiers resorted to corresponding with young women in the States as a means of combating loneliness and providing a brief mental escape from the male-dominated world of army life. Aching for his girlfriend, Private Charles P. Christian, a Sixth Cavalryman assigned to Camp Verde, Arizona Territory, sighed to her in a letter: "Often when walking post, pacing my lonely beat in a hostile region, you were by my side keeping me company. When laying down at night . . . hundreds of miles from any human habitation you were with me, always with me." Private Adelbert Butler, Second Cavalry, penned a note in 1877 excitedly announcing that he had begun corresponding with a young lady in Ohio "that I never have seen. She sent her photograph at me the other day & she is a screamer." The relationship apparently did not last, however. About a year later, after Butler's company transferred near the Crow Indian Reservation, he asked his sister to extend his regards to his male friends back home, adding optimistically: "Never mind the girls. There is plenty of them here, most of them dusky maidens but they are girls all the same."[5]

The more settled and populated areas in the West along railroads offered greater opportunities for soldiers inclined to interact with respectable classes of women. Salt Lake City, Utah, astride the main line of the Union Pacific, proved to have a bountiful supply of eligible women only too happy to enter into matrimony. A Thirteenth Infantryman posted at adjacent Camp Douglas in 1871 announced: "When the Seventh [Infantry] left for Montana the three companies stationed here took about twenty soldiers' wives with them, most of whom the 'boys' married while at this post, and mostly out of Mormon families, and now the Thirteenth is doing a lively business in the marrying line. Companies, C, E, and I brought only one soldier's wife with them when they arrived here last summer, and now their number is increased to fifteen." Nevertheless, many of those young women may have decided that marrying a soldier was an ill-considered choice when the regiment transferred to far-off New Orleans, Louisiana, three years later.[6]

Those men permitted to marry were usually wed at the post, often at some makeshift location because of the near-absence of army chapels for many years. An 1874 ceremony for Sergeant William Brinkman, Sixth Infantry, and his bride, the post quartermaster's cook, was conducted in the guard house at Fort Abraham Lincoln, Dakota Territory, with two of Brinkman's closest friends serving as witnesses. (Both were Seventh Cavalrymen, later killed in action at Little Bighorn.) At Fort Stevenson, Dakota Territory, an infantry musician married the sister of a company laundress in a "simple and primitive ceremony in keeping with our country and our position in the desert," according to the commanding officer. "She was in the employ of Mrs. [Second Lieutenant Frank R.] Walborn, in whose home the wedding took place." In this instance several officers were in attendance and the post adjutant performed the ceremony, after which "the company drank to the health of the newly-weds, who then withdrew into an apartment prepared for them for the night by one of the traders. . . . After a few gay remarks and insinuations, required by the event, everyone went home."[7]

Ever present were men who were hesitant to seek the company commander's blessing and married surreptitiously. Trumpeter Edward Botzer, Seventh Cavalry, fell in love with the daughter of one of the company laundresses and married her. His captain revealed in a letter to his wife: "They kept it a secret for about six or eight weeks, not even Mrs. Brush [mother] . . . being aware of their marriage! Poor Botzer, I think he might have done better." Having no alternative but to accept the situation as it was, the captain graciously authorized the issue of extra tents to the laundress-mother, adding: "She has quite a village for herself and son-in-law, and daughter, and little boy 'Charley' who gets . . . my spurs, sabre, and boots and keeps them in order for a slight compensation." Another Seventh Cavalryman, Corporal Jacob Horner, wed secretly at Fort Totten, Dakota Territory, in 1880, the news not becoming public for about four months after the nuptials were concluded. Horner donned sergeant's chevrons a short time later and, at his wife's urging, took his discharge about year after they were married. That was not surprising, because risking unauthorized marriage carried with it responsibilities and hardships not always foreseen, or at least realistically considered, by naive couples bound to tie the knot. Addressing this issue, the editor of the *Army & Navy Journal* observed:

> The unhappy families of the soldier married without leave . . . are left without lodging, light, fuel, or medical attendance. There is a certain tacit toleration of such marriages, or else the women and children would not be permitted to follow and to attach themselves to the regiment, even at their own expense; and yet . . . these poor pariahs of the army undergo an amount of suffering which, if it occurred amongst civilians, would give rise to indignation meetings all over country."[8]

Typical of rebellious teenagers immemorial, Bridget ("Biddy") Barrett, daughter of First Sergeant Thomas Barrett, Company B, Second Cavalry, became infatuated with a young private in the troop, much to her parents' distress. They refused to sanction the relationship. Leaving home at Camp Brown, Wyoming Territory, on two different occasions, Biddy threatened to run away to Omaha, to await her lover there until he was discharged. "The quarreling, occasioned by Biddy's persistent determination to marry the man she loved, reached the ears of everyone in the garrison," wrote the post surgeon. "Capt. Bates, commanding officer of the company, said he was heartily tired and wanted no more of it. . . . He told Biddy that there were quarters she could occupy and a ration as laundress . . . and that if she was going to marry Carter, he wanted her to do so and thus end the trouble." The outcome, unfortunately, was not recorded.[9]

Members of the noncommissioned staff seeking to marry were faced with challenges unique to their class. Not being attached to line units, their wives seldom had the opportunity to be appointed company laundresses, had they desired to do so. Most of those sergeants fully appreciated their elevated status, and the significantly higher salary of their grades usually obviated the need for their wives to be employed. The singular exception in some instances was the hospital steward, whose wife sometimes was appointed as matron to wash for the hospital. Stewards sometimes had a small house adjacent to the hospital, and at other times bachelors were simply assigned a room within the hospital. That was the situation at Camp Supply, Indian Territory, when Hospital Steward Seymour Kitching was about to be married in 1877. A lenient commanding officer, however, accommodated him by detailing men to down trees in a nearby canyon and construct a plain log abode for the couple. "But darling," a plaintive Kitching wrote, "they are fearful slow at it. I do wish they would hurry up so that it would be finished and I could start for you my own sweet darling. . . . I will then be happy and contented."[10]

Rarely employed was an exception to the regulations allowing the first-time enlistment of married men by special permission of the adjutant general of the army. One of those was Private John L. Hawkins, sworn into the Eighth Cavalry at Fort Union in 1870. Hawkins, with a wife and two children, had been a cattleman in the vicinity with the intention of marketing his animals at the railhead in Colorado when Indians made off with his herd of six hundred head. Having no other immediate means of supporting his family, Hawkins applied for enlistment at the nearby post. Captain Charles Hobart, commanding L Company, apparently sympathized with the earnest young man's plight. Being in need of a capable washerwoman for his company, he enlisted Hawkins and enrolled his wife as laundress. Bearing out the captain's positive instincts about the man, Hawkins faithfully served his full five years and was discharged as a corporal.[11]

Officers' wives and domestic servants notwithstanding, the only women officially recognized by the army at that time were hospital matrons (discussed in chapter 8) and company laundresses. Both were rationed and quartered on the justification of a single need, to wash for the men and sometimes officers too. In most instances white or black women or women of Mexican extraction performed that essential function. Until 1868 line companies were authorized to maintain as many as four laundresses, but a general order promulgated that year imposed a proration of one laundress for each nineteen and one-half soldiers, effecting a reduction of laundresses for most companies based on actual strength. A Second Cavalryman serving in the mid-1870s recalled that "ordinarily, about two enlisted men of each troop or company were allowed to marry and maintain wives at the post, with living quarters provided for them." Laundresses attached to the regimental band also washed for any bachelors among the noncommissioned staff, such as the sergeant major and post ordnance sergeant. Other enlisted men's wives not fortunate enough to be attached to a company sometimes resorted to hiring out to the designated laundresses to assist with the daunting task of washing and ironing for several dozen men.[12]

A further advantage for these company women was the allowance of the same daily ration authorized for soldiers, including army soap, augmented by a portion of the soap ration intended for the men. The washerwoman was nonetheless obligated to supply her own tubs, boilers, washboards, and other equipment. Her official status also qualified her to buy foodstuffs and other items stocked by the post commissary. The provision for drawing rations, however, was contingent upon her actually being present with her assigned company. When the company left the post on campaign or any other detached service, the captain had to remember to certify in writing the names of his laundresses to the post commander; otherwise they would be denied rations. The rule's real purpose, of course, was to prevent unauthorized women from misrepresenting themselves to the commissary as official laundresses, thereby obtaining free food to which they were not entitled.[13]

The matter of quartering laundresses apparently was left largely to the discretion of post commanders. At the more primitive stations, particularly during the immediate postwar years, the accommodations were hardly habitable, as described by First Sergeant Henry McConnell, Sixth Cavalry: "Situated on the outskirts of every military post may be seen a collection of huts, old tents, picket houses, and 'dugouts,' an air of squalor and dirt pervading the locality, and troops of shock-headed children and slovenly looking females of various colors completing the picture. These are the quarters of the married soldiers and of the laundresses, known in army parlance as 'Sudsville.'"[14]

Also variously called "soapsuds row," "laundry row," or simply "suds row," quarters for laundresses were not always so primitive but invariably occupied a location on the fringes of a post beyond the corrals or at best behind the rear of the barracks. The half-dozen log shanties aligned behind the barracks at Fort Custer was known by the colorful moniker "The Six Gun Battery." The quarters situated along the banks of the river at venerable Fort Laramie in 1868 were "of frame . . . 50 ft. long and 15 wide . . . divided into three sets of quarters." Sprawling

Fort Union, New Mexico Territory, uniquely claimed an unusually luxurious arrangement wherein the laundress quarters consisted of a score of one-room adobe apartments forming one side of the adjacent cavalry and quartermaster corrals, where wells conveniently provided water, though the residents had to share their backyards with the horses and mules. When permanent buildings were still under construction at Cantonment on Tongue River, Montana Territory (later Fort Keogh), during the winter of 1877, a soldier's son remembered:

> The tents of troop E, my mother and Mrs. Clancey, were pitched about 200 yards east of the troop quarters. We stayed in tents all winter, as no quarters had been built for the enlisted men's wives as yet. . . . Each married soldier had two 10 × 14 wall tents to live in. These were pitched one directly in front of the other and both topped by a large government tarpaulin. They proved to be comfortable and we lived in ours until the following spring, when log houses were put up for the laundresses. . . . This section of Fort Keogh was known to the soldiers as Tub Town or Sudsville, because most of the women who lived there were regular company laundresses.[15]

Signal Corpsman Will Barnes, stationed at Fort Apache, Arizona Territory, in the early 1880s, characterized the aging quarters there as "a line of nondescript structures of varied architecture and material, canvas, stone, log, and slabs; many were a combination of all these materials." Some commanders logically sited laundry row near a stream whenever it was possible to do so, and some lenient officers even allowed company women to keep a milk cow or chickens for the benefit of the troop kitchen.[16]

Soldiers routinely packed off their dirty laundry to the row every Saturday as part of the general company policing, picking up their clean clothes at the same time. Faced with a new pile of the malodorous if not lice-infested stuff, the laundresses prepared for another strenuous, disagreeable week's work. Winter in most regions of the West imposed even greater hardships, forcing the women to keep adequate quantities of water from freezing and to do both washing and drying indoors, stringing clotheslines within their already cramped living quarters. But government-provided housing, a monthly ration, and a regular cash income went a long way in mitigating the unpleasant aspects of the job.

Rates varied somewhat from one post to another, one dollar a month being the usual charge fixed by the post council of administration, a committee usually composed of three officers. The practice of establishing a monthly price avoided bookkeeping and guaranteed the washerwomen full payment at the pay table, the standard amount being deducted directly from each man's pay. But at some posts soldiers were charged a flat fee for army clothing, plus a price per piece for other items. "In each Laundress Quarters," a private in the Eighth Cavalry explained, "a card is tacked up with prices for each piece of washing . . . for one month's washing: Govt Cloth[e]s $1.00, for pants [probably civilian summer trousers] 25 [cents], white shirt 10, bed sack 10 cts. I wear white shirts all the time, but my laundress never charges me anything extra." Not all laundresses were so agreeable, however. The women at Fort Fetterman, Wyoming Territory, for instance, apparently rejected the prospect of washing all garments at the bulk price, insisting instead that they receive a dollar monthly for washing the men's underclothing alone, a grisly task by any estimation. Trumpeter Charles P. Christian, a Sixth Cavalryman posted at Camp Verde, informed his sister that his laundress-wife Annie was earning two dollars per dozen items, and "she washes something like 100 pieces a day for two or three days, then irons them, has them ready by Friday or Saturday." Industrious wives were thus able to earn a respectable income. When it was combined with a soldier's salary and ration, especially for a veteran noncom or company tailor, the couple enjoyed a financially comfortable existence, even when the accommodations left something to be desired.[17]

The proximity of camp followers, married or not, sometimes created problems because soldiers lacking feminine association readily consorted with any receptive laundresses or other women present. On one occasion the officer of the day making his usual nightly rounds at Fort Arbuckle, Indian Territory, discovered two noncoms and a private drinking at the laundresses' quarters at one o'clock in the morning. After reproving the men, he sent the sergeant and corporal to their quarters in arrest and jailed the private, but he could do little beyond rebuking the women for their behavior. Each of the soldiers was later fined three dollars for being out of quarters after taps. At

Fort McPherson, Nebraska, Private Patrick Moriarty, tailor for Company A, Ninth Infantry, became intimate with one of the laundresses, Mrs. Henry Boch, who was married to a man in the same company. Reputed to have exhibited licentious behavior with other soldiers on previous occasions, Mrs. Boch had never accused anyone of impropriety until this occasion, when her sister intruded on the amorous pair in a compromising posture. In another instance, the wife of Sergeant Barney McDougal, Twenty-Fourth Infantry, became the flash point of trouble when it was gossiped that a private in the same company wanted "to see if he could not get a little from McDougal's wife." Pistol in hand, the jealous sergeant sought out the interloper and fired several shots at him, apparently missing his intended target. McDougal nevertheless satisfied his honor but lost his stripes.[18]

Not all laundresses were married women or necessarily of the same race as the host unit. In the absence of married men in the company, it was sometimes a challenge for the company commander simply to find a woman willing and able to do the work at his particular station. Company A, Sixth Cavalry, employed a black laundress at Fort Richardson, Texas, in 1866, as did B Company, Second Cavalry at Camp Brown, Wyoming Territory, several years later. Working-class single women in the West had difficulty finding gainful employment of the respectable kind, especially in the sparsely peopled regions occupied by the army. Therefore securing a position as a designated laundress was a means of gaining a degree financial independence. How individual women may have conducted themselves in that role was due largely to their personal character and the level of tolerance exercised by officers.[19]

The majority of laundresses, insisted a Seventh Cavalryman, "were ladies in every sense of the word, and were respected by the common herd more than the wives of the officers." This was a commonly shared opinion. One spunky army woman, signing herself anonymously as "The Daughter of a Soldier and Laundress, the Sister of Soldiers, a Soldier's Wife, and a Laundress," expressed her pride in the profession by pointing out that no self-respecting soldier would submit to doing his own laundry "and even if they would, a man has no idea of the many changes of water and the care required to keep clothing soft, white, and in good condition. A woman understands it perfectly, and is always anxious to have the clothes entrusted to her for washing present a good appearance." Echoing that degree of self-respect, another laundress boasted that "the majority of them . . . try to outdo one another in the cleanliness of the clothing given them to wash." Eighth Cavalryman Matthews learned firsthand how difficult washing and ironing could be after he was detached to a subpost without a laundress. "My back aches, my arms and hands are sore, and I feel generally fatigued. . . . I never did begrudge paying my laundry bill, but will always pay more cheerfully for the future. . . . As a washerwoman I am not a success."[20]

An officer of many years' experience on the frontier characterized laundresses as "good, honest, industrious wives, usually well along in years, minutely familiar with their rights, which they dared to maintain with acrimonious volubility . . . and they were ever ready for a fight, yet they were kind of heart if rough in manner, always ready to assist in times of distress." Company women frequently helped each other, at times officers' wives, too, as midwives and nurses and at other times of family emergency. Bespeaking a degree of sisterhood among army women despite the great social chasm between officers' row and soap suds row, a cavalry laundress at Camp Apache obligingly took time away from her heavy workload to assist the wife of an infantry lieutenant following the birth of the officer's child.[21]

Not a few laundresses, in fact, considered themselves de facto members of the company, sharing a kinship with the soldiers and identity with the unit. Suffering from consumption at Fort Yuma, California, in 1870, an aged Mrs. Turley, laundress for Company D, Twelfth Infantry, was considered "a person of excellent character . . . respected by all and many of the men regarded her with almost maternal love." One of those with whom she shared an especially close relationship was Musician Thomas Rae, who had joined the regiment at age fifteen in 1862. Among laundress Turley's last requests before she passed away just prior to Christmas was that the veteran drummer be released from the guardhouse long enough to attend her funeral. Her wish was granted. Rae indeed marched in the procession accompanying her remains to the cemetery.[22]

First Sergeant John Ryan, Seventh Cavalry, related that some of the laundresses not only repaired and altered uniforms for the men but also earned extra income by "making pies for the enlisted men. The men used to call these pies pegged, cable-screwed, and sewed, as some of the women made better pies than others." (The slang ratings alluded to the various methods used for fastening the soles of army-issue boots and shoes.) A former Sixth Infantryman, R. Eugene Pelham, remembered that the wife of one of his comrades, Private John Mercer, then serving in his third enlistment, baked dried apple and cranberry pies, which she sold to the men at Fort Buford, Dakota Territory, for twenty-five and fifty cents, respectively. But even those pies came under the scrutiny of one by-the-book post commander, who insisted that laundresses could not sell pies made with ingredients purchased at the commissary, threatening to deny any future requests for baking supplies if they did. Just how he intended to enforce the rule can only be guessed, and the ladies undoubtedly devised shrewd ways to circumvent it.[23]

Still, problems abounded as a result of the laundress system, and some of them affected morale within the ranks. Writing anonymously to the *Army & Navy Journal*, a soldier complained that at his station:

> Out of fifteen sergeants there are no less than ten of them married. These sergeants seem to think that their duty consists in mounting guard every seven or eight days, and helping their wives to wash clothes and tend the babies the rest of the time. They have to do most of the washing, for . . . their wives must have time to curl their hair and talk gossip. . . . The men despise these "knights of the wash-tub" for their unmanliness, and the discipline of the company for the want of non-commissioned officers who would command the respect of the men.[24]

Invariably, Sudsville was a fertile spawning ground for rumor-mongering, sometimes vicious, among the women, who "are a great deal rougher in their language than we are," according to one soldier. It was not unusual for some of these strong-willed individuals to do pretty much as they pleased, even "disregarding edicts of the post council, they charge what prices they choose for washing, giving the unhappy possessor of dirty clothes the option of paying whatever they charge, or of washing for himself. . . . As a matter of course, they refuse always to wash for an officer who is not attached to the same company as themselves; and should a company commander attempt to exercise his authority, he is met with all sorts of excuses." The garrison at Fort Sanders, Wyoming Territory, witnessed such a conflict after word reached Captain William H. Powell that one of his laundresses had openly declared that "she would be damned if she would do any more washing for the Company Commander." Refusing to condone insubordination by anyone under his command, Powell dismissed her forthwith. Fortunate indeed was the company whose laundress was amenable to doing minor mending, while some adhered strictly to the regulation that they were "washerwomen" and nothing more. One bitter soldier, denigrating laundresses as "company plagues," groused that a man "must either . . . receive his clothes from his laundress in an unmended and buttonless condition, and often only half-washed, or he must wash them himself, which in this part of the country is almost next to an impossibility."[25]

More unscrupulous women schemed to defraud the government, some by deriving undue compensation by securing more than one official position simultaneously, such as being laundress for more than one company at the same time or being on duplicate rolls as a company laundress and as a hospital matron, thereby drawing double rations. Some also attempted to enroll their preteen daughters as laundresses for the same purpose. Perpetrating a more elaborate hoax, a bold woman "about forty-five years of age . . . [possessing] unmistakable traces of former beauty, although quite indifferently . . . dressed" approached Company Clerk John Spring on the eve of the Fourteenth Infantry's transfer from New York to California. Claiming to have a son in the regiment's second battalion at Vancouver Barracks, Washington Territory, and being temporarily without the means to travel to the West Coast, the woman petitioned pitifully to be appointed as a laundress so that she might be near her son. Swayed by the woman's heart-rending plea, and having only one laundress at the time, the captain assented, though Spring observed: "I do not know how much washing Mrs. Wilson performed, if any. She had frequent visits from the more decent men of the company during all hours of the day and evening until 'taps.'" Shortly after the regiment arrived at the Presidio of California, "Mrs. Wilson" resigned her position, whereupon Spring discovered that she was actually a rather well-known actress who had used her talent to dupe the army into paying for her travel to San Francisco for the purpose of advancing her career.[26]

"I am sure that every officer who has commanded a post will agree with me that one laundress is more trouble and annoyance to him than a company of men," declared one officer in a diatribe to the *Army & Navy Journal*. This was a widespread and not altogether unfounded view in army circles. Residing in such close association with each other, conflicts among laundresses were bound to arise. Those petty squabbles rarely became a matter of official record, but in one instance at Fort Fetterman laundress Annie Hessler, a first sergeant's wife, sought redress against her neighbor, a laundress for another company, complaining: "I am abused by her every moment I step outside my quarters." Mrs. Hessler named several witnesses who would support her accusation. Her company commander wisely chose to remain above the fray by simply assigning her and her husband to different, soon-to-be-vacated quarters.[27]

Despite the benefits that they brought to enlisted life, laundresses imposed financial and at times operational burdens on the government. Besides providing quarters, rations, straw or hay for bedding, medical care, and fuel, the army transported them and their families at government expense when their units made a change of station. The son of a Second Cavalryman related how a trumpeter's wife became an imposition as his father's troop transferred several hundred miles from Fort Sanders, Wyoming Territory, to Fort Keogh, Montana Territory. After the woman became so ill that she could not continue the journey, the frustrated commanding officer, having no transportation to spare, was compelled to leave his surgeon, a detail of twenty-five men, and another laundress to nurse her until an ambulance could be sent back from the post. During transfers it also aggravated soldiers when their officers ordered them to help erect and take down the tents of the laundresses, the men considering that sort of chore not to be in the line of duty.[28]

Inspector General Randolph B. Marcy wrote in his 1875 annual report: "It has often been said . . . that the baggage of four laundresses, with their children, generally amounts to more than that of all the enlisted men of the company." He added that for the previous three years the army had suffered reductions in its appropriation for housing, making it "impracticable to furnish comfortable or even habitable quarters for laundresses at many posts, and they and their children have suffered in consequence." Three years later General of the Army William T. Sherman weighed in, claiming that it cost the army no less than $150,562.50 annually to ration the authorized 1,650 women, further estimating that costs for quarters, fuel, and transportation would drive up the total to more than $300,000.00. The obvious solution, in his jaundiced view, was that marriage "should be universally prohibited to enlisted men attached to regiments and that captains of companies should provide for the washing of their men as they now do for the cooking." Some were of the opinion that the money devoted to supporting laundresses would be better spent on properly equipped post wash-houses, but Sherman likely calculated that laundry equipment could just as well be purchased from the soldiers' own company funds.[29]

A movement was clearly afoot, both in the army and in Congress, to end the service of costly laundresses, if not the headaches that all too frequently accompanied them. The ax fell in June 1878 in the form of a congressional act specifically prohibiting women laundresses from accompanying troops. Eliminated immediately were the positions encumbered by single women, although a discretionary grace period woven into the wording granted regimental commanders latitude to allow a laundress already married to a soldier to remain on the rolls until the end of the husband's current enlistment, conceivably up to five years from the date of the edict. The sometimes troublesome unmarried laundresses were sent packing immediately, while those who were married with whom commanders had experienced no significant problems enjoyed a temporary reprieve. Left unaddressed were those rare situations in which both the soldier and his laundress-wife may have posed nuisances, yet the army had ways of subtly ushering both out the door if it chose to do so. As to separate quarters for married men, the secretary of war clarified that "any right of married soldiers to separate quarters ends June 18, 1883, and that any allowance of such quarters after that date will be a matter of indulgence only . . . no expenditure of funds should be made on such quarters, which would not be needed were the quarters not occupied by women." Thus the existing buildings were allowed to deteriorate unless the husbands were able to find means to repair them.[30]

Caustic reactions by laundress-wives were not long in coming. To the majority of these women being a part of the military community was more than just a financial asset: it was a way of life. Wedded to the army, literally and figuratively, a plucky middle-aged laundress at Fort Lyon, Colorado, unflinchingly protested the decision:

> I have reared two boys, one has served eight years and one five, one during the war served three years and five since, and is still in the Army, and I don't think I have done the Army much

harm. You talk about the retirement of the existing laundresses and the discharge of their husbands in such a manner that injustice may not be done. I would like to know how that can be done after a man has served all his best days in the Army . . . , then . . . he must be turned out for no other reason than to save Government expenses.[31]

The army indisputably stood to lose capable, experienced men, not a few of them noncoms, as the result of phasing out laundresses. The only alternative for a married couple wishing to remain in the service was to adjust to an existence without her income, ration, and government quarters. But an even more serious personal and financial consideration faced married men—how to move their families when the company was ordered to transfer to another post. Reconsidering the directive in more humane terms, the secretary of war modified the official stance to permit married soldiers approaching the end of their enlistments who did not intend to reenlist simply because they had families to complete their terms by temporarily transferring to another company of their regiment that would be remaining at the present station or, failing that, to be discharged immediately. Even though army regulations did not exclude married soldiers from reenlisting, Sioux War veteran Brigadier General Nelson A. Miles, commanding the Department of the Columbia in 1882, advised against it because of "the hardship to those dependent upon them." Conceivably Miles saw in this situation an opportunity to contribute to the development of the West by urging that soon-to-be-discharged soldiers be specially furloughed so they might purchase land and take up residence or at least find employment in that developing economy. For those married enlisted men who elected to remain in service, changes of station imposed even greater difficulty, both financially and personally. An Eighth Cavalry captain remarked on the forced separations created by the epic overland march that his regiment made when transferring from the Texas-Mexican border to Dakota Territory in 1888: "It was a heavy expense to the Government, a heavy expense to the officers and married soldiers, some of whom had to leave their families for months in Texas, before they could save enough money to bring them north."[32]

As evidence that the army may not have been entirely insensitive to the plight of career noncoms, the adjutant general announced in early

1881 that "meritorious non-commissioned officers, who are married, may be re-enlisted within one month from date of discharge . . . provided it is understood their wives will be entitled to no privileges as laundresses, and that they will not make the fact of their being married a ground for discharge before expiration of their term of service." One suspects that the army's apparent concern may actually have veiled anxiety arising from the significant loss of that "bone and sinew" so vital to the organization. In any event, that tepid indulgence did little to boost morale among those directly affected. Typical of the class facing the crucial choice was First Sergeant William A. Curtiss, Seventh Cavalry, then in his third term and a veteran of both the Sioux and Nez Perce Campaigns. His wife, Kate, worked as a company laundress, at the same time managing the household and caring for their three children. Discouraged about their prospects for remaining in the army, the couple elected to leave the service a few months later to make a new life elsewhere. One sympathetic soldier penned a fitting tribute to the rough-hewn women residents of Sudsville: "If there is a religious wash woman in this Territory, your correspondent knoweth not, but religious or not, when they shuffle off their mortal souls, wring out the last Government shirt, fold their wash tubs and say 'adios' . . . to things earthly, they should be permitted to enter that land above where wash tubs and sick things are below par, for surely they have had enough punishment here below."[33]

In contrast to the hardships placed on some enlisted families, the abolition of company laundresses created a vacuum that afforded economic opportunity for other frontier entrepreneurs eager to better their own status. Within a year after the promulgation of the order, the commander of H Company, Sixth Cavalry, foresaw a coming crisis with the dwindling numbers of company women and therefore sought an alternative to traditional laundresses. Traveling from Fort Verde to the town of Prescott, Arizona Territory, he negotiated with two experienced Chinese men willing to wash clothes for his company and escorted them back to the post. The troopers cheered the captain's actions, one of them remarking of the company women: "They can't go any too soon to suit us. Certainly our clothes must be washed, but let Tang and Que do it. . . . The experiment has proved a great success. . . . They are neat and clean and give no trouble." When it was facetiously suggested that the popular duo ought to consider joining the army as "laundry soldiers," the Chinese deftly countered that enlisting "is not in affinity with our celestial views. . . . We haven't the remotest idea to bond our liberty and to jeopardize our rights as China-American citizens." As word of that business opportunity spread to other regions, consolidated post laundries privately operated by enterprising people of Chinese ancestry sprang up at forts across the West, including Fort Custer, Montana Territory, where Sam Lee and four or five helpers went into business, and even at remote Fort Bowie, perched high atop Arizona's Chiricahua Mountains. A former Ninth Cavalry trooper who served at Fort Robinson, Nebraska, during the late 1880s, recalled paying $3.00 a month to Chinese and Hispanic men and women operating a laundry camp on nearby Soldier Creek. Even though civilians necessarily had to charge soldiers higher prices for their services, the general quality of their work and the desire of the launderers to please their customers, and thus continue in business, combined for a mutually harmonious relationship.[34]

The attrition of authorized company laundresses continued unabated until the expiration of the five-year grace period in 1883. Repeated recommendations from various quarters for military-run laundries went unheeded by officials, the army continuing to suggest that soldiers could be detailed for that purpose, in the same manner that cooking and kitchen police were delegated. The army considered such facilities to be a needless expense, especially as garrisons were consolidated at fewer posts in response to the evaporating frontier and the proliferation of civilian communities. Officers throughout the chain of command were happy enough to see the exodus of laundresses and to be relieved of what many had long considered to be more nuisance than advantage. Perhaps none was more candid than Sherman's successor, General of the Army Philip H. Sheridan, as he sighed that "it is hoped they will never again be authorized."[35]

The presence of company women may have exerted an indirect ameliorating effect on tenor in the ranks, but religious activity remained a scarce commodity in the regular army of that era. Life in the regulars did not breed saints. "I had long since learned that there was 'no Sunday in the army,'" observed a first sergeant in the Sixth Cavalry. "No chaplains were stationed at any of the frontier posts in my time, no religious service was held on Sunday." Most soldiers recognized Sunday only by the suspension of fatigue and other routine activities, except weekly inspection and the incessant guard duty. Religion played little role in the day, however, regardless of a man's upbringing. Writing from Fort Sedgwick, Colorado Territory, in 1867, Private Maurice Wolfe, an Irish-Catholic immigrant, informed a relative: "We are living here like 'Hermits' but not doing penance for our sins, as there are no churches, or clergy within six hundred miles of us so that when a man dies or gets married it is the Adjutant that reads the ceremonies, which is very uncatholic. As for religion it's the last and least a man thinks of here." Another Irishman, Private Thomas P. Downing, a Seventh Cavalryman posted at Fort Totten, similarly admitted to his father that he had become "a careless Catholic" and had not attended Mass during his three years in the army. Private Eddie Matthews, reared in Maryland as a devout Protestant, informed his family that he had not been to church in nearly five years, not counting three graveside burial services that he had attended during that time. In his experience "a Christian in the Regular Army, excepting a few Chaplains, and they are even doubtful, would be as great a curiosity as one of Barnimes [Barnum's] Canibals [sic]."[36]

Coming from a strongly religious family, William B. Jett, a trooper in the Fourth Cavalry, confided in an oddly contradictory statement: "I had never gotten over saying my prayers and in spite of difficulties I said them (in my bed) amid . . . the rough talk going on around me. I also had a little Bible . . . and I made it my business to read as much as ten verses every day possible, though I was not a Christian." Jett added that he actually knew of only one private, an Irish Orangeman (Protestant), who professed to be a Christian. "The first night he was among us he got down on his knees beside his cot and prayed. Heads were raised in surprise at this innovation, all over the quarters, and shoes, boots, boot-jacks, canteens, clothing, and other missiles were thrown at him till he was about covered." The believer nevertheless persisted in his ritual every night and during the next ten days steadily won the respect of his comrades for his endurance, if not his faith. "Then . . . no one in the room of about fifty men would have dared to have thrown anything at Todd . . . any missile thrower would have been handled roughly."[37]

Comparatively few forts on the frontier had resident chaplains, invariably dubbed "Holy Joes," which accounted in some degree for the army's lack of emphasis on (if not concern for) the spiritual needs of soldiers. Addressing the issue in his inimitable gruff manner, General Sherman, whose wife regularly attended Catholic mass, growled: "The whole system is a farce. . . . If Congress wanted the army to have the influence of religion, it would allow the Commanding Officer of each [remote] post . . . to hire and pay for a minister . . . like surgeons. Of such posts there are nearly a hundred, whereas Chaplains are limited to thirty, say half of whom are sick, or don't like the isolation of Texas, Arizona, etc." The rule for assigning army chaplains, formerly one to each regiment, was modified a few years after the Civil War to coincide better with the fragmentation of regiments among widely separated posts. Congress, however, authorized only thirty-four chaplains, representing a variety of denominations, to serve the entire army—thirty assigned to designated posts, plus four more attached specifically to the four black regiments. All were required to be ordained ministers recommended by no less than five accredited ministers of the denomination represented by the applicant.[38]

However rare post chaplains may have been, there was still no assurance that the men would benefit much by their presence. A chaplain's basic duties called for him to hold services at least once on Sunday, to officiate at military funerals, and to submit monthly reports as to the "moral condition" of the troops. "There was a 'Holy Joe' who held services and took charge of funerals. Not many attended services," recalled Private James B. Wilkinson, who served in the Second Cavalry during the mid-1880s. As Sergeant Perley S. Eaton recalled of his service in the Third Cavalry at about the same time: "I don't think there were many soldiers that had any religion at all," thus accounting for the generally low attendance at services.[39]

In other instances an unmotivated chaplain was to blame. Trooper Jett remembered the chaplain at Fort Huachuca, Arizona Territory, failing to hold any services and associating only with officers and their families, though Jett conceded that on one occasion he did observe the chaplain assisting a drunken soldier back to his quarters. After complaining about the treatment of prisoners, thus arousing the ire of the post commander, the same chaplain was ordered to initiate services for the captive audience at the guardhouse. "The prisoners were placed under guard and made to attend those services at the point of a bayonet," according to Jett. "Many a time I, as guard, sat behind them and kept them in place and quiet while the Chaplain went through with what was to us worse than no service at all. . . . I never saw an officer at any of these services, nor did any of the soldiers attend save the prisoners and their guard." Tenth Infantryman George Neihaus attested that he did not recall the subject of religion ever being mentioned among the men in his company, claiming that "our post Chaplain had service on Sunday—then he spent the rest of the week indulging in liquor." While few post commanders seem to have exerted any particular emphasis on church attendance, an exception was Lieutenant Colonel Elmer Otis, successor to George A. Custer as second-in-command of the Seventh Cavalry following the Battle of the Little Bighorn. Otis ordered his first sergeants to publish a circular to their companies three times weekly announcing that Catholic masses would be conducted every Sunday and Monday. As an inducement for the men to attend, Otis dispensed with the usual Sunday morning inspection. Just how effective that may have proved was not entered in the record.[40]

In the absence of army chaplains, many posts were afforded limited religious exposure by itinerant ministers and priests sometimes posted at nearby Indian agencies. The Reverend Charles H. Cook visited Camp Bowie, Arizona Territory, in the early 1870s for two weeks as the guest of one of the officers. During that time he preached at least once a day, alternating between officers' row, the barracks, and the guardhouse, where his influence may have been needed most. It was reported that Reverend Cook was disappointed by the lack of enthusiasm shown by the few Third Cavalry boys who attended his sermon "Ten Virgins." When a French priest showed up at Fort Yuma, situated on the banks of the Lower Colorado River, the post surgeon noted with dripping sarcasm: "The men saw the priest dressed up in his bright colored vestments, surrounded by his other paraphernalia . . . heard him read the prayers and a mass, and after all was said and done, they had the privilege of contributing for this exhibition a sum of not less than seventy dollars. Truly a fine way of raising money." The surgeon rightly doubted that the men gained much from the experience, as the mass was said entirely in Latin. Likewise suspicious that the clergy may have had a financial motive in ministering to soldiers, the contract doctor at Fort Sill, Indian Territory, recorded shortly after an Episcopalian bishop visited the post: "There came two Sisters of Charity. They came in company with the Paymaster, a very good time to come, as everybody has money, and that is what the Sisters are after. They are collecting funds to build a hospital in Kansas City." The visits by the bishop and later a Catholic priest, he contended, were the only religious exposure the garrison had in two years.[41]

Army posts located conveniently near established communities, such as Fort Whipple near Prescott, Arizona Territory, sometimes enjoyed religious services provided by the local clergy on a regular basis, though it is doubtful that many enlisted men attended. A Fourth Infantryman at Fort Bridger, Wyoming Territory, commenting upon the arrival of a priest, hinted at the reason: "There are a great many Catholics here who were a long time going to Confession, and who were very reluctant in so doing, until such time as they would be out of the Service." Private Walter C. Harrington, who served in the Twenty-First Infantry, may have provided the best insight into the prevalent attitude among enlisted soldiers toward religion: "Not many attended church. Not many, practically none, of them indulged in the emotional phase, but they were right 'there' with their services and money in a deserving case." An example of "the boys" taking care of their own occurred when a recruit, accidentally shot through both knees, was medically discharged following his recovery. Concerned for the young man's welfare, his first sergeant collected more than three hundred dollars from among the men of his own and other companies and deposited it with the paymaster for the disabled man's benefit.[42]

If clergymen were a rarity at frontier forts, chapels were even scarcer. A few posts, such as Fort Davis, Texas, and Fort Randall, Dakota Territory, boasted dedicated church buildings, but the usual means for accommodating intermittent religious services was to utilize some other available space for the purpose. For a time at Fort Concho, Texas, services were held in one of the hospital wards and at other times in an unoccupied mess hall "used for a Chapel, reading room, & Court Room." The same could be said of the great majority of western posts, though a few garrisons had multipurpose halls used as a library, school, theater, and court, in addition to serving as a chapel when needed.[43]

Just as it largely ignored religious instruction, the army devoted little attention to providing traditional education for soldiers at frontier posts prior to the late 1870s, although it did provide means for funding post schools for children. An exception, however, were the black regiments organized after the Civil War, each of which was authorized its own chaplain responsible for developing an educational program for the men, because most had been denied educational opportunities. While various religious organizations and educational societies began establishing schools for freed blacks under the auspices of the Freedmen's Bureau, the army had its own reasons for doing so—literate noncommissioned officers were required to maintain the myriad records and other paperwork necessary for unit and post functions. Compounding the army's need was the high percentage of foreign immigrants in the white regiments, many of whom were barely able to communicate verbally in the English language, much less read and write it. In recognition that the army would directly benefit by educating its soldiers, an 1866 order directed all post commanders to provide some suitable building, or at least an adequate room, to serve school and church purposes.[44]

For a number of years, however, white soldiers were largely ignored and left almost completely to their own devices concerning education. Some line officers, initially convinced that it was not the army's place to educate soldiers and that it detracted from their availability for military duty, actively opposed efforts to educate enlisted men. An Eighteenth Infantry private at Fort Fetterman, Dakota Territory, informed his parents that he was attempting to improve himself in his spare time by the acquisition of a "Webster's dictionary, Davies new arithmetic, and the American orator. . . . These books are some I bought second handed, for the suttler keeps nothing but those every lasting novels which I do not allow myself to look at" (all odd spellings in the original).[45]

The situation exhibited signs of improvement by the early 1870s, as reflected in the increasing number of post schools, usually taught by qualified enlisted men, though civilian teachers were sometimes hired by the post council. By 1873 Fort Fetterman claimed a day school with sixteen young scholars, segregated into three progressive classes composed of both officers' and soldiers' children engaged in a curriculum of reading, writing, arithmetic, and geography. The teacher, Private John D. O'Brien, Fourth Infantry, was a native of Liverpool, England, and had been a clerk prior to joining the U.S. Army ten years earlier. That same year Fort Hays, Kansas, reported having three schools, two of them segregated by caste—one for officers' children, the other for the children of soldiers—and the third a Sunday school taught by the post surgeon's wife. No discrimination presumably was made among children attending Sunday school. At Fort Concho chaplain George W. Dunbar fulfilled his obligation by operating a night school for soldiers of the Twenty-Fifth Infantry. Dunbar taught classes two nights a week, from seven o'clock until tattoo, not only in the three Rs but also in United States history. Despite such advances in education for children and black soldiers, other enlisted men were still routinely deprived of formal education, except when they were inspired to be tutored by another soldier. One of those was Private Benjamin F. Brown, Seventh Cavalry, formerly a Kentucky farmer, who proudly composed a letter to his mother in 1875: "This is my own hand writing every word. I expect to be a clerk yet. When you write again, write it plain so that I can read it myself."[46]

Only in late 1877 did the matter of education for all enlisted soldiers come to the attention of the secretary of war, who convened a board of officers to consider the entire matter. In rendering its findings, the board acknowledged that the existing army budget would not permit the service to develop and execute a complete educational program but allowed that post funds could be used, with judicious management, to purchase books and other needed school supplies as currently provided in army regulations. Even though children's schools had been a legitimate expenditure of the post fund for many years, education was forced to compete at each post with the costs of operating the bakery and supporting the band, which was often the pet of the regimental commander. The board additionally pointed out a more serious deficiency in the lack of already scarce funds needed to construct school buildings, but the secretary pressured the quartermaster general to revise his program so that schools received a higher priority than they had before.[47]

The May 1878 general order directed that every garrison establish a post school for enlisted men, teaching "the common English branches of education and especially in the history of the United States." It further stipulated that all officers were obliged actively to promote the education of enlisted men. Teachers were to be detailed from among men in the companies; in instances when no qualified soldier was available, a post commander could request one through the Recruiting Service in the same way that companies obtained saddlers, musicians, and other skilled men. Responding to the challenge, Lieutenant Colonel Thomas M. Anderson, commanding the Columbus Barracks depot, initiated a normal school for the specific purpose of creating a pool of specially qualified men to fill requisitions for vocational teachers.[48]

Even though the men detailed as post school instructors received extra duty pay of thirty-five cents a day, some complained that the job imposed an unfair burden because "the army school master has not only his school duty to perform, four or five hours a day for the children, and two hours in the evening for the men, excepting Saturday and Sunday, but company duty also. He has to attend drill and dress parade, all company inspections, besides monthly inspection and muster, very often closing the school for half a day for that purpose." Another soldier lodged a similar complaint, adding that teachers, particularly those who were noncoms, were not even exempted from clerking, being charge-of-quarters, and attending NCO school. Rebelling against what they felt was unfair treatment, some soldier-teachers got drunk to avoid the duty. Then, too, questions were raised as to whether those specially requested soldier-teachers were to be assigned to companies, like other recruits, and if so whether they were liable to be transferred with those companies, possibly depriving the post of its only qualified instructor. General Sherman dispelled any uncertainty with a decision that in those circumstances the man should be transferred to another company of the same regiment, remaining at that station, or even to an incoming company belonging to a different regiment.[49]

Within a few months after the order classes for enlisted soldiers proliferated throughout the army. Nineteenth Infantryman Michael Pyne, a teacher before entering the service, was logically appointed as the first "Overseer of Schools" at Fort Lyon, Colorado, in August 1878. Pyne deftly developed a curriculum embracing geography, writing, spelling, arithmetic, grammar, and history. "The men comprising this class [averaging only 7 or 8] have had few educational advantages, but they desire to learn and have progressed rapidly," reported his successor after Pyne's promotion to sergeant major. "They have progressed through the geography of North and South America, are working . . . division of compound numbers, readily spell words of three and four syllables, write legibly, and are making good progress in the study of grammar." Sergeant James S. Hamilton, First Infantry, said that the first classes at Fort Meade, Dakota Territory, were "located somewhere in the quarters. . . . Usually some member of the company conducted the classes. I attended all classes possible and it was from one of these men I obtained a valuable little dictionary containing many obsolete words."[50]

Neither were the black regiments slow in responding. The post surgeon at Fort Concho boasted: "The new schoolroom is about 40 × 20, and is by far the best furnished room in the post. A very promising teacher was found in Sergeant Howell, of Co. A, 25th Infantry. He is very patient, and very ambitious, and will in due time, become an excellent teacher." Sergeant Samuel Harris related that officers of the Twenty-Fifth Infantry not only took an interest in the men's education but stepped up to teach night classes for soldiers. Even at an isolated subpost like Camp Pena Colorado, Texas, a Tenth Cavalry lieutenant was rather surprised to see that "there are quite a number of [Twenty-Fifth] Infantrymen in camp who are trying to learn to read. The Cavalrymen show few indications of a desire to improve their minds." But, he acknowledged, "This may be due to their being so much in the field and so hard worked in the post, that they have but little energy to devote to self-culture, but it is due to a greater extent to their officers not having taken any interest in their education."[51]

Unfortunately, not all officers shared a concern for elevating their men. Calling attention to an obvious breach of regulations, a soldier at Fort Elliott, Texas, complained that school had been suspended there as the result of having no teacher and the men being obligated to "furnish their books out of their scanty pay, if they wish to learn." The secretary of war was not unaware of such laxity in the enforcement of the 1878 directive and three years later found it pervasive enough to remind army officers of its provisions. The other side of the problem was that many soldiers simply were not motivated to go to school, even when it was offered, an element probably discouraging some officers from devoting much attention to the program. "The children of enlisted men are required to attend school unless excused by the officer in charge," observed a soldier at Fort Shaw, Montana Territory. "The fact that it has been optional with men to attend is exactly what has caused the present system to break down. At this post there are only eight men out of four companies and the band who attend regularly, or who take any interest in it." An officer examining the state of army education in the early 1880s determined that a significant factor detracting from its success was that "the exigencies of service at the far West prevent many from availing themselves of the school privileges."[52]

Despite those hurdles, educational opportunities steadily improved with the construction of schools at frontier forts or at least the dedication of adequate rooms for the purpose. In less than a year 935 enlisted men, not to mention a nearly equal number of children, were attending post schools. The secretary and the quartermaster general worked in concert to adjust construction priorities to remedy the shortage of school facilities and within three years the army had built fifty-two structures combining chapel, school, and library functions.[53]

In apparent contradiction to the limited funding for facilities, however, the new edition of *Army Regulations* adopted in 1881 specified that the schoolrooms at those garrisons where both white and black troops served would be separate for the two races, though of equal quality. If physical segregation was not enough, the regulations additionally stipulated that white teachers could instruct black soldiers but implied that the reverse would not be sanctioned. Among those puzzled by these new requirements was an anonymous soldier signing himself "Anxious Seeker," who queried the editor of the *Army & Navy Journal*: "Why this separation should be a necessity is a mystery to the unenlightened. Possibly the . . . [journal,] which is 'behind the scenes' in such matters, may be able to elucidate." No response was forthcoming, probably because the answer was only too obvious.[54]

Even though school attendance remained optional for soldiers, an increase in the percentage of American-born enlistees, higher enlistment standards, and the decline of field operations throughout much of the West by the late 1880s had the effect of enhancing school participation. In 1886 Fort Douglas, Utah, reported having an enrollment of 250 enlisted men but only 29 children. Sergeant Reinhold R. Geist, who entered the Eighth Cavalry a year later, said that his post had a school "to advance education for anyone who cared to go. I . . . took advantage of this." A cavalry trooper at Fort Custer, Montana Territory, proudly announced to a local newspaper that the post school was "in a flourishing condition. . . . Penmanship and book-keeping are specialties." That garrison was particularly fortunate, for both instructors at that time were soldiers who had formerly been schoolteachers in civil life and had been specially recruited for that reason. Many soldiers by that time became enthusiastic students, exemplified by Private Hartford G. Clark at Fort Niobrara, Nebraska, who wrote: "Went to school to day and got 100% in everything. Studying algebra now. . . . I have not been absent but twice and then I was on guard and could not get there." Yet there were a few men, like Hospital Corpsman Richard F. King, whose only motivation was to gain promotion. "I have got to go to school for a year ever[y] night," he lamented, "I do not like it but I haft to do it all the same but it will give me $25 a month then. I only get $13 now. . . . I will haft to pass well in ever[y] thing . . . to get my appointment [to hospital steward third class]" (all odd spellings in the original).[55]

The elimination of company laundresses may have seemed a blessing to the army, but it had the effect of greatly reducing the presence of both women and children at frontier posts by the latter 1880s. That may have been a good thing in the minds of many officers, but as might be expected many youths among the rank and file viewed it differently. There were the wives of officers, of course, and still some cooks and housekeepers along the officers' line, along with the families of a few senior noncoms, but the good old days of suds row were but a memory. At some posts women were almost entirely absent. Soldiers starved for feminine companionship at Fort Stanton, New Mexico Territory, enthusiastically accepted an invitation to attend a dance hosted by cowboys at a local ranch—but there was a catch. A Fourth Cavalryman wrote: "Each attendant paid five dollars . . . but this fee paid for a girl partner . . . two of the girls were chewing tobacco . . . [and another] was a very pretty girl and could rope a steer like a man. . . . The men all sat on one side of the room and ladies on the other." One trooper fortunate enough to secure a furlough in 1886 was caught unprepared when he arrived home in Baltimore and was greeted by a pretty girl hired by his father as a tutor for the younger siblings. Painfully aware that his social skills had degenerated in the army, he admitted: "I had no association with women during my five years in the West, and I was much embarrassed . . . when left in the sitting room alone with her. . . . I knew what to do with Indians, soldiers, Mexicans, cow-boys, teamsters, centipedes, tarantulas and rattlesnakes, but I did not know what to do with this young lady. . . . I contemplated jumping up and running from the room." Bemoaned another isolated soldier in 1889: "You know it is so lonsome [sic] out here that I almost go mad once in a while . . . I did not see one woman for a year and 2 months except the officers wifes [sic]." This lamentation was ironically reminiscent of the one expressed by the soldier in Colorado more than two decades earlier.[56]

The termination of company laundresses, however, did not necessarily mean an end to soldiers finding a mate, only that the financial and personal challenges became more daunting in the absence of the amenities formerly supplied by the army. The frontier had all but disappeared by that time, a factor enhancing the ability of lonely soldiers to meet young single women in the nearby towns budding all over the West. But impressionable young ladies dazzled by army blue and glittering brass buttons seldom realized what it really meant to embark on marriage to a soldier. A widow of experience wrote to the editor of the *Army & Navy Journal* admonishing girls what they might expect: "She has no quarters or roof under which to shelter. Where are her rations and clothing to come from? His $13 a month is not sufficient. . . . If she is fortunate enough to get a position in an officer's kitchen (if you call that fortunate) she may earn her own support." Still, that harsh reality was not always enough to deter true love.[57]

Shortly after his marriage to a domestic servant at Cheyenne, Wyoming Territory, in 1889, Private Howard A. Lyon and his company of the Seventeenth Infantry were ordered to the field for a month's training. Lovesick and concerned for the health of his young bride, Annie, Lyon encouraged her that "you are mine now and I don't want you to ware [sic] your self [sic] out working like a slave for other people. . . . I thank god the time will come when we shall not have to part." That time was, in fact, not far distant. Lyon would be discharged six months later, though the anticipated marital bliss was to be short-lived. Within a year after Howard's discharge from the army, Annie was left a widow.[58]

Sixth Cavalrymen stationed at Fort Niobrara in 1891 saw to it that girls in nearby Valentine, Nebraska, did not suffer any loneliness. After striking up a relationship with "a very refined young lady" who apparently had matrimonial designs, Private Hartford Clark confided to his diary that he "left her house at 2.15 in order to make the post by 3 o'clock as my pass expired at that time. . . . Miss Marshall wanted me to come down to the dance tonight, but [I] cannot stand the pressure." One of his friends, however, did find a mate, and "about fifteen soldiers (selected) went . . . to witness the marriage ceremony. . . . After the ceremony [at a local church] we went back to the [bride's] house to partake of ice cream, cake, lemon ade [sic] etc. . . . It was quite a nice little wedding for a soldier to have."[59] Indeed, both the West and the army were becoming quite different from what they had been a quarter-century earlier.

CHAPTER 10

"We Have Our Little Amusements"

Recreation and Pastimes

Soldier life on a frontier post was, more often than not, a decidedly boring existence marked by few diversions from the numbing routine of the garrison regimen. The average duty day—filled with fatigue, drill, guard, roll calls, and special details—left comparatively few hours that soldiers could call their own. Pastimes and recreational opportunities were few. "I am always thinking of home," lamented an immigrant sergeant in 1869. "Even with all the loneliness in Ireland I would rather be there than here, but I have cast my lot and must abide by it." This was the ubiquitous plight of soldiers serving in the West, particularly during the early years when forts remained isolated by distance, a paucity of towns, and, more often than not, slow, irregular communication with the States.[1]

The importance of mail to a soldier cannot be overstated. "What would our lives be without the mail?" queried a member of the garrison at Camp McPherson, Arizona Territory. "It is the only connecting link between us and civilization. . . . All last winter we were kept in a fever of excitement, owing to the detention of our letters by the overflowing of some river, or the impassability of the roads; and, to cap the climax, after the mail had surmounted all those obstacles, and was in a fair way of getting somewhere, the confounded Apaches gobbled it, wounding the mail-carrier and killing the escort." Even though mail coaches arrived and departed weekly, a trooper at neighboring Fort

Whipple informed his family in Maryland that "it takes about one month for a letter to come from home," when it arrived at all.[2]

Even along major overland routes, in advance of railroads, mail service could be unpredictable. The surgeon at Fort Fletcher, Kansas, a primitive cantonment situated on the Smoky Hill Route linking Kansas City and Denver, was exasperated to learn that while visiting Fort Ellsworth, some fifty miles east, one of their officers had noticed a mail bag marked for Fort Fletcher lying ignored at the sutler's store. "On inquiring into the matter, it appeared that this bag contained mails for us which had been sent to Denver. The P[ost] M[aster] there had sent it back to us, but the driver neglected to deliver it as he passed by us and carried it back to Ellsworth."[3]

More than a few posts, as exemplified by the three forts established along the Bozeman Trail in 1866, lay entirely off designated U.S. postal mail routes. Therefore the army was obligated to transport its own mail using relays of mounted or wagon-borne couriers. And while railroads began facilitating the mails to posts in proximity to the major transportation corridors, some of those in the far Northwest and the Southwest remained handicapped for years. At Fort Keogh, Montana Territory, a station reliant on steamboats for mail and supplies, a resident soldier informed the readers of the *Army & Navy Journal* that winter temperatures had ranged from twenty-five to fifty degrees below zero, so "no Eastern mails [were] received for 20 days at a time," and even then they came only by courier. On the nation's southwestern fringe, the territories of New Mexico and Arizona were not accessed by rail until the close of the 1870s and western Texas a few more years after that. Declared Private George S. Raper: "It would be hard for anyone who had not passed through the experience to realize the irksome sameness, or want of variety in a soldier's life in New Mexico, and especially at Fort Stanton, in the early 70s. The nearest point of anything that might be called civilization being Las Vegas, more than 150 miles away. . . . Mail once a week and taking from four to five weeks for a letter from as far east as Ohio."[4]

When not otherwise obligated to perform some duty, a soldier could do pretty much as he pleased with his spare time until tattoo sounded, so long as he did not venture farther than a mile from the flagstaff without a written pass. That restriction imposed little constraint on the men at most posts, simply because there was seldom anything worth seeing or doing so near a fort. Nearly all military reservations encompassed several square miles within which civilians were prohibited from settling or establishing businesses. As a result, soldiers commonly devoted their free time to loafing, visiting among themselves, playing cards (draw poker, twenty-one, and pinochle were popular), and, for those who were literate, reading or writing letters. "My time is passed mostly in reading, what little time I have to spare," Private George H. Cranston explained in a letter written at Camp Crittenden, Arizona Territory, in 1868. "But I am busy nearly all day, and in the evening I can not read much on account of candles, there being none at the post, only what are is[s]ued to us, and they last but a short time." It was just as well, perhaps, because the availability of reading matter was equally limited. A man stationed at Tucson, astride the Southern Overland Route, groused that despite triweekly mail delivery to that point "our papers seldom ever reach us, and our letters are from thirty-two to eighty-six days coming from New York. . . . The first person who meets the mail [about a hundred miles north at Maricopa Wells], carries it to the station, opens the mail, and distributes it according to the rider's wish. If the bag is heavy, they throw out a certain amount."[5]

Members of the rank and file, accordingly, were largely dependent on their own resourcefulness for recreation. Sergeant James S. Hamilton, First Infantry, affirmed that playing cards was the most popular activity, adding that a few energetic men sometimes engaged in footraces or a game of horseshoes, weather permitting. The post trader's complex was a popular gathering place: in addition to operating a small general store, he maintained a rude bar where soldiers could purchase liquor—cheap whiskey being the most prevalent drink prior to the availability of pasteurized beer in the mid-1870s. At an average cost of twenty-five cents a glass, whiskey offered the most alcohol for the price, but even so soldiers could not afford to buy very much. As one regular put it, "We had more free time than we had money."[6]

Only rarely during the early years were towns close enough to army posts to allow soldiers to frequent them in search of their preferred diversions—booze, women, and gambling. In Arizona Territory, Tucson was an exception, having been founded by the Spanish as a presidio nearly a century before the U.S. Army established Fort Lowell there. Despite its age and convenience to the garrison, Tucson offered the troops few amenities in 1869. A visitor described the place as a city of mud boxes, dingy and dilapidated, cracked and baked into a composite of dust and filth; littered about with broken corrals, sheds, bake-ovens, carcasses of dead animals, and broken pottery; barren of verdure, parched, baked, and grimly desolate in the glare of a southern sun. Adobe walls without whitewash inside or out, hard earth floors, baked and dried Mexicans, sore-backed burros, coyote dogs, and terra-cotta children; soldiers, teamsters, and honest miners lounging about the mescal shops, soaked with the fiery poison.[7]

The town showed no marked improvement eleven years later. Signal Sergeant Will Barnes, who passed through Tucson en route to Fort Apache, was astonished to see that "in each place a number of gambling games ran steadily the twenty-four hours round. There were faro, stud-poker, keno, roulette, monte, and straight poker. Everyone was either struggling to reach the bar for a drink or trying hard to get up to one of the games." First Cavalryman Maurice J. O'Leary related that soldiers posted in the Southwest also "went in strong for game cocks . . . and they sometimes cleaned up quite a little money on a good cock fight, and sometimes they got cleaned too."[8]

In other parts of the West boomtowns like Cheyenne and Laramie City, both astride the main line of the Union Pacific Railroad in Wyoming Territory, immediately became points for garrisoning troops and supplying regional military operations. Fortunate indeed were those soldiers stationed in such places, though a trip to town required a written pass granted by their company commander. Men selected as orderlies and members of the old guard were routinely rewarded with day passes (sometimes extending up to 24 hours) to be off post following their tours of duty. Mounted passes were often given to cavalry troopers to allow them to ride their horses to a town or other specified place. Fourth Infantrymen quartered at Fort Sanders were permitted to go into Laramie City, only three miles away, between "Retreat" and midnight, so long as they surrendered their passes to the sergeant of the guard upon their return as a means of accountability. At every post company officers, or the first sergeants, conducted a bed-check each night to ensure that no men were absent without authority.[9]

Civilians in the West generally tolerated, if not welcomed, the soldiers who patronized their towns and the whiskey ranches that invariably sprang up just beyond the reservation boundaries of forts distant from communities. For many, including business owners and those entrepreneurs who contracted to supply hay, wood, and beef cattle, the army represented a steady source of income. Moreover, westerners determined to establish themselves in business, ranching, or other ventures generally appreciated the army's presence for the protection the "boys in blue" afforded, especially in regions where Indian hostilities were prevalent. Even in formerly Confederate Texas inhabitants in the vicinity of Fort Richardson graciously accepted invitations to attend balls hosted by the soldiers: "and no friction ever occurred between the citizens and the soldiers as a rule," according to a Sixth Cavalryman, though he added that local Texans did not view all soldiers equally. "This don't apply to the colored soldiers, the citizens here had little use for the latter, and in fact, the white soldiers hadn't either." When a battalion of the Second Cavalry transferred to Montana in 1869, one of their officers commented that "the citizens of Virginia City are friendly and endeavor to make the best of everything. The people were anxious for us to remain over Sunday, but it is necessary to move on and get to Fort Ellis." The cordiality probably had a lot to do with the cash that the troops would leave behind, though trooper Eddie Matthews noted a similarly friendly reception when a patrol of the Eighth Cavalry paused in Trinidad, Colorado Territory, the same year. "The people of this town think a great deal of a Soldier," he wrote, "and do all in their power to make our stay as pleasant as possible."[10]

Nevertheless, the rough element populating the frontier—railroad workers, miners, cowhands, and toughs on the fringes of the law—could also make for volatile relationships, particularly when fueled by alcohol. "This is a wild reckless country for a man to live in," wrote a Thirtieth Infantry soldier at Fort D. A. Russell, Wyoming Territory. "A man will shoot another man upon the slightest provocation, as every man here [Cheyenne] carries his brace of revolvers and Bowie knife in his waist belt." Sadly, that was borne out all too often. In an affray typical of many, Private John Kimball, a Thirty-Fifth Infantryman stationed at Fort Bliss, Texas, was shot in the head and killed in the nearby town of Franklin in 1867. In a similar instance three years later a miner shot Private John Welsh, Third Cavalry, during a drunken row at Galisteo, New Mexico.[11]

The regulars enjoyed music in one form or another as a pleasant way to pass the time. "We have our little amusements, the post (Regimental) Band entertains us with choice music for an hour every evening," wrote a soldier at Fort Laramie, Wyoming Territory, in the summer of 1870. As enjoyable as such concerts may have been, they were all too rare for the majority of troops, each regiment having only a single band that without exception was garrisoned with the headquarters staff. The companies distributed among other posts were not so fortunate and had to make do for themselves. The ranks of nearly all companies included a few talented musicians who could play the common instruments. A Ninth Cavalryman, a self-taught guitarist himself, recalled that "soldiers played guitars and all kinds of banjos and fiddles. . . . Lots of fun." First Sergeant Henry McConnell said that among the men in his company were several good musicians who, along with a few from other units, formed a troupe "and with the aid of two violins, guitar, flute, and banjo, made really good music." In most instances such ensembles were initiated by the musicians themselves, but at Fort Union, New Mexico Territory, the post chaplain "called upon all who could sing or play any kind of instrument to meet at the Chapel. . . . several of the boys brought instruments such as violins, banjos, guitars, and brass horns. Mrs. Dr. Welden presided at the organ . . . and since that time we have had music and singing once each week."[12]

The inclination toward singing varied a great deal according to the individuals in a company at any given time, thus making generalizations difficult. According to Reynolds Burt, who spent his boyhood years at several frontier army posts: "There was no group singing in the evenings. . . . The enlisted men in general were too old (many of them professional soldiers of too long standing) to be interested in 'getting the gang going,' as it were. Occasionally, a more gifted soldier . . . would sing for his own contentment." Sergeant Perley Eaton, Third Cavalry, seconded that view, saying: "There weren't many singers in my company, at least I didn't hear them sing much." Nor did Sergeant Samuel Harris recall much singing in Company B, Twenty-Fifth Infantry. In the words of another infantryman, the lack of singing may have been simply because soldiers "were never that happy and no songs were sung unless they were slap-happy."[13]

Countering that impression, the members of some units were more musically inclined. First Sergeant McConnell was of the opinion that "if a fellow could sing at all, the bigger reprobate he was, the more addicted he would be to singing the most . . . sentimental songs." An officer serving with the Seventh Cavalry on the Kansas plains told of "the low sweet music of a violin, guitar, and flute owned in 'I' Troop—which was heard until long after midnight. . . . They have a glee club in 'I' Troop too, which is remarkably fine." The daughter of a Tenth Cavalry officer, Forrestine Hooker, recalled that "H Troop had a fine quartet, as one of the men . . . had a magnificent bass voice, and had sung with professional colored singers before he enlisted."[14]

Although patriotic Civil War camp songs steadily declined in popularity among the regulars, a few such as "Tenting on the Old Camp Ground," and "The Girl I Left behind Me" (of Irish origin) remained favorites throughout the era. As late as 1886, according to Corporal Peter Y. Black, Fifth Cavalry, the rousing "'Marching Through Georgia' always finds a ready audience." More frequently heard were the melancholy strains of "Annie Laurie" and "I'll Take You Home Again, Kathleen," along with songs expressive of a soldier's plight like "Home Boys, Home" and Harrigan & Hart's satirical "The Regular Army, O!" (complete with a sarcastic last verse composed by men of General George Crook's command following the Big Horn and Yellowstone Expedition). Foreign-born soldiers contributed songs from their native cultures. The Irish, never loath to entertain an audience, performed comical ballads like "Down Went McGinty" and "O'Riley's Gone to Hell." Another class of avid singers, though with a strikingly different repertoire, encompassed the Germans. "The Dutch members of our company have got together tonight and are making the camp fairly ring with their songs of 'My Faderland,'" wrote Private Eddie Matthews at Fort Bascom, New Mexico Territory. "Their favorite song is the 'Watch On the Rhine.' . . . It helps greatly whiling away the monotonous hours of camp life."[15]

At posts where winters were long and the days short, garrison life could be agonizingly monotonous, so any diversion was a godsend and enthusiastically supported. "For amusement the men of the Battalion got up a minstrel troop [sic], and there being one company room vacant, it was converted into a theater," Thirteenth Infantry Musician James Bothwell recorded of life at Camp Cooke, Montana Territory. "We had a performance several times every week, which helped the long winter nights along." Assistant Surgeon John Vance Lauderdale observed: "In every garrison there is some musical or dramatic talent among the ranks. That portion of our soldiery [Fourteenth Infantry] are now engaged in fitting up a stage whereupon to exhibit themselves. . . . They are engaged in erecting scenery and such other appurtenances as characterise [sic] the place of exhibition." Although an unoccupied barracks often sufficed as a theater, Lieutenant Colonel George A. Custer once allowed the men at Fort Abraham Lincoln, Dakota Territory, "to put up a place in which they could have entertainments. . . . They prepared the lumber in the saw-mill . . . the building was an ungainly looking structure . . . [and] the unseasoned cottonwood warped even while the house was being built, but by patching and lining with old torn tents, they managed to keep out the storm." The wives of married soldiers sometimes also joined in the effort, not only filling feminine roles on the stage but helping to fabricate costumes and sets. When women were unavailable, explained Private William H. White, a Second Cavalryman at Fort Ellis, Montana Territory, "all participants were soldiers of the post. For female parts the dress and general accoutrement was appropriate." Performances, usually limited to the winter months when troops were least active, were held weekly or bimonthly, with practices and other preparations serving as opportunities for social interaction during long dark evenings.[16]

The program typically followed the form known as varieties. The entertainment performed by the "Frontier Glee Club" at Fort Ringgold, Texas, consisted of minstrels, a magic lantern exhibition, song and dance pieces, three skits, and a vocal quartet, with music provided by the post band. The quality of the performances ranged along the full spectrum, according to available talent. A trooper at Fort Union opined: "There are a regular theatrical or Variety Troop [sic] here composed of soldiers, they give an entertainment once a week, have been twice. Don't think I'll go soon again, the performance is very poor." After attending a variety show at Fort Fred Steele, Wyoming Territory, during the winter of 1869, Corporal Lauren W. Aldrich tepidly endorsed it: "We have seen worse entertainments within civilization." Surgeon Launderdale, however, heartily praised the performance at Fort Yuma, California: "For three hours our boys kept the audience amused with songs, dances, and numerous plays of comic character. It is wonderful what dramatic talent we have among us. Maloney[,] . . . a patient under my care for several months . . . turns out to be an actor of much merit. While Corporal

Baxster bids fair to equal Geo. Christy or Billy Burch [*sic*]. The stage and drop curtain and the scenery generally was perfect."[17]

Soldiers fortunate enough to be stationed in garrisons located along railroads or overland stagecoach routes were occasionally treated to performances by professional troupes traveling through the country. "There is a regular Theatre here," Sergeant Maurice Wolfe announced while stationed at Fort D. A. Russell, Wyoming Territory. "The soldiers act. Sometimes there is a regular stock company here from the States. There is a circus here tomorrow." A Ninth Infantry soldier at Fort Laramie, situated on the Black Hills Stage Road, was less impressed with a second-rate troupe that paused there in December 1876: "There was a couple of shows here last week. Broken down actresses on their way from Deadwood to Cheyenne. It is also dull in that place." In other instances, however, the amateur groups formed among the troops became adept at their craft and were even permitted to perform off-post. One such troupe was the Fort Custer Comic Opera and Burlesque Company, which opened a twelve-performance season at the post in September 1885 and closed the following April, following a road trip across southern Montana Territory with additional appearances at Billings, Livingston, Bozeman, and Fort Ellis.[18]

There were also special occasions when shows were not done solely for entertainment purposes. Post players were known to contribute their talents in benefit performances for their disabled brothers in blue, even when the victim may have been a stranger in another company. After Private Lawrence Lea, Second Cavalry, had his leg amputated as the result of an accidental gunshot wound in 1883, the Fort Assinniboine Varieties voluntarily put on a show consisting of plays, minstrel acts, singing, clog dancing, and orchestral numbers. The performers donated all the gate receipts to a nest egg for the native Norwegian upon his discharge from the service. Further demonstrating that the army tended to care for its own, infantry and cavalry soldiers at Fort Niobrara, Nebraska, joined in sponsoring a minstrel show for the garrison and local citizens to raise money for a soldier "that got completely torn up in a belt or shafting in the saw mill at Fort Wingate, New Mexico. He is just alive, all crippled up." The performance garnered some three hundred dollars, noted Private Hartford G. Clark, "that will help keep that unfortunate fellow a good deal, though it will not replace what he has lost."[19]

Dances were always favored activities, though more often attended by younger soldiers than by the older ones, who tended to be nondancers or had lost enthusiasm for dancing. As in the case of theatricals, fall and winter usually occasioned such affairs because garrisons were more closely confined to their posts than during the more militarily active temperate seasons. Hops, the more informal variety of dances, were held irregularly at most posts, as opportunities presented themselves. An Eleventh Infantryman posted at Cheyenne Agency, Dakota Territory, in 1877 wrote: "We at present lead a very monotonous life here; the mail comes in twice a week. . . . Sometimes the 'Jolly Blues of Fort Sully' give a hop, when some of our boys go over to it, a distance of six or seven miles. Then, the 'Jolly Blues of Cheyenne' return the compliment." According to a First Infantryman, impromptu hops featured "jigs and square dances. Music usually consisted of a banjo or harmonica, once in awhile someone had a violin." At posts where a theater or vacant squad room was unavailable for such events soldiers pressed a mess hall into service as a dance floor. "The laundresses and women servants were the honoured guests at the dances, theatricals, and other entertainments given by the men," an officer recalled, "and the former responded with merrymaking in their own quarters, where the space was small but the enjoyment huge."[20]

Perhaps the greatest deterrent to dancing was a lack of female partners. "I don't care about attending dances where the women are so few as there is scarcely one woman to every 30 men at these dances," grumbled a Fourth Infantry sergeant at Fort Bridger, Wyoming Territory. Garrisons that had a village nearby could draw upon that source for a few women, but all too often there were simply none available, other than a few officers' wives, who were strictly off-limits to enlisted men. "This kind of soldiering gets very monotonous after a while," Private Ami Mulford wrote. "Then the boys get permission to have a stag-dance when we have fun all by ourselves and no officers to bother us. We dance all the popular dances and take turns being the opposite sex." The "female" partners would be identified by a white handkerchief or brassard worn on one arm. A lack of available women at Fort Laramie prompted Private George McAnulty to grouse: "It is very dull here, nothing like [Fort] Hartsuff, [where] an occasional hop [was] given by the soldiers. . . . There [sic] not like the ones we used to have." McAnulty obviously found Fort Hartsuff a more sociable setting because the North Loup Valley of eastern Nebraska was more heavily populated by civilians in 1876 than was Wyoming Territory.[21]

Soldier dances contrasted sharply with formal balls hosted by the companies or the noncommissioned officers of the garrison on holidays and at other times. Such social events reflected company esprit de corps and were conducted with all the propriety and decorum appropriate to the Victorian era. All officers on the post and their ladies and children, along with any prominent local civilians, were invited to attend. They all dressed in their finest for the occasion. Enlisted men appeared in dress uniforms (without headgear), waist belts, and white gloves. A correspondent to the *Army & Navy Journal* described a typical affair at Fort Hays, Kansas, in 1874:

> Company C, Sixth Cavalry, gave a complimentary ball at their quarters. . . . The ball room elaborately decorated with flags and evergreens. The regimental colors were displayed at one end of the room surrounded by flags, evergreens, rosettes, etc., and along the wall were sabres and carbines, helmets, guidons, and pistols, arranged in quaint designs, alternated with pictures. A large number of people from all round the country were present. Nearly all the officers of the garrison with their families participated in the festivities. The excellent band of the Sixth Cavalry gave the music, some of it composed for the occasion. . . . The supper was excellent, and a feast was set before the guests that could hardly be surpassed in the East. Full four hundred people were present, and the entertainment passed off in a manner gratifying to all.[22]

Dancing usually commenced at about nine o'clock on a Saturday evening and continued until midnight, when the mess hall was thrown open and a sumptuous supper served from heavily laden tables. With the meal concluded, the band or orchestra struck up once more. Dancing, lubricated with copious amounts of alcohol of all descriptions, continued until dawn or nearly so. Companies of the garrison, each taking its turn in sponsoring the balls, vied for honors as the most lavish and gracious hosts.

The army observed a number of officially proclaimed holidays throughout the year by suspending all but essential duties—guard duty and a few other necessary activities. In a letter to his niece, Hospital Corpsman Richard King described a traditional New Year's Eve party at Fort Union:

> We Soldiers gave a Ball, and it was just grand. It would have done you good to see the hall. We had it all trimmed in evergreen two roes all around the room, then we had each branch of the servis represented by decoration—that is we had each branch that is in the Post of which there are three—Infantry, Cavalry, and the Hospl. Corps. We had all the flags in the Post up on the walls besides we had Armes at different points about the hall. It all looked fine. The "Grand March" was lead by us Soldiers in full-dress. We had supper at twelve, lunch at 4, and went home at 5 o'clock.[23]

Holidays often were marked by the liberal consumption of alcohol, yet another soldier at Fort Union remarked that "New Year's day [1874] passed off quietly and was an exception to most holidays seen in the Army as no drunken soldiers were seen meandering about the Garrison." More often than not the highlight of the day was a special noontime meal. At Fort Yuma on New Year's Day 1869, for example: "The men had an excellent dinner served at their mess house today. Roast pig and everything in fine style—a regular feast. . . . I hear the men in the barracks finishing up their holy day with a breakdown dance to the music of a cornopean."[24]

Even though George Washington's birthday has since lost much of its former prominence, the army universally recognized February 22 for his service not only as the nation's venerated first president but also as the army's first commander. Post commanders throughout the country scheduled battalion formations and the firing of artillery salutes. "We had inspection, Parade, and Review at 11 o'clock A.M. which passed off very nice," wrote a soldier at Fort D. A. Russell. "There were a great many visitors present from the City of Cheyenne, which is about three miles from here." Regardless of whether a fort happened to be located near a town or was isolated in some remote region, the day nearly always justified a grand ball accompanied by a late-night feast.[25]

Then as now "the anniversary of Ireland's patron saint was duly observed by the men, regardless of nationality," wrote First Sergeant

Henry McConnell. "In fact, I now remember that two or three of the Germans in the command were the most enthusiastic celebrants of the occasion, and about a dozen of my men landed in the guardhouse." Although the army did not officially recognize St. Patrick's Day, soldiers, particularly Irish Catholics, universally embraced it as an excuse to engage in unbridled drinking, singing, and general revelry. Private Wilmot Sanford, a D Company, Sixth Infantryman posted at Fort Buford, Dakota Territory, in 1875, recorded in his diary: "Half of the Co[mpany] drunk. Deegan put in the mill and Co[r]p. McLoughlin put under arrest. . . . A lot of C Co. put in the mill." A Second Cavalryman similarly noted: "It's St. Patrick's day & the boys are making the old camp ring with patriotic songs, such as 'Wearing of the Green,' 'St. Patrick's Day Parade,' &c." At Fort Niobrara the post commander conceded to the inevitable by allowing the band to substitute a medley of Irish tunes to rouse the garrison in place of "Reveille," according to a Sixth Cavalryman, "in honor of St. Patrick or some other Micky and everybody is getting drunk and sporting green ribbons. I mean every Irishman and that is pretty near all the men of this post." In addition to the obligatory consumption of alcohol, companies all across the western frontier celebrated the day with variety shows, musical performances, and garrison dances. The *Army & Navy Journal* noted that at Fort Garland, Colorado Territory,

> the members of Company D, 15th Infantry . . . gave their second annual military ball, in commemoration of the birth of St. Patrick. It was from all accounts the most brilliant affair of the kind ever held in this part of the country. . . . Company D quarters were used for the occasion, one squad room for the dance hall, and one for the supper room. The ball room was beautifully decorated. . . . Dancing commenced at eight o'clock . . . and was continued until twelve, when supper was announced . . . dancing was resumed and kept up until reveille, when the ball broke up in good order.[26]

In 1868 the president declared the last Monday in May to be "Decoration Day" to honor the Union and Confederate dead as part of the national healing process. Within a short time the observance included not only placing flowers on the graves but also paying honor to surviving Union veterans of the war. The holiday seems not to have been widely celebrated at western military posts until the latter 1880s, however, perhaps because veterans previously had been so commonplace and only by that time had the conflict assumed the historical, even sentimental, aura witnessed in Grand Army of the Republic reunions and the widespread memorialization of eastern battlefields. One of the few Decoration Day observances by regulars coming to the attention of this study was touchingly recounted by Private James O. Purvis, First Cavalry, at Fort Custer, Montana Territory, in 1886:

> Decoration Day was observed here in a manner surpassing anything of the kind we ever saw in large cities or at first-class military cemeteries. . . . All the troops in the post escorted the veterans of the G.A.R. to the little cemetery on the bank of the Big Horn. Along the north, one large field piece boomed a salute. Man and horse vied with each other in steadiness of gait and seriousness of behavior as the band played well-chosen music for the escort. . . . Words cannot describe the beauty and grandeur of seeing that little band of veterans passing among the graves of their dead comrades bestowing upon each with reverent air the flowers gathered for the occasion. . . . While we thought of the dead and their sacrifice, we could not help also admiring the living members of John Buford Post, G.A.R. and the way they performed their duties yesterday.[27]

The most widely, and usually raucously, celebrated holiday of the entire year was the uniquely American tradition of Independence Day—the Fourth of July. Army regulations, in fact, required the day to be commemorated by the firing of a national salute (equal to the number of states) at every post and camp where an artillery piece and ammunition were available. Beyond that, the celebration could be as extensive as circumstances and the innovativeness of the garrison permitted.

During the early years when conditions remained fairly primitive at many frontier stations, the Fourth of July passed without much fanfare. At far-flung corners of the Union like the village of Tubac, Arizona Territory, over which several national flags had flown since its founding in the mid-eighteenth century, the day proved as dull as the native inhabitants were uninterested. As Thirty-Second Infantryman George Cranston laconically noted in 1867: "There was nothing going on but shooting big guns and rifles at a target"; otherwise the day was unexceptional. Even a station that had the requisite cannon did not necessarily guarantee a celebration in the early days, as reflected in the diary of a surgeon at Fort Rice, Dakota Territory: "Had Fourth of July sermon & a few ½ lb. cartridges fired off in the forenoon but no other attempts at celebration." The boys of the Seventh Cavalry, however, did not allow their isolation at a temporary camp twenty miles west of Fort Hays, Kansas, in 1868 pose a deterrent to making the most of the day. Lieutenant Albert Barnitz informed his wife: "We had a horse race—one horse from each troop—and a foot race, a 'sack race' and a 'wheelbarrow race.' Purses were made up so as to give $5. to the winner in every kind of race, and $2. to the company to which the winning horse belonged. The Suttler [sic] was allowed to sell beer and wine at discretion, and whiskey upon approval of the company commanders, and in consequence 13 casks of ale disappeared almost immediately and I don't know how many dozen bottles of other 'flooids.'"[28]

The commanding officer at Fort Laramie promulgated a typical order outlining the formal aspects of the observance: "The troops will be paraded at 8:30 A.M. All duty at the Post except the necessary guard & police & care of Public Animals will be suspended during the day. At reveille a Federal salute of thirteen (13) guns and at Meridian a National salute of thirty-seven (37) guns will be fired." (Some commanders dispensed with the federal salute recognizing the original thirteen colonies.) The adjutant detailed the post ordnance sergeant if present (otherwise an experienced company sergeant) in advance to form and train a gun crew, composed of former artillerymen to the extent possible in garrisons where only infantry and cavalry were present. Nonetheless, taking those precautions was not always enough to prevent accidents because firing muzzle-loading artillery, even with blank charges, was inherently dangerous. Crew members had to be thoroughly drilled in every movement in proper sequence and coordination with the others. An officer at Fort Stevenson, Dakota Territory, described the terrible consequences that could result from a single mistake:

> The holiday was clouded and saddened by a serious accident. One of the gunners who served the pieces which were firing the salute had his right arm shot off by the premature discharge of the cannon into which he was ramming the charge. Of course the accident happened through the fault of number three who had the responsibility of sealing the vent hermetically and who let the air get in through negligence or distraction. . . . During the war, he [the victim] served in the artillery. It is a real tragedy to have come through deadly battles only to be mutilated while firing a peaceful salute.[29]

That same day, far to the south at Fort Clark, Texas, Private George Grey, Ninth Cavalry, was handling the sponge-rammer when the gun accidentally discharged, blowing "away portions of both hands, tore several tendons from their origin, and superficially injured the arms above the elbow joints." After having both forearms amputated by the post surgeon, Grey lingered in a halting recovery, only to die from tetanus two weeks after the accident.[30]

Eagerly anticipating the Fourth, committees worked well in advance to plan a full program of activities. "The day was celebrated throughout very pleasantly," commented Corporal Emil Bode at Fort Sill, Indian Territory, in 1877. "[A] blind folded [sic] wheelbarrow race, sack race, and other laughable games were played in the forenoon, while in the afternoon a horse race took place between the Comanche and Kiowa Indians. In the evening the day was concluded with fireworks." With the Sioux War ended and the frontier rapidly shrinking by 1881, members of the garrison at Fort D. A. Russell sponsored an action-filled program in concert with their citizen neighbors in Cheyenne. The day's activities included a three-mile footrace around the parade ground; a hundred-yard dash; sack, mule, spoon, and wheelbarrow (blindfolded) races; standing and running broad jump contests; and a half-mile horse race, capped by a five-inning baseball game. Also reflecting the increasing expansion of western settlement, the Fifth Infantry band and garrison from Fort Keogh, Montana Territory, joined in the festivities and parade held in adjacent Miles City. A witness to the 1886 event at Fort Custer remarked that the day's program included not only the usual foot and horse races but football, a tug-of-war, and evening fireworks, after which the First Cavalry band performed a concert:

> Although this put the finishing touch to the festivities of the day, it by no means quenched the boys' thirst. They had now got all their prizes, consisting of sundry cases of beer . . . and lots of "Scads" [wagers]. The latter went to purchase more of that delicious beverage, "Schlitz," which enjoys a high reputation here (only 30 cents a bottle). All night long one could hear frantic and vociferous cheers that were loud enough to wake the dead. . . . Next day the hats, caps, and helmets did not all appear to fit their respective owners.[31]

By 1891 the region around Fort Niobrara was so peaceful that the "sports committee" ventured to appropriate fifty dollars to pay travel expenses "to bring some distant nine here the 4th to play us a game of ball. Good! Good!" Private Hartford Clark exclaimed. That entire Independence Day was crammed with events of all kinds, concluding in the evening with a fireworks display and a dance. With the minor exception that "only two serious accidents happened at the Horse races," Clark was immensely pleased with what had been a delightful July Fourth.[32]

Soldiers had nothing more of the sort to look forward to until the arrival of Thanksgiving in late November. Because the day had been set aside in 1863 by President Abraham Lincoln as an observance for "thanksgiving and prayer," the army recognized it officially by the customary suspension of nonessential duties. However, anticipating that the day would occasion more drinking than prayer among the men, Fort Laramie's commander took the precaution of directing that the post trader's store be closed at ten o'clock in the morning. At posts where weather permitted, the morning sometimes witnessed a few of the familiar athletic games, although nothing to compare with Independence Day. "The contests were open to all enlisted men," wrote a correspondent at Fort Lewis, Colorado, in 1884, "but the continual hard manual labor required consequent on building the post, deterred many from competing in the games."[33]

The primary focus of the day, of course, was on feasting. It was not uncommon for units to go to considerable effort and expense to provide a special dinner for the men, and some sent out hunting parties days before to bag wild turkey and other game to augment the victuals. "Thanksgiving & the men in general are filling up with good things," reported a solder at Fort Ellis, Montana Territory. In 1873 companies of the Fifteenth Infantry and the Eighth Cavalry combined resources to host an extraordinary soldiers' ball the night before Thanksgiving:

> At 8.30 nearly all the Officers and Ladies of the Post came in and opened the Ball for us, they danced one Quadrille and one Waltz, thanked us for the pleasure and departed. Soon as they made their exit, dancing commenced in earnest and was kept up until 12. Lunch in abundance consisting of Bread, Biscuits, butter, Ham, Tea, Coffee, Cake, Lemonade, Candy, and Cigars to wind up with . . . , then dancing kept up until 6 A.M. . . . Slept until 11 o'clock A.M., got up and dressed for Thanksgiving dinner. Had four roast turkeys, . . . two hams, fresh pork, biscuits, butter pickles, . . . coffee, bread, and for desert pudding and pies. There was only about twenty of us for dinner.[34]

The description of events at Fort Union, a large central supply post near the lower end of the Santa Fe Trail, contrasted sharply with a less glowing, and perhaps more typical, account of how the holiday was passed on the Dakota frontier in 1874. A Sixth Infantryman wrote: "Stew for breakfast. Extry for dinner, tomatoes, and apply pye [sic]. No fatigue. . . . A lot of the men on a drunk."[35]

"Come Christmas at the Fort a lot o' men felt sorta blue bein' so fur away from their folks. Some of 'em drank and raised hell jist to keep from thinking," recalled Seventh Cavalryman John Burkman. "I was all right 'cause the regiment was the only home I ever knowed" (all odd spellings in the original). Indeed soldiering was often a lonely occupation and Burkman captured the feelings of many regulars across the western frontier at that season. Despite the melancholy that descended on many soldiers at Christmastime, Musician Robert Greenhalgh at Fort Laramie assured his parents: "We had a pretty good dinner. . . . The rest of the Band drank pretty freely but I do not indulge myself." He was in the minority, however. In 1869 Surgeon Washington Matthews at Fort Rice claimed that the day was "a Christmas celebrated chiefly by the amount of whiskey drank at the post, soldiers having filed away whiskey orders and stored away the article itself for some time past in view of the approaching festival."[36]

The winter season, largely confining the men to their quarters, contributed in no small way to the overindulgence witnessed at Christmas, though they probably would have taken advantage of the day as an excuse to imbibe heavily as a matter of principle. Stationed at Fort Buford in 1876, Private Wilmot Sanford described a typical Christmas day for the rank and file: "Clear and cold 28 below. Came off guard in the morning and to the quarters the rest of the day. Having a good drink. Corn, peaches, jelly, butter, duff and roast beef and gravy and whiskey drinks. 3 galons [sic] to the Co[mpany] by the sutlers.... Half the company were drunk before night. No werk [sic] today. Took a sleep in the afternoon."[37] Some men, of course, could not wait until they were off duty to celebrate. A Seventh Cavalryman at Fort Riley, Kansas, noted in his diary on Christmas Day: "Private Butler of our Troop mounted Guard this morning and became intoxicated. His belt was taken off and he was put in the Guard House. Pvt. Lynch took his place on Guard."[38]

Without exception, the cooks made a special effort to prepare as elaborate a dinner as circumstances and the company fund permitted when the troops were in garrison. Even at a remote station like Fort C. F. Smith, Montana Territory, during the late 1860s the men were treated to a holiday meal "consisting of roast venison, soup, vegetables, &c." The members of Company L, Eighth Cavalry enjoyed Christmas 1870 with a dinner of chicken, wild turkey, roast pork, pies, plum pudding, and other trimmings. Some units practiced a custom whereby the officers and their wives called on the company on Christmas morning. Mrs. Frances Roe, wife of Second Lieutenant Fayette W. Roe, Third Infantry, described her experience at Fort Lyon, Colorado Territory, in 1871:

> From the chapel we . . . went to the company barracks to see the men's dinner tables. When we entered the dining hall we found the entire company standing in two lines, one down each side, every man in his best inspection uniform, and every button shining. With eyes to the front and hands down their

sides they looked absurdly like wax figures waiting to be "wound up." . . . The first sergeant came to meet us, and went around with us, there were three long tables, fairly groaning with things upon them: buffalo, antelope boiled ham, several kinds of vegetables, pies, cakes, quantities of pickles, dried "apple-duff," and coffee and in the center of each table, high up, was a cake thickly covered with icing. It is the custom in the regiment for the wives of the officers every Christmas to send the enlisted men of their husbands' companies large plum cakes. . . . The hall was very prettily decorated with flags and accoutrements. . . . General Phillips [*sic*: probably Captain and Brevet Brigadier General W. H. Penrose] said a few pleasant words to the men, wishing them a "Merry Christmas" for all of us. Judging from the laughing and shuffling of feet as soon as we got outside, the men were glad to be allowed to relax once more.[39]

By the mid-1880s, railroads were supplying many forts that had previously relied on contract wagon trains traveling overland or on steamboats plying the few navigable rivers in the West. The effect of enhanced transportation was evident in many of the available goods that had formerly been scarce, if not impossible to obtain, at frontier posts. As an example, Company G, Seventeenth Infantry, posted at Fort Abraham Lincoln, celebrated Christmas 1885 with a bill of fare featuring "turkey with cranberry sauce, roast beef, mashed potatoes, sauerkraut, pickled cauliflowers, tomato catsup, spiced ham, gravy a la mode, pickled cucumbers, pickled beets, chow chow, coffee and chocolate, mince pie, peach pie, pear pie, green apple pie, pound cake, sponge cake, marble cake, chocolate cake . . . pears, peaches, apples. Beer after dinner." The diners all the while were serenaded by their own coronet ensemble. In the aftermath of a similar feast at Fort Maginnis, Montana Territory, a trooper wrote to the *Army & Navy Journal*: "I think those big dinners are very injurious. At evening stables that day it was out of the question to expect the men to stoop in grooming their horses. They were not tight by any means, but their pants were."[40]

Christmas activities were sometimes supplemented with dances, when enough women were available, along with other amusements. Private Michael Vetter, a German immigrant in the Seventh Cavalry, described his first Christmas in the army: "We had good times and plenty to eat . . . we even danced after the Dinner. Since there are no girls on the Fort [Totten] some of our men dressed as girls and the Dance went on with lots of fun." At Camp Lowell, Arizona Territory, "A group of minstrels—blacked—made up from the different forts went around and gave entertainments," First Cavalryman Henry Yohn recorded. "They came here and gave an entertainment. . . . Everyone was crazy to go. They charged one dollar for admission. I was the only man in our party that had any savings. . . . I paid thirty dollars for thirty men." Although the regulars were not known for being compassionate, there were rare exceptions, such as the celebration for the children at Fort Washakie, Wyoming Territory. "I never saw more Xmas giving than there has been here," remarked the surgeon's wife. "The men have bought without limit. The Thomas children were loaded with beautiful things by the men of their father's company and laundress children too had no end of things." In another instance two members of the Fort Robinson, Nebraska, garrison drove a wagon some one hundred twenty-five miles to Sidney, the nearest rail connection, to take delivery of Christmas goods. During the return trip, however, the men encountered a blizzard that drove temperatures to nearly forty degrees below zero. Nevertheless, the two soldiers persevered in their mission, managing to return safely with the gifts to please the children on Christmas Eve.[41]

Christmas celebration varied to no great degree by the early 1890s, even though the towns in proximity to many forts may have afforded some luxuries and social interactions not available during earlier times. The religious significance of the day seems not to have occurred to most soldiers. Private Charles N. Hayden recorded that C Troop, Seventh Cavalry, then stationed at Fort Riley, hosted a masquerade ball in their mess hall on Christmas night. A merchant traveled there from Kansas City especially to rent costumes for the event. The majority of the men, however, passed the day in typical soldier fashion, much as they had the other holidays. A trooper at Fort Niobrara commented that he and his comrades enjoyed, "punches, brandy, nice whiskey, cigars, etc. all day long. . . . The band leader invited us all up to his house tonight to a blow out. We all had a nice time. . . . I put Ashton to bed. . . . Franze [was] on all fours." Thus passed Christmas in the regular army.[42]

Beyond drinking and playing cards, some enlisted men found recreation in limited athletic activities of various kinds during off-duty hours, although the practice was by no means universal. Climate, coupled with the amount of fatigue and drill, not to mention the ages of the men, affected their enthusiasm for athletics. Sergeant Armand Unger, for example, contended that the men in his troop of the Fifth Cavalry got all the physical exercise they desired during the duty day. Younger, more energetic soldiers, however, turned to sports as a pleasant alternative from military duty. Baseball, universally popular in America by the mid-nineteenth century, was unquestionably the soldiers' favorite sporting event during the era. Teams were usually formed along company lines, though in mixed garrisons the best players in one service branch or regiment, without regard to company, sometimes competed against another. In southern Arizona Territory during the late 1880s Tenth Cavalry troopers even invited their Apache scouts, who had taken an interest in watching the games, to join their teams, and some became enthusiastic ballplayers. Team names usually reflected the company identity, such as "The B Company Nine." Sometimes the name of the company commander or even the post commander was incorporated in the name, such as "Nolan's Red Stockings," named for Major Nicholas Nolan, commanding Fort Huachuca in 1883. With few exceptions, teams were composed of enlisted men. Company officers only rarely played but frequently served as coaches or referees. In the interest of fairness, an interested post surgeon or chaplain might be recruited to serve as an unbiased umpire.[43]

The army, of course, provided no athletic equipment, so bats and balls (no gloves were used at that time) were purchased from the company fund. By the mid-1880s baseball had become such a national passion that some army teams either made distinctive uniforms or ordered them from commercial suppliers, especially at posts where nearby civilian teams competed.

Other athletics indulged in by soldiers included the ever-popular footrace, a hundred-yard dash being the usual event, though occasionally races extended over longer distances. A former resident at Fort Laramie recalled an incident when overconfident soldiers were taken in by a dark horse contestant: "Suddenly . . . there appeared a tall, lanky, non-descript civilian who discreetly talked about foot-racing. A match with him and our best man was arranged. They ran the 100 yard dash; the stranger ran away from the soldier, with no effort at all. The 'stranger' faded out over-night, and I never learned any further details, nor how much money was bet."[44]

Private James B. Wilkinson, Second Cavalry, asserted that he experienced no organized athletic events, the nearest thing being "mostly fights among soldiers outside quarters." Young Lauren Aldrich, who had only recently joined his company from the depot, found himself engaged in such a match after he ran afoul of the company bully:

> Fighting was to be to a finish with bare hands in accordance with the Marquis of Queensbury Rules. . . . A ring of old soldiers and recruits was formed and the battle was on. There was nothing so remarkable about the scrap itself, but the results were quite amusing in so much as [I] was promoted from the ranks for breaking the slugger's jaw in two places. This very unusual promotion of a raw recruit was due to the old soldiers' extreme method of hazing and slugging new recruits.[45]

Unsanctioned bare-knuckle fighting and outright brawling behind the barracks gradually gave way to formal gloved boxing by the late 1880s. Grandison Mayo, who served in the Twenty-Fifth Infantry from 1885 to 1890, confirmed that both boxing and baseball were popular in his company. Near the end of the Indian campaigns, when field service had declined significantly, some posts constructed gymnasiums where boxing, wrestling, and other forms of physical exercise were available to the men.[46]

"Hunting was one of our most common diversions," declared Sergeant John E. Cox, First Infantry. "Many soldiers were keen and skillful sportsmen. I was not a 'professional' and yet I cherish many pleasant memories of the chase in Dakota." Soldiers hunted, and fished to a much lesser extent, both as a relaxing form of recreation and to supplement the company mess. Game usually became scarce near forts because it was depleted by hunting and scared away by human activity. "There are antelope and deer a few miles out but buffalo are scarce in this vicinity," wrote a soldier at Fort Laramie in 1870. "Fish are plenty and easily caught both in the Laramie and Platte rivers, they are mostly catfish and pike." Hunting parties made up of a few reliable men were granted passes to be away from the post, usually for ten-day periods.

Such passes were issued as special recognition to marksmen who had achieved the best score at company target practice or as a reward to soldiers for lengthy periods of good conduct. Occasionally a soldier with a proven record as a proficient hunter would be allowed latitude to go hunting alone. Buffalo, turkey, deer, antelope, and duck made welcome additions to the company's usual bill of fare.[47]

Moreover, such excursions were coveted by soldiers because they got away from the post, making a welcome break from the usual routine and constant discipline. First Sergeant John Ryan related that in the late 1860s Company M, Seventh Cavalry "had some pretty good shots. . . . These men would take a six-mule team and a few days' rations and forage with them, and on their way from camp they would pass through Hays City [Kansas] . . . the saloon keepers would furnish them with all the liquor they wanted . . . and they would proceed to the buffalo hunting grounds on the Smoky [Hill] River . . . and if they had good luck they would bring in a wagon load of buffalo hind quarters, tongues, livers, and humps." Eighth Cavalryman Frederick C. Kurtz stated that hunters near Fort Clark, Texas, were successful in returning with turkeys and wild hogs and that during the winter "we had about fifteen deer hung up in our cooking tent and we ate deer meat for breakfast, dinner, and supper for weeks."[48]

Scant, if any, consideration was given to conservation in a land where wildlife appeared in abundance. With game laws still in the distant future, army hunting parties sometimes unthinkingly contributed to the decimation of the seemingly limitless buffalo herds, though a few soldiers recognized indiscriminate killing beyond subsistence needs for the slaughter it was. A cavalryman in the field on the Staked Plains of Texas in 1872 expressed remorse after his party killed twenty-one animals, then "three were put in a wagon for our use, the remaining eighteen left on the plains. . . . It seemed a shame to kill those large animals merely for sport. The meat of those eighteen buffalo . . . would have been sufficient to keep that number of families for one year." In this same regard, Private Henry Hubman, an Eighteenth Infantry soldier posted at Camp Poplar River, Montana Territory, nearly a decade later informed his father: "We have lots of game around here, of Buffalo there are thousands. We kill lots of them every day[,] many are never touched. Just shot for fun. Yesterday I shot one and had to let him lay [sic] as it was to[o] far to carry to the Fort. I cut out the tongue and took that in." Despite the personal misgivings expressed by a few individuals, soldiers at the bottom rung of the army were hardly aware that they were actually helping to fulfill a strategy advanced by Lieutenant General Philip H. Sheridan, commanding the Division of the Missouri (and later the army) to deprive plains Indians of their natural commissary, thereby expediting the confinement of the tribes to reservations.[49]

Hunters were provided tents, cooking gear, and ammunition and were allowed to use their service arms, thus affording soldiers with practical experience that would prove valuable for actual field service as well as training in shooting at objects over unknown distances. Before the 1880s companies often purchased a shotgun or two with the company fund for hunting wildfowl and small game. Sergeant Cox, for example, recalled using a muzzle-loading shotgun to hunt rabbits and prairie chickens in the vicinity of Fort Randall, Dakota Territory, while First Sergeant Ryan paid thirty-five dollars for a personal shotgun. In 1881 the National Armory at Springfield, Massachusetts, began producing single-barrel twenty-gauge shotguns for issue to companies in the West especially for hunting purposes.[50]

Hunters were of course expected to apply themselves to the sport and to return with a respectable supply of meat, but some took unfair advantage of the opportunity. The members of Company D, Seventeenth Infantry, were heartily disappointed when a party sent out from Fort Yates, Dakota Territory, returned twenty days later with only five deer and a bear to show for their effort. Just what they had been doing all that time was not revealed. In a worse case, Sergeant Thomas White, Tenth Cavalry, was granted a hunting pass to be absent from Fort Davis, Texas, but instead spent several days on a lark with "disreputable women," for which he was tried and reduced to private. On another occasion at Fort Niobrara, diarist Private Hartford G. Clark revealed the reason why some hunters were prone to failure: "Behrman, Downer, and Lash, the trio that went out on a five days' hunting pass last Thursday, came back tonight feeling much broken up. . . . They claimed they shot a good many ducks but as they brought none home . . . I guess they done more drinking than shooting."[51]

Reading was a favorite pastime for literate men, who took full advantage of the library, sometimes termed a "reading room," that each garrison was supposed to maintain through the post fund. A soldier served voluntarily as an uncompensated librarian in his spare time. Some soldiers like Private Wilmot P. Sanford, Sixth Infantry, frequented the library nearly every evening during the winter when he was not on guard. Private Martin Andersen, a Danish immigrant, commented: "My recreation was mostly in the library studying.... I spent most of my time to learn the English language." The quality of libraries, however, often varied markedly from one fort to another. At some posts the commander failed to place any great importance on the library and its poor location and condition were deterrents to soldiers availing themselves of the opportunity. Representative of many, the library at Fort Laramie was "in the adjutant's office containing about 300 old, nearly worn out books. A number of papers and periodicals are subscribed for . . . and kept in the library room to which the enlisted men have access."[52]

A bandsman at another western fort grumbled: "I am stationed at one of the numerous military posts . . . which is unprovided with a decent library. Two companies, a regimental band and a detachment of recruits all are forced to seek for recreation in a library consisting of about twenty-five volumes, minus newspapers. . . . Some companies being poverty stricken, they have not even a ten cent novel for perusal. This is a serious privation at a frontier post . . . where we are completely lost to the world." Echoing similar dissatisfaction with the situation at old Fort Bascom, Eighth Cavalry trooper Eddie Matthews commented: "Our library consists of part of a *Democratic Advocate*, two or three New York papers and a small volume entitled 'The House of Seven Gables.' . . . Our's [sic] is a very literary troop, when any ten cent novels are to be had." To be sure, dime novels were universally popular with the men, but more extensive libraries, like that at Fort Ellis, offered titles such as Jules Verne's *Around the World in 80 Days* and *20,000 Leagues under the Sea*, along with Louisa May Alcott's *An Old-Fashioned Girl*. Some post commanders, often at the urging of the resident surgeon, made an effort to upgrade the library as an alternative to other less wholesome activities. Corporal Emil A. Bode found the library at Fort Sill housing "a great variety of weekly and monthly papers, besides useful books to enrich the mind a thousand different directions." In a few instances units elected to devote company funds to building small collections of books and periodicals to be kept in the orderly room or the barracks day room.[53]

While many soldiers on the western frontier may have felt that they were indeed lost to the world, they nevertheless thirsted for news from the States. The men responded enthusiastically to the arrival of newspapers, even though issues were usually weeks old by that time. Now and then a man was fortunate enough to have a relative or friend forward a hometown newspaper, which "was read by every man in the troop until entirely worn out [because] there was nothing to attract one's attention except the same old round of soldier duty, an unending sequence of guard, stable police, kitchen police, and fatigue, and then back over the same thing." Even foreigners like Seventh Cavalryman Michael Vetter who could not read English, at least not easily, desired to know what was happening in the rest of the world. Accordingly, Vetter wrote to his brother early in 1876 requesting a subscription to a newspaper published in German so that he might stay informed.[54]

Libraries gradually improved, commensurate with the army's increasing emphasis on education for enlisted men and the proliferation of post schools during the 1880s. The greater proportion of American-born soldiers possessing at least a rudimentary education by that time led to a demand for larger and better selections of publications at post libraries. The *Army & Navy Journal*, along with a counterpart, the *Army & Navy Register*, both catering to the military audience, were staples eagerly devoured by soldiers. Both publications served as media through which the men could express their opinions and grievances. As the curtain drew down on the era of Indian campaigning, a Sixth Cavalryman noted that the library at Fort Niobrara offered soldiers a wide selection of newspapers representing San Francisco, Detroit, Kansas City, St. Louis, and New York, in addition to the *Army & Navy Journal, Frank Leslie's Illustrated, Harper's Weekly*, and two German newspapers. Besides having the means to stay current on national and world events, the garrison could choose from among approximately six hundred books shelved at the library.[55]

Beyond reading and self-directed study, enlisted soldiers were rarely exposed to scholarly activities. A Sixteenth Infantryman recorded that he devoted some his off-duty time to collecting and pressing plant specimens growing in the vicinity of Fort Sill. A soldier posted in New Mexico developed a hobby of collecting scorpions, spiders, centipedes, and insects, while Sergeant John C. Appleby combated loneliness at Fort Bowie by capturing Gila monsters, birds, and small mammals.

Only rarely were lectures given at frontier posts, more often lyceums concerning military topics for the benefit of officers than offerings for enlisted men. An exception, however, was recorded by a soldier who attended an open lecture by the post surgeon at Fort Union in 1874:

> The monotony of garrison life was disturbed a little by the lecture delivered by Dr. Clark . . . this evening. Subject "A Trip to the Moon." The Hall was crowded, and every person anticipated a comic lecture for the subject would naturally impress one as being . . . rather flighty. . . . A sillier discourse I never listened too [sic], . . . nothing but the foolish ideas of an idiot who's [sic] brain was destroyed altogether from the influence of liquor.

By 1891, however, the younger and undoubtedly better educated soldiers at one post were inspired to form among themselves a literary and debating society.[56]

Some soldiers fought boredom by creating business opportunities of various sorts, including publishing their own post newspapers. Using portable presses turning out one sheet at a time, soldiers entertained themselves and the garrison by disseminating all the local news, tidbits, and unabashed gossip that came to the editors' attention. Not having access to a press, members of the Sixth Cavalry turned out weekly a single handwritten copy of the *Little Joker* at Jacksboro, Texas, in 1867. The paper would circulate around the post until it was literally worn out. Two years later the men at Fort Richardson produced six issues of *The Flea* by writing the copy and sending it to a commercial printer in Weatherford, Texas, for publication. Other examples of soldier newspapers were the *Regimental Flag*, published biweekly at Fort Union, New Mexico Territory, in 1873, and the *Apache Rocket*, distributed at Fort Davis, Texas, a decade later. All of these efforts proved to be short-lived as a result of being plagued with the same problems. The editors often found themselves strapped for capital, usually because subscribers failed to pay their debts or the men simply shared copies rather than buying their own. The demands of duty not infrequently interfered with soldier-publishers' time for pursuing such activities on a regular basis, or the unit was transferred to another station, thus curtailing the enterprise.[57]

Other business ventures served as diversions for the men, sometimes as a means of making extra money or simply as a pastime. One soldier devised a plan whereby he took orders from his comrades for pocket watches at inflated prices, which they paid in advance, with an officer holding the money in escrow until the merchandise arrived. The trooper then collected the money, sent the credited amount due the New York supplier, and pocketed the profit for his trouble. The art of photography was also a popular endeavor. Some men were self-taught, others served apprenticeships in their spare time under itinerant photographers who set up shop at frontier posts from time to time. One infantryman established a studio at Fort Buford to make and sell portrait photographs during his off-duty time. Private Oscar Bloom, Eighth Infantry, was a multitalented German immigrant who served as the extra-duty engineer in charge of the post waterworks at Fort Niobrara. In addition to his other activities, the energetic Bloom "put in a great deal of time studying," played in the post orchestra, and operated a photography studio.[58]

Despite the widespread propensity for drinking among regulars, the temperance movement of the mid-nineteenth century found some receptive converts in the frontier army. Foremost among the organizations dedicated to that cause was the Independent Order of Good Templars, an international society dating to the early 1850s that advocated abstinence from alcohol through group support and alternative recreational activities. "We have a very prosperous temperance lodge here, with about ninety members," reported a private at Fort Sanders, Wyoming Territory. "The officers have aided us in getting a room and an organ and taken great interest in our society, the object of which is to draw the men away from the sutler's drinking saloon to pass a cheerful evening at the lodge." For those garrisons numbering a few women, the temperance lodge provided polite association free of the raucous behavior and violence that often characterized the drinking establishments. In 1871 a soldier at Fort Randall proudly announced: "The Twenty-second Infantry Temperance Society gave their first ball, . . . one of the quarters having been very tastefully fitted up for the occasion . . . by numerous and brilliant displays of stars made from bayonets, very artistic and beautiful chandeliers, [and] neatly executed inscriptions illustrative of the Order of Good Templars. . . . Dancing was kept up until 2 o'clock in the morning." The movement found particularly fertile ground in the West among soldiers who had not been habitual drinkers prior to their enlistments and wanted to avoid the vice or had realized the error of their ways and elected to reform—going "up the pole" in army parlance. Fort Ellis boasted a Templars lodge of about a hundred members by the mid-1870s. By the end of the decade a veteran cavalryman at another post declared that 200 men out of a garrison of about 340 had pledged themselves to sobriety. "I know that it has wrought an incalculable amount of good," he observed. "When I joined the troop, in July, 1868, it was what is generally called in Army slang 'a hard crowd.' . . . Scenes of drunken dissipation, now the exception, were then the rule."[59]

Eager for any sort of social outlet, Fourth Infantrymen at Fort Fetterman, Wyoming Territory, invited members into a group dubbed the "Soldiers Dancing Club." Presumably there were enough women in the isolated garrison to make the effort worthwhile. Some First Cavalry troopers created a social club with the intention of attracting members of the fairer sex. Even though it was founded on principles of temperance, the plan backfired when the pious post chaplain denied use of the chapel for dancing. Some seventy-five women flocked to the organization, but "since none of the soldiers, or very, very few of them joined, it was mighty lonesome for the buck private."[60]

In an age when fraternal organizations abounded as a means of socializing and sharing common purposes, experience, or heritage, significant numbers of soldiers joined local chapters of the Masons and the Independent Order of Odd Fellows as a means of personal self-improvement. As early as 1869 immigrant soldiers at Fort Rice formed the "German Society" and hosted their first entertainment, consisting of "songs & supper and the drinking of a weak, home-made beer" (Pilsener lager) on Christmas Eve. The numerous Irishmen in the ranks, too, banded together in garrison clubs. In addition to an ethnically oriented Ancient Order of Hibernians, the array of organizations available at Fort Custer by 1886 included a Masonic Lodge, Good Templars, the Maennerchor [German] Club, the Custer Social Club, and Walker's Opera Company. Moreover, with so many former Civil War soldiers in the ranks during that era, it was not uncommon to find local posts of the Grand Army of the Republic, where the older men could share the fellowship of other veterans. Toward the end of era any soldier was eligible to join the Regular and Volunteer Army and Navy Union.[61]

No matter where they were, soldiers invariably accumulated a menagerie of pets to keep them company. Although dogs were by far the soldiers' favorite, almost any animal was eligible to become a mascot. When buffalo were still plentiful on the plains during the late 1860s, some soldiers took in calves and kept them until they either became nuisances or escaped to rejoin the herd. On one occasion an aging adult bull, banished from the herd, drifted into Fort Lyon, Colorado Territory. Third Infantryman John O. Stotts wrote: "We began feeding him and finally adopted him as our Mascot. In time he got fat and so tame that he would come up to the Fort and ramble over the parade ground. We named him Custer." After a sentry belonging to a passing unit shot the buffalo by mistake one night, Stotts recounted: "The next day the entire garrison of four companies turned out and with muffled drums beating the Dead Johnny March, we buried him, and fired the regulation salute over his grave." Individual soldiers frequently captured and tamed the little prairie dogs whose villages dotted the plains throughout the West. One soldier claimed to have as many as twenty at one time, while another related that his prairie dog Dick "became the pet of the garrison and was fed by everyone." Unfortunately, a well-meaning comrade indulged the critter by feeding him too many gingersnaps, resulting in his death. While stationed at Fort Sill, Indian Territory, the Fourth Cavalry band attracted and tamed a deer "who followed them like a dog through all their maneuvers," and a Sixth infantry sergeant somehow managed to catch a young antelope, though the animal survived only a few days in captivity. In Montana Territory troopers of the Second Cavalry at Fort Ellis not only tamed a bear cub but in true soldier fashion taught him to drink beer. "He would lap up the drippings from the taps at the EM bar," Private William H. White recalled. After the bear learned to turn the tap himself, tragically, he drank himself to death.[62]

First Sergeant Henry McConnell attested: "One of the soldier's predilections is his love for dogs, and his propensity for them was such that every detail returning from the settlements was accompanied by a new lot of curs that they had induced to come with them. Our regiment [Sixth Cavalry] was always overrun with dogs. . . . At the sound of the bugle every dog would set up a howl, until at times the nuisance would become epidemic." They were not the only ones to acquire dogs from civilians or Indians, as revealed by a Fourteenth Infantryman in 1866. As his battalion marched overland from California to take station in Arizona Territory, Private John Spring noted: "From the time that we had reached the Pima villages, and principally during our stay in Tucson, quite a number of our men had enticed stray dogs away from their habitats and brought them to [Fort] Bowie."[63]

Dogs belonging to enlisted men tended to be classified into three groups—company dogs, guardhouse dogs, and dogs at large. "Every outfit had a dog. But the dog had no master. And God help the man that abused the dog," declared Corporal Maurice O'Leary, First Cavalry. Company dogs may not have acknowledged a particular master, but they usually bonded with one or two soldiers in the unit as bunk mates. Ninth Cavalryman Simpson Mann recalled that Dick, the F Troop dog, slept on a pillow in the squad room. In another instance a dog belonging to Company D, Sixth Infantry, shared a bunk with one of the men. Known for their unquestioning loyalty to those who treat them well, dogs often identified closely with the unit that they considered home. A tawny dog of mixed collie breed, named Coyote, recognized "only those who wore the uniform of the cavalry . . . he would not allow any advances or permit an undue familiarity, save from those for whom he lived," a company member asserted. He further claimed that the dog was a valuable security asset because he "could tell an Indian as far as he could see him, which he indicated by a deep growl, pointing the direction. . . . There was no mistaking what he meant. . . . A lone sentinel in the night could not be surprised, nor could a scouting detail be ambushed." Private Arthur S. Wallace, Fifth Cavalry, noted in his diary that his dog became so exhausted while trying to keep up with the unit during a rapid march in northern Wyoming that he had to be abandoned at a ranch. Four days later Wallace was astounded when the dog found him in camp, after trailing the troop over ninety miles.[64]

Such attributes contributed to company pride and kind treatment of its dogs. "There was many a heated but good natured argument on the subject of dogs, one company claiming that their dog was a better one than another company," recalled a Seventh Cavalryman. "Our dogs would sometimes get [cactus needles] in their paws and it would be fun to see a dog trying to pull a needle out of his paw. . . . He would hold up his paw as much as to say that he needed help, and one of our men would dismount and pull the needle out. He would then take him up on the saddle in front of him and carry him for a mile or two, then he would hand him over to some other man, and in this manner the dog would be carried all day." Private Edgar Hoffner, Company G, First Cavalry, related that in another instance: "Sport, our company dog, which followed the supply train from Boise Barracks [to find the troop] . . . ran . . . through the hot ashes [of a forest fire] getting up on a log now and then to ease his feet. The poor brute was badly burnt when he at last sat up on his haunches and set up a piteous howl. One of the boys picked him up and carried him in front of him on his saddle."[65]

In a bizarre incident in 1873, a dog actually contributed, though not willingly, to saving a couple of men belonging to Company K, Twentieth Infantry. After a corporal and a private serving with the escort for the Northern Boundary Survey became lost during a hunting trip, a company member recounted: "The third day, when their stock of [prairie] chickens was out and no more could be procured, they hit upon a novel plan of sustaining life for awhile without killing their 'setter'—a dog they thought much of. They cut his tail . . . close, roasted and eat [sic] it giving the bone to the dog. They concluded to eat the dog next day, but luckily struck the trail the same evening. . . . Inquiries being made in camp about the dog's tail, they told many stories of bears biting it off, etc., until at last the truth was extracted from them."[66]

For reasons known only to dogs, some attached themselves to the guardhouse and the prisoners. Old Taylor, a large, shaggy yellow dog, followed a prisoner to the guard house at Buffalo Springs, Texas, in 1867, where he became a fixture thereafter. The next year he accompanied the prisoners of the Sixth Cavalry to Fort Richardson and remained at the guardhouse there for the next three years. "When the headquarters and first six companies of the regiment proceeded to Kansas . . . [in 1871]," a witness recalled, "he took up his line of march . . . trudging along the road for seven hundred miles and keeping right with the guard and prisoners all the while." Observing the peculiarities exhibited by Old Taylor, a soldier noted that the dog would lie in front of the guardhouse every day, until fatigue call sounded, when he would follow the prisoner work details to and from their assignments. He became quite attached to the prisoners, who shared their food with him during their incarceration, particularly those who served lengthy sentences. Once they were released and returned to duty, however, the dog had nothing more to do with them.[67]

Another guardhouse dog, Old Bum, was a character that attached himself to the First Cavalry at Fort Walla Walla, Washington Territory. "He would follow the prisoners all day, but when the bugle sounded retreat, and the big cannon was fired, Old Bum would make a bee-line for town, as would many of the officers and enlisted men," recounted a trooper. "He would slip under the swinging doors of the saloons . . . and would lap up the stale beer that dripped from the faucet into a bucket. After visiting two or three places, Old Bum, swaying from side to side, would toddle back to the guardhouse. He was the worst booze hound in the regiment."[68]

The numbers of dogs at frontier posts became cause for concern on several levels for post commanders. Besides making for a generally unmilitary appearance, unrestricted dogs contributed to both sanitation and health problems. The post commander at Fort Omaha, Nebraska, for example, issued an edict prohibiting the men from allowing dogs in their quarters after tattoo. Pointing up a more serious situation, a correspondent wrote from Fort Hays complaining: "Cases of hydrophobia are uncomfortably frequent in this vicinity . . . the greatest danger is from the packs of useless curs that infect military posts, and disgrace small villages." In an effort to reduce the number of dogs at Fort Fetterman, the frustrated commander imposed a five dollar tax per head, threatening to kill any untaxed dogs remaining on the post, as well as all female dogs still running at large, taxed or not. A corporal's patrol of the guard thus became dogcatchers charged with shooting loose animals that could not be caught, although one questions whether stray dogs or stray bullets posed the greater danger to the inhabitants.[69]

Indeed companies grew quite attached to their mascot dogs, sometimes keeping them for years and considering them to be bona fide members of the unit. A company of the Twenty-Third Infantry adopted a mascot named Chum born in a litter at Fort Leavenworth, Kansas, in 1876. The dog constantly accompanied the unit in field and garrison until his death at Fort Brady, Michigan, a decade later. G Troop, Sixth

Cavalry, adopted a dog recovered in the vicinity of the Sioux massacre at Wounded Knee. The men grew quite attached to him and were outraged when "some mean damn fool shot Mig our dog this afternoon out by the target butts. A two legged dog is far below a four legged one in my opinion. Poor Mig never bothered anybody." The loyalty developed between soldiers and their dogs was mutual. When Coyote, the Second Cavalry dog mentioned previously, was killed in action with Indians, "there was not a single man in that party who did not owe his life directly or indirectly . . . to the intelligence and devotion of the faithful Coyote. . . . We buried Coyote where he had fallen." The epitaph that Sergeant Thomas Sullivan penned for Coyote probably expressed the feelings many soldiers held for their canine companions: "To mark a friend's remains these stones arise, I never knew but one, and here he lies."[70]

If recreational opportunities for soldiers were limited, obtaining furloughs to go elsewhere to escape the tedium were even more so. Even though army regulations provided for twenty-day furloughs, soldiers seldom availed themselves of the privilege for several reasons. While company commanders may have been inclined to grant furloughs to their men now and then, the authority rested with the post commander and could be "prohibited at the discretion of the officer in command." In other words, the request could be denied for no particular reason. Further discouraging men was a limit on the post commander's authority to approve travel only within the geographic department in which his station was located. Twenty-Fourth Infantry musician Alexander Hatcher commented that it was senseless to bother taking a furlough at Fort Huachuca, Arizona Territory, because the only town in the vicinity was the rough little mining community of Tombstone, which lay twenty-five miles away. With towns generally few and far between in the West, Sergeant James S. Hamilton summed up the situation: "Most of the time we did not have any place to go so did not take regular furloughs."[71]

Virtually all of the military departments embracing frontier posts lay west of the Mississippi River, some of them considerably distant from the States. A soldier posted in Montana and wishing to visit his home in New York, for example, would be required to submit his request to his post commander, who forwarded it through Department of Dakota headquarters in St. Paul, Minnesota, for endorsement, whereupon it would be kicked up to the Division of the Missouri commander in Chicago for approval. If soldiers actually succeeded in obtaining a furlough, frontier transportation being what it was, they would find it difficult to reach almost any place in the East and return within the time allowed, much less spend any meaningful time at their chosen destination. Generals commanding military departments and divisions could approve extended furloughs of two and three months, respectively, yet enlisted soldiers reluctant to request approval by a post commander were even less inclined to buck the red tape involving a higher office.[72]

If those hurdles were not enough to deter soldiers from applying for furlough, the travel costs probably were. Each man was financially responsible for paying his own expenses to and from his destination, and those could be considerable. Regulations did provide that if a soldier had insufficient funds to pay his travel when "special urgency" could be adequately justified, a department commander could authorize the Quartermaster Department to charge the expenses against the man's pay. Having been granted an emergency furlough in 1883 to go to Albany, New York, to settle some real estate matters, Private John G. Brown, Thirteenth Infantry, attested: "After my return to Fort Wingate, I rec'd. no pay until I made good $84.50, the amount [illegible] from N.Y.C. to Ft. Wingate, N. Mex." Such a debt could impose a serious hardship on a soldier whose gross earnings may have amounted to no more than $15.00 a month.[73]

Four years into his enlistment, a disgusted but wiser Private Eddie Matthews claimed that the recruiting officer had promised him a thirty-day furlough annually if he would sign up. "It is the same as everything else with the Regular Army *viz*: 'a fraud.' . . . A man enlists with the expectation of receiving that furlough . . . but in case he applied for it ten chances to one he would be put in the Guard House for having the presumption to ask."[74] Conditions had improved somewhat by about 1890 as the result of army reforms, but furloughs always remained elusive. Matthews's complaint certainly lent credence to the words in Harrington & Hart's sarcastic army ballad:

> And if you want a furlough, to the colonel you do go.
> He says, "Go to bed and wait 'til you're dead,"
> In the Regular Army, O!

Apart from the amusements that they could improvise for themselves in garrison, the regulars at frontier forts were extremely limited in their recreational opportunities and were largely confined to their isolated stations. Small wonder that many, by character, background, or desperation, succumbed to finding other outlets for boredom, pent-up sexual energy, and the aggravations that came with living in close quarters with other men of every character imaginable.

CHAPTER 11

"The Moral Condition Is Very Poor"

The Seamy Side of Enlisted Life

Having few recreational alternatives in the immediate postbellum years, soldiers, not unlike other frontiersmen in the West, usually turned to drinking, gambling, and other vices as diversions from an otherwise stark, tedious existence. But those activities required money, and cash was often in short supply except for a few days following payday. Whether or not the paymaster arrived on time—and he usually did not—payday was an occasion for letting off steam, with predictable results. And while the officers indulged the men to some extent at those times, drunkenness, disobedience, and worse spawned a range of problems and such behavior was dealt with harshly.

"At the post located here, the troops now present . . . have not been paid for four months . . . there is a strong probability that they may have to wait still another two months," complained a regular in 1869. Troops were to be mustered for pay every two months. Not receiving their pay on time was understandably a major source of discontent among the rank and file. "I am mustered for five months and three weeks pay," groused a trooper at Fort Whipple, Arizona Territory. Some garrisons had to wait as long as seven or eight months.[1]

When the long-anticipated day finally arrived, the boys were more than ready to make the most of it. "Payday," said Corporal Emil Bode, "was always a holiday and duly celebrated by all concerned. Buying necessary articles, spending foolishly, or on whisky and gambling." Many of those with any money left after settling up with each other, the trader, and laundresses attempted to increase their purses through games of chance in the barracks. Most companies included a member or two known as "boss gamblers," or "sharps," who took full advantage of payday, and their comrades. "Long rows of gambling tables were prepared for the event," Bode related. "The habitual gamblers luring a few suckers and greenies into a chuck-a-luck game; further on a faro and keno game in full blast, while in a corner twenty-one and monte played by an anguished crowd. Groups of four had blankets spread over the bunkboards, indulging in quiet games of poker."[2]

Indeed draw and stud poker were the most popular card games engaged in by soldiers, though Mexican monte and blackjack were also favored. Cribbage and shooting crap (then a singular noun) also had their enthusiasts. Gambling, ostensibly illegal on military posts, was generally overlooked by the officers simply because they too enjoyed a good poker game in quarters or the officers' club room. According to a Ninth Cavalry trooper, "Many soldiers wouldn't have any money 15 minutes after the paymaster had paid them . . . some men won a lot of money." When cash ran out, soldiers gambled for almost anything of value: tobacco, clothing, cartridges, pies—even pickled pigs' feet, according to one man. Markers were sometimes accepted against future pay, at least among trusted comrades. So long as cash or other valued goods held out, the games continued unabated, unless a strict post commander ordered the officer of the day to enforce "lights out" after taps. Undeterred, the gamblers then moved elsewhere. "The windows of outhouses [were] darkened with blankets, the tailor shop filled with men anxiously awaiting their luck at monte, [while] others took possession of the post bakery or butcher shop, and others went into the woods," a soldier at Fort Sill, Indian Territory remarked.[3]

A Second Cavalryman who served at Fort Bidwell, California, contended: "There were men in the fort, who I think were professional gamblers, who would actually enlist just for the opportunity to gamble. They'd put the money in a bank; then they'd serve their time or desert." The sharps tended to be hard men simply out to make money. One of them, a soldier named Pate, "had won all the money from a man who had sold the shoes off his little girl's feet to gamble with." When the loser's wife begged Pate for enough money to buy food for the child, he coldly turned her down, saying: "Not a cent. Your husband would have won mine if he could." A devil-may-care gambler named Campbell, about to be discharged at Fort Ellis, Montana Territory, was feeling particularly lucky. With five hundred dollars to his credit, he bet anyone to play him one hand of seven-up for the entire amount. "If I lose, I'll re-enlist. If I win, I'll go away," recounted one of his comrades. "The game was played the following day [after his discharge]. . . . It was carefully supervised. . . . At its end, Campbell walked away with a thousand dollars and an honorable discharge in his pocket."[4]

Paydays were universally marked by rampant drinking. "The drunkard, keen to get whiskey after a prolonged spell of enforced abstinence, at once began to make up for lost time by either congregating in the sutler's store or quietly and surreptitiously going off by himself with a supply," wrote First Sergeant Henry McConnell. Thirsty soldiers, now having money in their pockets, immediately overwhelmed the enlisted men's bar, which was usually the nearest place to obtain a drink. There was standing room only, such places seldom being furnished with tables and chairs anyway. Sixth Cavalryman Anton Mazzanovich described a typical scene:

> The sutler store at Fort Grant was sure a great institution, and on paydays the troopers lined the bar three deep, liquoring up. Hambler and Barney Norton had them trained not to call for any fancy or mixed drinks, consequently everyone had to drink their favorite brand straight. It did not require much time for the troopers to squander the two months' pay. . . . The bar had to close when taps sounded, 9:00 P.M.[5]

Whiskey, either rye or bourbon, was the soldiers' preferred drink for a decade after the Civil War, if for no other reason than it was universally available and was impervious to varying climatic conditions. It was, according one man, "the soldier's curse; a soldier who does not drink is rare; and if he does not on entering the army his good principles are soon overcome." Shipped by distillers in wood casks, kegs, and barrels, whiskey could be dispensed by the glass directly from the cask at the bar or into unlabeled bottles for package sales. Chaplain George G. Mullins, Twenty-Fifth Infantry, was of the opinion that drunkenness was not so much attributable to the quantity of whiskey as to its quality. "The small quantity of ardent spirits consumed could not be pronounced a serious evil, were it not frontier and Texas whiskey," Mullins contended. He suggested that post traders ought "to keep the purest and most costly liquors for sale and mete them out in small quantities." He may have been correct in his view, but it ignored the economics of the situation. Cheap whiskey was just that, and a soldier with very limited funds could buy more of it than he could of the better quality liquor stocked for officers.[6]

Lacking regular alcoholic beverages, or the money to buy them, some soldiers, particularly chronic alcoholics, resorted to other alternatives. Referring to the Eleventh Infantry garrison at Cheyenne Agency, Dakota Territory, a correspondent to the *Omaha Daily Bee* observed: "It is apparent that soldiers will have strong drink, and if they could not get whiskey they would take to a substitute in the shape of pine alcohol, Jamaica rum [*sic*], and even bay rum, mixed with blacking and Tripoli, etc." At least one brand of patented Jamaica ginger, Sanford's, contained 90 percent alcohol. Flavoring extracts, which also have high alcohol content, were popular for a quick buzz. Vanilla and lemon were readily available through both traders' stores and commissary sales.[7]

Even so, the irregularity of paydays could impose long dry spells on cash-strapped soldiers, a real hardship for chronic drinkers. Desperate for alcohol, a noncom and two privates of the Sixth Cavalry conspired to break into the hospital storeroom at Camp Buffalo Springs, Texas, and absconded with several cases of medicinal liquor. The thieves were later arrested after a black laundress confessed that they had given her one of the thirty-two-ounce bottles, possibly in exchange for sexual favors. Corporal Emil Bode, Sixteenth Infantry, cited the case of a man in his company who would no sooner get out of the guardhouse for drunkenness than "he would examine his box for clothes or new shoes or try to draw some from the company in order to sell them for whiskey." A soldier in D Troop, Fourth Cavalry, according to Private William B. Jett, earned the nickname, "'Booze' because he spent all his money for drink and drank all any others would give him. When all the other men were out of the quarters and he was 'room orderly,' I have seen him going up and down between the rows of bunks sniffing as he went till he located liquor hidden in some man's bunk, and drinking it till he not only could not walk but until he could hardly sniff." Some men cached liquor in the squad room according to Private Simpson Mann, Ninth Cavalry, who admitted that he had been a drinker prior to joining the army and often kept a gallon of whiskey in his foot locker.[8]

The theft and sale or barter of government firearms to civilians, usually for liquor, constantly plagued the army. The problem became so acute at Fort Laramie, Wyoming Territory, in 1870 that the post commander was compelled to direct the captains to take every possible measure to prevent the men of their companies from disposing of arms and ammunition. The widespread theft of arms across the Department of Texas resulted in orders for the arms of every company to be secured in a rack or locked room closely supervised by a noncommissioned officer, yet the problem persisted throughout the service until the army adopted standard locking gun racks for both long arms and revolvers in 1880.[9]

Officers, often heavy drinkers themselves, conveniently overlooked drunkenness among the men unless their conduct got out of hand, necessitating intervention by the guard. As a result of the evil effects that spirits had on some men, however, commanders devised various means to control the amount of alcohol available to soldiers. As a Seventh Cavalryman recalled, when liquor was sold by the drink at Fort Rice, Dakota Territory:

> Every man in the company who was in the habit of getting liquor had his name posted up along side of the bar. If a man whose name was on that board . . . got a drink . . . there was a pin put in the hole opposite his name . . . [so] there was a certain number of pins opposite his name, which indicated that he had received so many drinks. He could obtain no more drinks until after a certain time.[10]

A more common practice called for post or company commanders to issue written permits for individuals to purchase whiskey, usually no more than a pint at a time. But even that failed to restrict some men, according to Captain Albert Barnitz, Seventh Cavalry, who wrote in a letter to this wife:

> Hitherto I have refused for several months to sign any "whiskey orders." But having been so frequently importuned . . . by both privates and non-commissioned officers of the company

for permits, and finding that by some means they obtain whiskey at any rate . . . I have therefore endeavored to reconcile matters . . . so that temperate men . . . may not be entirely debarred from the privilege of paying the trader $12 a gallon for an inferior article . . . , while the intemperate men will be restrained from excesses."[11]

Nevertheless, when restrictions were imposed, enterprising civilians were only too happy to assist soldiers with getting booze. While his company was being transported by rail from Fort Sill to Fort Gibson, Indian Territory, in 1880, an infantryman told of an accommodating vendor who boarded the train during a stop and passed through the cars offering to sell oranges for twenty-five cents each. Or for a dollar the soldiers could purchase a "special" variety, which they discovered were injected with whiskey. In another instance, Private William J. Slaughter related that when the Seventh Cavalry, bound for Pine Ridge Agency, detrained temporarily at Beatrice, Nebraska, some of the men made directly for a nearby hotel having a bar. Knowing full-well the potential effect on his command, the colonel immediately placed the building off limits and posted a guard at each entrance. "The enterprising proprietor, not to be outdone, had three or four men carry a couple of quarts of tangle-foot apiece and sell it on the quiet to those who had the money, and when the money ran out, he had them swap a quart for an army blanket."[12]

An anonymous soldier at Fort Laramie wrote: "The moral condition is very poor, but better since the sutler has been prohibited selling whiskey, which was the worst I ever tasted; and at the moderate price of twenty-five cents per drink." In other instances, some post commanders attempted to ban alcohol altogether. A Thirty-Sixth Infantry private, John D. Laird, wrote in a letter to his father that "it is not allowed that the post suttler [sic] sell any kind of liquors to soldiers or citizens belonging to the fort [Sanders, Wyoming Territory] without an order of the Commanding Officer and he would not give it if you ask him."[13]

A significant scientific advancement not only benefited the field of medicine but also altered soldiers' drinking habits. French chemist Louis Pasteur's pioneering work in microbiology proved that fermentation in some beverages resulted from the growth of bacteria already present in them. For this reason, the lager beers of low alcoholic content that became widely popular in the United States during the 1860s could not long be preserved, usually only a few days. Consequently such beer could not be transported any great distance from the breweries, and certainly not to the western frontier. As alternatives to whiskey, soldiers consumed large quantities of ale and stout, both containing considerably higher alcoholic content than beer and therefore having a longer shelf-life. Pasteur developed a process whereby various liquids were heated to specific temperatures, thus killing most bacteria. The bottling industry concurrently invented a method for mass-producing air-tight, nonporous glass bottles, as opposed to ceramic, that would greatly extend the keeping qualities of lager beer.

In 1873 St. Louis brewer Adolphus Busch recognized the potential for combining pasteurized beer with the improved containers. The concept proved to be an economic bonanza for Busch and a godsend to soldiers. Not only did the majority of men prefer beer to whiskey and find it more thirst-quenching, but it also cost less. A twenty-four-ounce bottle of beer initially sold in the West for about thirty-five cents, but tap beer, put up in five- and ten-gallon kegs, was only ten cents a glass. Almost overnight Busch transformed the mostly whiskey-drinking soldiery into prodigious consumers of lager beer, much of it marketed under Busch's own labels, "St. Louis Lager Beer" and "Budweiser," although "Schlitz," brewed in Milwaukee, Wisconsin, also became extremely popular by the 1880s.[14]

The use of narcotics among soldiers, while comparatively uncommon, was not unknown. Opiates were readily available on the open market, without prescription, in the form of numerous proprietary medicines, most of them sold as remedies for pain, cough, diarrhea, or whatever ailment a person might have. Some of those products, one popular brand being "Davis' Vegetable Pain Killer," boasted all-natural ingredients but consisted primarily of alcohol and opium. Regardless of the label or the manufacturer's claims to the product being a "wonder drug," most were essentially laudanum camouflaged with various flavoring additives. The occasional archeological recovery of opium vials at western fort sites suggests its use in concentrated form, but whether by soldiers, officers' families, or Asian immigrants and to what extent is unclear. But it is certain that at least a few soldiers, such as Private John F. James, Sixth Cavalry, abused opiate drugs. James died at Austin, Texas, from an overdose of laudanum. It might be expected that stewards or nurses assigned to hospitals, with ready access to drugs, would have easily fallen victim to abuse, yet only one recorded case has been noted. Writing to his journal at Fort C. F. Smith in 1867, Lieutenant Colonel Luther P. Bradley recorded: "Hospital Steward Simmons was reported crazy today. Think it is from the effects of opium." In view of the limited available evidence, it is apparent that soldiers acquired readily available opiates in the form of patented pain-killing concoctions, perhaps to avoid going the hospital or simply for the resulting effects.[15]

Drinking and gambling may have been uppermost in the minds of many soldiers. But human nature being what it is, the need for sex was not far behind. "I lived a disgraceful life . . . in the army," one man candidly confessed. To be sure, army life on the frontier in that era did not breed saints. Private Henry Hubman assured his brother: "About my fretting for the flesh pots of Egypt . . . a Soldier can get more of that out here than he wants." However, the degree of moral looseness was directly related to the availability of women, at least of the immoral stripe, in the vicinity of forts. A lack of women was an often-voiced complaint, depending on the degree of isolation from what passed as civilization on the frontier.[16]

Under the circumstances, particularly prior to the adoption of single bunks, one might imagine that homosexual contacts were common. Yet the historical record is all but silent regarding same-sex behavior among postwar regulars. It existed, certainly, but societal norms of the day rendered the topic deeply hidden. If people were reluctant to discuss homosexuality, they wrote about it even more rarely. In one instance, Private Wilmot P. Sanford, Sixth Infantry, revealed in his diary that two men in his company were caught in the act of sodomy. The two soldiers, Privates James Costigan and Elmore Bradley, had both enlisted in July 1875 and apparently formed a relationship while at the recruiting depot, because they arrived at Fort Buford, Dakota Territory, in the same draft about a month later. The twenty-eight-year-old Costigan was tried and dishonorably discharged, while Bradley, six years his junior, deserted several months later while his company was in the field.[17]

An infamous and even more scandalous case is well documented. At least four firsthand accounts referenced the same event at a time when homosexuality was a forbidden topic, which suggests that public exposure of such liaisons was highly unusual, at least in the army. First Sergeant John Ryan captured the essence of the story:

> There was . . . a woman in this camp [Fort Hays] that was called "The Mexican" and her real name was Mrs. Nash. She was very tall and dark skinned and always kept a handkerchief tied around her lower lip and chin and the rumor got around camp that she used to shave. I understood from some of the men at that time that she drove a six-mule team from New Mexico to Kansas with the 5th U.S. Infantry in 1866 or 1867. This woman was married two or three times while in the 7th Cavalry, and I found out afterwards that there was one sergeant belonging to one of the companies who committed suicide on account of her and she turned out to be a hermaphrodite.[18]

Shortly after her arrival in Kansas, "Mrs. Nash" attached herself to the Seventh Cavalry as a laundress and was able to form relationships with a series of male partners, moving from one to another as men either were discharged or died. Her last "husband" was Corporal John Noonan, L Company, who accompanied his unit in the field for several months during 1878, while his "wife" remained at Fort Abraham Lincoln, Dakota Territory. About a month before Noonan returned, however, a shocking revelation became public:

> Mrs. Sergeant [sic] Noonan, who died last night, turns out to be a man. Mrs. Noonan was a laundress at the post and a most popular midwife. She was married three times and was one of the widows of the Custer massacre. Her husband . . . is now in the field. There is no explanation of this unusual union except that the supposed Mexican woman was worth $10,000 and was able to buy her husband's silence.[19]

By the time Noonan's company returned to the fort near the end of November, the post was ablaze with lurid gossip. The episode came to an abrupt and tragic conclusion a few days later when Noonan, unable to cope with the embarrassment and ridicule heaped upon him, walked to the stables and shot himself through the heart. It will never be known how many other soldier suicides and desertions may have been attributable to similar sexual exposure. The observation that one authority has made concerning soldiers during the Civil War would seem to apply equally to the later regular army: "Both the psychology and true incidence of homosexuality . . . appear to be mysteries."[20]

Prostitution was a prevalent and mostly unregulated industry throughout the West, supplying the needs of townsmen, cowboys, miners, railroaders, and every other class. With prostitutes vastly outnumbering "respectable" women on the frontier, the profession was simply considered a necessary evil. Unconsciously recognizing the law of supply and demand, Sergeant Charles Johnson summed up the state of morality among enlisted soldiers: "With 400 unattached men, you can bank on there being 50 unattached women and about the same consequence as in any similar condition anywhere." Although it was atypical to find so many prostitutes in the immediate vicinity of military posts, sporting women managed to seek out the troops or follow them to most locations. These "soiled doves" or "bankers' daughters," now past their prime, had descended the professional ladder from commanding higher wages in cities to its lowest rung, the army. Soldiers were notorious for having little money, so therefore the prices for services remained low, commensurate with the status of the women. The "Sage Hen's Ranch," near Fort Niobrara, Nebraska for example, was considered "a low place" operated initially by a disreputable madam from Yankton, Dakota Territory, whose successor recruited his prostitutes in the dives and on the streets of Omaha.[21]

Houses of ill-fame near western forts, commonly called "hog ranches" by soldiers, were primitive and the existence was difficult. An officer at Fort Laramie, Wyoming Territory, wrote in 1877:

> Three miles out there was a nest of ranches, Cooneys and Ecoffey's and Wrights, tenanted by as hardened and depraved a set of wretches as could be found on the face of the globe. Each of these establishments was equipped with a rum-mill of the worst kind and each contained from three to a half dozen Cyprians, virgins whose lamps were always burning brightly in expectancy of the coming bridegroom, and who lured to destruction the soldiers of the garrison. . . . I have never seen a lower, more beastly set of people of both sexes.

As a member of a party of fresh recruits being conveyed to Fort Grant, Private John Stokes was initiated to the term when the sergeant in charge pointed out the hog ranch within sight of the post. As Stokes later admitted, "We thought that was where the soldiers got their pork." Beyond plying their trade, it was incumbent on resident prostitutes to help with the chores necessary to operate the place—washing laundry and dishes, cooking, carrying water, and cutting firewood. Addiction to alcohol and/or opiates seemed to go with the profession, making hard women—often the victims of abuse or abandonment—even harder. Transient whores were only slightly more advantaged by following the paymaster to a fort and "each day the prostitutes would come to the saloons outside the post and stay there until the soldiers' money was gone," according to Private Thomas E. Gutch.[22]

Soldiers made a distinction between a "hog ranch" and a "whiskey ranch," a crude store with a saloon primarily for drinking, which may have offered prostitutes intermittently. A Second Cavalryman explained: "The 'ranches' as we knew them on the old trails were not farms in any sense. . . . The ranch was simply a store which offered for sale everything from flour to guns and ammunition, for which they exacted extortionate prices from the passing immigrants. Their principle stock consisted of a vile quality of gin and whiskey. . . . Ranches were few and far between, and usually found only within a few miles of some fort on the frontier."[23]

Not all of those dives, in fact, were situated off-post. A notable exception developed in a large abandoned earthwork on the plain immediately adjacent to Fort Union, New Mexico Territory. The army had constructed the bastioned star fort in 1861 as a stop-gap defense against an anticipated Confederate invasion of the territory, but its defeat by Union troops near Santa Fe a year later precluded any further necessity for such a work. By 1867 the post commander had decided to demolish the place in order to break up illicit trade occurring within its recesses and to salvage the lumber therein for other purposes. Upon inspecting the old fort, First Lieutenant Granville Lewis discovered "three rows of partially underground structures . . . [occupied] by citizens employed by the Depot Quartermaster's Department who have Mexican women whom they represent to be their wives. . . . Gambling, drinking, and prostitution seems to be the principal use to which many of the rooms are appropriated, and soldiers are enticed and harbored there to carouse all night." The operation was broken up, only to move elsewhere.[24]

Ever aware of the arrival of a paymaster, transient prostitutes even trailed behind him to far-flung outpost camps in order take advantage of freshly paid soldiers. Captain Gustavus Doane, Fourth Cavalry, commanding a picket camp at Bowie Station, Arizona Territory, penned a graphic description of one such caravan:

> The old strumpets—white, Mexican and Negro—follow up the Paymasters from camp to camp—in wagons, carryalls and in every other conveyance—with regular camp equipage. One lot of seven wenches have a large carnal house which is portable . . . and they do their own work . . . & drive their own train. They are a hideous lot of regular corn-fed wenches. . . . A second lot of five (the same kind) are in an old empty shack. The white ones stay in the saloon and deal faro, sing, play the guitar, etc.

At other locations prostitutes established themselves in squalid tent camps just outside the boundaries of military reservations and beyond army jurisdiction. To say that such operations were primitive would be an understatement. Some even lacked the basic facilities usually associated with the trade. "Those hideous old sluts . . . are humping soldiers out in the brush in reliefs." Doane confided in a subsequent letter to his wife. "If you could see their performances by moonlight once or hear their howls and jokes with the men at a distance of a few hundred yards . . . you would probably be as disgusted as I am."[25]

Between paydays, when cash was scarce, some men resorted to bartering to satisfy their sexual urge. An inspecting officer commented: "This is especially the case at Fort Abraham Lincoln. Directly opposite the Post . . . are located houses of low character where I understand enlisted men find it easy to dispose of Government property. In winter particularly [when the river was frozen] there is no difficulty in evading the sentinels and crossing the river." Such nocturnal antics were commonplace, with predictable results. "Between taps (10 P.M.) and reveille (4.30 A.M.)," another officer reported, "the men would steal out of camp, run the post guard in the dark, visit these places, and return before daylight. As a matter of course, they were heavy-eyed, stupid, and not up to their work the next day." It was not uncommon for some of those escapades to end tragically, such as when an inebriated Private John Smith staggered back toward Fort Laramie on a cold night in December 1874 after visiting a hog ranch three miles away. The following day soldiers found him lying frozen stiff and comatose where he had passed out along the road to the post. Smith died in the hospital without regaining consciousness.[26]

The frontier never lacked entrepreneurial spirits who survived by catering to army garrisons. At times so many congregated in one place that they constituted a sordid village. Near Camp Thomas, Arizona Territory, the short-lived town of Moxey became a soldier hangout offering gambling joints, a dance hall, and, of course, several saloons. Located on Beaver Creek, about a mile from Fort Assinniboine, Montana Territory, was a "settlement . . . bossed over by a white man . . . a squawman, a double-hearted and treacherous scoundrel who would harbor and shield rum runners . . . he was a man who would buy and sell good-looking, dark-featured Indian women, [and] would commercialize in fair-looking, half-breed girls yet in their teens." After the demise of the old star fort operation at Fort Union, Loma Parda, a sort of permanent substitute with two or three streets rose seven miles away, outside the reservation. Writing in 1870, an Eighth Cavalry soldier portrayed it as featuring "several drinking saloons and two dance halls . . . and plenty of Mexican women. . . . The Third Cavalry had two or three men killed over there by Mexicans." A Tenth Infantryman serving there a decade and a half later attested that Loma Parda was still the main attraction for soldiers and that in order to have time to walk there and back they formed dummies in their bunks to cover them for a check roll call by the first sergeant. However, such villages, whose economy was totally reliant on the army trade, quickly died out when the garrisons were eventually withdrawn.[27]

In other places hog ranches gave birth to what later became respectable civilian communities. One of the most notorious was San Angela (later San Angelo), adjacent to Fort Concho, Texas. Describing the village in 1875, a civilian wrote:

> It consists of about two doz[en] mud and stockade buildings, or rather hovels. Everything in the place is a whiskey shop or

something worse. . . . Its population is almost a hundred, said to be very bad subjects. . . . The males are Mexicans or Americans, and the females are all Mexicans. . . . The former are said to earn their wages by enticing the negro soldiery into their dens, and depriving them of their money at the card table. . . . The women appear to be such creatures as would naturally be attracted to such men.

Even in formerly remote northern Wyoming Territory, white occupation had gained a foothold little more than a decade after the old Bozeman Trail had been ceded to the Sioux. When his troop of the Fifth Cavalry was camped temporarily near Fort McKinney in 1881, Private Arthur Wallace happily noted in his diary that "a little town has sprung up here called Buffalo City & contains about 14 Ranches & one fine store. . . . The females at this town were imported from Denver, Col."[28]

Other raw-boned towns sprouted rapidly along water and rail transportation routes apace with the expansion of commerce, agriculture, and mining. When military posts happened to be in the vicinity— and they usually predated the establishment of permanent towns—they contributed significantly to the local economy, though frequently at a high cost to good order and military discipline. A soldier stationed at Fort Hays, Kansas, in 1871 observed that in nearby Hays City "there was always a large number of mule skinners, bull punchers, freighters, also cowboys, besides six companies of soldiers only half a mile away. . . . All these people spent their money freely, so that the one hotel, one general store, three dance halls, and 15 saloons—all running 24 hours per day, seven days in the week, certainly did a thriving business." Miles City, just east of Fort Keogh, Montana Territory, laid claim to no less than thirty-two saloons, six whorehouses—and one church. Similarly, Cheyenne, Wyoming Territory, was a wide-open town frequented by soldiers from Fort D. A. Russell, as well as cattle drovers, railroaders, and prospectors. One soldier visiting the place commented that he

> found the town hid . . . with three years['] collection of rubbish . . . in the center of the streets was a miscellaneous collection of tin cans, old boots, broken crockery, barrels, etc.,

enough to choke up the road. I was informed by a bystander that the city authorities were discussing with becoming gravity the question [whether] to clean the streets, or move the town. . . . Vice and filth go hand in hand; keno and faro are played openly. . . . Prostitutes parade the streets at all times of day and night, flaunting their gay dresses, and smiling and leering as only that class can do.[29]

Frontier towns were much the same, regardless of region, although some of the older ones were becoming somewhat more sophisticated (at the risk of abusing the word) by the 1880s. Sixth Cavalryman Anton Mazzanovich related that he and his comrades would obtain twenty-four-hour passes from Fort Lowell, Arizona Territory, in order to walk a few miles into Tucson "and squander our two months' pay over at the Congress Hall, Palace Hotel, or Fashion Bar. And many would buck the tiger, or Mexican monte game. Some of them would put too much Cowboy's Delight under their belt and get tanked up and overstay their passes." As late as 1891, a few months after the tragic affair with the Sioux at Wounded Knee, the little community of Valentine, Nebraska, near Fort Niobrara was overrun by thirsty, sex-starved soldiers when the assembled force was dissolved prior to returning to their home stations. Private Walter C. Harrington, a Twenty-First Infantryman, recalled that his unit marched to the railhead where they were to entrain. "About a mile outside their village (which itself was pretty orderly) was some sort of a 'joint' called the 'Hog Ranch.' All the men had plenty of money . . . and made a hike en-mass [sic] to the 'joint' referred to. They held up the train we were to take about 30 hours before they could be rounded up."[30]

Predictably, alcohol, gambling, and women, singly or in combination, were catalysts for a multitude of troubles ranging from health and disciplinary problems to theft and violence, often resulting in injury, even death. "The habits of the men are not good, judging from the considerable number of venereal diseases, and the wounds and injuries occurring in drinking and bawdy house quarrels," reported Fort Concho's surgeon Jean V. DeHanne.[31]

Indeed venereal disease was so much accepted as a natural hazard associated with indiscriminate sexual relations that one officer claimed that army doctors of that era had nothing more to do than "confine laundresses and treat the clap." That was an exaggeration, of course, but it was nonetheless indicative of the scope of the problem. However, compared with other maladies of the day, such as typhoid fever and smallpox, venereal diseases were not especially deadly. Statistics compiled during the Civil War indicated that death resulted in less than 2 percent of the reported cases of syphilis and a negligible number of gonorrhea patients.[32]

Those figures seem consistent with the postwar regular army, although a direct comparison is difficult. Prior to the 1880s the Surgeon General's Office was lax in publishing breakdowns of the various diseases suffered by the troops. In the past much has been made of frontier soldiers' association with prostitutes, yet it should come as no surprise that garrisons east of the Mississippi River, where soldiers were in close proximity to cities, experienced considerably higher rates of venereal diseases than did those in the West. This is not to imply that soldiers differed much in their sexual proclivities—they did not—but indicates only that those stationed on the frontier had less access to women. Even so, statistics indicate that permanent settlements and adjacent Indian reservations provided ready sources of women willing to fraternize with the troops. Fort Davis, Texas, as an example, was relatively isolated in the Trans-Pecos region, yet in 1884 its garrison had the highest rate of venereal diseases among the thirty-one posts embraced by the surgeon general's South Plateau and Mountain Region, no doubt as a result of the town situated at the fort's doorstep. In the north, Fort Custer, guardian over the Crow Indian Reservation, tied that rate, while Fort Assinniboine, near the Cree Reservation, experienced the highest venereal rate in the entire West by a wide margin and nationally was second only to the recruiting depot at Columbus Barracks, Ohio.[33]

Army doctors voiced a common complaint that upon arrival at their assigned commands a large percentage of recruits were found to be already afflicted with syphilis or gonorrhea. A lack of knowledge about the actual causes of the diseases limited physicians to treating only the external symptoms by applying calomel, irrigating solutions, and mercurial salves. Although those methods were fairly effective in correcting the manifestations of the diseases, they usually failed to result in permanent cures. The long-term effects—insanity and sometimes death—occurred years later.[34]

An unspoken rule among soldiers was that a man's locker and other personal property were to be respected. Most soldiers abided by that code of honor, considering their company a big family. "You will hardly ever find one old soldier who will steal from another, i.e., clothing or the likes of that," declared First Sergeant John Ryan, Seventh Cavalry. "I do not mean to say that they would not steal turkeys or chickens or pigs or things like that from each other" (those being considered as fair game particularly between different companies). Another soldier candidly attested that not much theft occurred for the simple reason that "there wasn't much to steal." Even so, sometimes dishonesty, at times aggravated by the delay between paydays or by gambling debts, outweighed both conscience and unit loyalty. Whatever the motive, theft was not tolerated and the culprit was often subjected to soldier justice. Ryan claimed that theft of personal belongings routinely peaked upon the arrival of a batch of new recruits. In one instance when a recruit was caught stealing clothing and blankets, the men did not bother turning him over to higher authority:

> The company was immediately roused and each man took his [carbine] sling belt or saber knot and proceeded to the stable. Caw was taken down and was made to run the gauntlet . . . men lined up in two rows facing each other. . . . Caw was ordered to take off his clothes. . . . He was obliged to run down the length of these two rows and as he went by each man gave him a stroke with one of these belts. . . . One of the men had a haversack full of rations . . . and this man Caw was given this haversack and then escorted by a squad to the center of the parade ground and then he was ordered to leave.[35]

One can imagine that Private Hartford G. Clark was not speaking of official action when he recorded in his diary that "Boyd and Sayers were confined tonight for breaking in a man's box. They will suffer severely." When the first sergeant of Company A, Thirteenth Infantry, caught a private going through his effects in the orderly room, the sergeant meted out justice immediately by shooting the thief on the spot. In some instances, thefts were more complex, requiring official intervention. At Fort McKinney, for example, Private Andrew Davis stole a gold watch and chain from one of his Ninth Cavalry comrades then pawned them to a prostitute in town. Upon being tried and convicted, Davis was sentenced to three years' hard labor and sent to the Kansas State Penitentiary. Swift and certain retribution served notice to other would-be offenders, and at the same time rid the company of undesirables, thus contributing to unit cohesiveness.[36]

Crimes by enlisted men against officers were infrequent, probably because of the gulf between the two classes, the lack of opportunity, and the perception, if not the reality, that offenders would be dealt with harshly. After being tried for stealing a government Springfield rifle from his colonel's quarters then selling it to a civilian, Private Walter L. Melus, Fourth Infantry, was confined to the guardhouse at Fort Omaha at hard labor for six months, at the end of which he was dishonorably discharged and forfeited all retained pay. On another occasion near Fort Sanders, Wyoming Territory, Lieutenant William W. Bell, Eighteenth Infantry, reprimanded Private James Brown for being drunk, insolent, and absent from camp without leave. Just as the lieutenant relented and gave Brown permission to return to the company, the armed soldier raised his rifle and "shot the Lieut[ant] dead, the ball entering his right side near the lungs and passing out through the spine." The Canadian-born officer had served as an enlisted man with the regiment throughout the war and was universally admired by the rest of the men, who peremptorily elected to shortcut the judicial process. Before returning to the post, "the private was shot [dead] by the Co[mpany] before the officers in command could stop them." No charges were filed against those involved and, justice having been served to everyone's satisfaction, the matter was quietly dropped.[37]

Whiskey also contributed to the needless death of a Third Cavalryman in 1878. Two men belonging to different companies, both under the influence, were engaged in a trivial quarrel when a third trooper approached from "behind his victim & struck him a crushing blow on the back of the head felling him to the ground with the back of his head crushed in. He lived one hour." The murdered man was Private Edward Olwill of Co. F, an Irish immigrant who had enlisted in the army only five months earlier.[38]

During an affray at Fort Niobrara, two Sixth Cavalrymen argued over a black prostitute, described by another soldier as "the most troublesome and abusive brute with the presence of which this town [Valentine] is cursed." Apparently, Corporal John R. Carter and Trumpeter Dixon were competing for the woman's attentions when the situation turned hostile. Just as the forty-year-old Carter, then in his second enlistment, exited the rear door of the barracks, Dixon accosted him, saying: "Carter you are no man." At the same instant he shot the corporal through the abdomen with his .45-caliber service revolver. Though mortally wounded, Carter managed to grab and hold Dixon until the guard arrived. Carter lingered until about noon the following day. A comrade described them both as fine, popular men, but Dixon's flaw "was his association with low women. He very seldom was seen drunk though was under the influence of alcohol last night . . . [and] feels very broken up over the affair. Poor Carter is dead and the country is less a good, yes better than good soldier."[39]

Regulars may have fought with each other, even killed each other on occasion, but those disagreements were considered to be within the family. When civilians threatened soldiers, it was another matter. The honor of the cloth demanded that soldiers face external threats with closed ranks and that hostile acts perpetrated on "the boys in blue" be avenged. Jules Ecoffey operated a whiskey ranch on the North Platte River downstream from Fort Laramie, described as "a vile den, the resort of the worst characters in the country . . . a grog shop, faro bank, and billiard saloon." During Fourth of July revelry in 1867 some of the hard cases hanging around the place murdered Corporal William Tyrrel, Second Cavalry. Upon receiving the news, the post commander sent a detachment of soldiers to investigate, but the civilians involved had already fled farther downstream hoping to escape. The pursuing detail nevertheless managed to capture one of the perpetrators. While conducting him back to the fort, the soldiers vented their anger by pillaging the joint and burning it to the ground.[40]

A penniless soldier craving sex at Fort Yates, Dakota Territory, visited the home of a nearby prostitute known only as "Mrs. Woods," where he bartered his army-issue buffalo overcoat for her favors. Knowing that the man would face serious consequences for disposing of government property, some of his friends, headed by Private Thomas Stallard, an Englishman in his third enlistment, attempted to recover it before the theft was discovered. Even after Stallard offered to reimburse Mrs. Woods and her father the five dollars that they had credited to the soldier, they refused to redeem the coat. Proceeding inside the house, the parties continued a combative exchange until the disreputable woman drew a revolver from her dress and threatened to shoot "the first —— —— —— who steps outside the house." Private Stallard raised the Springfield shotgun that he was holding and fired. The full blast struck Mrs. Woods in the right eye and tore away part of her head. A coroner's jury later determined that Stallard had acted in self-defense, whereupon he was restored to duty.[41]

Fortunately, some encounters with civilians ended on a lighter note. An inebriated soldier from Fort Assinniboine appeared on the streets of the Missouri Riverfront town of Fort Benton in 1882 offering to fight any civilian game enough to accept his challenge. One of the local characters, "Pegleg Tom," likely also under the influence, quickly stepped up to accommodate the "warrior bold," peeling off his clothes as he did so, and saying that he would fight the soldier in any manner he might choose. The local newspaper reported: "There was a great deal of dressing and undressing between the two, accordingly, as the hopes of victory fluctuated in the mind of the Assiniboine [sic] knight, and just as war was ready to be waged in earnest, a sergeant appeared and the blood-drinking boy in blue was escorted to camp under guard."[42]

At some locations where black troops formed all or part of a garrison, race became a factor in confrontations with civilians. When eight troopers of the Ninth Cavalry attended an evening dance at San Marcial, New Mexico Territory, a village on the Rio Grande a few miles above Fort Craig, they were informed that as a precaution all guns had to be turned over to the bartender before the men could enter the dance hall. Seven of the men immediately surrendered their Colts, but one refused, sparking a riot with the local citizens. After the soldiers were ejected from the saloon, the owner refused to return any of the arms, whereupon the troopers returned to their barracks and quietly aroused the rest of the troop. Mounted and fully armed, the company rode back to the village, surrounded it, fired two carbine volleys in the air, and demanded the pistols be returned. When two women meekly emerged with the revolvers within a few minutes, "their heroes and defenders had disappeared, not a man in sight."[43]

In an infamous affair at Fort Concho the common bond of military brotherhood trumped racial differences. After citizens in the notorious little town of San Angela wantonly murdered Private Hiram E. Pinder, Sixteenth Infantry, and a short time later Private William Watkins, Tenth Cavalry, no action was taken to punish the perpetrators.

The troops opted to exercise soldier justice. On the night following Watkins's killing, most of the men belonging to Pinder's company, along with a few from Watkins's, armed themselves and proceeded into town. They took the sheriff prisoner and demanded that the guilty parties, one of whom was the constable, be turned over in exchange. The incident was temporarily diffused when the post commander dispatched most of the guard and some officers to compel the men to return to their quarters. Tensions nevertheless remained high. On February 3, 1881 black and white soldiers jointly published the following ultimatum:

> We, the soldiers of the U.S. Army, do hereby warn cow-boys & c. of San Angela, and vicinity to recognize our right of way, as just and peaceable men. If we do not receive justice and fair play, which we must have, some one [sic] must suffer, if not the guilty, the innocent.
> U.S. Soldiers
> One and All[44]

The sheriff finally arrested the constable and transported him to the county seat jail to preclude his friends from attacking the San Angela facility to free him. However, by that same evening, the prisoner was reported back in town again. A party of civilians later opened fire on the picket guard that had been posted at the river crossing between the fort and the village. With their patience at an end, about seventy men, most of them belonging to the three companies of the garrison that had not been involved up to that time, broke into the barracks gun racks and made a rush on the town. Despite numerous shots being fired, only one citizen was wounded before the guard detail arrived and the men evaporated to return to quarters. The timely arrival of a company of Texas Rangers, in cooperation with the army, finally quelled the incident. Colonel Benjamin Grierson saw to it that three noncommissioned officers and two privates, identified as ring leaders, were arrested and charged. In doing so, however, he felt compelled to point out to his superior: "In addition to the cold blooded murdering of soldiers . . . lately, a great many others have been killed by citizens and up to this time the murderers have invariably escaped punishment, which the records will show that soldiers are constantly arrested and severely punished for slight offenses by the civil authorities." While Grierson made no excuse for the actions of his men, he added that he made the statement "simply to show under what difficulties the officers are placed to control the men when their comrades are shot down without any punishment being inflicted on the guilty parties."[45]

Troopers of the Fourth Cavalry at Fort Walla Walla, Washington Territory, reacted to the senseless murder of one of their own by a gambler in 1891 by plotting a coordinated raid on the adjoining town. Stealing into town late at night, a portion of the troops deftly cordoned off the courthouse square, while another party forced its way into the jail, overwhelming the guards and extracting the prisoner. Once outside, several troopers summarily shot the man to death as he lay on the courthouse lawn. Even though six men eventually were tried for the crime, all were acquitted, mainly because the sheriff was unable to distinguish one soldier from another in the darkness and their comrades remained loyal to the code of solidarity by not divulging their identities.[46]

Soldiers could be subject to military or civil law, or both, depending on the nature of the offense. Courts-martial exercised exclusive jurisdiction over violations of Army Regulations, general and special orders, and the Articles of War, while the respective state and territorial civil tribunals retained jurisdiction over capital crimes. In such cases commanding officers were mandated to surrender accused soldiers to civilian authority for confinement and trial. If convicted, the man was dishonorably discharged from the army and served sentence in a civilian prison or was executed.[47]

In its broadest interpretation, military law encompassed almost every situation imaginable. It was a rare soldier who was able to avoid appearing before a court-martial during his five-year enlistment. "We have had as high as eighteen out of sixty in the guard house at a time and there is but a few men in the company for duty," grumbled a private at Camp Grant, Arizona Territory. He added that it was nothing for citizens to murder each other because little civil law enforcement existed there in the late 1860s. When a soldier shot another, he was only court-martialed. General courts-martial, involving from five to thirteen officers, were convened by order of a department commander to try officers or enlisted men charged with capital offenses. Punishments ranged from mere reprimands, forfeiture of pay and allowances, and various periods of confinement to being incarcerated for various periods. Solitary confinement was the punishment for hard cases, sometimes on bread-and-water diet, though neither of those could be imposed for continuous periods of more than fourteen days. Depending on the circumstances, some prisoners were assigned to hard labor. General courts also were vested with authority to impose dishonorable discharge from the service or even the death sentence (but only in times of declared war, which the Indian campaigns were not). Some deference was shown noncommissioned officers who erred, the most common punishment being reduction to the ranks.[48]

Less than capital violations were heard by either regimental or garrison courts. Because regimental courts were authorized to judge only cases involving members of that regiment, and the officers available at a post often represented other units, trials in regimental courts were comparatively rare. The garrison court-martial, however, could be authorized by any commanding officer at a station whose garrison included elements of different regiments or branches of service, the usual situation on the frontier. This inferior court, sometimes referred to as a field officer's court, composed of three commissioned officers, was limited to imposing sentences of not more than thirty days' general confinement or fourteen days solitary, either of which could be compounded with bread-and-water diet and/or forfeiture of up to one month's pay. With regard to noncoms, the garrison court could do nothing more than reduce them to the rank of private.[49]

It was not unusual for soldiers to bear a grudge against garrison courts for treating them unjustly for relatively minor offenses that should have been within the province of company punishment. Writing to the *Army & Navy Journal* from Fort Davis, a soldier claimed that garrison courts were a primary cause of desertion. "For example, a soldier misses roll-call, is . . . sentenced to forfeit five or ten dollars. . . . Another fails to stand 'at attention,' or his blouse is unbuttoned; straightaway he is marched to the guardhouse . . . the ubiquitous court adjusts the matter by entering up a fine of ten dollars against the offending party." Adding insult to injury was the rather lengthy time that a soldier could be confined until his case was heard.[50]

According to the type of court hearing the case, those convicted were classed as either "general" or "garrison" prisoners. Prior to the mid-1870s soldiers convicted by general courts of capital offenses or serious breaches of military law were sentenced to serve long periods of confinement, often at hard labor, in post guardhouses. Lacking uniform building standards, department and post quartermasters designed prison facilities ranging from only fair to barbaric. Commenting on the insufficient ventilation of the adobe guardhouse at Fort Yuma, California, where summer temperatures averaged 105 to 113 degrees, Assistant Surgeon John Vance Lauderdale wrote in 1868: "I know those fellows must have had a hot time of it in there during the last heated term. I will suggest that their cage be punctured with a few more air holes and have them a little nearer the floor. Men do not deserve roasting alive." The majority of guardhouses featured only a single general confinement room, at times augmented with manacles chained to one wall for restraining particularly vicious prisoners, and a couple of solitary confinement cells partitioned from the main room. The post surgeon at Fort Laramie decried the conditions he found: "The practice generally is to crowd all the prisoners indiscriminately into one prison room; those who have been tried and sentenced for murder, felony, desertion etc. are brought into direct contact with and forced to be the immediate companions of innocent men or men who are presumed to be innocent since they have not been proven guilty."[51]

Exceptions to the norm were at Alcatraz Island, California, and at Fort Union, which frequently served as headquarters for the District of New Mexico. Two jail facilities were erected at Fort Union, one a regular guardhouse where garrison offenders were incarcerated and a second, designated a military prison for general prisoners, incorporating a block of ten stone cells enclosed within an adobe building. Long-term general convicts from other forts in the territory were sent there to serve their sentences in the presumably more secure jail or held as transients until they could be forwarded to a state penitentiary. But even the iron-barred stone cells proved not to be escape-proof for determined hard-cases. Shortly after eight general prisoners were incarcerated at Fort Union to serve their sentences, they disappeared. "As there were no troops but infantry at the Post and very few of them," a soldier related, "the prisoners had nothing to fear from pursuit." Alcatraz Island, occupied by the army since 1850 as part of the defenses of San Francisco Bay, functioned as a central collection point for incarcerating long-term prisoners convicted of serious crimes in the Division of the Pacific owing to its great distance from other state institutions. Located in the bay and distanced from any shore, Alcatraz was ideally suited to house prisoners with maximum security at minimal expense.⁵²

Before 1875 the army often imprisoned men convicted of serious military crimes in state penitentiaries through contractual arrangements with various state governments. That proved less than satisfactory because of the variations in the quality and security of facilities and prisoner treatment from one institution to another. To rectify the situation, Congress authorized the construction of a dedicated U.S. Military Prison at Fort Leavenworth, Kansas, thus providing a facility that was more administratively efficient than keeping general prisoners in post guardhouses or distributing them among various penitentiaries. At an army facility long-term inmates ostensibly would be treated according to uniform policies and rules and could be rehabilitated in more humane living conditions through training and meaningful work in prison shops manufacturing army footwear, mule harness, tinware for kitchens, and barracks furniture.

A visitor to the U.S. Military Prison in 1882 described what he saw:

> Before its portals are reached, the prisoner . . . has generally ceased to be a soldier. Adjudicated to be not worth keeping in the army, and for the sake, too, of simplifying the company books, he had been written off his regiment as "dishonorably discharged." . . . Once inside the prison, his hair is left to him and he is assigned quarters in an airy barrack-room, far more comfortable than the tent or adobe hut which . . . he had been occupying when with his company. Here he has his bed from the first night, and the liberty of unrestrained conversation with his fellow-prisoners. His food is the liberal ration issued to the American soldier . . . supplemented in season by the produce of the prison garden. . . . The labor to which he is put is some handicraft, the practice of which . . . may furnish him an honest livelihood when again he shall be a free man.⁵³

Some of the arbitrary punishments imposed at the garrison and company levels were as old as the army itself, perhaps inherited from the British. Soon after joining the Fourth Cavalry in 1865 Private James

Foley was repulsed to witness "a man whipped out of camp with a wagon whip. He was tied up to a tree and the lashes were laid on his bare back." Because an officer could be brought up on charges for directing such extreme punishment, whipping was rare. Unofficially, however, the men themselves sometimes saw fit to subject a man to it, such as when a company of the Seventh Cavalry "had 56 lashes with a whip administered to one of their men for stealing their hard tack." The officers, undoubtedly aware of the incident, apparently elected not to interfere, probably considering it rough justice for an offense perpetrated against the unit by one of their own.[54]

Extreme cases of drunkenness on duty, particularly those involving violent behavior, were punished through an array of diabolical means of long tradition. Bucking-and-gagging was an experience not soon forgotten by anyone subjected to it. First Sergeant John Ryan, Seventh Cavalry, vividly recalled:

> It is simply putting a stick across a man's mouth, and tying a string to the ends of the stick, and tying it at the back of his neck, which prevents him from speaking or moving his mouth. The bucking part consists of sitting a man on the ground, tying his arms together, also his feet, sliding his arms over his knees, and putting a stick under his knees and over his elbows so that he is unable to move hands or feet without falling over. They remained in this position until they fell asleep when they were unbound and ungagged and allowed to remain in the guard house.[55]

Two other harsh lessons imposed for drunkenness involved suspending a man by his thumbs or wrists, with his toes just touching the ground, for several hours at a time. As Sergeant Perley S. Eaton remembered: "When the soldier got drunk and got so bad that you could do nothing with him, I have seen them make a spread eagle of him." The severity of such inhumane treatment was not lost on an Eighteenth Infantry soldier who saw a man spread-eagled at Fort Reno, Dakota Territory: "At the guard tent four stakes were driven into the ground and the drunken soldier was stretched at full length and tied to them. . . . The sun was beating down on him when I saw him and I thought he was dead. Flies were eating him up and were running in and out of his mouth, ears, and nose." A Third Infantryman claimed that some of the men became drunk after securing a keg of whiskey at Fort Lyon, Colorado Territory. But, true to the soldier's code of loyalty, all refused to divulge the source to their officers. "In order to force them to tell they tied some of them up by the thumbs and spread eagled others. The orders were to leave them there all night. . . . We had to do guard duty that night, but when the officers went to look the men over in the morning, all they saw was the stakes and ropes that they were tied to. We cut them loose during the night."[56]

The wooden horse was occasionally employed for drunkenness but more often when a trooper abused his mount. After a Fourth Cavalryman had been caught sitting sideways on his horse while on herd guard, Private William B. Jett declared, "a log was put in the crotch of two forked stakes driven in the ground, and the soldier was made to sit astride of this for ten days, with his feet dangling above the earth." The excruciating pain inflicted by such punishment was calculated to serve as a permanent reminder to the offender to respect the well-being his horse at all times.[57]

As time passed and a degree of enlightenment dawned in the army, the service became less indulgent of egregious abuses of authority over enlisted soldiers. In one notable example, at Fort McKavett, Texas, Captain Theodore J. Wint, who had formerly served in the ranks as a state volunteer, had Private Patrick Murray placed in handcuffs then chained chest-high to the stable wall. Murray was kept in that position, unable even to sit down, for a period of forty-five hours, except for meals and calls of nature. For more than eight hours nightly, the prisoner was left alone and "no precautions were adopted for his being taken down in case of sudden illness, or to attend the calls of nature." Upon completion of this torture, Murray requested to see the surgeon for treatment, but Wint allowed him only a twenty-four-hour respite to "cure himself" before returning to full duty. Wint was subsequently charged with having denied Murray due process of law and with illegally punishing him, yet the captain received only a reprimand.[58]

If a general court-martial had any benefit to the soldier over the garrison court, it was that the proceedings had to be forwarded to the department commanding general for review. He did not often question the findings or mitigate the punishment, except in a few rare cases. One of these involved Private Stanislaus Johnson, Company G, Fourth

Infantry, charged with theft and the catch-all "conduct prejudice of good order and military discipline." The court acquitted Johnson of the first more serious charge, yet, not unexpectedly, found him guilty of the second, sentencing him to be dishonorably discharged and to serve one year in prison. Reviewing the record, Brigadier General Christopher C. Augur and his staff at Department of the Platte headquarters considered the punishment excessive for the offense. Augur therefore reduced the sentence to six months' forfeiture of pay and six months in the guardhouse. Recognizing that Johnson had already been jailed that long awaiting trial, Auger remitted the unexecuted portion of his time. Happily, the man was fully vindicated a month later with his promotion to corporal.[59]

In the absence of any requirement formally to charge offending soldiers, company officers and noncoms exercised latitude and arbitrarily took various disciplinary measures against the men for minor offenses. Infractions like talking back to a noncom, unruliness in quarters, being tardy, or failing to pass inspection were penalized by extra duty assignments to kitchen police, blacking stoves, sawing wood, or other menial tasks about the barracks. After the army adopted reloadable metallic cartridges in 1881, some companies, according to Private John C. Ford, Seventeenth Infantry, used the making of ammunition for target practice as company punishment. Most of these light measures were tasks that needed to be done in any event. Some cavalry units went so far as to place men under informal company arrest to clean stalls or carry a log for a few hours under supervision of the stable guard.[60]

Discipline was constant and exacting; seldom was any infraction overlooked. Private William J. Burke probably considered himself lucky when he appeared before a garrison court in 1881 and was fined only fifty cents for failing to attend a reading of the Articles of War. Lieutenant John Bigelow, Tenth Cavalry, made an example of Private Brady Jewell, an old soldier in his third enlistment and formerly a first sergeant, by placing him in the guardhouse because he was assigned as room orderly but left the squad room without permission by the charge-of-quarters. Even though Jewell was later acquitted, after serving a few days in jail, Bigelow had made his point. Punishments for other petty violations of discipline, such as missing or being late to drills or roll calls, usually resulted in short-term confinement in the guardhouse, ten days being typical, and a nominal fine (or "blind," as soldiers called it) of five or ten dollars deducted from the soldier's next pay. When a man was said to have received "ten and ten," for example, it translated to ten days confinement and a ten-dollar fine.[61]

Sentences for more serious offenses—drunkenness, disorderly conduct, insubordination, or any combination thereof—usually ranged from one to three or four months, plus a levy on the soldier's pay, though never all of it. Private Edmund Thornton got three months' hard labor and a ten-dollar fine for each of those months for refusing his first sergeant's order to proceed to the guardhouse. Thornton turned on the sergeant, challenging him to "take me to the guard house, you son of a bitch" and began pummeling him while continuing to curse in "vile and opprobrious language" until a duty sergeant stepped in to help subdue the man. Before going to the "mill," however, a Sixteenth Infantry soldier advised, it was best to have empty pockets because "he would be taken care of by a kindhearted guard and fellow prisoners. The latter would go through him and take all the money the sirens missed."[62]

Soldiers in confinement continued to be fed by their companies, the food being the same as that given the other men, unless the sentence called for a bread-and-water diet. The kitchen police of the respective companies delivered meals to the guardhouse and returned later for the containers. The guards nevertheless had to be alert because some prisoners, especially those with little else to lose, would take any opportunity to win their freedom. One transient convict at Fort Union, facing a four-year sentence in a penitentiary, saw his chance just after dinner and daringly "took up lot of pans and walked out of the Guard House, past the Sentry on duty," making his escape. In all probability, the inattentive guard quickly found himself behind bars.[63]

A brief stint in the guardhouse was not taken very seriously by most soldiers, perhaps even looked upon as a rite of passage. The work was not very different (if distinguishable at all) from company or old guard police when no prisoners were available. For example, company commanders at Fort Laramie were informed that "owing to the small number of general prisoners, and the large amount of general work to be performed, Company Officers must have their own wood cut and policing done by the fatigue details from their own companies." Prisoners not sentenced to hard labor performed routine police duty under the supervision of the provost sergeant during the normal fatigue hours, typically collecting garbage with the slop wagon or cart, clearing snow from walks, hauling water, gathering litter, and pulling weeds on the parade ground. But, according to a sarcastic Private William F. Zimmer, Second Cavalry, there were compensating benefits: "You have a guard with you with a loaded carbine to keep off mad dogs, and at night you are locked up so there's no danger of your being stolen."[64]

A sentence including hard labor, however, could be a different matter. A man considered himself fortunate to be assigned only to cutting wood all day to supply officers' kitchens and quarters. More typical was a sentence calling for the prisoner to carry a twenty-five-pound log while walking beat with Sentinel No. 1 at the guardhouse, two hours on and four off between reveille and retreat. A variant method required the prisoner, under the eyes of a guard, to walk a prescribed circle carrying the log. Guards belonging to the same company as prisoners, especially if they happened to be friends, might do what they could to alleviate some of the heavy work and discomfort. Sergeant John Cox of the First Infantry told of an occasion when he was ordered by the officer of the day to take charge of two men who were to walk around the barracks carrying "the largest sticks in the wood pile" on their shoulders. Cox, confident they were good soldiers, chose two old dry-rotted cottonwood logs missing most of their cores. When out of sight of the officers' quarters, the prisoners danced a jig and performed other antics, but as they came around in view, "the efforts required to 'tote' those 'logs' were truly painful. Two hours passed, and the boys were evidently almost exhausted. They staggered rather than walked. . . . I could see the officer and his good wife were interested spectators of the performance, and so . . . encouraged the boys to persevere, as I believed . . . that victory would soon rest on our banner." Before long the inexperienced lieutenant indeed relented and directed the sergeant to release prisoners. Cox added, however, that an older officer would not have been so easily duped.[65]

It was long recognized that whiskey, gin, and other hard liquors were the bane of the army. While many soldiers drank only moderately, and some not at all, liquor consumption was a primary and constant source of disciplinary problems and crime. Alcohol accounted for great loss to the service from inability of soldiers to perform duty because of illness and needless injury, incarceration, chronic alcoholism, discharges, and death. Some laid partial blame on the officers for setting the example for their men, "like master, like man. If an officer drinks he gives his men orders on the sutler for whiskey. . . . Cannot the Military Committee in Congress . . . do something for the cause of morality . . . to suppress this curse?" insisted a temperance advocate writing to the *Army & Navy Journal*. Some officers did take personal action to try to dissuade their men from falling victim to alcohol. Among them was Brigadier General Oliver Otis Howard, nicknamed "the Christian Soldier," who visited Fort Lapwai, Idaho Territory in 1876 and "gave a little service in the Infantry Barracks . . . , nothing more than a little temperance talk to the men—but the whole thing was very pleasant." Here and there a post commander took individual initiative to curtail the introduction of alcohol of any kind on his military reservation, at least without special permission.[66]

In an effort to combat the abuse of alcohol, soldiers in some garrisons took the initiative to organize local chapters of the Independent Order of Good Templars. Meetings were conducted regularly, featuring inspirational talks, alcohol-free punch or other refreshments, and good fellowship encouraging abstinence. "I try to be moderate in my habits," First Sergeant Frederick Stortz informed his father. "I still am a good Templar and now hold the highest office in the [illegible] of the lodge. . . . We ought all to thank God for what he has made me." At posts lacking a formal temperance organization, those soldiers desiring to stay sober sometimes took it upon themselves to form a pact. Quartermaster Sergeant Maurice Wolfe, Thirtieth Infantry, announced in a letter written at Fort Fred Steele, Wyoming Territory: "I am saving all my pay now as I don't drink any kind of liquor. The Quartermaster drew up a pledge and got all his clerks to sign it, and to make it more binding the first man that breaks it has to pay 50 dollars fine." Other men possessing self-discipline simply learned the hard way to avoid drinking. One of those was Sergeant George Neihaus, who confessed that as a young soldier he made the mistake of overindulging in Mexican muscatel wine: "I . . . was tied up for 2 days and never drank again in my life."[67]

Through the efforts of a number of religious and other groups, the temperance movement steadily gained momentum across the nation. Unable to effect any sudden change in the habits of the general population, temperance societies focused on the army. Shortly before leaving office in early 1881, President Rutherford B. Hayes, purportedly influenced by his wife, directed that an order be issued by army headquarters prohibiting the sale of intoxicating liquors at all military posts, under the impression that soldiers would thus be compelled to abstain. While some vocal adherents of temperance in the army praised General Orders No. 24 as a great stride forward in reforming the service, others were not so enthusiastic. Lieutenant General Philip H. Sheridan, whose command of the Division of the Missouri encompassed the great majority of the stations west of the Mississippi River, dared to ask for clarification of the definition of "intoxicating liquors." The adjutant general informed him that his understanding was that the order applied only to "ardent spirits," such as whiskey, gin, brandy, rum, and other liquors of high alcohol content. Beer, light wine, cider, and ale were unaffected. That news was of some relief, as beer and ale had become the favorite beverages of the rank and file anyway. Besides, as a correspondent to the *Army & Navy Journal* pointed out, those who desired stronger refreshments had only to go outside the military reservation. The order was effectively nullified because it "simply takes the selling of liquor out of the hands of the regulated trader, and transfers it to the irresponsible sellers of poisoned decoctions who are within reach of every Army post, and beyond the control of the post commander." Colonel George A. Forsyth, formerly an aide to Sheridan and later commander of the Fourth Cavalry, succinctly described the ramifications:

> Within three months from the enforcement of said order just outside of the post reservations . . . all over the country, little shacks or shanties began to make their appearance. These shacks soon became known as "hog ranches," and at first consisted of a lean-to (a long room), one man, two or three tin cups, and one or two four-gallon jugs of vile whiskey. Within three months they were enlarged to two or more rooms, held a bar that had behind it whiskey by the barrel, and in the room outside of the bar were two or three card tables, and possibly a faro layout. Within two or three months there were two or three bedrooms built on to the ranch and two or three of the most wretched and lowest class of abandoned women . . . could be seen in the doorway or heard singing and shouting at the bar.[68]

The temperance order nevertheless heralded an era of reformation that benefited the enlisted men of the army and the service in general. Soldiers serving during the 1880s, in the wake of the order, attested that drunkenness and related problems on-post were far less common than they had previously been. When hard liquor was consumed, it was obtained at establishments outside the military reservation. In fact men acquiring reputations as heavy drinkers became less common. Rejecting the popular impression that most soldiers were drunkards, an experienced regular wrote in 1883 that "the fact is that they don't drink as much as the same number of healthy young citizens. Being in uniform, their drinking is prominent and a few men in uniform can give an unjust notoriety to all." Even though whiskey continued to be available at civilian-owned saloons in nearby towns and "ranches," the banning of its sale at forts did in fact make it more inconvenient for soldiers to obtain. That factor alone seems to have had a mollifying effect in reducing occurrences of extreme intoxication and attendant problems. As First Cavalryman Richard F. Watson, pointed out, "Most of the men knew how to drink and it did not interfere with the performance of their duties." Soldiers were soldiers, and most of them drank, but the higher recruitment standards and generally better character of the men enlisting during the 1880s, combined with restrictions on alcohol, mitigated the abuses experienced earlier.[69]

A viable alternative to the off-post saloon and the whiskey-dispensing post trader was the "canteen" adopted from the British Army. The concept was a self-sustaining club room operated by and for the men where they could obtain snacks, light lunches, and refreshments. One of the earliest examples in the United States Army was at Fort Abraham Lincoln, Dakota Territory, where in 1873 Company A, Sixth Infantry organized a canteen after the British model. This experiment, however, differed in a few important aspects from those created later. Unlike its successors, access was restricted to members of that company, including officers, and only by paid membership. Still, it was a significant step in the right direction.[70]

By 1881, so-called coffee canteens, only for enlisted men, were operating at Fort Vancouver, Washington Territory, and at Fort Keogh, Montana Territory. There a soldier could enjoy a sandwich and a cup of coffee for the price of only five cents, a real boon for soldiers accustomed to being gouged by post traders and other civilians. Of further advantage to cash-strapped soldiers was the creation of a credit system used at both places. The men could charge up to a dollar a week, with the amount entered in a ledger, and be given a corresponding sum in five-cent printed tickets. The beneficial effect on enlisted soldiers was immediately apparent to one garrison resident, who wrote that "where formerly the men would congregate around the trader's bar, they crowded into the coffee canteen."[71]

Colonel Henry A. Morrow, Twenty-First Infantry, proved to be a pioneering spirit promoting the canteen movement. He was the one, in fact, who had initiated the Fort Vancouver canteen while posted there. Shortly after his regiment was transferred to stations in the Department of the Platte, he encouraged the battalion at Fort Sidney, Nebraska, to continue the program. Thus, an "amusement hall" for the men opened its doors in December 1884. A correspondent notified the editor of the *Army & Navy Journal* that the room was "filled with billiard and card tables, and has also a lunch counter where the soldiers can get a glass of first class beer or a genuine ham sandwich at five cents each. Everything is quiet and orderly, and as the soldiers themselves have taken a pride in the matter, the scheme is a great success so far. Nobody gets drunk, and the boys can have all the fun they want in a quiet way."[72]

As idyllic as that seemed to be, the canteen was not without its opponents in the form of local saloon owners in the town of Sidney, only a quarter mile away. Indeed the sudden decline in military clientele forced one saloon to close its doors. Other owners hung on, threatening legal action against Morrow on the ground that the State of Nebraska had never ceded jurisdiction to the army; therefore the post commander had no authority to operate a competing business. The challenge failed, of course, simply because the canteen was open only to soldiers, not the public, and the men were still free to go into town if they pleased. For the army, the canteen was a huge success. Guardhouse confinements dropped by some 62 percent immediately after the canteen began operation.

Enemies of another class also resisted canteens, and not without justification. Post traders, who were licensed exclusively to operate stores and bars at the forts for the convenience of the troops, were directly and adversely affected by soldier-managed canteens. By 1886 a number of posts boasted such canteens, which were expanding services to include sundries used by the soldier, including cigars, pipes, cigarettes, and tobacco, in addition to beer, wine, and lunches. Having no overhead costs, building space provided by the government, and no profit margin to maintain, the canteens could invariably keep prices far below those of the merchants. The traders also rightly claimed that they were assessed a head-tax for the exclusive privilege of doing business on military reservations and, moreover, that canteens operated without any specific authority granted by the War Department.

Those challenges quickly attracted official attention at the highest levels, prompting a series of restrictions to be imposed on canteens in 1888. When the secretary of the treasury discovered that canteens were selling tobacco products and malt liquors tax-free, he immediately insisted that the revenues be collected at the point of sale. Likewise, the army's own Subsistence Department complained that canteens were purchasing supplies, such as pickles, ham, and tobacco, at the special rates authorized for the personal use of army personnel and civilian employees. The commissary general subsequently determined that the regulations governing those sales did not allow for canteens to be profiting unfairly by the sale of government supplies. Finally, in an edict portending a death blow to the canteens, the secretary of war announced that the sale of beer and other alcoholic beverages, even though permitted by the 1881 Hayes order, were henceforth banned at canteens because those sales violated the legal rights of the traders. Sutlers had traditionally relied on the sale of alcohol as an underpinning of their business. The secretary thus decreed in October that, despite the recognized advantages afforded by canteens, they must not "infringe on the vested rights of the post traders." These decisions virtually negated the benefits produced by canteens. An officer at Fort Robinson complained in December: "Breaking up the canteen has sent the garrison back to the old pay day times, filling the guardhouse to its utmost capacity. The men will drink, and now must go off to get it. Rows and drunks are largely increased. The desertions have more than doubled since the canteen was closed by the Secretary of War."[73]

By the late 1880s, however, not all military posts still had licensed traders. The West was becoming a different place than it had been when sutlers were considered essential for providing garrisons with many items, including liquor, not furnished by the government. No longer were the majority of "frontier" forts considered isolated, making post traders less relevant. At many locations the very presence of army garrisons had given rise to local communities presenting direct competition to the traders. Towns also sprang up as a result of a growing western agricultural industry and the ever-expanding rail network, supplementing existing stage and star mail routes. Moreover, the army's effort to reduce the number of posts, particularly those not located on major lines of transportation or communication or conveniently near Indian reservations, had been abandoned or soon would be. This combination of factors served to thin post traderships directly or by attrition, as sutlers' resigned because of declining profits. Times were changing, and traderships simply were not the lucrative ventures they once had been.

Not all officers, however, favored establishing canteens if it meant the demise of the traders. A private at Fort Meade, South Dakota, revealed what in his opinion were the selfish motives of many officers: "What they want is a place where they can gather, a place of rendezvous, and the sutler's store is the only place at the present. . . . Now, what prevents the Government from erecting canteens for the enlisted men and clubhouses for the officers at the frontier posts?" Recognizing that the trader would not quietly surrender "the golden stream that flows into his till every month after the paymaster makes his appearance," the soldier conceded that the traders would soon cease to exist if the government would only provide separate clubrooms for officers and enlisted men.[74]

The conflict of interest between post traders and canteens presented an ongoing conundrum for the army, which recognized the disadvantages of the trader's bar while continuing to be hamstrung by the law. After another year of searching for some compromise solution that would satisfy both the traders and the canteen advocates, Army Headquarters promulgated General Orders No. 75 in September 1889. The carefully crafted wording walked a fine line with the traders by allowing them to continue selling alcohol but restricting such sales to beer and light wine only "in unbroken packages to officers and to canteens" (only in sealed bottles, not by the drink) and at prices competitive with distributors in the local market. While the order recognized the traders' exclusive right to trade on the reservation, canteens were specifically exempted from that rule, being permitted to sell not only alcoholic beverages by the drink to soldiers but "such articles as may be deemed necessary for their use, entertainment, and comfort; also for affording them the requisite facilities for gymnastic exercises, billiards, and other proper games." Predictably, the post traders were infuriated with that outcome and petitioned for reconsideration. However, in reviewing the order, the judge advocate general determined that it did not *legally* infringe on the traders' rights (though it certainly did in a practical sense). This was the final straw for many frustrated traders, who began closing their army businesses in favor of other pursuits. Going a step further early the next year, the secretary of war granted a blanket authorization for canteens to be established at all posts that did not have trader's stores.[75]

By 1890 the benefits of the canteen system, and its influence in drastically reducing drunkenness and disorderly conduct at posts, were obvious to all, particularly to officers at many western posts, where recreational opportunities often remained limited. Colonel Alexander McD. McCook, commanding the Sixth Infantry, was representative of a score of officers who wrote to the editor of the *Army & Navy Journal* enthusiastically supporting the canteen idea:

> There is no doubt that the canteen, its sales, etc. has improved the discipline of the post and more contentment exists among the enlisted men. The sales of beer and light wines at the canteen, under proper restraint, induces temperance among those formerly slaves to drink. Should this sale be prohibited at the canteen, whiskey dens will spring up in number around the reservation, from which vile decoctions of liquor will be exchanged for money, clothing or other Government property that can be stolen and concealed.[76]

Still, rigid temperance advocates inside and outside army circles opposed the dispensing of any kind of intoxicants on military posts, apparently in the misguided belief that such a move would reform soldiers by depriving them of alcoholic beverages altogether. It was hardly a realistic expectation. True to McCook's prediction, the commander at Fort Bowie, where a canteen had not yet been established, reported his reasons for unilaterally authorizing the sale of beer at his post:

> To enforce that order before a canteen was established, would bring a colony of whiskey ranches with their usual compliment

of prostitutes, gamblers, etc. to the borders of the Reserve, where sales of liquor (and that of the vilest kind) could not be controlled, exposing the enlisted men to a temptation too strong for many of them to resist, with the usual results; as well as to venereal diseases etc. Within the past year, one such resort near here has been broken up . . . and I hear of several other parties, who are waiting for the enforcement of that order, to set up their establishments near here.[77]

At Fort Bowie and elsewhere, post canteens exclusively for enlisted men subsequently proliferated. As a minor concession to the temperance movement, however, wine was officially stricken from the menu. But the selling of lager beer by the drink was reinstated based on the reasoning that "giving to the men the opportunity of obtaining such beverage within the post limits has the effect of preventing them from resorting for strong intoxicants to places without such limits, and tends to promote temperance and discipline among them."[78]

The editor of the *Army & Navy Journal* hailed the post canteen as "no longer an experiment; its success was established months ago, and its growth has been so rapid since, notwithstanding the many elements of opposition the [War] Department had to contend with, that the system may be regarded as a permanent feature of the military establishment." His prediction was correct. Within another three years, the number of traders and their influence declined to the point that the secretary of war announced that current traders' licenses would not be renewed and no further appointments would be made. The antiquated sutler concept would linger awhile and eventually die by attrition.[79]

The year 1890 also witnessed two other important reforms that brought greater justice to the common soldier. Congress passed legislation authorizing the president to define uniform sentencing guidelines to be used by general and garrison courts during peacetime. No longer could officers of the court hand down "traditional" or capricious punishments inconsistent with the offense. Congress also was aware that general and garrison courts-martial were cumbersome because of the time required for the required complement of officers to be assembled and the number of cases to be heard. Prisoners, guilty or not, had been subjected to lengthy periods of confinement before ever being brought to trial. Not uncommonly, a soldier arrested for some petty offense served a longer period in the guardhouse before receiving a hearing than the sentence eventually prescribed. In keeping with the jurisprudence of a speedy trial, Congress authorized the so-called summary court to hear cases involving minor offenses, a process formerly taking weeks or even months. Only one officer, the second ranking at the respective garrison, conducted the summary court within twenty-four hours after a man's arrest, but even then the accused could elect to have his case be heard by a regimental or garrison court.[80]

By the end of the era army paydays occurred with a great deal more regularity as a result of the disappearance of a defined frontier and expanding transportation systems in the West. Soldiers continued to drink, of course, and some overindulged, but thankfully the day of the sutler's monopoly and his rotgut whiskey had passed. As a practical-minded officer at Fort Sully, South Dakota, expressed it: "I . . . wish that total abstinence could be enforced, but I believe that half a loaf is better than no bread." Certainly saloons continued to operate where towns existed at the fringes of army posts, but at least soldiers had a convenient alternative. The canteen, offering billiards and other non-gambling games, afforded a decent environment apart from duty and vigilant officers where the men could relax and socialize with each other, without necessarily having to indulge in alcohol. Beer now dominated as the soldier's drink, and the canteen rationed even that. Gone were the turbulent paydays witnessing wholesale drunkenness, debauchery, and often violence at or near army posts that filled guardhouses to overflowing. There can be no doubt that the movement to establish post canteens, coupled with enlightened reforms in military justice, had a beneficial effect on discipline and morale throughout the service.[81]

As a symbolic concession to the prohibitionists, however, someone in the hierarchy conceded to redesignating canteens as "post exchanges," which presumably sounded less like drinking establishments, because they indeed provided the little necessities that were formerly the province of the trader. Post exchanges proliferated rapidly, quickly becoming a standard feature at the surviving western army posts and across the nation. One of the legacies of the frontier regular army even to the present day is evidenced in a "PX" at virtually every American military installation.[82]

CHAPTER 12

"There Are a Great Many Deserting from Our Regiment"

The Problem of Desertion

Desertion was not unique to the postbellum regulars; it had always plagued the army. The causes were many, some of them universal, others unique to a particular event or period. Two factors, tyrannical treatment by superiors and low pay, were perennial complaints of peacetime soldiers prior to the Civil War. Never popular, conscription was resorted to in times of war, but even when men volunteered, they often resented surrendering personal freedom in exchange for strict discipline, a hard life, and often poor food. The government took a dim view of desertion; Congress imposed harsh penalties on those who skipped out. Until it was outlawed in 1812, flogging (fifty or one hundred lashes laid on with a whip) was the most common corporal punishment for deserters, after which they were formally drummed out of the service. Execution by hanging or shooting could also be imposed at the discretion of a court-martial. The death penalty, however, was restricted to wartime beginning in 1830, but whipping was reinstituted three years later and remained legal until the outbreak of the Civil War.[1]

During the war many states offered monetary bounties as an inducement for men to volunteer to meet federal quotas, and draftees were legally permitted to hire substitutes to serve in their stead. The trouble was, unscrupulous men made a career of taking the bounties offered, then went "over the hill," as desertion was commonly termed, only to repeat the process. By late 1863 these elements, compounded by the horrendous casualties suffered by the Union Army, made desertion rampant. The army had no hesitation in executing numerous deserters, usually by firing squad, in an unsuccessful attempt to curb the problem.

Men joining the regulars in the postwar era either adapted to army life—some even found that they enjoyed it—or let it get the better of them in one way or another. Soldiers commonly found temporary escape in drunkenness. When things became unendurable, they simply left. Predictably, their foremost complaints echoed those heard for as long as the army had existed.

The predominant justification for desertion was the work demanded of soldiers. Fourteenth Infantryman John Spring, who served during the late 1860s, insisted: "All this unpaid labor, carried on from day to day, from month to month, by men enlisted for military service, created almost universal dissatisfaction and desertions became frequent." Critically assessing the situation, an officer offered the following explanation:

> The root of the difficulty lies in the War Department, where an established usage prevails for the employment of enlisted men as carpenters, blacksmiths, road-makers, and laborers. One way to lessen desertions would be to allow a soldier to do a soldier's duty by omitting the clause "with the labor of the troops," from all orders requiring much manual labor at military posts. The difficulty is not with the War Department, but with Congress. The War Department has no funds to pay for citizen labor.[2]

Even if funds had been available, the remoteness of many posts on the western frontier for more than a decade after the Civil War made it impractical, if not impossible, to contract the work to civilians.

It was not that the work was so hard in many instances; much of it was not, especially for men of the nineteenth century accustomed to physical labor. Rather, soldiers complained as a matter of principle; some even considered it a breach of contract on the army's part. Major William B. Royall, serving with the Fifth Cavalry at Camp Lowell, Arizona, in 1875, pointed out that the amount of work assigned to the men seriously detracted from the development of military skills: "Drills are almost unknown here, for the reason that after the details for laborers are made for the day, there are no men left, and I am of the opinion that dissatisfaction and the cases of frequent desertion are attributable to the fact that soldiers are not used as they expected to be when enlisting in the Army, most of them enlisting to be soldiers, not laborers." Another seasoned line officer, First Lieutenant Henry Romeyn, Fifth Infantry, went further by addressing the economic effect of labor on desertions:

> If they wish to live on laborers' pay, and do the work of the "farm-hand," the "navvy," or the street laborer, they can do it without enlisting. If a man is a mechanic, and sober and honest, he can make better wages working at this trade out of the army than in it. When enlisted his trade is noted on his descriptive list, and if he had any skill that can be of use to the quartermaster, even if it be only ability to drive a team, he, in five cases out of six, has been but a few months with his company before he finds himself taken from most of the duties of a soldier and ordered to report for labor, as an "extra or daily duty man," all allowances included, one dollar and twenty five cents per day, when mechanics in civil life, at work at the same calling . . . can earn from two to three times that sum.[3]

Romeyn's reasoning is logical, of course, but ignores the reality that soldiers' extra pay was unencumbered, whereas civilians were obliged to absorb their own basic costs of living. Nevertheless, the men felt that the government was taking unfair advantage of them. Compounding soldiers' grievances in this regard was the burdensome grind of routine duty at small posts, accentuated by the various fatigues. A First Cavalryman posted in Arizona Territory grumbled: "Out here on the frontier . . . duty becomes so hard that it becomes work, and very hard work—scouting, escorting, herding, going after firewood, building quarters, stables, for the last year being in camp a few days in every month, and when in camp, only one or two nights in bed between every tour of guard." "It may be set down as an axiom," concluded the editor of the *Army & Navy Journal*, "that where soldiers are used almost exclusively as laborers, without rest or intermission and without drill of any description to instill habits of obedience and discipline, there you will find desertion."[4]

Some soldiers, especially native-born Americans, found the discipline inherent in the regulars to be particularly onerous. "A lot of fellows from the citys [sic] and eastern towns could not stand the discipline and taking orders from noncoms," explained Private Louis Ebert, Sixth Cavalry, implying that men from rural backgrounds adjusted more readily. Based on long tradition, discipline and unquestioning obedience were the hallmarks of the regular army. The near-absolute authority vested in officers and noncommissioned officers sometimes degenerated into tyranny, particularly when the company commander allowed his first sergeant too much discretion in managing the daily affairs of the company. One soldier contended that his first sergeant had constantly abused him. When the private requested permission to speak with the captain, the first sergeant refused. The frustrated private then resorted to appealing directly to the captain, whereupon the officer sent him back without redress for not following the chain of command. Several witnesses overheard the first sergeant threaten the soldier that he would "make it hotter than hell for him if he remained, and if he would leave he would see that he was not hunted for." The deserter, accidentally recognized and arrested six months later, was sentenced to two years in a penitentiary, yet the first sergeant who allegedly encouraged the act went unpunished. It was reported that of fifty-three deserters imprisoned at Alcatraz Island in 1872, twenty gave harsh treatment by noncoms, particularly first sergeants, as their reason for deserting.[5]

Officers of higher rank also sometimes allowed themselves to descend into that frame of mind. Captain Albert Barnitz, in the newly formed Seventh Cavalry, recognized that his commanding officer, Lieutenant Colonel George A. Custer, was fast making a reputation for being excessively hard-nosed and abusive to the men. In one instance Custer made an example of six men by having their heads half-shaved and further humiliated by marching them under guard through camp. Their only offense had been to leave the bivouac for less than an hour to walk to nearby Fort Hays to purchase canned fruit. During their brief absence they had missed no roll calls or other duty. Some months later Barnitz informed his wife: "If Gen'l. Custer remains long in command, I fear that recruiting will have to go on rapidly to keep the regiment replenished!"[6]

The dismantling of the volunteer forces during 1865–66 released a surge of veterans eager to go west in pursuit of more lucrative ventures than the East afforded. In fact, a high percentage of those enlisting immediately after the Civil War, knowing that virtually all of the mounted regiments were posted in the West, specifically requested assignment to the cavalry, thereby obtaining free transportation to the frontier. Brigadier General John Pope, commanding the Department of the Missouri, recognized that

> the rapid settlement of the new States and Territories, the construction of numerous lines of railroad, the opening and working of rich mines and prospecting for others—in short, the wonderful enterprise and activity everywhere prevailing, occasion such a demand for men, and open such avenues to prosperity and success, that the inducements to desert the service are almost irresistible to a soldier stationed in this region. A sober and industrious man, even without a trade, is welcomed everywhere and every position is within his reach.[7]

Indeed many enlistees, intending their association with the army to be as brief as possible, went west in hopes of reaching one of the rich mining regions in Colorado, Arizona, Montana, or elsewhere. In one instance late in 1866 fifteen troopers of the Second Cavalry escorted a supply train from Fort Phil Kearny to Fort C. F. Smith, Montana Territory, where they overnighted prior to returning to their home station. Four of the fifteen deserted after dark, probably attempting to reach the goldfields in western Montana Territory. For others, according to an officer, "the inaction and routine of garrison duty and, too, the strict discipline hastened their determination to get to the mines." Gold fever drove desertions to appalling levels—26 percent in 1867 and 16.4 percent the next year. While encamped near Fort Hays, Captain Barnitz wrote that wholesale desertions "are of nightly occurrence! As many as 10 non-commissioned officers and privates have left in one night, with horses and arms! . . . I sent out a detail of 1 sergeant and 3 privates the other day, to shoot buffalo, and they all forgot to return!" (Fort Hays was situated near the Smoky Hill Trail leading west to Denver.) The lust for riches was irresistible. "Gold to most men means sudden wealth, big times, whiskey and gambling and women . . . adventure and all the things they never had," recalled Private Charles Windolph. "The gold fever is like taking dope . . . we had it bad." Inspector General Randolph B. Marcy acknowledged in 1874 that the great demand for mine laborers, and the considerably higher wages paid, continued to induce large numbers of soldiers to desert. Mine owners, moreover, afforded protection to known deserters from detachments sent in pursuit.[8]

Economic conditions also influenced a less industrious class of men to find a home in the army, albeit a temporary one. Alike in their goal of traveling west at government expense, these drifters were essentially "tramps . . . desirous of no fixed labor or station, but seeking change for change's sake. These men . . . were recognized . . . as 'Snowbirds,' hunting out a recruiting office in the fall, and relieving the Service of their presence in the spring following." Recalling the infusion of batches of recruits with several such malingerers, First Sergeant John Ryan blamed them for "a good deal of the stealing going on in the company, especially clothing, a thing that was never known to be done until we got recruits from the states, then it would begin." With the return of fair weather, and a stock of extra clothing, these slackers would be "carried off with the spring fever."[9]

Army food posed a constant source of complaint by soldiers, and rightfully so because it had a great deal to do with their overall morale and well-being. A few months after enlisting in the Second Cavalry, Musician Robert Greenhalgh informed his parents: "There are a great many deserting from our regiment just now on account of the Humbug they receive from the Officers and rations are too small for healthy young men to live on, consequently they clear out and leave." One "guardhouse lawyer" justified desertion on the basis that providing an adequate ration was a commitment made by the government when he enlisted, so the inadequacy was a breach of contract by the army. "I hold that if these solemn promises of the Government are broken, we have the same right to break ours and nearly all that have deserted from this cause think the same." The army disagreed, of course. Although some groused about the insufficiency of the ration, most of those who deserted because of the food later cited the poor quality of the cooking as their real grievance. One thoughtful enlisted man considered the ration plentiful but suspected that pilfering and graft in the supply system accounted for food shortages at the soldiers' end. "The great trouble is it has to pass through so many different Depots and Commissaries and like our Congressmen, each makes a grab . . . by the time it is . . . issued to the men there is nothing left." He calculated that his company of the Eighth Cavalry suffered 103 desertions in less than seven years, and another had lost 300 men during the same period.[10]

In 1871 a veteran of twenty years raised other food-related issues with more foundation. He claimed that the majority of company commanders failed to take sufficient interest in the meals being served to the men and contended that the company funds were too often mismanaged, specifically citing the separate messes maintained by the noncoms in many units, to the detriment of the rest of the men. A decade later Private Henry Hubman, Eighteenth Infantry, confided in a letter to his brother: "We only get $13. a month and after we pay out expenses and buy something to eat there is nothing left. . . . If I could save money I would get out of [here?] quick but Uncle Sam has what the Spaniards call the Sincha [*cincha*] on us here." The obvious fault with food preparation was the army's custom of rotating cooking duty among the men, most of whom previously had little or no exposure to the craft.[11]

Even though soldiers groused about the food and being overworked, they seldom complained about their pay per se, except for a few years in the early 1870s. In its continuing effort to pare down expenditures for a peacetime army, Congress in 1869 reduced the monthly rate for a private from $16.00 to $13.00, a cut of 18.75 percent, to take effect the following year. As Private George S. Raper of the Eighth Cavalry correctly assessed the situation: "That did not set very good, and the result was the army lost many men by refusal to re-enlist and by desertion." During 1872 alone, his regiment lost 118 men to desertion. Noting that the rate skyrocketed from 9.4 percent in 1870 to 32.6 percent the next year, the inspector general of the army conceded: "There are doubtless many men who enlisted prior to the time the reduction went into effect who were under the impression at the time of enlisting that they were to receive $16 per month during the entire term of their service, and they now profess to regard the reduction as a violation of contract on the part of the Government, which . . . they plead in extenuation of their desertion." Just how many men may not have understood that condition, or were intentionally misled by recruiters, will never be known, but the effect was clear, for the desertion rate remained at about 30 percent through 1873.[12]

Loss of pay only intensified soldiers' frustrations with the humdrum life that they experienced much of the time. An officer serving with the Fourth Cavalry during the early 1870s was of the opinion that epidemic desertions were caused by

> the terrible monotony of the life without amusements or recreation of any kind, no athletics or competitions, no libraries, infrequent mails . . . no theaters or concerts, nothing but the dreary monotonous grind of guard and police duty, detached service, and the rather questionable pleasure they got out of some saloons and gambling halls which generally landed them "broke" and subjects for the guard house and disciplinary measures, and more forfeiture of pay, hard labor and other punishment.[13]

Deserters attributed their taking "French leave" to myriad other reasons, including homesickness and the near impossibility of obtaining furloughs. In that same regard, a great many men found that a five-year enlistment could be an excruciatingly long time, especially without a furlough, under the conditions experienced on the frontier. Responding to Congress's decision to increase the term from three to five years, a soldier at Fort Reynolds, Colorado Territory, inquired in 1870: "Had they ever shouldered a musket in their time, or ever been reduced to poverty, they would have done far different. Why were not three years long enough to suffer upon these deserts away from all society and civilization?" The irony is not that so many deserted but that so many stayed.[14]

A few of the more ambitious men also cited the lack of any mechanism for promotion beyond the ranks. "There is just one dead, dreary level lying before the soldier in the line on his entering the service," declared Colonel Wesley Merritt, Fifth Cavalry, "with only a step or two in the way of advancement that breaks the monotony of a lifelong experience, separated by a chasm of appalling dimensions from the rank of the commissioned officer, which few . . . can ever hope to overcome." Merritt also argued in favor of significantly increasing the pay of noncommissioned officers as an inducement to attract and retain capable individuals in those positions.[15]

Contributing to the high rates of desertion were repeat offenders, similar to the wartime bounty jumpers. Inspector General Marcy observed: "It is not an uncommon thing to find men in the ranks who have deserted four and five times, and in some few cases as many as six or seven times." In assessing the overall rates of desertion, one must consider that these "repeaters," as they were known, formed a percentage of the totals, although there is no way to determine precisely what that may have been. Not all deserters had fled the army. Every now and then soldiers were revealed to have deserted from other military services and to be hiding in the army under assumed names. Private George K. Attwood (aka George Torrens), for example, was a veteran of two enlistments in the U.S. Marine Corps when he deserted in 1871. A little over two years later he was discovered in the ranks of the Seventh Cavalry and surrendered himself. When Private John Valentine, Eighteenth Infantry, divulged his true identity at Fort Assinniboine, Montana Territory, in 1881, he confessed to having previously deserted from the U.S. Navy.[16]

Although some men availed themselves of serendipitous opportunities to go over the hill, often as a result of payday sprees, the majority schemed in advance to make their escape. One key to success was having some money to purchase food, civilian clothing, and perhaps transportation. It came as no surprise, therefore, that the period immediately following payday experienced peak desertions. When long lapses occurred between paydays, as they often did at frontier posts, "the men who received seven months' pay . . . do not have to worry about money if they wish to desert," declared Colonel Philippe Régis De Trobriand, Thirteenth Infantry. Particularly susceptible were those recruits who either had reflected on their decision to join the army or simply wanted to get out west. The editor of the *Army & Navy Journal* opined: "On the frontier the first payday after a detachment of recruits arrive the majority . . . who intend to go desert, at the second payday the remainder of those who intend to leave desert. It will probably be found that the last party received but little money at the first payment [after the army deducted initial costs for clothing, mess gear, and so forth] and waited until the second in order to have money to desert with."[17]

Not many deserters announced their intentions prior to leaving. An exception was Third Infantryman James C. Blackwood, who wrote to his mother in 1880 that "three years is a long time yet. I would not mind so much if it was not for seeing how much better I could do outside here. I could get fifty or eighty dollars per month here, in fact I have been offered $20. per week in Helena [Montana Territory]. I only want to be at liberty to take it." Eight months after writing that letter, he took the liberty. Weighing the potential consequences, Private Henry Hubman, who had impulsively left his New York farm after a disagreement with his father, moaned: "I am going to get out of the Army if I have to Desert. If I get caught I will only get 2 years in Prison, which will be better than staying here."[18]

Active Indian campaigning also induced men to take off. The mere prospect of a campaign sometimes was enough to motivate men to leave, while others became either weak-kneed or fed up with conditions in the field; still others endured but returned from campaigning so disheartened and exhausted—perhaps half-starved and ill—that they desired only to get away from the army as quickly as possible to avoid any repetition of the experience.

When soldiers lacked cash, particularly in the field, and sometimes even when they had money, they absconded with arms, ammunition, and horses. Taking fully equipped troops into the field, especially when they were untried, was an ever-present risk. "Officers are afraid to send any of the new men . . . recruits on the road for fear they will desert," wrote Private Eddie Matthews, Eighth Cavalry. "And take horse, carbine, revolver, and equipments with them. When they desert from the Garrison they can only take their carbines with them. As the horses are in the Corrall [sic] and revolvers are in the 1st Sergeants room." All of this equipment, particularly arms, ammunition, and horses, was easily bartered to civilians on the frontier in exchange for money, food, shelter, and different animals. Deserters skipping out while on campaign in hostile territory usually took their arms for personal defense, only to trade them off when safely back in the settlements. In some instances, such as when a Sixth Infantry soldier deserted one night during the 1876 Sioux Campaign, he took his own rifle and ammunition, along with the cartridge belts of two other men for good measure. To ensure a rapid escape, the man also commandeered a small boat belonging to one of the officers and floated down the Yellowstone River.[19]

Private Edward Williams, Second Cavalry, recorded that two troopers belonging to his company deserted soon after his unit took the field in the spring of 1877: "They took a horse a piece [sic], two Colt's Revolvers, one Carbine, and all the ammunition they could get ahold of. This morning two more deserted. . . . A good many will scip [sic] yet." Making off with horses was facilitated when two or more men conspired to leave then waited for their chance until one would be assigned as picket line guard after dark.[20]

Despite the loss to the government, such thefts could nonetheless be used to advantage by company commanders and imaginative first sergeants. "Arms were more difficult to drop from property records than any other type of item," explained First Sergeant Henry McConnell. "Deserters were often charged with having taken arms (or other property) that the company first sergeant could not otherwise account for. This was an easy way to clean up the books. A deserter often proves a godsend to a company commander, who is enabled to get even on articles he is short of, by charging them to a deserter, for even if the deserter is apprehended and brought back, he has placed himself in so bad a fix by his crime that the 'affidavit man's' testimony cannot be impeached and the company papers are cleared of a lot of old stuff." An "affidavit man" was an indispensable character in the company possessing a "wonderful and convenient memory; he could forget an incident or remember it at will, and this 'mind power' always moved in the 'proper channel' . . . so far as the 'papers' of the officer accountable for the property were concerned." In short, the man would swear to anything as a witness, whether or not he had any knowledge about it.[21]

In garrison the officers sometimes resorted to various measures to discourage desertion, the most common being the check roll call. Private Ami F. Mulford described the procedure: "Sometime during the night, the Captain or a Lieutenant would come to the Company quarters and with the First Sergeant, would go from bunk to bunk, waking up those asleep, and require each man to give his name, which would be checked off as 'present.'" Another soldier claimed that in addition to checking on the men personally some officers cultivated informants in the company to report any desertion-related conversations that they might overhear.[22]

Deserters taking off in frontier regions stood a fairly good chance of making good their escape if they were able to survive the elements and did not encounter unfriendly Indians. Three soldiers at Fort Fetterman, Wyoming Territory, made an ill-advised decision to desert in January 1870, during what an officer's wife described as "the coldest weather we have had the whole winter. Water barrel freezing solid in the kitchen . . . they [deserters] will certainly freeze to death if they are not captured." Private William F. Zimmer told of a Fifth Infantryman who had deserted from Tongue River Cantonment who gave up at their camp at the western edge of Dakota Territory's Black Hills. "He had a horse & rifle but his chuck had run out some time ago. He had killed one deer & was obliged to eat it raw, as he had no means for starting a fire." Eighteenth Infantryman Henry Hubman declared his intention to desert at all costs yet expressed reservations about leaving Fort Assinniboine: "It is a pretty risky piece of business as we have to go through 200 miles of hostile Cree Indian country, but I am willing to risk anything to get out of this hole." He knew well the odds; just six months earlier three of his comrades had deserted. "One of them was killed by the Crees and is supposed the wolves eat [sic] the others as some of their clothes were found by the Grovan [Gros Ventre] Scout."[23]

Soldiers inclined to desert enjoyed a special advantage, and greater chances of a successful escape, when they happened to be stationed at forts near the international borders. "We were payed [sic] off about a week ago," wrote Private George H. Cranston at Camp Grant, Arizona Territory. "Fifteen of us calculated to strike out for Senora [sic] in New Mexico [sic], a distance of about two hundred miles . . . we are all here yet, and I am glad of it." That was probably just as well, since they were apparently confused as to their proposed destination. Even two decades later a soldier at Fort Davis, Texas, located less than one hundred miles from Mexico, indicated the ease with which deserters could cross the border to Chihuahua City: thus "the land of Montezuma gains a citizen, and the United States loses a soldier." Canada likewise beckoned to those posted in the northern tier of territories. Private Hubman, for example, made good his escape across the border into Saskatchewan, where he found refuge with friendly Indians.[24]

As soon as men were missed, their absence was reported. Post commanders invariably sent out mounted detachments, taking advantage of Indian scouts when available, in pursuit of deserters when there was any hope of catching them. That frequently depended on whether the men had gone overland, either on foot or mounted, or by some conveyance, as well as on the diligence of the officer or noncom in charge of the party. Sergeant Eddie Matthews, for example, said that he was the second-ranking member of a detachment led by a lieutenant that remained out for twelve days, traveling approximately four hundred miles from Fort Union, New Mexico Territory, into Colorado Territory, and successfully captured eight deserters. Even though soldiers dispatched to find and bring back deserters may have sympathized with them, duty was duty. "I pitied the poor boys," Matthews wrote, "but I could not help catching them." Lieutenant Robert G. Carter, Fourth Cavalry, told of an occasion when Colonel Ranald S. Mackenzie was determined to track down some deserters from Fort Richardson, Texas, at all costs. Mackenzie ordered Carter to go in pursuit with a detail of thirteen men. If the deserters were able to reach a railroad ahead of him, Carter was to drop his detachment, taking one noncom with him, and continue the chase "even if they went to Galveston, New Orleans, or even N[ew] Y[ork] C[ity]." The colonel advised his subordinate to comply with all local laws in that event, and in the meantime he would issue a blanket order covering the lieutenant for all contingencies.[25]

At other times, according to Private William White, Second Cavalry, "pursuit of the unauthorized quitters was extremely lax. . . . If he took with him some distinctly-valuable government property—a rifle, a revolver, a saber, a blanket, or some other such article—he would be followed until captured. . . . If he took nothing but his uniform, he had simply to keep on going until he got entirely out of sight and out of hearing distance." A first sergeant of the Seventh Cavalry confirmed that in his experience "we were not very particular about capturing deserters. I recollect cases where non-commissioned officers with a detail of men would take a few days' rations and forage with them and leave the forts . . . proceed several miles . . . and not finding the deserters, would go into camp . . . remain there and after their rations and forage were gone would report back to camp saying they could not overhaul the deserters." For this reason, such detachments were drawn from companies other than the one to which the deserter belonged, though that was not always possible in small commands. Regardless of whether deserters evaded capture or were allowed to escape, the company was often grateful to be rid of undesirables.[26]

As the West developed, would-be deserters with easier access to public transportation unhesitatingly took full advantage of whatever might be available. At posts along the Upper Missouri River, "they can easily find a way of getting on the steamboats which may stop for the night anywhere near by," affording a means of quickly getting either to Omaha and civilization or to the goldfields of western Montana Territory. Railroads also offered a ready means of escape. The Union Pacific station at Medicine Bow, Wyoming Territory, provided the most convenient mail connection for Fort Fetterman. Just after the garrison was paid in May 1874, seven bold men out of a twenty-three-man mail detail simply bought tickets, boarded the train, and were gone. Major Alexander Chambers, commanding the post, later allowed that "some arrangement might be made [with the railroad] by which soldiers should in addition to paying their fare, show some paper authorizing them to travel." The railroad network was well developed by that time, so by traveling east they could rapidly traverse great distances in a short time and quickly meld into urban populations, making apprehension difficult.[27]

The government offered a reward for the capture of deserters, but the bounty remained minimal for years, thus frustrating efforts at apprehension. Until the early 1860s the reward was a mere five dollars, from which the person turning in the deserter had to pay all travel, jail, and other attendant costs. With so little incentive, it was no wonder that citizens seldom bothered to make any effort to identify and capture army deserters. That changed with the war and a sharp increase in desertion. In July 1862 the army began reimbursing captors for reasonable expenses, in addition to the reward. Still, considering that physical descriptions recorded at enlistment were so basic and no photographs were available (fingerprinting was still in the future), relatively few deserters were caught. As "Solomon" expressed it in the *Army & Navy Journal*: "If there was more danger of recapture, there would not be so much desertion. At present it is what the bounty jumpers used to call a 'regular give away.'" Insufficient though the reward may have been, the army recovered the amount, plus the expenses incurred for his arrest, by charging them against the deserter when convicted.[28]

Even after the reward (including expenses) was increased to thirty dollars in the 1870s, civilians on the frontier had little incentive to report deserters; indeed they were more inclined to assist them. As the recipients of the government property stolen by deserters, civilians stood to profit more handsomely by that than by going to the trouble of turning in the man and collecting the reward. An officer addressing this reality wrote:

> In many localities the man who should apprehend the deserters . . . would be looked upon as intermeddling in affairs that did not concern him, and the arrested party as a martyr to a harsh and cruel despotism; and the culprit, once away from his post . . . is comparatively safe. . . . It is not at all difficult for the absconding soldier to dispose of his arms, or even his horse, to many men on the frontier who would resent . . . any doubt of their honesty.[29]

Furthermore, many members of the laboring class—not a few of whom had been in the army during or after the Civil War and may themselves have been deserters—sympathized with a soldier's plight in going over the hill.

Thus men skipping out in frontier regions, and remaining there, often stood a better chance of avoiding arrest than those who returned to the States. The adjutant general's office made a practice of publishing deserters' descriptions in their hometown and area newspapers and alerting local U.S. marshals, surmising they might return to familiar haunts. Some keen-eyed eastern detectives, and a few in western cities, made a business of surveilling railroad stations and other likely places in the hope of collaring deserters and collecting the rewards. A detective in Council Bluffs, Iowa, when asked why so many deserters were arrested there, replied: "It is simply because no effort is made to catch them further west." There was even one recorded instance of an ex–first sergeant of the Tenth Cavalry turning to bounty-hunting for deserters following his own discharge. There could be drawbacks, however, because what might seem obvious was not always so. Ex-private John Bergstrom related that after his discharge he found a job with the railroad but continued wearing his army blue shirt and trousers as work clothes. A lawman spotted him and attempted to make an arrest, assuming Bergstrom to be a deserter. Not for nothing were discharged soldiers advised to protect their discharge papers and keep them handy.[30]

Once caught, the deserter was fitted with a ball and chain to discourage any further attempt to go over the hill while awaiting trial. "A ball and chain consists of either a round iron ball probably weighting ten or twelve pounds [*sic*: twenty-four] . . . ," one soldier attested, "with a chain about seven or eight feet long attached to it. This chain is fastened to an iron band which is clasped around the prisoner's ankle and an iron rivet put into it. . . . This ball and chain must remain attached to the soldier's leg day and night." In those instances when a man was considered prone to flight under any circumstances a blacksmith hot-riveted shackles on both ankles, connected by a short chain, not over a foot long, to restrict the length of his stride. Another chain, approximately six feet long, was riveted at one end to a link midway between the two shackles and on the other to a ball weighing approximately twenty-four pounds. The prisoner, under close guard, was obliged "to work standing still, or he had to pick up the iron ball and carry it to the next stopping place."[31]

Following trial and conviction of the charge, the offender was first given a dishonorable discharge from the service then "drummed out" of the garrison. The ceremony, though not included in the tactics manuals of the day, was nonetheless universally familiar and conducted with only minor variations. The deserter was first stripped of all insignia identifying him as a soldier, leaving him only shirt, trousers, and shoes (and perhaps his overcoat, absent the buttons), after which the officer of the day had the man's head shaved. Some commanders preferred to shave the hair from only one side of the head as being more distinctive. It was not unusual for a placard labeled "DESERTER" (or other offense) to be hung around the man's neck.[32]

Thus prepared, as First Sergeant John Ryan recounted, "these men were laid down on their left side, their right hip exposed, and an iron brand an inch or more in diameter was heated and these two men branded with the letter D on the right hip." Most accounts indicate that the letter "D" measured one and one-half inches high and was applied to either buttock using a hot iron or for those more fortunate by indelible tattooing using India ink. Either method permanently identified a deserter in the event he tried to reenlist. Sometimes even that was not a deterrent. "We know of a man who was marked for desertion," wrote a correspondent to the *Army & Navy Journal* in 1868, "attempting to enlist after having figures tattooed on both hips, adroitly bringing the letter D into a figure as a proper portion of it." Apparently an alert doctor rejected the applicant after detecting slight differences in the tints and ages of the tattoos.[33]

With the entire garrison formed on the parade, the adjutant read aloud the sentence imposed by the court, whereupon the prisoner was conducted down the length of the formation by a detail composed of two musicians and two armed guards marching in front, arms reversed, followed closely behind by two more guards with loaded rifles or carbines held at "charge bayonets." In that fashion, Private William Murphy recalled, "they were marched around the fort with a fife and drum playing 'Poor Old Soldier' [The Rogue's March], and then drummed out." He noted that at the time "it was suicide to go a mile from the Fort [Phil Kearny] for the Indians watched the road constantly, but this did not seem to matter." Thus disgraced, the man was released some distance from the post to go his own way. More importantly, the ordeal served notice to the rest of the troops what they could expect should they be inclined to leave.[34]

For some, however, success mollified the disgrace. An army wife at Fort Wingate, New Mexico Territory, described the time when two defiant soldiers, one an American, the other an Englishman, were shaved and drummed out of the garrison. "When the two deserters had reached the boundary line . . . the Englishman doffed his cap, turning the shaved side of his head toward the spectators and gave a mocking salute and a bow, shouting out that he 'hoped we would all meet again.' The other man said nothing . . . and we saw them no more." Albeit by an ignominious method, the two had nevertheless achieved their aim of getting out of the army.[35]

Not all deserters were released immediately, however, no doubt to their disappointment. The court had the option of ruling that a convicted deserter would be dishonorably discharged then imprisoned for a defined period. A soldier serving at Fort Union recorded that the sentence given to a deserter "was two years at hard labor, wearing a twelve lb. ball, with a chain four feet long attached to the left leg, to be dishonorably discharged . . . and branded on the left hip with the letter D, one and one half inches long."[36]

The practices of branding and tattooing, considered barbaric by many in the civilian community, came under congressional review and were abolished by law in 1872. A drawback was that after branding was outlawed it became extremely difficult for recruiting officers to detect repeaters. Thus the issue was revisited from time to time, though branding was never reinstituted.[37]

With a desertion rate averaging over 31 percent during the early 1870s, the army was compelled to do something to retard the illegal outflow of personnel and reduce the costs attendant on their loss. President and old soldier Ulysses S. Grant elected to authorize a general amnesty for deserters. Expressed as General Orders No. 102 of 1873, the amnesty offered a full pardon to those who would surrender themselves to military authorities on or before January 1, 1874. Those turning themselves in would forfeit all pay and other allowances due to them during their unauthorized absence, but they would be restored to duty immediately in their former units without trial or punishment, provided they continued to serve faithfully. The proclamation had the desired effect. "They are flocking in from all parts of the country," announced a soldier at Fort Union. "Four men in our Company now, one of them a Sergeant and a married man besides, have surrendered as Deserters from different branches of the service. . . . Eleven all told have surrendered at this Post."[38]

Despite the return of hundreds of men who had fled the army, Grant's leniency proved to be of only marginal value. By the time the numbers were compiled and reconciled in late 1874, the adjutant general lamented: "Only about one-fourteenth of the whole number surrendered were an actual gain in number to the Army; the rest have all been discharged or have again deserted." Adding salt to the wound, the editor of the *Army & Navy Journal* sarcastically observed: "It seems that this order has only resulted in returning to the Army the most thoroughly worthless of material, the same which during the civil war became so notorious under the name of 'bounty jumpers.'" Others raised questions as to the disposition of charges for other crimes, chiefly the theft of all those arms, horses, and other material, related to a man's desertion. Apparently those too were dropped under the definition of full pardon, lest offenders be discouraged from surrendering themselves.[39]

Although hot branding unquestionably had been excessive and cruel, the army was plagued for years with repeaters after the amnesty, confounding recruiting officers by their inability to identify those men. Some thought that a return to marking deserters in some way was the only solution. "As every enlisted man is previously examined by a surgeon, a slight indelible mark would be detected," wrote one correspondent in 1883. Legitimate objections were raised, however, to "placing a mark of infamy upon an American citizen." Moreover, the marking of deserters would be of advantage only in those cases when they were actually captured and tried; it would do nothing for the majority who went over the hill without ever being apprehended. A few whose consciences got the better of them eventually surrendered themselves, and some repeaters gave themselves away through a careless comment or, more rarely, were recognized by a former comrade. However, as one writer expressed the scope of the problem: "The five hundred inmates of Fort Leavenworth are only a feeble proportion of the grand total. . . . They are but the unlucky ones who get caught." An officer addressing the subject claimed that hardly more than 10 percent of those deserting were ever captured.[40]

The tradition of drumming out deserters was seldom used after the early 1870s, though it remained on the books as a legal punishment. Prisoners were still subjected to wearing a ball-and-chain from the time of their capture until they were eventually transferred to the U.S. Military Prison at Fort Leavenworth, Kansas, or to Alcatraz Island, California, according to whether they had been stationed east or west of the Rocky Mountains. The sentences handed down, usually three to five years in prison for those dishonorably discharged, invariably lasted longer than the time a man would have served to complete his enlistment. Sergeant Perley S. Eaton, Third Cavalry, remembered two men with only four months left to serve foolishly fleeing from Fort Verde, Arizona Territory, in the early 1880s. The men were caught and sentenced to four years' hard labor at Alcatraz. In those comparatively rare cases when a soldier was not first dishonorably discharged, the sentence imposed could be no longer than the remainder of his enlistment.[41]

A detail normally composed of a sergeant and two to four reliable men escorted convicts to the prison, wherever that might be. The party took public transportation whenever available, though an army wagon or ambulance might be used to convey the party from the post to the initial connection with a stage or rail line. The guards would be rationed, or per diem commutation of rations would be authorized, for the expected duration of the trip. Such journeys afforded the guards a welcome break from garrison routine and were a small reward for good behavior.

Desertion rates declined steadily during the mid-1870s due in part to the economic Panic of 1873 and the resulting five-year depression that diminished job opportunities on the outside. The economic climate, ironically, worked to the army's benefit by creating a larger number of quality recruits and influencing those already in the army to remain there. Apart from the economic incentives, though conveniently dovetailing with them, were efforts by the Recruiting Service to secure men of higher character through closer screening of applicants for enlistment.

Just when the army thought that it had found a partial solution to the problem, the desertion rate again spiked in 1877 in response to a knee-jerk reaction by Congress to the Seventh Cavalry's defeat at Little Bighorn. With the nation shocked by the deaths of Custer and more than two hundred fifty men of his command, Congress in mid-1876 voted to augment the cavalry immediately by temporarily increasing the strength of companies to one hundred men. Consequently recruiting officers, anxious to fill quotas, simply did not look very closely at the men showing up at their stations late in the year. The pressure was on to bolster the cavalry as rapidly as possible to take reprisals against the Sioux. That meant pushing substandard recruits through the depots in a very short time (one or two weeks being the norm), creating ersatz soldiers entirely unprepared to play any effective role with their units. Another factor not to be underestimated as a powerful element in the fervor to enlist was that the gold-rich Black Hills were now undefended by the Sioux and ripe for the picking. First Lieutenant Charles King, in the field with the Fifth Cavalry in Dakota Territory, witnessed firsthand the arrival of a batch of such replacements:

> If a police force of our large Eastern cities were at a loss to account for the disappearance of a thousand or more of their "regular boarders," a flying trip to the Black Hills on this 12th day of October, '76, would have satisfied them as to their whereabouts. Where there were ten "good men and true" among the new-comers, there were forty who came simply with the intention of deserting when they got fairly into the Hills and within striking distance of the mines.[42]

And desert they did: over 2,500 men, many of them recent recruits, along with others who had their fill of campaign hardships, departed within a few months. It should be noted, however, that it was not the fault of the men alone. Congress also failed the army by not passing an appropriation bill that year, so the men were serving without pay. In their minds, the army had breached the contract. The resulting exodus compelled Adjutant General Edward D. Townsend to confess: "The 2,500 men thus specially authorized to be raised were so urgently needed, and the time for recruiting them so very short, that the usual precautions to avoid enlisting any but good men had to be relaxed. The result was, increased desertion and a large number of discharges on the plea of minority." The army's experience with the "Custer Avengers" prompted a reversion to enforcing the more stringent recruitment standards adopted in 1874. The formula successfully employed earlier in the decade, combined with a prolonged economic depression, served to retard desertions over the next few years.[43]

Although the early 1880s no longer experienced the soaring desertion rates of a decade earlier when army pay was cut, desertion now rose in reaction to a more robust national economy. It was the same old story; when soldiers saw better job opportunities outside the army, many left. And, correspondingly, fewer men were motivated to enlist. General of the Army William T. Sherman was confident that the situation was a temporary reaction to current conditions:

> affording better employment to the class of men who generally enlist; but winter and hard times will soon enable us to fill our ranks with a good class of men, and re-enlistments will increase by reason of the advantages the Army now holds out in the schools, in the better condition of the frontier posts, more abundant food and clothing, and the vastly diminished labor of the past by the completion of railroads to regions hitherto inaccessible except by long marches across arid, desolate plains.

Increased desertion also created a great and constant demand for recruits to keep regiments up to adequate strength. As usual, the hard-pressed commanders of the principal depots were burdened with turning out poorly trained recruits in an effort to keep up with requisitions. For several years the adjutant general pled, to no avail, to have the army supplemented by a thousand men, specifically to maintain a constant pool of recruits in training sufficient to meet demands.[44]

Some who examined the problem saw two other principal causes for so much desertion. First the thirty dollar reward, to include expenses, was hardly sufficient inducement for citizens to apprehend deserters. The overarching reason, perhaps peculiar to Americans, was

> the undoubted fact that desertion is not in reality regarded as a crime by the public in general or by the soldiers themselves.... The only class out of the 65,000,000 people composing this great nation which looks upon desertion as a crime will be found in the 2500 officers of the army ... the mass of the one class ... simply look upon the act as a venial breach of contract or simple infraction of military rules, and the convicted deserter as an unfortunate victim.[45]

In consequence, civilians were largely indifferent to whether deserters were caught or not and in fact harbored and shielded them from arrest. Related to this was a considerably more lenient way of dealing with deserters who had merely skipped without committing other crimes. When a man was captured, or voluntarily surrendered himself to authorities, he could be permitted the opportunity to "make good his time," as it was termed, in those instances when his superiors considered him salvageable based on his previous conduct. Even though he lost all pay and allowances for the period of his absence, the man was restored to his previous status in his unit and was to be treated like any other soldier of good standing. Officers wisely decided in many instances that giving a man a second chance was better for the individual and the service than losing him altogether, besides being more economical. But the individual was obligated to compensate the army for the time lost by faithfully serving an equivalent period beyond his enlistment, whereupon he would receive an honorable discharge.[46]

Inspector General D. B. Sacket pointed out that in practice "the sentence usually given or approved for soldiers sent to the military prison is for a less term than they would have had to serve had they not deserted." Moreover, he added:

> There is a saying among the enlisted men at Fort Leavenworth that "if a soldier wishes to be comfortable and well cared for, he must become an inmate of either the military prison or the national cemetery," . . . that [there are] letters sent by convicts to men serving with their companies, advising them to desert, . . . [stating] that they would have a much easier time, with less work, more comforts, and would get out of service months, if not years sooner than they otherwise would.

Sacket agreed that deserters, particularly repeaters, were being shown too much leniency and that the army would do well to increase the bounty to one hundred dollars in order to convince civilians of the seriousness of the crime and gain their cooperation in capturing deserters. As for the maximum sentence prescribed by Article 48, Sacket appreciated the near-impossibility of altering an Article of War but urged a return to punishing deserters with confinement at hard labor and wearing the ball and chain (both of which remained legal punishments) at their posts for the balance of their enlistments. Assigning them all the dirty work and drudgery of the garrison would at the same time relieve other soldiers from having to do it, thereby alleviating one of the most often voiced complaints. These were practical, perhaps even potentially effective, solutions, yet they were out of step with societal reforms of the times.[47]

The continuing problem of desertion prompted several army officers to undertake thoughtful studies of the subject in search of the central cause. Some were confident that interviewing convicted deserters would surely identify the root motive, yet the results were less than enlightening. In 1883 the principal reasons given were "intemperance, impatience of the restraints of military service, a desire to obtain better wages, and dissatisfaction with the food provided[,] . . . the excess of manual labor . . . [and] enlisting in the East for no other purposes than to get a free ride to the west and then desert." Tabulating the causes for desertion in the Department of the Platte the following year, Lieutenant Colonel Edwin C. Mason arrived at similar conclusions, with the exception of one startling anomaly. Of a total of 466 cases investigated through boards of survey, 53 percent of the men could offer no particular reason for skipping out.[48]

Also absent from both surveys, interestingly, was the accusation of abuse by officers and noncoms. That was probably a reflection of the better overall quality of the rank and file (both privates and noncoms) by the mid-1880s, resulting in less necessity for sergeants to enforce discipline with their fists and officers to employ physical punishments. It was widely recognized by that time that noncoms were "the prominent enemies of the dishonest and the worthless. That a rascal should find life unpleasant and desert is to be expected and when apprehended . . . will claim he was persecuted by the non-commissioned officers when he might with more truth claim the privates were rude to him." When soldiers performed their duty well and received even-handed treatment by their superiors, desertion on that count ceased to be a factor.[49]

In the end Lieutenant Colonel Henry W. Closson, Fifth Artillery, probably came closest to the mark when he concluded "The prime reason after all being the worthlessness of the deserter." In truth, many men enlisted on a whim, with no thought of becoming professional soldiers, and ducked out just as readily. They were, in the words of another officer, "restless, roving individuals incapable of remaining long in one place or occupation . . . the discontented, dissatisfied nature of these men drives them to abscond from the service so soon as their uncontrollable restlessness seized them." An Eighth Cavalryman, Private William G. Wilkinson, was not alone in his opinion regarding the transients: "In most cases they were men whom the Army could well do without." The reliable ones stayed.[50]

Significantly, a portion of the army did not suffer from heavy desertions. In contrast to white units, the four black regiments maintained reputations throughout the Indian Wars era for having drastically lower desertion rates. In fact, recruiting for the black regiments was actually suspended during the early 1880s, as it had been from time to time previously, because of their low rates of desertion and high retention of quality veterans. The black regiments sustained those enviable levels, in part, by reenlisting only those soldiers rated with good or better service records, thereby winnowing out the undesirables.[51]

The reason for lower black desertion rates was not because black regiments had easier duty or served in more hospitable regions, for they did not. All four regiments were posted in western Texas and the territories of New Mexico and Arizona throughout all but the last few years of the Indian campaigns. In 1876–77, for example, each of the eight white cavalry regiments lost an average of 156 men to desertion, while the Ninth lost only 6 and the Tenth 18. During the same period 7 men deserted from the Twenty-Fourth Infantry and 9 from the Twenty-Fifth, as opposed to an average of 33 for each of the other regiments. Those proportions were not exceptional; rather they were typical throughout the era. The adjutant general reported in 1880 that the black regiments suffered the fewest desertions in the entire army, an average of 22 for the cavalry and only 16 for the infantry, compared with 76 and 43, respectively, for white regiments. Even at posts with racially mixed garrisons where conditions were identical, far fewer black soldiers went over the hill than did their white counterparts. When the Third Cavalry and Fifth Cavalry were posted with the Twenty-Fourth Infantry in Indian Territory in 1885, the cavalry units lost 104 and 99 men, respectively, while the Twenty-Fourth suffered a loss by desertion of only 3 men during the same period.[52]

The secretary of war reported in 1889 that the first eight regiments of cavalry (white), as well as the twenty-three white infantry regiments, had desertion rates averaging 12 percent, while the four black regiments lost only 2 percent. The editor of the *Army & Navy Journal* remarked fittingly: "When the colored man enlists he evidently intends to stay." Examining the reasons for this phenomenon, Quartermaster General Samuel B. Holabird concluded:

> Without absolutely knowing, it seems fair to attribute it to the fact that the colored man is better satisfied with his position than the white man who enlists. The colored man's expectations are more nearly met; his relative condition is better. He feels a pride that is new to him. The uniform in his eyes sets him aside as a conspicuous man among his kind. If the white man could be made to view things in a similar light he would hold on to his engagement in the same way.[53]

Unlike whites, who often turned to the army as a last resort or a temporary refuge, or for free transportation west, black men often tended to view the army in light of limited opportunities available to them in civil life. Not only did the black soldier receive pay, clothing, and food consistent with that furnished to white troops, but his overall condition generally improved from what he might have experienced on the outside. Beyond the material factors, however, was the self-respect that a black man gained as a full-fledged United States soldier. He often realized a sense of belonging that he had not previously experienced, perhaps stronger than that of many of his white counterparts. Consistent with that, regardless of army discipline, was a newfound degree of self-determination. What the soldier made of the opportunity relied on his own initiative and conduct. Unlike much of civilian society at the time, the army gave black soldiers, particularly those from laboring and uneducated backgrounds, the opportunity to attain what they considered to be a respectable profession, and many did. The Tenth Cavalry serves as an example. Of 105 noncommissioned officers in the regiment in 1897, 19 had already served ten years or more. A like number were serving in their fourth enlistments. Of these NCOs 6 were credited with at least twenty years' service and 6 others had been in the regular army more than twenty-five years. Incredibly, 11 were truly old soldiers, having honorably worn the blue for at least thirty years at the time the roster was compiled.[54]

Even though the army may not have discovered a central thread of discontent in the ranks, it nevertheless implemented or at least considered a number of reforms aimed at improving the lives of enlisted men in the hope of stemming the flow of deserters. Many officers had long viewed the bimonthly payday as a problem, because the men engaged in drinking sprees, sometimes resulting directly in desertion or indirectly in poor discipline and violent behavior. They also suspected that receiving two months' pay at one time provided enough cash for soldiers bent on deserting to escape the tedium of barracks life. But as Lieutenant Henry Romeyn concluded in his study of the subject, "the man who is ready to desert has, as a general thing, but few scruples of conscience, and any failure of funds for his purpose . . . would be made good by the sale of his arms, horse, or clothing, or those of his comrades. . . . It is true that desertions are generally looked for after 'payday,' but a change to any shorter period would only bring 'deserter day' so much more frequently." He was exactly right; therefore the army had to look elsewhere to effect changes that might discourage desertion.[55]

Years earlier enlightened officers had expressed concern about the lack of career opportunities for those intelligent enlisted men having the ambition to become officers. The positions of commissioned officers in the regulars had traditionally been filled by two means: from graduates of the U.S. Military Academy and, less frequently, from civil life. Prior to 1878 it was almost impossible for a man in the ranks to cross the invisible chasm separating the two classes. Recognizing that some noncoms demonstrated superior skills and intellect, Congress passed legislation granting higher priority to consideration of men demonstrating potential for attaining higher rank. Key to this was modifying the selection process.

Positions for second lieutenants continued to be filled first from among the West Pointers, but second priority for remaining vacancies was reserved for meritorious noncommissioned officers. To ensure that such opportunities were made available, regulations called for company commanders annually to submit the names of qualified noncommissioned officers in their companies who "by education, conduct, and services, seem to merit advancement." Candidates were required to be single, between the ages of twenty-one and thirty, and have at least two years' service in the army. The regimental commanders forwarded those applications, along with any nominations from among their noncommissioned staff, to department headquarters, where a board of officers periodically reviewed the applications. Those endorsed were submitted to the secretary of war by the first day of June so that vacancies might be filled immediately after the graduating cadets had been assigned.[56]

One of the men who gained a commission by this process was Henry White, a Vermont native and former clerk who enlisted in 1881 and served with the First Cavalry. White soon proved his superior abilities and was promoted to sergeant-major of the regiment before his first term was out. A few months after reenlisting, White applied for a commission, a move that his comrades enthusiastically supported. "White is a way up soldier, and every way qualified to fill the honorable position he is looking for," one of them wrote. White achieved his goal of donning shoulder straps two years later.[57]

By the mid-1880s soldiers were reaping the benefits of high-level decisions aimed at improving their lives. Educational opportunities through post schools were enhanced, and official emphasis on a marksmanship program saw men out at the range on a regular basis in a healthy, competitive atmosphere vying for badges denoting their skill levels. Although the basic army ration remained essentially unchanged, the Subsistence Department had added to its inventory canned items such as milk, corned beef, and baked beans. Additionally, companies could purchase from the commissary almost any type of canned vegetable or other product available on the open market. Inspector General Sacket proudly declared: "The rations were never better nor the variety so large as now issued. . . . The soldier lives far better than the laboring class about him and . . . infinitely better than he ever did before he enlisted. . . . The manner in which he is fed certainly should not be advanced, as it frequently is, as a cause for his desertion."[58]

More than the food itself, poor cooking had long been identified as a chief complaint among soldiers. In an unsuccessful attempt to justify adding cooks to the table of organization, Commissary General Robert Macfeely said of the typical company cook who had never worked in a kitchen before that "his fellow soldiers are the sufferers from his ignorance." The designation of specially trained company cooks would not become a reality until the end of the nineteenth century, but Adjutant General Richard C. Drum did take a step in that direction in 1881 by ordering that each of the four new graded companies of instruction at the depots were to assign three men for instruction as assistant cooks. When determined to be competent, those men would be distributed to line companies as needed.[59]

The retirement of Quartermaster General Montgomery C. Meigs, who had headed the department more than twenty years, and his subsequent replacement by the forward-thinking Brigadier General Samuel B. Holabird in 1883, cleared the way for numerous modern innovations. Barracks became somewhat more comfortable by the addition of lard oil lamps, spring bunks, and muslin sheets and pillow cases. The quality of uniforms in both fit and materials increased markedly, and they were better adapted to hot and cold climates. Sacket was of the opinion that the American soldier had never been better and more comfortably outfitted.[60]

Adjutant General Drum likewise sought to improve the readiness of recruits to perform basic duty by insisting that only men from the most advanced companies (those who had been at the depot at least four months) be assignable. A self-satisfied Drum boasted: "The recruiting service has, under the impulse of the new system, furnished the Army with excellent men, who are prepared at the depot to at once enter upon company duty as soon as they join the regiment . . . instead of . . . having to undergo the setting up process at posts and, possibly, in the field."[61]

But just when conditions in the army were improving, and desertion was again declining, a Supreme Court decision rendered in late 1885 actually had the effect of encouraging desertion. Civilian peace officers and citizens, the justices determined, had no legal authority to arrest or even detain a deserter without express direction from an army officer. The editor of the *Army & Navy Journal* announced three years later:

> According to the ruling . . . it is only necessary for a soldier who wishes to desert to walk out of the post whenever he feels so disposed. If he succeeds in eluding pursuit until beyond the reach of his immediate command, he is perfectly safe in any part of the country . . . as he will not be recognized by military authorities elsewhere, and civilian and civil officers are prohibited from arresting him without a military warrant or order. We are told that at a certain post near a large city previous to its publication the guardhouse was constantly filled with deserters from nearly every regiment and detachment . . . delivered up by policemen who in each case received the legal reward for his apprehension. Immediately afterwards this ceased . . . and the guardhouse is empty.[62]

Evidence of his statement was found in sharply elevated rates of desertion for the years 1887 through 1889, at a time when soldiers should have been the most content—Indian campaigning was virtually over, living conditions were better, and physical labor, though not absent, was quite unlike what it had been in former times. Routine jobs such as policing, painting, cutting wood, and cleaning stables were still a part of army life, but major building construction and its attendant arduous tasks like cutting and hauling timber, sawing lumber, burning lime, making and laying adobe bricks, and carpentering were practically nonexistent. All of that had been accomplished by soldier labor years earlier when western forts were proliferating and there was no one else to build them. Now those posts were being abandoned and turned over to the Interior Department, or returned to private lessors when the army had no further use for them and could no longer justify the expense of their maintenance. At posts being retained for a while longer, soldiers still made temporary repairs to dilapidated structures that had seen better days. In time they too would be dropped from the army's inventory. A few strategically located posts lived on and were expanded, while some new ones, such as Fort Logan at Denver, Colorado, would be constructed by local contractors.

Relegated to the past were events like Sunday morning inspection, often the only thing marking the Sabbath at an army post. And in 1889 the traditional tattoo roll call was dispensed with; the bugle call would still be sounded, although there would be no formation. "Unnecessary restraint should be removed and the soldier's life in post be made as comfortable and pleasant as possible," advocated the secretary of war. "A check roll call has recently been substituted for tattoo, so that men are no longer required to run out at 9 P.M. in cold or storm." Similarly, the sounding of taps was standardized throughout the army at eleven P.M., followed by a walk-through inspection of the squad room by the first sergeant, with lights extinguished fifteen minutes later.[63]

Contributing to the quality of the rank and file, as well as the army as a whole, were rigidly enforced standards for recruits and more thorough physical examinations. A visitor to a New York City recruiting station in 1888 commented: "A man may be all right in a social sense, and be rejected for physical causes, and of these there are not less than forty-three bodily blemishes [such as scars, tattoos, moles, etc.], any one of which would render acceptance impossible." By 1891 about 74 percent of applicants were being rejected for one reason or another.[64]

Statistics gathered by the army over many years determined that desertion occurred most frequently during the first three years of a soldier's enlistment. Within that period, according to a newspaper correspondent: "The novelty has worn off, the routine duties have been learned, and the wearying monotony begins. Then for three years the temptation to desert is always present. . . . After a service of three years the soldier's life has become so familiar, so part of the man's nature, that restlessness has worn off, and comparative contentment begins." Contentment, however, may have been confused with a soldier's knowledge that his retained pay and unused uniform allowance would be lost if he deserted. By the end of three years, those usually amounted to a considerable nest egg. As a further inducement for soldiers to remain loyal to their oath, the Pay Department began withholding four dollars monthly from their first year's pay as additional insurance against desertion.[65]

In one stroke the army issued two general orders in mid-1890 that had a greater effect on reducing desertion than all of the other measures and good intentions combined. General Orders No. 80 provided that any soldier who had served faithfully for three years could apply to his department commander for a furlough of up to three months, an unheard of "vacation" in former times. The furlough, with travel at the soldier's own expense, was intended to afford a discontented man a legal means for getting away from the army for a while and time to consider his options. At the end of his furlough, the man could either return to his unit to serve out the remainder of his enlistment or request discharge, so long as his time in service totaled three years and three months. If he elected to be discharged while absent on furlough, he could apply by mail. Once approved, his certificate and final statement would be sent to him.[66]

A related order issued concurrently granted soldiers serving in the second year of enlistment, or the first six months of their third year, the opportunity to purchase their discharge. During that eighteen-month window a disenchanted soldier could apply directly to the adjutant general of the army stating forthrightly (and verified by his company commander) his reasons for wanting out. The initial price for such a buy-out was $120.00 in the first month of the second year. As an inducement to remain, the price was reduced by five dollars monthly thereafter.[67]

Predictably, scores of soldiers, especially men who had enlisted on impulse, availed themselves of these opportunities to leave the army honorably. For many others who stayed, these measures afforded the peace of mind of simply knowing that legal mechanisms existed for getting out if they chose to do so. As a result of these changes, combined with the various reforms instituted during the previous decade, the early 1890s witnessed the lowest desertion rates that the army had ever experienced. As the editor of the *Army & Navy Journal* noted: "The extensive display of service chevrons worn in the ranks of our regiments shows that a large percentage of the men are now serving a second and third enlistment and gives the best evidence of their content."[68]

CHAPTER 13

"I Will See Some Real Wild-West Life"

Preparing for Field Service

The very nature of service on the western frontier demanded that soldiers, particularly the cavalry, spend a great deal of time in the outdoors away from their posts. Scouting and active campaigning might occupy much of their time from spring through fall, depending on their location and proximity to tribes considered to be hostile at any particular time. However, many routine duties common to all posts required men to be in the field for varying periods year-round in all kinds of climates and weather.

Prior to joining the army the majority of regulars had never been any great distance from home, although those who were Civil War veterans had seen something of the eastern and southern parts of the country, and still others had emigrated from other nations halfway around the globe to reach the United States. Almost none of the first-time enlistees, however, had experienced the West or knew much about the extensive region beyond the Mississippi, other than impressions gained through hearsay and the hogwash dispensed in dime novels. This land was unlike anything they had known previously and required adaptation. To most it was a grand adventure. One of the neophytes was a twenty-four-year-old New Yorker, Private Adelbert Butler, Second Cavalry, who confided in a letter to a hometown friend: "I tell you when I . . . heard you relate your travels, I never imagined that I would myself traverse almost thrice the distance, but here I am Soldiering in a country far from home." That country was the Sweetwater mining district in western Wyoming Territory. Private Butler indeed had traveled a long way.[1]

Corporal Maurice H. Wolfe had emigrated from his native Ireland, an island somewhat smaller than the state of Maine, and was clearly impressed with what he saw as his unit transferred from Utah to Fort Sedgwick, Colorado Territory. Wolfe was challenged to describe to his cousin back home the stunning magnificence of the American West: "You may be sure I saw grand sights on the route, which was about 1600 miles. I passed the snow-capped peaks of the Rocky Mountains and the fertile Valley of Utah, where stand the City and the Great Salt Lake. It is as beautiful and rich a country as I ever saw." Those previously unaccustomed to the West at first found it difficult to comprehend the seemingly limitless Great Plains, commonly likening the experience metaphorically to being at sea. "For perhaps thirty miles its vast reach was unbroken by a tree—we were 'out of sight of land,' sky and grass meeting on every side," exclaimed Sixth Cavalryman Henry McConnell.[2]

But not all soldiers appreciated the plains, simply because the region stood in such stark contrast to the environment from which they had come. Upon his initial exposure to the Great Plains, an Eighteenth Infantryman stated flatly: "It seems as though this country was made for the Indians, what us[e] it is to the United States I have not seen eny [sic] yet." A soldier hailing from Pennsylvania described the country that he passed through on his way to Fort Laramie, Wyoming Territory, in 1870 as "all sand and gravel, hardly any vegetation, a short wiry grass without apparent sap, a few varieties of stunted cactus constitute the catalogue." Although he considered most of the country north of Cheyenne, where they had disembarked from the train, as flat and uninteresting, he did allow that "the scenery between the fort and Chug [mail] station is very grand, a line of bluffs rising ninety to one hundred and fifty feet in height, running for miles . . . like some old Castle of medieval times, crumbling into ruins."[3]

Like many others of that time, a soldier passing through Dakota Territory saw only a barren landscape and moaned: "Dakota I do not like at all. We [went] right through the center of it, and what they claim is the best part, it is all a level prairie as far as the eye can reach. There is not a tree in sight. You do not know how to appreciate a tree till you get where there is none." Nevertheless, where some perceived only emptiness on the northern Great Plains of Dakota, others found solitude, even beauty. Seated on a bluff above Fort Abraham Lincoln on the eve of the 1873 Yellowstone Expedition, Private Thomas N. Way was deeply affected by the grandeur of the scene stretching into the distance. "I can see the grand Missouri winding its course as far as the eye can reach," he penned in his journal. "On the opposite banks lay the town of Bismarck, a pleasant looking little place which I have no doubt that one day to come will be a large city. The view makes one . . . feel that they are near to civilization again. In the distance trains of rail road cars go and come." By that time the Northern Pacific Railway had indeed built track as far as the Missouri River, where a lack of funding would delay its completion for several more years. Way clearly appreciated that he was witnessing with his own eyes the nation's westward expansion and that the frontier was only a temporary phenomenon.[4]

Soldiers serving in the West never failed to be impressed by the abundance of wild game, especially the enormous herds of buffalo thriving there during the late 1860s, before they were separated into northern and southern divisions by the railroad corridors advancing across Nebraska and Kansas. Another decade would see the rapid decimation of the stately beasts. In 1866, as a battalion of the Second Cavalry passed through the Republican River watershed, "for four days we marched thru immense herds, and camped in their midst night after night; there were millions of them, and that is not a figure of speech. . . . They covered the rolling prairie from horizon to horizon. They did not disturb us." A private who served with the Seventh Cavalry in western Kansas during 1867–68 challenged readers to imagine "standing one day's march from Fort Larned due south . . . and looking to the extreme left, out on the horizon, and seeing apparently a black line running entirely around it from said point to your extreme right; and knowing they were buffalo, the mind might grasp the immense quantity of them that there must be in that vast space." Shortly after his enlistment, a Third Infantryman crossed the plains via the Santa Fe Trail through Kansas and Colorado to reach his first station. Buffalo were so numerous, he asserted, that "in several instances we had to cut our wagon train in two to let them pass us for be it understood that when a big herd of buffalo was stampeded nothing could stop them."[5]

Soldiers whose travels took them into the Rocky Mountains encountered a natural wonderland. Even while participating in an active campaign against the Nez Perces in 1877, Trumpeter Isaac H. Sembower, First Cavalry, could not resist commenting on the beauty of the country in the vicinity of Yellowstone National Park. "[We] traveled over the mountains all day. Crossed Dades Creek and came to the Yellowstone falls. Big Horn mountains in sight. Magnificent [sic] scenery." Writing two years later during the Sheepeater Campaign, Private Edgar Hoffner, another First Cavalryman, gave a glowing description of Idaho Territory, at the same time foretelling its promising future: "Good timber here, fine angling in the river, an abundance of fresh water clams, ducks, sage hens, deer, antelope, jack rabbits, and grizzly bears. This is a good place for a stock ranch . . . in case a railroad passes near, a fortune awaits the man who makes this a resort." But as soldiers will, Hoffner could not resist commenting on his surroundings in a more practical sense as they related to his personal comfort. "The surrounding mountains covered with timber, and snow . . . 'snow, snow, beautiful snow.' Let him rave whom it suits. I hate it because it soaks thro' my boots." A Thirteenth Infantry corporal in New Mexico Territory offered a more positive view of field service in the Southwest, an opinion shared by the majority of men only too happy to be away from garrison duty. "It is fine and healthy to be out here tramping through the mountains and altogether our rough and ready way of living should be appreciated. I like it and I think that nearly all of us enjoy it."[6]

Although Indian campaigning is usually looked upon as the principal form of the frontier army's field service, it was actually the least frequent of the many activities requiring troops to be away from their posts. Forts located in regions experiencing hostile interaction with Indians, or the potential for it, included one or more cavalry troops in the garrison. Because of its inherent mobility, the cavalry virtually always had responsibility for patrolling, or scouting as it was commonly called, while the doughboys usually drew more static duty securing strategic passes and springs and guarding supply camps. The size of scouting parties and the frequency of patrols depended on the particular circumstances, the tribes involved, and the proximity of a garrison to those Indians. Because the number of men available for duty in a single company might be inadequate for the requirements of the mission, it was not uncommon for scouting detachments to be composed of soldiers drawn from two or three companies at a post. Raiding within the local district might prompt an immediate pursuit at any time at the forts protecting the routes of overland travel. "We were comfortably quartered in the barracks at Fort Sedgwick [Colorado Territory]," remembered Private Albin H. Drown, Second Cavalry, "when at midnight of Jan. 21, 1867, the clear note of the bugle from the adjutant's office sounded 'Boots and Saddles.' The thermometer registered 10 to 20 below zero. . . . At the sound of the bugle all was hurry and bustle, and 37 comrades lined up in front of the quarters, all that were able for duty." A trooper at Fort Custer, Montana Territory, described the more common tedium of the duty when he asserted: "I go out on a scout to day [sic], come back in two or three days and go out in some other direction the next day. . . . I sleep as well as I would in a feather bed." Scouting parties might be in the field for periods of a few days up to several weeks.[7]

Indians in the Southwest, particularly the various Apache tribes, were more fragmented and compelled by the environment to move about in smaller numbers. Cavalry there routinely engaged in extended scouts of two or three hundred miles. Water was the vital key. Service in desert regions tended to be a cat-and-mouse game of locating and monitoring springs, attempting to intercept and follow fresh trails and to strike concealed Apache rancherías, before the Indians either vanished or reversed the tables by striking first. The challenge was not so much fighting Indians as it was finding them. And soldiers did not always possess a great deal of enthusiasm for doing that. "We are out on what is supposed to be a scouting expedition," a corporal leading a detachment recorded, "but as we haven't lost any Indians, we are not going to put ourselves out of the way to hunt for them."[8]

For more than a decade following the Civil War only three east-west railroads traversed the Great Plains: the Union Pacific, the Kansas Pacific, and the Atchison, Topeka and Santa Fe. Whereas the U.S. Mail had been transported by contractors via stagecoach along interterritorial and transcontinental routes until about 1869, extended rail service along those same corridors rapidly reduced the distances from railheads to other points. Only in the Southwest, not accessed by rail until 1879–80, did the Post Office Department continue to let contracts for the long haul from Texas and New Mexico to California.

Mail contractors operating the stage lines constructed relay stations along their routes, usually at intervals of about twenty miles, according to the availability of water and forage for the teams. Depending on the current Indian threat, the stations and civilian employees along officially designated mail routes were protected by small detachments of soldiers, usually ten to fourteen, commanded by a noncom, on a rotational detail of thirty days. These station guards were almost always infantry, though in a few rare instances cavalry served as mounted escort, keeping pace with the coaches. A cavalryman writing to his parents from Fort Union, New Mexico Territory, in 1873 announced that he had volunteered "to take a ride of fifty-six miles tomorrow [to Cimarron] for exercise. An escort is sent out with the mail now, since the last Indian scare." Infantry parties were kept constantly busy providing escorts for the coaches passing in either direction. The common practice was to place two or three doughboys aboard the coach at each station to ride as far as the next station, where they would be relieved, and so on. The men would return to their home stations by escorting the next stage traveling in the opposite direction. Samuel Gardner, a private with the Fifth Infantry posted at Fort Wallace, Kansas, recounted his experience:

> The Indians in Colorado and Kansas were all on the warpath in 1868. We were stationed out on the mail and stage line, and we had some hot times with the Indians. We were placed 10 men and [a] Sergeant or Corporal at the different stations . . . [on the Smoky Hill Trail]. The stage company did not carry any passengers, only the mail. Every stage that went out had four or five of us boys on it as an escort. . . . The run from one station to the next was about 20 to 25 miles. . . . We had "needle" guns and plenty of ammunition, and . . . we made it hot for the Indians when they got close to us, but they hardly ever came very close; they would try to kill our mules or get them to run away.[9]

Sergeant John O. Stotts, posted on the Santa Fe Trail in Colorado Territory, explained how the station detachments were resupplied: "The commander sent for me and told me . . . to take rations and ammunition and in fact supplies of all kinds to several stock ranches.

Those ranches were 10 miles apart . . . and at each ranch 10 soldiers under a corporal was kept as guards. . . . At each ranch we left the men supplied for 10 days. When we got to the end of the line we drove back empty."[10]

Stage stations, constructed of sod, stone, adobe, or logs depending on the materials locally available, were often fortified to some extent. Some featured loop-holed stockades enclosing the mule corral, while others had embrasures in the walls of the house itself. In other locations defenses were more primitive. For example, at Eagle Spring Station on the Southern Overland Route in western Texas, the guards built rude stone breastworks atop nearby hills to serve as sentry posts and firing positions if needed. (Apaches in fact attacked this station several times.)[11]

Depending on the isolation and vulnerability of stage stations, especially on open plains where terrain afforded little natural protection, the troops constructed more elaborate defenses. Unique to the Smoky Hill Trail on the high plains of western Kansas was a type of bunker dubbed the "prairie monitor," which was inspired by the curious armored gunboat made famous during the Civil War. The concept was an adaptation of the so-called bomb-proofs employed at Petersburg and elsewhere during the conflict and would have been familiar to veterans later serving in the regulars. A newspaper reporter traveling the road in 1868 was so intrigued by the monitors that he saw at several of the stations west of Fort Hays that he inspected and described them in detail:

> The process of building one of these ingenious little defensive works was first to dig a hole ten feet square or more according to the number of men to be accommodated, and about breast deep. The soil, being very compact, made excellent walls. Upon the surface a sod breast, about eighteen inches thick and a foot high, was built on each face of the square, and overhead a plank roof was thrown, covered with a thick mass of earth, rendering the top bullet-proof. In the sod walls and angles a number of loop-holes were cut, allowing free scope of firing in every direction. These works were reached by subterranean passage, with the entrance as much as thirty feet distant.[12]

An army contract surgeon, W. Thornton Parker, remembered the monitors having an appearance not unlike the gunboat: "The structure was hardly noticeable a short distance away, as it was elevated only about sixteen or eighteen inches above the surrounding level, or just high enough to afford loopholes for the rifles of its garrison." Completing the defenses at some of the stations, according to another witness, were two additional bunkers so positioned around the station as to make the trio mutually supportive. "They had underground passages that connected the stables to the bomb-proofs," First Sergeant John Ryan explained, "so if the Indians should attack the stations, they could run from the stations through the passages to the bomb-proofs. . . . They also had in these bomb-proofs plenty of provisions and water in case of attack."[13]

The troops erected even more extensive field fortifications at some places where they anticipated attacks by greatly superior numbers of Indians. One such outpost, although not a regular stage station, lay along the military road between Fort Dodge, Kansas, and Camp Supply, Indian Territory. Captain Richard T. Jacob, Sixth Infantry, described a fifty-foot-square redoubt that he and his doughboys built at the crossing of Bear Creek in 1871:

> The interior wall was built of burlap bags, filled with earth. Loose earth was filled about fifteen feet wide. The wall or embankment was about ten feet thick at the base. Bastions were built at diagonally opposite corners. There was a stable for the mules on the inside of the enclosure, built against the wall on the western side. On the eastern side there was a living room and kitchen built for the men. Both of these structures were of "hackall" or stockade, the earthen embankment forming one wall of each. The roofs were covered with earth and were a foot or two lower than the walls, so that they could be occupied for defensive purposes in case of an attack. A well was dug on a high creek bank . . . outside the gate.[14]

Aside from authorized mail routes, the army was usually responsible for carrying the mail from one post to another using mounted couriers or light wagons. Even though steamers transported mail to the posts along the Upper Missouri River in Dakota Territory, soldiers, usually operating in pairs, had to relay it to more far-flung posts on the plains. Troops from Fort Stevenson, for example, constructed small log cabins at intervals along the open road to Fort Totten to shelter the mail carriers at night and during storms. This was lonely and sometimes treacherous duty. An army wife who had lived at Camp Apache, Arizona Territory, remembered: "The mail was brought twice a week [from San Carlos Agency] by a soldier on horseback. When he failed to come in at the usual time, much anxiety was manifested. . . . Only a short time before, one of the mail-carriers had been killed by Indians and the mail destroyed." As rail lines advanced, the Post Office Department contracted with the companies to carry mail along their routes, but other means had to be resorted to for getting it to forts located away from the main lines. In one such instance during the late 1860s details were sent from Fort Laramie, Wyoming Territory, to the railhead at Cheyenne to collect the mail for that post and Fort Fetterman, situated farther up the North Platte River. Small three- or four-man infantry details, armed and rationed, then conveyed the mail by wagon to and from the upper station. The establishment of the Cheyenne and Black Hills stage line to Deadwood, Dakota Territory, during the mid-1870s, created weekly and twice-weekly service from the railhead through Fort Laramie, though its more isolated sister post remained dependent on the courier system for the duration of its existence.[15]

By the mid-1870s, if not before, the majority of western posts were connected with the nation by telegraph. Posts located near railroad routes gained immediate access, either directly or by branch lines, while other more isolated stations eventually were connected through the U.S. Military Telegraph operated by the Signal Corps. "We get this news as soon as you do. Their [sic] is a telegraph runs into this post so you see we are pretty well fixed for news," wrote a trooper at Camp Stambaugh, Wyoming Territory. The troops constructed and maintained the military lines under the supervision of a post signal officer or a Signal Corps sergeant assigned to manage the station at the post, train soldiers in the basics of line repair, and record weather data. Among a detachment sent out to build a line between Forts Sill and Reno in Indian Territory, Corporal Emil A. Bode explained: "About sixteen men were detached from the two infantry companies . . . with crowbars and shovels. . . . We moved along in pairs to the designated spots for the holes, here digging in loose sand, there in solid sandstone or gravel. . . . It was altogether a very dry and tiresome piece of work. . . . We were soon as well acquainted with handling a crowbar as we were in the manual of arms or any other military exercise." When a break occurred between posts, details of three or four men and a noncommissioned officer were sent out from either end to find the damage and repair it as quickly as possible. Besides restoring communication, such assignments tested the self-reliance, efficiency, and leadership abilities of junior noncoms.[16]

The myriad other noncombat activities requiring soldiers to be in the field for varying periods in all types of climate and weather are nearly incalculable. Regardless of the purpose, the majority of soldiers viewed such duty as a welcome break from the garrison regimen. Small details, usually of cavalry when available, routinely escorted paymasters and inspectors general from one post to another in the conduct of their duties. Fourth Infantryman Emmet G. Latta stated that "one of our duties was to escort [supply] trains going from one post to another. This was more interesting than garrison duty . . . a few others of like mind volunteered for escort duty at every opportunity." Larger parties—twenty-five or more men—cut timber and fuel for the garrison at detached camps in the mountains and operated lime kilns, often located some miles from a fort. Such detachments were always armed and equipped for the field and those remaining out at the timber camps or other camps for prolonged duty took along tents and cooking gear.[17]

During times of Indian activity army detachments protected railroad construction crews and sometimes stood watch even after trains were operating on a regular schedule. Corporal William Murphy, Twenty-Seventh Infantry, recalled: "My company [in 1868] . . . was detailed to guard the U. P. Railroad from Sidney, Nebraska, to Cheyenne. Six men and a 'non Com' were at each station with head-quarters at Pine Bluffs. . . . I had charge of six men at Buford Station about thirty five miles from Cheyenne, Wyoming, and west of there." Troops also commonly accompanied various scientific expeditions into minimally explored regions of the West, notable examples being a paleontological expedition from Fort Laramie to the Black Hills in 1874 and another expedition, with an entourage of no less than ten companies, to examine the Black Hills geologically in 1875. Regardless of the purpose of the mission, the men enjoyed the outing and company commanders took advantage of these opportunities to provide practical field experience for the soldiers, especially for recruits, to condition them for active campaigning.[18]

Troops might be ordered out in response to Indian raiding or movement at any moment, the reaction being much the same regardless of location. "Just after midnight, there was a loud knocking at the door of D Company, Fifth Infantry," Sergeant William Gurnett related. "We heard the headquarters orderly tell the first sergeant to turn out the company for a 30 days scout in light marching order. Fort Keogh was soon in a buzz for an Indian campaign." Major campaigns and other planned expeditions received their marching orders somewhat in advance, yet the event always occasioned similar excitement. In the spring of 1876, for example, several commands were ordered to take the field in a converging movement against the Sioux in the Big Horn River country of Montana Territory. A Third Cavalryman at Sidney Barracks, Nebraska, Private Louis Zinser, captured the moment: "The garrison is in an uproar. . . . An expedition is to be formed, and everybody is hustling to pack up. All are to go . . . , only the sick remaining in camp. . . . I . . . will see some real wild-west life."[19]

Much had to be done in a short time. "The first sergeants of each company had commenced to get all of the arms and equipments of the men, also the saddles and saddle equipments . . . in readiness for a campaign. This was always done before starting out, as a great many arms and equipments . . . that could be used at a fort would not answer on a campaign," First Sergeant John Ryan declared. Every available officer and noncom quickly sprang into action to ready the company to take the field. Arms and equipment found not to be fully serviceable were replaced. Company quartermaster sergeants drew and distributed rations and ammunition according to the directive issued to the command; cavalry blacksmiths and farriers went to work examining and reshoeing all the horses, while the other men sorted clothing and individual equipment, deciding what should be taken and what would only be excess baggage. The old hands stepped in to advise the rookies as to what they would find useful and practical, leaving behind the rest. As one soldier noted: "We were not to take anything but a change of clothing, all to be carried on the saddle, and a good soldier will make his load as light as possible."[20]

With that accomplished the men stripped the barracks, placing their dress uniforms and any personal items in their foot lockers and packing up all company property that would be unneeded in the field—mess hall cooking gear and dishes, books, records, spare arms, and garrison accouterments, along with the men's extra clothing, dress caps and helmets, and bedding. Experienced first sergeants kept a number of empty crates on hand for this purpose; otherwise details had to scurry about the post warehouses collecting any boxes they could find. This helped secure the property during the company's absence, because there was no certainty that the company would return to the same quarters, or even the same post, upon termination of the campaign. It was sometimes necessary to forward the containers to wherever the unit might be assigned several months hence. When a movement had to be executed hastily, and time did not permit the packing to be completed, a noncom and a private or two would be left behind to finish the task and to look after the quarters. For this duty the first sergeant often selected family men or individuals too old or incapacitated for active field service.[21]

Amid the bustle of preparation for an active campaign, company commanders took advantage of any spare moments to conduct the skirmish drill and target practice that all too often had been slighted up to that time. All of those routine garrison duties that had taken precedence over training suddenly became less important. "We have been very busy in this camp," remarked Private Maurice Wolfe, Thirtieth Infantry, "drilling and target practice all day, preparing for an expected Indian campaign which I am sure will come off very soon, as the Redskins are showing a very hostile front." Drill was especially critical for the new men, some of whom had been with their companies only a few weeks or even days. Encamped south of Fort Dodge, Kansas, in fall 1868, the Seventh Cavalry received approximately five hundred recruits who had to be drilled and taught how to shoot even as the regiment was embarking on a winter campaign against the Cheyennes. Private Jacob Horner, who enlisted early in April 1876 and was among a draft of recruits dispatched less than a month later to fill up the Seventh Cavalry prior to the Sioux Campaign, claimed that before beginning the march he received no instruction in how to fire his carbine. Following the Battle of the Little Bighorn, the Seventh was strapped with a large number of "Custer Avengers," the raw recruits who had been rushed through the depots and assigned to bolster the cavalry. A harried Lieutenant Jonathan W. Biddle wrote: "We have reveille at 5 A.M. . . . There is drill for recruits only in saddling, bridling, mounting and dismounting. . . . 10 A.M. drill for recruits with carbine. 3 P.M. squad drill for recruits in marching, all three of which drills I have to conduct, each lasting one hour."[22]

Other units faced similar challenges. Ordered from Fort Leavenworth, Kansas, to the northern plains immediately after Custer's defeat, the Fifth Infantry rode the cars to Yankton, Dakota Territory, then boarded a steamboat to travel up the Missouri River. During the voyage officers and noncoms drilled the recruits (many of whom joined en route) on the decks, conducting target practice and battalion skirmish drills ashore for all companies whenever the boat paused to replenish wood supplies. In the meantime other troops were marshaled from posts all across the plains in response to the emergency. A Fourteenth Infantry soldier watched agape as a load of rooky cavalrymen detrained at Fort D. A. Russell, Wyoming Territory, to begin their march to the front:

> After unloading the cars then came a trying time for the recruit horsemen, the trying time for the poor rider, many of them never having rode a horse before, the horses many of them having no person on their backs before. It was a pitiable sight to see the many mishaps that befell them. You could see guns, hats, caps, and blankets strewn along the road. Even the men themselves were often thrown off and the horse went scampering over the prairie, some of the old hands would have to catch them again.[23]

The frontier army may have closely emulated the armies of Europe at dress parade, but its field garb represented a stark contrast that was purely American. The men were plainly garbed in a fatigue blouse worn over a woolen shirt, trousers, canton flannel drawers, and shoes or boots. "My ideas of the dashing trooper going out to war, clad in gay uniform . . . faded into nothingness before the reality," wrote a disappointed Elizabeth Custer upon seeing the Seventh Cavalry ready for the field. Nor was there any particular distinction among units. "When you have seen one regiment of our soldiers in the field," observed a newspaper correspondent, "you have seen them all . . . as for uniform, the absence thereof is a leading characteristic of the service." Although some men chose to wear their oldest garments to the field, knowing that they would be worn out by the time they returned, an Eighth Cavalry officer cautioned: "It is a great mistake to wear old clothes into the field. Rough field service is hard on clothes. You should start with new ones." He may have had a point, but most soldiers ignored the advice. Perhaps the nearest they came to doing so was during the late 1870s when the Quartermaster Department was trying to rid its inventory of obsolete patterns of clothing, some of it dating back to the Civil War. Garments designated as "old pattern" were sold at reduced prices to induce the men to draw them for work garments or to use in the field. The motley effect of these variants, most frequently blouses and hats, was readily apparent in any column bound for the field, but that was of no concern to anyone.[24]

Even after the improvements and greater uniformity of army clothing during the 1880s, soldiers in the field continued to dress according to their personal whims and preferences. A civilian observing troopers of the Fourth Cavalry in 1881 commented: "What in the British army is known as 'smartness,' was here clearly no object . . . as the appearance of slovenliness wore off, it became apparent that to the minutest detail everything was contrived for and subordinated to practical utility." Writing to his journal in 1886 during the Geronimo Campaign, First Lieutenant John Bigelow described the appearance of his Tenth Cavalry troopers:

> Most of the men ride in their blue flannel shirts, their blouses strapped to their saddles, one big sergeant wears a bright red shirt. . . . Some of the men take off their blue shirts and ride in their gray knit undershirts. There are all sorts of hats worn, of American and Mexican make, the most common being the ugly army campaign hat of gray felt. Some of the men wear over their blue army trousers the brown canvas overall, intended to be worn only on fatigue; some wear blue civilian overalls. There are few trousers not torn or badly worn, especially in the seat.[25]

Even though the Ordnance Department prescribed particular arms and field kits for infantry and cavalry, veterans carried only the practical necessities, and the new men soon followed suit. The commander, regardless of the size of the operation, specified the quantity of ammunition per man, the ration, the expected duration of the mission, and what was to be taken in the way of bedding and tentage. The usual practice called for men to be in "light marching order," carrying on their persons from one hundred to one hundred fifty rounds of ammunition for either rifle or carbine, depending on the expectation of combat; rations for two to four days carried in the haversack or saddle bags; and a canteen, a quart tin cup, mess gear, one blanket, and either an overcoat or shelter half. Some officers left to individual preference the choice of taking either a shelter half or a poncho. Tents and rubber blankets or ponchos, when not carried, usually were relegated to wagons, as were additional ammunition, rations, blankets, and buffalo robes during winter operations on the plains. In lieu of the bayonet, for which there was no use on an Indian campaign, soldiers almost always provided themselves with a simple butcher or hunting knife for camp chores, as did cavalrymen.

Refusing to embrace the various patterns of unwieldy knapsacks officially adopted by the army, doughboys universally employed the simple and comfortable blanket roll popularized by soldiers of both sides during the Civil War. While in the field during the 1876 Sioux War, Captain Samuel J. Ovenshine noted that his Fifth Infantrymen were "reduced to one piece of shelter tent, one blanket, a change of underclothing, and two pairs of shoes each." An officer of the Seventh Infantry explained that the roll was formed "by each man spreading his blanket and rolling therein a change of under clothing, simple toilet articles, and the overcoat. The experienced old timer carried less than the new man. He had learned by the ache-and-blister experience system to travel light. The rookie . . . frequently overloads himself . . . , but he quickly learns to cut out every ounce in excess of what his marching, camping, fighting and eating make necessary, not merely desirable." The ends of the roll were then brought together and tied, forming a sort of horseshoe that could be worn over the shoulder.[26]

Cavalry troopers had the comparative luxury of carrying everything but their weapons and cartridge belts attached to their saddles. As Private William O. Taylor recounted, "Rolled up and strapped to the saddle, was carried a blanket, piece of shelter tent and an overcoat." The cavalryman, unlike his infantry counterpart, was burdened with additional items necessary for his mount, beyond his saddle, bridle, and halter. Strapped atop the overcoat was a cylindrical canvas grain sack containing two days' ration of oats or corn. Elsewhere on his saddle were a nose bag, lariat and picket pin, brush and curry comb, and set of sidelines for securing the animal when put out to graze. Each trooper carried in his saddle bags two spare horseshoes, prefitted for his animal's front and hind feet, respectively. When the horse lost a shoe on the march, the troop blacksmith could quickly and easily set a replacement without the necessity of a forge.[27]

Doughboys were armed with one of the various models of the Springfield rifle, .50 or later .45 caliber, fitted with a leather sling to enable the soldier to wear the weapon muzzle-down in foul weather. The habitual manner of carrying the rifle on the march was on one shoulder or the other or perhaps cradled in the elbow. The cavalryman's primary weapon was the short-barreled carbine, either a Spencer or Sharps prior to 1874, and the .45-caliber single-shot Springfield thereafter. Regulations prescribed that the carbine be suspended from a wide leather carbine sling, worn across the body, to prevent its being lost or separated from the soldier in combat. The weight of the carbine constantly hammering on a man's shoulder while on the march caused troopers to seek relief in various ways. Lieutenant Bigelow left a vivid description of what he observed in two companies of the Tenth Cavalry:

> The carbines are variously carried; some according to regulations, hung by a sling over the left shoulder, the muzzle steadied in a socket behind the right leg; some in a boot or holster under the leg; some strapped, muzzle downward, to the cantle or the pummel [sic] of the saddle; some loose in the hand in front of the body. . . . In K Troop [Bigelow's] the carbines are all carried according to regulations. . . . The non-commissioned officers are armed with a Colt's revolver, in addition to the carbine. The trumpeters . . . are armed like the privates, and have no trumpets.[28]

Traditional cavalry armaments also included the saber and revolver. However useful the saber may have been for conventional warfare, it was seldom served any purpose in Indian fighting. With few exceptions, engagements with Indians were conducted at rather long range with troopers afoot and armed with carbines; only very rarely did mounted cavalry close with tribesmen so that a saber might be brought into play. "The saber is virtually done away with in our service . . . ," insisted an officer in 1874. "It is simply an encumbrance. . . . When a cavalry command is about to start on a scout their sabers are carefully packed away and left behind, and in some cases are never again unpacked." Major Louis H. Carpenter, a veteran of seventeen years' frontier service with the Tenth Cavalry, reinforced that view: "It is very seldom indeed that the mounted Indian will meet the soldier in a hand to hand conflict, though it is sometimes necessary to charge through villages, and the revolver would be sufficient for such emergencies." On those occasions when sabers were carried, soldiers found practical uses for them. During a long overland march while changing stations from Texas to Dakota Territory, Sergeant Frederick C. Kurtz explained: "These cavalry ornaments often came in handy in cutting down grass, chopping wood, digging out tarantulas, and knocking the heads off rattlers."[29]

The revolver had somewhat greater potential for use in combat than the saber, though not by a wide margin. Like the saber, it was a secondary weapon intended for use while the trooper was mounted. Its only advantages over the blade were that it had a longer range and could therefore play an offensive role in a charge. As some officers pointed out, however, the revolver, unlike the saber, was useless for close-quarters fighting after all the cartridges were expended. It was nearly impossible for a soldier to reload a revolver in action while mounted on an excited horse. Moreover, until the late 1880s, even less attention was devoted to pistol practice than to carbine target practice, thus relegating the revolver to a defensive role at point-blank range. The decision whether or not to carry revolvers in the field usually rested with company commanders, many of whom preferred to leave them behind, especially when scouting, rather than carry the weight of the revolvers and their ammunition with little possibility that they would be needed. An experienced Second Cavalry officer and veteran of the Sioux War advised that "a soldier had better carry its [the revolver's] weight in carbine ammunition. I look upon it as a useless weapon liable to do much mischief."[30]

"We will have a big expedition this summer, Indian fighting until further orders," Corporal George C. Brown scribbled to a friend back home. "We are now camping near Fort Lincoln . . . I am writing this letter on my knee." Forewarned of a coming campaign and faced with the prospect of being in combat, many soldiers felt compelled to contact relatives or friends, provided they had any. Those individuals who were illiterate sometimes asked a comrade to write a missive for them. Sergeant Charles Scott was also in the camp of the Seventh Cavalry in that spring of 1876. Recognizing the possibility that he might not return, Scott informed his sister: "We air maken big preperishins for a big indian fight this summer . . . we air [going] to what is cauld the Big Horn River. . . . If I get kild this summer I will have a bout 50 dollars coming to me. . . . If you get a lawyer to wright to genral Gorge A. Couster of this post you can get the money, and if I don't I gess I can come home this next fall my self" (all odd spellings in the original). (Scott did not return home. He was killed in action.) Nearly all the men anticipated going to the field with some degree of excitement. Despite potential dangers, "All had rather endure the hardships of an active campaign, and take the chances of being killed by an Indian," asserted Trumpeter Ami F. Mulford, "than remain in quarters and be abused by stiff-necked officers during the summer."[31]

The day of departure was marked by a final inspection of the outbound troops. Kept on the move for days prior to the march, Seventh Cavalryman John F. Donahue was so tired the night before that "it was too late to undress, so I laid down fully attired, spurs and all on. When the call was sounded [next morning], I jumped up quick and hurried to the parade ground, and being a little late could not wait to disengage my 'pup' tent from my spur and so dragged the same with me. For this I was ordered to 'carry a log.'" Lieutenant Charles King described the final formation: "Officers ride slowly along their commands, carefully scrutinizing each horse and man. Blanket, poncho, overcoat, side-line, lariat, and picket pin, canteen and haversack, each has its appropriate place and must be in no other. Each trooper in turn displays his 'thimble belt' and extra pocket package [cartridges], to show that he has the prescribed one hundred rounds." Some officers concluded the inspection with a pep-talk aimed at bolstering morale. Just before his company left Fort Klamath, Oregon, in 1877, Private Isaac H. Sembower, First Cavalry, related that "Captain [James] Jackson made a short speech to the Company stating that we had a reputation second to none in the Army and he hoped we would preserve it during the coming Campaign, to which the boys responded with three hearty cheers. We then moved out."[32]

Scouting and escort parties routinely left a post without any particular fanfare, other than a few wives watching longingly from a distance as their husbands went out, perhaps for the last time. Major expeditions, however, sparked a different atmosphere. Private Theodore Ewert recorded in his diary the exodus of the Seventh Cavalry en route for the Black Hills in 1874:

> At 8 o'clock the 2nd day of July, the companies wheeled by fours into line of march, guidons flying in the breeze, the band playing our battle quickstep, "Garry Owen," the officers dashing up and down the column with an air of importance, the men cheering and full of chatter, and as we cast our eyes for the last time on Fort A. Lincoln up the valley, we saw the ladies of our command (the wives of officers and men) waving their scarfs and handkerchiefs in sad farewell and just as we left the last ridge that overlooked the valley the men gave three hearty cheers.[33]

An old army tradition called for departing commands to be played out of the post to the strains of an ancient Irish melody "The Girl I Left behind Me." Many men, like First Sergeant John Ryan, recalled the occasion with great emotion. Just after his regiment marched out of Fort Abraham Lincoln to begin the 1876 campaign, "we made a halt for a short time, and the officers and men were allowed to go back and say good-by to their wives and sweethearts. 'Mount' and 'Forward' were sounded and our band struck up 'The Girl I Left Behind Me.'" Private Charles Windolph, also riding in that column, described the feeling of excitement shared by many of the men:

> You felt like you were somebody when you were on a good horse, with a carbine dangling from its small leather ring socket . . . and a Colt army revolver strapped on your hip; and a hundred rounds of ammunition in your web belt and in your saddle pockets. You were a cavalryman of the Seventh Regiment.

You were a part of a proud outfit that had a fighting reputation, and you were ready for a fight or a frolic.[34]

Later that summer the Fifth Infantry was ordered to join the expedition against the Sioux. "The chartered special train stood puffing and steaming on the track [at Fort Leavenworth]," wrote an officer's wife. "The hour had come for farewells and tears from the wives and sweethearts of the departing troops. The train was packed with soldiers within and without, on the roofs of the coaches and hanging to straps to catch the last glimpse of the dear ones left behind. To the strains from the band of 'The Girl I Left Behind Me,' the train pulled out."[35]

Field service, whether or not the troops expected to engage Indians, invariably posed unforeseen dangers for soldiers. Combat, if it came, only increased the risk. Nevertheless, the troops left their stations in high spirits and thirsting for adventure.

CHAPTER 14

"More Than I Ever Thought I Could Bear"

Life in the Field

Military field operations differed dramatically according to region. In the Southwest, populations of nomadic Apaches, which often moved about in bands of extended familial groups, were limited by their environment and by the numbers of people the land could sustain in any given place and time. Similarly, the troops scouting for or pursuing Apaches relied on those same widely separated and undependable sources of water, causing strike forces to be smaller and more mobile than those employed on the plains. Forts, generally being more prolific throughout the desert regions, added to the widespread use of comparatively small, more nimble forces. Troops operating in mountainous regions of the north, while not limited by a lack of water, also were restricted in size and mobility by rugged terrain and trackless forests. Wagons, if taken at all, had to keep to the valleys, while troops seeking Indians were dependent on pack trains. On the Great Plains, conversely, especially in the far north and the southern regions, posts were comparatively few to nonexistent. Plains tribes of the buffalo culture migrated in considerably larger groups than desert dwellers, not infrequently in combined tribal bodies, within their respective ranges. Those factors compelled the army likewise to respond when necessary with larger forces against those tribes. The gentler terrain and more plentiful water sources of the plains nevertheless facilitated operations by those larger bodies of troops.

Heavy columns sent into Indian country, whether as strike forces, for exploration, or as escorts to railroad surveyors, were well-organized endeavors that relied on being well supplied with everything that the command might need for several weeks or even months.

The essential centerpiece of any major expedition was the wagon train, operated and manned by civilian contractors. Several of them might accompany a column, depending on the particular circumstances. Individual trains were composed of twenty-four heavy freight wagons drawn by mules to transport tons of rations for the troops and forage for hundreds of cavalry horses as well as the draft animals. Additionally, two army wagons were assigned to each of the companies (though only one might be taken into the field) for use in hauling extra arms and ammunition, troop picket ropes, cooking gear for the officers, and a limited quantity of equipment from company stores to replace any that might be worn out in the field. When permitted by the expedition commander, a few of the larger "A" and wall tents might also be stowed in the company wagons. Being a teamster in garrison was considered good duty but was not popular with some men when active field service loomed. Private August Hettinger groused: "I was detailed to drive the four-mule ammunition wagon. That sure got my goat . . . here was a likely campaign . . . for which I had waited for years, and I was told to drive mules."[1]

First Sergeant John Ryan pointed out that as the contractor's wagons "became lightened by the use of forage for the horses and rations . . . for the troops, one wagon was sent to each company and then the men could put in their blankets and such articles as were not required on their saddles, and it was carried for them." Infantrymen likewise eagerly took advantage of empty wagons whenever available by shedding blanket rolls and haversacks, retaining only their rifles, cartridge belts, and canteens.[2]

The troops were arranged in a prescribed order of march, according to circumstances and the units present, to protect and keep pace with the slow-moving supply train. Lieutenant Edward S. Godfrey described a typical regimental formation used during the Washita Campaign of 1868:

> The Seventh Cavalry was organized with four squadrons, two troops each. Troop K . . . was detailed as Headquarters guard

and escort. Two troops had the advance, two on each flank and two as rear guard. The infantry loaded in wagons was at the head of the wagon train.... The wagon train was formed two abreast and the cavalry was to regulate its march on the wagon train. The General [Alfred Sully] in his ambulance, followed by his escort, rode at the head of the train.[3]

Private William D. Nugent recalled that during the 1873 Yellowstone Expedition, escorting surveyors for the Northern Pacific Railroad, the train of some four hundred wagons traversing wide open plains "was being driven eight wagons abreast, with ten companies of infantry on the left flank and ten on the right. Six companies of cavalry were in the advance, and two companies were acting as rear guard, with two companies deployed as flankers." Each of the flanking battalions, termed "wings" and commanded by field officers or senior captains, provided defense against possible attack. As further security, the flanking units detailed several mounted vedettes to shadow the column on either side at a distance of a quarter-mile or more to provide early warning of anyone approaching the column. A force of cavalry (at least one company) trailed the column at some distance as the rear guard and to prevent straggling. The rear guard was also charged with assisting any wagons that might become stuck or otherwise need help. The order of march almost always rotated daily to distribute the duties equitably.[4]

Moving cross-country with wheeled vehicles where no roads existed could be difficult at best. A separate party of so-called pioneers was composed of two or three men detailed from each company, or at times an entire company, according to the size of the command and the obstacles anticipated. The pioneer force, commanded by an officer detailed for the duty, operated between the advance guard and the main body to grade stream banks, remove large rocks and downed logs, and even fell trees, thereby enabling the wagons to pass. "Now and again we'd hit a bad creek or river crossing, and pioneer troops would have to build a temporary bridge," a cavalryman explained. "We had two light wagons filled with axes, picks, and shovels, and bridge timbers and planks." Pioneering was strenuous, requiring much physical labor (especially in mountainous terrain) and was not looked upon with great favor by the men assigned. First Sergeant Ryan offered a vivid description of the difficulties encountered:

> Our pioneers were obliged to cut lots of those large trees out of the way so that we could get through. . . . Some of the hills were so steep that it was impossible to get our wagon trains over their tops. We had to build roads winding around the sides, taking dirt from the upper side and throwing it on the lower side of the trail. We also were obliged to throw ropes over the tops of the wagons, and as the mules drew them up the sides, we had to hold on to them on the upper sides to keep them from tumbling down.[5]

Private Peter Thompson related that while the Seventh Cavalry was engaged in constructing a wagon road through a particularly difficult area in Sioux country "a company of infantry, for the country was almost impassable to horses, was deployed on both sides of us as skirmishers." Anticipating an unusually arduous job to extricate the command from a timbered pocket in the Black Hills, Second Cavalryman John P. Slough and his comrades were elated when they discovered "an easy path . . . a few hundred yards on the road we came down yesterday. . . . Co. I in particular full of jollity as usual, but more so today from the fact that they had no pioneering to do, thereby having the last laugh on the rest of the command."[6]

During active Indian campaigns the army was always disadvantaged by its reliance on adequate supplies, usually transported by sizable wagon trains. Unlike Indians in their native habitat, large bodies of soldiers were far less able to survive on what nature provided. Nor could their animals, horses, and mules (accustomed to being fed grain) maintain adequate strength on grass alone. As one officer metaphorically expressed the constraints, military expeditions were like a chained dog, "within the length of the chain irresistible, beyond it powerless."[7]

On the plains, where large expeditions often were employed strategically to corral the highly mobile tribes and bring them to bay, officers soon learned the advantage of establishing base camps where trains could stockpile supplies and return to posts for more, while strike columns advanced farther into hostile country seeking the Indians.

Steamboats, too, were utilized where possible, notably on the Yellowstone River in Montana Territory, to replenish rations and other material as needed at central field depots. The infantry and green cavalry recruits, often detached from their units as being more hindrance than help to a strike force, were assigned to guard the camps.

Brigadier General George Crook, operating against the Tonto Apaches in the rugged terrain of northern Arizona Territory in the early 1870s, learned the practical advantages afforded by pack mules. With each animal able to carry up to three hundred pounds, small patrols with a couple of mules could transport supplies sufficient to last a few weeks. Moreover, mules were hardy, intelligent, and able to go anywhere that Indian and cavalry horses could go—and some places they could not. Mules readily proved their worth in the mountains by transporting the rations, blankets, and reserve ammunition for infantry and even dismounted cavalry when the going became too rough and broken for horses to negotiate. Showing obvious respect for the animal, Private Edgar Hoffner, First Cavalry, related an incident during the Sheepeater Campaign when "one mule lost its footing, and rolled end over end about three hundred feet down the side of the mountain. The pack came off, Sir Mule gained his feet, shook himself, faced the pack, flopped his ear, gave a wink and walked off to graze. A bruised eye and cut on his chest were the only injuries."[8]

Pack trains were managed either by experienced civilian packers under contract or by the soldiers themselves. In large expeditions, according to Sergeant Fred Platten, "several packers, under a head packer who was the boss of the pack train, were assigned to each unit." Those mules accompanying strong columns often belonged to the contractor, being specially selected and well trained for the task. The chief packer for Crook's Big Horn Expedition in 1876 offered an expert's description of such a train:

> It consists of a lot of medium sized mules on which to carry supplies for the army, when we cut loose from the wagon trains. We could then keep up with the command, let the soldiers go when and where they would travel as fast as they wished. The pack-train was right at their heels, with their provisions, blankets, ammunition, tents, or feed for the horses. A pack train usually consists of about sixty pack and ten riding mules, led

by one bell mare horse. . . . Keep the bell horse in hand, and Indians will get very few mules in case of a stampede.[9]

In other instances, government mules were employed. "Each troop has two packers and ten or twelve pack mules," a Second Cavalry trooper explained. "On a scout or rapid campaign movement there were helpers for each pair of troop packers [detailed for the purpose]. The helpers took care of the mules in camp, herded them for pasturage, brought them into camp for use, blanketed them and put on saddles. The packers then began their work." A typical load, according to one trooper, consisted of two fifty-pound boxes of hardtack, one lashed on either side of the animal, with a thousand-round crate of ammunition placed on top between the two, or a two-hundred-pound canvas sack of bacon was substituted for the ammunition. Packers also used heavy canvas panniers (bags) hung from the saddle to contain loose items such as blankets, medical supplies, and cooking gear. Private Anton Mazzanovich, Sixth Cavalry, acknowledged that learning the craft of packing required training and time, in his case about two months' experience, after which he "became as good at the game as any hombre in the outfit."[10]

Many times, in order to pursue or strike Indians, it became necessary to form pack trains in the field using novice soldiers and team mules borrowed from the wagons at the field depots. Private Charles Windolph described the results he witnessed early in the Sioux Campaign:

> Here at the mouth of Powder River we started training pack mules and we had a lot of fun doing it. They were the ordinary wagon mules. We had a few experienced [civilian] packers with us, but I think they must have been pretty disgusted with trying to teach us how to throw the Diamond hitch. The mules were just as green as the men. But both of us learned. We first tried out our mules with sacks of grain and water kegs, and we had a lot of fun laughing at the other fellow.[11]

Windolph added that the makeshift packers caused so much trouble by their loads coming loose and impeding the march that the commander, Lieutenant Colonel George A. Custer, was forced to assign responsibility for the train to an experienced junior officer. Embarking on what was predictably a hostile situation, Custer also assigned a reinforced company to protect and help manage the train.

Once on the march, things became somewhat less formal, although when bugle calls were permitted the "General" signaled the breaking of camp, and all tents were dropped simultaneously on the last note. Immediately after packing up, the first sergeants had the men fall in under arms and called the rolls to account for everyone and allow officers to inspect the weapons and ammunition. Then, recalled a cavalryman, "before mounting the companies form single lines. Each man, commencing at the head of the company calls out in turn his number; one, two, three, four, and so these are repeated until the company is all numbered into sets of fours." Infantry counted off in similar fashion, though sometimes in sets of twos, the companies being smaller and the Number Four men not being a tactical necessity as in the cavalry. According to the manner in which the men were ordered to count off, the units marched in columns of either fours or twos, though the type of terrain encountered might cause the formation to be altered en route.[12]

In the absence of any urgency, troops taking the field usually made easy marches the first few days out. This shakedown period permitted larger columns to resolve any problems that might arise with wagon or pack trains and allowed recruits, as well as garrison-softened soldiers and animals, perhaps inactive for months, to become conditioned. As Colonel John Gibbon's column moved from Fort Ellis, Montana Territory, down the Yellowstone River at the beginning of the 1876 Sioux Campaign, an officer observed:

> Sick call, according to a fashion that the boys have fallen into, was received with cheers and groans all over camp that deterred many a poor devil who needed treatment for sore limbs and feet from presenting himself at the doctor's tent. But the march had told upon the men unaccustomed to it as they were, and there was a pretty respectable attendance at the hospital of men too badly off to care for ridicule. . . . But the men are toughening to their work, and will be all right in a few days.

Nor were the cavalry of Gibbon's command in any better physical shape. One of them, Private Fred Munn, Second Cavalry, recalled: "Nearly all the men were in bad condition, saddle-chafed and sore, particularly the recruits which consisted of about 120 men."[13]

At those times when the command included infantry, the doughboys established the pace and distance, usually not more than ten miles a day initially. As a battalion of the Seventh Infantry left Fort Shaw, Montana Territory, during the month of March, wrote Private Eugene Geant: "There was about a foot of snow on the level and we marched about 8 miles the first day . . . the weather freezing hard. . . . Rather a little rough experience for the boys for their first expedition." Then, resigning himself to the inevitable, Geant added: "I suppose we will get used to it." The habitual distance thereafter increased to "the usual fifteen-mile doughboy trek," according to Private Samuel Gilpin. After their first five days' shakedown march from Fort D. A. Russell to Fort Fetterman, Wyoming Territory, a distance of approximately one hundred and twenty miles, Fourteenth Infantry sergeant John Zimmerman declared: "From this [day?] forward all the new hands were drilled tolerably well in the misfortunes of camp life," adding a half-hearted positive note: "Things began to look more cheerful."[14]

In an emergency, however, infantry might be called upon to march considerably farther, an ability that was no small source of pride to the veterans, as attested by Private Luther Barker describing the departure of a battalion of the Fifth Infantry from Fort Keogh, Montana Territory, at the outset of their involvement in the Nez Perce Campaign: "The twenty-five mile march this first day was only exercise for the train guard. The next day we marched thirty miles. No one seemed to notice the extra five miles, except a few recruits that had never been on a real campaign. We were camping each night with the mounted men." In response to the Ghost Dance craze among the Sioux in November 1890, four companies of the Eighth Infantry and two companies of the Ninth Cavalry were ordered out in heavy marching order on six hours' notice, to proceed from Fort Niobrara, Nebraska, to the Pine Ridge Reservation. "A forty-mile march is no particular feat for an infantry command to make after they are two or three days on the road," claimed Private August Hettinger. "But to make forty miles under heavy packs the first day out can only be accomplished by the American doughboy."[15]

Roused well before dawn, the men (with the cavalry first feeding their horses) brewed their indispensable coffee over small fires, when permitted, and were soon on the march. Private Lawrence R. Jerome, Fourth Cavalry, remembered chasing Apaches in New Mexico. "With the earliest streak of dawn we were again underway hot on the trail. The usual program was to breakfast on a piece of bacon, a slice of bread [hardtack], and a cup of coffee before daylight; as soon as there was light enough to take up the trail and follow until it was too dark to see, never stopping for dinner." Veteran noncom Frederick C. Kurtz recalled: "Everybody had a canteen full of water and a few hardtack, just to keep the stomach from growling." Cooking breakfast was a luxury seldom allowed in the field simply because it required too much time. Rookies quickly learned to fry their next day's meat ration the night before so that it could be consumed cold before taking up the march or carried and eaten later in the day. When closely pressing a war party, commanders usually ordered a "dry camp" with no fires to be made wherever darkness overtook them.[16]

Ideally, during summer troops marched only until midday before going into camp to avoid afternoon heat or sometimes rain. When it was necessary to go farther, the commander might allow the men to take a "nooning" of a few hours then continue the march until dark, depending on sources of water. Private George Cranston, a Thirty-Second Infantryman stationed in Arizona Territory, attested that the usual way of moving across the desert was "to march nights and sleep days." Routine hikes were "regulated into one hour marching and ten minutes rest," Corporal Emil Bode stated, "the leading companies of the column changing daily. . . . The dull time of the march passed with the men singing and joking." Even though the usual day's march for infantry averaged fifteen miles, once conditioned the doughboys often trekked up to thirty miles when demanded during active campaigning. Cavalry keeping pace with its wagon train traversed the same distances, of course, but the advance guard and flankers might cover considerably more ground in the course of their duties. Neither was it uncommon for cavalry in emergencies to make forced marches of forty, fifty, or even more miles in a day, although the officer in command had to manage his animals judiciously to avoid exhausting or injuring them. Cavalry leading worn-out horses was worse off than infantry.[17]

River crossings posed the greatest obstacle—and inherent danger—to troops marching cross-country. "We had a great deal of trouble getting the wagon train through mud holes and over creeks," grumbled Private Thomas N. Way, a member of Colonel David S. Stanley's 1873 Yellowstone Expedition. The men assigned as pioneers often performed back-breaking work to move the heavily loaded wagons past such obstacles, as Trooper Louis Zinser noted in his diary. "Our first work this morning was to pull our wagons across the creek . . . then we marched twenty-seven miles." Getting wheeled vehicles across small streams could be laborious and aggravating, but cavalry and even infantry generally negotiated them with relatively little difficulty.[18]

Major watercourses were another matter and downright treacherous for both men and animals. On its way to establish posts along the Bozeman Trail, the Eighteenth Infantry encountered unforeseen problems getting across the South Platte River near Julesburg, Colorado Territory. "In places the water would be only two or three inches deep," remembered Private William Murphy, "while a few feet away there would be seven or eight feet of water. Two of our men got caught in the quick-sands and were drowned. We finally crossed by having a long rope stretched from man to man, strapping our guns and equipment to our backs, and holding to the rope." A corporal of the Fourteenth Infantry witnessed the dangers experienced by General Crook's column when crossing the swollen North Platte River in spring 1876: "Each man must ride his own [horse] over no matter how deep . . . all the wagons must cross in the water. Often the horses would drift downstream a mile or more, the wagons would sometimes turn over, baggage and all going downstream losing a portion of it."[19]

When Colonel John Gibbon's column attempted to ford the Yellowstone River in Montana Territory, Second Cavalryman Edward Williams recorded that the cavalry unsaddled and placed all their equipment aboard recently arrived steamboats, but "after a hard struggle we succeeded in getting two horses across at a time, and so we got about 8–10 horses across." The men then unsuccessfully attempted to drive the remainder of the horses into the water, but the herd bolted and stampeded back to camp. By the end of a long, frustrating day the men had succeeded in getting only one company of cavalry to the opposite side, drowning five horses in the process. Private Arthur S. Wallace related that when crossing the Powder River he and his Fifth Cavalry comrades were instructed to head their mounts upstream and to swim alongside, but most of the men slid back and hung on to the horses' tails to be pulled across. That worked well enough, so long as the horse possessed a natural ability to swim, but not all did. "Many of the horses cannot swim," insisted another trooper. "My horse left me in the water and if it had of been over my head, I would have drowned." Some cavalry units employed a different technique for crossing rivers. Faced with traversing the 300-yard-wide Rio Grande in New Mexico Territory, several troops of the Eighth Cavalry first stripped their horses of all equipment then crowded the animals into the water, with the men of each company forming a human chain. "One of D Co., a private, volunteered to ride his horse over in front of the others, so they would follow. . . . The soldier and his horse . . . made the other bank, but not togeather [sic] . . . as they struck the swift current the soldier was washed off the horse. He had quite a struggle in the water and was pretty well exhausted when he reached the other shore."[20]

Not surprisingly, the infantry generally had more difficulty negotiating rivers. Men shod in leather-soled shoes easily slipped and fell on smooth rocks while trying to resist the force of the current, sometimes losing their rifles or other equipment. Serpentine watercourses often forced columns moving along the valleys to ford the same stream numerous times. Corporal John Zimmerman offered a detailed account of the doughboys' plight as he experienced it during the Sioux Campaign:

> The cavalry rode through the water good enough, but the Infantry had to march and wade right through, sometimes breast high other times knee deep. . . . All took off their shoes and stockings, after crossing put them on again and continued the march to the next fording place. At the third crossing, our feet began to get sore from the sharp rocks and sand. We were then told that there were more than a dozen such crossings before us yet for this day . . . after this we marched into the river removing nothing, and not delaying the march, never thinking of changing any more.[21]

In those instances when streams were shallow enough for the horses to remain on their feet rather than swimming some expedition commanders, particularly infantry officers, considered the welfare of the men by transporting doughboys more rapidly and safely using the cavalry mounts or wagons. "Colonel Gibbon usually sent part of the cavalry ahead and had one of the cavalrymen lead about three horses back, so that in that way we infantrymen got over dry shod," recounted Private George C. Berry, Seventh Infantry. When infantrymen were permitted to hitch a ride aboard the wagons, related Seventh Cavalryman Peter Thompson, "they would climb onto the wagons like bees on a hive." Doughboys always appreciated being able to avoid the chaffing caused by marching in wet socks and shoes.[22]

Winter campaigning presented its own particular challenges to crossing streams. A Fifth Infantry private, Edwin M. Brown, related that when separate battalions of his regiment rendezvoused on the Yellowstone in 1877 "ice was floating all along the river; it seems the place where we crossed [on the ice] was very tough as it was in a bend, but on either side of this the ice was much broken. They made rafts and crossed the mules, wagons, and luggage, afterwards crossing the command." Depending on recent temperatures, the ice on frozen rivers might support the weight of a man, but not a horse. Captain Francis Moore, Ninth Cavalry, a practical-minded Scot who had begun his career on the plains as an enlisted man in the First Colorado Volunteer Cavalry, was confronted with a frozen river while on a march in Indian Territory. Knowing that the ice was not thick enough to support the troop's horses, Moore had the men "cut holes in the ice and with tin cups and camp kettles flooded the ice for a width of about 30 feet and extending across the river. This water froze quickly . . . and finally had an ice bridge over which he could cross in safety." However, Second Cavalryman William F. Zimmer noted that even in winter river crossings might offer certain benefits. After several troopers lost their seats during a crossing and emerged from the stream thoroughly soaked and shivering, the surgeon administered liberal doses of medicinal whiskey to revive them. "I think more would have got wet had they known that whiskey would be dealt out to the wet ones," Zimmer opined.[23]

At the conclusion of a day's march the troops bivouacked on the most favorable ground available, preferably in the open to discourage surprise attack. Scouting detachments dispensed with formality and spread their blankets wherever they found a reasonably comfortable spot to lie down, though always in close proximity to each other for security and nighttime guard reliefs. Army tactics manuals prescribed the arrangements of infantry and cavalry camps, differing principally in the placement of the officers' tents in relation to those of the men. In practice, however, terrain often dictated the actual layout and degree of formality.

When tents were used, and suitable ground was available, infantry companies erected their tents in two rows facing each other, perhaps forty feet apart, thus forming the company street. Officers' tents stood at right angles some distance from one end of the street and facing it. Rifles might be stacked (in freestanding tripods) on a line a few feet in front of each row of tents when not in enemy territory. The usual practice for maintaining a state of readiness and protecting the weapons from night dampness called for each man to sleep with his rifle or carbine and carry it with him to roll calls.

The presence of horses dictated a camp plan unique to cavalry. The foundation of the bivouac was the picket line, as described by Private Louis E. Hills, Seventh Cavalry:

> At night the wagons [two] would be placed about one hundred and fifty feet apart and a large rope would be stretched from the hind wheel of one wagon to the hind wheel of the other, thus making a picket line to tie our horses to. . . . When we first went into camp, we would stake our horses out to feed where there was good grass, then just before dark bring them in, and tied to the picket line and give them their oats.

With the picket line thus established, troopers pitched their tents along a parallel line about fifteen yards in front of the horses. The men kept their arms in their blankets and equipment in or immediately adjacent to their respective tents. In semipermanent camps where timber was available, the men sometimes erected a line of saddle racks in front of the tents to keep their equipment off the ground and readily accessible. Cooking fires, never large, were placed in shallow trenches parallel to the line of saddles but nearer the tents, though wind direction might dictate that they be positioned elsewhere for the safety of the camp. Although regulations called for the sinks, in the form of slit trenches, to be located some distance beyond the tents, First Sergeant John Ryan remembered a more practical arrangement: "There was erected on the left of each company on the line of their tents at quite a distance off a Sibley tent [over the slit trench] for each company that was used as the company sink."[24]

Large expeditions established a wagon park (the vehicles being aligned with military precision) as well as a bivouac for the pack train, if present, and the civilian employees. Distinct grazing areas and picket lines were established for the mules, and the drivers and packers provided their own guards.

Upon arriving in camp, members of the infantry first dropped their gear and cavalrymen unsaddled and groomed their horses, after which the first sergeants directed everyone, except the Number Four horse holders, out to gather fuel for cooking fires. In wooded regions that was not difficult, but finding fuel on the plains was problematical. When wood was available at one night's camp, an experienced first sergeant would see that an initial supply was loaded aboard a company wagon to be hauled to the next stop, where fuel might not be available. Operating on the treeless Staked Plains in the Texas Panhandle, a column of Fourth Cavalrymen presented an appearance not unlike lancers after retrieving lodge poles abandoned by their Comanche enemies. "It was a most singular sight to see a long column of five hundred troopers, each with two or three fourteen-foot poles raised right in the air over their shoulders," a lieutenant remembered. "[Colonel Ranald S.] Mackenzie . . . suspecting a joke, or that they were being carried along as relics, was about to seriously order them to be thrown away when somebody suggested their possible utility for fuel instead of buffalo chips." Mackenzie thus narrowly avoided becoming the most unpopular man in his regiment.[25]

On the Great Plains the native buffalo provided a ready source of fuel in the form of dried dung, commonly referred to as "chips" because of their pancake-like shape. As Private James Lockwood recalled: "Each soldier, upon coming into camp after a day's march, was expected to take a sack and go around over the prairie and collect it full of 'buffalo chips' . . . and empty it down by the fires of the cooks." Commands accompanied by wagons used empty grain sacks for this purpose, while cavalry units operating independently sent the men out in pairs with saddle blankets, with a trooper supporting either end, to gather chips. "These chips make a very good fire, but the odor arising after they burn sometimes does not smell as sweet as 'new mown hay,'" offered an Eighth Cavalryman. Twenty-Second Infantryman Anthony Gavin expressed himself more candidly regarding dung that was not fully cured: "Oh what a stench it used to make!" Buffalo chips nevertheless produced heat and that was what really mattered, although Musician James C. Bothwell explained that chips had another advantage in that they did not "make a very bright fire, and being in a hole could not be seen by the Indians." Weary at the end of a day's march, reflected another soldier, the men gratefully filled their cups and stood or squatted around their buffalo chip fires staring into "the dull glow of coals as you waited for coffee."[26]

Field cooking sometimes benefited by combining the rations and having company cooks prepare the food in bulk, but that was possible only when commanders authorized camp kettles, large mess pans, and other paraphernalia to be hauled in the wagons. Much of the time soldiers cooked individually or shared the task with their bunkies, using issue field mess gear—a quart-size tin cup and two-piece meat can forming a plate and skillet. (Prior to 1875 the army provided no individual mess equipment, so the soldiers were responsible for purchasing their own tin cups, plates, and light sheet-iron skillets.)

Because there was no means for food preservation beyond salting, the daily basic field ration consisted of a pound of hard bread, universally known to soldiers as hardtack; twelve ounces of salt pork or bacon; and coffee. "We now have a change of diet," announced a Seventh Cavalryman, "hard-tack, bacon, and coffee for breakfast; raw bacon and tack for dinner; fried bacon and hard bread for supper." Soldiers referred to this no frills diet as "government straight." On occasion, the ration was supplemented with small quantities of dry beans or rice, sugar, and perhaps a few casks of vinegar. "We drank vinegar to keep scurvy away and saw no fruit for over two years while campaigning," recounted Private Gavin.[27]

A hardtack was nothing more than an unleavened white flour cracker approximately three inches square and three-eighths to half an inch thick. Put up by government contractors in fifty-pound wooden boxes, fourteen or fifteen crackers were a day's ration. The word "hard" was no exaggeration. "At supper last night we had a piece of hard bread, very hard and dusty," Private Edward Williams complained, "and as I took a bit[e] of it, I broke one of my front teeth in two." Most, if not all, of the hardtack issued during the Indian Wars came from stocks left over from the Civil War. One thoughtful soldier even concluded that "no one but an Egyptologist could decipher" the marking impressed in each cracker, suggesting that it "evidently dated from the Pharohs [sic]."

Cavalry trooper Eddie Matthews complained in 1872 that age and poor storage had left it musty and "full of worms . . . old hard bread which undoubtedly had been baked in some mechanical bakery during the first part of the late war." Sixteen years after Matthews penned that comment, another Eighth Cavalryman, Private Frederick C. Kurtz, was equally suspicious, claiming that "the hardtack was full of little black bugs, a sort of weevil. We used to dip the hardtack in water first, so as to let the little fellows creep out before eating. The hardtack was of a grayish color, no doubt from age, and we often wondered if it was not remnants of the War of the Rebellion."[28]

Because biting through a cracker was nearly impossible, soldiers usually resorted to first breaking it into pieces using a gun butt, rock, or any other handy implement. Not infrequently the job had already been accomplished when partial quantities remained in a crate and the crackers were reduced to shards after jolting all day in a wagon or on the back of a pack mule. Eating hardtack thus broken up was the prevalent way to consume it on the march, but other methods might be resorted to in camp. Provided sufficient water was available, crackers could be soaked in a cup of water, pulverized, then fried in bacon grease and topped with sugar, if available, to form a sort of pastry. "We older men had learned that five of these hardtack fried in bacon grease made a good meal with the addition of the bacon and huge tin cups of coffee," declared Private Theodore W. Goldin, Seventh Cavalry, "but the poor recruits had not yet learned this and we often found them eating all their hardtack at a single meal."[29]

Issued in great quantities during the Civil War, salt pork, dubbed "Cincinnati chicken" by soldiers, was far less popular among regulars, at least as a field ration. Contractors packed the meat in thick salt brine, two hundred pounds to the barrel. Without first being soaked for a few hours or parboiled to remove the preservative, it was practically inedible, nauseating at best. Nevertheless, Seventh Cavalryman Jacob Horner claimed that one of the "delicacies" for which he acquired a taste was "raw sow belly dipped in vinegar and sprinkled with salt." Unless forced, units on the frontier often refused to draw pork from the commissary because of its age and the generally poor storage that it had received. In garrison the stuff could be properly boiled and utilized in beans, soups, or stews, but in the field soldiers had little choice but to fry it or perhaps wrap it around a green stick and broil it over coals.

Even so, the heavy wooden barrels were cumbersome to handle and difficult to transport in the field.[30]

Soldiers by far preferred bacon as a meat ration. Smoked, lightly salted, and double-sacked for storage, the slabs were lighter and more easily hauled, especially on pack mules. Like other commodities issued to the troops, however, bacon was almost always war surplus. Some of it had become rancid, even wormy, some merely "rusty" with fungus accumulated on the surface. Even though "the hard tack had bugs in it and bacon had worms," Sergeant Perley S. Eaton sighed, "anything was good enough for a soldier in those days." The huge chunks were removed from their sacks, cleaved into hunks approximating the daily ration, and issued to the men. Upon receiving his ration, a trooper of the First Cavalry closely examined it: "Being interested in said piece of bacon, I unsheathed my knife and scraping a portion of the rust off of it, discovered the letters B. C. Truly a venerable piece of meat to feed men." The men usually fried bacon in their skillets, thereby saving the grease for hardtack, or sometimes varied that by broiling bacon on a green stick. Yet cooking was not always possible. When no fires were permitted, "for fear of being spotted by the Indians," Private Lines P. Wasson remarked, "raw bacon and hardtack was all we had, but we thought it pretty good at that time."[31]

The unrivaled mainstay of the ration was coffee, "which a soldier longs for more than food," contended Sergeant Adam Fox, Second Cavalry. Brazilian "Rio," the army standard for many years, was issued green in the whole bean, so it was necessary to roast and grind it before use. A company cook might have a mess pan available in which to roast a quantity of beans over coals, but most of the time the men resorted to their cups or mess tins to parch their own rations. "It would seem as though this were roughing it in earnest to friends in the East," observed Private George Howard, "with only a spoon, tin cup, and knife be expected to parch coffee." Now and then, when troops were accompanied by wagons, each company might bring along a coffee mill from its kitchen to facilitate grinding. But the usual practice, as explained by Private Louis Zinser, Third Cavalry, was for each man to "put a portion of it in a bag and take two rocks and pound it, thereby grinding it sufficiently." The soldier's quart tin cup served for both boiling and drinking. Receiving a fresh issue of coffee in the field during the Nez Perce Campaign, a soldier noted smugly that the label indicated it was "Old Java, we are getting hightoned now, Rio Coffee won't do anymore."³²

In some circumstances flour was hauled aboard the supply wagons or steamers and provided to the troops in lieu of hard bread or as a supplement to the regular ration. "We have run out of hardtacks and will have to bake our own bread," conceded Private Winfield S. Harvey in 1868 on the plains near Fort Cobb, Indian Territory. Officers sometimes charged company cooks with converting bulk flour into bread, when a few days' halt permitted, but with little equipment and often less knowledge of the craft the effort did not bode well. During an extended scout for Comanches in Texas, Private Matthews expressed his disappointment with the results of field baking: "At breakfast this morning I was handed something which from its color and weight I presumed must part of a brick, but was told by the cook that it was my ration of bread. . . . I politely . . . declined eating any of his fresh bread, preferring 'hard tack.'" Having a portion of flour ladled into his tin cup, the soldier was faced with what to do with it. The men usually had to rely on their individual resourcefulness. "Taking a tin cup and partly filling it with wheat flour," recalled a Seventh Cavalryman, "we would add water and make a paste, and then add a piece of pork, and cook the mess. It was difficult to dig it out of the cup." Those soldiers equipped with the two-piece meat can, incorporating a skillet and plate, were somewhat better prepared to make pancakes. Observing the cooking operation, however, a distressed medical officer explained that "the men were compelled to make a kind of thin cake of the flour by use of baking powder. These cakes were cooked in a frying pan, when they could procure them, or . . . in tin plates or split canteens. These cakes being fried over a quick fire, were merely browned on the surface, the interior being but uncooked dough." A few experienced men, like Private Edgar Hoffner, a second enlistment veteran, prided themselves on knowing how to make the best of primitive living conditions. "Today I traded vennison [sic] with one of the boys for flour, then baked bread," he explained. "First kneaded dough on a poncho . . . then dug a hole in the ground large enough for a mess pan . . . then put in hot coals and heated hole, then placed dough on a tin pan, turning mess pan over it placing coals over all, and baked til done. We had salt and baking powder. . . . We then made gravy of flour, water and bacon grease. With vennison steak and coffee, we had a fine supper." Only in the 1880s did the Subsistence Department finally begin providing cast-iron Dutch ovens for baking bread in the field, though of course the heavy articles could only be transported by wagon or pack mule.[33]

Campaigning afforded few luxuries in the way of food, but soldiers understandably availed themselves of special items when an opportunity presented, particularly when a sutler was allowed to accompany an expedition. A member of the 1876 Powder River Expedition, Private William E. Smith, related that he and other orderlies detailed to Colonel Ranald S. Mackenzie's headquarters pooled their money "and made up a nuff to bye a lot of cand [canned] stuff sutch as corn and tomatoes . . . we did a feast while this stuff lasted" (all odd spellings in the original). Another soldier, after subsisting on half rations and finally being able to purchase commercial foodstuffs, exclaimed that he was "living high. Bought some potatoes, butter, and peaches. This is the first square meal I have had for some time." Some officers concerned for their men's welfare ensured that company supplies included a few boxes of evaporated apples, which would become a welcome treat after a steady diet of bacon and hardtack. After the army added canned fresh beef, corned beef and baked beans to commissary stores in about 1880, these items became staples in the field whenever it was possible to take them along. In winter operations, however, canned food had a significant drawback. During the Sioux Campaign of 1890–91 in South Dakota, "We had to thaw [it] out before we could eat it," complained First Sergeant Charles N. Jansen.[34]

Troops involved in active campaigning frequently experienced moderate to severe food shortages when columns outdistanced their supply lines. Hardtack, and short rations at that, was often the only thing available, yet it was better than nothing. A soldier with Custer's 1869 pursuit of tribesmen in Indian Territory wrote that the men had been getting by on just two crackers a day for more than a week when a supply train finally reached the command. On another occasion, after the pack train failed to catch up with their column, and having had nothing to eat for thirty-six hours, a First Cavalryman wrote: "Every man wearing an elongated visage. A stranger coming into camp would think that we had lost a favorite dog." On the Powder River in 1877 men of the Second Cavalry trailing the Sioux were destitute of any food when they finally arrived in camp one night. Whereas there was usually no love lost between the cavalry and the infantry, those attitudes were often mollified with the reality of shared hardships. Private William F. Zimmer noted in his diary that he and his cavalry comrades "would have went hungry to bed only for the infantry. They gave us 4 hardtack apiece & some coffee, but no sugar." Bleak fare it may have been, but the hungry troopers nevertheless appreciated and remembered this compassionate act.[35]

Troops often foraged for game and other food either by choice or by necessity. Game was plentiful in most areas of the West, so many species of animals and fowl became welcome sources of fresh meat. When conditions permitted hunting, a few designated individuals or at times larger detachments were sent out to bag whatever the country provided. Numerous soldier accounts relate that hunters brought in buffalo, elk, deer, antelopes, rabbits, wild turkeys, prairie chickens, and even bears to supplement the larder and vary the diet. During Colonel Richard I. Dodge's 1875 expedition to the Black Hills, for example, a soldier exclaimed: "Eight deer [killed] today. . . . The one hundredth deer [was] roasted and disposed of with all the pomp and ceremony worthy of the event. The feast a genuine Nimrod affair."[36]

Fish, especially trout, also were eagerly sought after by the men, many of whom went to the field prepared with hooks and lines hoping for an opportunity to test their skill. Willow sticks (the preferred material when it could be obtained) or other types of branches served as rods and grasshoppers or even bits of bacon as bait. In a few instances experienced men had the forethought to take along seines for greater efficiency. "We pulled out a hundred and sixty of the prettiest mountain trouts I have ever saw [sic] . . . and we are having a fine supper," a Third Cavalryman wrote. Indeed under many circumstances life in the field could be an enjoyable summer outing.[37]

Regardless of the region in the West, intense summer sunlight beating down on white tents increased interior temperatures dramatically, making occupancy during daytime almost unbearable. Even after nightfall the heated canvas continued to radiate heat. But the solution was both simple and universal among frontier troops at any camp where they expected to remain for any length of time. "All the men fixing a shade to their tents," Sixth Infantryman Wilmot P. Sanford noted in his 1876 diary. Constructing a makeshift arbor was accomplished by first setting four tree branches, preferably with forks in the upper ends, upright in the ground, with cross pieces joining the tops.

Smaller poles and a covering of leafy branches or brush were then laid over the framework to form a shade a few feet above the tent, allowing a generous space for air flow above the tent. Known as ramadas in the Southwest, such structures were widely used by both Hispanic and Indian populations as shades under which to cook and lounge. Sometimes soldiers pooled labor and materials to build a single continuous ramada extending over an entire row of tents. The men found that such shelters not only cooled the canvas but had the added advantage of breaking the force of torrential rains and hail.[38]

Corporal Clarence Chrisman, a Thirteenth Infantryman in the field during the Geronimo Campaign, admitted that even when the men had shelter tents they did not always bother to erect them. "Thinking that it would be a pretty night . . . we slept on them. During the night it commenced to rain and we almost got drowned out. It was a comical sight to see the fellows waking up as they got wet and rustling around . . . in the drenching rain to get their tents up."[39]

Soldiers were not always afforded the relative comfort of being under canvas. Tents were left behind during forced marches and when scouts were conducted from established camps. Their absence could make for a decidedly dismal bivouac, as Private John P. Slough lamented in his Black Hills journal: "Command [a scouting command] have no tents, were slightly out of luck as a rain set in just after we made camp and continued until some hours after dark. Wet blankets followed as a consequence." Soldiers adapted to circumstances as best they could, however. "In these cases of travel without tents, the soldiers fashioned willow dome shelters, copying the Indian way," explained Private William H. White, "and covered them with the poncho rain-capes. Two or three men joining themselves together in one structure would make for themselves a good temporary shelter in this manner." But the men did not always carry even ponchos. A Third Cavalryman groaned: "It rained all day, and as our willow house only protects against the sun, we go to sleep tonight on a wet bed." The small shelters shared by a couple of soldiers sometimes featured circular bases, but a cavalry officer described in detail a more common design employed during the Great Sioux War: "Six or eight withes were sharpened at the heavier end and forced into the ground in two parallel rows about two and one-half feet apart. The tapering ends, being brought together and interlaced, formed a support about three feet in height for a blanket whose sides came to the ground and were fastened down with wooden pegs. . . . One end of this semi-cylindrical tepee was closed by an overcoat, a saddle blanket, or a piece of shelter tent." Soldiers trenched around the perimeters of their tents or shelters when there was a prospect of rain.[40]

Following a hard day's march in fair weather, most of the men were content simply to wrap up in a blanket and go to sleep. Soldiers in the field slept in their clothes, perhaps removing only their shoes or boots, though a participant in the 1876 Big Horn Expedition observed that "several men did not have their boots off for two weeks, at least." The blouse, when not needed for warmth, might be rolled for use as a pillow; otherwise the head could be propped on the haversack or saddle. "The only bedding that we have is a saddle blanket and overcoat, with some pine twiggs [sic] for mattress and the canopy of heaven for shelter," wrote Private Edgar Hoffner, First Cavalry. Indeed some soldiers were inclined, when time permitted, to make hard ground somewhat softer by loosening the soil beneath the hips with a knife, or laying down a bedding of grass, pine boughs, or other available foliage. At semipermanent camps inventive soldiers sometimes fabricated more elaborate beds using materials at hand. At a Sixteenth Infantry bivouac near Fort Sill, Indian Territory in 1878, Corporal Emil A. Bode described theirs: "Four wooden forks [were] driven into the ground with crosspieces for the foot and headboards. . . . Willow pieces [were] placed on top of this and fastened lengthways to the crossbars. We then cut enough prairie grass with our knives to make a good foundation on which to spread our buffalo robes and blankets. Our bed was completed with overcoat for a pillow, where we slept as warm and comfortable as in a brownstone house."[41]

When tents were pitched, bunkies joined their shelter halves to make the proverbial "dog tent." If nights were cold, they likewise combined their blankets and overcoats, along with body heat, for warmer sleeping, as described by an infantryman: "The blankets were put together by two or three men and one bed made of them. A rubber blanket or piece of canvas with a buffalo robe and some woolen blankets were used for the bedding, while one to three blankets, according to the atmosphere outside, were used as covering . . . in the morning . . . the whole rolled into a bundle for convenient transportation."[42]

Winter field service imposed even more daunting challenges and hardship. Sent in pursuit of a war party that had attacked some woodcutters sixty miles from Fort Sedgwick, Colorado Territory, in January 1867, a trooper of the Second Cavalry remembered that "the snow was so deep that we formed a line two deep and made a continual 'right-about-wheel' until the snow was trampled down. Many of the comrades were unable to dismount and had to be lifted out of their saddles. Here we remained until morning, stamping our feet to keep from freezing to death." A veteran Seventh Cavalryman described a practice when wagon-borne tools were available: "We would take some shovels and shovel the snow from a place about five or six feet square and build a fire on the ground. After the ground got thoroughly dried and warm we would shovel the snow away from another place and move the fire on to that place." Under those circumstances three or four men combined their blankets, overcoats, and shelter halves if they had them to make for relatively comfortable sleeping. Cavalry troopers also had the saddle blanket for added warmth. Private John Hechner, a Fifth Infantryman serving in the Texas Panhandle in late November 1874, during the latter part of the Red River War, told how he and a couple of other soldiers with access to spades "dug a hole & covered it with a wagon sheet and had a pretty good night's sleep." He noted that they made dugouts at every opportunity because getting themselves below ground was the best protection from winter winds and that a wagon sheet staked over the top aided measurably in retaining body heat. Thus infantrymen were advantaged when assigned to escort the trains.[43]

The Quartermaster Department did furnish larger tents, but troops on campaign seldom took them into the field. The common or "A" tent, derived from its shape like the letter, was quite popular for use in permanent camps because of its height, closed ends, and capacity for accommodating four or five men. However, weighing in at about twenty pounds and requiring poles, it was too heavy for other than wagon transportation. Although conical-shaped Sibley tents, eighteen feet in diameter, and sheet-iron tent stoves were available throughout the era, only infrequent references are made to their use in the field, other than during the Sioux Campaign of 1890–91. The obvious reason was they were bulky and extremely heavy. Fortunately, the Pine Ridge Reservation, the seat of war, was situated reasonably close to the railhead at Rushville, Nebraska, where such equipment could be shipped and then hauled by wagon to the troops.[44]

The amenities of camp life depended to a great degree on how much time the troops spent at any particular place. Halts were usually only a night or two during scouts and the demands of active Indian campaigning, which did not permit indulging in many creature comforts. But when the need for movement was not urgent commanders allowed their men brief respites. During summer 1874 Lieutenant Colonel George A. Custer's Black Hills Expedition paused along the creek in Prospect Valley. "We lay over and the 'boys,' nearly six hundred in number, were scattered along the banks of that creek for the time being converted into laundresses and busy as bees rubbing, scrubbing and splashing their 'linen?' in a genuine washwoman style," Private Theodore Ewert recorded in his diary. "This proved very welcome as we, of the rank and file, had only brought one change of underclothing . . . and both changes having been worn one week, we stood in need of a rest day." While clothes hung on branches and spread over bushes dried in the breeze, most men also took advantage of the opportunity to bathe before donning their freshly laundered garments. A Seventh Cavalryman in camp along the Yellowstone River late in the 1876 Sioux Campaign commented that camp was "all quiet here today. Have just had a good bath at the river, also a shave—a great luxury in this barren, uncivilized country." Bathing and doing laundry in the field undoubtedly had a refreshing effect on everyone, though "there was one great drawback to the common laundry, a dearth of soap." Nevertheless, a cold water wash of both body and clothing was infinitely better than living with one's own grime and sweat and the stench of others.[45]

Motivated officers concerned about the combat readiness of their men took advantage of layovers to conduct skirmish drill as well as some close order drill to reinforce discipline, lest the men become too lax. During the Geronimo Campaign a corporal commented that some of his Sixteenth Infantry comrades "lounged beneath trees and were instructed in identifying bugle calls and drilling by calls" to further prepare them, especially recruits, for combat.[46]

"Everybody in camp wants some tobacco and there is not an ounce in the train," lamented Private Edward Williams, Second Cavalry. For those soldiers who used tobacco, and the great majority did, being in the field for long periods could impose a real hardship when soldiers exhausted their individual supplies. As one soldier contended: "It was the wead [sic] that a soldier likes eaven [sic] better than he does

Whiskey." Some smokers became so desperate, according to Private James B. Frew, Fifth Cavalry, they were "crazy for tobacco" and were "smoking coffee grounds." The few nonsmokers, meanwhile, often quietly reserved their plugs, assured that sooner or later their stock would command high prices. A couple of days after tobacco became scarce in his troop during the Nez Perce Campaign, First Cavalryman Isaac H. Sembower noted that the users began paying $2.50 a pound and the next day $4.00. Only three days later demand drove the price to $10.00, nearly a month's pay. Pulverized dried tree leaves sometimes provided a degree of satisfaction. Also, "the bark of the tender shoots of the willow made a good substitute" for pipe tobacco, according to one man. The chewers were no better off. Private Luther Barker, Fifth Infantry, recounted that immediately following the Battle of Bear Paw Mountain in 1877 the destitute men in his rifle pit "hadn't had a chew of tobacco for so long that we could not smile anymore." The degree to which soldiers in the field valued their tobacco is reflected in the anger expressed by Private Hoffner when he discovered that a packer had stolen his supply. "If cussing could kill, there would be a vacancy in [the] packers ranks," he wrote. "We consider the loss of the tobacco the greatest as we are two hundred miles from our base."[47]

Mail was prized almost as highly as tobacco, although deliveries on campaign were always as irregular as they were uncertain. When mail did arrive, it sparked a great clamor among news-starved soldiers hungry for any word from the outside world. "There is a dead run after Newspapers in camp . . . ," a Second Cavalryman wrote, "they are so particular with them that there is some time more a riot in camp." Nevertheless, those troops at locations accessible by steamboat received mail rather reliably, along with supplies to prolong the expedition. Escorts for supply trains operating between forts and field depots also conveniently doubled as mail carriers. Independent expeditions, however, usually relied on civilian scouts or soldier-couriers conveying official dispatches among field commanders and their superiors. The trouble was, they did not always know where to find mobile commands in the unsettled and often poorly mapped regions of the West. A First Cavalry trooper involved in the pursuit of Sheepeater Indians in the mountains of Idaho recorded that two messengers carrying mail for the command searched for more than two weeks before finding it. Traversing hostile territory posed particular dangers for messengers. When

Private Henry Hubman and another soldier were dispatched with the mail from their field command in Montana Territory, he informed his brother: "We had to carry it 120 miles right through their [Cree] country and a pretty tough time we had of it as they set the prairie on fire and it drove us over the Milk River. We made it in 3 nights and 2 days starting at night."[48]

Marching, whether afoot or horseback, left the men with little energy or enthusiasm for recreation in camp. After establishing a bivouac, gathering fuel, cooking, and tending horses, those men not detailed for guard or picket duty were content simply to rest. Sergeant Perley S. Eaton related: "After supper we would sit around the camp fire and smoke our pipes, then unroll our blankets and spread them on the wet ground always using our overcoats for a pillow. . . . That was the way it went from day to day." During layovers in semipermanent camps where little or no enemy contact was expected, the men naturally fell back on some of their usual garrison pastimes: "playing cards[,] . . . singing religious, sentimental, & comic songs, reading, telling stories." Some soldiers, alone or in parties of two or three, went hunting both for sport and to supplement the larder with wild game. Now and then a horse or foot race, accompanied with betting, might be gotten up between companies as an exciting diversion. In areas like the Black Hills of Dakota Territory all other forms of recreation became secondary to panning for gold, to which soldiers avidly devoted themselves during every off-duty moment. When camped in gold- and silver-rich regions of the Southwest, many soldiers likewise spent their free time running "over the mountains in search of minerals, while some secretly worked with pick and shovel in lonely places expecting to strike it rich and become millionaires." Some of the more curious and adventuresome, especially in mountainous areas, undertook sightseeing hikes to promontories or other points of geological interest in the vicinity of camp.[49]

Regardless of where troops might be in the field, guards were always posted at night. The designated officer of the guard selected the specific guard posts or beats and made them known to his noncoms. Typically, depending on the size of the command, two noncommissioned officers and three reliefs made up the detail of the main guard. The members were inspected in an informal detachment guard mounting to ensure that arms and ammunition were in order. Those men not actually walking a beat remained together at a designated tent or other location somewhat apart from the main bivouac. As in garrison, guards were required to remain dressed and equipped at all times to be prepared for an emergency, but Private William B. Jett admitted that when relieved during one particularly cold, wet night in New Mexico Territory he "did what was positively contrary to orders. I took off my ammunition belt and then removed my wet clothing and got my two pieces of underclothing from my saddle pockets, put them on . . . and turned in for the next four hours. When I did all this I had reached the point of desperation and did not care what happened to me." Private William E. Smith, with Mackenzie's command in 1876, noted that when the old guard was relieved in the morning the members were responsible for straightening tents and gathering firewood for the regimental headquarters.[50]

Soon after the troopers arrived in camp the horses were groomed, watered, and conducted under an armed herd guard to wherever pasturage might be found near camp when no enemy presence threatened. When in a hostile situation, each horse would be tethered with picket pin and lariat and sidelined so that it might graze but not be stampeded. When the layover was of any duration, the horses were permitted to graze some distance away from camp all day and were brought to camp before nightfall. The herd guards were responsible for keeping the horses from drifting away from the ground selected and to be brought to camp at the prescribed time. The men on herd guard usually remained mounted and vigilant, especially in enemy country, to sound alarm and ward off any attack on the herd.[51]

As in garrison, each cavalry company additionally assigned men in three reliefs under an NCO to act as stable guards on those occasions when the horses were kept in camp and tied to the picket line for safety. Stable guards walked the picket lines in front of the tents to ensure that horses remained securely tied and did not become entangled and that none were taken from the line without proper authority. The stable guard went on duty at retreat—sunset—when the horses were gathered and brought in from grazing.

A command operating in hostile territory customarily established one or more picket posts in the vicinity of camp to serve as early warning of an approaching enemy. During daytime the picket was located some distance from camp, preferably on an elevation providing a view of both the surrounding countryside and the bivouac. At night the sentinel withdrew to a prearranged lower point at the rear of that eminence, the better to see an approaching enemy in relief against the horizon, while remaining nearly invisible to the enemy. Private Thomas N. Way, Seventh Cavalry, captured the loneliness of the assignment when he was placed "on picket duty two miles from camp dismounted. Not very pleasant a place to be in an Indian country, but duty must be done so I must not complain." Just as in garrison, every member of the company, with the possible exception of cooks, took a turn at guard. A Fifth Cavalryman remembered that a corporal in his troop equitably assigned reliefs by scratching the numbers "1, 2 or 3 on cartridges and reaching into his hat for your night trick." The corporal or sergeant of the guard awakened each relief and accompanied him to the outpost to execute the change. An infantryman at a semipermanent camp in New Mexico Territory explained that they arranged their outposts in the form of "small forts or redoubts [were] erected as breastworks . . . pickets were thrown out every night in the ravines and different approaches to the camp, in addition to a permanent guard on top of one of the hills."[52]

When the threat was great and the camp large, several picket posts of three men each might form a "chain guard" entirely around the bivouac or between two points, such as a protective arc covering a riverside camp. The soldiers assigned to each post were responsible for managing their own reliefs in a system known as a running guard, making certain that at least one man at each outpost was awake at all times. Ensuring that was the job of the officer of the day. "I am Officer [of the] Day, have 21 privates and 5 non. Com Officers on picket which gives me all the exercise I want to visit them," wrote Captain Gerhard L. Luhn, Fourth Infantry, with Crook's column. "It takes me 1½ hours to make the round on horseback, each picket has a company designated to support it in case of firing, but our men are getting so well used to picket duty, that we have very few false alarms."[53]

Nevertheless, false alarms were bound to occur. Sometimes nervous, inexperienced sentries fired at noises or perceived enemies in the night. At a sentinel's shot, the NCO and other members of the guard double-timed to that outpost immediately, while everyone else in the camp turned out under arms and fell in as companies. For tired, chilled men, as one soldier recounted, the experience was never pleasant. "While you are standing there shivering and yawning, five, ten, fifteen, and possibly sixty minutes elapse 'till finally the corporal . . . rides in and reports to the commanding officer that the alarm was a false one and that [it] . . . on closer inspection turned out to be 'bunches of grass.'" Other intruders were real enough. At a Third Cavalry camp in the Black Hills in 1877, Private Edward D. Barker exclaimed: "We were awaken[ed] this morning by a very rapid fireing by the centinel on duty. All jumped up in a hurry and seized our guns. We thought the Indians had made an attacked on the camp, but . . . the cause of all the racket was a deer. . . . The centinel could not resist the temptation . . . and we had some venison fore breakfast" (all odd spellings in the original). Had the sentry missed the deer, he would not have been forgiven so easily.[54]

The trooper firing that shot should have considered himself extremely fortunate to have escaped punishment for his impetuous act. Even though life may have been less regimented in the field, discipline in the regulars was no less strict. An unwarranted shot by a sentinel, particularly during the early morning hours when attacks traditionally occurred, was a serious breach of discipline seldom overlooked by the officers. Private Ami F. Mulford recounted an event during the Nez Perce Campaign when "two men on picket duty fired their guns at jackrabbits, and were ordered brought in. They were taken before [Lieutenant] Colonel [Elmer] Otis, who lectured them and placed them in charge of the guard, with orders that the culprits be required to walk during the marches for a whole week." Although Mulford did not identify these men, they were likely among the ill-trained recruits hurriedly dispatched to the cavalry following the Battle of the Little Bighorn. He added, however, that the punishment Otis meted out was probably not harsh enough to make the desired impression, one of the errant men quipping that they "got two rabbits and are to have a vacation for a whole week." In another instance two thirsty Second Cavalrymen left their column without permission to get a drink of water during the Jenney Expedition and were given light punishment in the form of walking the rest of the way to camp.[55]

Sentencing cavalrymen to march on foot, under guard, at the rear of the column was commonplace when units were on the move, giving individuals ample opportunity to consider the consequences of disobedience. Yet some officers devised harsher variations for violations of "good order and discipline." An errant Fourth Cavalryman on the regiment's march from Arizona to New Mexico in 1881 had a lot of time for reflection when he was forced to walk two hundred miles while carrying a thirty-pound log. Farrier Winfield S. Harvey, Seventh Cavalry, related that substitutions for weights were made when logs might not have been readily available. He wrote that at a camp near Medicine Bluff, Indian Territory, "three men of our Troop had to carry saddles for not being out for [Sunday] inspection at the first call."[56]

A soldier might well have been abused, but the cavalry had no tolerance for the mistreatment of horses. One man, for example, was taught a hard lesson after he failed to water his mount at the proper time. At water call for several days thereafter he was made to wear a halter and was led to the creek with the horses. When Captain Thomas H. French happened to see one of his Seventh Cavalry troopers striking his mount during the 1873 Yellowstone Expedition, he punished the man by ordering him to dismount and lead his horse at the rear of the company. Defiant, the soldier sat on the ground and refused to walk. The captain thereupon ordered a member of the stable guard to fasten one end of his lariat to his saddle, placing the other around the man's neck, and to drag him if he would not walk. After being dragged along on the ground for a short distance, the soldier decided that walking would in fact be better.[57]

More serious offenses like drunkenness or attempted desertion were rewarded with confinement, but in the absence of a guardhouse that usually called for some creative thinking by the officers. A Seventh Cavalry trooper described Custer's improvised, and rather elaborate, facility for holding prisoners at an established camp on Big Creek, near Fort Hays, Kansas. It consisted of "a circular hole in the ground about twenty feet deep and at least thirty or forty feet wide. He had a large butt of a tree erected perpendicularly in the center of the hole, so the crotch of the tree extended a little over the level of the ground . . . [with] logs laid across to answer the purpose of rafters. . . . Then had hay and bagging put on top of that and covered . . . over with several feet of earth, having left a hole in the center of it . . . for a door." The more common form of restraint, especially when troops were on the march, was simply tying their hands and feet. A Seventh Cavalry soldier, for example, was kept tied up all day for being dirty on guard mount inspection at a field camp. Wagon wheels also served as convenient devices for "spread-eagling" men by tying their wrists to the rim at opposite points. In December 1876, as Colonel Mackenzie's regiment was moving from Fort Fetterman, Wyoming Territory, to Camp Robinson, Nebraska, one of his men wrote: "The boys in my tent were on gard [sic] and they made a raid on a whiskey wagon that was near. Some of the boys goot tide [sic] up to wagons." Trees also served the purpose.[58]

During a cold winter march, with two feet of snow on the ground, Second Cavalryman William F. Zimmer related that after some soldiers of the rear guard obtained liquor and arrived in camp drunk one man "got his ear broke by the corporal for refusing some duty," while another man "was riding his horse around like some Irish duke. He got tied up to a cottonwood tree for 3 hours to freeze sober." On those occasions when wagons or trees were unavailable, two or three offenders might be tied together and left that way for twenty-four hours. Such stern disciplinary measures, however, did not necessarily have a positive effect on morale among the rank and file. During the 1873 Yellowstone Expedition, Private Way grumbled: "The men are getting dissatisfied with the treatment they receive by the company officers. One man was tied up for a mere nothing today."[59]

Long periods of field service wore down officers and men alike, physically and psychologically. Simply contending with the natural environment on daily basis was tedious, aggravating, and sometimes dangerous. Private John O. Stotts said that the men became so accustomed to prairie rattlesnakes while marching across the plains that "we paid little attention to them. . . . Taurantulas [sic] we saw nearly [every] day and those are dreaded worse than snakes." Rattlesnakes of one species or another were commonplace throughout the West, and soldiers learned to be alert to their presence. In one instance, upon arriving in camp in New Mexico Territory and lying down for a few minutes rest, a cavalryman jumped up when he discovered a four-foot rattler under his blanket. Although snakebites were remarkably rare, considering the number of men in the field over the years, they did occur. First-aid training was nonexistent at that time, but accounts suggest that common knowledge dictated constriction of the blood flow above the wound, followed by lancing to drain the poison. In one instance, however, Sergeant George S. Howard recorded that when a snake struck an Irishman in his troop, "the doctor . . . burned the wound and poured ammonia on it. McManus enjoyed the whiskey to kill the pain. He will live." Soldiers also occasionally suffered bites by scorpions and tarantulas in the deserts of the Southwest but seem not to have considered them any more serious than a bee sting. Ants, too, were pervasive and could create real discomfort when someone became careless, as related by a Fourteenth Infantryman who spread his blanket on an inviting patch of grass. "I felt about a dozen of the most excruciating bites on my body and legs . . . ants had crawled under my clothing and next to the skin in a way that made me wince."[60]

More annoying than snakes and other critters were mosquitoes. They could be particularly aggravating on the plains and in the Rocky Mountains, where, according to one soldier, they were "as thick as redheaded children in Utah." He added that mosquitoes, "like the creditor, put in their bills at the most unreasonable moment." Private George McAnulty, Ninth Infantry, swore that the mosquitoes in Wyoming Territory were "almost big enough to stand on the ground & drink out of a tea cup." Warm nights could be torture and seemingly endless for soldiers bivouacked in tents, where the whining insects tended to collect, only to disappear with the morning sun.[61]

Regardless of the region in which troops were operating, adequate sources of potable water were of paramount importance for man and beast. Without it, military operations quickly devolved into struggles for survival. In July 1877 a platoon of the Tenth Cavalry struck out upon the southern Staked Plains in pursuit of Comanche raiders. As the detachment rode farther into that trackless region, and one after another of the predicted waterholes proved to be dry, the commander finally turned back. After covering a circuitous route of 440 miles, and existing the last eighty-six hours without water, the black troopers finally staggered back to their original base camp. Flowing streams and springs usually provided good water, but sluggish creeks and mere waterholes were frequently brackish and alkaline. Private William W. Jordan of the Fourteenth Infantry described Pumpkin Creek in eastern Montana Territory as being "about the color of yellow ochre, and as thick as mud. . . . We could not make coffee with it, or at least when made it had not the slightest taste of coffee." Upon arriving at a camp, a Second Cavalry trooper recorded in his diary: "We are . . . at a large basin of water, & the water is so bad that it nearly gags one to drink it." Sometimes the only water available was water accumulated in holes in rock formations or depressions on the prairie. Happy at finally finding even that sort of water during a scout in Wyoming, First Sergeant James S. McClellan assessed it as "thick with mud but it seems the best water I ever drank."[62]

The men often resorted to drinking stagnant water collected in buffalo wallows and other pools from which thirsty horses and mules would turn away. Predictably, the men suffered terribly from diarrhea and dysentery brought on by the combination of polluted water and poor diet. Intestinal cramping and frequent calls of nature quickly eroded morale, causing men to straggle and even discouraged cavalrymen from riding their horses because of the frequent need to dismount. A Second Cavalry sergeant, after consuming tainted water, experienced painful cramps and reported to the expedition surgeon hoping "to get a snifter [whiskey] but is fooled. The Dr. prescribes a pill instead." Army doctors, when accompanying troops at all, usually dispensed opium pills to mitigate the effects of severe intestinal disorders, but one contract doctor refused to do even that. Private Theodore Ewert described the plight of one of his Seventh Cavalry comrades: "Cunningham was taken with acute dysentery about the 13th and went on the sick report. The doctor ? . . . marked him for duty, . . . The disease becoming worse, he went on again the 17th. . . . [The doctor] marked him for duty again. [On] the 18th . . . Cunningham, through weakness and loss of blood, fainted and fell off his horse." Although the doctor, whom the soldiers dubbed "Butcher Allen," went to look at the trooper, he did nothing. Private Cunningham died later that day.[63]

Rapidly moving commands that sacrificed tents or ponchos, or both, in favor of saving weight often had pause to regret that decision after they were in the field. During an extended scout in the usually arid Texas Panhandle in the summer of 1872 Private Eddie Matthews described the plight of the Eighth Cavalry: "The rain continues to fall making it rather disagreeable for us, as we have no tents. All we have to do is stand out and weather the storm. . . . I imagine that I feel the effect of this exposure in my bones, but suppose it will soon pass away." Indeed many men developed severe rheumatism either during their military service or later in life as a result of the exposure that they had experienced. More immediate afflictions included inflammation of the joints, head and chest colds, fever, and catarrh, but when no ambulances or wagons were available, wrote Private Eugene Geant, "any man who took sick was out of luck."[64]

Winter only compounded those conditions, snow blindness being a common affliction. Besides causing intense pain, "the eye became very much inflamed," a First Cavalry officer attested, "some being so swelled up as to be entirely closed, and the men's horses had to be led on the march. As many as could procured goggles . . . and instructions were given for every man to keep his face blackened with burnt cork, which will relieve the eyes from the terrible glare of the sun and snow." Ice and snow created slippery footing, causing horses to fall on their riders, sometimes breaking their arms or legs. Moreover, when troops clad only in regulation woolen overcoats and mittens were compelled to be in the open, exposed to wind and subzero temperatures, frostbitten ears and extremities could hardly be avoided. While making a march from the Canadian border to Fort Shaw in 1871, Company B, Seventh Infantry, was caught in a blizzard, resulting in numerous frozen hands and/or feet. One sergeant later had both his hands and feet amputated.[65]

Of all the hard service that soldiers experienced during the Indian Wars era, one event stands out above all others as the most horrendous—the Starvation or Horse Meat March. General George Crook's disheartening stern chase of the Sioux in late summer 1876, following the army's reversals at the Battles of the Rosebud and Little Bighorn, embodied the worst conditions, save perhaps freezing temperatures, that soldiers might encounter in the field. After tarrying in his Goose Creek camp for weeks awaiting reinforcements after the Rosebud fight, Crook eventually took up the Indian trail hoping to trap the hostiles between his force and that of General Alfred Terry, which he had been informed was on the Yellowstone. Crook's column, now bolstered to nearly 2,300 men, including some 1,800 cavalry and infantry soldiers, 250 allied Indians, and 200 packers and other civilians, moved cautiously north down Rosebud Creek. In early August the two columns formed an unexpected juncture, but the bag was empty. Sitting Bull had eluded both. The combined forces, with Terry's adding over 1,600 troops to the total, ponderously snaked eastward following the hostiles' trail over the divide to Tongue River. It became quickly apparent to Terry that Crook's method of relying on pack animals was more sensible than taking wagons. He therefore converted draft mules to carrying his supplies and sent his train with unneeded baggage and part of the infantry back to a steamer-supplied depot on the Yellowstone to await developments. Marching twenty miles down the serpentine course of Tongue River on August 6, Private Richard Flynn noted in his diary that they had "crossed the . . . river 13 times. . . . The Infantry was not allowed to make any delay in crossing . . . and in consequence of fording with their shoes and stockings on the men were most exhausted after to[day's] march."[66]

But the army's challenge in chasing down the Sioux was to become infinitely more difficult. Weather on the northern plains is notoriously unpredictable, and August 1876 proved to be no exception. Whereas the days had been hot and dry, and much of the march had been through prairie left fire-blackened by the Indians, rain began falling on August 10 and continued without interruption. With cooking fires out of the question much of the time, hardtack and raw bacon became standard fare. Private William W. Jordan, a member of Company C, Fourteenth Infantry, described the camp on Tongue River: "Has rained steadily for forty-eight hours. . . . No shelter of any kind. Stood up all night with blankets over our shoulders, and soaking wet." Jordan was nevertheless impressed with a man in his company, Private Andy Shuttles, who had previously been shot in the nose and snored loudly as a result of his wound. Jordan claimed that Shuttles was "the first man I ever saw who could lie down in a pool of water . . . and sleep like a top."[67]

The wind-driven downpour continued unabated. Already difficult marching was compounded by sticky mud. "Some of the newly-enlisted infantry grew desperate," recorded newspaperman John Finerty, who accompanied the expedition, "their feet bleeding and their legs swollen from the continuous tramp—and refused to move a step." These were mostly unconditioned recruits belonging to the Fifth and Twenty-Second Infantry, who had ridden aboard steamers to join Terry's column a few weeks previous. Those truly too lame to walk were hoisted onto the ponies of the Indian allies. In the meantime Crook's undernourished cavalry horses began to falter; those unable to continue were abandoned or shot. Yet conditions would become much worse.[68]

Crook's doughboys, however, were the exception. "Chambers' astonishing infantry," as the journalist dubbed the battalion composed of elements of the Fourth, Ninth, and Fourteenth regiments, having previously walked overland all the way from Fort Fetterman, endured "the full march, and not a man fell out of the ranks."[69]

By mid-month, with the column still struggling through rain and mud, a disheartened soldier noted in his diary: "Our rations are mixed with sand, our blankets look like sheets of mud . . . will not get any rations for three days. That isn't very encouraging." They made another twenty miles that day, with the horses staggering so much that most troopers dismounted and led their animals. When one fell and could not be coaxed to stand, the saddle and other equipment had to be either loaded on a mule or abandoned along the trail. All of the extra led horses that had been brought along as replacements had already been pressed into service. Only on August 22, after having left the valley of the Tongue, crossed over to Powder River, and descended to its mouth, did the Big Horn and Yellowstone Expedition finally find plentiful grass and the steamer *Far West* awaiting them with supplies. The rain still continued with hardly a break. After one particularly hard storm, as men working in pairs assisted each other in wringing out overcoats and blankets, journalist Finerty overheard an Irishman roundly condemning whiskey for leading him into the army. Attempting to strike a more positive chord, his bunkie chided: "Now, George, wouldn't you just wish you had a little drop to mix with all this water?" Water they would continue to receive in abundance; whiskey would be only a fond memory for weeks to come.[70]

Realizing that their large force was unwieldy and unsustainable, the generals decided to part company—Terry circling north beyond the Yellowstone in hopes of thwarting any Sioux attempt to move toward Canada and Crook dogging the trail leading eastward toward the Little Missouri in Dakota Territory. Crook's men persisted, with the horses sinking up to their knees in mud; "soldiers' shoes were pulled off in trying to drag their feet through the sticky slime" of accumulated clay mud and grass that balled to enormous proportions on their feet. The deluge on the treeless plain was unremitting. One two-hour storm was made all the more punishing by a prolonged pounding with "hail stones about the size of duck eggs," according to Private Richard Flynn, Fourth Infantry. The men's only protection was to cover their heads and shoulders with folded blankets. Horses could only turn tails into the wind and lower their heads seeking relief. Resigning himself to the hellish conditions, a twenty-two-year old cavalry trooper from

Bellville, Illinois, expressed the sentiment of many soldiers in that column: "I am bearing more than I ever thought I could bear when I left home." Some surely considered desertion, but the abominable conditions would not have changed—besides there was nowhere to go.[71]

By early September the troops were reduced to half rations of coffee and hard bread. Their only remaining cooking utensils were their quart tin cups; everything else had been lost or jettisoned. "The infantry are becoming desperate and we are wondering when this will end," wrote a Second Cavalryman. "Our horses are dropping every day, and this weather rots and decays them, but we are compelled to eat." Cavalry horses, deprived of grain and unable to find much grazing, weakened and died by the score, their riders and the doughboys immediately carving off pieces of their flesh where the animals lay. Unable to build fires much of the time as a result of the lack of wood and only sodden chips to be found, Private Oliver C. Pollock wrote that "we partook of raw horseflesh," at times seasoned with gunpowder emptied from soldiers' cartridges.[72]

Upon finally reaching the headwaters of the Heart River, Crook had to make a choice: either trek another 160 miles farther east to Fort Abraham Lincoln on the Missouri River or turn south toward the Black Hills in the vain hope of intercepting Indians returning to the safety of the agencies in northwest Nebraska. In either event he had only enough half rations to last two and a half days, and those would have to be stretched to last a week. Crook calculated that he would lose at least two weeks' time, and most of his remaining horses, by going to Fort Lincoln. Better to go south, he concluded, and perhaps salvage something of the campaign and his reputation. The mining settlements of Custer City and Deadwood presented sources of resupply. The troops, however, received that news with considerable disappointment and growling. "I firmly believe from my general knowledge of the American soldier," declared Sergeant John Powers, "that there would not have been a murmur of disaffection . . . had there been a show of a cause for . . . such a state of affairs, but it was merely to satisfy a fleeting fancy of General Crook." Observing that the general's beloved packers seemed not to experience the same food shortages as the troops, someone in the ranks vented his frustration by composing an additional sarcastic verse to the popular Harrigan & Hart ballad:

> But 'twas out upon the Yellowstone we had the damndest time,
> Faith we made the trip wid Rosebud George, six months without a dime.
> Some eighteen hundred miles we went through hunger, mud, and rain,
> Wid backs all bare, and rations rare, no chance for grass or grain;
> Wid "bunkies starvin'" by your side, no rations was the rule,
> Sure 'twas ate the your boots and saddles, you brutes, but feed the packer and the mule.
> But you know full well that in your fights no soldier lad was slow,
> And it wasn't the packer that won ye a star in the Regular Army, O![73]

After a portion of the command attacked and captured a small Sioux village at Slim Buttes on September 9, the troops retrieved several tons of dried buffalo, elk, venison, and other foodstuffs. "This was a Godsend," remarked Private George S. Howard, Second Cavalry. "Besides the meat, the Indians had immense quantities of dried berries and plums put up in bags for transportation." Surviving on captured food, in fact, was not at all uncommon. Commenting on the quality of similar food found in a camp later that year, a Twenty-Second Infantryman thought that it "was disgusting stuff to eat, but I tell you we were mighty hungry and glad to get it. We ate it with relish."[74]

Captured Indian ponies offered another source of sustenance. One cavalryman quipped that "the old sore backed [cavalry] horses are at a discount since we got the indian [*sic*] ponies to eat." Taking advantage of a brief break in the weather, another soldier in that miserable column was cheered to report: "We were living in style this morning . . . [on] fried horse meat, stewed bull berries, and choke cherries as desert, and coffee. My bunky surprised me this morning. He had two hard tack hidden in his saddle pocket, but for fear that it would be stolen, he divided them, and not a crumb was left." Despite the slight improvement in the fare, the wretched conditions continued to exact a horrible toll on the men. Just a few days later the same trooper despondently wrote:: "Still raining and almost exhausted. All of our infantry are not with us yet, but marching was too much for some, cavalry dismounted. The suffering is very great. They had to send back a detachment to pick up stragglers. . . . No one seems to fear death, as we might just as well be dead as living the way we are now."[75]

A few days later a battalion of cavalry that had pressed ahead to secure supplies returned with a civilian train bearing flour and vegetables along with a herd of cattle. But, as it turned out, some of the food was not free, even for Uncle Sam's famished warriors. Private Jordan described the reaction when soldiers, having reached the limits of physical and mental exhaustion, heard the announcement of profiteers who had tagged along. "One Jew wanted to sell it [bread] at $1 per loaf, but the other demurred, saying, . . . 'let tem [sic] pay $2 for it.' While the row was in progress the moneyless soldiers overturned the wagon, drove the Jews off with stones, and made short work of the bread and provisions it contained." Sympathetic officers, no better off themselves, turned a blind eye. Making camp on the Belle Fourche River, the troops gorged themselves on flapjacks, bread, and fresh beef roasted on willow sticks held over open fires. "Such a time cooking," wrote a Fifth Cavalryman, "Boys cooked till near midnight."[76]

The worst was behind them at last. Taking note of the men around him, Third Cavalryman Zinser observed: "None of us have shaved for this whole trip. We have long hair, look wild in appearance, ragged and some are barefooted." Despite now having food, the troops still had to limp some one hundred and fifty miles farther south to reach Fort Robinson, Nebraska, where the expedition would disband. From there they would return to their home posts. By that time most of the men had already been in the field for more than four months and had marched an average of 1,400 miles.[77]

To a man, soldiers were always eager to return home, wherever that might be. "It was near sunset when we rode into Fort Klamath, our garrison," recounted a First Cavalryman returning from the Modoc War. "This small and ancient fort, located in the very heart of the Cascade Mountains, looked forlorn and with nothing to spare—but it was our home." Sergeant John Cox, First Infantry, who had left Fort Randall, Dakota Territory, on a summer expedition to the Black Hills in 1874, expressed his joy at once again seeing the post: "As I came limping back, after a thousand-mile march, I thought the old garrison was almost paradise."[78]

After spending months in the field, the men coming back into the posts bore little resemblance to their soldierly appearance at the time they had left. Typical were three companies of the Thirteenth Infantry marching back into Fort Wingate, New Mexico Territory, after a year spent pursuing Apaches. Corporal Clarence Chrisman was among them. "The only way you could detect that we were Regular army soldiers was by examining our arms and equipment," he declared. "Aside from that, I must say that we looked more like tramps than soldiers. . . . We returned almost literally covered with buckskin, scarcely a patch of blue to be seen and had on all sorts of hats, boots, or shoes, or what was left of them. . . . One thing we had in plenty, and that was whiskers, and sunburned." Some commanders at headquarters posts turned out the band "so as to brace us up, and enable us to come in more like soldiers than stragglers," recalled Private E. W. Pagel, a Sixth Infantryman stationed at Fort Buford, Dakota Territory. More often than not, the welcoming band struck up a traditional Civil War air, "When Johnny Comes Marching Home." With or without fanfare, Private Edgar Hoffner wrote: "A more pleased lot of men would be difficult to find . . . weuns [sic] having got back to home quarters."[79]

One of Pagel's comrades was comforted to find the company assigned to its former barracks, whereupon he happily noted that he "moved into our old quarters and my old place" in the squad room. "This day will be long remembered," lamented another soldier now grateful for small pleasures. "We entered our winter quarters the first time in six months, to live under a roof and sleep in a bunk all to myself."[80]

Most men immediately underwent a remarkable transformation by shedding and burning their filthy rags, along with any resident lice, drawing new clothing, bathing, and getting a shave. As one trooper remarked: "We hardly know one another." Refreshed and somewhat revived after coming in from the field, many of the boys, according to a Second Cavalryman at Fort Laramie, indulged in "a day and night of beer, wines, and jollity . . . most all hands visit the Hag [sic] Ranches, much shooting but no one hurt." Others, particularly the older men, were simply too spent to have any enthusiasm for celebrating or prostitutes. "I remember Sergeant Thomas Gray had prepared D Company a good dinner" upon its return to Cantonment on Tongue River, recalled Private Luther Barker, "but we would rather sleep than eat." When the first sergeant entered the squad room to announce that Colonel Nelson Miles had excused the company from duty for three days, Barker's Irish bunkie lay back contentedly and sighed, "Bless Paddy Miles." The boys were home.[81]

The nature of field service began changing during the 1880s as active scouting and Indian campaigning diminished. On the southern plains army expeditions had crushed the Comanches, Kiowas, and Southern Cheyennes, compelling them to submit to the reservations in Indian Territory. The Great Sioux War of 1876–77 finally sputtered out after a series of mostly small engagements with the scattered roamer bands, forcing them too to accept reservation life. Crazy Horse had been killed, and Sitting Bull eventually returned from his haven in Canada to surrender. Other briefer but nonetheless arduous campaigns had been prosecuted against some of the northwestern tribes: the Nez Perces, Bannocks, Paiutes, and Sheepeaters. In 1878 the Northern Cheyennes made a desperate bid to dash from the Indian Territory to their homeland in the Powder River country and in doing so managed to evade the numerous troops fielded against them. To be sure, hard service continued intermittently for a few years against the recalcitrant Mescalero, Warm Springs, and Chiricahua Apache tribes in the Southwest, but this was largely sporadic hit-and-run warfare not involving the heavy columns seen during the previous two decades.

Aside from the troops directly involved in those operations at any particular time, however, the army in the West settled into the routine of garrison life with few interruptions. As time passed, only a relatively few old-timers in the ranks remembered the days of "real soldiering" on the Great Plains and in the Yellowstone country. Retired Lieutenant Colonel George A. Forsyth, Civil War veteran, hero of the 1868 Battle of Beecher's Island, and experienced frontier cavalry officer, observed: "Sometimes in uneventful days, the monotony of barrack life slowly breeds discontent, no matter how comfortably housed nor how well fed the troops might be. . . . A shrewd commanding officer will find some field duty for all the men who can be safely spared from garrison." Indeed many post commanders followed that advice by sending out details, or even whole companies, to improve roads, construct telegraph lines, and map the surrounding country. During fair seasons battalion-strength bodies, often equipped in heavy marching order, were ordered out on practice marches over designated routes to establish bivouacs at predetermined locations offering the basic necessities of wood, water, and grass. Once there the troops might spend a couple of weeks conducting target practice, drilling in tactics, and being instructed in camp security, signaling, and other practical exercises. As Forsyth accurately predicted: "The result is that in two or three weeks, the men return to the post . . . perfectly content and glad to be back to the comforts of barrack life once more."[82]

These "outings," as one officer referred to them, increased in popularity and were adopted by numerous post and regimental commanders as annual events. Private Eugene Frierson, Tenth Cavalry, explained that the exercises in which he participated were "for the purpose of giving 'recruits' (young soldiers) an idea of field service, a knowledge essential to the duties of a soldier in time of actual warfare, and to give older soldiers more practice and experience in the duties and knowledge pertaining to the same." Brigadier General Nelson A. Miles, who had campaigned extensively and successfully on the plains and in the Southwest, went a step further by instituting a training program involving practical field maneuvers in the Department of Arizona. He directed that all troops, except for skeleton garrisons left at each post, were to be placed on field duty during the months of September and October, during which they would be schooled in all aspects of field service. Moreover, they participated in war games in which the garrisons of the various posts competed with each other in sham exercises rooted in Indian tactics.[83]

Penning a letter to the editor of the *Army & Navy Journal* in 1887, Second Lieutenant Abner Pickering, Second Infantry, urged that "a large 'camp of instruction' be established in every Department to be composed of the majority of the troops from each of the organizations in the Department." With the curtain all but closed on Indian fighting, even the likes of General Crook perceived the advantages of getting the troops out of garrison and the companies of the various regiments assembled in at least battalion strength, many of which had not served together for many years. These exercises also brought together the various arms of service—infantry, cavalry, and sometimes even artillery—for tactical training in conventional warfare methods.

The staff branches, including the Signal Corps and the newly authorized Hospital Corps, also participated.[84]

Crook's concept, shamelessly adopted from Pickering's, was to concentrate the troops at some designated location, usually for a month in early fall, where line organizations would drill as battalions in combined arms exercises. Further specific instruction was provided in marksmanship, scouting, signaling, treatment of the wounded, and constructing rifle pits. In 1889 the Department of the Missouri conducted a camp in the Cherokee Strip, in present-day Oklahoma, involving two regiments of cavalry, a brigade of infantry, and three batteries of light artillery practicing "formations for attacks and defense, the disposition for security and information, and the operations of hostile contact . . . in accordance with proper military principles." The camps of instruction, particularly on Miles's plan of guerrilla tactics, would have been a step in the right direction had they been inaugurated a quarter-century earlier, but that would have been virtually impossible under the circumstances. As it was, field training came too late to benefit soldiers for the Indian-fighting role in which they had been cast on the western frontier. They had needed to learn the hard way, by experience.[85]

CHAPTER 15

"Our Orders Were to Go after Them"

Regulars and Red Men

The relationship between American Indians and the blue-clad regulars is popularly viewed only as a hostile one in the context of continuous unrelenting warfare throughout the Trans-Mississippi West. That misimpression ignores the realities that the U.S. government maintained favorable relations with all but a relatively small number of Indian tribes and that most soldiers of the post–Civil War era, except for those in the cavalry prior to the mid-1880s, rarely encountered a so-called hostile. During the quarter-century following the Civil War the army recorded fewer than 1,100 engagements with Indians, and all but 134 of those occurred before 1880. When compared with the number of men who served in the army during that same period, the percentage who experienced combat was relatively small, but those who did never forgot it. Contrasted with that, many men never even saw an Indian, in action or otherwise, during a five-year enlistment. One bitter cavalryman expressed a common frustration upon returning from the field in 1872: "The scout as a 'failure' was a decided 'success.' We accomplished nothing, and the cost of the expedition will greatly add to the 'National Debt.'"[1]

Opinions held by the rank and file regarding Indians stemmed from several sources and in not a few instances were later modified as a result of actual association with Indians in the West, falling under the influence of other soldiers after entering the service, or witnessing or being told of Indian atrocities. Coming to grips with real conditions on the frontier and experiencing combat personally also shaped their views. That is to say, there can be no universal characterization of how soldiers felt about Indian people.

The American public, at least those who were able to read, were indelibly influenced by the popular literature of the day. The five-novel series Leatherstocking Tales by James Fenimore Cooper, the prolific New York novelist of the early part of the nineteenth century, created a strong impression of some of the tribes inhabiting the Northeast during the previous century. Cooper's idyllic image of Native Americans, notably portrayed in *The Last of the Mohicans*, cemented in the minds of many white Americans the notion of the "noble savage" or conversely an impression of a fierce, merciless enemy. Mid-century witnessed the rise and proliferation of the dime novel, many of them set in the "wild West," which found an enthusiastic following, especially among school-age boys. Once in the army and coming in direct contact with Indian people, however, soldiers were sometimes immediately disillusioned. As his batch of recruits steamed up the Colorado River en route to their first assignments in Arizona Territory in 1869, Private Eddie Matthews observed curious Yuma Indians lining the banks: "They look anything but civilized. Why do people call them noble . . . what can there be noble in a miserable, dirty, lousy, thieving piece of humanity, which all the Indians I have seen are[?]" The reaction of this native Marylander, in the army a mere two months and having never before set foot in the West, was not unusual. In the early 1880s Fourth Cavalryman William B. Jett, posted at Fort Stanton, New Mexico Territory, commented on visitors from the nearby Mescalero Apache Reservation: "The Indians, male and female, were often in our quarters and as I came in contact with them, I came to the conclusion that all the type of J. Fenimore Cooper Indians were dead. They were the dirtiest people in their apparel and in their eating I have ever seen."[2]

The cultural differences between the peoples posed a stark contrast to each other and usually were misunderstood by soldiers new to the frontier. "There are very near 6,000 friendly Indians here getting food and clothing from the government," remarked a Fourth Infantryman at the Shoshone Agency in central Wyoming Territory. "The men are the most lazy set of beings I ever saw, as they do nothing but hunt and fight, while the women do all the work." Without realizing it, he had accurately synthesized the normal division of labor practiced in Indian society.³

Some newcomers in the West were immediately intimidated by the tales that they had read about Indians or had been fed by old soldiers in their companies, who were ever willing to take advantage of the "fresh fish." One soldier who experienced this was a young Eighteenth Infantry drummer, Alson B. Ostrander. Marching up the Bozeman Trail in 1866, he confided: "As we got farther into the Indian country, I found that the enthusiasm for the wilds of the West I had gained from Beadle's dime novels gradually left me. . . . My courage had largely oozed out while I listened to the blood curdling tales the old-timers recited." A disgusted post commander in Dakota Territory, similarly reported that "many of the new soldiers, thoroughly frightened by ridiculous reports and absurd commentaries on the Indians, have become accustomed to considering them so dangerous that they think more of avoiding them than of fighting them." Permitted to go fishing not long after his arrival at Poplar Creek Agency, Montana Territory, in 1881, recruit Henry Hubman was startled when a hand grasped his shoulder. "Looking up, I saw the ugliest Sioux that you can imagine. I jumpt [sic] about ten feet and done some of the liveliest running I ever did." Back at camp, the warrior may have enjoyed a good laugh with his friends over the incident.⁴

Other inexperienced men demonstrated a certain naiveté regarding Indians, even when a degree of caution would have been fully warranted. The army established Fort C. F. Smith, Montana Territory, astride the Bozeman Trail in defiance of Lakota Sioux claims on the area east of the Bighorn Mountains. As a result, the Sioux kept the garrison constantly under surveillance and made it hazardous for anyone to venture far beyond the stockade. In an incredible coincidence, Private Albert Carter, a member of the Twenty-Seventh Infantry posted at the isolated fort, joined a friend to go fishing along the Bighorn River on the very day the Sioux attacked the nearby hay camp. Hearing gunfire, Carter said that he "went to look around the bend. One glance was all I wanted. The whole hay bottom was covered with mounted Indians and as we had left our guns at the Ft., we concluded it was no place for us to stay any longer." That two soldiers could have elected to leave the post unarmed under those conditions defies every precept of common sense. They were extremely fortunate to have lived to tell about it.⁵

Soldiers uninitiated to Indian culture often found their customs and behavior difficult to understand and at times resented Indian advances even though they intended no harm. When the Third Infantry took station on the plains in late 1866, Private John Stotts recounted the reception that he and some comrades received when they visited a village (probably Southern Cheyenne) near their route of march along Santa Fe Trail in Kansas. "We were surrounded by a howling mob of squaws and children of all ages. They began to beg for money, tobacco, or any kind of trinkets. We gave them all the small change we had and some [of] the boys even gave them pocket knives." Then the women began cutting the brass buttons from the men's blouses. "I happened to have my dress coat on, which had lots of buttons." Stotts remarked. "It was the only [one] I had and no chance to get another." After pushing away an old woman wielding a knife, Stotts was struck and nearly knocked down by a headless arrow loosed by a young boy attempting to defend her. Just as an older boy began stringing a war arrow, Stotts jumped, knocking the youth over the creek bank and sparking a general uproar. Retreating rapidly toward their own camp, the unarmed soldiers were saved in the nick of time by a platoon of cavalry dispatched to rescue them.[6]

Soldiers learned that begging was commonplace among most of the tribes, though it was frequently resented when carried too far. Near Cimarron, New Mexico Territory, a detachment of Eighth Cavalrymen paused at a familiar ranch for milk and fresh bread, which the old German couple living there always proffered freely to passing patrols. As the troopers rode up, they found the owner's wife alone and badly frightened by a group of Jicarilla Apaches from the nearby reservation who had arrived previously and were demanding more food than she could provide. One of the men related: "We took our carbines off our saddles and told the Indians to leave. They did not seem to care about going. One of our party raised his carbine and fired over their heads. That frightened them, and off they ran. . . . We fired about twenty rounds after them . . . [and] we were very careful not to hit any of them."[7]

When posted on the fringes of Indian reservations, soldiers were inclined to a more tolerant view of the Indians, though usually looking upon them as inferiors, and associated with them rather freely. "Most men who were not in active campaigns felt friendly toward the

Indians," declared Sergeant James S. Hamilton, First Infantry. "Some even learned their language, attended their pow-wows and dog feasts. We bartered and traded with them for their hand-made articles and many interesting and beautiful things were obtained and sent home to our families." A Seventh Cavalryman present at the Medicine Lodge Treaty negotiations in 1867 innocently traded a dozen Spencer carbine cartridges to two Indian women "for a beautiful tanned buffalo skin or robe, which had colored Indian markings all over the inside of it and was soft as a chamois skin." In his eagerness to acquire the robe, however, the soldier neglected recently issued orders not to barter or sell arms or ammunition to Indians, a mistake that earned him a court-martial and imprisonment.[8]

The garrison at Fort Ellis, Montana Territory, near the Crow agency on Stillwater Creek, got along well with their Indian native neighbors, who were traditionally friendly with whites and had provided a number of scouts to the army at various times. Having just received a load of firewood at their quarters, Private George C. Berry recollected that two Crow women "going past asked for a couple of axes and soon had the wood ready for the cook stove a lot quicker than we could have done it ourselves. We offered to pay them for their work, but they only asked for some soap which we supplied them with." Indicative of the amicable relationship between the army and their old allies, Private Fred H. Toby remarked that a band of about two hundred Crows paid a visit to a Seventh Cavalry camp on the Yellowstone River. "During the evening, they donned their war dress and mounted their war ponies and gave us a sample of their fighting qualities in the shape of a sham battle."[9]

It was not unusual for soldiers and Indian people traditionally friendly with whites to treat each other with mutual respect and courtesy. First Sergeant Herman Werner, First Cavalry, recounted an experience in December 1884 when his troop was ordered out of Fort Assinniboine, Montana Territory, to intercept and turn back several hundred mixed-blood French-Canadian Indian renegades invading U.S. territory and threatening peaceful Assiniboines on the American side. With the thermometer standing well below zero, Werner and his men, bundled in buffalo overcoats, fur gauntlets, and sealskin caps covered with canvas hoods, approached an Assiniboine village in the hope of finding shelter from the icy winds knifing across the open plains. The troopers were cheered at the sight of the village, he said, and "most welcome was the friendly disposition of these Assiniboine Indians when they invited our men into their fairly warmed-up wigwams, and it was soon after that, all of us, excepting the ones on guard, crowded into the wigwams.... We cooked our evening meal over the fires ... and we shared generously with these friendly people."[10]

In some instances army personnel demonstrated exceptional compassion toward Indians, particularly the children who became the innocent victims of total warfare. In one example, following an 1870 cavalry attack on a Tonto Apache camp in eastern Arizona, virtually all the adults were killed, leaving two boys about twelve years of age in army custody. Facing the problem of what to do with them, a unit involved in the fight, B Troop, Third Cavalry, informally adopted one of the boys. The other child, given the name "Sunday," for the day of his capture, found a home with K Troop, First Cavalry. Private B. S. Bivenour, a member of that company, recalled that "Sunday was still with the company when I was discharged at Klamath, Oregon, in 1873." Sergeant Timothy Dougherty, Twenty-Third Infantry, took in another orphaned Apache boy also captured in northern Arizona during the Tonto Campaign. Dougherty, who must have been married, shared his home with the boy until spring 1876, when he met his death in a skirmish with Sioux in the sand hills region of Nebraska.[11]

Soldiers who had not personally suffered at the hands of Indians or who had not lost friends to a particular tribe in combat were sometimes inclined to overlook former animosities. Shortly after fighting subsided with the Sioux in 1877, a large party of Sioux returning to the Nebraska agencies passed by a bivouac of cavalry serving as escort to surveyors marking the eastern boundary of Wyoming Territory. "Some of them stoped [sic] at our camp to trade and then went their way well satisfied with their bargains," Private Edward D. Barker noted in his journal. A Sixth Infantryman at Fort Buford, Dakota Territory, related that peaceful Lakota Sioux camped near the post "would sally forth every day and make a raid upon the company kitchens for the regular hand out" and the cooks would oblige them. First Sergeant Charles Maurer, Fourth Cavalry, was temporarily posted at the Cheyenne-Arapaho Agency in Indian Territory, where he befriended the former war chief Black Wolf by giving him foodstuffs because the man was too proud to beg. "The morning we broke camp, Black Wolf and many of the other Indians called to bid us good bye," Maurer recorded. "Later in the fall . . . he came over to me and shook hands and invited me to call on him at the Indian camp just outside the Agency. . . . If I did not call on him at least once a month, he came over to see if I was sick."[12]

Predictably, frontier soldiers far from home and craving feminine companionship looked to Indian women to fill the void and were not very particular about tribal affiliation. Riding with Custer's column into Indian Territory a few months after the Battle of the Washita, Private Winfield S. Harvey, a farrier, remarked: "We traveled through the entire Kiowa Indian Camp this morning and also the Comanche Camp. I saw some very pretty Indian women; a very pretty sight for one who had never seen an Indian." The Seventh Cavalry established camp on Medicine Bluff Creek and within only a few weeks Harvey reported that he had made friends with a Plains Apache chief, who had offered him the company of a nice woman. Harvey was only too happy to accept. Even though Private Emil A. Bode thought that the Cherokee and Chickasaw women he encountered in Indian Territory were of remarkable beauty, he reserved highest praise for Comanche women as "the most bewitching beings I ever beheld. . . . I was head over heels in love with one of them. I really felt sick in the region of my heart and was convinced that Cupid had sent an arrow clear through the old rusty armor of my bachelorhood." Bode added that the Comanche women were neat and clean, taking daily baths, and that they "used paint, not unlike their civilized sisters, only they used red instead of black paint for the lids of their eyes." Lakota women also adorned themselves with paint, according to a soldier at Fort Laramie, Wyoming Territory, who associated closely with a band of Brulés that had inhabited the area for years. "They are considered to be in the height of fashion with their faces and part of their hair dubbed [sic] profusely with Chinese vermillion. They may be found at any time around the company mess house and the Subtler [sic] Store, waiting to receive all that may be offered."[13]

A trooper of the Fourth Cavalry serving in the Southwest offered a contrasting opinion of Apache women, contending that "the only good looking Indian girl I ever saw was at this Mescalero Apache Indian Agency. . . . high cheek bones, flat noses, and broad faces prevented beauty." Beauty was in the eye of the beholder.[14]

Like young men and women everywhere, of all eras, the sexes found ways to overcome racial and linguistic barriers. Accompanying a force of Crow scouts who joined General Terry's column encamped on the Yellowstone in August 1876 were some young women, probably brought along to cook and perform camp chores. While on picket duty the next day, Private Fred Toby wrote that he "had a visit from an Indian squaw, fair and dusky and for a wonder rather clean.... I entertained her with a German picture paper, which she seemed quite pleased with." He was not the only man impressed with the Crow women. Second Cavalryman William H. White related: "Various Crow girls drew my admiring attention.... The native shyness of the girls gradually disappeared to the extent that they would come and sit on the ground outside our soldier tent, there to visit with us. We would spread a blanket and play cards with them.... We could not talk Crow. They knew nothing of English. Nevertheless, smiles, laughter and other universal modes of human expression brought mutual understanding. Oh, what delightful recollections of that summer!"[15]

A Fifth Cavalryman of German origin stationed at Fort McKinney, Wyoming Territory, was "deeply smitten" by a Crow woman when "he went to the well for a bucket of water and she stood there and greeted him with a pretty smile and a mumurous [sic] giggle.... She was fair to gaze upon, and he grew amorous." His comrades teased the lovesick man unmercifully, one of them even composing a fitting doggerel verse:

> Glue your lips mit me, mein squaw, mein squaw,
> Und squeeze of your lofer's hand,
> Und fly mit him now, mein squaw, mein squaw,
> Far from der prairies land.
> Come where the schooners is cheap und pig,
> Und notings at all is der kraut,
> We will ride away quick on my fiery steed,
> Und your mother don't know you was oudt![16]

On a cold winter's night a first sergeant of the First Cavalry fell victim to the lure of keeping company with an Indian woman when one of the men rushed into the orderly room to announce that an Indian had been seen behind the troop bath house. The amorously charged sergeant hurried out to investigate, found the woman there wrapped in a blanket, and immediately invited her into his quarters where it would be warmer. To his surprise, the "woman" exclaimed in guttural English, "Me no squaw, me buck," drew a large knife, and began slashing the air. The sergeant beat a hasty retreat to the barracks and never did find out that "his Indian friend was none other than Shorty Grant, a Trumpeter of his own troop and the knife was a long bladed breadknife from the troop kitchen."[17]

The attention that soldiers paid to Indian women sometimes also aroused the very human emotion of jealousy among their tribal suitors. Some Ninth Cavalrymen at the Pine Ridge Agency in Dakota Territory "were fooling around the Cheyenne women . . . more than some of the bucks liked," resulting in shots being fired by one party or the other "and probably someone got hurt over it." Private Hartford G. Clark, a Sixth Cavalryman also at Pine Ridge in 1891, commented that he found in the Sioux camp "an awful pretty squaw, about seventeen years old, that kept looking at me, and I smiled with her several times . . . and went up and talked with her until her masculine relations or friends got so close to me I thought I would leave her. . . . She could talk [sic] good English, as she had been to the Carlisle school in Penn." Not all Indian women were so socially inclined, sometimes for good reason. As Private Walter C. Harrington and his friend Carter walked across the grounds at Rosebud Agency, Dakota Territory, "we passed a fine appearing young squaw. I raised my cap; like a flash and without a sound she made a slash at me with her knife; Carter caught the movement before I did and gave me a shove. She missed me." The soldiers later learned that the woman's husband had been killed at the Wounded Knee Massacre, making her reaction understandable.[18]

Some of the relationships formed between Indian women and soldiers evolved into genuine romances that sometimes led to marriage. Private Henry Hubman, for example, informed his brother that he was sending him a photograph "of an Indian girl that lives near the Fort [Assinniboine] by the name of Laughing Eyes. Ain't she a beauty . . . [and] how would you like to spark her?" In a subsequent letter written about two weeks later, Hubman revealed that the girl had offered him twenty ponies if he would desert and go to Canada to live with her, and he did. The Cheyennes, also reputed for having attractive women, according to one soldier, "frequently marry whites, especially soldiers, or the better young and pretty squaws were sold by their mothers to soldiers at a price of $20 per year. The mother kept the money and the soldier provided his young wife with shelter and provisions and, if soft-hearted, for the whole family." The Cheyennes acknowledged this arrangement as a legitimate marriage. Trooper White, who had enjoyed such memorable hours with the Crow girls at Fort Ellis, later married a sixteen-year-old shortly after taking his discharge in 1878. They spent the next fifty-seven years together until her death.[19]

When troops were stationed near agencies or reservations, where they had prolonged association with Indian people, they were sometimes surprised to discover that their preconceived opinions had changed. As time passed, in fact, the army was more often called upon to settle internal tribal disputes and to protect Indians from white encroachments and thievery than to subdue them. A Tenth Infantry sergeant, George Neihaus, who had been posted adjacent to the Ute agency in Colorado, attested: "My opinion was the soldiers did not hold hard feeling about the Indians. I could always make friends with them, when they were treated right." Upon his unit's transfer from Fort Sill, agency for seven Indian nations (including three with whom the army had formerly been at war), Corporal Emil Bode observed that the men of his company looked back "at the place we entered three years ago with the firm conviction of finding wild men . . . on the same level with beasts, but instead were welcomed by a race who in every respect were equally intelligent to the Caucasian." Private Simpson Mann, Ninth Cavalry, may have summed it up best when he said of Indians with whom he had had contact: "They were just people."[20]

Prior to entering the army, enlisted regulars may not have been aware of the government's contradictory Indian policy that vacillated between feeding and fighting western tribes, but they soon learned that their lives were directly influenced by decisions made in the nation's capital as well as in the various military division and department headquarters. By negotiating treaties, the government's inevitable goal was to gain land concessions and Indian promises that they would not oppose transportation corridors, exploration, expanded settlement, mineral extraction, or a combination thereof, according to current perceived needs, within traditional or even previously granted Indian lands. In exchange, the government nearly always stipulated the confinement of Indians to ever-shrinking reservations, where they would be provisioned and otherwise cared for by the Indian Bureau and therefore become wards of the government.

The president appointed Indian agents. He sometimes awarded the positions to representatives of various religious denominations and at other times handed them out as political plums. To each tribe the government granted a monetary allotment, which their assigned agent was supposed to spend on behalf of the people. Therein lay the inherent problem. As one observer explained: "These appointments were nearly all made upon political considerations, and . . . where political considerations have a controlling influence, personal integrity and capability are but little thought of." Admittedly, agent positions suffered from low pay, and when the incumbent had no sponsor the expenses for getting himself (and often his family) to the agency fell upon his own resources. The circumstances were enough to test the integrity of honest men, much less those inclined to line their own pockets at the expense of their charges. Indian agents, as a class, became infamous for corrupt activity, especially during Ulysses S. Grant's presidency. Far removed from Washington, D.C., and with unilateral authority over their appropriations, some agents enhanced their income by withholding a portion of the rations and clothing intended for the Indians, the difference being written off as damaged or covered by falsified invoices. Agents diverted some of the goods to their own use then surreptitiously sold the rest at low prices back to unscrupulous contractors, who were often personal friends, and pocketed the illegal proceeds. The contractor then resold the same goods to the agent at high prices, thus doubling his profits. Another scheme of mutual collusion involved contractors agreeing to supply food and clothing of inferior quality, rather than that for which they had been paid, then splitting the profits with the receiving agents who approved the shipments.[21]

Such illicit activity became an open secret, even among the army's rank and file, and was the source of Indian trouble most often cited by soldiers at the time. A keenly observant Private Herman S. Searl was convinced that the agents "get a large sallery [sic] for cheating them [Indians] besides all the Government presents he keeps which is enough to make eny [sic] one man rich, but as I am only a private soldier . . . it will not do to say much." Writing from Camp Brown, Wyoming Territory, in 1870, Quartermaster Sergeant Maurice H. Wolfe echoed that the agents were "a damn pack of rascals. Indians can live very well when they are on the war path . . . but when at peace they have to live on game, and what the Indian Agent gives them (which is very little) besides their hunting ground being very restricted." A few years later a Seventh Cavalry recruit posted at the Standing Rock Agency, Dakota Territory, was initiated to the political realities of the so-called Indian problem. "After supper we walked down to the Infantry quarters and spent a very pleasant evening with the men. It was here that I learned much of the way that Indian agents rob the Indians and cause most of the Indian wars."[22]

Blame lay not with the Indian Bureau alone. Whites encroaching upon or usurping Indian reservation lands for mining or agriculture accounted for much Indian animosity, while whiskey peddlers and gun runners operating around or on reservations also contributed mightily to creating trouble. In other instances, recalcitrant Indian leaders, notably Sitting Bull of the Lakotas and later the Chiricahua Apache Geronimo, used their stature and influence to encourage their peacefully inclined followers to join in armed resistance, sometimes resorting to coercion through threats and intimidation.

Not to be overlooked were false alarms of Indian depredations sounded by greedy white inhabitants who thrived financially from the army's presence in settled regions. Freighters, beef and hay contractors, and others stood to profit from government business, especially in depressed markets, regardless of whether troops had a valid reason for being in the vicinity. Responding to a purported Indian raid on a cattle herd in Idaho, Private Edgar Hoffner's company of the First Cavalry left Boise Barracks and rode all day to reach the scene of the incident. "My private opinion is that the party was whites," the veteran trooper confided after examining the evidence. "They had left too much of the beef behind them [to be] Indians. . . . I have been in contact with Indians, Apaches in Arizona, Modocs in northern California and southern Oregon, Piutes in Nevada, and Sheepeaters in Idaho, and know their methods. My opinion is that citizens in the valley having grain and hay to dispose of and no market near, hit on this plan to make a few dimes." Neither was it unheard of to blame Indians for livestock thefts, even murders, that whites actually committed in order to mask the real perpetrators. Soldiers considered the protection of citizens and their property to be a primary duty, but they clearly resented civilians who took unfair advantage of the troops by sending them on fruitless missions in search of phantom raiders or against local Indians innocent of the reported wrongdoing.[23]

Resentment against the government's contradictory Indian policy, manifested in the Indian Bureau, ran particularly high among soldiers who realized that, while some Indians indeed took the warpath for their own reasons, those who had accepted reservation life were often subjected to unendurable conditions that forced them back to the free-roaming life. The army had no authority within the reservations—though many argued it should—unless the agents officially requested its intervention, sometimes to quell intratribal conflicts. Once the Indians bolted from bureau jurisdiction, however, the agents absolved themselves of responsibility and relinquished the refractory elements to the army. An officer writing to his mother in 1879 candidly synthesized the situation: "It is the old story, unjust treatment of the Indians by the Gov't., promises broken, treaties violated and the Indians moved from one reservation to another against their will, until finally they break out and go on the warpath and the army is called in to kill them. It is hard to fight against and shoot down men when you know they are in the right." A band or tribe considered friendly one day might well be the target of a military operation the next. Regardless of any personal opinions held by soldiers in the ranks, Twenty-Second Infantryman John Gibbert said that it came down to one thing: "We were fighting them and of course considered them our enemy."[24]

This is not to imply that all Indians of the western plains and mountains were peacefully inclined. Warfare was an essential cultural ingredient, particularly of Plains tribes, as well as that of some Indian nations in other regions. The primary virtue of manhood was successfully fulfilling the role of the hunter and warrior. It was a system established long before the army or in fact whites appeared in the West. The successful hunter sustained the tribe's existence by providing food for all the people. The skins and bones of the animals killed were converted to clothing, bedding, shelter, tools, and other useful objects. Through combat and raiding he distinguished himself and proved his worth to his people as both provider and protector. Counting coup (approaching an enemy close enough to strike or touch him while alive and surviving to tell about it) demonstrated courage of the highest order. Touching or scalping a dead enemy also counted but for less than if he was alive. Stealing horses, women, and children from enemy tribes to augment one's own people was standard practice in the culture. As one authority on the Sioux has observed: "War was an all-pervading contest against himself, his fellow men, and his adversaries." That applied as well to most of the other tribes with which the army came into conflict. So-called peace commissions treated with the various nations and separate tribes from time to time to quell warfare among the Indians and with whites, to establish specified hunting territories, and often to define reservations to which identified tribes would be confined, supported, and educated (retrained as farmers) by the government. That concept, however, was foreign to western Indians and clearly at odds with their culture.[25]

A commission formed in 1865, and obviously frustrated with its limited success, rightly concluded that Indians could not conceive of universal peace. "The idea of a general peace seemed to the Indians 'quite preposterous, and they accepted this clause of our treaties with great misgiving as to its success.'" It would take another quarter-century of conflict and bloodshed to arrive at the inevitable outcome.[26]

The ways in which western Indians conducted warfare contrasted sharply with the methods of a conventional army. The army failed to embrace this idea formally; it had to be learned through experience. Conflicts with Indians had gone on intermittently since Europeans first came to North America. So far as the army was concerned, each outbreak could well be the last. Therefore both officers and men were schooled in conventional tactics in order to be prepared for the next war on the European model. Stand-up battles with Indians seldom occurred during the era and were rarely initiated by the Indians. Hit-and-run raiding, attacking numerically inferior foes from ambush, and occasionally laying siege to isolated stations or small enemy parties constituted the Indian art of warfare, though specific practices sometimes differed according to tribal custom, population, and environment. Characterizing the nature of Indian warfare in a contemporary treatise, Second Lieutenant Edward S. Farrow wrote that the Indian was "like the flea, 'put your finger on him and he is not there.' Living off the land and with no lines of retreat to cover, he is enabled to withhold himself from combat, unless he finds himself very superior in number and position." It was guerrilla warfare in its purest form.[27]

Some uninitiated soldiers looked upon the Indian way of combat as cowardly, but, as French-born Colonel Philippe Régis De Trobriand accurately perceived, "bravery for them does not consist in exposing themselves to danger for a difficult or uncertain result; their exploits are, on the contrary, counted the more brilliant if they have gathered many scalps or stolen many mules or horses with the least possible risk. So, they proceed by ambush and abstain from attacking openly." Unlike conventional armies that had only to recruit more soldiers, warriors had to be reared from birth, so they were too valuable to sacrifice for uncertain gains. This basic factor accounts for the rarity of walled or stockaded posts on the western frontier. "The Indians never attack military posts to occupy them in force," De Trobriand continued. "They would lose too many warriors. They limit their effort to drawing out a small detachment and then luring it into an ambush."[28]

Many tribes used that tactic against U.S. soldiers with varying degrees of success throughout the era. The quintessential example occurred at Fort Phil Kearny in 1866, when Captain William J. Fetterman pursued a decoy party of warriors beyond a ridge and out of sight from the fort. Once his eighty-man detachment of infantry and cavalry had reached a point beyond any immediate help, a greatly superior force of Sioux and Northern Cheyenne warriors suddenly emerged from ravines where they had been concealed and overwhelmed Fetterman's command. The subsequent notoriety of this event served as a lesson to make other army officers more aware and cautious.

Defense of static positions was generally not of great concern to the army. The challenge lay in finding and coming to grips with a highly mobile enemy thoroughly familiar with the surroundings. It was not unusual for Plains Indians to move about in bands of about fifty up to perhaps two or three hundred warriors, along with their families, yet the areas to be searched were vast. "You might as well hunt a needle in a haystack as to hunt Indians in small parties," opined Private William F. Zimmer. At times these bands might congregate in considerably larger tribal numbers for purposes of hunting or for ceremonial observances. In rare instances multiple tribes might assemble in one or more villages at a particular location, but only temporarily. "It was impossible for large bodies of Indians to hold together for long periods of time," an experienced plainsman asserted. "Subsisting mainly on game, they were forced to scatter and live in small villages." Because each warrior possessed several ponies, the herds associated with large gatherings could find adequate grazing in the vicinity of the villages for only a few days at best.[29]

Apaches, generally encompassing a number of distinct tribes inhabiting the desert and mountainous regions of the Southwest from western Texas to Arizona, were more severely limited in the numbers of people who could be supported at any one place in such an arid environment. Sources of water, food, and grazing for animals worked to keep assemblages small, usually with fewer than sixty or so warriors and often far less. They nevertheless took every advantage of the desert terrain. Apache raiders proved especially difficult to corral, a Fourth Cavalryman contended. "The Indians traveled on fast broncos in the lightest marching order possible and ate whatever they could lay their hands upon among tame, or wild animals without, necessarily, cooking the food. And a dog meant good meat to them when pushed for food." Water was critical to survival, and Apaches knew the locations of every water source, no matter how small or secluded. When trailed by the army, they usually made for the nearest mountain range. "The Indians here always fight in the mountains, and never until they are ready, that is, when they have an immense advantage of the troops," wrote an officer of the Ninth Cavalry. Although Apaches rode horses, they did not prize them as highly as people of the buffalo culture, being perfectly willing to abandon the animals and proceed on foot over the most difficult and inhospitable terrain imaginable to evade their pursuers. As Private Lawrence R. Jerome (alias Laurence Vinton) recounted of a typical chase: "We were pressing them very closely and, on arriving on the summit of the Sierra Azul, they killed all their stock . . . and branched out in several small parties on foot."[30]

That habit of scattering was a cat-and-mouse technique generally employed by Indians regardless of tribe simply because it was so easy and effective. Before splitting up, of course, the warriors agreed upon some distant point familiar to all at which they would rendezvous. "We were not able to overtake those Indians after they scattered in small bands," admitted a Seventh Cavalryman. A single pony trail might have been difficult enough to follow, but villagers or a war party would divide to shake off pursuers, forcing the troops to decide which group to follow or whether to split into two parties. Indians sometimes employed that tactic even more effectively by subdividing into several smaller parties themselves, detouring over the roughest terrain available, making it useless to follow any particular one.[31]

Because the army was comparatively unfamiliar with most areas in which it operated, it overcame that deficiency through the aid of Indian scouts from tribes willing to cooperate with whites. Numerous army commanders made use of Indian scouts, notably Brigadier General George Crook (who employed them extensively in field operations in Arizona and on the northern plains), Colonel Ranald S. Mackenzie, and Lieutenant Colonel George A. Custer. Indians had been in conflict with other Indians through the tradition of mutual raiding, horse stealing, and the kidnapping of women and children, and in competition over their respective hunting territories long before Europeans entered the picture. That situation was only intensified by the interlopers crowding Indians into an ever-shrinking area, who merely took advantage of those old animosities. Thus the army distinguished between "friendlies" and "hostiles." The most effective scouts were those knowledgeable of the area of operations who understood the habits of the opposing tribes, though in some instances scouts had to be procured from more distant reservations. At the very least, the army procured Indian or white scouts adept at tracking and plains lore. They were not necessarily obligated to fight, if it came to that, but most Indian scouts expected to engage in combat against hereditary enemies as a means of proving themselves in accordance with the warrior code.

The nature of the conflict in the West approached total warfare, and it could hardly have been otherwise in view of the northern expansion of New Spain and the subsequent inheritance of the region by Mexico, followed by the Americans pressing inexorably westward during the nineteenth century. The combined result was two centuries of uninterrupted conflict with the Apaches. The concurrent American expansion across the plains and beyond the transmountain region to the Pacific Northwest was accompanied by transportation and communications routes cutting across Indian hunting territories vital to their existence. Later the establishment of settlements and towns, along with mining and agricultural activities, often blatantly disregarded the Indian inhabitants. It came as no surprise that the affected tribes resisted these invasions, considering all non-Indians as enemies, regardless of race, sex, or occupation. Accordingly, in this no-holds-barred clash civilians (emigrants, settlers, and travelers) were considered intruders with no right to be there.

The killing of civilians, especially women, made indelible impressions on most soldiers. Sergeant William Miller, Fourth Cavalry, was in a detachment sent out from Fort Griffin, Texas, during the 1870s to investigate the report of a raid on a ranch sixteen miles distant. Upon their arrival, the troops found "the ranch was burned down and . . . in front of it stood two trees with the remains of a daughter hanging head downwards, scalped and the unborn babe cut from her. The father lay in the ruins, also horribly mutilated. The daughter, who was a school teacher down in the settlements, was spending her vacation with her parents. . . . It was the most horrible sight ever a man looked on." Such atrocities hardened attitudes, even among those soldiers who had previously harbored no particular antipathy for Indians. During the 1873 Yellowstone Expedition with the Northern Pacific Railroad surveying party, Sioux warriors descended upon and killed two civilian men riding only a short distance from the main column. German immigrant Private Charles Windolph confided that "the thing that stuck in our craw long after we got back to our winter quarters was the brutal killing of Doctor Honsinger, our old German-born vet who everybody loved, and our subtler [sutler], Mr. Balarin. . . . Their murder ranked in our hearts. The whole regiment swore some day we would get revenge."[32]

In another instance an infantryman in Wyoming Territory was present when the bodies of three local citizens were found near South Pass. "The men were fearfully cut up," he wrote. "They were full of arrows. Their sides and limbs were chopped up from knives and hatchets. Their eyes were dug out and laid in front of them. One man . . . had an iron wagon hammer driven through his head which took two men to extract. . . . I never saw such a horrid spectacle in my life." A young soldier who had been in the army only a few months when a hunter's mutilated remains were discovered along a road in Arizona Territory moaned: "Who would have sympathy for a race of barbarians like they are."[33]

Casualties among soldiers, conversely, were to be expected in combat. Although it was never easy to lose one's friends, soldiers vehemently resented acts of mutilation perpetrated on corpses, and even more on the wounded. Private David W. Luce (alias Charles Newton),

Seventh Cavalry, vividly described the deaths of two of his bunkies killed on the Kansas plains in 1867: "One lost his life by the arrow of an Indian, which pierced his abdomen, coming out at the back, while the other was found some distance away . . . with his heart cut out, scalp taken, tongue cut out, and gashes cut in his thighs. . . . When he was found his flesh was yet quivering." No stranger to battlefield casualties, an Eighteenth Infantry soldier, Sergeant David Kerstetter, who had served throughout the Civil War as a member of that regiment, said of the soldiers killed in the Fetterman Fight in December 1866: "All were killed, scalped, and horribly mutilated. . . . Men were butchered in the most indescribable manner—throats cut, arms and legs cut off, eyes cut out, and in a dozen other ways mutilated. . . . All were stripped and scalped. Their acquaintances could hardly recognize them."[34]

Scalping and occasional mutilation of enemy bodies were timeless traditions largely confined to the plains tribes and were not peculiar to the Indian-white conflict. Scalping was the most common form of mutilation among Indians, though not necessarily universal among all the peoples. By the 1870s the Nez Perces, for example, allegedly avoided all forms of mutilation, due in part perhaps to early Christian influence, yet the similarly acculturated Modocs of Oregon killed a soldier captive, leaving the body nude. "The toes were cut off at the second joint, the scalp was torn off the head, and finally his brains were dashed out by a jagged rock," according to Private P. W. Hamont, Fourth Artillery.[35]

Lieutenant William Philo Clark, a Second Cavalry officer who devoted himself to intensive study of western Indian culture, interviewed numerous Indians during the 1870s and early 1880s and found that almost all tribes practiced scalping as evidence of warrior skill in combat. According to the many interviews he conducted, Clark learned that the custom arose from some warriors making false claims of Indian enemies killed. Taking a man's scalp and bringing it back to camp was incontrovertible evidence of his accomplishment and by extension his bravery. Tribes of the buffalo culture took scalps as temporary trophies, merely as proof of male feats in combat. Upon their return from battle, warriors turned over the scalps to wives or mothers, who fastened them to poles to be displayed during scalp dances proclaiming victory. After the grisly trophies had served their purpose, they were usually discarded.

Among some tribes, enemy scalps were attached to a special buckskin war shirt signifying the man's stature among his peers. "The popular superstition that it's only a small lock is a mistake," related Lieutenant Charles L. Hammond, Third Cavalry, speaking of the Sioux. "They take the whole top of a man's head off if they have the time." The scalp lock among Plains Indians was intended as a dare to their enemies—"take it if you can." Begun for males during early childhood, the lock was formed by braiding the hair contained within roughly a two-inch circle on the crown of the head. The hair was then parted to either side through the middle of his head, with the part terminating at the scalp lock. Rather than simply taking the lock, as was widely believed, warriors usually took the entire scalp. The lock merely served as verification that the scalp was genuine, taken from a warrior. Elaborating on the process as he had witnessed it at Fort Phil Kearny, Private William Murphy confirmed: "They ran a knife around the edge of the hair and took off all the scalp. Some tribes cut the scalp up in small pieces and [up to four men] braided it in with their own hair making a 'scalp lock' as a further badge of courage. The lock was, of course, considered the 'choice cut' and was kept by the principal warrior making the kill." Clark noted that during intertribal warfare the Sioux were known to decapitate a slain enemy and take the head to the first night's camp, where the entire scalp along with the still-connected ears could be carefully removed to preserve earrings and other ornaments, making it a particularly fine trophy.[36]

Victims were not always dead when scalped, as borne out by the Minneconjou Lakota White Bull's statement that after clubbing an Indian enemy he "grasped the man's hair with his left hand . . . cut the skin of his head all around, and jerked off the scalp. The man was still alive . . . [and] this wounded enemy got up and staggered away." There were in fact numerous recorded instances in which victims of scalping survived the ordeal.[37]

Apaches, in contrast to popular belief, rarely engaged in scalping their enemies. "I have seen hundreds of people killed but not scalped," attested a former member of Victorio's Mescalero band. A Chiricahua Apache who fought with Geronimo stated that "Apaches did not practice the custom of scalping a fallen enemy." Yet he allowed: "There may have been exceptions to this but they were very, very rare." John C. Cremony lived among the Apaches prior to the Civil War and later served with the California Volunteers in Arizona, New Mexico, and Texas. He attested that on some occasions Apaches retrieved only one or two scalps from those they killed, as trophies to be used a few days afterward for a religious ceremony.[38]

While Apaches usually refrained from scalping, they did engage in other barbarous acts. Two of the most popular were tying their victims to wagon wheels and burning them and binding and suspending hapless captives by their feet over a slow fire to roast their brains. During a treacherous revolt by enlisted Apache scouts at Cibicu Creek, Arizona Territory, in 1881, the scouts unexpectedly shot down an officer and five Sixth Cavalrymen. A short time later a party was sent out to recover the temporarily interred bodies, but upon their arrival they found that "the Indians . . . had desecrated the graves . . . and there on the polluted ground were extended in mutilated, unrecognizable hideousness the bodies of the once stalwart . . . Captain Hentig . . . and four [sic] soldiers. An attempt had been made to cut them into pieces."[39]

Northern Cheyenne historian John Stands In Timber offered another perspective on why soldiers were not always scalped. His people, he asserted, "preferred fighting with other Indians to fighting with white men, because if they won and took scalps the scalp of an Indian was worth much more. A white man's hair was clipped short most times. . . . A man might take the scalp all right, but he did not bring it into camp because he would be criticized; it did not really count." Warrior scalps, he contended, were considered much more prestigious because the long hair or braids were adorned with feathers and metal ornaments. Soldiers nearly always had their hair cut short prior to taking the field simply because it was less bothersome and easier to wash when men were afforded the opportunity. Tenth Cavalry blacksmith James Tucker added another possible explanation for soldiers cropping their hair when they anticipated being in action with Indians. Finding the bodies of two of his comrades killed by Cheyennes in western Kansas, Tucker observed that one had been scalped, but "they didn't scalp the other man because his hair was too short, and they didn't scalp short-haired people." Some soldiers may have cut their hair short to avoid the possibility of being scalped, especially while still alive, which supports Stands In Timber's view.[40]

Indians, in accordance with long practice, sometimes performed acts of mutilation on the bodies of dead enemies. In the late eighteenth century an experienced French trader observed that mutilation was common among the tribes of the Middle Missouri River country. "I have seen these furious old hags . . . cut off the hands, limbs, [and] virile parts of the dead enemies, hang them around the neck and at the ears, and dance thus at all the lodge doors of the village. . . . In the scalp dance it was customary for women to stand in the center displaying the trophies their husbands or other male relatives had taken in the recently concluded action." After a combined force of Assiniboines and Crees attacked a Piegan (Blackfoot) village at the American Fur Company's Fort McKenzie in 1833, "The Blackfoot warriors left much of the revenge to the women and children, who mutilated the one Assiniboine at the fort to such an extent the corpse hardly resembled a human body." Mutilation was not carried out among the Blackfoot and perhaps some other tribes, however, if there was no specific motive for revenge.[41]

A persistent myth generated in the nineteenth century suggested that mutilation was a practice based on a religious belief that a disfigured enemy would reside in the hereafter in the same physical condition. Lieutenant Clark concluded from his many interviews that "no superstition exists that by scalping or other mutilation the progress of the spirit towards the happiness of life after death is thereby interfered with. . . . It should be distinctly understood that however mutilated a person may be who has been killed in . . . battle, he (as an Indian said to me) 'goes by the most direct and easiest trail . . . to the Happy Hunting Ground.'" Thus enemy bodies sometimes were mutilated to avenge the death of a relative or friend at the hands of that foe or at other times simply out of anger and hatred for an enemy. As in other conflicts—some of them among "civilized" peoples in modern times—enemy bodies were mutilated for no other reason than the psychological effect that the perpetrators hoped this would have on those who found the remains, as a warning. It had the desired effect. Barracks talk among soldiers was often intended only to feed the "fresh fish," but not always. Private James B. Wilkinson, who served with the Second Cavalry during the mid-1880s, claimed: "We were told we would be killed after being tortured. 'Old timers' told us not to be taken prisoner, but to save the last shot for ourselves." Combat-wise veterans understood the nature of this no-holds-barred conflict.[42]

Western Indians used a wide variety of traditional weapons and fire-arms throughout the era, although the traditional weapons were more prevalent in the immediate postwar years. "Most all of them . . . are armed with bows and arrows and lances. Some with fire arms," wrote Private George H. Cranston in 1867 when describing the Apaches in the vicinity of Camp Grant, Arizona Territory. The state of Indian armaments was similar throughout the Great Plains region. Private Emmet G. Latta, who served on the northern plains in the late 1860s, wrote: "About half the bucks [Lakota Sioux] carried short bows, with a quiver of metal-pointed arrows; others had lances, war clubs of different kinds, and about one in five had a fire-arm of some kind."[43]

"In the '60s the arrow was the favorite weapon of Indian warriors," declared an army surgeon. "Swift, silent, accurate and deadly. . . . By our soldiers stationed on the frontier . . . it was regarded with the greatest aversion, the most dreaded of all missiles to which they were exposed." A veteran Seventh Cavalryman who had experienced combat on several occasions told why: "There is a barb on the arrow point, and in pulling it out it has to tear the flesh. If it is shot into a person it must be withdrawn as soon as possible, for, if not, the sinew that fastens the point . . . to the shaft will become moistened and is liable to stick, and when the shaft is pulled out the head or point . . . remains" (assuming, of course, that the victim survived long enough have the missile extracted). An Eighteenth Infantryman related that he and his comrades were greatly impressed with a bow shooting demonstration by Sioux youths at Fort Laramie, Dakota Territory, in 1866: "The young boys could hit a button, pencil, or any small article at about thirty yards," he claimed. Accuracy with a bow was a skill finely honed from early childhood, as proven by a young Kiowa man at his agency in 1880. Some Sixteenth Infantry soldiers, out to take advantage, offered the warrior a coin for every coin tossed in the air that he could hit with an arrow. "He did better than we expected and we discontinued the coin shooting as a bad investment on our side," one man grumbled.[44]

Private Latta emphasized, however, that even though "the bow and arrow is a dangerous weapon at close quarters, and they could discharge their arrows much faster than we could fire our Springfield breech-loaders. . . . They could not shoot any closer than a good ballplayer could throw a baseball." According to some sources, the maximum accurate range was approximately one hundred fifty yards. Besides their limited range, arrows were very susceptible to wind, an ever-present factor on the plains. Nevertheless, unlike firearms, Indians could supply themselves with bows and arrows, both of which could be readily fabricated from locally available materials.[45]

A cavalry officer serving in western Kansas in 1867 was surprised to learn that Cheyenne warriors had attempted to improve their native weapon by combining it with white technology to produce incendiary arrows. It was discovered that after attacking stage stations along the Smoky Hill Route the Indians "had attempted to burn them with a kind of torpedo arrows—made by placing a percussion cap on the point of the arrow blade, and encasing the same in a little cotton sack, containing about a thimble full of gun powder!" He examined some of the projectiles and found that even though the caps had split the charge had failed to explode.[46]

Many tribes encountered by the army employed the lance to a greater or lesser extent. The weapon could be used for thrusting or thrown as a missile. The Comanches and Kiowas inhabiting the southern plains were famous for their ability in the use of lances. During a skirmish with Comanches on the Staked Plains in 1874, a civilian scout recorded that warriors "hurled a spear at my companion [a Delaware scout] but slightly missing its aim, the staff of the spear which was six feet long, knocked him senseless from his horse, which they ran against, knocking him completely from his feet." The effectiveness of the lance, when it did find its mark, was evident when soldiers found the body of a teamster killed by Kiowa warriors near a camp in Texas. "The spear had gone clear through him," recalled First Sergeant Henry McConnell. Lances were generally similar in form, regardless of tribe. Private George Cranston described typical Apache lances as "made of a piece of steel about two feet and a half long and an inch and a half wide, sharpened on both sides. This is set into a long wooden handle about six feet long."[47]

Indians acquired an almost infinite variety of firearms from numerous sources. Among the most popular arms used throughout the era were muzzle-loading muskets, rifles, shotguns, and pistols simply because ammunition in the form of bulk powder and cast lead balls or shot was more versatile and easier to obtain than fixed metallic cartridges. The regulars resented nothing more about government Indian policy than the Indian Bureau's providing firearms to its charges on the justification the Indians needed them for hunting purposes, when those same people had been using traditional weapons for hunting game quite successfully for centuries. In one instance, upon the signing of the 1868 Fort Laramie Treaty, a soldier present at the time saw "a train load of supplies distributed among the Indians, including several cases of muzzle-loading Lancaster rifles." Most soldiers considered feeding the Indians one thing but arming them quite another.[48]

While the Indian Bureau supplied guns to agency Indians, nontreaty tribes and bands were able to obtain them from any number of other sources. One of those, naturally, was by capture from army or civilian casualties or looting from coaches, ranches, and stage stations attacked by war parties. Apaches took advantage of opportunities in both Mexico and the United States. A former volunteer officer having extensive experience in the Southwest wrote in 1868 that "they have a considerable number of Henry's, Spencer's and Sharp's [sic] rifles, with some of the fixed ammunition required by the two first mentioned. . . . These weapons have been obtained gradually by the robbery and murder of the former owners, and not a few have been bought in the frontier Mexican towns, where they were sold by immigrants to obtain food and other supplies while crossing the continent." Even enlisted soldiers were keenly aware that civilians were not averse to supplying arms to Indians actively engaged in opposing the army. "It may seem very strange to you how these Indians procure these arms and ammunition," Private Eddie Matthews informed his parents in a letter written at Fort Bascom, New Mexico Territory, in 1873. "But to us it is as plain as rolling off a log. These territorys [sic] are infested with a lot of scoundrels who trade with the Indians. I have no doubt for one gun: twenty head of cattle would be given in exchange." His regiment, the Eighth Cavalry, was at that time at the forefront of the government's efforts to curtail the illicit commerce being conducted by New Mexican traders, known as Comancheros, with the Comanches and Kiowas roaming the Texas Panhandle.[49]

The problem was prevalent throughout the West. Private George App, who served in the Third Infantry in Montana Territory during the 1870s, similarly claimed that "traders who looked only for profit readily equipped the Indians with the best rifles of the times in return for furs [buffalo robes] which were in great demand in the east." A soldier writing to his hometown newspaper in Pennsylvania reported that the Lakota warriors he had seen "are all well-armed with revolvers, carbines and rifles; they nearly all also carry a bow and a knife." Colonel John Gibbon compared the situation with "a colossus. In one hand it holds a scourge, from the other is dispensed to the Indian the best improved means of resisting this scourge. Every trader at an Indian agency, every little frontier town, or country store, is an arsenal where Indians . . . can purchase the most improved firearms and any quantity of metallic ammunition that they can pay for."[50]

The defeat of the Seventh Cavalry at the Battle of the Little Bighorn brought the matter of Indian armament to public attention when it was widely reported that Sitting Bull's warriors had been better armed than the troops. Custer's men were indeed outgunned, as has been established through archaeology, though the Sioux and Northern Cheyenne warriors were not universally armed with Winchester repeating rifles, as was widely rumored in the wake of the battle. Evidence suggests that approximately one-quarter of the warriors were armed with lever-action magazine repeaters and another one-quarter with a plethora of older muzzle-loading and single-shot cartridge weapons. The remainder, or about half of those engaged, probably used traditional weapons, primarily bows and arrows. Expressing a widely held belief among the rank and file, Sergeant James S. Hamilton was convinced that "the Indians had better rifles than our own men. When they [the Sioux] were disarmed at Standing Rock [Agency], they had cap and ball Colts, plus various kinds of rifles, but for the most part they carried good Winchester rifles." His impression was countered, however, by Private William F. Zimmer, who witnessed a cache of surrendered Sioux weapons at Cantonment on Tongue River in 1877: "It's quite a curiosity to . . . see the different kind of firearms the Indians turned in. Some of the first ever invented, muzzle-loading shotguns & rifles with flintlocks, others with caplock, some old rifles with barrels as large around as a chair leg. . . . Besides [these], they had some of the latest breech-loaders for metallic shells."[51]

Lieutenant James Worden Pope, a veteran of the Sioux War, may have arrived at the best reason for soldiers to believe Indians were better armed than the troops when he opined that "many ideas of the superiority of Indian arms are acquired in action . . . when to the best of men an arm that has whizzed a bullet close to the ear seems an excellent weapon."⁵²

The marksmanship ability of Indians has sometimes been discredited, falsely it would seem, considering contemporary evidence to the contrary. By the time of the Civil War, guns were nothing new to western Indians. The tribes of the northern plains began acquiring muskets primarily through the British fur trade as early as the mid-eighteenth century. By 1800 the proliferation of firearms, combined with the acquisition of horses from the Spanish, had altered both the culture and dynamics of the Great Plains. Addressing the effect guns had on Indians, a veteran army officer explained:

> He soon discovered it was more reliable, and accurate, and safer than his bow and arrow; that it brought down his game and enemy at longer distances, and with ordinary precaution was not affected by wet weather. Still he had to become skilled in its use, for he discovered that he who was the most skilled killed the most enemies and got the most game, and at the longest, and, for himself, safest distances. As improvements went on in our arms, we kindly transferred them to him; and as the arms improved so did his marksmanship, for his livelihood and safety depended upon it.⁵³

The smoothbore musket required only flints (later percussion caps), loose powder, and ball, which made it easy to use and well adapted to the Indians' sources of supply on the frontier. Whether in the hands of Indians or other peoples, however, the musket was an imperfect tool, leaving much to be desired in the way of accuracy. Fitted only with a small front sight blade for lateral alignment, it was essentially a point-blank proposition effective to only about seventy-five yards. Still, as Indians acquired more advanced arms, warriors learned the purpose and use of gun sights. One frontiersman commented: "At an early period they understood fully the value of double sights on any weapon carrying a ball, and the old old-fashioned single-barreled shot guns [fowlers and trade muskets] . . . were invariably sawed into with a knife to the depth of one-eighth of an inch, a few inches from the breech, when the thin sliver was raised above the barrel and carefully notched for the rear sight." As time passed and firearms technology advanced, so too did warrior skill. Observing Plains Indians, Colonel Gibbon noted: "They are as much at home in the use of firearms on horseback as they are on foot, although not so accurate in their fire, . . . [but can] at full speed alongside of a buffalo, and, generally at the first shot, from revolver or carbine, kill or mortally wound . . . game." During a fifteen-mile running fight with black Thirty-Eighth Infantrymen near Fort Hays, Kansas, in 1867, Cheyenne warriors fired an estimated two thousand rounds without causing any casualties among the troops. Amazed at this outcome, an officer offered: "The only reason I can give for their being such poor marksmen is that they had not become accustomed to the use of our new firearms. The most of them seemed to be armed with the improved Spencer carbine, others with rifles and revolvers." He referred to the latest .50-caliber Model 1865 Spencer carbine, with which the cavalry was then armed. Regardless of the guns that came into their hands, warriors adapted and became relatively proficient marksmen simply through practical necessity. "This process of instruction in the use of firearms has been going on from father to son for nearly three-quarters of a century," Gibbon further opined in 1879, "the arms improving with the marksman and marksman with the arms, until at the present day an Indian who cannot hit an object the size of a man at a distance of four or five hundred yards would be ridiculed by his comrades and laughed at as a squaw." Gibbon was amply qualified to make such a statement considering his experience with Nez Perce sharpshooters at the Battle of the Big Hole.[54]

The regular army was ill suited to fight a guerrilla-style conflict against an unconventional yet capable foe. Frontier warfare consisted of isolated small engagements, punctuated occasionally with sporadic organized campaigns against Indians of different nations or separate tribes and often of distinctly different cultures, practicing their own tactics. Moreover, the army could seldom be certain where or when or with whom the next emergency might arise. With few exceptions, Indian warriors were skilled horsemen who were highly mobile and adept at fighting on horseback. Contemplating the army's situation not long after the termination of the Civil War, Colonel Phillip Régis De Trobriand was convinced that the cavalry is the only arm of the service that can be used effectively in pursuing Indians. Unfortunately, nothing can be accomplished for a number of reasons: the superabundance of recruits who are not horsemen and are only awkward children in points of horsemanship when compared with the redskins . . . the task of transporting grain, shoeing equipment, and supplies to pursue an enemy who had no need of these impedimenta. . . . The Indian pony . . . can cover . . . sixty to eighty miles [a day], while most of our horses are tired out at the end of thirty or forty miles.[55]

Indian ponies that always foraged on grass and tree bark were clearly advantaged over the larger and initially more powerful army horses accustomed to subsisting on an abundance of grain and hay. As grain rations dwindled, or ran out completely, so too did the stamina of the mounts. As a civilian with General George Crook's column in midsummer 1876 complained: "The poor horses looked supremely miserable. Even those of the newly arrived Fifth were completely played out by the scout in pursuit of the Cheyennes. . . . As for the animals of the Second and Third Cavalry, they had had no grain or corn since the beginning of June, and at least a third of them looked well fitted for the boneyard."[56]

Such was the dilemma of cavalry in the West. Pursuing a highly mobile foe across the extensive distances encountered on the frontier was only a part of the problem. Whereas every male Indian became one with a horse at a very early age, riding and hunting every day if not engaging in mock combat, depot drill sergeants did well to teach recruits elementary horsemanship before the men left to join their units. Under ideal circumstances recruits were exposed to further mounted drilling, riding over rough terrain, and becoming properly conditioned. The problem was, conditions were not always ideal. Captain Thomas McGregor, for example, reported that twenty-odd recruits were assigned to his company of the First Cavalry literally on the eve of his departure on an Indian expedition. "These recruits were immediately . . . furnished with equipments for themselves and horses, and next day started on the expedition," he complained. "Not one fourth of these men knew how to saddle a horse, and in case the company had got into action, they would not only have been unable to inflict any injury on an enemy, but would have been an incumbrance [sic] to the other men."⁵⁷

It was exactly this factor of encumbrance imposed by recruits that caused some experienced commanders to segregate inexperienced men from the ranks when the prospect of combat appeared imminent. This is exemplified by the Seventh Cavalry as it prepared to advance up Rosebud Creek during June 1876. According one researcher's figures, the regiment had begun the campaign with some 7 percent raw recruits with less than six months' service, some of whom had joined their companies only during the month prior to the expedition. Custer prudently detached the bulk of these men and left them behind at the supply depot on the Yellowstone River, even though the decision reduced the effective strength of his regiment. Analyzing the First Cavalry's defeat at White Bird Canyon the following year, one officer claimed that participants in the fight, both officers and men, were "convinced that they had not the power to cope with an equal number of Indians. . . . The men had not been drilled, could not manage their horses, and knew little of the use of their arms. They had . . . been leading a comfortable, easy life at their posts, with an occasional drill, few inspections and a large proportion of men on extra and daily duty." This was undoubtedly an effect of the large influx of recruits to the cavalry in late 1876 and 1877, combined with short stints at the depot, resulting from congressional authority to bolster the cavalry after the Battle of the Little Bighorn.⁵⁸

The tactical doctrine of the day made the frontier cavalryman a second-rate mounted combatant at best and an indifferent one when dismounted. First Sergeant Henry McConnell, Sixth Cavalry, recognized the inconsistency of training and experience in his remark that "the Indians greatly preferred to fight cavalry . . . to fighting infantry, for the obvious reason that, owing to their superior and, in fact, unequaled horsemanship, they had their enemies at a very great disadvantage." Plains Indians had become particularly adept at using war clubs and hatchets in mounted combat against other Indians. There was therefore a good deal of truth in a widespread belief that "if a soldier gets near enough to an Indian to use a saber, it is an even chance as to which goes under." By the conclusion of the Civil War the greater range of the rifle-musket and the proliferation of breech-loading arms had rendered the traditional saber charge all but obsolete because cavalry formations could be decimated long before they clashed with infantry. Cavalry armed with breech-loading carbines, consequently, usually dismounted to fight on foot in skirmish order. During the subsequent Indian campaigns the near absence of close-quarters combat further reinforced the practice of fighting dismounted.[59]

Not a few cavalry officers were of the opinion that their men should never fight mounted. Therefore training men in the use of saber was neglected, as was firing the carbine and revolver while mounted. Also, cavalry horses, unlike Indian ponies used for buffalo hunting, often became frightened and unmanageable at the sound of gunfire. Cavalry became hardly more than mounted infantry, with the horse merely serving as the mode of transportation, and not effective for several reasons.

Tactics called for troops to maneuver in sets of four men each, trooper Number Four being the designated horse holder. When a unit dismounted to fight on foot, the Number Four man linked his own horse with those of the other three men of his set and withdrew with the animals to a point in the rear designated by the company commander. Meanwhile the other three soldiers assumed positions five yards apart on the skirmish line. Cavalry could perform such a deployment very rapidly with practice. A significant disadvantage not lost on Indians was that a cavalry force's effective strength and firepower was immediately reduced by 25 percent at the outset of a skirmish, while disciplined warrior ponies remained ground-tied behind a convenient hill or in a ravine.

Cavalrymen were further handicapped by their short-barreled carbines, which fired less powerful cartridges than infantry rifles. The smaller carbine was more convenient to handle and carry while the trooper was mounted, but at the same time it possessed shorter range. Thus United States cavalrymen, who were usually not armed with sabers, fighting afoot, with one-fourth of their number holding horses in the rear, and armed with less effective carbines, had transformed into a hybrid arm of uncertain identity. According to a correspondent to the *Army & Navy Journal*: "Our cavalry now is not cavalry, nor hussars, nor dragoons; exactly what it is will never be told."[60]

The infantry, more limited in speed and marching distances, often was relegated to garrisoning the forts during the cavalry's absence on campaign, escorting supply trains in the field, or guarding field depots from which the cavalry operated. Colonel John Gibbon, testifying before a congressional committee in 1878, conceded that the cavalry had the advantages of being able to travel much farther and faster, while the infantry was limited by human endurance. He added, however, that

> under favorable circumstances . . . as where the Indians are encumbered with their villages, infantry can sometimes overtake them and strike them in their camp. . . . The infantry is, in my opinion, far superior to the cavalry, and I think the Indians dread them more than they dread the cavalry, because they are well aware that as horsemen they are the superiors of the white men and that they are better shots on horseback than the white men possibly could be.[61]

Gibbon was not simply prejudiced in favor of his own branch of service: Red Horse, a Minneconjou Lakota veteran of the Custer fight, also attested to the warriors' respect for the "Walk-a-Heaps." Having kept the surviving two battalions of the Seventh Cavalry besieged on the bluffs above the Little Bighorn River for two days, the Sioux and Cheyennes sighted the Terry-Gibbon Column approaching up the valley. "A Sioux man came and said many walking soldiers were coming near," Red Horse related. "The coming of the walking soldiers was the saving of the soldiers on the hill. Sioux cannot fight the walking soldiers, being afraid of them, so the Sioux hurriedly left." Red Horse appreciated that infantry not only fought on foot, unencumbered by horses, but carried rifles that were dangerous at much longer ranges than were the short guns of the cavalry. As an unnamed correspondent, likely an army officer, expressed it in the *Cheyenne Daily Leader*: "The long infantry rifle is the thing to lift the Indian off his feet, wherefore the Sioux dread the 'walk-a-heaps' . . . unembarrassed by scary horses, much more than they do our showy cavalry. . . . The carbine is a pretty weapon, but compared with the musket . . . it is a mere military toy, excellent for dress parade, but damnable for active service." Indians, especially when mounted, were reluctant to approach within range of an infantry skirmish line and, when defending a village, also recognized the steadiness and inexorable quality of the attacking doughboys.[62]

Colonel Nelson A. Miles successfully demonstrated that his Fifth Infantry could operate against the Sioux at the most advantageous season of the year, winter. Indians normally moved to protected winter camp sites along streams where they remained sedentary until the following spring. During winter their ponies subsisted on tree bark and whatever grass they could find by pawing through the snow, until the new spring growth replenished their energy. When the cavalry occasionally moved against the Indians in early spring or late fall, enormous quantities of forage had to be hauled along in wagons to keep the cavalry mounts from starving, and even then the supply might be depleted. Miles proved in the Battle of Wolf Mountains (January 1877) that his doughboys could march, fight, and win under the extreme winter conditions in southern Montana Territory, at a time when the Indians least expected the blue coats.[63]

Field commanders were not oblivious to the special demands imposed by Indian fighting in the West. The dilemma was how to bring the infantry's longer range rifles and steadiness to bear against the Indian foe. The army had faced a similar problem prior to the Civil War when the mounted force consisted of only two regiments of dragoons armed with sabers and short smoothbore musketoons. In 1846 the army sought to combine the advantages of cavalry and infantry in what became known as the Regiment of Mounted Riflemen, intended for service exclusively on the western frontier, initially along the Oregon Trail. Horses provided the men mobility, but they fought on foot using infantry tactics and rifles of moderate length rather than carbines or muskets. Wartime demands caused the regiment to be transformed into a third cavalry regiment in 1861, yet the concept remained sound with regard to Indian fighting.

The regular army's return to the frontier after the war renewed the need for "mounted riflemen." In some instances, such as at posts like Fort Phil Kearny, Dakota Territory, where there was either no cavalry or a force too small to meet the demand, the post commander organized a detachment of infantry primarily for scouting purposes. Usually mounted on mules borrowed from the quartermaster or horses in a few cases when they were available, they were outfitted with regulation horse equipment. Corporal Lauren W. Aldrich, Thirtieth Infantry, was detailed to such a detachment at Fort Fred Steele, Wyoming Territory, in 1868. The twenty picked men of the detail were armed with Colt Army Model .44-caliber revolvers, along with their breech-loading Springfield rifles, and were permitted to wear buckskin outfits rather than the regulation uniform. They assumed something of an elite status and were together in the field constantly. Aldrich said: "Every man in our Mounted Infantry Scouts was great for sport as well as for active service and the ties of true friendship that bound them together were unbreakable of which no one but the soldier can fully understand." Despite the army reorganization the following year, the detachment remained intact and became a component of Company H, Fourth Infantry. Besides scouting, men of the detachment served as mail carriers from Fort Fetterman, Wyoming Territory, until they met and exchanged bags with the cavalry coming from Fort Laramie.[64]

Commanders continued to utilize mounted infantry from time to time, occasionally in the Southwest though more frequently on the northern plains. General George Crook, ever the pragmatist, not only converted many of his team mules to carry packs during the Sioux Campaign of 1876 but also devoted the rest as makeshift mounts for some two hundred doughboys of the Fourth and Ninth Infantry. Crook's head scout, Frank Grouard, witnessed what he referred to as the first circus ever held on the later site of Sheridan, Wyoming:

> Many of the infantry (Walk-a-heaps, as the Indians called them) had never been in a saddle in their lives, while none of the mules had ever had a saddle on their backs. . . . The [Goose Creek] valley for a miles in every direction was filled with bucking mules, frightened infantrymen, broken saddles and applauding spectators. Having nothing else to do, the entire command took a half holiday to enjoy the sport, and some of the most ludicrous mishaps imaginable were witnessed. But the average soldier is as persevering as the mule is stubborn and in the end the mule was forced to surrender.[65]

The employment of mounted infantry peaked during the campaigns of the late 1870s. The most enthusiastic advocate of makeshift cavalry was none other than Colonel Nelson A. Miles, commanding the Fifth Infantry. One of his officers explained why:

> This regiment campaigns altogether mounted on Indian ponies captured in former Indian wars. Miles perceived some time ago that Indians could catch us when they pleased, and that when it served their purposes to retreat, we were unable to follow them up. . . . The little animals are fat and frisky on the small amount of grain they occasionally receive . . . their ancestors for many a generation back have never known more luxurious provender than grass and sage brush, and the amount of forage required to keep an American horse in condition would cause two Indian ponies to die.

Obviously the ponies thrived in the luxury of a small grain ration, yet when necessary they could exist very well, as they always had, on grass alone.[66]

As would be expected, cavalrymen took advantage of the situation to poke fun at mounted infantrymen. Preparing to set out after the Nez Perce in 1877, Private William F. Zimmer and a group of Third Cavalrymen "went to the bank of the river to see a co. of infantry drill mounted on Indian ponies. . . . The sight was very amusing." The snickering troopers thereupon facetiously dubbed this battalion of the Fifth Infantry the "Eleventh Cavalry." Jokes notwithstanding, those same mounted doughboys eventually caught up with the Nez Perces at Bear's Paw Mountain in northern Montana Territory and, in the words of one of their officers, "dismounted and leading their ponies the men went right up to the edge of the bluffs and settled down to work. We held this position all the time, and we were about 300 yards from the centre of the village." Those latter day "mounted riflemen" thus proved their worth.[67]

Even as late as 1890, during operations against the Sioux on the Pine Ridge Reservation, the First Infantry was summoned to travel by rail from its stations in California to add its weight to controlling the rebellious Lakotas. The regiment's commander, Colonel William R. "Pecos Bill" Shafter, insisted to his superiors that the concept of mounted infantry be revived. "So the government ordered cow ponies for us," exclaimed Corporal Joseph Monnette, "and as a result our men had broken arms, and jaws and numerous other injuries." It did not take long for the hapless First to be accorded the moniker "the Eleventh California Dragoons."[68]

But the walk-a-heaps did not always walk or even ride horses or mules. In a few rare circumstances infantrymen rode into action aboard wagons. Such transportation was not any faster than good infantry could walk, if as fast, but the advantage lay in conserving their strength and perhaps providing a mobile firing platform. According to the statement of a Sixth Cavalryman who had served on the plains, the method was effective. "It took our people a long time to find out that a dozen infantrymen with 'long toms,' riding in a six-mule government wagon, were more dreaded by the Indians than a whole squadron of cavalry." In a brief 1876 encounter at Warbonnet Creek, Nebraska, two companies of doughboys were concealed in company wagons as escort to a supply train being watched by a large Cheyenne war party. "They were Indians who had seen our wagons and now were preparing an attack to win an easy victory," recounted Private Christian Madsen, Fifth Cavalry. "They thought this was a group of settlers, not knowing that under the tarpaulins infantry companies were hiding and that over one thousand horsemen were waiting for the signal to rush out." After a brief skirmish, the surprised warriors turned and retreated back to their agency, with the troops closely dogging them all the way. Two years later during the Dull Knife Outbreak, the post nearest the northward-passing Cheyennes, Fort Dodge, Kansas, had no cavalry in its garrison. Anxious to assist elements of the Fourth Cavalry then in pursuit of the Indians, the commanding officer ordered two companies of the Nineteenth Infantry loaded into six-mule wagons in what proved to be a successful tactic to intercept the Cheyennes temporarily.[69]

Regardless of the reasons for sending troops against Indians or the means, even a high private in the rear rank accepted that in the end the job of resolving the situation with arms would fall to him and his comrades. Seventh Infantryman Homer Coon, a participant in the Nez Perce War, expressed feelings typical of many regulars of the era. "None of us felt very hostile towards them," he lamented. "But our orders were to go after them." That unquestioning discipline, no matter what the mission, was the hallmark of the regulars. A first sergeant who had also served in the volunteers observed: "Each man loses his identity and becomes part of a machine. . . . Therein, in fact, lies the superiority of regular troops."[70]

CHAPTER 16

"The Government Pays You to Get Shot At"

Combat

In the broad scope of the military-Indian conflict in the Trans-Mississippi frontier, Indians for decades resisted Euro-American expansion, both civilian and military, into their claimed homelands and hunting territories. By the very nature of the conflict, the army was placed in the position of waging offensive operations against the tribes opposing the interlopers. That resulted in a great deal more scouting and marching on fruitless pursuits than actual combat. Engagements, when they happened, were mostly skirmishes, commonly characterized by ambushes and hit-and-run raids, only rarely punctuated by comparatively large-scale actions.

In the territories of the Southwest, already dotted with numerous towns and settlements dating from Spanish-Mexican occupation, military posts were established to protect thriving mining and agricultural areas as well as significant travel routes. Apaches in relatively small numbers initiated raids and ambushes on ranches, travelers, stagecoaches, and even military patrols, prompting the army to attempt to chase down the raiders and force them into a decisive fight. Such actions usually involved a detachment or company, less frequently battalion-sized forces. Occasionally the troops were persistent enough to locate and destroy Apache camps secluded in the mountains or canyon recesses. In only a couple of instances during the 1880s did the army marshal fairly large numbers of troops against the remaining Apache renegades, not because a pitched battle was anticipated but rather to control and check their movements throughout vast desert regions until they were worn down with no remaining sanctuary. In the words of Sergeant George Neihaus, Tenth Infantry: "It was a war of who lasted longest."[1]

On the plains and in the mountains of the North and Northwest, where the tribes encountered were larger and often more distanced from military posts, the army organized multiple strike forces, each numbering from several hundred to more than a thousand troops. The strategy for contending with these self-sufficient nomads was first to locate them, usually through Indian informants and white frontiersmen familiar with the haunts of the targeted people, then devise a strategy whereby the separate columns converged on the general area in which the Indians were believed to be. The Indians' mobility, however, seldom made it practical for the army to coordinate any specific actions very far in advance. The most that might be envisioned was that one or two columns might serve as "beaters" to drive the Indians into collision with another, or a column might find and launch a surprise attack on an unwary village. The overriding concern of field commanders was that the Indians would elude them and escape without drawing them into a telling battle and/or forcing them back to a reservation.

Inflicting defeat on Plains Indians, or even catching them, during summer was highly problematic because the tribes rarely remained in one place for very long. Buffalo and other game were plentiful, and grass was available in abundance to maintain the ponies in prime condition. Hunting and scouting parties ranging for miles in all directions from the camps reduced the chances that any approaching force would get close enough to attack without first being detected.

Campaigning in winter, even though it imposed special logistical problems for the army and greater suffering for the troops, proved a more successful strategy. In that season the Indians congregated in camps along streams where the valleys and timber sheltered them from frigid winds. During the peak season the people stockpiled enough food to see them through winter to the following spring, necessitating only minimal hunting. Their ponies, weakened by lack of grass and malnutrition, subsisted as best they could by pawing through the snow and foraging on tree bark. For the army's part, a surprise dawn attack on a sleeping village offered the most promising results.

Regardless of the time of year, the army found it necessary to wage total war against the tribes against which it was sent. A close friend of the Oglala Sioux, pioneer-rancher James H. Cook, explained the tactics employed: "No matter in what form an encampment might be approached by soldiers, whether mounted or on foot, opening fire upon the occupants of the encampment, regardless of the age or sex of those fired upon, was the usual procedure. To capture the horses of the band and kill as many of them as possible, and to secure some women and children as prisoners, was regarded as a most successful termination of a campaign."[2]

Indeed the brutal nature of Indian warfare could hardly have been prevented. Warriors avoided engaging in pitched battles with troops, if possible, unless they had a clear superiority in numbers over their enemy and terrain of their own choosing. That reluctance to fight on the army's terms was simply prudence on the part of the Indians. Unlike conventional military forces, Indians calculated to fight only when the odds favored their success, with the least possible loss to themselves. Their hit-and-run tactics had been honed to a fine art at least since the coming of the horse, perhaps longer. For the army to succeed, it had to strike the Indians when and where they were most vulnerable: in their villages, destroying their shelters, food supplies, arms and munitions, and virtually everything that enabled them to continue resistance. In that process noncombatants (women, children, the elders) were bound to become casualties either by accident or by intent. As early as 1871 a correspondent to the *Army & Navy Journal* recognized the army's dilemma: "The situation of the troops posted on our Western frontiers, and especially those placed in garrison in the hostile Indian regions, is very unenviable, as they are between two fires. If they do any real service they are denounced by the pseudo-philanthropists; if they fail for any reason to do all that may be expected of them, they are accused by settlers and travelers of inefficiency."[3]

Regardless of the politics of the particular situation, rank-and-file regulars fully appreciated that they would be the pawns called upon to risk their lives to enforce the government's will in settling the conflict. They were well aware, for instance, that a new war with the Sioux was approaching in early 1876. Evidence of their recognition of the forces placing the Indians on a collision course with national economic interests and their own disinterest in the matter can be found in this revelatory inscription that soldiers left on a board nailed to a tree near Custer City in the Black Hills:

> Our Sentiments
> We soldiers have got the blues—
> Cause the d--d infernal Sioux;
> We know the miner boys are bricks,
> But we obey Commander Mix.
> We know the time is not afar
> When we will see an Indian war;
> We know our efforts are as vain,
> As to make this creek run up again;
> We know the miners, too, are right,
> So let the reds and miners fight.
> Some Boys in Blue.[4]

Expeditions specifically aimed at finding and striking Indians created a different atmosphere than garrisons might have experienced prior to a routine summer escort or exploration. Private Peter Thompson, a Seventh Cavalryman posted at Fort Abraham Lincoln, Dakota Territory, in the spring of 1876, recalled that "after Custer's return [from Washington, D.C.], we were not long in doubt as to our future plan of action. We were put to work and kept busy overhauling stores, sacking grain, etc. Wagon trains also began to arrive from other posts to be loaded with grain, food, ammunition, tents, pack saddles and such other articles as are necessary for a campaign." As one of his comrades, Private William A. Lossee, predicted: "We expect to be out four or five months and have some fighting to do this summer for the Indians have all broke lose [sic]." Of course the men had no voice in the matter, yet at least some of them perceived the real motives for Sioux defiance and the impetus for the coming campaign. "This is one of the greatest Indian wars . . . ," contended Private Marion Horn, "and it is all on account of their being forced out of their rations and the miners going in the Hills and their possessions."[5]

Increased training in target practice and skirmishing were certain indicators that a campaign was imminent. Commenting on the mounting excitement, Sergeant William B. Cashan of Company L wrote to his cousin on May 6, 1876 (prophetically as it turned out):

> We are . . . all fitted out for war. . . . Every man is well armed with 100 rounds of aminition always carried. Their is a large

wagon train. Their will be about 2000 men in all. . . . This expedition is going to the big horn and is a different one from anyey that ever went out in this Contrey. . . . This is a war mission and Sutting Bull the Sioux Cheef must submit to Uncl Sam or kill the 7 Hors[e]. . . . I have eighteen months to serve. . . . I will be lookey anough to get this thrue. I will be a feerefull warrier.[6]

It was natural for most soldiers facing the potential danger of combat to experience some degree of apprehension. A veteran cavalryman, learning of a recent fight involving other troops of his column, confided in his journal: "I must lean on my Savior . . . for I do not know at what time I may fall or die." He indeed saw action a week later and survived the experience. No doubt some who had not previously embraced religion were suddenly inspired to do so. Others felt a need to reconcile with those that they had offended or experienced problems. First Sergeant Frederick Stortz, who had joined the army against his parents' wishes, wrote to his father on the eve of the Nez Perce Campaign: "If I should fall in Battle this summer . . . think kindly of me and forgive my past follies and believe as I do that my lot is cast for the best." All things considered, however, Private Charles Windolph best expressed the attitude of the average soldier in the ranks: "We knew there'd be some hard fighting, but a soldier always feels that it's the other fellow who's going to get it. Never himself."[7]

Morale often came down to the regulars' discipline and self-confidence. "We had orders to move and overtake those devils," declared a Twenty-Second Infantryman, "so with high spirits and determination, we boarded the old flat-bottomed steamer." Similar enthusiasm was evident when Company G, First Cavalry, received orders at Boise Barracks, Idaho Territory, to take the field against a band of Sheepeaters accused of murdering several Chinese prospectors. Closely observing his fellow soldiers making preparations, Private Edgar Hoffner recorded in his journal: "The boys are whetting their knives on their boots, their eyes snapping fire. The few hairs on the head of my Bunkie [are] standing on end." The men generally demonstrated a strong desire to be with their companies when there was a prospect of combat. No one wanted to be left behind. Learning that their units were being ordered out to control Apache insurgents, three troopers hospitalized at Fort Apache, Arizona Territory, coerced the surgeon to release them from sick report and return them to duty. While reluctantly signing the forms, the surgeon allegedly mumbled that theirs was "the most remarkable recovery in the history of the post." Two of those men were later killed in action.[8]

As the expectation of an engagement drew closer, stress affected men in different ways, some demonstrating determination, come what may; others humor; many experiencing varying degrees of fear. After dogging the trail of the Sioux for months Private Anthony Gavin said: "We wanted to have one good hot scrap with them. . . . If we could just get a fight, we thought that . . . would settle it." On the Staked Plains of the Texas Panhandle, as a battalion of the Eighth Cavalry closed the distance with Comanches for whom they had been searching, Private Eddie Matthews commented that he "knew what had to be done in case we met the Indians, my own life was at stake . . . and I was willing to risk that life with the rest, but not foolishly. . . . As we rode along I occupied my mind for a time by scanning the faces of the greater part of our Troop. Some looked stern and resolute, while others were wreathed in smiles called forth no doubt by some humorous remark of some of the wits . . . , but taken all in all a kind [of] stillness prevailed throughout the entire command." The reality of personal danger came home to twenty-one-year-old Private Jesse G. Harris during the Ghost Dance rebellion on the Pine Ridge Sioux Reservation. Harris, who had been in the army only seven months at that time, was ordered to ride as a flank guard some distance from the column during its approach to the Sioux camp. He was instructed that "if he saw any Sioux, to shoot and then fall back to the regiment. . . . I saw no Sioux. If I had, it wouldn't have taken me long to fall back. I was scared."[9]

As troops moved into enemy territory, the officers directed certain precautions to be taken, both to minimize detection and to maintain a state of heightened security and readiness to repel an attack. "Orders were given that no bugles were to be blown, no loud noises was [sic] to be made, and double pickets were to be placed around our camp," a trooper remembered. Experienced officers quietly assembled their companies at retreat to inspect the condition of arms and ammunition, and cavalry officers instructed the noncoms to ensure that the men repacked their saddles to be ready for instant use. "One night on the Yellowstone I will never forget," recalled Sergeant John Zimmerman,

Fourteenth Infantry. "It was a continual pour all night, and not the least shelter for anyone. . . . I was on picket with a squad of four men about five hundred yards from camp. All of us except one would sit together on some brush or rocks while the other would be out further to the front on watch." A member of Brigadier General George Crook's 1876 Big Horn Expedition claimed that when scouts warned the column that it was nearing the Indian village that they sought there was "a cold drizzling rain all night, with thurmometer [sic] said to be 30 below zero. Guards on the bluff crests above camp were told not to walk their posts. Must lie on the snowy ground and keep watch without moving, only the slightest turn of the head to detect any hostile approach." Second Cavalry private William White confirmed that "guards and pickets were wide awake. The night guards were ordered to shoot at once without waiting to challenge if any human form should be seen among the horses along the picket line at night." To defend against the possibility of a dawn attack, according to Seventh Infantryman Eugene Geant, "Every morning the whole command turns out at 2 o'clock and forms a skirmish line around and 500 yards from camp, remaining there until broad daylight."[10]

Guard duty in enemy country always posed risks to friends as well as foes. Making an ill-conceived decision, Colonel John Gibbon insisted that his Seventh Infantry pickets whistle twice, rather than challenge intruders in the usual manner. One of his officers considered it "an abominable system . . . [that] seems to be based upon the fallacy that an Indian will have more compunction about putting an arrow into a whistler than a man who talks out in his mother tongue." The sentries had standing orders to shoot if they failed to receive a response. The procedure had predictable results. "We were all startled . . . in the night by the discharge of a gun in the vicinity of camp," the wagon master for the Diamond R train recorded in his diary. "One of the guards had shot the Sergeant of the Guard in the head. Rather a sad affair to so lose one of our men." Sergeant Bernard Belicki, a bespectacled German serving in his third enlistment, had been making his rounds when he presumably meandered outside the lines and failed to hear the sentinel's whistle. He was buried the next morning on Little Timber Creek, Montana Territory.[11]

Pickets served a vital purpose by providing early warning and a buffer between themselves and the encampment. When an enemy was detected, the sentries were to offer resistance then fall back on the main body. Sergeant William Miller, Fourth Cavalry, participated in a campaign against the Comanches in the Texas Panhandle in 1869. He recalled that while the command (composed of several companies of the Ninth Cavalry and the Twenty-Fourth Infantry in addition to his own) was camped along a stream "we were surprised on towards night by a band of Comanche and Kiowa Indians who drove in our pickets and tried to stampede our horses, but were driven off." The following day the troops struck and destroyed a small village in the fluid sort of warfare that typified the Indian Wars. An Eighth Cavalry private described his experience being assigned to a picket post with green men and their reaction when an alarm sounded: "Soon as the shot was fired all hands (excepting myself) ran in. I would have been in soon as any of the others, had I only heard the shot. I talked pretty plain to those men who slept near me, for running in and leaving me sound asleep . . . I am not very courageous, but if [I] dreaded the name of Indians as much as a great number of our command, I would never soldier a day on the frontier." Seventh Infantryman Thomas H. Wilson informed a friend that his first experience of being shot at occurred when he was a picket on post about two miles from camp. Sighting what he correctly assumed were Indians approaching his position, Wilson mounted his horse and waited until the figures were within about four hundred yards. "Then I let blaze into them and started for camp. The red devils let blaze after me and let their war whoop. It was worse than the bullets. I thought I was a gone gosslen [sic: gosling]." Despite his fright, Private Wilson remembered his instructions and performed his duty by alerting the camp in time for his comrades to turn out and repel the attack.[12]

Unsurprisingly, plains Indians practiced their time-honored tactic of raiding in various forms against the army, as they had always done against other Indians. Raiding camps and successfully escaping with horses or mules, even though the practice involved risk, was challenging, exhilarating, and a means of proving warrior prowess. Such attacks were lightning quick, affording no time for soldiers to prepare mentally for imminent danger. Private Isaac H. Sembower, a First Cavalryman, described a typical dawn raid during the Nez Perce War. "The Indians stampeded the pack mules and jumped the camp at break of day. We gave them a couple of volleys and they left. As soon as it got light enough to see, we saddled up and started after them." In this instance, the three companies caught up with the raiders and engaged them in a five-hour skirmish. Even though they recovered some of the stolen mules, the troops paid a high price—one man killed and three wounded, two of whom died that night.[13]

Indians had a disconcerting habit of showing up when and where they were least expected. A troop of the Third Cavalry searching for straggling Sioux bands in the Black Hills in 1877 broke camp one morning and rode all day without finding any signs of the enemy. Shortly after they arrived back at their bivouac on the Belle Fourche River and were boiling up coffee, however, the Indians suddenly attacked them. "We droped [sic] our coffee and went fore [sic] our horses and saddled up in a hurry," Private Edward D. Barker recorded in his journal. "We routed the Indians and chased them until dark when we gave up the chase. We filled our canteens with water and struck the trail of the Indians without eatin[g] anything and followed it all night and at day light we went into camp and I was sent out too [sic] miles on picket." Such a ploy, keeping the enemy under surveillance all day then raiding their camp unexpectedly, was typical of the Indian way of war.[14]

Not all ambushes were so benign; in fact they could be quite the opposite. In June 1885 a Fourth Cavalry detachment from Fort Huachuca, Arizona Territory, while guarding a supply camp near the international border with Mexico, became complacent by assuming that Chiricahua Apaches would not attack a soldier camp, and certainly not in broad daylight. Several of the men were eating dinner when the recruit posted as guard over the grazing horses unexpectedly showed up in camp. Having previously expressed a great desire to see an Indian fight, the man abruptly had his wish granted. Just then "we were surprised by a thundering volley from the nearby hills, none of us had our guns with us as we had left them with the wagons a few yards away," confessed Private William B. Jett. "At the first volley, Neihaus, right by my side, was killed by a bullet in his forehead. He fell with a biscuit and a piece of meat in his mouth and did not move again." The negligent sentry, armed only with his revolver, immediately bolted for cover but was cut down. Two other troopers turned tail and ran for safety in nearby hills, leaving a sergeant and three men to fend off the Apaches. Jett continued: "The surprise was so great and I was so shocked at the death of my old friend Neihaus [sic] that the only thing . . . I thought of was to run to the wagon and get my gun as the others did. When we four were left alone and firing from behind the wagons . . . I was very much scared. . . . I was terribly afraid to die, as I knew I was no Christian." The sergeant's leadership in putting up a determined defense for several hours saved the rest of the party, although, after being wounded three times, he was killed by a fourth fatal shot.[15]

Contrary to widespread belief that Indians never fought at night, some most certainly did when it was to their advantage, like a Comanche raiding party that struck a cavalry camp on the Staked Plains at about one o'clock in the morning. Suddenly jolted awake, one trooper exclaimed that

> it sounded to me like all the devils incarnate and all the demons of hell had issued forth in that one lonely spot to make the night hideous with their orgies. . . . I was only a moment in getting a cartridge in my carbine, and with revolver in one hand and carbine in the other with only my shirt and pants on I ran to the right of our troop. . . . I could see the Indians by the light of the moon riding in a circle near our lines. . . . I discharged my carbine at the first Indian I saw, and never taking time to notice with what effect I reloaded and fired as fast as I possible [sic] could.

The officers then advanced a skirmish line that continued firing to drive off the warriors. At dawn the command took stock and found that one man had been wounded and two mules killed. "A number of the wagons bore bullet holes in there [sic] canvas, showing that the Indian fire was too high," the soldier added. "It is impossible now to tell the loss of the Indians, as they left none of their number behind."[16]

Determining the number of Indian casualties was always problematical for that very reason. A mark of warrior bravery in battle was to retrieve the wounded and dead, usually on horseback, and carry them from the field, even if it meant exposing the warrior to great danger. The greater the risk, the greater the honor. Only those falling within or in immediate proximity to troop positions were sacrificed. Army reports of Indian casualties therefore were estimates at best, relying as they did upon what officers and men saw, or thought they saw, and bloodstains on the ground as well as any bodies left in their possession.

Army marksmanship training, as discussed previously, was woefully inadequate prior to the 1880s and depended to a great extent on the degree of emphasis applied by the regimental or post commanders. Even so, the parsimonious amount of ammunition allowed for target practice, coupled with elementary instruction in shooting, was insufficient to make most soldiers more than poor to mediocre shots under the best of circumstances. Colonel John Gibbon counseled: "In fighting Indians good marksmanship is the first requisite. . . . We cannot expect to compete by the employment of men, many of whom never looked through the sights of a rifle six months before they are called on to shoot Indians!" Only during the early 1880s did the training curriculum finally include limited practice involving moving targets and firing as skirmishers at unknown distances, and that only for men classified as marksmen. The rest continued to fire at bull's-eye targets at fixed ranges. Practice in volley firing, which had been the norm when troops had been armed with muskets, was nonetheless continued.[17]

The army took it for granted that soldiers would indeed use their weapons when the time came, but there were individual exceptions. Some men simply were not psychologically prepared to kill another human being. In one instance, some infantrymen sneaked up on a party of Indians. Having an Indian in his sights only forty yards away, a corporal took an inordinate length of time aiming yet did not fire. When another soldier inquired about it later, the corporal admitted that it was because "that Indian had no earthly chance whatever and the trigger finger on my gun hand would not make the final touch." His comrade responded sardonically: "I didn't know you was so blamed chicken hearted." Many, like Seventh Cavalry recruit Peter Thompson, were both inexperienced and poorly trained. While lagging alone behind his battalion as it advanced on a huge Indian village situated on the Little Bighorn River, Thompson was suddenly confronted at a distance by five warriors. Only when he threw his carbine to his shoulder did he remember that it was not loaded. Fortunately for Thompson, the perplexed Sioux moved off, leaving him unharmed.[18]

Faced with his first combat situation, Private George Cranston thought "how queer it seemed to draw up and blaze away right at the yelling redskins, but it had to be done." If the great majority of soldiers had any moral conflict about killing other men, they apparently kept it to themselves and adjusted mentally. Coming under Indian fire for the first time, Signal Corpsman Will C. Barnes probably reflected a common emotion when he exclaimed: "Everybody blazed away at them, hoping by some bit of good luck to hit one. . . . Can you imagine the thrill I was getting? My first Indian fight! What a joyful experience! . . . I was a constant reader of yellow-backed dime novels . . . and I was living them all over again."[19]

In a stand-up fight both infantry and dismounted cavalry deployed in skirmish lines. The tactic had been employed during the Civil War as a light screen of soldiers deployed at a distance before a main battle line to initially engage their enemies, either offensively or defensively, to reveal their position and gauge their strength, whereupon the skirmishers fell back on the main body. During the Indian Wars, however, the skirmish line became the principal combat deployment, given the usually small forces involved and the nature of Indian tactics. The advent of breech-loading rifles and carbines likewise made massed troops unnecessary, because more soldiers in extended order could deliver a greater volume of aimed fire over longer distances. Such a formation had the flexibility to be deployed to the front or on either flank and could advance or retire over uneven terrain, be extended or contracted according to circumstances, be quickly shifted either right or left on the same line, or be wheeled on an axis to meet a threat from a different direction. The first and second sergeants were posted on the right and left flanks of the line, respectively, with the other sergeants positioned a short distance behind to act as file closers to maintain the prescribed intervals and prevent any soldiers from leaving the line without orders. The officers positioned themselves several yards behind the file closers to maneuver the line and direct the firing.

Private Anton Mazzanovich, an Austrian-born immigrant serving in F Troop, Sixth Cavalry, left a vivid description of the quintessential Indian fight that might have occurred anywhere in the West. Spotting the troops well in advance of their arrival at the mouth of a canyon wherein lay his village, Geronimo laid an ambush as a delaying tactic to occupy the troops until his women and children could safely escape. As they began receiving fire, the cavalrymen were ordered to dismount and count fours, and the designated holders led the horses to the rear. Mazzanovich continued his narrative:

> We then spread out in a long line about fifteen feet apart, and commenced to advance toward the mouth of the canyon. . . . When the Indians first opened fire on us we were . . . about 400 yards from them, and when the skirmish line was formed, the distance to the mouth of the canyon was about 1500 yards. The order was to advance in double-quick time until we were within 1000 yards. . . . By this time I was calm and collected. That peculiar feeling I had undergone when we were first fired on, had all disappeared. We could locate none of the Indians, as they were all under cover; so the only thing to do was to watch for a puff of smoke and fire at that. When the Indians would begin to get a bead on our line, we would advance fifteen paces forward [to alter the range]. It was evident that they were peppering away at our horses in the rear, as they made a good target. . . . Orders were given to save our ammunition, as each man had only sixty rounds and the officers did not know when the pack train would overtake us. . . . We were fully exposed to the fire of the Indians for the ground was level. . . . I can't say how close the bullets were dropping, but they certainly made a most ugly sound. . . . It was queer how the men would duck their heads. From time to time we moved slowly forward. Our officers were back of the line, moving to and fro, so the Indians could not get a bead on them. . . . Bu[r]ford, our [acting] first sergeant, who was on my right, fell. . . . [Mazzanovich was then ordered back to replace one of the horse holders.] During the time I was on the skirmish line I fired thirty rounds of ammunition, and I wondered if any of the bullets had found a mark. . . . We had been fighting the foe all the afternoon without a fair chance of hitting an Indian because they were all under cover and concealed from view.[20]

The pack train with additional ammunition having come up, the combatants continued exchanging fire until it was too dark to see well enough to shoot. By that time the Indian women signaled that they had reached a safe distance. After firing a few parting shots, the warriors too slipped away into the night. Sergeant Burford's body was taken back to Fort Grant, Arizona Territory, for burial.

When Indians stampeded from the Cheyenne-Arapaho Agency in Indian Territory and occupied a commanding hill south of the Canadian River, a force composed of two troops of the Tenth Cavalry, one of the Sixth, and a company of the Fifth Infantry was ordered to bring them back. A sharp fight ensued, typical of the nameless actions of the Indian Wars, as recalled by Corporal Perry A. Hayman, Tenth Cavalry:

> As the first set of fours crossed the river, Captain Steven T. Norvelle of M Troop formed the line and gave the command to dismount to fight on foot. . . . The next was the order to charge. We charged them and dislodged them, our captain now giving the command to take cover. . . . While [I was] rolling around on the ground my rifle [*sic*: carbine] got some sand in the . . . breech. I had to get a stick to clean it out, and in doing so I got in full view of the Indians. . . . I got shot in the right side. I laid down behind a stump, and again those Indians fired a number of shots. . . . Some came so close to me that they threw sand in my face. . . . Laying [*sic*] as if I was dead, the Indians gave up shooting at me."

Hayman's presence of mind while being targeted undoubtedly saved his life.[21]

Once a village had been located and reconnoitered, usually through the aid of friendly Indian scouts, the informal tactical doctrine called for a strong column to be divided into at least three battalions, usually but not always composed of cavalry. When at all possible, two or more companies or battalions would attack from as many different directions, with another assigned to scoop up and drive off the pony herd. Indian scouts often participated in the latter task on the promise of being allowed to take their pick of the captured ponies.

The element of surprise was all-important, so attacks were launched in the grayness of early dawn when movement was masked and villagers still lay asleep, yet the steadily increasing daylight would be of advantage to the attackers. A Second Cavalryman involved in the

Reynolds Fight at Powder River related that the troops halted in a ravine about three miles from the Indian village "for two long eternal-like hours . . . hunger, frost, and want of sleep held us fast. Scouts return at day and the sluggard, faded and half alive column moves off." As Fourth Cavalrymen approached a Cheyenne village in the Bighorn Mountains of Wyoming Territory in late 1876, "strict orders were given against loud talking and no smoking or lights were permitted. We moved forward with the utmost secrecy, under cover of darkness," related First Sergeant Charles Maurer.[22]

After making a long trek over the mountains in pursuit of the Nez Perces in western Montana Territory, the Seventh Infantry came within striking distance of the Indian camp in the Big Hole Valley. Private Homer Coon described the preparations when the column was still five miles away: "All of us left behind anything that would hinder us in a fight such as overcoats, blankets, etc. . . . Every man was issued 100 rounds of ammunition. Most of the men left their blouses behind. There were no unnecessary orders given for what one was to do because every one of us had some Sioux Campaign experience the year before. Company commanders had their orders and we only waited to get them. . . . Everything was done quietly without any kind of noise."[23]

With combat imminent, the men settled into the serious business at hand. A Fourth Cavalryman about to enter his first combat wrote that he "began to think what I was about to get into." He was certainly not alone in those thoughts. Another trooper remembered that a somber mood descended over his company of the Seventh Cavalry as the column rode toward the combined Sioux and Northern Cheyenne village on the Little Bighorn. It was obvious that every man appreciated the gravity of the situation. "We knew right enough that this was *the* day. This was *IT*. This was what we had been training and working for all these years. . . . [Captain Frederick] Benteen used to say: 'The government pays you to get shot at.'" They were about to experience, in spades, just what that meant.[24]

Private William G. Wilkinson told how two of his officers inadvertently relieved the tension just before going into combat on a cold winter's morning. "Capt. [Edmond G.] Fechet told us to try and get our fingers limbered up as we would be in action in a few minutes," Wilkinson recalled. "We were so numbed from the cold, we could not have pulled the trigger. . . . He also told us to take off our overcoats. We were in pretty low spirits . . . and that did not help any. Lt. [Edward C.] Brooks said, 'Capt[ain] I think we could die just as well with our coats on.' The capt., who was inclined to profanity, said, 'Well —— keep them on.' That created a laugh, and raised our spirits somewhat."[25]

Because Indians did not customarily post night sentries, disciplined troops cautiously approaching camps usually gained the advantage of surprise. Beyond the possibility of a young man or boy out tending the ponies, no one in a village stirred at that early hour. "The first thing we did was to capture the ponies, which was easily done, as they were grazing leisurely," wrote Private Louis Zinser, Third Cavalry, describing the attack on a Sioux village at the Battle of Slim Buttes. "We mounted our horses, making a charge, and yelled as though the earth was coming to an end. The Indians were surprised. . . . We made short work of it, captured everything they had and took possession of the village." Success did not always come that easily, however. Sergeant Charles N. Loynes recalled the Seventh Infantry's charge at the Big Hole River: "The shouts of the soldiers, the war whoops of the Indians, the screeching of the squaws, who with Winchesters in their hands were as much to be feared as the bucks. Our attack was a complete surprise." But as Private Homer Coon elaborated: "We fired several volleys into their tepees from across the river then plonged [sic] into the water and attacked. . . . It took us only a short time to capture the two camps which were held for about 20 minutes. The smoke from our rifles settled to the ground in the early morning light everything looked very hazy."[26]

Fights that started at dawn sometimes unexpectedly lasted well into the day or even longer when Indian resistance proved to be more stubborn than anticipated. At Slim Buttes the initial attack cleared the village, but as Private Richard Flynn, Fourth Infantry, recorded in his diary: "16 Indians including 11 squaws and papooses concealed and entrenched themselves in a ravine . . . and opened fire on any one [sic] who happened to come within range. After a brisk firing from our Command, we succeeded in killing and wounding three of the bucks, and the rest having fired all their ammunition away now begged for quarters. . . . In the ravine were found the bodies of . . . a prominent chief and 3 squaws, who had fought to the death, rather than be taken prisoners."[27]

When women took up arms, soldiers were left no choice but to treat them as combatants. DeBenneville Randolph Keim, a newspaper correspondent present at the attack on Black Kettle's Cheyenne village on the Washita River, observed: "A number of squaws also participated in the fight, and were seen firing with all the energy and precision of warriors." Also in that village was First Sergeant John Ryan, who witnessed the killing of a woman simply for revenge. "An Indian squaw had a white child and was trying to make her escape with that child . . . and when . . . she saw that this white child was about to fall into our hands, she immediately seized a butcher knife and plunged it into the child's body, killing it instantly. She had no sooner committed this act than the whole side of her head was blown off by our men." Other evidence, however, suggests that the light-complexioned child may in fact have been her own and that she killed it in panic to prevent the child from falling into the hands of the attackers.[28]

The necessity of attacking villages in order to defeat the warriors inevitably resulted in women, children, and elderly men and women becoming casualties. Prior to going into action, some officers instructed their men to spare noncombatant villagers if at all possible. A Seventh Infantryman attested: "We were told not to shoot the squaws and I honestly can say it was not done on purpose." Wooden Leg, a Northern Cheyenne warrior participant in the Reynolds Fight on Powder River, related that in the panic of the attack a blind elderly woman inadvertently had been abandoned by her people as they fled. That night some of the men returned to the devastated camp looking for any ponies that might have survived. Wooden Leg said: "At the destroyed camp we saw one lodge still standing. . . . There was the missing old blind woman. Her tepee and herself had been left entirely unharmed. We talked about this matter, all agreeing that the act showed the soldiers had good hearts." But even when troops exercised restraint, conditions did not favor such discrimination. Poor light, haze created by gun smoke and dust, and hundreds of shots being fired in all directions (not to mention ricocheting bullets), compounded by the confusion attendant to such an attack, virtually assured that some family members would become casualties.[29]

Others, however, attempted no distinction. A prevalent attitude among the rank and file was expressed by Sixth Cavalryman George Whittaker: "When at peace everything was fine, but when at war, it was kill them all." In a circumstance almost identical to that related above, a Second Cavalryman involved in the Dull Knife Fight entered a lodge and discovered an elderly woman wrapped in a buffalo robe and holding a pipe. When the woman refused to give up the pipe, the trooper noted that "I stuck my pistell in her fase [sic] and she did not like the looks of it." The soldier claimed the pipe as a souvenir, yet did not molest the woman. Returning to the same lodge a few hours later, however, he "saw the old squaw shot all to pieces. I found afterwards that some of the boys in my company had done it for to get the Bufflow [sic] robe."[30]

Indian fighting always had a few traits in common: intensity, danger, and brutality. With regard to his experience fighting the Modocs in the Lava Beds of Oregon, Private Maurice Fitzgerald said: "They expected no quarter, and none was given." That rule applied universally, regardless of the tribes or the army units involved. Soldiers knew that being captured was not an option. As the Twenty-Seventh Infantrymen at the Wagon Box corral prepared for an onslaught by a vastly superior number of Sioux and Cheyenne warriors, Samuel Gibson, then a private, was stunned to see two veterans "fixing their shoestrings into loops to fit over the right foot . . . thence to the triggers of their rifles for the same purpose Sergeant [Frank] Robertson had done—to kill themselves when all hope was lost." Private Samuel H. Bentley, Fifth Cavalry, corroborated that view: "We always put one cartridge where we could get it, for if we were captured by the Indians we knew what our fate would be." That unwritten axiom was widely understood and accepted among the frontier regulars.[31]

Few engagements with Indians approached the magnitude of true battles, yet in some instances relatively large numbers of troops and Indians clashed in open combat, testing the mettle of both sides. "There was no flinching on the part of anyone," Private William O. Taylor remarked of the beginning of the Battle of the Little Bighorn. "To most of us, it was our first real battle at close range . . . a strange new experience to sit up as a human target to be shot at." One of his Seventh Cavalry comrades, Private William C. Slaper, recalled that "bullets began to whiz about us. . . . This was my first experience under fire. I know that for a time I was frightened, and far more so when I got my first glimpse of the Indians riding about . . . firing at us and yelling and whooping like incarnate fiends." That wild yelling and whooping, remembered by so many combat veterans, was not without psychological purpose; it not only unnerved the soldiers but also bolstered the courage of Indian warriors.[32]

Inexperienced recruits sometimes failed to appreciate the danger that they were in by unconsciously exposing themselves to enemy fire. At the 1873 Allen Creek Fight in Montana Territory the Lakota and the Seventh Cavalry were exchanging continuous fire across the Yellowstone River. As Trumpeter Louis E. Hills later admitted: "I laughed when [Private John] Tuttle shot an Indian, and General Custer . . . told someone to take that boy [Hills] and put him behind a tree and make him stay there. Pieces of leaves were then dropping like rain from the bullets passing through the trees overhead." A green Fourth Cavalry headquarters orderly in his first combat action related: "We were standing still once and the boolets were flying thick. When . . . one of the orderleys rode up to me and says, 'move around . . . or you will git shot.' This is something I had never thought about before, for I was to[o] much excited looking at some of the rest of the boys gitting shot" (all odd spellings in the original).[33]

The conditions encountered in actual combat immeasurably complicated effective shooting, particularly for the poorly trained men with no previous combat or hunting experience. Private William Earl Smith enlisted in the army on February 1, 1876, and barely nine months later was engaged in the Dull Knife Fight in the Bighorn Mountains of northern Wyoming Territory. Experiencing combat for the first time, Smith assumed a prone position and began firing "at some Indians I saw about 1 thousand yards off. I fired the shots I had in my belt and then, as I was lying there on my belley [sic] I feel [sic] asleep." If his estimate of the distance was even close to being correct, Smith may as well have gone to sleep, because the enemy was far beyond the effective range of his .45 Springfield carbine. Sixth Cavalryman Fred Platten participated in the 1882 Battle of Big Dry Wash, the last major engagement in which the army was pitted against Apaches in Arizona Territory. Lying along the canyon rim, Platten's troop commenced firing at a range of several hundred yards. "Strain my eyes as I did, I couldn't see anything to shoot at, and couldn't figure out what the others were shooting at," he confessed. "'I can't see any Indians,' I called out to the soldier on my right. 'Me neither!' he yelled back. But that didn't stop him; he proceeded to take several shots at trees and rocks across the wash. I entered into the spirit of things and fired a few shots myself, at nothing in particular." An Apache warrior nevertheless spotted Platten. "Wham! A slug tore into the tree trunk, about three inches from my face, throwing bark and slivers all over me. I ducked plenty fast."[34]

It was in combat that the veterans truly proved the worth of their experience and discipline. One of those was Private Thomas F. O'Neill, who had served in the volunteer infantry during the Civil War and afterward in both the regular artillery and infantry prior to joining the Seventh Cavalry. During the initial stage of the Battle of the Little Bighorn, as one of the soldiers on Major Marcus A. Reno's skirmish line, he recalled: "The men were in good spirits, talking and laughing and not apprehensive of being defeated." A new man, Private William C. Slaper, said that the behavior of the veterans, exemplified by a soldier in his company known as "Happy Jack," had a calming effect on him and the other recruits. "During all that leaden hail that fell about us," Slaper remarked, "I could hear "Happy's hearty laugh ring out at a distance . . . I didn't see anything to laugh at; but it cheered me and made me feel a bit braver." In the thick of the fighting, Lieutenant Winfield S. Edgerly's attention was drawn to Private Charles Sanders, a third-enlistment man in his company. "I noticed a broad grin on his face, altho' he was sitting in a perfect shower of bullets. I didn't have time to question him then, but the next day after the firing had ceased, I asked him what he was laughing at at such a time. He replied, 'I was laughing to see what poor shots those Indians were; they were shooting too low.'"[35]

That devil-may-care spirit so often evident in the frontier regulars is reflected in the diary entry of Private Louis Zinser made immediately following the Battle of the Rosebud. A strong force of Lakotas and Northern Cheyennes suddenly descended on Crook's midday bivouac along both sides of the creek. Once the cavalry recovered from its initial surprise and formed in line, Zinser recorded: "We were ready for a good time . . . something we were looking for! We were ordered to take a hill on the opposite side [of the creek] to keep them from surrounding the camp. Companies C and G were in for that, while other companies were ordered in other directions. We had four men wounded in taking our position, but none killed. We found five dead Indians on the hill." The battle continued to seesaw back and forth across a wide swath of hills throughout the day, with some of the fighting becoming hand-to-hand. "[Sergeant] William W. Allen . . . died as such a soldier might be expected to," wrote a witness. "His horse was shot twice and he was dismounted. . . . He turned upon them, determined to sell his life as dearly as possible. . . . The brave fellow fought, standing all the while and firing cooly with his carbine until the Sioux, coming in on either side, shot him down. Allen then tried to draw his pistol, but one of the Sioux, clubbing his carbine, struck the poor fellow over the head." Private Thomas Lloyd, Third Cavalry, exclaimed: "It was one of the hottest places I ever was in. . . . . The company was surrounded by Indians and [it was] only that we stuck together and give [sic] them the best in the shop; they would have got away with our scalps. They stood and fought us within 100 yards, until we got 6 volleys into them and commence[d] to drop them and their ponies. They . . . fell back into the hills . . . trying to coax us to follow, but we knew too much of Mr. Sitting Bull for that." A civilian who observed the intense fighting at first hand commented on the behavior of the regulars: "The whistling of the bullets could not induce them to forget that they were American soldiers. Under such conditions it was easy to understand how steady discipline can conquer mere numbers."[36]

The Dull Knife Fight offers another premier example of a pitched battle during the western Indian campaigns. While some of the cavalry's advances were conducted as mounted charges, much of the fighting with the Cheyenne tribesmen was executed in the prevailing dismounted fashion. A participant in the battle, First Sergeant James S. McClellan, Company H, Third Cavalry, provided a detailed contemporary account of Indian combat:

> We charged them on foot and the bullets flew as thick as hail. Lots of men fell on both sides as we run in on them. They broke and ran. One of them being about 15 yards from me, I shot him through the small of the back. He fell on his face. I run up and gave him a few pistol shots, took his gun, a Sharps carbine and as I was doing so a Pawnee [scout] came up and took the coup. I could not scalp him as it looked so bad for a white man to commence to mutilate the dead in that way. . . . The company stood fire like a brick and we had some hard fighting. We were on the skirmish line from daylight until dark, 9 hours.[37]

The common idea that Indian combat marksmanship was poor because of a lack of understanding about trajectory and the use of long-range rifle sights is a generalization that bears reexamination. Certainly not all warriors were competent riflemen, any more than were all soldiers. First Lieutenant Oskaloosa M. Smith, Twenty-Second Infantry, considered the Sioux to be poor marksmen because they had wounded only three of his men during a skirmish lasting several hours. In contrast, Second Lieutenant Charles L. Hammond, Third Cavalry, was clearly impressed by the shooting of Northern Cheyenne warriors that he encountered at the Dull Knife Fight. A few months after that experience he wrote to a friend informing him: "They are such deuced fine shots & chipped the sage brush around your head so constantly . . . that it's a wonder they were not more successfully [sic]." When the Sioux and Cheyennes opened fire from several hundred yards on General Crook's camp on Tongue River in early June 1876, newspaper correspondent John Finerty observed: "The savages were rapidly getting the range of our camp and making things uncomfortably warm. . . . Their guns carried admirably, and made loungers who thought themselves comparatively safe, hop around in a very lively . . . manner."[38]

About two weeks later those same warriors inflicted extremely heavy losses on the Seventh Cavalry at the Battle of the Little Bighorn. Although Indian marksmanship in the Custer fight can hardly be evaluated, considering the circumstances, the two-day siege of the Reno-Benteen battalion does offer a reasonable measure. A private of A Company remarked that he had just taken cover behind a makeshift barricade when an Indian warrior a few hundred yards away began firing. "The man next to me on the left [packer Frank Mann] . . . raised his head just enough to take a shot when a bullet struck him right between the eyes. . . . He had been quite noticeable for his continuous firing . . . and he was finally located by an Indian sharpshooter and put out of business." Lying next to a comrade in a shallow rifle pit, Private Charles Windolph recalled that "Jones said something about taking off his overcoat, and he started to roll on his side so that he could get his arms and shoulders out. . . . Suddenly I heard him cry out. He had been shot through the heart." Minutes later Windolph himself received a flesh wound from a ricochet, and another bullet shattered the stock of his carbine. On the opposite side of the troops' position, Company M was similarly targeted by another sniper. First Sergeant

John Ryan attested that "he fired a shot and killed the fourth man on my right. Soon after he fired again and shot the third man; fired the third time and shot the second man. . . . He fired again and wounded the man next to me . . . [and] I thought my turn was coming next." At a signal Ryan and a half-dozen others arose and returned a volley at the warrior's position, silencing him. Meanwhile the Indians drew the fire of the troopers by jumping up then immediately falling flat on the ground before the troopers could take proper aim or holding up a headdress or blanket as a decoy target: "and we'd blaze away, until we learned better," Windolph confided.[39]

When Sitting Bull's Lakotas made a night-time attack on a combined camp of infantry and cavalry on the Yellowstone River, Sergeant Fred W. Mixer recalled that "the war whoops plainly showed that a good sized band were before us. . . . Their aim, however, was wild, they firing over us every shot, and they showed no disposition to charge." As Mixer's company lay prone on the ground, bullets began striking closer, some of them splattering mud and grass in his face. His company commander, Captain George L. Browning, lying beside him and noting the obvious, dryly remarked that "they seem to be firing lower." Browning, a veteran of Gettysburg and other battles, had been an enlisted man and later a line officer in the Regular Division throughout the Civil War.[40]

The Nez Perces gained a well-deserved reputation for being superior marksmen. They had long been friendly with whites and had been in close association with them on their reservations in Idaho and northeastern Oregon. Consequently they came into possession of quite a number of firearms, including repeaters and fine single-shot hunting rifles. When a portion of their reservation was abolished and the people were forced to relocate, the "nontreaty" Nez Perces made a bid for freedom, prompting the government to send the army against them. At the Battle of Camas Meadows a Nez Perce bullet ripped through a Second Cavalry officer's buttocks, which according to one of his men "caused us to realize that we had no ordinary Indians to deal with." A First Cavalry trooper, Private John P. Schorr, claimed that in a subsequent fight with the same warriors a particularly skilled Indian sharpshooter killed or wounded a soldier every time he fired.[41]

After attacking Chief Joseph's village on the Big Hole River, Colonel John Gibbon underestimated the determination and fighting skill of the Nez Perces and suddenly found himself on the defensive. Private Homer Coon recalled: "We re-crossed the stream and made for the wooded side of the mountain. . . . We used trowel bayonets and we began to entrench our position at once. The Indians soon had us surrounded." The thick pine woods provided excellent concealment and protection for the warriors as well as an elevated shooting position for one of their sharpshooters. "They were quite successful in this as they got about seven of us, including Lieut. English, before we found the sniper," Coon declared. A sergeant finally spotted the warrior and dropped him from his perch. But many other Indian marksmen continued the fight in the woods. They recognized the insignia of rank and concentrated their fire on officers and noncoms. After penning up the troops until late that night, by which time the Indian families were safely away, the warriors broke off the fight. They had killed twenty-three soldiers and six civilians. One of the soldiers, lamented a comrade, was "First Sergeant Frederick Stortz with the glaze of death coming in his light blue eyes." Stortz was the man who had written to his father on the eve of the campaign asking for forgiveness.[42]

In the final episode of the Nez Perce War the troops finally corralled Joseph and his people at Bear's Paw Mountain in north-central Montana Territory. This time it was the Nez Perces who were besieged in a position from which there was no escape. Still, the warriors continued to peg away at any soldier who exposed himself in the surrounding positions. Private Luther Barker, Fifth Infantry, recollected that Corporal John Haddo announced that he was going out on the firing line to take a few shots at the Indians. Selecting a good position "and raising his shoulder a little higher to get a better view of the Indian stronghold, he received a rifle ball through the center of his chest and sank down dead, without getting a single shot at the Indians."[43]

The regulars generally had confidence in their officers and noncoms, especially those veterans with combat experience in the Civil War or in western service. One of the most notable examples was Captain James Powell, who commanded a detachment of Twenty-Seventh Infantrymen at the beleaguered wagon box corral near Fort Phil Kearny in 1867. Surrounded by several hundred Lakota and Cheyenne warriors, Powell, according to Sergeant John M. Hoover, calmly instructed his men to aim for the middle of the body as the best way to ensure a disabling wound. Powell had also taken the precaution of supplying his men with some seven thousand rounds of ammunition for their new .50-caliber Springfield breechloaders. The captain knew his business, having served as a private and noncommissioned officer in the infantry and dragoons for many years before the Civil War and as a line company officer throughout it. Powell's cool demeanor and grim determination to put up a spirited fight served to inspire his men, several of whom were also wartime veterans. "There was no thought of wavering," one of them said later. They stood their ground.[44]

In New Mexico Territory later that year Captain Francis H. Wilson led a detachment of the Third Cavalry from Fort Union in pursuit of some Mescalero Apaches who had run off stock from a local ranch. Wilson, a regular officer, had served with both the Fifth Infantry and the Third Cavalry in the territory since 1861. When he and his men caught up with the raiders, however, the band had grown to several hundred, far outnumbering the troops. "We were compelled to retreat . . . dismounting and number four leading the horses," explained Private John R. P. Foster. "We had five more men wounded and killed, which left about 30 men to do the fighting. If our Captain had not been a grand old Indian fighter there would not have been one man left to tell the story." In this instance Wilson's men admired his prudence in withdrawing from a fight that they obviously could not win.[45]

Captain Frederick W. Benteen was a thoroughly seasoned combat officer, having served in the volunteers throughout the war and on the plains with the Seventh Cavalry since its organization in 1866. During the hilltop fight at Little Bighorn, Benteen was calmly walking along behind his company's line observing the Indians and directing the fire of his men. Just as he passed a sergeant lying in a rifle pit, the man raised his head slightly and a bullet pierced the crown of his hat, without touching the man's head. Benteen immediately dressed him down: "Damn you, I told you to keep down; now you do it." The sergeant grinned and retorted: "Why don't you keep down, Captain?" To which Benteen replied: "Oh, I am all right; Mother [his wife] sewed some good medicine in my blouse before I left home, so they won't get me." The witness who related the story commented that the captain's example and his courage throughout the fight did much to boost the men's confidence.[46]

Wounded during the Battle of the Big Hole, Colonel John Gibbon directed his senior captain, Charles C. Rawn, to form his company and advance on a threatening warrior force firing from brush some eighty yards away. "Then the discipline of the regular soldier showed itself," remarked Sergeant Charles N. Loynes. "The company formed under fire and advanced toward the Indians. On they went, over dead and wounded soldiers and Indians." The sense of duty instilled in the regulars and unquestioning fidelity to that duty on all occasions, no matter how great the hardship or danger, was the normal expectation.[47]

Combat action sometimes brought out the best in individuals. As Captain Benteen had impressed on his men, getting shot at went with the job. One who accepted that, and represented the essence of the frontier regular, was forty-three-year-old Sergeant Daniel Conn, a five-foot six-inch transplanted Hibernian from Cork. By 1882 he was serving in his fourth enlistment and had become a fixture, if not something of a stock character, in the Sixth Cavalry. While on the firing line at Big Dry Wash, Conn took an Apache bullet through his neck, the slug narrowly missing his jugular vein but nicking a vertebrae and making an exit hole the size of a silver dollar. His captain, standing close by and seeing him fall, remarked sadly: "Well, I'm afraid they got poor Conn." But the sergeant later regained consciousness and, while under the care of the surgeon, was heard to say: "Sure, I heard the Cap'n say I was kilt. But I knew I was not. I was only spa-a-achless!" (odd spellings in the original). Conn survived, but the wound nevertheless ended his army career nine months later when he was compelled to take a disability discharge.[48]

Some soldiers displayed courage under fire by taking the initiative to perform seemingly minor yet dangerous acts, such as during the early stages of the Wagon Box Fight when the men realized that their tents had been left standing beyond the corral, thus providing a screen for the Sioux warriors shooting at them. Private Samuel Gibson, a nineteen-year-old native of Nottingham, England, saw two men sprint out to pull them down. Suddenly the man next to him, Private John Grady, yelled "'Come on kid, let's help,' As he jumped over the box, I followed him, with the bullets zipping about our ears and the arrows swishing past and striking the ground on all sides of us." All made it back to the corral safely. In actuality the American-born Grady was only a year older than Gibson and had a month's more service.[49]

Sergeant David Marshall, Third Cavalry, went down with a bullet through his face at the Battle of the Rosebud. Three men picked up the still-alive sergeant and began carrying him to the rear when Private Phineas Towne of his company saw them struggling with Marshall and lent a hand. A number of warriors rode over a nearby hilltop about that time, causing the men to drop Marshall and make for their horses. Towne alone remained to defend the wounded man. The sergeant urged Towne to save himself because he was dying anyway. Ignoring the sergeant's plea, the plucky private shouldered him: "I carried my comrade until it was useless to carry him any farther, for he was dead." Towne laid the body down and sought cover.[50]

Numerous acts of courage by enlisted men went unnoticed or were not recorded officially by officers. Prior to the Civil War meritorious acts in combat could be recognized officially in two ways. The most common was by citing men in regimental orders read out to their commands at parade. The other was the granting of a "Certificate of Merit," an impressive velum document signed by the president and the secretary of war. The certificate was first authorized in 1847 as a means of materially rewarding private soldiers: the honor carried bonus pay of two dollars a month. Initially intended to recognize courageous acts by soldiers during the Mexican-American War, the award was allowed to go dormant until being revived through petition of army officers in 1877. Still, the award had two inherent problems: it could be granted only to privates, and the extra pay ceased if the man was promoted. Those rules, accordingly, excluded noncommissioned officers and at the same time discouraged the recipients from accepting promotion. Those restrictions were not lifted until 1891, after the Indian Wars had effectively ended.[51]

In those days the army awarded only one decoration: the Medal of Honor, first authorized by Congress in 1862 in recognition of most distinguished gallantry in action and other soldierly qualities. No lesser decorations existed for heroism in combat and the early criteria were rather broadly defined, so a comparatively large number of Medals of Honor were awarded during the nineteenth century. The first of those issued to regulars during the post–Civil War era came in 1868, with a total of 367 awarded through 1891.[52]

A disproportionate number of Medals of Honor were awarded to noncommissioned officers, not only because they were more prone to demonstrate initiative and leadership in combat but for the more practical reason that they were excluded from receiving the Certificate of

Merit. First Sergeant Thomas H. Forsyth, for example, served with the Fourth Cavalry and distinguished himself at the Dull Knife Fight by exposing himself to heavy, close-range fire. Despite receiving a gunshot wound to the head, he inspired other troopers to remain with him to prevent the body of their dead lieutenant from falling into the hands of the Indians. At the time Forsyth was nominated for the Medal of Honor, his company commander attested: "I know that Col. Mackenzie wished him to have one [Certificate of Merit] and preferred to recommend for that instead of a Medal of Honor because the certificate carried extra pay with it, and the Sergt. being a married man needed the money." That statement alone reflects Mackenzie's high regard for his sergeant and the welfare of his family, yet he did not recommend Forsyth for the medal. Mackenzie did, however, promote Forsyth to the prestigious rank and higher pay of regimental sergeant major in partial recognition of his "distinguished gallantry." Forsyth eventually received the medal sixteen years after the event, just prior to his retirement at the rank of post commissary sergeant.[53]

Recipients of the Medal of Honor performed their deeds in engagements all across the western frontier. Some of those fights are well known, many others all but forgotten. The citations for most, like that for Sergeant John F. Rowalt, L Troop, Eighth Cavalry, are brief: "Gallantry in action with Indians" at Lyry Creek, Arizona Territory, October 14, 1869. Although the record is silent about the details of how this former Ohio farmer distinguished himself, it was not the only time when the sergeant demonstrated his pluck. Three and a half years later, while commanding a detail of three other soldiers and six civilians pursuing Kiowa raiders near Fort Bascom, New Mexico Territory, Rowalt caught up to them and led an assault against the party numbering seventeen. In the sharp skirmish that followed, Rowalt's men killed five warriors and wounded three, with no loss to themselves. The civilians involved enthusiastically commended the behavior of the four soldiers in a letter to their company commander. Unit pride was clearly evident in a comrade's announcement: "The Lieutenant brought the letter over to the Troop and read it to the men. . . . Three cheers for our little party was given by all hands. The citizen who brought the letter was one of the party in the fight and he said he never saw men behave better in a fight than our boys did. Said they were no more excited than they would have been hunting rabbits." Sergeant Rowalt was not decorated for this second action, but he and the other participants were later cited in department orders for "gallant and meritorious conduct," an honor shared by the entire troop.[54]

The highest number of Medals of Honor awarded for a single engagement (though not the greatest percentage for the number of troops involved) was for the Battle of the Little Bighorn. None, of course, were granted to men in Custer's battalion, which had no survivors, but twenty-four medals were awarded to enlisted men of the combined battalions of Major Marcus A. Reno and Captain Frederick W. Benteen. (There was no provision at that time for posthumous awards.) Seven of those went to noncommissioned officers. Fourteen men were cited for volunteering to obtain water for the wounded by descending the face of a barren bluff to the river and were exposed to fire for approximately a quarter-mile. Four others performed courageously by providing a base of covering fire for the water carriers and in so doing diverted the Indian fire from the carriers to their own position.[55]

Sergeant Richard P. Hanley, then thirty-three years old and in his third enlistment, particularly distinguished himself, although by his own admission his bravery may have been more inspired by a sense of responsibility than by intentional heroics. Late in the afternoon of June 25, 1876, after the battalions had taken up a defensive position atop the bluffs, Hanley saw an ammunition-laden mule named Barnum break from the rest of pack mules and start trotting east toward the Indian lines. The Sioux and Cheyennes would have been only too happy to receive the two thousand rounds of .45-caliber ammunition that the traitorous Barnum was carrying. Hanley, the quartermaster for Company C and a member of the train detachment, "felt responsible for the mule and thought he would be blamed if the mule got away." Quickly mounting his horse, the sergeant rode out, revolver in hand, trying to either catch the animal or shoot him before he reached the enemy. Hanley spent some twenty minutes trying to capture the headstrong mule, with Indian bullets zipping by and kicking up dirt all around him. Finally, when the two circling contestants had progressed nearly halfway toward the Indian positions, the sergeant succeeded in heading off Barnum and driving him back to the herd. Hanley miraculously survived the ordeal unscathed.[56]

The Apache wars also accounted for a number of incidents in which regulars performed in an exemplary manner. Two Ninth Cavalrymen distinguished themselves in a hard-fought confrontation with a band of approximately fifty of Chief Nana's warriors near Cuchillo Negro Creek in southern New Mexico Territory during August 1881. Troop I, operating from Fort Craig, pursued the Apaches into the foothills some forty miles southwest of the post, when the warriors turned and put up a determined fight against the black cavalrymen for approximately two hours. One of the officers suffered two wounds, two soldiers were wounded, and six horses killed. Second Lieutenant George R. Burnett, the officer wounded, later cited First Sergeant Moses Williams

> for his bravery in volunteering to come to my assistance, his skill in conducting the right flank in a running fight of three or four hours [sic], his keensightness [sic] in discouraging the Indians in hiding, which probably prevented my command from falling into a trap, for the skill and ability displayed by him rallying my men when I was dismounted, . . . and lastly for his coolness, bravery, and unflinching devotion to duty in standing by me in an open position under a heavy fire from a large party of Indians at a comparatively short range.

Burnett also commended another of his men, Private Augustus Walley, for his courage under fire, "for he was always to the front, ready, willing, and anxious to do his full duty—and even more." Walley was conspicuous for mounting and riding out between the lines, under heavy fire, to rescue a wounded comrade and bringing him back safely, the men riding double. Both Williams and Walley received Medals of Honor for their conduct in the engagement.[57]

In contrast, the reality of combat, or sometimes just the imminent prospect of fighting Indians, occasionally exposed weaknesses of human character. A Sixth Cavalryman told of a man in his company who became so completely incapacitated by fear when Indians threatened their camp at Jacksboro, Texas, that he had to be disarmed. This former schoolteacher, who obviously lacked the basic instincts for soldiering, subsequently deserted, surrendered, then deserted a second time. At Fort Stevenson, Dakota Territory, Corporal George E. Wilson and four men were on herd guard near the post when a dozen Lakota warriors appeared. Seven of them made a dash toward the grazing mules. The exasperated post commander exclaimed: "On seeing them appear—just seeing them appear—the corporal . . . and the four men—without firing a shot . . . abandoned the mules and cowardly ran to hide themselves like sheep behind the slope of the bank." The corporal was summarily stripped of his rank and the other men punished by being taken off extra duty pay. "The only thing such cowards are good for is making mud for adobe," added the thoroughly disgusted colonel.[58]

Some men lost their nerve when combat dangers loomed. On the eve of the Sioux Campaign in 1876, Second Cavalryman William F. Zimmer noted in his diary that "last night Gould of our co. shot off 2 joints of his trigger finger while on guard. It's strange that so many trigger fingers get shot off & always accidental. This is the third one I've known of." About three months later, during the Battle of the Rosebud, a small party of troopers became surrounded and the fighting became hand to hand. Proving the adage that surrender was not an option when fighting Indians, Captain H. R. Lemly confided just after the battle: "One poor lad, a recruit, with an insane idea of surrender . . . calmly gave up his carbine, handing it to the nearest Sioux and was brained instead by a blow from its butt." A Seventh Cavalryman who showed the white feather at the Battle of the Little Bighorn was ever-after stuck with the nickname "Cracker Box Dan" because he sought the dubious protection of an empty hardtack crate placed over his head. The man was so mercilessly ridiculed by the other members of his company that he later deserted. Further evidence that cowardly behavior was not tolerated is found in the journal of an enlisted man kept during the Sheepeater Campaign of 1879. Just before an anticipated action, Private Edgar Hoffner, a second enlistment man, and his First Cavalry comrades learned of a veteran infantryman in the command who had hidden out all day. To discourage any of their own men who might be similarly inclined, Hoffner wrote: "A couple of Cavalry men drew their revolvers and threatened to shoot any who ran during the fun."[59]

There can be no doubt that major engagements, particularly defeats, had their effects on the morale of the army's rank and file. A Seventh Infantry soldier who had helped bury the more than two hundred dead of Custer's battalion following the Battle of the Little Bighorn was clearly shaken. Expressing his trepidation in a letter to his brother a few days after that gruesome experience, he wrote: "Things look very bad. There are ten Indians for one of us, and they are whipping us every time they meet us. There have been over 450 soldiers killed here this summer. There is no use denying the fact[,] Ed, but I think I have seen the states for the last time." This soldier's enlistment ended about a month later. Having seen enough, he was only too happy to board a Yellowstone steamer to return to the tranquillity of his Illinois home.⁶⁰

The treatment that Indians accorded enemy dead and wounded who fell into their hands during and after battle often defied description, given the societal sensibilities of the late nineteenth century. Although some tribes, as discussed previously, did not engage in much if any mutilation of enemy bodies, the Sioux and Cheyennes were infamous for doing so. Private Phineas Towne, Third Cavalry, a participant in the Rosebud battle asserted that "they captured one other comrade of mine by the name of Bennett, of L Troop . . . and completely cut him in pieces. His remains were buried in a grain sack." Second Cavalry trooper William H. White, who arrived on the Little Bighorn battlefield a couple of days after the engagement, observed:

> All of the bodies . . . were stripped to utter nakedness. Faces and hands were hacked, Bodies and limbs were slashed. Chests and abdomens were wide open, with viscera protruding. In some instances heads were missing. A hand, or a foot, or an arm or a leg, or both, or some of these or all of them, were gone from most of the body trunks. These extreme mutilations, supplemented by the effects of the warm weather, made recognition of individuals a difficult or impossible attainment.⁶¹

Another cavalryman present at the time noted sadly that "their hatred extended even to the poor horses, they cut and slashed them before the[y] were dead." Such scenes did nothing to engender sympathy for Indians among soldiers, but did give a man pause to consider his chosen occupation. "It is a grand thing to look on to see a brave fellow killed or wounded in battle," Irish Private Francis O'Toole wrote to the *Pittsburgh Leader*, "but when you come to look on your comrades and friends butchered and cut up the way they were . . . it makes a man think of the position he holds in this grand army of our great republic."⁶²

Indians may have intended such scenes to intimidate their enemies, but more often than not brutalizing the dead generated just the opposite reaction among soldiers. Private Louis Zinser described the aroused spirit that pervaded the troops in Crook's column, now committed to fight come what may: "All of the boys would rather kill Indians than eat these days, in order that they may avenge General Custer."[63]

Neither were soldiers immune to scalping and otherwise abusing enemy bodies in combat situations. First Sergeant John Ryan recounted his experience taking a scalp at the Battle of the Washita. Suddenly encountering a dismounted Cheyenne warrior firing at another trooper, Ryan spurred his horse, nearly running over the Indian.

> As I went by, I fired and dropped him with [my] first shot. . . . I wheeled around and put two more bullets from my Spencer carbine into him and then emptied my Colt six shooter into him. . . . I immediately dismounted, turned the Indian over on his face and . . . put my left foot on the back of his neck, and raised his scalp. I held the scalp to Egan, saying, "John, here is the first scalp for M Troop." . . . [After collecting the warrior's weapons] I hung this scalp on the saber hook of my waist belt . . . on the way back I noticed that the skirt of my overcoat was covered with blood from the scalp and I threw it away.

Ryan added that when his company commander asked how he felt about having taken a scalp, he replied that he "felt a little relieved about the heart."[64]

In another instance, a twenty-man detachment of the Fourth Infantry had a skirmish with a party of about twenty-five Indians near Fort Fred Steele, Wyoming Territory, in 1869. One of the members of the detachment, Private Charles Lester, informed his sister by letter: "We only killed three of them and the rest escaped. We took the scalps of the ones we killed and let them lay [sic]." Scalping was not universally condoned, however, as reflected in Tenth Cavalryman Reuben Waller's admission: "Our soldiers also scalped some of the Indians, but we soon put a stop to that kind of barbarity." Much of the scalping that did occur was perpetrated by allied Indian scouts, according to a Fourteenth Infantryman: "They jumped right in among them [Sioux], commencing to scalp them, flinging the scalps high in the air, hooting and howling. This is the only time I ever saw any scalping done by any one [*sic*]." In some circumstances, nevertheless, soldiers did not limit themselves merely to scalping. Incensed by the treacherous murder of Brigadier General Edward R. S. Canby during a peace conference with Modocs in 1873, Private Maurice Fitzgerald declared: "I remember distinctly seeing the head of a Modoc severed from the trunk, perhaps by some soldier. . . . Passing troopers generally saluted it with a vicious kick."[65]

Although scalping and other savage acts by soldiers were the exception, American soldiers have always had a penchant for collecting other trophies of war in the form of souvenirs. After the 1875 fight on Sappa Creek in Kansas, Sixth Cavalry sergeant Fred Platten returned to inspect the body of a Cheyenne who had come near killing him but was shot by another trooper. He took the warbonnet as a memento of his close call, but later one of his officers borrowed it, ostensibly to show friends in New York. Platten never saw it again. In the aftermath of the Battle of the Little Bighorn, soldiers rummaged through the abandoned Indian village looking for any keepsakes they might find. A Second Cavalryman revealed that the corpses of Sioux and Cheyenne warriors killed during the fight and reposing in still-standing lodges were readily looted for souvenirs. "I took about half a dozen pairs of moccasins from the surplus of such foot wear beside the bodies, which had been placed thus in accordance with Indian customs as extra supplies." Writing to his diary in 1891, Private Hartford G. Clark may have sensed that the massacre of the Lakotas at Wounded Knee may have signaled the end of the plains wars and thus opportunities for obtaining trophies: "Today I managed to get holt [*sic*] of an indian's scalp, which a Cheyenne scout brought in, and I will hang it up over my bed." Two days after making that entry he noted that his troop had ridden across the battleground, strewn with the bodies of men, women, and children. "I got a pair of leggings of[f] one of the warriors legs—every-body [*sic*] was looking out for relics."[66]

Burials in the field often were "simply a respectful gesture," in the words of one soldier. Digging implements were always in short supply unless the command happened to be accompanied by a wagon train, resulting in only the most rudimentary graves. When circumstances permitted, the body of the deceased was wrapped in his own blanket or overcoat, or occasionally sewn up in a canvas shelter half, and interred in a shallow grave. A single trench sufficed when it was necessary to bury several bodies. "The dead soldiers were buried at twilight and all in one grave," recalled Private William O. Taylor, referring to the three men killed during the Seventh Cavalry's August 11, 1873, fight with the Sioux on the Yellowstone River. "The burial was conducted with all the impressive ceremonies incidental to a soldier's funeral. The troops parading with reversed arms and forming a hollow square in the center of which was the grave, and then 'Taps' was blown. It was quite a solemn affair." It was customary for one of the commissioned officers to read a burial service, or at least scripture passages, over the deceased. In at least one instance, however, not a single Bible could be found in a Fifth Cavalry command, so a lieutenant stepped forward to recite the Episcopal burial service from memory, which was "a distinct compliment to his early religious training," a trooper remarked. Such acts elevated the esteem soldiers had for their officers and contributed to the professional bond.[67]

When troops were in enemy territory, graves were obscured to every extent possible to prevent Indians from disinterring the remains for the purpose of looting and mutilating the corpses. After Crook's command suffered a loss of eight men killed in action at the Battle of the Rosebud, Sergeant John Zimmerman described the most common procedure used to accomplish this: "A large hole was dug in the ground right in the main trail, all of them laid in it, covered with their blankets, then with canvas, filling up the hole as nearly as possible. A fire was then built on top of this, the ashes afterward scattered about the place, [and] all the command, horses and men, then marched over the spot, obliterating all signs of breaking the earth." An alternate method called for the cavalry picket line to be stretched across the grave site immediately after the burial so that by morning trampling by the horses hooves left the grave unrecognizable. Yet a third method was to locate the grave within the bivouac, level the mound and carry away the excess backfill, and then build a large fire on the site, leaving only ashes.[68]

Combat conditions frequently precluded any sort of formality, resulting in burials that were both hasty and minimal, if that. In at least one instance the "burial" of two Third Cavalrymen killed in action at the Powder River fight consisted only of disposing of the corpses by slipping them beneath the ice on the frozen river. When two companies of the First Cavalry clashed disastrously with Nez Perce warriors at

White Bird Canyon, Idaho Territory, they lost an officer and thirty-three enlisted men. Private John P. Schorr recalled: "We had no chance to bury our comrades until a week later, and it was a painful duty to perform. We did not at the time bury them, but simply covered the bodies with rocks to keep the coyotes from mutilating the bodies."[69]

In other extreme circumstances, such as the situation after Little Bighorn, where the survivors needed to bury more than two hundred and fifty bodies, Private William C. Slaper declared: "All we could possibly do was to remove a little dirt in a low place, roll in a body and cover it with dirt. Some I can well remember, were not altogether covered. But the stench was so strong from the disfigured, decaying bodies . . . that it was impossible to make as decent a job of interring them as we could otherwise have done." Having only a few spades, supplemented with tin cups, hatchets, and axes to loosen the soil, First Sergeant John Ryan lamented: "We simply dug up a little dirt aside of the bodies and threw it over them. In a great many instances their arms and legs protruded out." Only those burials made upstream at the site of the Reno-Benteen siege came near being adequate simply because the rifle pits dug for protection during the fight came into use as graves for the dead. It would be more than a year before the army sent troops to make more proper burials, but even so it was too little, too late. By then many exposed bones had been carried off by animals, and some of the first graves could not be found.[70]

The dead were sometimes buried at or near where they fell, particularly in the case of infantry or when the officers did not anticipate Indians revisiting the site. At other times corpses were removed by tying them on the backs of horses or mules to be buried at more distant locations considered to be less vulnerable to desecration. But even that precaution could not guarantee that the bodies might not be exhumed and misused. An example of this occurred after the wounded of the Seventh Cavalry were transported aboard a steamer down the Yellowstone River for return to Fort Abraham Lincoln. Nearing death by the time the boat arrived at the supply camp situated at the mouth of Powder River, Private William George was left there and expired soon thereafter. The Sixth Infantrymen guarding the depot buried George with military honors but later were called away for other duty. When the doughboys returned a few weeks afterward, they discovered that the Sioux had destroyed the deposited grain supplies and dug up the soldier's body.[71]

The men wounded in action more often than not faced a grim prognosis. Medics trained and equipped immediately to treat casualties on the battlefield would not become a reality until decades after the Indian Wars. Small units in the field almost never benefited by having a surgeon or even a hospital steward. The soldier "was not taught anything about 'first aid' and was not furnished anything for first aid," Private William Murphy declared. "Men were sent out on escort . . . and if wounded had nothing to bandage the wound or stop the bleeding. . . . Often it would be several days before the wounded man could see a doctor." Similarly, a man wounded during an engagement could not rely on anyone to remove him from the line of fire, unlike the risks taken by modern-day combat medics. Private Peter Allen, Seventh Cavalry, told how he was wounded during a retreat, "one bullet crushing my left arm from the elbow to wrist, another passed through my belt and clothing, grazing my skin on my right side; and a third bullet passing through my hat, plowing a furrow through my hair across the top of my head, which rendered me unconscious for a short time." When he awoke, Allen found that he was between the lines and called to the man nearest him on the skirmish line to hold his fire long enough to permit him to crawl to safety. Allen later counted nine bullet holes in his overcoat, yet he survived.[72]

A Second Cavalry trooper, Private John Lang, wounded at the Powder River fight in March 1876, related the typical experience of a casualty: "I, with other wounded, received such aid as was available, and [was] made as comfortable as a campfire, blood-soaked blanket, and hot coffee would afford." Recovery from wounds often depended on the health of the victim, pure grit, and considerable luck. Sixth Cavalryman Louis Ebert took a bullet through his thigh while carrying dispatches, but fortunately the missile did not strike bone. When his sergeant told him that the wound must be disinfected, Ebert asked him what with, as they had no medical supplies. "He took a big chew of tobacco . . . pulled the wound wide open and spit the nicotine into it, then kept working until blood and chew ran out below—then took part of my shirt for a bandage and helped me in the saddle." They rode another ten miles to reach an infantry camp, where the wound was properly dressed. Ebert claimed that he never saw a doctor and never missed a day of duty as a result.[73]

One or more army surgeons, either career professionals or contract doctors, accompanied major expeditions, because accidental injuries and combat wounds were to be expected. The medical component of the short-lived Big Horn and Yellowstone Expedition consisted of six surgeons in all, with their supplies packed on two mules. Each doctor additionally carried a small quantity of common medicines and dressings on his own mount for emergency use. Still, the means were primitive by any standard. The medical officers agreed that the seriously sick and injured would be collected in some spot designated as "the hospital" at the end of each day's march, "but for this purpose there was but one tent fly, no bedding except four blankets, and no cooking utensils but the tin cups of the men, and one frying pan borrowed from the packers." Another army surgeon fortunate enough to be allowed an ambulance reported that the vehicle served as his hospital during the daytime marches and dog tents sufficed at night.[74]

Bullet wounds in the head and torso frequently proved fatal, if not immediately then later as a result of shock, blood loss, uncontrolled infection, or a combination thereof. The large-caliber soft lead projectiles of the day caused horrific wounds by taking a path of least resistance and creating great tissue damage, particularly when they encountered bone and became deformed. Such bullets, moving at relatively low velocity, striking an arm or leg bone nearly always shattered the bone, necessitating amputation of the limb. In a scene reminiscent of the Civil War, New York newspaper correspondent Finerty described the medical facility on the Rosebud battlefield: "The hospital was established under the trees down by the sluggish creek, and there the surgeons exercised their skill with marvelous rapidity. Most of the injured men bore their sufferings stoically enough, but an occasional groan or half-smothered shriek would tell where the knife, or the probe, had struck an exposed nerve." Even with chloroform as an anesthetic, operations were inherently dangerous. "Kennedy was wounded in the knee, so badly that amputation was necessary," wrote Sergeant John A. Kirkwood after the fight at Slim Buttes, Dakota Territory. "He died while being operated on. I was in the hospital at the time."[75]

Almost miraculously, some seriously wounded men managed to defy the odds and survive. Following the attack on the Cheyenne village on Red Fork of Powder River late in 1876, First Sergeant James S. McClellan, Third Cavalry, recorded in his diary that he "was up to the hospital to see the wounded. Found them in good spirits. Holden is the worst. They have not got the ball out of his shoulder." The bullet struck Private Henry Holden, pitcher for the Company H baseball team, between the shoulder blades then passed down his spine before lodging in his back. Surgeons eventually removed the ball some months later, and Holden served out the remainder of his enlistment. Whether or not he was still able to pitch a baseball was not recorded.[76]

Transporting the wounded in the field occurred more as an afterthought than by preplanning. Unlike the Civil War, where battles took place in populated regions with farms and villages and transportation was readily available to convey the wounded to homes and field hospitals, engagements on the frontier almost without exception occurred far from civilization, often hundreds of miles from the nearest army post. Small units without benefit of either medical personnel or wheeled vehicles, which was usually the plight of troops operating in the Southwest, had few choices. After the fight at Cibique Creek, Arizona Territory, a soldier related: "The four wounded men were placed on gentle horses, with a soldier riding behind each man to support him" during the more than forty-mile return trip across broken terrain to Fort Apache. First Sergeant Charles Maurer noted that after the Fourth Cavalry's engagement with Geronimo's band at Horseshoe Canyon in western New Mexico Territory "there were no stretchers or ambulances with the command. The wounded Sergeant of 'C' Troop who had been shot above the heart was carried in an improvised litter by men of his troop. It took these men practically all night to reach the camp.... The [other] three wounded men had no other alternative and rode the ten miles on horseback, suffering horrible pain."[77]

Small lightweight army ambulances with a capacity of no more than four patients were always in short supply, even when medical officers accompanied large expeditions. When the number of casualties exceeded ambulance space, army supply wagons were pressed into service if available. But, as one observer commented, making a comparison with the medieval torture device: "A sick man might as well be stretched upon the rack as in an army wagon." Obviously wagons with no springs intended for transporting tons of materiel over the roughest terrain were not well adapted for carrying injured soldiers, though better than nothing when provided with grass bedding and blankets.[78]

In the absence of wheeled vehicles other more primitive means were resorted to for moving the wounded. Following the Battle of the Little Bighorn, it became necessary to move some fifty wounded men about fifteen miles downstream to rendezvous with a steamer than had somehow managed to reach that point. Initially the medical officers thought that the casualties could be transported by the simplest means available—hand litters consisting of blankets. Private William H. White remembered the ordeal: "Each litter had four carriers, a man at each corner. The carriers were afoot. . . . The litter-bearers had to stop for rest every fifty to seventy-five yards. The putting down of the litter beds for these rest periods was distressful to the patients." Distressful hardly described the agony suffered by wounded men carried doubled up in a hammock-like blanket with the bearers stumbling over uneven ground in the dark.[79]

A slightly better conveyance often employed in the West was the travois adopted from the Indians, who used it to move their camp goods and the infirm from one place to another. A medical officer authoring a study of the subject claimed that this well-known method for transporting the wounded had been used as far back as colonial times and during the Lewis and Clark expedition. The device consisted simply of two long poles, often lodge poles salvaged from Indian villages, with the forward ends fastened on either side of a horse or mule. The splayed trailing ends of the shafts were coupled by two cross-braces (spreaders), to which were fastened a hide or canvas bed for the patient. Thus only one man was required to lead the animal and make sure that the wounded man was not spilled on the ground. Even though the travois was easy to construct in the field and could traverse uneven terrain fairly well, Trumpeter Ami F. Mulford called it "a crude device and a source of constant torture to a patient as it is jolted along," while a sergeant in the Second Cavalry cursed the travois as "a wretched and barbarous fixture."[80]

An only slightly better invention was the two-horse or two-mule litter described by Sergeant John Zimmerman, Fourteenth Infantry:

> The wounded were carried in this way, two mules for one man, one in front, one behind the patient; two poles were tied, one

on either side of the mules thus made fast to the mules at both ends, making them on a level. A blanket was then stretched across the center between the mules and left [to] sag down a little. On this the wounded were conveyed as gently as possible, as we were in a very hilly country, sometimes straight up, sometimes down, over ditches, gullies, creeks, mud and slush, sometimes miring down the mules. It was anything but pleasant for a wounded man.

A Seventh Infantryman involved with transporting the wounded down the valley of the Little Bighorn explained how it was done:

> It had been the intention to carry them to the steamer, but we had to give it up. The distance was too great and we were all played out, so we went into camp at 2 A.M. . . . The [next] day was occupied constructing litters to be carried by two mules. . . . The litters were made of cottonwood and rawhide . . . got from dead horses, skinning them and cutting the hides into long strips. It was a nasty job, but had to be done. There were three men to a litter, one man holding the front mule, the second leading the rear mule and the third man steadying the litter.[81]

In the far reaches of the northern plains and mountains just getting wounded men to better means of transportation often involved long, arduous journeys, and even that did not necessarily assure their survival. Army surgeons were always in short supply in the field but did their best to provide for the wounded, yet the task was frequently beyond their capabilities. Only two surgeons, for example, accompanied the force that corralled the Nez Perces at Bear's Paw in remote northern Montana. They were charged with caring for the four officers and forty-six enlisted men wounded in the battle, and it was still necessary to travel a long distance to reach river steamers on the Missouri. A Fifth infantry veteran of the engagement commented: "Some that were shot through the body died that first night on the steamer, after relaxing their energy. These men's wounds had not been dressed since the beginning of the battle" twelve days earlier. Even after reaching hospitals at distant posts, some of the wounded died weeks or months later.[82]

The wounds suffered by some men were not visible but nonetheless incapacitated them. With psychology still in its infancy, the medical community had not yet identified the condition that would become known as shell shock in World War I, combat fatigue in World War II, and post-traumatic stress disorder in more recent conflicts. It also affected soldiers in earlier times, as evidenced in the comments of Seventh Cavalryman William O. Taylor:

> While lying in this camp Captain Lewis Thompson, of the Second Cavalry, committed suicide. . . . No reason was known for the rash act, unless as it was believed by many . . . that the hardships of the campaign and the horrors of the Custer battlefield had, as it undoubtedly had done to others, unsettled his mind. It was not an uncommon thing to happen on the summer's campaign. Private Crowley, of A Troop, and another private of D Troop . . . were sent home on that account from this camp. Two soldiers . . . from General Crook's command went completely crazy after being chased by the Indians.[83]

Sergeant George S. Howard, Second Cavalry, also recorded that extreme stress caused one of his comrades, Sergeant Oscar R. Cornwell, to become "insane from fright and suffering" during the 1876 campaign. Cornwell, a second enlistment man, failed to recover and not too surprisingly deserted a few months later. In the Fifth Cavalry, an officer recorded, "ten soldiers . . . were pronounced incapacitated by the examiners and ordered to return" to their posts. News of Custer's overwhelming defeat, he related, had so preyed upon one man's mind "as to temporarily destroy his intellect . . . [yet] it was an open question whether Caniff . . . was downright insane, or only shamming . . . and got away from the danger he dreaded." The corporal in charge of the returning detachment later informed the officer that by the time they passed Bismarck, Dakota Territory, on their southward voyage down the Missouri, however, the man appeared completely normal.[84]

Men coming off a hard scout or campaign without exception were happy to return to their home stations and be out of danger, for the moment anyway. Leaving his company a few days before reaching Boise Barracks, Idaho Territory, a captain of the First Cavalry directed his men to push on and march the remaining distance in three days. "But on reaching the summit," a relieved soldier wrote, "we met a courier with orders to take it easy, as we were to stay in barracks after getting there. This caused a general smile." Everyone looked forward to "warm quarters, shelter from the bleak mountain winds, well cooked meals and a good wash," offered an infantryman.[85]

If "the boys" had not been veterans when they left on a combat scout or campaign, they were now—if they survived. Arriving back at Fort Ellis, Montana Territory, at the end of the Nez Perce War, Private William F. Zimmer took stock of the toll on Company F, Second Cavalry. "When we left this fort there was 90 men & 100 horses. Today there is but 50 horses (and some of them unfit to ride. One of ours dropped dead just the other side of Bozeman) & 58 men. . . . Two were killed, some were wounded & left along the route along with a large number of sick. 10 have been discharged, their time being out." Sergeant Howard intentionally understated the situation when he penned in his diary: "Arrived at Fort Sanders Nov. 4 [1876] after being out 8 mos. and 19 days and in the saddle 2600 miles, a pretty fair summer campaign."[86]

Just as it was customary for the band to play troops out of a post when leaving on campaign, the musicians similarly gave them a rousing welcome home, with the entire garrison turning out for the occasion regardless of weather. Fifth Infantryman Edwin M. Brown recalled his regiment's return to Cantonment on Tongue River following its victory at Wolf Mountains: "All hearts, save those forever stilled by the missiles of death, throbbed for very joy at the sight of the dear old Post, and enthusiasm knew no bounds when the ringing sound of the 5th Infantry Band greeted our ears coming far out over the flat to break the monotonous tread of the boys in blue."[87]

One regular aptly synthesized the essence of soldiers' attitudes about Indian campaigning. Private Thomas Lloyd, Third Cavalry, who had experienced the Horse Meat March and survived three major combat actions during 1876 (the Reynolds Fight on Powder River and the Battles of the Rosebud and Slim Buttes) confessed in a letter to his cousin: "I don't want any more of Indian fighting. I don't mind the fighting part, but the hardships we had to go through and starvation."[88]

CHAPTER 17

"Thank God I Am Done Soldiering"

Enlistment's End

Army service on the western frontier was demanding by any measure. The unrelenting routine, the strict adherence to duty, and the constant and sometimes harshly imposed discipline—aside from combat and grueling hardships often experienced in the field—demanded the most of a man's endurance. "I am resigned to it now but do not like it & never intend to soldier any more if I live to serve this term out," swore Private George McAnulty, adding: "I do not know what possessed me to enlist." Tenth Cavalryman James Tucker declared that he "soldiered with men out of the Civil War and also out of the Navy, and they say that the Indian War was the hardest service they ever served." Perhaps the great majority felt as did Private Charles Lester, a Fourth Infantry soldier stationed at Fort D. A. Russell, Wyoming Territory. Lester, as anxious as the next man for his enlistment to end, meanwhile resigned himself to the life as it was: "I have got just one year from tomorrow to serve and thank god then I am done soldiering in the regular army. I don't believe there is a thing worse than being in the regular army and out of civilization, but I have got use[d] to it now and don't mind much." Every man was a volunteer, and those who remained loyal to their oaths adapted and endured, despite the conditions and privations. As an introspective Third Cavalryman recognized: "No one is to blame for my being here, but my own self."[1]

Enlisting in the army had begun as a great adventure for thousands of men who had not contemplated that they would be disaffected from family and all that was familiar for a long period. Some men, away from home for the first time and thrust into a drastically different environment, regretted that their time in the service influenced them in not so beneficial ways. Former Fourth Cavalryman William Jett confided that he became "a different man . . . in many respects not conducive to my welfare or to high ideals. I ate different food, wore different clothes, slept under different covering, formed different habits, acted differently toward others and for some time had absolutely no communication with anyone in the East. . . . I was in the army five years. I was dead for that period of time to all my past." For others, the time passed rather quickly despite recurrent struggles with homesickness. "When discharged I was three years older than I was the day I began to wear the blue," reminisced John O. Stotts, who had served on the central plains in the late 1860s. "And even yet it don't seem possible that three years had passed so quickly. . . . There were many times and places that I became homesick and wished for home and my people, but something would always happen to cause me not to think too much about home."[2]

Like soldiers at any time, stated Private Jesse G. Harris, "Some men liked it, others didn't. I did." He was not alone in that sentiment: many concluded that army life actually had some benefits. Many like Private George Cranston recognized in retrospect that military service developed maturity. Writing to his sister, Cranston offered: "I don't think I am the boy I was when I left home, and by the time I get home I hope to be a man in mind as well as years." Those who had joined the army to see the West were not disappointed. Not a few would have agreed with former Illinois farm boy R. Eugene Pelham, who served on the central and northern plains as a member of the Sixth Infantry. "Five years in the Regular Army . . . gave me a splendid opportunity to see and travel over this vast territory extending from the Missouri River to the Rocky Mountains and from the British possessions to the borders of Texas," he remarked.[3]

The roster of any company was never static for very long. Even though batches of recruits had arrived together at the regiments, nearly all of them had enlisted on different dates and had to be discharged accordingly. Contributing to the constant turnover were those men who either had enlisted in the regiment or had reenlisted directly in their old companies and elected discharge. Anticipating his exodus from the service, Musician Robert Greenhalgh calculated that "one of the Band will be discharged next September, then three more seven months after him, then two more shortly after them, then I come next. . . . That's the way it is in the Regular Army—coming and going all the time." At any particular time approximately 10 percent of a company's members were approaching discharge. A private in the Eighth Cavalry, counting down the days he had left to serve, could hardly conceal the envy that he had felt as other men were discharged: "Since I joined the company, [I] have seen three different detachments of men discharged from it . . . and to bid those men good bye [sic], knowing they would soon be surrounded by their friends, while I was compelled to remain in this country was the hardest of all for me to bear, but now comes my turn." According to Sergeant Frederick Kurtz, merely surviving a five-year enlistment was no small feat. "From the original seventeen recruits assigned to my troop in 1883, just three returned after serving their full five years' enlistment in August 1888, including myself. Some died of fever, some were wounded or injured . . . and some were killed; a few deserted."[4]

"If a soldier's life is such a dog's life, why is it that so many re-enlist?" inquired a correspondent to the *Army & Navy Journal*. Reflecting the old adage about the grass being greener on the other side, many soldiers grumbled continually about the army and what they would do when they got out. Then, according to James G. Morrison, formerly a First Cavalry trooper, those who had wanted out so badly suddenly wanted back in. "Most of 'A' Troop were old soldiers," he noted. While many men complained of poor food and the amount of physical labor demanded of soldiers, sometimes even citing those as excuses for their desertion, former Twenty-Fifth Infantry sergeant Grandison Mayo commented: "I liked it & most of the men in my Co[mpany] did, to a point they didn't go home on leave." The feeling that a man's company indeed was his family was prevalent among the regulars. "Next to my own folks, I'm prouder of the Seventh Cavalry than anything in the world. And I'm especially proud of Troop H," declared Charles Windolph many years after his army service. There was "a nice feeling of loyalty" among the men, according to ex-private Joseph Kuhn, Second Cavalry. That camaraderie, mentioned by many Indian Wars veterans, bonded the men during and beyond their army days.[5]

The ranks of the regular army were filled with veterans who served multiple enlistments. This was the class that had found their niche as "professional privates," thoroughly familiar with their duty and the ropes of the service. More often than not, these were men who shunned rank and the greater responsibility that came with it. Shortly before leaving the army, a Third Infantryman made a copy of his company's muster roll so that he might remember the names of his comrades. He recorded that seven of the seventy-seven men in the company at that time had from fifteen to thirty years of service to their credit. Only one of those was a noncom, while the others were privates. Sooner or later, even some of the veterans who had provided cohesion to the ranks for so long finally had their fill of military life. Typical of those was Private John G. Kimm, a Seventh Cavalryman who had survived the Battle of the Little Bighorn and served out his final term. Having enlisted in the volunteers in 1864, Kimm spent the rest of the war as a light artilleryman and subsequently enlisted in the regular army in September 1865. After serving enlistments in the Second Infantry and Twelfth Infantry, he transferred to the First Cavalry. His last term was in the Seventh. Nearing the end of twelve years of service late in 1876, without ever having been home since the end of the war, he groused in a letter to a friend that he had enough. "I am coming as soon as I can get away from this outfit for I am disgusted with anything that looks like a soldier." When his term expired, Kimm took his discharge to marry his sweetheart and enter into partnership with his father in the printing and bookbinding business.[6]

Posted at Camp Verde, Arizona Territory, Trumpeter Charles P. Christian, Sixth Cavalry, wrote to his sister expressing his desire to leave the army to begin a new venture when his term of enlistment ended a year and a half hence. "I am making money fast and holding on to all I can get as I am determined, ferociously determined, to stay out of the army when my time is out. I bought a cow, a heifer, the other day as my intention at present is to remain in Arizona and make it my home, . . . the end of a career of 13 years of soldiering." Making good on his vow, Charles, his wife, Annie, and their four-year-old son settled on a homestead near Fort Grant, where he found work as a government teamster. Getting married while in service, in fact, became a consideration for many men when it came time to make a decision about reenlisting. Jacob Horner said: "I liked the army and would have stayed in . . . , but my wife objected. . . . She wanted a permanent home of her own, and children."[7]

Leaving the army to get married was a common expression of a most human desire. "I had a girl—so I wished to marry and resume civilian life," explained ex-sergeant James S. Hamilton. "Life in the army in those days was too rugged for a woman. I was offered a promotion if I would stay but refused." A former Eighth Infantry sergeant, Washington McCardle, reflected that view, stating that he "was going to get married and didn't want to take a woman into the fort." These experienced men appreciated only too well that the army made almost no allowances for wives of enlisted men and that subjecting their wives to those conditions would result in distinct hardships on their families, if not stress on their marital relationships.[8]

Married men and those intending to marry recognized that the army held scant promise of a successful future. Writing to his niece in 1889, hospital corpsman Richard F. King weighed the advantages and disadvantages of the potential opportunities in the army's new medical organization. "If I study for 3 years I can get $50 per month so long as I live . . . but if I can get along out of the army after my two years that I have left to serve the $50 can go to ——— and I will stay whair [sic] I can do as I like." Personal freedom, stability, and a better financial outlook were strong inducements for men to leave the army. Ninth Cavalryman Simpson Mann, posted at Fort Robinson, Nebraska, said flatly that he was "tired of it" and wanted to marry a girl in the nearby town of Chadron, and he did. George Whittaker, formerly a Sixth Cavalryman, commented that he desired "better employment. There is no future in the service, nothing but retirement." After serving in the Third Cavalry from 1881 to 86, ex-sergeant Perley S. Eaton determined that he "couldn't afford to stay in the service any longer for the pay they were giving. Another reason was I didn't like the confinement."[9]

When the much anticipated last day finally arrived for a man not intending to reenlist, he turned in his weapons, personal equipment, and any other accountable property he might have in his possession, such as his horse equipment, buffalo overcoat, and shelter half. The first sergeant and the company clerk would have his discharge certificate and Final Statement ready in the orderly room. The company commander would have already signed the discharge and penned a character rating for the soldier at the bottom, unless he was a disreputable sort, in which case the captain would "bobtail" the parchment certificate by cutting off that section to prevent a bad rating from being altered. The captain usually made a point of being present to bid farewell to the discharged man.

The Final Statement was all-important to the departing individual. The wise soldier examined it carefully, because it was a financial accounting of his last pay, including the amount that had been retained as compulsory saving throughout his five years' service, and settlement of his clothing allowance. If he had overdrawn his allowance, the amount was shown as a deduction from the money owed him; otherwise the balance to his credit was added. When Private Alson Ostrander took his discharge from the Twenty-Seventh Infantry, "we found, as expected, that I was overcharged on my clothing account. The error amounted to about ten dollars." Ostrander claimed that his first sergeant held a grudge against him and intentionally miscalculated the amount due. The same thing happened to Private William H. White in reprisal for his helping to expel his first sergeant from the Good Templars Lodge at Fort Ellis, Montana Territory. By White's computation, he was due approximately $250.00, "but I learned the books showed less than half that sum. Intensive inquiry . . . brought out that the First Sergeant of our troop had juggled the book in my case. He had done the same with others of his men. . . . Anyhow, I had to accept what the books showed." White knew that the man had previously been a sergeant but had been busted to the ranks for some misconduct. As a result of this new offense, however, he was dishonorably discharged. When a paymaster happened to be available, the discharged soldier could get his final papers cashed immediately. Otherwise, he had to wait until the paymaster's next visit or sell his account at an 8 or 10 percent discount to the post trader or someone else with the required amount of cash on hand or somehow find his way back to the States, where he could cash his statement with a paymaster there.[10]

Regulations required that the soldier had to be present at the time of his discharge. That is to say, he could not be granted a furlough terminating with his last day of service; nor could his discharge and final statement be mailed to him elsewhere. Until the 1880s the effective hour of discharge varied somewhat. Fair-minded company commanders often released a man late in the afternoon on the last day of his term, while sticklers considered him to belong to the army until midnight. In those instances discharged soldiers were given their papers the next morning. For many years there seemed to have been no standard procedure; apparently the practice varied from one regiment to another or was a matter of convenience. In 1879, however, a general order stipulated that discharge would occur on the last day of the soldier's term of service.[11]

Terminating his ten years in the Seventh Cavalry, First Sergeant John Ryan related the emotions that he experienced on his last day at Fort Abraham Lincoln, December 19, 1876:

> I went to the stable and gave my horse a through good grooming, an extra feed of oats, patted him on the neck and said goodbye. If it had not been for that horse, I would not be here today. . . . I rode him ten years on every skirmish, engagement and campaign that Custer was on. . . . My last act was to shake hands with all the men whom I left behind me. . . . While I did not have an opportunity to have Christmas dinner with the boys of the company, I wished them all sorts of success and happiness. I felt as if I had the blues when leaving the company and old friends whom I had served with for 10 years, and especially my horse. I rode . . . to the nearest railroad station, which was at Bismarck, in order to get the last train that left that part of the country for the winter.[12]

Soldiers serving in the field when their terms were about to expire were faced with a choice of either reenlisting wherever they happened to be or notifying their company commanders that they wanted to be discharged. The army was obligated to return the man to his place of enlistment, but that was often impossible, or nearly so, when the soldier's command was on the march or in some remote area. In that event he was presented two options. Either he was retained in service, with pay, until the command reached a place from which he could be transported or groups of soldiers whose enlistments were ending soon were returned to their station, usually aboard an empty supply train or a steamer, where they would be discharged at the appropriate time. When a soldier's discharge was delayed as a result of circumstances beyond his control, the actual date and reason were recorded on his papers.[13]

Elated at last to be out from under the strict authority of officers and at liberty to be themselves, recently discharged men commonly felt as if they had been released from prison. Exercising his newfound freedom at Fort Huachuca, Arizona Territory, ex-private William B. Jett recounted:

> The next day I met the Commanding Officer . . . and the Quartermaster on the parade ground. I had been saluting officers for five years and I was tired of it and . . . felt I could stand on equal terms with an officer . . . so I passed on without saluting or otherwise letting them know I saw them. . . . So when he said, "You are the first man discharged from my regiment that did not salute as he met me." I replied, "If I had thought you wanted to be saluted very badly I would have done so." He then said, "The best thing you can do is to get off this Reservation as soon as possible." [I told him:] "I am going right now, sir."

Jett added that a few days later he received a note from the post quartermaster on behalf of the colonel expressing his regrets for the incident and stating that Jett was welcome to visit the post at any time. Jett was admittedly relieved, because he intended to settle in the area and hoped to sell milk to the garrison.[14]

Leaving the army and returning to the States was not always an easy journey, particularly during the late 1860s and early 1870s before western railroads were well developed. Regulations provided that discharged soldiers be given travel pay and rations (or commutation of rations) to reach their places of enlistment. The trouble was, there was often no public transportation available. Sergeant Major David Kerstetter, Twenty-Seventh Infantry, took his discharge in February 1867 at Fort Phil Kearny. Having no other way to get home, and not eager to stay at that isolated northern post until spring, he and eighteen other discharged soldiers formed a party and left on foot. "We made a mid-winter trip of 640 miles across the plains, reaching North Platte City, Nebraska, then the terminus of the Union Pacific Railroad on March 31 with the mercury at zero. Many times on the trip the weather was far below zero and we made our beds in the snow." If nothing else, these doughboys had learned how to march long distances and survive in the field.[15]

Soldiers discharged in the Southwest faced similar distances, but opposite extremes of nature. At the time Private Henry I. Yohn was discharged from the First Cavalry at Camp Lowell, Arizona Territory, in mid-summer 1868, the paymaster had not been there in months and he and five discharged companions were broke. "I borrowed $53 and we six started to walk to Los Angeles," Yohn recalled. "We made Yuma on foot [approximately 250 miles], and then, starting the long stretch over the Colorado desert, we threw all our belongings into the Colorado River as we realized that we would have to travel light. . . . We walked at night, clad only in our underclothes. The day heat was something like 132 degrees in the shade. . . . At Corrizo, when 125 miles of the desert had been covered, we ran into the paymaster with our money."[16]

Private John O. Stotts was somewhat better off being stationed at Fort Lyon, Colorado Territory, on the Santa Fe Trail. "There were no railroads [1869] and the only means of getting to civilization was by stage. They charged 8 c[ents] a mile to ride that. The soldier . . . was allowed the measly sum of 5 c[ents] a mile to the place of his enlistment." Travel pay for discharged soldiers was based on the mileage of the shortest mail route between the respective points or, in the absence of mail service, on the shortest practical route. The ration allowance was computed at the rate of one day's rations for every twenty miles. If the trip took longer, the man was obligated to fend for himself. Considering it out of the question to go by stagecoach, Stotts hitched a ride with a slow east-bound bull train.[17]

Stotts was not alone in his distress at trying to get home without depleting his own resources. A soldier in Idaho Territory complained that he and many of his comrades had enlisted at New York City and "all they get to pay their fare home is $145 in currency including commutation of rations, just about enough to take them one-third of the way across the Plains. . . . The only conveyance is the overland stage, the fare from Boise City . . . to the nearest Pacific Railway station is something like $300 . . . to get to New York by the cheapest route costs at the very least $360 . . . unless a soldier has . . . saved a great deal of his pay he must either re-enlist or settle in the mining regions."[18]

Soldiers stationed at posts along the upper Missouri River benefited by steamboat service in the warm seasons but found themselves stranded after the river froze in late fall or early winter. In the absence of steamers at Fort Stevenson, Dakota Territory, wrote an officer, "the men released from service this month are hurrying to put the finishing touches on the . . . Mackinaws in which they will go down river in a few days. Seven of them are actually going to embark in a long canoe made of an enormous tree trunk hollowed out. . . . The impatience of these liberated men to see civilization again . . . is such that I believe that for lack of anything better they would board a raft rather than wait two months for the return of the first boat." Others of his men had acquired Indian ponies to ride "rather than to prolong their stay here until navigation is open on the river."[19]

As transportation systems improved in the West, discharged soldiers found it more convenient to return home or wherever else they may have elected to go. At least one man intending to start a ranch in Arizona Territory worked the angles for an economical way to visit his parents in Maryland by obtaining a furlough shortly before his discharge. As required, he reported back to his post just a week before his enlistment ended to collect in person on his Final Statement. Traveling at his own expense, but at the lower rates extended to active duty soldiers, he profited by collecting in cash the greater amount of travel pay allowed for the trip to Baltimore had he gone there after being discharged.[20]

For those who elected to "take another blanket" immediately and had a decent character rating, reenlistment was a simple process handled at the company level or in the case of regimental and staff noncommissioned officers by the colonel or the adjutant general of the army, respectively. On the day of his discharge, after being notified that his papers were ready, the soldier simply reported to the orderly room of his company to receive them, take the oath of allegiance, and sign new enlistment forms in triplicate. The number of his new term (second, third, and so forth) would be noted on the forms to permit him to receive the authorized amount of reenlistment pay. A discharged soldier had a period of thirty days during which he might reenlist and still qualify for the bonus. Some men used that time in lieu of a furlough to go back east or to some other destination then reenlisted at the nearest recruiting station before their time was up. Perhaps the majority, especially those posted at remote forts, reenlisted on the day of their discharge or within a few days if they wanted to experience a taste of freedom at or near the post.

The record suggests that comparatively few corporals reenlisted, probably because that was something of a probationary grade and most men had either advanced to sergeant or reverted to private by the end of their enlistments. Sergeants frequently signed on again because they found that they liked army life and that at the journeyman level they could escape some of the drudgery experienced by privates. Sergeant Maurice Wolfe, a company quartermaster in the Fourth Infantry, wrote from Fort D. A. Russell to his family in Ireland: "I know ye were all against me for joining the Army of the United States for the second time, but I don't dislike it at all. I am far more independent here than I would be in any other walk of life. . . . I have a very good and honourable Captain. . . . I could not wish for better times than I had in my last enlistment." Noncoms were afforded the same thirty-day grace period, but only those in good standing with the company commander who reenlisted immediately were assured of retaining their current rank. Regulations prohibited reenlisting a noncom at his former grade if he had a break in service. In that case the captain was required to recommend the man's promotion and issuance of a new warrant approved by the colonel, if the vacancy still existed. Otherwise the man rejoined as a private. A captain might be inclined to hold open a position, appointing a lance sergeant to fill in temporarily, but was not permitted by regulations to exceed the prescribed thirty-day limit. The usual tactic for circumventing the regulations (relying on mutual trust) for either a private or a noncom called for the company commander to grant the man a furlough of more than thirty days beginning *after* his reenlistment. In this way he retained his grade, position, and bonus pay.[21]

Personal situations and economic conditions not uncommonly influenced men to treat the army as a revolving door, as in the case of John Henley, who served during the Civil War as a private in the Forty-Third Indiana Volunteer Infantry. Within two weeks after his discharge in 1865, Henley enlisted in the regulars and was assigned to the Thirteenth Infantry, which was later merged into the Twenty-Second Infantry. Discharged in 1868, he thought that he had experienced enough of army life and worked as a carpenter for two years. Then, at age twenty-two, he enlisted again and served with the Seventh Cavalry for five more years. Upon his discharge as a sergeant in 1875, he took a position as a post trader for the next three years but in the spring of

1878 reenlisted directly in his old company for another five-year hitch. He finally quit the army for good in 1883 as a first sergeant.[22]

Another of those individuals was Fred Platten, a private in the Sixth Cavalry, 1871–76. Following his discharge, he related: "I headed for Colorado where I planned to establish a ranch. . . . I took up a homestead and preemption near Las Animas [where he built a house] . . . and after making several other improvements I rented out my place on shares and went to work punching cows." Platten was laid off the ranch at the end of summer 1877. "Then with nothing to do I went along with two companions for a trip on horseback. We ended up at Fort Bowie [Arizona Territory], where I immediately re-enlisted in the Sixth Cavalry. . . . It seemed pretty good to be back in harness." After putting in another five years, he was discharged as first sergeant of his troop.[23]

There were always some men who simply wanted a more comfortable situation elsewhere or sought a better climate than in the locality where they were currently posted. First Sergeant Charles N. Jansen served with the Tenth Infantry, 1885–90, and at the end of his enlistment declared: "I had had all the Indian chasing I wanted and came out to Angel Island [California] hoping to forget some of the hardships of the Apache campaign." After reaching San Francisco he enlisted in the recently arrived First Infantry with the idea of enjoying soft duty in a pleasant environment in California. "But no sooner were we located than the Sioux outbreak occurred in South Dakota," he grumbled, "and . . . we were fitted out for field service in that cold and frozen north and started out for Dakota."[24]

By the 1880s the ranks were sprinkled with old soldiers, some of whom made a career of the army. The adjutant general reported in 1884 that 25 percent of the 1,300 men reenlisted during that year were noncoms. Of the total army roster, 3,451 men were serving a second enlistment, 1,840 a third; 119 claimed more than twenty years' service in the regulars; and 49 had over thirty years. Wedded to their ways, and inclined to be disdainful of the evolving service and its reforms, these professional soldiers made no secret of lamenting the passing of the "old army" in which they had learned the soldiering craft. An officer of the Fourth Cavalry described the type that he knew so well:

> It was a fine sight to see one of these old men on muster or monthly inspection. Erect and soldierly . . . his white hair cut

close, his arms and accoutrements shining, not a wrinkle in his neat-fitting uniform, nor a speck of dust about him, his corps badge, and it may be a medal, on his breast, he stood in the ranks among the others like an oak tree in a grove of cottonwood saplings. [When his colonel, with whom he had served on the Utah Expedition prior to the war, confronts him]. . . . "Well, Blank, how are you getting along?" asks the colonel. Blank's hand in salute slaps against his rifle sharply enough to make the bands rattle. . . . "Fairly well, sir. . . . The hash mornings has got a sight more potatoes than meat in it." The honour of the cloth forbids an unqualified approval of treatment. "Well this is different from Camp Floyd in '57, isn't it?" the colonel continues. "Yes, sir. There was soldiering in those days."[25]

First Sergeant Thomas Ross was representative of the quintessential image. Having migrated from Ireland to the United States as a young man on the eve of the Civil War, Ross enlisted in the Eighty-Eighth New York Volunteer Infantry, part of Brigadier General Thomas Francis Meagher's famed Irish Brigade in 1864. Wounded at the Battle of the Wilderness, Ross was later declared unfit for field service and was transferred to the Veteran Reserve Corps to serve out his term. Strangely enough, his wound did not prevent him from joining the regulars in the fall of 1865. A clerk by trade, he remained with the General Service Infantry at Fort Columbus, New York, until his discharge three years later. He thereupon reenlisted immediately for a line company and was assigned to Company B, Twentieth Infantry, in which he remained a fixture until his retirement in 1893 at age fifty-five.[26]

In some families military service became a tradition. An exceptional, possibly unique, case was that of the Seventh Infantry's Rogan and McLennon families. Patrick Rogan emigrated from Ireland prior to the Civil War and was mustered into the Seventy-Sixth Pennsylvania Infantry as a substitute for a draftee who paid him $625 for fulfilling his obligation. Following his discharge during the summer of 1865, Rogan returned briefly to civil life but joined the regular army a year later. That was the first of what would eventually total seven enlistments, all of them in Company A, Seventh Infantry. In 1869 Rogan married Margaret McLennon, daughter of ex-sergeant Michael McLennon, who had been a member of the same company from 1852 to 1867. Patrick and Margaret Rogan eventually had twelve children, five of them boys, three of whom later enlisted in their father's company. He was by then first sergeant. Two years after his marriage to Margaret, Rogan's brother-in-law, John McLennon, followed his father's footsteps and enlisted as a drummer in Company A in 1871. Both Sergeant Rogan and Musician McLennon received Medals of Honor for gallant conduct during the hard-fought Battle of the Big Hole in 1877. Tragically, John McLennon, who had risen to sergeant, died in 1887, during his fourth enlistment, probably from the effects of alcoholism. But the four Rogans, the father and three sons, went on to briefly serve together for a few months prior to Patrick's retirement in 1894. Once posted at Camp Pilot Butte, Wyoming Territory, Rogan and his wife, Margaret, settled in Rawlins after retirement. There Patrick found employment as a Union Pacific Railroad watchman for the next fourteen years.[27]

In June 1886 the garrison at Fort Shaw, Montana Territory, paraded to honor the memory of First Sergeant James Fegan, Third Infantry, who died in service with thirty-five years to his credit. Also an Irish immigrant, Fegan had enlisted in the regular army in 1851 and served his adopted country continuously from that time until his death at age fifty-nine. A sergeant for nearly all that time, he had been awarded the Medal of Honor in 1868 for single-handedly repulsing a band of desperados who attempted to free a deserter in Fegan's custody and to set fire to the government supply train that he commanded at the time. In tribute to his old sergeant, his captain eulogized: "He was exemplary in this habits, honest, truthful, slow to anger, conscientious, respectful, and soldierly in his demeanor to officers, a tower of strength among the men." During the funeral, Fegan's son, James, stood in the ranks of his father's company. He had emulated his father by enlisting as a musician at age seventeen in 1874 and had risen to noncommissioned rank. "The singular spectacle of father and son both serving as sergeants in the same organization thus presents itself," wrote the company commander. Son James took the last of six discharges in 1900.[28]

Until the mid-1880s no formal provision existed for the retirement of enlisted men who were not infirm. The most any man might anticipate was admission to the Soldiers' Home in Washington, D.C., although there was no guarantee of acceptance. His company commander was responsible for preparing a justification and sending it through channels to the adjutant general of the army for review. If deemed acceptable, the application was forwarded to the Soldiers' Home's board of commissioners for consideration of the man's case based upon "old age and long service . . . or disability contracted in the line of duty." While medical conditions had to be thoroughly documented in a surgeon's Certificate of Disability, old age and long service were much more subjective in the board's judgment. Once granted tentative approval, the soldier was sent to the home to undergo a thorough physical evaluation to reach a final determination of his eligibility for admission. If he was found not to qualify, the soldier was returned to duty at his former station. But if he was accepted the board recommended that he be immediately discharged from the service and retained at the home, where he would be provided lodging, food, medical care, and other basic necessities. Although that did not offer a particularly promising outlook, all other discharged soldiers, without regard to their length of service, were on their own.[29]

Not all disabled veterans elected to reside at the Soldiers' Home; nor were they required to do so. Ami F. Mulford, the trumpeter who as a recruit had roundly rejected the prospect of eating mush, had been seriously injured when his horse fell with him during the Nez Perce Campaign. Near the end of December 1877, after being hospitalized for months, he was medically discharged as "incurable." On one hand, the idea of being out of the army appealed to him: "No longer Drill! Drill! Drill! No more hard-tack and bacon!" he proclaimed. On the other hand, the reality of his situation was grim. "I would now have all I could do to keep up on crutches." He chose to return to his home in Corning, New York, informing his commanding officer that he could die as well in one place as the other. After leaving the army, Mulford married twice within a few years, while his condition steadily worsened. Soon unable to work to support his wife and himself, he found he was qualified for an invalid pension, and small wonder. His physician described his condition: "This applicant is confined to his bed, bolstered up in a half-sitting posture, with his legs drawn up, and supported by a pillow under his knees." Nevertheless, Mulford made use of his convalescence to write one of the classic accounts of enlisted life in the regulars, *Fighting Indians in the 7th United States Cavalry*, first published in 1878. By 1889 Mulford was diagnosed with "paralysis of the bladder and of the bowels and partial paralysis of the left arm," requiring full-time nursing care and daily visits by a doctor. He died the following year at the age of thirty-six, though his story lives on, as vibrant and humorous today as it was when he related it.[30]

Only in 1885 was the law changed to allow older yet physically able soldiers to retire after thirty years' service in the army, the Marine Corps, or a combination of the two. Service in the field during the Civil War or active wartime service with the Marine Corps or U.S. Navy counted double in calculating a man's total time. Once his application and verified service record were approved by the adjutant general, the man received his discharge and was placed on the army's retired list at 75 percent of his final rate of pay, including the bonus for longevity. He also received travel pay and a subsistence allowance for the journey to his home or to the Soldiers' Home, at his discretion.[31]

While some of the army reforms—such as retirement—had the desired effect of reducing desertion and retaining good men, however, they had a corresponding negative side. In 1888 Adjutant General Richard C. Drum noted that the army on the whole was aging, with 72 percent of the average enlisted strength of 18,000 men having more than three years' service. In that year nearly 4,000 were in their second enlistments and the number of those with twenty or more years' service had risen to 423. He reported that the average age of a cavalryman was twenty-three, an infantry soldier thirty, and an artilleryman thirty-four. Reviewing statistics for the rank and file of the army three years later, his successor, Brigadier General J. C. Kelton, argued that he considered those mean ages to be too high for an efficient army, and he was right. The demands of field service and combat were for young men in good physical condition. Kelton opined that the "old professional soldier" should be eliminated because too many men were living in the army for one term after another with no other aspiration. He urged that the maximum age for enlistment should therefore be reduced from thirty-five years to thirty, that privates should be retained no more than fifteen years, and that only men with noncommissioned rank should be allowed to retire. As the final curtain came down on the Indian campaigns, his first recommendation was implemented, but not the other two.[32]

Perhaps the majority of discharged soldiers were anxious to return to familiar surroundings and meld back into the civilian populace. A former Twenty-Fourth Infantryman, Jacob Clay Smith, settled in the nation's capital and became a real estate broker, while James B.

Wilkinson returned to farming in Ohio. William E. Morris, an ex-Seventh Cavalry trooper who carried a bullet wound from the Battle of the Little Bighorn and was later discharged as a private of worthless character, earned a law degree and served as a municipal judge in the Bronx, New York, for twenty-one years. Two other survivors of that battle, John Ryan and Thomas F. O'Neill, were Civil War veterans prior to joining the regular army. Ryan subsequently served ten years in the regulars, O'Neill nearly twenty-five. Both men spent the rest of their lives as policemen in eastern cities, both rising to the rank of captain in their respective departments. Others became firemen. George Neihaus, for example, had served in the Tenth Infantry against the Apaches. He joined the Indianapolis Fire Department, where he worked for thirty-five years until retiring in 1931. Still others returned to the East and Midwest, where they attended college. First Infantryman John Cox, who had deftly evaded the sentries to visit his girlfriend at Fort Randall, Dakota Territory, attended theological seminary and became a minister. The majority followed an endless variety of occupations common to America in the late nineteenth and first part of the twentieth centuries: as railroad and street car conductors, machinists, mail carriers, carpenters and builders, watchmen, storekeepers, and businessmen. William "Eddie" Matthews, who had anxiously counted the days left to his discharge, rejoined his old company after less than four years as a civilian. He later returned to Pennsylvania and spent the rest of his life as a cigar maker.[33]

A few individuals even turned experience gained in the army into postservice livelihoods. After his discharge in 1870, former First Cavalryman John H. Cady found work as a cook with a railroad construction crew building a short-line in California. He liked it so well that he got hired as a chef at the Bella Union Hotel in Los Angeles and parlayed that into his own venture, eventually owning a restaurant, hotel, dance hall, and liquor distributorships in Phoenix and Tucson, Arizona. A Minneapolis man, John Gibbert, who had been the tailor in Company H, Twenty-Second Infantry, returned home to take up the trade in his own shop. Veterans who had been on extra duty as butchers during their army days found that to be useful experience too. One who made a career of it was Martin Andersen, who wound up in Omaha, Nebraska, and worked in a meat packing house until 1939. Another man who had spent ten years in the Second Cavalry took advantage of his practical education as a baker to fill that role at an Indian trading post in Arizona. He found he liked the country and the Navajo people so well that he later bought the place and operated it until 1942.[34]

The lure of the American West proved a recurrent motive drawing men to the regular army. Once there, regardless of their reasons for enlisting, many formed a lasting bond with that land of grand vistas and fresh opportunities. Some quickly took to the goldfields or other mining interests to get rich, or so they hoped. After leaving the army ex-private John L. Hubbard indulged his wanderlust by going to Alaska for ten years. German immigrant Charles Windolph, who also suffered a wound at Little Bighorn but lived to be the last white survivor of that battle, went to the mining district in the Black Hills, where he spent forty-nine years as a blacksmith for the Homestake Mine at Lead. The railroads that were rapidly shrinking the nation and developing the West afforded a variety of jobs. William F. Hynes had come to the frontier with the Second Cavalry. After his discharge as a sergeant at Fort D. A. Russell, Wyoming Territory, in 1869, he was hired as a track supervisor with the Union Pacific Railroad. Ex-commissary sergeant James W. Foley, a veteran of the Civil War and eight years in the Fourth Cavalry, took his final discharge in 1883 to settle in Medora, Dakota Territory, where he was hired as an agent for the Northern Pacific Railroad.[35]

It is perhaps not surprising that some men who had enjoyed their service did not stray far from the army after being discharged. Anton Mazzanovich left the Sixth Cavalry at Camp Grant on a disability discharge but found work immediately as a "counter jumper" (clerk) and part-time bar tender at the post trader's store. Later he hired on as cook for the government packers at the fort, who taught him the trade and subsequently promoted him to that job. Another former Sixth Cavalryman, Fred Platten, credited with two enlistments, related that he devoted his first three years of civilian life to cattle ranching near Camp Verde, Arizona Territory, then took an additional job as a packer for the Tenth Cavalry. "There's something about army life that gets in one's blood—or in mine anyhow," said Platten. "I was in almost daily contact with the troops at Camp Verde and was often on the verge of joining up again." He resisted that urge but continued to work as an army packer all through the 1890s and was reassigned to the train of the First U.S. Volunteer Cavalry (Roosevelt's "Rough Riders") in Cuba during the Spanish-American War. He eventually terminated his association with the army in 1902, settling in Flagstaff, Arizona, where he worked as a U.S. Forest Ranger until 1917. Former cavalry trooper George Whittaker found a similar occupation as an army scout in Yellowstone National Park patrolling for wildlife poachers. Danish emigrant Christian Madsen served with the Fifth Cavalry from 1876 until 1891, most of that time as a noncom, then joined the Rough Riders in 1898 and went to Cuba as regimental quartermaster sergeant. Another who could not sever his tie to military life was Martin Welsh. After serving two consecutive enlistments in the Third Cavalry, he enlisted in the U.S. Marine Corps for five years. After trying civilian life for a time and finding it not to his liking, he enlisted in the army Ordnance Department in 1898 and put in another fourteen years.[36]

The Apache wars veteran who got caught up in the 1890 Sioux uprising, Charles N. Jansen, left the service in 1891. When the U.S. declared war on Germany during World War I, however, he could not resist being left out. Based on his prior regular army experience as a first sergeant, Jansen secured a commission as a captain in the Quartermaster Corps and served nearly two years overseas with the American Expeditionary Force. Another old soldier who wanted in the fray was William G. Bowen, formerly of the Eleventh Infantry. After nine years in the ranks, the experienced Bowen had taken his discharge and quickly moved up the ladder in the New York National Guard, eventually holding the rank of major. "Tiring of the play of soldiering," he recounted, "I helped to raise and equip a gun co[mpany]." By the time World War I necessitated a general call-up of guardsmen, Bowen was informed that he was too old, by one day, to accompany his unit overseas.[37]

Quite a number of ex-soldiers viewed the vast western grasslands as an invitation to establish themselves as cattle ranchers. New York native George Cranston transformed into a full-fledged westerner after leaving the army. Working as a teamster for a time in Arizona, he later traveled to Texas, where he became a cattle drover to the Kansas railheads then worked as a cowboy and horse trader near Uvalde, Texas, before opening a saloon. Two men discharged at Fort Apache, Arizona Territory, Sergeant Major Victor Gomez and Signal Sergeant Will Barnes, formed a partnership in the livestock business in 1882.

William B. Jett and a Fourth Cavalry comrade, William Kane, were discharged at about the same time and also combined their resources to start a small ranch in southern Arizona. Realizing only marginal success, however, they had to take turns working at other part-time jobs for cash income. Finally, Jett, the man who fought Geronimo's warriors at Guadeloupe Canyon and thanked the Almighty for sparing him even though he was not a Christian, returned to Virginia in 1888. There he entered college and was later ordained a minister, eventually becoming an elder in the Methodist Church.[38]

Henry Frith and Edward W. Dunne became bunkies while serving together in the Eleventh Infantry during the mid-1870s. Frith, a native of Scotland, was a second enlistment man who had served previously in the same unit from 1868–71 but took his discharge at Fort Concho, Texas, and worked for two years "in the various occupations incidental to the cattle industry in the southwest at that time." Things apparently did not go well for the twenty-eight-year-old Frith, prompting him to enlist again at Fort Richardson in 1873, specifying that he wished to be assigned to his old company. Back in the ranks, he formed a friendship with Dunne, a former waiter who had joined the army at Baltimore, Maryland, about the same time. The two received their discharges a few months apart at Fort Custer, Montana Territory, in 1878 and quickly followed through on a plan to homestead east of Billings. They remained fast friends for more than five decades thereafter, Frith eventually becoming a government referee in bankruptcy cases and Dunne the Yellowstone County assessor. A former first sergeant of the Twenty-Second Infantry, Rasmus Pilgard, worked seven years as a section foreman for the Great Northern Railway then settled on a homestead that he farmed for the next twenty-eight years.[39]

Business partnerships among old comrades were not at all uncommon. Two discharged Tenth Cavalrymen pooled their resources and immediately opened a store near the Mowry Mine, south of Tucson, Arizona Territory, in 1885. "They keep liquors and cigars and a small stock of clothing—the equivalent of a small sutler store," observed their former company commander. Demonstrating continuing interest in the welfare of these veterans, as well as his troopers, he added: "I believe I have convinced them that it is more to their interest to keep good whiskey . . . than to keep poor." Other ex-soldiers, too, made use of their experience by becoming saloon keepers and bartenders, although John Bergstrom, who owned his own saloon in the 1890s, later turned to a more respectable life, saying that he preferred not to recall that earlier period.[40]

Former Ninth Infantryman George McAnulty left the army in 1880 after one enlistment, married the girl with whom he had corresponded as a soldier, and began what would be a sixty-year farming career near his former station, Fort Hartsuff, Nebraska. McAnulty developed a passion for local history and often spoke publicly about his army service. Late in his life, even though he had not enjoyed his time in the army, McAnulty was elected president of a local citizens' association formed to preserve the old fort.[41]

During the first half of the nineteenth century the few veterans' organizations that existed in the United States consisted of former and current officers representing the American Revolution, War of 1812, and the Mexican-American War. The smoke had hardly cleared after the Civil War before veteran officers formed a new fraternal organization, the Military Order of the Loyal Legion. While male lineal descendants and even selected civilian men could gain membership, former enlisted soldiers were excluded. Just a few months later, the Grand Army of the Republic (GAR) came into being, embracing all Union veterans, commissioned and enlisted alike. Like other veterans' groups, the GAR adopted a distinctive badge for the purpose of identifying its members and promoting camaraderie. Wartime veterans serving in the regulars during the Indian campaigns were permitted to wear the badge, as well their former corps badges, on the dress uniform at parade as marks of distinction. The quarter-century following the Civil War witnessed the formation of a plethora of fraternal organizations composed of Union veterans of specific branches, corps, and armies. By 1891 the GAR boasted well over 6,000 posts nationwide and a membership of more than 400,000.[42]

The horrendous losses incurred during Civil War left thousands of men crippled or invalided and women, often mothers, widowed. As time passed, many of the smaller veterans' groups melded with the GAR to form a politically powerful advocacy organization that proved highly successful in influencing Congress to pass legislation favoring disability pensions for Civil War veterans and their survivors.

Regular army veterans of the postwar era, however, received little notice and had no organization representing their interests. Only in

1888 was there movement in that direction with the organization of the Regular Army and Navy Union. Membership was open to any honorably discharged officer or enlisted man of the army, navy, or Marine Corps. Unlike other associations, the Union welcomed membership by active-duty men with at least one year's service. Still, it continued to be a comparatively small organization, with only about 4,500 members by the turn of the twentieth century.[43]

Not until the eve of the Spanish-American War did a group emerge that was devoted exclusively to veterans of the Indian campaigns. However, like similar predecessor groups, membership in the Society of Veterans of Indian Wars of the United States was limited to current or former officers who had actually served during an Indian war or the lineal male descendants of those officers. The only exceptions made for enlisted men were recipients of the Medal of Honor or a Certificate of Merit. Obviously, that rule excluded the great majority of former frontier soldiers. The group had barely launched when for reasons that remain unclear it was reconstituted as the Order of Indian Wars, a fraternity confined to active and retired officers who could claim service in the field or in engagements against hostile Indians. The number of members, accordingly, was never large: fewer than four hundred at its peak in the early 1930s.[44]

Even though a few regional groups, composed mainly of militia veterans, organized to bring attention to the issue of pensions for participants in conflicts against Indians, their fragmented nature meant that they lacked the political clout to effect congressional action. That effort took a significant step forward in 1909 with the creation in Denver, Colorado, of the National Indian War Veterans Organization (later changed to Association: NIWV) under the leadership of a former Fifth Cavalryman, Charles R. Hauser. The seal of the NIWV bore the legend "The Men Who Protected the Frontier," clearly distinguishing this class from all other veterans. The NIWV focused its attention on securing pensions for regular and militia veterans who had served on the western frontier between 1866 and 1891. The combined lobbying efforts of some five hundred members paid off in 1917 when Congress enacted legislation to extend monthly pensions of twenty dollars to qualified veterans age sixty-two or older and twelve dollars a month to widows.

Resting on its laurels, the Denver chapter of the NIWV languished and dissolved after World War I as national attention was drawn to the returning veterans of that conflict. In the mid-1920s the San Francisco chapter filled the vacuum by assuming a more prominent leadership role and coalescing several smaller West Coast chapters. Concurrently, George W. Webb, a former member of the Third Infantry who had served on the southern plains, made significant contributions to the NIWV as a talented national commander. Webb renewed the effort to improve pensions for ex-soldiers and widows of the Indian Wars era by circulating a petition among thousands of veterans and dependents under the motto "One for All, All for One." To attract additional members, and thus enhance the strength of the NIWV, Webb created and published a monthly tabloid titled *Winners of the West*, the self-proclaimed sobriquet adopted by those who had served in the West during the post–Civil War years. The value of this popular periodical in unifying thousands of ex-regulars and state and territorial volunteers under a single banner cannot be overstated. Not only did it give a voice to the thousands of men who passed through the army, only to return home or to pursuits elsewhere unsung and for the most part anonymous, but it provided a forum to share their experiences and in some instances to reconnect with former comrades.

By the late 1920s the NIWV claimed some 1,300 members. During the next two decades from twenty-two to forty-four chapters, called "camps," were active at various times in major cities across the nation. The meetings held periodically by each chapter gave the members opportunities to formalize their needs and desires for congressional recognition regarding pensions, which could then be funneled to the national headquarters, Camp No. 11 at St. Joseph, Missouri. Typical of those was the plea of John Rovinsky, who had served enlistments in the Eighth Cavalry and the Seventh Infantry: "We stood as targets to the enemy, when our country needed us, and it should now do something for us in our declining days. We, of Indian Wars, are proud of the service we rendered our country, and should not be humiliated and disgraced now before our fellow civilians. . . . We should be placed on an equal with veterans of all other wars." More than that, the chapters provided renewed camaraderie and opportunities to compare notes with other veterans who had mostly served in diverse parts of the frontier and at different times. One of those local chapters, Abraham Lincoln Camp No. 30 at San Antonio, Texas, was segregated exclusively for former members of the Ninth and Tenth Cavalry and the

Twenty-Fourth and Twenty-Fifth Infantry. Members in rural areas or otherwise unable to belong to one of other camps could affiliate with the St. Joseph chapter.[45]

The NIWV experienced a revolt during its 1928 annual convention after a significant portion of the membership became dissatisfied with Webb's domination of the organization in reaction to a motion by his supporters that certain officers' reports critical of Webb should not be read into the minutes. When the motion came to a vote and the opposition faction lost, members of several camps stomped out of the convention. Reorganizing under their own constitution, this faction formed what was known as the United Indian War Veterans (UIWV) of the United States and claimed almost half of the NIWV membership as its own. The two rival entities co-existed as the NIWV thereafter steadily declined until its demise in 1944. The UIWV remained active for more than two decades longer. Its last meeting was held in 1968 with just four veterans in attendance.

The western United States had changed rapidly and dramatically by the early twentieth century. The Indians, the old nemesis of the frontier army, were all peacefully confined to reservations as wards of the government trying to adapt to the new order. Relatively few of the old frontier forts active during the Indian Wars were still garrisoned; most lay abandoned and neglected or had been razed to the ground by local residents salvaging building materials. Networks of rail lines and roads now crisscrossed the entire region west of the Mississippi River, connecting farming and ranching communities with markets in larger towns and cities. The West was a far different place than Alson Ostrander had first seen as a teenaged soldier going up the Bozeman Trail in 1866. "As an old man, [I] am living in a small flat in a large Eastern city with little hope of ever seeing this wonderful transformation," he remarked. "Still it is a source of satisfaction and great delight to me to think that I am one of the thousands of boys and men who in those days 'did their bit' to make it possible." That sense of identity and pride in fulfilling the then-prevailing national concept of Manifest Destiny became increasingly prevalent among veterans as they accrued perspective on their lives and as the unpleasant memories of army life dimmed.[46]

Veteran William Murphy opined on the regulars of his day and what he viewed as their thankless service:

> They were . . . shot at and abused. Their deeds were in a country little known and against an enemy that was not a national menace as in other wars. . . . They traveled through snow and cold without shelter and were expected to do the impossible. . . . The popular idea was that they were no good anyway. If the settlers that now enjoy their ranches in . . . all of the western states would stop and think, they would find that at least one Indian War Veteran lost his life for every township in the entire territory described.

Exaggerated though his claim for casualties may have been, Murphy's words reflected a view generally shared among his former comrades-in-arms.[47]

Some of those veterans who had not remained in the West after their army service later experienced an irresistible desire to see once again the places of their youth as "boys in blue." Visiting the site of old Fort Buford, North Dakota, in 1913, R. Eugene Pelham, formerly of the Sixth Infantry, recalled the day in 1876 when he had taken his discharge and boarded a river steamer down the Missouri. "Little did I think . . . that 37 years later I would find myself on the same spot where I left them [his comrades] standing on that day, or that I would ever see that part of Uncle Sam's domain again," he sighed. "On reaching the ground where the old garrison had stood I found but one building remaining." Absent were not only the buildings but the troops, the bugle calls, the steamers, the buffalo, the Indians—all of the frontier world that he had known. As a former Fourth Cavalryman nostalgically related in later years: "I would not like to go back to the mistakes and foolishness and sinfulness of my past life . . . but the call of the plains and mountains with their accompaniments and the rough experiences of those long gone years is still upon me as I write, and I feel that I would like to live them all over again."[48]

Writing to the *Winners of the West* in 1924, ex-private William Gurnett recounted with obvious pride the day half a century earlier when six companies of the Eighth Infantry disembarked from a steamer at Omaha, Nebraska, after spending several months in the field:

> We were ragged and dirty, the tails of our blouses had been cut off by the cartridges in our home made thimble belts, and the

brims of our hats were gone, the result of a hail storm in Montana. As we waded through the yellow mud from the boat to the nearest street the people gathered about us and jeered. The 9th Infantry band came down from the barracks to meet us and wheeled in on the right. We fell in, counted off, and broke to the right in fours. The band played, "Home Again," and as we came to the next corner we formed company front, wheeled into a leading street like six toll gates. There was a silence on the sidewalks, the jeering had ceased, and one of the natives shouted, "By God, they are soldiers all right!"[49]

And they were. They would be soldiers at their core for the rest of their lives, wherever they went, whatever they did. The U.S. Army has never seen a more diverse collection of men—native-born Americans, both white and black; immigrants from around the globe; good men often rough in manner, toughs and misfits, characters of every stripe—but volunteers all. Many deserted, yet the good ones stayed. Discipline molded them; shared experience tempered and bonded them. For better or worse, they were the frontier regulars.

APPENDIX A

1872 Army Pay Table

PAY OF ENLISTED MEN OF THE ARMY UNDER ACT OF MAY 15, 1872.

Head Qrs. 6th Infantry

RANK. (Alphabetically Arranged.)	SERVICE.	First Enlistment	Re-Enlistment (Retained Pay not Included)			
			First Re-Enlistment	Second Re-Enlistment	Third Re-Enlistment	Fourth Re-Enlistment
*Artificer	Artillery and Infantry	15	...	...	...	...
Blacksmith and Farrier	Cavalry	15	17	19	20	21	22
*Chief Musician	Artillery, Cavalry and Infantry	60	...	...	...	...
Chief Trumpeter	Cavalry	22	24	26	27	28	29
Corporal	Artillery, Cavalry and Infantry	15	17	19	20	21	22
Do	Engineers and Ordnance	20	22	24	25	26	27
First Sergeant	Artillery, Cavalry and Infantry	22	24	26	27	28	29
*Hospital Matron		10	...	...	...	...
Hospital Steward	First Class	30	32	34	35	36	37
Do	Second Class	22	24	26	27	28	29
Do	Third Class	20	22	24	25	26	27
*Leader of Band	(At West Point)	75	...	...	...	...
Musician	Engineers, Artillery and Infantry	13	15	17	18	19	20
Do	First Class (At West Point)	34	...	...	...	...
Do	Second Class (do)	20	...	...	...	...
Do	Third Class (do)	17	...	...	...	...
Ordnance Sergeant	Of Posts	34	36	38	39	40	41
Principal Musician	Artillery and Infantry	22	24	26	27	28	29
Private	Artillery, Cavalry and Infantry	13	15	17	18	19	20
Do	First Class Engineers and Ordnance	17	19	21	22	23	24
Do	Second Class Engineers and Ordnance	13	15	17	18	19	20
Quartermaster Sergeant	Artillery, Cavalry and Infantry	23	25	27	28	29	30
Do	Engineers	36	38	40	41	42	43
Saddler	Cavalry	15	17	19	20	21	22
Saddler Sergeant	do	22	24	26	27	28	29
Sergeant	Artillery, Cavalry and Infantry	17	19	21	22	23	24
Do	Engineers and Ordnance	34	36	38	39	40	41
Sergeant Major	Artillery, Cavalry and Infantry	23	25	27	28	29	30
Do	Engineers	36	38	40	41	42	43
‖ Superintendents of National Cemeteries		...	...	...	...	...
Trumpeter	Cavalry	13	15	17	18	19	20
*Veterinary Surgeon (Senior)	do	100	...	...	...	...
Do (Junior)	do	75	...	...	...	...
*Wagoner	Artillery, Cavalry and Infantry	14	...	...	...	...

* Not changed by Act of May 15, 1872. No pay retained in these cases.

† These rates are due soldiers serving in a first term of enlistment, and to those who have served a previous term, or terms, without ever re-enlisting under provisions of act of August 4, 1854. The same rate is payable for each year of first term; the increase provided by Sec. 2, Act May 15, 1872, for third, fourth and fifth year is treated as retained pay due only upon discharge. See General Orders, No. 51 of 1872, from Adjutant General's Office.

‡ These rates are due soldiers who having heretofore re-enlisted under act of August 4, 1854, have since been honorably discharged, and are serving a new term of enlistment. This includes the class of men referred to in par. 98 (6th and 7th lines), also par. 102, Paymaster's Manual, June, 1871. $1.00 per month additional for all grades paid on discharge, on the conditions explained in General Orders, No. 51 of 1872.

§ These rates are due soldiers who are serving in first, second, third, or fourth continuous term of re-enlistment under provisions and with benefits of act of August 4, 1854.

‖ Superintendents of National Cemeteries [not enlisted men] "shall receive for their compensation from $60.00 to $75.00 per month to be determined by the Secretary of War." Not entitled to clothing or rations or money in lieu of either. See General Orders 51, par. 12, War Department, Adjutant General's Office, June 22, 1872.

CLOTHING—Due soldier, paid only on final discharge. Due United States, settled 30th of June and 31st December of each year, or on final statements if sooner discharged.

OFFICIAL :

(signed) Benj. Alvord
Paymaster General, U. S. A.

Printed at the Surgeon General's Office.

Received August 31st 1872

P. M. G. O. July 1, 1872.

APPENDIX B

Glossary of Army Slang

affidavit man soldier who would give his oath and sign his name to almost anything

awkward squad raw recruits at the most basic level of instruction.

baby herder officer's servant.

banker's daughters prostitutes.

batch party of depot recruits assigned to a regiment.

beat short for "deadbeat," one who shirks duty.

biscuit shooter company cook.

bit portion of a year, usually used in reference to a soldier's enlistment, as in "three years and a bit to serve."

blanket reenlistment, as in "take another blanket." Derived from the fact that a soldier was issued a new blanket upon reenlistment.

blind fine levied against a soldier's pay.

bloodhounds Seventh Cavalry survivors of the Little Bighorn who continued to pursue Sitting Bull in 1876.

blue or **blues** army service, as in "wearing the blue" or "the blues." Derived from the dark blue uniform coats and blouses and sky blue trousers.

bobtail discharge certificate with the character section cut off: dishonorable discharge. Also used as a verb: "He was bob-tailed."

boiled shirt white cotton or linen civilian shirt.

bounty jumper (1) someone who enlisted during the Civil War merely to receive the cash bounty then promptly deserted to do it over again under another name; (2) nickname for the belt support bolsters on the back of the 1855 cavalry jacket: a nuisance.

boys   universal soldiers' term for themselves, usually "the boys."

boys in blue   U.S. soldiers.

bull doze   (1) to put down or disparage; (2) to haze or abuse one's authority.

Bullring or **Bull Ring**   the mounted training arena at the cavalry recruiting depot.

bunk fatigue   off-duty loafing in quarters.

bunkie   someone with whom a soldier shares his bunk, tent, or blankets, usually considered to be his closest friend and confidant.

butt   a little more than; used in connection with the short or stub end of one's enlistment, as derived from a partially smoked cigar, as in "a year and a butt" or "six months and a butt."

buzz   to hang around and flirt with a girl, as a bee does with a flower, as in "to buzz a girl."

buzzard   army discharge certificate, referring to the eagle surmounting the document.

calaboose   jail, usually referring to a civilian prison. Corruption of the Spanish word *calabozo*, meaning a dungeon.

catch   used in the sense to take or win, as in to "catch" orderly in the guard mounting competition. Also past tense, as in "to have caught orderly before."

cavee yard   horses or mules being freely herded.

chain guard   sentries posted within sight of each other at intervals around a camp.

chasing prisoners   daytime duty for members of the reserve guard assigned to oversee prisoners at work.

chow   mess or a meal.

chuck pile   food.

Cincinnati chicken   salt pork. Derived from the labels on packing boxes and barrels. The meat was put up in Cincinnati, Ohio, a major processing center.

coffee cooler   loafer or shirker.

Company Q   guardhouse prisoners.

count-off   the process of soldiers in ranks counting off by numbers one through four (or occasionally two) to determine the sets of fours (or twos) for marching; in the cavalry the designation of horse holders (no. 4).

cracker machine U.S. Military Academy.

croak to die.

crumby lousy dirty or otherwise unfit to pass inspection.

cup the prize. To take the cup was to be named orderly during the guard-mounting competition.

Custer Avengers new men who filled the depleted ranks of the Seventh Cavalry during late summer 1876, so-called by the citizens of Bismarck, Dakota Territory.

cut to be among a group of finalists, such as for orderly, as in "he made the cut."

daisy synonym for "dandy," something or someone cool.

daisy smasher infantryman.

Dance Jack definition uncertain, perhaps meaning a corporal.

dandy someone concerned with presenting a smart soldierly appearance.

dead list excused from duty by the surgeon, implying that someone had to be dead or nearly so to be excused.

dog robber soldier hired as an officer's servant.

dog tent shelter tent for two men, implying that it was only big enough for a dog.

double up to share blankets in the field for additional warmth, "to double up."

doughboy infantryman.

dude company company whose members took special pride in their appearance, often adopting distinctive off-duty dress, such as white summer trousers.

Eleventh Cavalry trooper's term for mounted infantry.

fagged physically exhausted.

finals final statement of clothing and pay accounts given to each soldier at discharge.

firewater inferior whiskey; rotgut.

floater man having no permanent residence, drifter. A term applied to men who enlisted with no intention of remaining in the army, taking advantage of the service for transportation to the West or for food and shelter during winter.

footpads infantry.
fresh fish green recruits.
fried collar starched white linen collar for a dress shirt.
German battery beer.
goose wine water.
go over the hill to desert.
government ghosts cavalrymen dressed in white canvas stable outfits.
government straight regulation field ration consisting of coffee, hardtack, and salt pork or bacon.
government workhouse fort, with reference to the amount of fatigue that soldiers had to perform.
gravel pusher infantryman.
greenies new recruits.
guardhouse lawyer soldier who established himself as a legal authority, based upon experience gained from his own indiscretions, confinements, and trials.
haybag uncomplimentary term for a laundress, implying a woman of easy virtue. Derived from the army bed sack filled with hay.
hightoned sophisticated, upscale.
hike field march, especially for infantry.
hitch term of enlistment.
hocks horses.
hog ranch rural house of prostitution, a low, vile place also serving rotgut whiskey.
Holy Joe chaplain, priest, or minister.
hook own responsibility, as in "being on his own hook."
hunky dory satisfactory.
jag drinking spree or being drunk.
jamboree drinking spree.
jaw-bone unsecured loan by one soldier to another until payday, as in "to put it on jaw-bone."
jim-jams delirium tremens.
Jonah someone cursed with bad luck; also a habitual bungler.
jump (1) an attack by Indians, as in to "jump a coach"; (2) to desert.
kick to complain.
kick the bucket to die.
knight-of-the-washtub married soldier who assisted his laundress wife.

lit up   drunk.

Lo (also Poor Lo, Mr. Lo, and Lo, the Poor Indian)   nickname for American Indians, used more frequently on the northern plains. Originated in the line "Lo, the poor Indian whose untutor'd mind Sees god in clouds" by Alexander Pope (*An Essay on Man; in Four Epistles to H. St. John, Lord Bolingbroke* [New York: Clark & Maynard, 1867], p. 8).

long tom   breech-loading Springfield rifle used by the infantry.

mill   (1) guardhouse; (2) fistfight.

needle gun   breech-loading Springfield rifle, usually applied to the Model 1866, with reference to its long firing pin.

night-in   day without guard duty (being able to sleep in one's own bunk).

nobby   stylish.

noncom   noncommissioned officer.

Number Four   designated horse holder in dismounted cavalry deployments.

old army   the antebellum army, as used by regulars who had served before the Civil War.

old man   term of respect used for the company commander.

old soldier   experienced soldier usually, but not always, with more than one enlistment to his credit. The term was sometimes applied to a relatively new man once he became well posted in all of his duties.

overland trout   bacon.

pile driver   coffee.

play off   to feign illness.

polishing up   cleaning up; used in conjunction with preparing the uniform, arms, and accouterments for inspection or policing up around the quarters, post, or camp.

pony soldiers   Indian term for cavalry.

pup tent   shelter tent for two men. See also "dog tent."

racket   drinking spree.

rawhiding   being made fun of by one's comrades.

read out   addressed in orders read to the company or garrison, such as a promotion, demotion, citation for bravery, or special assignment, as in "Private Larson was read out tonight as corporal."

recruit   (1) new man; (2) to recuperate; (3) new horse, as used in the Ninth and Tenth Cavalry.

reds or **red devils**   Indians.
redskins   nearly universal term for Indians.
repeater   chronic deserter.
rooky   inexperienced soldier.
running guard   separated picket posts usually composed of three mean each, who relieve each other in rotation to ensure that at least one is always awake to maintain constant vigilance.
Saturday night   civilian dress shirt.
shaky-day   the day after payday, when soldiers were recovering from drunkenness.
shavetail   (1) recruit; (2) young, inexperienced second lieutenant. Both meanings derive from the term used for inexperienced mules, whose tails were shaved halfway down for ready identification until they were trained.
shavies   recruits.
shove up   to sell or barter one's equipment or clothing.
Siwash   Indians (used in northern Montana).
skalljaw   coffee.
skip or skip out   to desert.
slum   army stew.
slung dung   pudding.
smokewagon   artillery piece, cannon.
snowbird   man who enlisted only for food and shelter in winter then deserted in spring.
soldiering-on-the-job   working at a slow pace.
soldier name   alias used by a man while in the army.
soldier straight   basic army field ration—coffee, hardtack, and salt pork or bacon. See also "government straight."
sore ass   infantry term for a cavalryman.
spiflicated   drunk.
squad room   barracks dormitory.
squaw man   white man married to an Indian women.
the States   the organized portion of the United States, as opposed to the western frontier.
striker   soldier hired as an officer's servant.
Suds Row   laundress quarters.
Sudsville   laundress quarters.

sutler post trader. Although technically incorrect after ca. 1869, soldiers often continued to use this term.
swell someone who dressed fashionably, applied to a soldier who wore tailored uniforms supplemented with civilian apparel when off duty.
tack short for hardtack.
take French leave to desert.
take on to enlist in the army.
top nickname for the first sergeant, as in "top sergeant."
top pusher first sergeant.
top sergeant first sergeant.
trick guard relief: a two-hour turn at walking post every four hours.
troop cavalry company.
Tub Town laundress quarters.
Uncle Sam's watch and chain ball and chain worn by prisoners.
vegetable police company gardener.
walk-a-heaps Indian term for infantry.
walking a ring punishment, coupled with carrying a 25– to 30-pound log on the shoulder for several hours at a time.
whack-up to divide proceeds, settle up.
windjammer bugler.
wooden overcoat coffin.
young soldier new recruit, as used in the black regiments.

APPENDIX C

Selected Regular Army Ballads

THE REGULAR ARMY, O!

Words by Ed. Harrigan. Performed by Harrigan & Hart. Music adapted and arranged by David Braham. Published by W. A. Pond & Co., New York, 1874.

> Three years ago this very day, we went to Governor's Isle
> For to stand forninst the cannon, in true military style.
> Seventeen American dollars, each month we surely get,
> For to carry a gun and bagnet with a regimental step.
> We had our choice of going to the army or to jail,
> Or it's up the Hudson river, with a "copper" take a sail!
> Oh we puckered up our courage, wid bravery we did go;
> Oh we cursed the day we went away wid the Regular Army O!
> *Chorus*:
> There was Sergeant John McCaffery and Captain Donahue,
> Oh they make us march and toe the mark in gallant Company "Q."
> Oh, the drums would roll, upon my soul, this is the style we'd go,
> Forty miles a day, on beans and hay, in the Regular Army O!
>
> We wint to Arizony for the to fight the Injins there;
> Came nearly being made bald-headed, but they never got our hair.
> We lay among the ditches, in the yellow dirty mud,

And we never saw an onion, a turnip, or a spud.
Oh we were taken prisoners, conveyed forninst the Chafe,
Oh he said "We'll make an Irish stew," the dirty Indian thafe.
On the telegraphic wire we walked to Mexico,
We bless the day we skipped away from the Regular Army O!
Chorus

We've been dry as army herrings, And as hungry as a Turk;
Oh the boys along the street cry out, "Soger, would you work?"
We'd ship into the Navy for to plow the raging sea,
But cold water sure we couldn't endure, t'would never agree wid me.
We'll join the politicians, then we know we'll be well fed,
Oh we'll sleep no more upon the ground, but in a feather bed.
And if a war it should break out, they call on us to go,
We'll git Italian substitutes for the Regular Army O!
Chorus

We've corns upon our heels, my boys, and bunions on our toes;
From lugging a gun in the red-hot sun, puts freckles upon our nose.
England has its Grenadiers, France has its Zoo-zoos,
The U.S.A. never changes, they say, but continually wear the blues.
When we are out upon parade, we must have our muskets bright,
Or they'll slap us in the guard-house to pass away the night,
And, whin we want a furlough, to the Colonel we do go;
He says, go to bed, and wait till you're dead, in the Regular Army O!
Chorus

[*Verse added by Brigadier General George Crook's soldiers, 1876*]
But 'twas out upon the Yellowstone we had damndest time,
Faith, we made the trip with Rosebud George, six months without a dime.
Some eighteen hundred miles we went through hunger, mud, and rain,
Wid back all bare, and rations rare, no chance for grass or grain;
Wid bunkies starvin' by your side, no rations was the rule;
Shure 'twas ate your boots and saddles, you brutes, but feed the packer and the mule.

But, you know full well that in your fights no soldier lad was slow,
And it wasn't the packer that won ye a star in the Regular Army, O.
Chorus

ME BUNKIE AND I [TO THE TUNE OF "SWEET BETSY FROM PIKE"]

He joined us at Russell and didn't know beans,
Took on in St. Louis—no cash in his jeans;
He drilled with a shovel, a pick and a hoe,
And "struck" for the "top's" wife, first house on the row;
Scrubbed tins in the kitchen and wrestled the pots,
Policed in the stables with old Baldy Watts;
I "fell for his tin type," yet never knew why—
We're one loop and toggle, me bunkie and I.

He pulls a strong wire with the post's "Holy Joe,"
The Bible holds nothing that "Chump" doesn't know;
From cover to cover he "saveys" the "sharps"
That raised Cain down here, but are now playing harps;
He is sand, grit and ginger, and red pepper, too;
A soldier, a scrapper, a sport through and through;
I'm "stuck on his mug," still I couldn't tell why,
We soldier together, me bunkie and I.

One day big Tim Fagan—his Irish was up—
Called bunkie a "psalm-singin'," craw-thumpin' pup.
Old bunkie said nothing, I fixed it they'd meet
Just back of the canteen right after retreat;
He walloped Tim Fagan behind the canteen,
Such scrappin' as that I never have seen;
Tim's gang tried to rush us—I'll tell you no lie—
We dusted their jackets, me bunkie and I.

He doesn't touch liquor, he hasn't a guile.
He's always on deck when I'm broke for a "smile,"
Guard mornings, just after I'm back from a spree,
Me kit's there all ready and shining for me;

He never forgets the old folks in the East,
But sends them each pay day six "cart wheels" at least;
He's white through and through and as straight as a die,
We're same as two brothers, me bunkie and I.

He's sober and steady and decent and strong,
I booze and go absent, "dead beat," get in wrong;
They've busted me often—I've had my last show—
He never has asked me to stop or go slow;
I know that he knows that I know I must drink,
He never has hinted to brace up and think;
Now that's why I like him—no preaching, that's why,
We pull well together, me bunkie and I.

Some things men must smother way down in their souls,
'Mid ashes and cinders that fill up the holes
Burn't deep by a fire and that once flamed in the night,
But now hide the scorch of the turf in the light.
Spent fires of the heart mid your ashes and dust,
Why count o'er the nails of your wood now all rust—
Perhaps bunkie "saveys," he never asked why—
That's just why were chummy, me bunkie and I.

I'll stand by me bunkie through thick and through thin,
With jag on or sober I'll back him to win;
You can't get him rattled, he'll never "dead beat,"
But soldiers it straight from "First Call" to "Retreat":
He stands up for me—with but two years to serve—
Though everything's gone that I've had but me nerve;
I'm "stuck on his mug," he's a man and that's why
We hang out together, me bunkie and I.

O'REILLY

O'Reilly was a soldier man—the best in Comp'ny "B";
There wasn't in the regiment a better man than he.
A ranking duty non-com, he knew his business well,

But since he "tumbled down the pole" O'Reilly's gone to hell,
Chorus:
O'Reilly's gone to hell, since down the pole he fell;
He drank up all the "jag juice" the whiskey man would sell.
They "ran him in the mill." They've got him in there still,
They'll hand him out a "bobtail" sure, O'Reilly's gone to hell.

O'Reilly hit the whiskey route—with six months "up the pole,"
He blew himself at Casey's place and then went in the "hole,"
He drank with all the rookies, and "showed his face" as well—
The whole outfit is on the bum. O'Reilly's gone to hell—
Chorus

O'Reilly "swiped a blanket" and shoved it up I hear,
He shoved it for a dollar bill and blew that in on beer.
He licked a "coffee-cooler" next—the buggar said he'd tell—
He's ten days absent without leave. O'Reilly's gone to hell—
Chorus

When they try him by Court Martial he will never get a chance
To tell them how his mother died, or some such "song and dance,"
He'll soon be down in Comp'ny "Q" and sleeps night in a cell,
A big red "P" stamped on his back. O'Reilly's gone to hell—
Chorus

MCCARTHY OF TROOP "G"

Where the prairie winds are blowing and the gramma grasses growing
By the stretches of the Laramie, lives McCarthy of Troop "G."
He was born in Tipperary, but the glamor of the prairie
Held him captive in its fetters—we were "bunkies" him and me.

He'd a heart big as a mountain, overflowing like a fountain,
With the sap of love and kindness for the law-bound human race.
Mount him up behind the guidon of Troop "G," and he would ride on
To the flagstaff of Inferno; slap the "clootie" in the face.

Out of one post and another, we both "chased" the painted brother,
From Assiniboine to Wingate, from Wingate down to Brown.
Thirty years we served together in the warm and freezing weather;
Sheltered by a rubber poncho when the rain came swishing down.

At Slim Buttes I found him crying, where a Sioux papoose lay dying
Close beside its wounded mother–shot in running dodging fight.
There he sat, both of them nursing, and between his sobs kept
  cursing
At the white man's greed and grasping, and his self-established
  "right."

Once a "red" had got me under, and the knife of "Rolling Thunder"
Was about to sign my "buzzard" and relieve me of my hair;
When I heard a horse come dashing, then a saber blade went
  flashing,
Said a voice, "Get up there, Smokey." Mac of "G" sat grinning there.

After years of soldier starching, guard, fatigue, and marching,
We retired, and Mac located where the Platte and Lar'mie meet;
While my fool steps I directed, just as all the Troop expected,
To a six-by-ten hall bedroom in a crowded city street.

Here amid a whining rabble talking strange, unmeaning gabble—
Do I live alone unheeded by this lucre-loving corps;
Cursed by fate and early teaching to an everlasting reaching
For the wealth of one another, as their fathers did before.

Here I'm thinking of the prairie and the man from Tipperary;
Of the startled cattle "bunching" as a wolf goes slinking by;
Of the perfume of the grasses, of the foothills and their passes;
Of the swales and draws, and coulies where the prairie chickens lie.

God of joy, disperse my sorrow, for I'm going back tomorrow
To the stretches of the Lar'mie, where a man's a man and free.
Take this miasmatic gutter, where men plot and scheme and
  mutter—
Give me back the rolling prairies with McCarthy of Troop "G."

APPENDIX D

Enlisted Soldiers Whose Personal Accounts of Service Were Consulted for This Book

Adams, Jacob (7th Cav.)
Albrecht, Ernest F. (1st Cav.)
Aldrich, Lauren W. (30th Inf.)
Allen, Clarence H. (7th Cav.)
Allen, Emerson A. (1st Inf.)
Allen, Peter (7th Cav.)
Andersen, Martin (4th Arty.)
App, George (3rd Inf.)
Ashdown, Charles (1st Cav.)
Ashkey, Herman P. (2nd Cav.)
Bailey, Harry L. (7th Inf.)
Bailey, John A. (7th Cav.)
Bangerd, John G. H. (7th Inf.)
Barker, Edward D. (3rd Cav.)
Barker, Luther (5th Inf.)
Barnes, Will C. (Signal Corps)
Bayliss, George E. (8th Inf.)
Becker, Henry B. (7th Cav.)
Beckley, William (18th Inf.)
Bentley, Samuel H. (5th Cav.)
Bergstrom, John (22nd Inf.)
Berry, George C. (7th Inf.)
Bingham, Wallace E. (23rd Inf.)

Bivenour, Bernard S. (alias Henry Wilson) (1st Cav.)
Blackwood, James C. (3rd Inf.)
Blaut, Jacob (5th Cav.)
Bode, Emil A. (16th Inf.)
Bothwell, James C. (13th Inf.)
Bowen, William G. (11th Inf.)
Boyer, H. B. (Signal Corps)
Bradley, Reginald A. (4th Cav.)
Branch, William (25th Inf.)
Briggs, Andrew (4th Arty.)
Brinckerhoff, Henry M. (7th Cav.)
Brinkman, William (6th Inf.)
Brown, Alexander (7th Cav.)
Brown, Alexander (18th & 27th Inf.)
Brown, Benjamin F. (7th Cav.)
Brown, Edwin M. (5th Inf.)
Brown, John George (13th Inf.)
Brush, Charles A. (2nd Inf.)
Buckow, Herman (16th Inf.)
Burns, Richard T. (2nd Inf.)
Butler, Adelbert (2nd Cav.)
Cady, John H. (1st Cav.)
Cahill, Luke (3rd and 5th Inf.)
Carter, Albert (27th Inf.)
Casey, John F. (10th Cav.)
Cashan, William (7th Cav.)
Cashin, Herschel V. (10th Cav.)
Charlton, John B. (4th Cav.)
Chrisman, Clarence B. (13th Inf.)
Christian, Charles P. (6th Cav.)
Ciscel, Harvey J. (8th Cav.)
Clark, Hartford G. (6th Cav.)
Cline, Isaac M. (Signal Corps)
Coleman, Thomas W. (7th Cav.)
Comfort, Will L. (5th Cav.)
Connelly, James (8th Cav.)
Connelly, James N. (2nd Cav.)
Cook, Charles (24th Inf.)

ENLISTED SOLDIERS   617

Coon, Homer (7th Inf.)
Cox, John E. (1st Inf.)
Courville, Louis (7th Cav.)
Cranston, George H. (32 Inf.)
Curran, Stephen H. (1st Inf.)
Dahlgren, Axel (13th Inf.)
Davis, Harry J. (2nd Cav.)
Delemont, John C. (5th Inf.)
Demarest, Samuel A. (21st Inf.)
Dewel, Fritz (6th Cav.)
Dickson, Archibald (3rd Inf.)
Dolan, John (7th Cav.)
Donahue, John F. (7th Cav.)
Donath, Ralph (17th Inf.)
Dose, Henry (7th Cav.)
Drown, Albin H. (2nd Cav.)
DuBois, George B. (8th Cav.)
Dugan, Lawrence (4th Inf.)
Dunne, Edward W. (11th Inf.)
Eaton, Perley S. (3rd Cav.)
Ebert, Louis (6th Cav.)
Eisele, Charles J. (21st Inf.)
Ertberg, Harry L. A. (1st Cav.)
Evans, Samuel (7th Cav.)
Ewert, Theodore (7th Cav.)
Farley, John F. (3rd Cav.)
Fensch, Albert (19th Inf.)
Fetter, William (6th Inf.)
Fitzgerald, Maurice (1st Cav.)
Fitzpatrick, Bartholomew (18th Inf.)
Flynn, Andrew M. (7th Cav.)
Flynn, Richard (4th Inf.)
Foley, James W. (4th Cav. & Comm. Sgt.)
Ford, George W. (10th Cav.)
Ford, John C. (17th Inf.)
Forsyth, Thomas H. (4th Cav. and Comm. Sgt.)
Forte, Edward (7th Cav.)
Foster, John R. P. (3rd Cav.)

Fox, Adam (2nd Cav.)
Fox, John (7th Cav.)
Frascola, Antonio (5th Cav.)
Frew, James B. (5th Cav.)
Frierson, Eugene P. (10th Cav.)
Frith, Henry A. (11th Inf.)
Gaffney, George (7th Cav.)
Gallenne, Jean Baptiste D. (7th Cav.)
Gardner, John P. (8th Inf.)
Gardner, Samuel (5th Inf.)
Gavin, Anthony (22nd Inf.)
Geant, Eugene (7th Inf.)
Geist, Reinhold R. (8th Cav.)
Gibbert, John (22nd Inf.)
Gibson, Samuel (27th Inf., 4th Cav., 16th Inf., 22nd Inf., Ord., 22nd Inf.)
Gibson, Thomas V. (13th Inf.)
Gilpin, Samuel D. (13th Inf.)
Goldin, Theodore W. (7th Cav.)
Goodenberger, Charles (9th Inf.)
Gould, Clarence S. (1st Cav.)
Greenhalgh, Robert (2nd Cav.)
Grover, Sylvester (4th Cav.)
Gurnett, William (5th Inf.)
Gutch, Thomas E. (1st Cav.)
Guthrie, John (2nd Cav.)
Guy, Theodore E. (1st Cav.)
Hall, Earl (3rd Cav.)
Hamilton, Edward (9th Cav.)
Hamilton, James Starr (1st Inf.)
Hamont, P. W. (4th Art.)
Harbers, Herman (3rd Inf.)
Hardin, Charles B. (1st Cav.)
Harrington, Walter C. (21st Inf.)
Harris, Jesse Grant (7th Cav.)
Harris, Samuel (25th Inf.)
Harrison, Thomas W. (7th Cav.)
Harvey, Winfield S. (7th Cav.)

Hatcher, Alexander (24th Inf.)
Hayden, Charles N. (7th Cav.)
Hayman, Perry A. (10th Cav.)
Hechner, John (5th Inf.)
Heidelberger, Frank (6th Cav.)
Henley, John (7th Cav.)
Henry, Lawrence J. (7th Cav.)
Herron, Leander (3rd Inf.)
Hetler, Jacob (7th Cav.)
Hettinger, August (8th Inf.)
Hildreth, Charles M. (5th Cav.)
Hills, Louis E. (7th Cav.)
Hoffner, Edgar (1st Cav.)
Horn, Marion E. (7th Cav.)
Horner, Jacob (7th Cav.)
Howard, George S. (2nd Cav.)
Howerton, John (10th Cav.)
Hubbard, John L. (3rd Cav.)
Hubman, Henry (18th Inf.)
Hunteole, William (1st Cav.)
Hynds, Hugh (20th Inf.
Hynes, William F. (alias Wm. Jones) (2nd Cav.)
Jansen, Charles N. (10th Inf.)
Jenkins, John W. (6th Inf.)
Jepson, Soren (8th Cav.)
Jerome, Lawrence R. (4th Cav.)
Jett, William B. (4th Cav.)
Johnson, Charles (8th Cav.)
Johnson, John (8th Inf.)
Jordan, William W. (14th Inf.)
Kennedy, Francis Johnson (7th Cav.)
Kerstetter, David M. (18 & 27 Inf.)
Kimm, John G. (7th Cav.)
Kincaid, James B. (4th Cav.)
King, Richard F. (10 Inf. & Hosp. Corps)
Kingsbury, George W. (12th Inf.)
Kirkwood, John A. (3rd Cav.)
Kitching, Seymour (Hospital Dept.)

Knight, Frank B. (5th Inf.)
Kolarik, Charles (1st Cav.)
Krause, Frederick C. (8th Cav.)
Kuhn, Joseph (2nd Cav.)
Lacher, Peter (4th Cav.)
Lally, John N. (1st Inf.)
Lanahan, John (7th Inf.)
Lang, John (2nd Cav.)
Langley, Henry (7th Cav.)
Latta, Emmet G. (4th Inf.)
Lattman, John (7th Cav.)
Lautenschlaeger, Edward (5th Inf.)
Lea, Lawrence (2nd Cav.)
Lester, Charles (30th & 4th Inf.)
Lewis, Thos. E. H. (alias John Sharpe) (18th Inf., 27th Inf.)
Lisk, George K. (5th Cav.)
Lockwood, James D. (18th Inf.)
Lowell, Frank (5th Cav.)
Loynes, Charles N. (7th Inf.)
Luce, David W., Jr. (alias Charles Newton) (7th Cav.)
Lynch, Dennis (7th Cav.)
Lyon, Howard A. (17th Inf.)
Madsen, Christian (5th Cav.)
Maher, James (1st Arty.)
Mann, Simpson (9th Cav.)
Marshall, John (10th Cav.)
Matthews, Wm. Edward (8th Cav.)
Maurer, Charles (4th Cav.)
Mayers, Edward (7th Cav.)
Mayo, Grandison (25th Inf.)
Mazzanovich, Anton (6th Cav.)
McAnulty, George W. (9th Inf.)
McBlain, John (2nd Cav.)
McCardle, Washington (8th Inf.)
McClellan, James S. (3rd Cav.)
McConnell, Henry H. (6th Cav.)
McGrath, Hugh K. (2nd Cav.)
McKay, Barney (24th Inf.)

ENLISTED SOLDIERS 621

McVeigh, David (7th Cav.)
Meddaugh, Samuel L. (6th Inf.)
Miller, William (3rd Cav., 4th Cav.)
Mixer, Fred (2nd Cav., 7th Inf.)
Molchert, William (7th Inf.)
Monnette, Joseph (1st Inf.)
Morris, William E. (7th Cav.)
Morrison, James G. (1st Cav.)
Mulford, Ami F. (7th Cav.)
Murphy, John E. (12th Inf.)
Murphy, William (18th Inf., 27th Inf.)
Neifert, William W. (Signal Corps)
Neihaus, George (10th Inf.)
Neville, John J. (1st Cav.)
Nihill, John (5th Cav.)
Nixon, John R. (7th Cav.)
Norman, Robert C. O. (3rd Inf.)
Nugent, William D. (7th Cav.)
O'Brien, John (soldier's son)
O'Brien, Timothy (18th Inf.)
Ofdenkamp, Henry F. (6th Cav.)
O'Leary, Maurice (1st Cav.)
O'Neill, Thomas F. (7th Cav.)
Ostrander, Alson B. (18th Inf.)
O'Sullivan, Michael M. (7th Inf.)
O'Toole, Francis (7th Cav.)
Pagel, E. W. (6th Inf.)
Patterson, Eugene (5th Cav.)
Pauly, Emil (4th Cav.)
Pelham, R. Eugene (6th Inf.)
Persons, Charles C. (1st Cav.)
Phillips, Dorsey (7th Cav.)
Pickard, Edwin F. (7th Cav.)
Pickens, William H. (5th Cav.)
Pierce, Charles W. (6th Cav.)
Pilgard, Rasmus (22nd Inf.)
Platten, Fred (6th Cav.)
Pollock, Oliver C. C. (3rd Cav.)

Prescott, F. G. (27th Inf.)
Purvis, James O. (1st Cav.)
Rallya, Clinton (7th Cav.)
Raper, George S. (8th Cav.)
Reid, Elwyn S. (7th Cav.)
Rhymer, James H. (2nd Cav.)
Richey, Stephen R. (Signal Corps)
Roque, Emanuel (12th Inf.)
Rovinsky, John (8th Cav.)
Ryan, John (7th Cav.)
Sanders, John D. (6th Inf.)
Sanford, Wilmot P. (6th Inf.)
Schall, Lafayette (3rd Inf.)
Schoeni, Arnold (4th Cav.)
Schorr, John P. (1st Cav.)
Schreiber, Phillip (18th Inf.)
Schuldt, Henry (4th Cav.)
Scott, Charles (7th Cav.)
Searl, Herman S. (18th Inf.)
Selander, Ernest A. (2nd and 5th Cav.)
Sembower, Isaac H. (1st Cav.)
Settle, Green A. (7th Cav.)
Shannehan, Arthur W. (alias Arthur S. Wallace) (5th Cav.)
Shropshire, Shelvin (10th Cav.)
Siefert, August (7th Cav.)
Sivertsten, John (7th Cav.)
Slaper, William C. (7th Cav.)
Slaughter, William J. (7th Cav.)
Sloan, Wolsey A. (4th Cav.)
Slough, John P. (2nd Cav.)
Smit, Frederick (37th & 3rd Inf.)
Smith, James D. (2nd Cav.)
Smith, John M. (23rd Inf.)
Smith, William Earl (4th Cav.)
Snepp, James E. (3rd Cav.)
Sniffin, Frank (7th Cav.)
Snow, Fred (7th Cav.)
Sommer, Christian F. (23rd Inf.)

Souter, Edward (6th Cav.)
Spring, John A. (14th Inf.)
Stafford, John (1st Cav.)
Stance, Emanuel (10th Cav.)
Stokes, John T. (1st Cav.)
Stortz, Frederick (7th Inf.)
Stotts, John O. (3rd Inf.)
Stringham, Alonzo (7th Cav.)
Sturr, Frank (7th Cav.)
Suttles, John J. (5th Cav.)
Taylor, William O. (7th Cav.)
Terwilliger, Jasper N. (1st Cav.)
Tetzel, Karl (3rd Cav.)
Theis, Daniel (13th Inf.)
Thompson, Peter (7th Cav.)
Tinkham, George F. (3rd Cav.)
Toby, Fred H. (7th Cav.)
Topping, Grant C. (6th Cav.)
Towne, Phineas S. (3rd Cav.)
Tucker, James (10th Cav.)
Turhune, Louis P. (21st Inf.)
Unger, Armand J. (5th Cav.)
Vetter, Michael (7th Cav.)
Von Hammerstein, Herbert (2nd Cav.)
Von Ostermann, Georg F. (8th Cav.)
Walker, W. H. (4th Cav.)
Wallace, Arthur S. (5th Cav.)
Waller, Eddie (13th Inf.)
Waller, Reuben (10th Cav.)
Walsh, John (7th Cav.)
Wasson, Lines P. (9th Inf.)
Watkins, William (25th Inf.)
Watson, Richard F. (1st Cav.)
Way, Thomas N. (7th Cav.)
Weber, George (27th Inf.)
Weber, Martin J. (5th Cav.)
Weihe, Henry Charles (alias Charles White) (7th Cav.)
Welsh, Martin (3rd Cav.)

Werner, Herman (1st Cav.)
White, William H. (2nd Cav.)
Whittaker, George (6th Cav.)
Wilkinson, James B. (2nd Cav.)
Wilkinson, William G. (8th Cav.)
Wilks, Jacob (9th Cav.)
Williams, Edward (2nd Cav.)
Willis, Albert (4th Cav.)
Wilson, Charles William (18th Inf.)
Wilson, James E. (20th Inf.)
Wilson, Thomas H. (7th Inf.)
Windolph, Charles (7th Inf.)
Wolfe, Maurice H. (30th Inf.)
Wood, Edwin D. (3rd Cav.)
Yohn, Henry I. (1st Cav.)
Zimmer, William F. (2nd Cav.)
Zimmerman, John K. (14th Inf.)
Zinser, Louis (3rd Cav.)

Abbreviations

AAG	Assistant Adjutant General
AAS	Acting Assistant Surgeon
AG	Adjutant General
AGO	Adjutant General's Office
AHC	American Heritage Center
AHS	Arizona Historical Society Library
ANJ	*Army & Navy Journal*
ANR	*Army & Navy Register*
ARSW	*Annual Report of the Secretary of War*
BBHC	Buffalo Bill Historical Center
BHNB	Big Hole National Battlefield
BL, YU	Beinecke Library, Yale University
BPL	Billings Public Library
BYU	Brigham Young University
CC	Camp Collection
CHL	Chavez History Library
CO	Commanding Officer
DPL	Denver Public Library
DU	Duke University
ECP	Ellison/Camp Papers
FLNHS	Fort Laramie National Historic Site
FUNM	Fort Union National Monument
GCMO	*General Court-Martial Orders*

GO	*General Orders*
GTC	Groenewold-Triplett Collection
HL	Huntington Library
HQ	Headquarters
HR	House of Representatives
IWWP	Indian Wars Widows Project
JNEM	Jefferson National Expansion Memorial
LBBNM	Little Bighorn Battlefield National Monument
LR	Letters Received
LS	Letters Sent
M	Prefix for numbered microfilm publications, National Archives
MHS	Montana Historical Society
ML, UU	Marriott Library, University of Utah
MSHSL	Missouri State Historical Society Library
MSU	Montana State University
NARA	National Archives and Records Administration
NL	Newberry Library
NPHP	Nez Perce Historical Park
OHS	Oklahoma Historical Society
QM	Quartermaster
RC	Rickey Collection, U.S. Army Heritage and Education Center
RE	Register of Enlistments
RG	Record Group
RP, DPL	Rickey Papers, Denver Public Library
SC, DU	Special Collections, Duke University
SC, UAL	Special Collections, University of Arizona Library
SHS	State Historic Site
SO	*Special Orders*
UCB	University of Colorado (Boulder)
UIWV	United Indian Wars Veterans
USA	United States Army
USAMHI	U.S. Army Military History Institute, U.S. Army Heritage and Education Center
USCL	University of South Carolina Library
WSA	Wyoming State Archives

Notes

Book epigraph source: Summerhayes, *Vanished Arizona*, 63.

INTRODUCTION

1. Hoffner diary, Aug. 20, 1879, Brown Papers, CU. Harry Egan was killed in action with so-called Sheepeaters, renegade Bannock and Shoshoni Indians. His remains lie buried somewhere along Big Creek in the remote River of No Return Wilderness of Idaho's Salmon River Mountains; Second Infantry Returns, August 1879, Returns from Regular Army Infantry Regiments, M665, RG 94, NARA.

2. One source records the total casualties as 923 officers and enlisted men killed in action. McDermott, *Guide to the Indian Wars*, 28. Perhaps the figure most closely approximating an official tally is 85 officers and 875 enlisted men, though even the combined lists therein are not completely reliable. As an example, the entry for the Salmon River fight on Aug. 20, 1879, lists no casualties. Yet we know that Private Harry Egan was mortally wounded and buried there. *Chronological List of Actions & c. with Indians from January 15, 1837 to January, 1891.*

3. Reese, *Sykes' Regular Infantry Division, 1861–1864*, 377–80. All of the regular regiments served east of the Mississippi during the war, except for the Fifth Infantry, which remained in New Mexico Territory, and the Ninth, stationed in California throughout the conflict. During 1862 it played a significant role in several actions against Confederate troops thrusting up the Rio Grande from Texas. Rodenbough, *Army of the United States*, 471–72. In 1861 the two regiments of U.S. Dragoons and the Regiment of Mounted Riflemen were combined with three regiments of cavalry, with the six regiments thereafter to be designated as cavalry. Urwin, *United States Cavalry*, 112, 118, 120; The Third Cavalry, also posted in New Mexico Territory at the outset of the war, remained there during 1861–62 and also saw action during the Confederate invasion. Late in 1862, however, the regiment was transferred to the eastern theater and did not return to the West until 1866. Rodenbough, *Army of the United States*, 201–3.

4. *ARSW*, 1866, 17.

5. The actual strength of the army in 1865 is based on a compilation provided by the Adjutant General's Office and published in Prucha, *Guide to the Military Posts*, 144. Figures used here and elsewhere in this discussion reflect the total strengths of the army as authorized by Congress. Heitman, *Historical Register*, 2:604, 608, 610–11, 612–13. Another useful compilation, showing the actual strengths for any given year during the period of this study, is found in Weigley, *History of the United States Army*, 567.

6. *ARSW*, 1866, 28. The term "Buffalo Soldiers" has been applied to the black regulars, particularly the Ninth and Tenth Cavalry, since the 1880s. Perhaps the earliest printed reference to the name was made in 1872 by Roe, *Army Letters*, as referenced in Schubert, *Voices*, 47–49. Black soldiers themselves, however, seem to have seldom if ever used it during the nineteenth century. In researching the present volume, I found the nickname used in only two firsthand soldier accounts, both of them left by white men. Entry for Jan. 12, 1891, Private Hartford G. Clark diary, Jan. 12, 1891, f. 11, box 9, RP, DPL; John G. Brown to Viola Ransom Wood, Mar. 23, 1933, box 1, RC, USAMHI. The term may even have been considered derogatory to black soldiers in that time. A Tombstone, Arizona Territory, resident, George W. Parsons, made reference in his journal on Oct. 6, 1881: "One company or two of Negro, or Buffalo Soldiers as the Indians call them, are in this command. The Indians deride them, the hostiles I mean [as opposed to Indian scouts with the command]." Bailey, *Tenderfoot in Tombstone*, 183. The moniker was popularized with the 1967 publication of William H. Leckie's landmark book by that title. Since that time, the term "Buffalo Soldiers" has been applied universally to all of the black units active during the Indian Wars, connoting "elite." I contend that, except for generally lower desertion rates, these units were no better and no worse than the other regular regiments of that time. A cogent discussion of this topic is found in Dobak and Phillips, *Black Regulars*, xvii. A persistent myth suggests that the black regulars were subjected to discrimination by being issued worn-out equipment, substandard weapons, and obsolete clothes, rather than first-class materiel on a par with that of their white counterparts. This is a false notion. The Tenth Cavalry, for example, was among the first four regiments to receive the new Model 1873 Springfield Carbine and the Model 1873 Colt Army Revolver in early 1874. Moreover, eight companies of the regiment drew the new weapons, compared with only one or two companies each of the Second, Fourth, and Six Cavalry. The record indicates that infantry regiments were issued the new .45-caliber rifles in the order of their numerical sequence, beginning with the First Infantry. Accordingly, the higher-numbered regiments, upward of fifteen, did not receive Model 1873 rifles until the first months of 1875. Prior to the new issue, black infantry, like all other foot regiments, had been uniformly armed with Model 1868 and Model 1870 rifles. Summary Statements of Quarterly Returns of Ordnance and Ordnance Stores on Hand in Regular and Volunteer Army Organizations, Records of the Chief of Ordnance, RG 156, rolls 3 and 8, M1281, NARA. Official reports rendered to the adjutant general early in 1875 substantiate that the Ninth and Tenth Cavalry and the Twenty-Fourth and Twenty-Fifth Infantry were provided clothing and individual equipment equal to that being issued to all other units of the army at that time. For instance, the men of Company E, Tenth Cavalry, posted at Fort Richardson, Texas, had already received the 1874-pattern blouse, officially adopted just two months earlier. 2nd Lieutenant George H. Evans, Tenth Cavalry, Fort Richardson, Texas, to post adjutant, Feb. 20, 1875; additional documentation is found in Colonel George L. Andrews, Twenty-Fifth Infantry, Fort Davis, Texas, to AG, USA, Feb. 25, 1875; and Captain Edward G. Bush, Tenth Infantry, Fort Stockton, Texas, to AG, USA, Feb. 27, 1875; all in Papers Relating

to the Army Equipment Board, 1878–79, LR, AGO (Main Series), 1871–80, RG 94, rolls 435 and 436, M666, NARA.

7. *ARSW,* 1869, 25–26.

8. House of Representatives, Report No. 384, *Reorganization of the Army,* at iii (1874).

9. Foley, "The 4th U.S. Cav.," *National Tribune,* June 5, 1915 (quotation); Wooster, *The Military and United States Indian Policy,* 14. The adjutant general reported in October 1872 that the whole of the Seventh Cavalry, two companies of the Sixth Cavalry, and five entire infantry regiments were posted in the southern states, making a total of over 17 percent of the available infantry and cavalry assigned to Reconstruction duty. The artillery was not included in the calculation because the various units were posted routinely in permanent fortifications along the seacoasts. *ARSW,* 1872, 20–33.

10. *ARSW,* 1866, 17.

11. Ibid., 19.

12. Ibid., 31.

13. Although a few incidents occurred after Wounded Knee, they involved individuals or very small parties of "outlaw" Indians, not tribal entities. The pursuit of the "Apache Kid" in Arizona serves as a case in point.

14. *ANJ,* April 26, 1890, 654.

15. With reference to the actual strength of the army line, Sherman observed:

> We have 852 men unassigned to any regiment or organization, engaged in the recruiting service. That may be in excess of propriety, but it seems to be the result of experience . . . Then we have 299 men charged as general service men; men who are employed at the War Department, at the Headquarters of the Army and in the different military divisions and departments, who are in fact clerks, and nothing else . . . the Ordnance Department, which never sends a man into the field . . . has 355 men enrolled . . . we have 230 men at West Point to aid the young men there . . . we have 236 hospital stewards . . . they do not take muskets . . . 151 commissary sergeants . . . 66 men as prison guard for Fort Leavenworth, and 237 recruits who are available may be sent forward. This makes nearly 3,000 men out of your 25,000.

ANJ, Aug. 12, 1876, 10. Except for infrequent occasions when a few companies were dispatched to Indian country, the five regiments of artillery saw no western field service either.

CHAPTER 1. "TAKING TO SOLDIERING"

1. David W. Luce, "Indian War Campaigning," *National Tribune,* Sept. 18, 1921.

2. Clarence Allen, "My Experiences," f. 57, box 8, RP, DPL (first quotation); Forsyth, *Story of the Soldier,* 86 (second quotation).

3. Lockwood, *Life and Adventures of a Drummer Boy,* 118–19.

4. McConnell, *Five Years a Cavalryman,* 17 (first quotation); Robert Greenhalgh to Father and Mother, Oct. 8, 1865, Greenhalgh letters, RP, DPL (second quotation); Forsyth, *Story of the Soldier,* 370.

5. Barnard, *Ten Years with Custer,* 16.

6. Anonymous, "With Custer in 1876," *National Tribune,* Sept. 13, 1923.

7. Barnard, *Ten Years with Custer,* 18 (quotation); John W. Jenkins, "One Who Helped Many Years in the Hard Work," *National Tribune,* May 26, 1919. The law stated: "No

person who has served in any capacity in the military, naval, or civil service of the so-called Confederate States, or of either of the States in insurrection during the late rebellion, shall be appointed to any position in the Army of the United States." The intention was to exclude former rebels from being appointed as commissioned officers, but technically it also applied to noncommissioned officers. As a result, some privates known to have been Confederates were denied promotion. In other instances, southerners had been appointed as noncoms but were in danger of losing their rank if the law was strictly enforced. A bill was introduced in 1884 to repeal the earlier statute. HR No. 1855, 46th Cong., 1st Sess. (1884).

8. McConnell, *Five Years a Cavalryman*, 106–7. The term "dog robber" was army slang for a soldier who hired out as an officer's servant. An article published in 1881 noted that "The Germans come in increasing numbers, and are proner [*sic*] than men of any other nationality to make a career of the American army. The old-fashioned Irish sergeant . . . is said to have become rare" (Forbes, "The United States Army," 136). This trend was reflected in an 1883 statistic showing that 40 percent of cavalry recruits were American-born, 27 percent German, and 22 percent Irish (*ANJ*, Jan. 26, 1884, 524).

9. *ANJ*, Jan. 19, 1884, 502; HR Misc. Doc. No. 105, 44th Cong., 1st Sess. (1876); *ARSW*, 1880, 41–43; *ANJ*, Jan. 14, 1884, 501 (quotation). Recruiting reports submitted annually by the adjutant general record percentages ranging between 30 and 40 for the period 1880 to 1891, which likely reflect the ebb and flow of immigration to the United States and economic conditions generally during that period. *ARSW*, 1888, 73; 1889, 92; 1890, 68, 1891, 82.

10. Hebard and Brininstool, *Bozeman Trail*, 2:73, 83.

11. Christian Madsen, "Five Years on the Prairies," MS, BBHC (quotation). Norman arrived in the United States in 1890 and served three years in the Third Infantry. Robert C. O. Norman questionnaire, f. 95, box 9, RP, DPL.

12. Windolph, *I Fought with Custer*, 3–4.

13. 1886 *Billings Gazette* article reprinted in Upton, *Fort Custer*, 81.

14. QM Sergeant Maurice H. Wolfe to Cousin Maurice, Nov. 16, 1868, Wolfe letters, FLNHS.

15. James W. Foley, "The 4th U.S. Cavalry in Texas," *National Tribune*, Sept. 18, 1913 (quotation); Gustafson, *John Spring's Arizona*, 6–11.

16. Cady, *Arizona's Regiment*, 15–16; John O. Stotts reminiscence, Spencer collection (quotation).

17. *ARSW*, 1866, 2; Nankivell, *History of the Twenty-Fifth Infantry*, 6–7.

18. *GO No. 125*, AGO, Dec. 15, 1870.

19. General Guy V. Henry quoted in Adams, *Class and Race*, 183. Henry had extensive experience serving with black soldiers, having been a major in the Ninth Cavalry, 1881–92, and colonel of the Tenth, 1897–98. Heitman, *Historical Register*, 1:523.

20. Reuben Waller, "History of a Slave," in *Battle of Beecher Island*, 86.

21. Richardson, *West from Appomattox*, 29.

22. Schubert, *Voices of the Buffalo Soldier*, 53 (first quotation), 86 (second quotation).

23. McChristian, *Frontier Cavalry Trooper*, 2 (first quotation), 286; QM Sergeant Maurice H. Wolfe to Cousin Maurice, Nov. 7, 1872, Wolfe letters, FLNHS (second quotation); James S. Hamilton questionnaire, f. 52, box 9, RP, DPL (third quotation).

24. *ANJ*, May 3, 1873, 600 (first quotation); *ANJ*, Dec. 16, 1882, 437 (second quotation).

25. Washington McCardle questionnaire, f. 82, box 9 (quotation); William Hunteole questionnaire, f. 63, box 9; RP, DPL.

26. McDonald enlisted in the U.S. Navy at Boston in 1867 and served three years. Shortly after his discharge, he joined the army and served three enlistments in the First and Seventh Infantry, taking his final discharge in 1885. Bryan McDonald, June 1867, U.S. Naval Enlistment Rendezvous, 1855–1891, Ancestry.com (2014); Register of Enlistments, M233, rolls 36, 39, 42.

27. *ARSW*, 1880, 44–45.

28. Romeyn, "Desertion: Some Causes and Remedies," 671.

29. Evidence of the effect of continuing uncertain economic conditions is found in a report that a Boston recruiting officer enlisted forty men in less than a month "due to the recent strikes and labor troubles." The officer claimed that this was a larger number than he had recruited during any previous month. *ANJ*, July 3, 1886, 997. Cox admitted in his narrative that he was only twenty years old, although a young man had to be at least twenty-one to enlist without written parental consent. His enlistment record shows his age as twenty-one, indicating that he gave a false answer to that question. Cox, *Five Years in the United States Army*, 6–8 (quotations).

30. Munn, "Fred Munn, Veteran of Frontier Experiences," 51 (first quotation); Armand Unger questionnaire, f. 34, box 10, RP, DPL (second quotation); Walker, "Reluctant Corporal" (pt. 1), 4 (third quotation); "Old Soldier Residing Here," Montana Scrapbook, Billings Library (fourth quotation). The relics attributed to Cody likely came from the 1876 skirmish at Warbonnet Creek, Nebraska, in which he had been a participant, rather than from the Little Bighorn.

31. Grandison Mayo questionnaire, f. 45, box 9, RP, DPL (first quotation); Greene, *Indian War Veterans*, 26 (second quotation); Wallace Bingham, "Early Days On the Frontier," f. 72, box 8, RP, DPL (third quotation).

32. "Captain Bivens, Veteran of Many Wars," *Billings Gazette*, Mar. 2, 1930, vertical files, Billings Library.

33. Bradley's outfit included "a .44/40 Winchester rifle and six-shooter that used the same ammunition." Reginald A. Bradley interview, f. 76, box 8, RP, DPL.

34. Lawrence J. Henry to Viola Ransom Wood, UIWV, Aug. 15, 1934, f. 83, box 10 (first quotation); Alexander Hatcher questionnaire, f. 58, box 10 (second quotation); William G. Bowen, f. 2, box 9 (third quotation); Walter C. Harrington, f. 78, box 9; John G. H. Bangerd, f. 69, box 8 (fourth quotation); William G. Wilkinson, f. 44, box 10 (fifth quotation); all in RP, DPL.

35. McChristian, *Frontier Cavalry Trooper*, 169 (first quotation); George Neihaus questionnaire, f. 95, box 9, (second quotation); Samuel Evans questionnaire, f. 30, box 9 (third quotation); Joseph Kuhn questionnaire, f. 71, box 9 (fourth quotation); all questionnaires in RP, DPL.

36. Anonymous veteran to E. A. Brininstool, June 1935, in Carroll, *Seventh Cavalry Scrapbook*, 11 (first quotation); Simpson Mann interview, f. 79, box 9, RP, DPL (second and third quotations); Theodore E. Guy questionnaire, f. 51, box 9, RP, DPL.

37. Bell, *New Tracks*, 64 (first quotation); Private Henry Hubman to Brother Herman, Oct. 1, 1881. and Nov. 19, 1881, Hubman Letters, James Mountain files (second and third quotations); Thomas P. Downing folder, Seventh Cavalry File, LBBNM.

38. George Cranston to Gertrude Cranston (sister), Oct. 27, 1866, f. 2, box 1, Cranston Letters, SC, UAL (first quotation); Harvey J. Ciscel questionnaire, f. 9, box 9,

RP, DPL (second quotation); *ANJ*, Aug. 14, 1880, 29; Custer, *Following the Guidon*, viii (third and fourth quotations).

39. *ANJ*, Sept. 19, 1885, 997.

40. The Mounted Recruiting Service was assigned a separate headquarters at Jefferson Barracks, Missouri, in 1886. *ANJ*, July 3, 1886, 1001.

41. A station operated in Atlanta, Georgia, during 1877, apparently without much success. Rendezvous attracting significant numbers of black recruits were located in Nashville and Memphis, Tennessee; Louisville, Kentucky; and St. Louis, Missouri. *ARSW*, 1877, 44; 1879, 33; 1880, 38; 1887, 83.

42. The sergeant noted that nearly twice as many blacks as whites were attracted to the army. *ANJ*, Dec. 10, 1887.

43. The San Antonio station was discontinued in 1881, after all but one of the black regiments had left Texas. *ARSW*, 1881, 45.

44. Recruiting officers in the Division of the Pacific were prohibited from enlisting black men. This was simply a matter of practicality, because none of the black regiments were stationed on the West Coast. Enlisting blacks would have necessitated transporting them at government expense to the eastern depots and thence back to regiments in the West. *ARSW*, 1872, 120.

45. *ARSW*, 1869, 151; 1873, 80; 1878, 28; 1879, 34.

46. Smaller cities in predominantly rural areas that were tried were Pittsburgh and Harrisburg, Pennsylvania; Springfield, Illinois, and Troy, New York. The station at Denver was also designated as a subdepot for the purpose of providing basic training to recruits, who were then sent directly to regiments in the West and Southwest. *ARSW*, 1883, 56; 1884, 55; 1890, 67 (quotation); 1891, 78–79.

47. Nelson, "Davids Island," 509. Line companies not infrequently suffered from a lack of leadership as a result of so many officers being absent for recruiting duty and myriad other reasons. The choice of locations for recruiting assignments was based on an officer's seniority according to the date of his commission. *ANJ*, Aug. 16, 1879, 21. An example was Private Thomas Ross, who entered his third enlistment at Fort Columbus, New York Harbor, in fall 1868. He had previously served in the Irish Brigade during the Civil War, was wounded, and transferred to the Veteran Reserve Corps. Both his second and third enlistments were in the General Service Infantry, though he afterward served five more enlistments in the Twentieth Infantry, from which he was discharged at the rank of first sergeant. Thomas Ross Pension File, RG 15, NARA, copy in author's files.

48. "Will He Enlist?" 1641.

49. White, *Custer, Cavalry, and Crows*, 14.

50. Brininstool, *Troopers with Custer*, 35 (first quotation); Walker, "Reluctant Corporal" (pt. 1), 4 (second quotation).

51. Perley S. Eaton questionnaire, f. 24, box 9, RP, DPL (first quotation); Cozzens, *Eyewitnesses*, 2:117 (second quotation); Cox, *Five Years in the United States Army*, 9 (third quotation).

52. *ANJ*, June 6, 1874, 682 (first quotation); Walker, "Reluctant Corporal" (pt. 1), 4–5 (second quotation; this man may have been set up by a recruiting party needing to bolster its statistics); Hubman to Father, July 10, 1881, Hubman letters, James Mountain files (third quotation).

53. *Revised United States Army Regulations of 1861*, 130. The revisions for enlistment made in 1863 are found on 519.

54. Ibid., 519. An 1864 law prohibited the enlistment of musicians younger than sixteen, and then only with parental permission. *ARSW*, 1866, 52; *ARSW*, 1868, 150; *Regulations of the Army, 1881*, 73. In 1884 the maximum weight was increased to 190 pounds for foot soldiers and 165 pounds for cavalry. *ANJ*, Jan. 26, 1881, 518. At the end of the Indian Wars era, Adjutant General J. C. Kelton noted that the average age of cavalrymen was twenty-three, infantrymen thirty, and artillerymen thirty-four. He recommended that the maximum age for enlistment should be lowered from thirty-five to thirty to reduce the number of older men in the ranks. *ARSW*, 1891, 83.

55. *Revised United States Army Regulations of 1861*, 130; *ANJ*, Aug. 12, 1871; *ARSW*, 1871, 87; *Circular*, AGO, Dec. 14, 1874, published in Billings, *Circular No. 8*, vii.

56. *ARSW*, 1876, 72 (first quotation); Brininstool, *Troopers with Custer*, 36 (second quotation); Adams, *Class and Race*, 23.

57. *ANJ*, Oct. 16, 1880 (quotation). A circular dated Jan. 31, 1867, from the AGO attempted to reduce the number of illegal enlistments by making careless or imprudent recruiting officers personally liable for the government's expenses in such cases. In practice, however, the rule seems not to have had much effect. *Regulations of the Army, 1881*, 73.

58. White, *Custer, Cavalry, and Crows*, 14 (first quotation); Martin Andersen questionnaire, f. 59, box 8, RP, DPL (second quotation); Liddic and Harbaugh, *Camp on Custer*, 155 (third quotation); Schubert, *Voices of the Buffalo Soldier*, 183 (fourth quotation).

59. Bivenour to W. M. Camp, Feb. 10, 1921, microfilm reel no. 2, Camp Papers, BYU (first quotation); *ARSW*, 1877, 46 (second quotation); Nichols, *Men with Custer*, 394–95; James B. Kincaid, "Served as Companion to Indian Scout," *Winners of the West* July 1939 (third quotation).

60. *Revised United States Army Regulations of 1861*, 354.

61. *ARSW*, 1869, 26; McChristian, *Frontier Cavalry Trooper*, 2 (quotation).

62. *ANJ*, Jan. 23, 1875, 378 (first quotation); *ANJ*, May 16, 1879, 21–22 (second quotation).

63. Walker, "Reluctant Corporal" (pt. 1), 4 (first quotation); Windolph, *I Fought with Custer*, 4 (second quotation).

64. Maurer and Maurer, *First Sergeant*, 4 (first quotation); *ANJ*, Jan. 23, 1875: 378 (second quotation). The Cardiff Giant was an elaborate hoax perpetrated in 1869 in which a ten-foot stone figure of a man was buried then "discovered" and claimed to be a petrified human.

65. In rare instances, such as when a man enlisted at a depot or when the stock of uniforms had been depleted at a station, recruits began their training in civilian attire. This situation is suggested in Nelson, "Davids Island," 509; Hedren, "Campaigning with the Fifth U.S. Cavalry," 135; Mulford, *Fighting Indians*, 11; *ANJ*, Jan. 23, 1875 (first quotation); Greene, *Indian War Veterans*, 18 (second quotation).

66. Regulations prescribed that recruits were to be sent to the depots every ten days or sooner, so long as the party numbered more than three men, but this seems to have been fairly flexible in practice. *Revised United States Army Regulations of 1861*, 132; Walker, "Reluctant Corporal" (pt. 1), 5 (quotation).

67. Barnard, *Ten Years with Custer*, 34–35.

68. *GO No. 126*, AGO, Nov. 20, 1874 (quotation). By the 1880s, at a time when the frontier was becoming more heavily populated, some western military departments began establishing their own recruiting stations. The Department of the Missouri, for example,

designated Fort Bliss, Texas; Fort Lewis, Colorado; and Forts Bayard, Craig, Stanton, and Wingate, New Mexico; as well as the district headquarters in Santa Fe, as recruiting rendezvous where enlistments and reenlistments could be accepted for any unit posted in that department. The only exception was the Twenty-Fourth Infantry, for which only reenlistments of black veterans of good character could be accepted. *ANJ,* Nov. 19, 1881, 339. The army began taking identification photos ("mug shots") and fingerprints of each enlistee in 1906. The assignment of an identification number unique to each soldier would not be instituted until World War I. *Compilation of General Orders,* 395–97.

69. John O. Stotts reminiscence, Spencer collection (quotations); Rodenbough, *Army of the United States,* 447–48.

70. Hills, "With Gen. George A. Custer," 50.

71. Smith, *A Dose of Frontier Soldiering,* 15–17.

72. Mulford, *Fighting Indians,* 6–8.

73. *ANJ,* Jan. 23, 1875.

CHAPTER 2. "WE ARE KEPT PRETTY BUSY"

1. Carlisle Barracks, established during the Revolutionary War and used throughout the late eighteenth and early nineteenth centuries as a training school for all arms of the service, was designated exclusively as a depot for the mounted service from 1838 to 1842. It was again used for training dragoons for several years following the Mexican-American War then lapsed into a small infantry garrison until it was destroyed during the Confederate invasion of Pennsylvania in 1863. Shortly thereafter Carlisle Barracks was rebuilt and used exclusively for a time as the army's only mounted recruiting depot. Fort Leavenworth was designated as a general depot for both infantry and cavalry during 1869–70 but was replaced by the Cavalry Depot at St. Louis, Missouri. Gruber et al., *Preliminary Inventory,* RG 393, 114; Rodenbough, *From Everglade to Canyon,* 245–46; *GO No. 46,* AGO, April 26, 1869. First known as Pagganeck and later as Hutten Island, Governors Island was settled originally by the Dutch. From 1756 until the mid-1770s it was home, successively, to six New York governors: thus the name. The Americans fortified the island in 1775 and later, in response to a threatened French invasion, constructed Fort Jay there in 1794. Fort Columbus was established in 1806, with Castle William completed in 1811. The "castle" was used to house Confederate prisoners during the Civil War. "Garrison Life," 594–95. Newport, originally established as an arsenal in the early nineteenth century, later became Newport Barracks and was headquarters for the General Recruiting Service, Western Department in 1833. It continued in use as a depot until the Civil War intervened. The depot was reestablished in 1866. Gruber et. al., *Preliminary Inventory,* RG 393, 428. The system of recruiting depots was maintained until 1894, when that function was eliminated at all three. Thereafter recruits went directly from stations to regiments whenever there were vacancies to be filled. Only when the regiments were filled to capacity were recruits retained temporarily at the three former depots and at Fort Sheridan, Illinois, all of which were designated as rendezvous. *ARSW,* 1894, 185. The army altered and standardized the terminology for recruiting stations, which had formerly been "places where recruits are enlisted," as recruit rendezvous, which were now "designated posts at which general service recruits are collected for distribution to regiments." *Regulations for the Army, 1895,* 112.

2. Carlisle Barracks continued in use as a cavalry subdepot for a few months during 1871, when it too was discontinued as a needless expense. *GO No. 125,* AGO, Dec. 15,

1870; *ARSW,* 1871, 253; *ANJ,* Nov. 16, 1872: 212; *ARSW,* 1878, 28. Following an order to close the depots on the Pacific Coast, a small subdepot for cavalry continued at Benicia Barracks until finally disbanded in 1875. *ARSW,* 1872, 120; *ANJ,* May 8, 1875. The Army Organization Act of 1866 provided that two companies of each of the five artillery regiments would be light (or mounted) batteries, while the rest would be foot. When the army was reorganized in 1869, only one light battery was authorized for each regiment. A light artillery school was established at Fort Riley, Kansas, that same year. Recruits intended for light batteries took their basic training at one of the cavalry depots then proceeded to Fort Riley for specialized artillery training. Those for the foot (heavy) artillery companies went to one of the general service depots and thence to their units. Heitman, *Historical Register,* 2:605, 607; Rodenbough, *Army of the United States,* 325.

3. Gruber et al., *Preliminary Inventory,* RG 393, 428; Post Returns, Columbus Barracks, Ohio, Sept. 1875, RG 94, NARA.

4. "Garrison Life," 599 (quotation), 602; Nelson, "Davids Island," 509. The abandonment of Governors Island as a recruiting depot actually was prompted by the relocation of the headquarters, Division of the Atlantic from New York City, to the island July 1, 1878. Major General Winfield S. Hancock, commanding the division, petitioned for additional space "required for himself and staff," so the depot was moved. *ARSW,* 1878, 27.

5. Stephen R. Richey diary, June 29, 1883.

6. Hynes, *Soldiers of the Frontier,* 7 (first quotation); Ostrander, *Army Boy,* 245–46 (second quotation); Cox, *Five Years in the United States Army,* 10 (third quotation).

7. These terms were the official nomenclature, but General Service Infantry and General Service Cavalry also commonly appear in the record; Hospital Steward David Robertson, a native of Scotland, first enlisted in 1854 at age twenty-one. He was stationed at Governors Island from about 1856 until after the Indian Wars ended. In fact, he enlisted for the sixteenth time at the age of seventy-six in 1910, faithfully completing his last three years. "Garrison Life," 597; Register of Enlistments, M233, roll 24, NARA.

8. Rodenbough, *From Everglade to Canyon,* 249.

9. Private William Kane took a disability discharge in 1879, went to the U.S. Soldiers Home in Washington, D.C., and died there a few months later. All information concerning Kane was found in the Register of Enlistments, RG 94, AGO, NARA. The term "depot detachment" was adopted in 1881 in conjunction with a decision to abolish permanent parties. Beginning that year, eight sergeants of the line (two from the cavalry and six from the infantry) were chosen by regimental commanders to be detailed as drill masters at the general depots for one year. This measure was offered as compensation to "faithful and deserving non-commissioned officers serving at distant stations . . . to promote the efficiency of the recruiting service." *ANJ,* May 28, 1881, 889.

10. McChristian, *Frontier Cavalry Trooper,* 7.

11. Ibid. (quotation). "As a rule, a company officer will keep open a good sergeant's place for him for a month after the expiration of his term of enlistment. If he re-enlists within that time, he continues to wear his chevrons." Nelson, "Davids Island," 509.

12. McConnell, *Five Years a Cavalryman,* 12 (first quotation). Frank E. Woodward, a reporter for the *St. Louis Post-Dispatch,* enlisted in the army for the sole purpose of writing an exposé on the treatment of recruits at Jefferson Barracks. *ANJ,* Sept. 17, 1889, 25 (second quotation).

13. *ANJ,* Sept. 17, 1889, 25. Enlistment papers were filled out in triplicate, one of which the NCO in charge delivered to the depot adjutant. A descriptive list was a physical

description of the enlistee, noting age, previous occupation, and color of eyes and hair, along with complexion and height. Also recorded were the details of his enlistment. The descriptive list, maintained on every man throughout his term of service, formed his personal history.

14. Nelson, "Davids Island," 509.
15. Billings, *Circular No. 8*, xvi-xvii.
16. Ibid., xvi (first and second quotations); McChristian, *Frontier Cavalry Trooper*, 4 (third and fourth quotations).
17. Kolarik, "Comrade Kolarik Talks" (first quotation). Kolarik's memory regarding the wooden bunk slats was faulty. They measured six inches wide by six feet ten inches long. The two outer ones were one inch thick and the two in the middle were three-quarters of an inch thick. Specifications for iron bunks are in *U.S. Army Uniforms*, 12; Cox, *Five Years in the United States Army*, 12 (second quotation); Munn, "Fred Munn, Veteran of Frontier Experiences," 51 (third quotation). Obsolete war surplus clothing was issued well into the 1870s, especially to recruits, to dispose of stocks before current-patterns could be issued. McChristian, *U.S. Army in the West*, 144–45; *ANJ*, Sept. 17, 1889 (fourth quotation); Walker, "Reluctant Corporal" (pt. 1), 7 (fifth quotation).
18. McChristian, *Frontier Cavalry Trooper*, 5 (first quotation). Sutler's checks were tokens in various denominations signed out as credit against the recruit's first pay; McConnell, *Five Years a Cavalryman*, 12 (second quotation). Seventh Cavalryman Peter Thompson recalled buying an identical mess outfit at Jefferson Barracks late in 1875 for $4.00 and was assured that it was the regulation pattern. He later learned that the same items were available in nearby St. Louis for $1.50. When he joined his company a few months later, he was ordered to surrender his mess gear and draw the new regulation articles. Magnussen, *Peter Thompson's Narrative*, 33–34. Beginning in 1881, the Ordnance Department issued at no charge to soldiers, including recruits, a complete mess outfit, consisting of a two-piece meat can, utensils, and tin cup. *GO No. 14*, AGO, Feb. 7, 1881.
19. Smith, *A Dose of Frontier Soldiering*, 124 (first quotation); McChristian, *Frontier Cavalry Trooper*, 10 (second quotation); Private Henry Hubman to Father, July 10, 1881, Hubman Letters, James Mountain files (third quotation). By the end of the Indian Wars, according to one source, recruiting officers were rejecting 75 percent of the applicants for enlistment, indicating "not only the care in the selection of those who are accepted, but also the low character of very many of the applicants." Nelson, "Davids Island," 509; Forsyth, *Story of the Soldier*, 87–88 (fourth quotation); White, *Custer, Cavalry, and Crows*, 14–15 (fifth quotation).
20. *Revised United States Army Regulations of 1861*, 139.
21. Medical History, Fort Laramie, W.T., April 1871 (typescripts in library, FLNHS) (first quotation); Telegram, CO, Fort Fetterman, Wyo. Terr. to CO, Fort Sanders, Wyo. Terr., Mar. 18, 1873, Telegrams Sent & Received, Fort Fetterman, W.T., RG 393, NARA (second and third quotations). In addition to the initial physical examination at the recruiting stations, army regulations required each recruit to be examined twice at the depot, once upon arrival and again prior to being transferred from the depot to a regiment. Post surgeons were obligated to inspect recruits again upon arrival at their stations. *Revised United States Army Regulations of 1861*, 139. A persistent story of questionable authenticity concerns Private William Cathey. A black woman, Cathay Williams, later claimed to have served two years in the Thirty-Eighth Infantry posing as this man. While it makes an intriguing tale and may speak to the superficial nature of some army physical examinations, one must bear in mind the requirement for four such exams,

with the patient stripped naked. In addition, a number of examinations of Cathey were allegedly made by post surgeons during routine treatments. It stretches the imagination to believe that any army doctor, much less several, could have overlooked an individual's sex. Troubling gaps in the available evidence, not to mention unaddressed questions relating to the reality of barracks life, call for considerable leaps of faith. If the story is true at all, it seems far more likely that the woman was fraudulently attempting to collect a disability pension. Blanton, "Cathay Williams," in *Buffalo Soldiers in the West*, edited by Glasrud and Searles, 101–13; Schubert, *Voices of the Buffalo Soldier*, 33–34: *ARSW*, 1878, 28 (fourth quotation).

22. McConnell, *Five Years a Cavalryman*, 14.

23. Green A. Settle to Ralph Donath, Feb. 28, 1936, f. 9, box 10, RP, DPL. The rules were changed in 1876. Former soldiers of creditable character who enlisted within thirty days after being discharged could be reenlisted at bonus pay. *Regulations of the Army, 1881*, 260. Capable noncommissioned officers reenlisting immediately at the unit level usually maintained their former rank. Those who might enlist elsewhere for general service started over as privates, though accorded the status of old soldiers; Lafayetter Schall to Mary J. Arthur, n.d., UIWV files, f. 108, box 10, RP, DPL. Schall also served a third enlistment in the Fourth and Sixteenth Infantry, taking his final discharge in 1897. Register of Enlistments, M233, roll 48.

24. McChristian, *Frontier Cavalry Trooper*, 7.

25. This is supported by Dobak and Phillips, *Black Regulars*, 48–49.

26. Post Returns, Jefferson Barracks, July 1887, RG 94, NARA.

27. Post Returns, Cavalry Depot, Jefferson Barracks, October 1883, RG 94, NARA; Nelson, "Davids Island," 512 (quotation).

28. Mulford, *Fighting Indians*, 10–11 (first quotation); Private Arthur S. Wallace to Dan, n.d., FLNHS (second quotation).

29. Ostrander, *Army Boy*, 24.

30. McChristian, *Frontier Cavalry Trooper*, 5 (first quotation); Walker, "Reluctant Corporal" (pt. 1), 7 (second quotation); Forsyth, *Story of the Soldier*, 88 (third quotation); Register of Enlistments, M233, roll 40, NARA.

31. *Revised United States Army Regulations of 1861*, 501.

32. McChristian, *Frontier Cavalry Trooper*, 4–5 (first quotation); McConnell, *Five Years a Cavalryman*, 14 (second quotation).

33. Cox, *Five Years in the United States Army*, 11 (first quotation). "Upton" refers to the system of infantry tactics developed by Lieutenant Colonel Emory Upton first adopted by the army in 1867. The basic commands and formations of Upton's tactics were later assimilated for the cavalry and artillery. Jamieson, *Crossing the Deadly Ground*, 6, 9; *ANJ*, Jan. 8, 1881, 450 (second quotation).

34. Mulford, *Fighting Indians*, 9–10 (first quotation); Custer, *Following the Guidon*, 226 (second quotation). I heard these same lyrics sung by ex-first sergeant William H. Brown, who served in the Eighth Cavalry, 1916–21.

35. McChristian, *Frontier Cavalry Trooper*, 4 (first quotation); Cox, *Five Years in the United States Army*, 11; Ostrander, *Army Boy*, 19 (second quotation). Low-quality depot food was not peculiar to the Indian Wars era. In fact other accounts suggest that poor food was the norm. For example, a recruit at Fort Columbus in 1846 described breakfast as "six ounces of bread, a slice of salt pork, and a basin of bean soup. . . . I have seen some strange and rather uninviting dishes both before and since, but never anything so utterly unpalatable as the bean soup of Governors Island." This man had formerly served in the

British Army. Ballentine, *Autobiography of an English Soldier*, 23; Private Henry Hubman to Father, Aug. 17, 1881, Hubman letters, James Mountain files (third quotation); Mann interview, f. 79, RP, DPL; *ANJ*, Sept. 17, 1889 (fourth quotation): 25; Walker, "Reluctant Corporal" (pt. 1), 7 (fifth quotation).

36. Walker, "Reluctant Corporal," pt. 1, 7–8 (quotations); Ashburn, *History of the Medical Department*, 97. Common childhood diseases also ravaged the depot garrisons when men from varied populations were thrown together. For example, an epidemic of measles broke out among the 500-man garrison at Columbus Barracks in 1881. *ANJ*, June 11, 1881: 935.

37. Billings, *Circular No. 8*, xxxii (first quotation); Ostrander, *Army Boy*, 22 (second quotation); McChristian, *Frontier Cavalry Trooper*, 10 (third quotation).

38. Kolarik, "Comrade Kolarik Talks."

39. Thompson, *Narrative*, 32 (first quotation); Kolarik, "Comrade Kolarik Talks" (second quotation).

40. *ANJ*, July 30, 1887. By 1887 two the three recruiting depots had adopted the concept of general mess halls. *ARSW*, 1887, 83. 6; Nelson, "Davids Island," 512 (quotation).

41. QM Sergeant Maurice H. Wolfe to Cousin Maurice, June 7, 1870, Maurice Wolfe Letters, FLNHS (first quotation); Nixon, "Memories" (second quotation); Arthur S. Wallace to Dan, n.d., FLNHS (third quotation).

42. White, *Custer, Cavalry, and Crows*, 16; Walker, "Reluctant Corporal" (pt. 1), 8 (quotation).

43. Private Henry Hubman to Father, Aug. 17, 1881, Hubman Letters, James Mountain files (first quotation); *ANJ*, Sept. 17, 1889 (second quotation).

44. Ostrander, *Army Boy*, 250–52 (quotation); Reg. of Enlistments, M233, roll 8, NARA; *ANJ*, Jan. 31, 1874.

45. Ostrander, *Army Boy*, 249–50 (first quotation). Ostrander largely paraphrased, even plagiarized, Meyers, *Ten Years in the Ranks, U.S. Army*, for most of what he wrote about his experience at Governors Island. Meyers enlisted in 1854 and met Sergeant Henke at that time. Ostrander must have considered his own experience so much like Meyers's that he simply copied the earlier work. *ANJ*, Jan. 31, 1874, 394 (second and third quotations). In a most unusual circumstance, Moore was unilaterally promoted to the rank of second lieutenant, Ninth Infantry, in 1869 when his son, First Lieutenant Charles E. Moore, was posted at Governors Island. Rumor had it that the army promoted Michael Moore to place father and son on an equal footing as a favor to the faithful old soldier. Indeed, Moore retired from the army on Dec. 15, 1870, and lived until 1897. *ANJ*, Jan. 31 1874; Heitman, *Historical Register*, 1:721, 723; Ostrander, *Army Boy*, 250–52. Charles Henke died at Fort Columbus on Jan. 14, 1872, at the age of seventy-two. He was in his eleventh enlistment. Register of Enlistments, M233, roll 36, NARA.

46. Arthur S. Wallace to Dan, n.d., FLNHS.

47. Signal Corpsman Stephen Richey noted that his detachment was issued carbines, a waist belt and cartridge box, a cartridge belt, and a "gun swab." He privately purchased a saber, which probably was not an arm authorized for his branch, in nearby Washington, D.C. Because the Signal Corps was a small, specialized branch, recruits also were issued a "service kit" consisting of a haversack, canteen, and signal equipment. Richey diary, July 7 and Aug. 27, 1883, WSA; Windolph, *I Fought with Custer*, 4 (quotation).

48. McChristian, *Frontier Cavalry Trooper*, 7–8.

49. Walker, "Reluctant Corporal" (pt. 1), 8.

50. Nixon, "Memories."

51. Private Henry Hubman to Father, Aug. 17, 1881, Hubman Letters, James Mountain files (first quotation); Walker, "Reluctant Corporal" (pt. 1), 8 (second quotation); Henry Schuldt service record, f. 34, box 10, RP, DPL.

52. Ostrander, *Army Boy*, 18 (first quotation); Memoir of an unidentified trumpeter, MS, MSHSL (second quotation).

53. Prior to 1874 the Signal Corps had no personnel of its own, other than the chief of the bureau. In that year Congress authorized it to have 400 enlisted men, 180 of whom were corporals and sergeants because of the educational requirements and nature of their duties. The Signal Corps was primarily responsible for conducting and providing training to other soldiers in military signaling and for operating and maintaining the Military Telegraph System in the West, where no commercial lines yet existed. The men, attached to posts, also observed and recorded meteorological conditions. Heitman, *Historical Register*, 2:612–13; Rodenbough, *Army of the United States*, 147–48; H. B. Boyer reminiscence, Interviews with Signal Sergeants, box H, Indian Wars veterans, J. A. Greene files (quotations); Richey diary, July 3, 1883, WSA.

54. H. B. Boyer reminiscence, Interviews with Signal Sergeants, box H, Indian Wars veterans, J. A. Greene files.

55. Brininstool, *Troopers with Custer*, 39.

56. McConnell, *Five Years a Cavalryman*, 15.

57. In a few instances when recruits were badly needed for campaign service, mounted training was abbreviated or neglected entirely. Merritt, "Some Defects in Our Cavalry System," 559; Nixon, "Memories" (first quotation); Clarence Allen, "My Experiences," f. 57, box 8, RP, DPL (second quotation).

58. Marshall P. Crocker enlisted in the Fourth Infantry in 1866 at age twenty-three. His second enlistment, and perhaps a third (no record found), was in the Second Cavalry. He thereafter served a term in the Eighth Infantry and two more in the General Service. He was forty-six years of age when he retired at Columbus Barracks in 1894. Register of Enlistments, M233, rolls 31, 36, 41, 44, 46, NARA; Allen, "My Experiences," f. 57, RP, DPL (quotation).

59. Arthur S. Wallace to Dan, n.d., FLNHS (first quotation); Frederick K. Kurtz in Greene, *Indian War Veterans*, 32 (second quotation).

60. *ANJ*, May 8, 1869, 599.

61. Memoir of an unidentified trumpeter, MS, MSHSL.

62. Walker, "Reluctant Corporal" (pt. 1), 8.

63. Nelson, "Davids Island," 512 (first quotation); Private Henry Hubman to Herman (brother), Aug. 2, 1881, Henry Hubman letters, James Mountain files (second quotation).

64. McConnell, *Five Years a Cavalryman*, 16 (quotations). Enlistees at Philadelphia were more fortunate than most. With one of the major army clothing manufacturers located at the city's Schuylkill Arsenal, recruiting sergeants took new recruits directly to the depot, where they were measured for blouses and trousers. A few days later they returned for final fitting and thus obtained tailored uniforms by the time they went off to the recruiting depot. For further discussion about the fitting of uniforms for recruits, see McChristian, *Uniforms, Arms, and Equipment*, 1:88–89.

65. Moore, *Dakota Cowboy Soldier*, 9 (first quotation); Maurer and Maurer, *First Sergeant*, 42; Robert Greenhalgh to Mother, Oct. 8, 1865, Greenhalgh letters, RP, DPL (second quotation).

66. Ostrander, *Army Boy*, 19.

67. McChristian, *Frontier Cavalry Trooper*, 8; Nelson, "Davids Island," 512; Richard F. Watson questionnaire, f. 37, box 10, RP, DPL: Schubert, *Voices of the Buffalo Soldier*, 155. Isaac M. Cline enlisted in the Signal Corps in 1882. E-mail attachment, Pete Scarafiotti to Jerry Greene, Mar. 30, 2009, J. A. Greene files.

68. Private Henry Hubman to Father, July 10 and Aug. 17, 1881, Hubman letters, James Mountain files (first quotation). McChristian, *Frontier Cavalry Trooper*, 3–4 (second quotation).

69. *ANJ*, Aug. 26, 1882, 526 (first quotation); Brininstool, *Troopers with Custer*, 36 (second quotation); Private Henry Hubman to Herman (brother) Sept. 12, 1882, Hubman letters, James Mountain files (third quotation). Trooper William White said that he waited two years before sending a photograph of himself to friends in Indiana. It was the first intimation they had that he was in the army. White, *Custer, Cavalry, and Crows*, 35.

70. Hedren, "Campaigning with the Fifth U.S. Cavalry," 132.

71. This topic is elaborated in McChristian, "Custer's Avengers."

72. Cozzens, *Eyewitnesses to the Indian Wars*, 2:548 (first quotation); *ARSW*, 1876, 72–73 (second quotation).

73. *ARSW*, 1877, 48 (first quotation); *ARSW*, 1879, 32 (second quotation); *ANJ*, Oct. 16, 1880, 206 (third quotation). Inspector General D. B. Sacket noted as well that "the assignment of cavalry recruits to regiments and companies before they are properly instructed at depots . . . is an unfortunate necessity." *ARSW*, 1881, 79.

74. Lawrence Lea, "Chronology of Service," f. 42, box 2, IWWP, JNEM. Cavalrymen used three arms: the carbine, revolver, and saber. Whether or not recruits received any training with revolvers remains open to question. However, I found no reference to it in any contemporary account, which suggests that familiarity with that weapon was done at the company level. As late as 1883 the adjutant general reported: "Many men are annually lost to the Army by being sent to regiments too soon after enlistment to acquire any but the most rudimentary knowledge of the service." *ARSW*, 1883, 57 (quotation); *ARSW*, 1886, 81.

75. Lafayette Schall to Mary J. Arthur, UIVW, n.d., f. 108, box 10, RP, DPL (quotation); Greene, *Indian War Veterans*, 42. The adjutant general noted in 1890 that not only were recruits being kept at the depots for at least three months but detailed instructions governing the management and treatment of recruits had been provided to depot commanders. He claimed that these reforms had already resulted in a marked improvement in morale among the new men. *ARSW*, 1890, 68

76. Permanent parties at the three principal depots numbered a total of 1,710 enlisted men not belonging to any field command; nor were they organized as a regiment, yet they represented a body larger than any three infantry regiments in the service. *ANJ*, Mar. 20, 1880. It can only be wondered why it did not occur to the army command to augment the line with these soldiers at a much earlier date, particularly in 1876, when the need was so urgent. By order of the adjutant general in 1881, permanent parties were disbanded and replaced by "depot detachments" composed of six sergeants for each of four companies of instruction, plus the necessary clerks, bandsmen, cooks, and extra duty men supporting the depot. Recruits were organized in Companies A, B, C, and D, graded for training purposes in descending order of four months down to one month in service. House of Representatives, Report No. 1403, 47th Cong., 1st Sess. (1882); *ARSW*, 1881, 46; *ANJ*, Jan. 29, 1881, 530.

77. *ARSW*, 1881, 46.

78. *ANJ*, Jan. 29, 1881. Traditional recruiting depots were discontinued in 1894, when the army determined that training at the regimental level was preferable to central depots. Experiments with regimental recruiting beginning in 1890 proved to be more advantageous because recruits were sent directly to their units. On those occasions when the number of recruits exceeded current regimental requirements, the surplus was sent to one of the three former depots, redesignated general recruiting stations, and to Fort Sheridan, Illinois, for training until a regimental requisition was received. *ARSW,* 1894, 185.

79. *ARSW,* 1873, 88 (first quotation); Private Henry Hubman to Herman (brother), Aug. 2, 1881, Hubman letters, James Mountain files (second quotation). Hubman probably exaggerated the ranges at which he was shooting in order to impress his brother. Target practice usually began at distances of 100 and 200 yards, after the soldier had been instructed in aiming drills. It seems unlikely that recruits would have fired at longer distances. McChristian, *Army of Marksmen,* 43, 45–46.

80. An example is First Lieutenant J. F. Weston to Adjutant, Seventh Cavalry, May 21, 1872, Order Book, Co. L, Seventh Cavalry Letter Book, Baird collection. A consolidated request for recruits, including such skilled men as carpenters, masons, clerks, tailors, and shoemakers, is found in Lieutenant Colonel George A. Woodward to Adjutant, Fourteenth Infantry, Mar. 16, 1872, Telegrams Sent, Fort Fetterman, Wyo. Terr., RG 393, NARA.

81. McChristian, *Frontier Cavalry Trooper,* 7 (first quotation); Lowell, "Indian Fighter Recalls Eventful Days," 4 (second quotation); McConnell, *Five Years a Cavalryman,* 19 (third quotation).

82. Cox, *Five Years in the United States Army,* 12–13.

83. Another reference to the issue of "tin cups, haversacks, and three days rations" is found in McConnell, *Five Years a Cavalryman,* 17. Beginning as early 1875, recruits bound for their regiments were issued 1874-pattern clothing bags, stenciled "RECRUIT." These bags, larger than the haversack, were commodious enough to contain the recruit's few extra clothing articles and rations. Upon arrival at their permanent stations, the recruits turned in the bags to the post quartermaster, who sent them to an arsenal for cleaning, after which they were recycled back to the depots. Jett, "Autobiography," MS, SC, UAL (first quotation); McChristian, *U.S. Army in the West,* 208–9; Clarence Gould, account of service, f. 76, box 10, RP, DPL (second quotation).

84. McChristian, *Frontier Cavalry Trooper,* 14. Desertions increased with the news of regimental assignments. Henry McConnell, for example, noted: "There were several names that failed to respond when called, the owners having 'skipped out' on the eve of departure." McConnell, *Five Years a Cavalryman,* 19.

85. Within only a few months the regiment was transferred to New Mexico. John G. Brown to Viola Ransom Wood, Nov. 23, 1933, box 1, RC, USAMHI (quotation); Rodenbough, *Army of the United States,* 583–84.

86. *ANJ*, Jan. 23, 1875, 378 (first quotation); McConnell, *Five Years a Cavalryman,* 20 (second quotation).

CHAPTER 3. "DON'T GRIEVE AFTER ME"

1. Jett, "Autobiography," MS, SC, UAL.
2. White, *Custer, Cavalry, and Crows,* 15.

3. McChristian, *Frontier Cavalry Trooper*, 14, 12. Permanent party soldiers belonging to the destination regiment who had requested transfer back to the line sometimes traveled with the recruit draft for convenience. An example is found in McConnell, *Ten Years a Cavalryman*, 19.

4. Templeton diary, April 25, 1866, NL.

5. McConnell, *Ten Years a Cavalryman*, 19 (quotation). In some instances, temporary noncoms were not selected until later. William E. Matthews mentioned: "At Omaha we were put in companies [sic] with Sergeants and Corporals appointed to take charge till we arrived at this place [Angel Island, Calif.]." McChristian, *Frontier Cavalry Trooper*, 16.

6. *ANJ*, Oct. 16, 1880, 206.

7. White, *Custer, Cavalry, and Crows*, 16 (first quotation); McConnell, *Five Years a Cavalryman*, 39 (second quotation).

8. *ANJ*, Nov. 19 1881, 339 (first quotation); McConnell, *Five Years a Cavalryman*, 39 (second quotation); White, *Custer, Cavalry, and Crows*, 16 (third quotation); *ANJ*, Mar. 9, 1889, 563 (fourth quotation). As an example of the army's increasing effort to screen out unsuitable men before they got into line units, recruits bound for Fort Sill, Oklahoma, in 1891 were given another medical examination when they passed through Fort Riley, Kansas. Hayden diary, Dec. 30, 1891, LBBNM.

9. White, *Custer, Cavalry, and Crows*, 16.

10. Ibid., 17.

11. R. Eugene Pelham, "The Passing of the Frontiers," *National Tribune*, Dec. 12, 1918.

12. F. G. Prescott interview, f. 133, box 1, series 4, ECP, DPL.

13. Mulford, *Fighting Indians*, 20, 23.

14. William C. Slaper, "A Trooper's Account of the Battle," in Brininstool, *Troopers with Custer*, 40–41 (first quotation). If Slaper's memory was accurate, this represents a rare instance in which recruits had been issued arms prior to taking public transportation. It is more likely that the sergeant induced the recruits to trade their blankets. McChristian, *Frontier Cavalry Trooper*, 24 (second quotation).

15. McConnell, *Five Years a Cavalryman*, 19–21.

16. Lockwood, *Life and Adventures of a Drummer Boy*, 130 (first quotation); F. G. Prescott interview, f. 133, box 1, series 4, ECP, DPL (second quotation).

17. Lauren Aldrich, "Brief Reminiscences," HM65817, HL.

18. Hynes, *Soldiers of the Frontier*, 14 (first quotation); Albin H. Drown, "A Blizzard Campaign," *National Tribune*, Mar. 13, 1913 (second quotation).

19. *ANJ*, May 8, 1869: 599 (first quotation); David W. Luce, "Indian War Campaigning," *National Tribune*, Sept. 18, 1921 (second quotation). Platten was among the last recruits to pass through the old cavalry depot at Carlisle before its closure in 1871. Way, *Sgt. Fred Platten's Ten Years*, 4 (third quotation). Seventh Cavalryman John Ryan, an infantry veteran of the Civil War, also mentioned being trained briefly at Fort Leavenworth after passing through Carlisle in 1867. "After being there [Fort Leavenworth] a few days doing the regular fatigue duty and drilling pertaining to a cavalry recruit, which was something new to me at that time, about three hundred of us in a batch started for Fort Riley." Barnard, *Ten Years with Custer*, 17. Infantry recruits from both Fort Columbus, New York, and Newport Barracks, Kentucky, often were forwarded to Fort Leavenworth, where they were armed and equipped before moving on to their assigned regiments. For examples of many such references, see *ANJ*, Jan. 15, 1870, 834; Oct. 1, 1870, 104; Oct. 8, 1870, 120; Oct. 15, 1870, 136; John Farley, "Veteran of the Indian Wars," *National Tribune*, Mar. 19, 1936; Greene, *Indian War Veterans*, 313 (fourth quotation).

20. Gustafson, *John Spring's Arizona*, 27.

21. McChristian, *Frontier Cavalry Trooper*, 19.

22. Lowell, "Indian Fighter Recalls Eventful Days," 4 (quotation); Dinges, "New York Private," 57 (second quotation); Lauren Aldrich, "Brief Reminiscences," HM65817, HL (third quotation).

23. Returns from Regular Army Infantry Regiments, First Infantry, Sept. 1876–April 1877, M665, NARA.

24. John Farley, "Veteran of the Indian Wars," *National Tribune*, Mar. 19, 1936.

25. Eighth Cavalryman George Raper mentioned that the recruits were issued arms when they detrained at Kit Carson, Colorado Territory. Greene, *Indian War Veterans*, 19 (quotation). For many years the nearest railhead for travelers to New Mexico was at Kit Carson. From there they proceeded overland via a trail leading to the Arkansas River near Fort Lyon then followed the Mountain Branch of the Santa Fe Trail to Trinidad and Las Vegas, New Mexico.

26. Ashburn, *History of the Medical Department*, 97–98 (quotation). Recruit parties usually were not armed until reaching their destinations, but an exception to the normal practice was noted when replacements bound for the Fifteenth Infantry at Fort Stanton, New Mexico Territory, were issued arms at Fort Marcy prior to the final leg of their journey. This was probably because of the perceived danger posed by renegade Apaches at that time. *ANJ*, Mar. 16, 1878, 501.

27. Peter Allen, "Military Expedition," f. 10, box 2, ECP, DPL.

28. White, *Custer, Cavalry, and Crows*, 16 (quotation). White recalled that the recruits were given dismounted drill for about six hours a day while at Fort Sanders. Munn, "Fred Munn, Veteran of Frontier Experiences," 52–53. One of the so-called Custer Avengers, who enlisted at Jefferson Barracks on Aug. 24, 1876, related that he was sent to the Fourth Cavalry's headquarters at Fort D. A. Russell, Wyoming Territory, where he stayed for about thirty days before being forwarded to his company at Camp Robinson, Nebraska. Presumably he received some training at the former post. Private William J. Murphy, in Greene, *Indian War Veterans*, 9.

29. Private Henry Hubman to Father, Mother, and Brothers, Sept. 10, 1881, Poplar Creek Indian Agency, Montana Terr., Hubman letters, James Mountain files.

30. Mulford, *Fighting Indians*, 19.

31. White, *Custer, Cavalry, and Crows*, 15.

32. Greene, *Indian War Veterans*, 360.

33. Hynes, *Soldiers of the Frontier*, 10.

34. Lockwood, *Apaches and Longhorns*, 4.

35. Service record, Emanuel Roque, box 1, RC, USAMHI.

36. Mulford, *Fighting Indians*, 9, 12. A heel-ball was a ball of beeswax mixed with lamp black used for polishing shoes, leather belts, and other accouterments; Post Returns, Fort Leavenworth, Kansas, Sept. 1876, NARA.

37. Mulford, *Fighting Indians*, 11, 16.

38. R. Eugene Pelham, "The Passing of the Frontiers," *National Tribune*, Dec. 12, 1918.

39. *ANJ*, Jan. 23, 1875: 378 (first quotation); Mulford, *Fighting Indians*, 25 (second quotation); Smith, *Dose of Frontier Soldiering*, 123–24 (third quotation); King, *Campaigning with Crook*, 161–62 (fourth quotation).

40. Mulford, *Fighting Indians*, 25 (first quotation). Recruits arriving at the headquarters post late in the day were distributed overnight among the various companies of

the garrison for purposes of meals and sleeping arrangements. McConnell, *Five Years a Cavalryman*, 48; Suttles, statement of service, f. 28, box 10, RP, DPL (second quotation).

41. "William W. Neifert of North Kingstown," *[Providence] Journal*, Mar. 6, 1947, copy in box 1, RC, USAMHI.

CHAPTER 4. "DEPLOYED AS SKIRMISHERS"

1. Utley, *Life in Custer's Cavalry*, 44 (first quotation); *ANJ*, Sept. 16, 1876, 90 (second quotation).

2. McChristian *Garrison Tangles*, 60, 82 n. 54. When ten companies of the Fourth Cavalry rendezvoused at Fort Richardson, Texas, for a campaign in 1871, it was the first time that many had assembled since the Civil War. Carter, *On the Border with Mackenzie*, 106; Phelps, "From Texas to Dakota," 858 (quotation).

3. Captain Joseph H. Dorst to Rogers, Feb. 19, 1890, Dorst Biographical File, AHS.

4. "Memorandum of Edward Williams," MS, LBBNM. A "coffee cooler" was army slang for a loafer.

5. McChristian, "Shot Like a Dog," 56 (first quotation); Private Hartford G. Clark Diary, Mar. 31, 1891, f. 16, Box 1, IWWP, JNEM (second quotation).

6. "Squadron" was used to designate companies in the 1841 *Cavalry Tactics* manual, a term that Cooke continued to use in his version. Cooke, *Cavalry Tactics*, 1:3. Even though "squadron" was not used in the tactics manuals of the 1870s and 1880s, some older cavalry officers accustomed to the term continued to use it in every day parlance as a synonym for "battalion." An army reorganization act effected on March 2, 1899, officially organized cavalry regiments in three squadrons of four troops each. Heitman, *Historical Register*, 2:602.

7. Sherman also stipulated that the term "battery" would apply only to those artillery units actually provided with guns and horses. *GO No. 5*, AGO, June 20, 1873 (quotation). Percival G. Lowe, who served with the First Dragoons in the early 1850s, freely used the term "troop" throughout his classic account of antebellum enlisted life. Lowe, *Five Years a Dragoon*. Conversely, James A. Bennett, another soldier serving in the same regiment during the same period, consistently used "company" in his diary. Brooks and Reeve, *Forts and Forays*.

8. *ANJ*, Oct. 29, 1881, 278 (first quotation); *ARSW*, 1881, 34 (second quotation). Like the army of the time, herein I use "company" for infantry and either "company" or "troop" indiscriminately for cavalry.

9. Colonel Robert H. Hall, Fourth Infantry, *ANJ*, May 16, 1896, 678 (first quotation); *ANJ*, Nov. 15, 1884, 311 (second quotation); Hammer, *With Custer in '76*, 140 (third quotation). An alternative but less credible origin for the term is found in *ANJ*, April 25, 1896, 615; Lt. Col. George Custer applied another nickname to infantrymen when he referred them as "web feet" in an 1873 letter to his wife. The term likewise connoted the foot soldiers' lot of marching through mud and water. Merington, *Custer Story*, 254. Other contemporary enlisted men's references to "dough boy" noted here are found in Robert Greenhalgh to Father and Mother, Aug. 27, 1865, Greenhalgh letters, RP, DPL; Smith, *Sagebrush Soldier*, 28 (1876); Smith, ed., *A Dose of Frontier Soldiering*, 143 (1880). As late as World War II infantrymen were often still referred to as doughboys or simply "doughs."

10. Finerty, *War Path and Bivouac*, 74.

11. *ANJ*, June 14, 1884, 943.

12. Summerhayes, *Vanished Arizona*, 15 (first quotation); James Foley, "The 4th Cavalry," *National Tribune*, Sept. 18, 1913 (second quotation). The Fifth Infantry was stationed in New Mexico Territory from 1860 to 1866, which probably accounts for Foley's statement that many of its members could speak Spanish. In some instances commanders resorted to other means for augmenting the band. For instance, Trumpeter Francis Brocard, Troop E, Seventh Cavalry, was detailed to the band on daily duty, which meant that he would not be carried on the rolls of the band or draw the additional pay authorized for extra duty. *SO No. 14*, Headquarters, Battalion of Seventh Cavalry, April 28, 1873, *General and Special Orders, and Circulars Issued*, 1873–74, Seventh Cavalry, RG 391, NARA. A group photograph of the Third Cavalry Band depicts the regimental saddler sergeant, whose regular duties were light, serving in the capacity of bass drummer. Langellier, *Drums Would Roll*, 35.

13. Private Herman S. Searl to Dear Parents, Nov. 5, 1867, Herman S. Searl letters, WSA (first quotation); De Trobriand, *Military Life in Dakota*, 276 (second quotation); Windolph, *I Fought with Custer*, 38 (third quotation).

14. Barnard, *Ten Years with Custer*, 95 (first quotation); Faust and Randall, "Life at Post," 80–82; Hedren, "Eben Swift's Army Service," 152 (second quotation).

15. Forsyth, *Story of the Soldier*, 126–27 (first quotation). George A. Forsyth was particularly well qualified to author this volume. He had served thirty-one years in the army, retiring in 1890, before he wrote this classic work on the regular army. During his career, he served through the entire Civil War as a line and field officer, rising to the brevet rank of brigadier general of volunteers. Entering the regulars in 1866, he was appointed to the new Ninth Cavalry. His most famous exploit was that of commanding a unit of fifty civilian scouts at the famous Battle of Beecher's Island in 1868. As a lieutenant colonel, he served four years as military secretary to Lieutenant General Philip H. Sheridan, commanding the Division of the Missouri. From 1878 to 1881 he was Sheridan's aide-de-camp. For the remainder of his career, he served with the Fourth Cavalry. Heitman, *Historical Register*, 1:430; Reynolds J. Burt Boyhood Data, box 2, RC, USAMHI (second quotation).

16. Robinson, "Brigadier General George Crook's Horse Meat March," 48 (first quotation); Lieut. Jonathan W. Biddle, to Mother, April 28, 1877, Biddle Letters, copy in J. A. Greene files (second quotation). The officer referred to was Lieutenant Colonel Elwell S. Otis, Twenty-Second Infantry. Cozzens, ed., *Eyewitnesses to the Indian Wars*, 5:319 (third quotation).

17. Simpson Mann interview, f. 79, box 8, RP, DPL (first quotation). A few statements that came to my attention show that not all soldiers felt this way. Private Ami F. Mulford, for example, wrote that he and some of his cavalry comrades "walked down to the Infantry quarters [at Standing Rock Agency, Dakota Territory] and spent a very pleasant evening with them." Mulford, *Fighting Indians*, 48. Another Seventh Cavalryman, who participated in the Sioux Campaign of 1876, noted in his diary upon his company's return to the base camp at the mouth of Powder River: "Back again with our old friends the 'doughboys.'" Cozzens, *Eyewitnesses to the Indian Wars*, 5:320; John O. Stotts reminiscence, Spencer collection (second quotation); Reginald A. Bradley questionnaire, f. 76, box 8, and Harvey J. Ciscel questionnaire, f. 9, box 9, both in RP, DPL.

18. The strength of cavalry companies declined from ninety-nine men to eighty-one in 1869 and to seventy-seven in 1870. The congressional acts of 1874, 1875, and 1876 increased them slightly to eighty men, but they were again reduced to only sixty-six in

1889. Heitman, *Historical Register*, 2:604–5, 608–9, 610–11, 612–13, 614–15; Reginald A. Bradley questionnaire, f. 76, box 8, and Harvey J. Ciscel questionnaire, f. 9, box 9, both in RP, DPL.

19. Robert Greenhalgh to Father and Mother, Dec. 7, 1866, Greenhalgh Letters, RP, DPL (first quotation); White, *Custer, Cavalry, and Crows*, 21 (second quotation).

20. Fitzgerald, "Sixteen Young Men," 12.

21. Fort Laramie, Wyoming, May 1871, Medical History of Posts, RG 94, NARA (first quotation); Chappell, "Surgeon at Fort Sidney," 425 (second quotation).

22. Kolarik, "Comrade Kolarik Talks," 3.

23. Munn, "Fred Munn, Veteran of Frontier Experiences," 53.

24. Kautz, *Customs of Service*, 138, 140. Soldiers were held individually responsible for the arms and equipment issued to them. The cost of any items lost, stolen, or seriously damaged through their own neglect would be deducted from their pay. The Ordnance Department periodically published a current price list of all items. *Revised United States Army Regulations of 1861*, 20–21, 398, 402.

25. Maurer and Maurer, *First Sergeant*, 4.

26. The company clerk also recorded the combat actions in which the soldier was engaged. *Revised United States Army Regulations of 1861*, 20.

27. *ANJ*, Feb. 15, 1890, 477.

28. Forsyth, *Story of the Soldier*, 134.

29. McConnell, *Five Years a Cavalryman*, 49 (first quotation); Cox, *Five Years in the United States Army*, 14 (second quotation); McChristian, *Frontier Cavalry Trooper*, 28 (third quotation).

30. Mulford, *Fighting Indians*, 27 (quotation); Rickey, *Forty Miles a Day*, 84.

31. Clarence S. Gould, Account of Service, f. 76, box 10, RP, DPL.

32. McConnell, *Five Years a Cavalryman*, 13, 30. The three old soldiers referred to had served prior to the Civil War in the dragoons, mounted rifles, and infantry, respectively. Munger died in Arizona Territory while his troop was in the field during the Geronimo Campaign. He was buried at a campsite at the base of the Dragoon Mountains, where his comrades, with the full support of the troop commander, erected a stone memorial over his grave. Lt. Gustavus Doane to My Darling Wife, July 5 and 31, 1886, Doane Papers, MSU.

33. Lockwood, *Life and Adventures of a Drummer Boy*, 119.

34. Account by Musician James C. Bothwell, Thirteenth Infantry, author's files (first quotation); Annual Record of Events for the Year 1866, Eighteenth Infantry, Returns of Regular Infantry Regiments, AGO, RG 94, NARA, Washington, D.C.; Greene, *Indian War Veterans*, 90 (second quotation); Windolph, *I Fought with Custer*, 50 (third quotation). It should be borne in mind that the term "old soldier" was applied to men because of their experience and maturity, not because they were aged in years. Civil War veterans were still relatively young men at this time.

35. James W. Foley, "4th U.S. Cavalry," *National Tribune*, June 5, 1915 (first quotation); Dinges, "New York Private," 70. Henry McConnell also claimed that the majority of Fourth Cavalrymen in 1866 were "bounty jumpers, blackguards, and criminals of various degrees, or at any rate, men who had sought the army as an asylum from the punishments that the law would have justly meted out to them." McConnell, *Five Years a Cavalryman*, 13 (second quotation). The term "bounty jumper" referred to a man who accepted a monetary reward for enlisting in the army during the war but then deserted in order to reenlist and collect another bounty. Many of these scalawags, often foreigners,

had no interest in the Union cause but made a profitable profession of bounty jumping. Billings, *Hardtack and Coffee*, 167.

36. *ANJ*, May 19, 1883: 957 (first quotation); Smith, *Dose of Frontier Soldiering*, 124 (second quotation); De Trobriand, *Military Life in Dakota*, 60 (third quotation); John Henley's account in Liddic and Harbaugh, *Camp on Custer*, 37 (fourth and fifth quotations).

37. Greene, *Indian War Veterans*, 47–48.

38. Comfort, *Trooper Tales*, 31 (first quotation). Even though this man served in the Fifth Cavalry in the late 1890s, his experiences could not have been far different from those of men who served during the Indian campaigns. Lauren Aldrich, "Brief Reminiscences," HM65817, HL (second quotation). The McReynold conversation was overheard by Lieutenant John Bigelow, who paraphrased it in rawer form in his journal in 1879, and is quoted in Kinevan, *Frontier Cavalryman*, 214 (third quotation); Maurer and Maurer, *First Sergeant*, 7 (fourth quotation).

39. Armand Unger interview, f. 34, box 10, Rickey Papers, DPL (first quotation); Reinhold R. Gast questionnaire, f. 37, box 9, RP, DPL (second quotation); Lawrence J. Harvey to Viola Ransom Wood, UIWV, Aug. 15, 1934, f. 83, box 10, RP, DPL; (third quotation). The actual strength of Company C going into the battle was forty-nine, of whom thirty-six were killed in action. Gray, *Centennial Campaign*, 289; David W. Luce, "Indian War Campaigning," *National Tribune*, Sept. 18, 1921 (fourth quotation).

40. Hynes, *Soldiers of the Frontier*, 54.

41. James Foley, "4th Cavalry," *National Tribune*, Sept. 18, 1913 (first quotation); F. G. Prescott interview, f. 133, box 1, series 4, ECP, DPL (second quotation).

42. QM Sergeant Maurice H. Wolfe, to Cousin Maurice, Sept. 11, 1870, Wolfe letters, FLNHS (first quotation); McChristian, *Frontier Cavalry Trooper*, 98 (second quotation).

43. QM Sergeant Maurice H. Wolfe to Cousin Maurice, June 7, 1870, Wolfe letters, FLNHS. This is just one example of several letters that Wolfe wrote in which he mentioned encountering Irishmen from his home area.

44. Nelson, "Davids Island," 512 (first quotation); *ANJ*, Feb. 17, 1883: 659 (second quotation); George Whittaker questionnaire, f. 42, box 10, RP, DPL (third quotation). An Eighth Cavalryman who served in the early 1890s evinced some ethnic strife by relating that he and his comrades referred to the Germans in the troop as "squareheads." Harvey J. Ciscel questionnaire, f. 9, box 9, RP, DPL; King, *Campaigning with Crook*, 8 (fourth quotation).

45. Barnard, *Ten Years with Custer*, 116 (quotation); Dugan, "Real Service," 6.

46. James S. Hamilton questionnaire, f. 52, box 9, RP, DPL (first quotation); William G. Wilkinson questionnaire, f. 44, box 10, RP, DPL; James B. Wilkinson questionnaire, f. 43, box 10, RP, DPL (second quotation).

47. Former volunteer John D. Billings, who had been a member of the Tenth Massachusetts Artillery, devoted a full chapter to this class of soldiers, providing detailed, timeless descriptions of beats and Jonahs as he experienced them during the Civil War. Billings, *Hardtack and Coffee*, 87–107.

48. *ANJ*, May 24, 1873, 647.

49. *ANJ*, April 11, 1868, 538 (first quotation); Gustafson, *John Spring's Arizona*, 28 (second quotation).

50. Walker, "Reluctant Corporal" (pt. 1), 19; Clarence Allen, "My Experiences," MS, RP, DPL (first quotation); Zinser, *Indian War Diary*, 31 (second quotation); no guardhouse was available, so the saddler was punished by having to carry his saddle while

leading his horse around camp for twenty-four hours under guard; Wooster, *History of Fort Davis, Texas*, 284–85; Carroll, *Seventh Cavalry Scrapbook*, 12 (third quotation).

51. Kolarik, "Comrade Kolarik Talks," 3 (first quotation); Theodore E. Guy questionnaire, f. 51, box 9, RP, DPL (second quotation); "Memorandum of Edward Williams," MS, LBBNM (third quotation); Private Hartford G. Clark diary, Aug. 9, 1891, f. 16, box 1, IWWP, JNEM (fourth quotation); Simpson Mann interview, f. 79, RP, DPL (fifth quotation).

52. Cozzens, *Eyewitnesses to the Indian Wars*, 4:344.

53. For an official example of soldier numbering, see Third Cavalry Returns, January 1868, Returns from Regular Cavalry Regiments, M744, roll 30. Among numerous references, nicknames were drawn from Barnard, *Ten Years with* Custer, 74 (first quotation); Greene, *Indian War Veterans*, 42; Windolph, *I Fought with* Custer, 4–5; Lockwood, *Apaches and Longhorns*, 65; Thomas N. Way journal, July 10, 1873, J. A. Greene files; Taylor, *With Custer*, 44; Jesse G. Harris questionnaire, f. 56, box 9, RP, DPL; Walter C. Harrington questionnaire, f. 78, box 10, RP, DPL; Perley S. Eaton questionnaire, f. 23, box 9, RP, DPL (second quotation).

54. "Commanding Officers of Companies D, K, G, F, 4th Infty. will without necessary delays arm and fully equip the Recruits assigned to their respective Companies. All old Soldiers in the Detachments will be placed on duty as soon as possible." *Circular*, Nov. 20, 1870, Fourth Infantry Order Book, FLNHS.

55. Hynes, *Soldiers of the Frontier*, 37 (first quotation); Fitzgerald, "Sixteen Young Men," 12 (second quotation); Mulford, *Fighting Indians*, 29 (third quotation).

56. *Circular*, Oct. 27, 1880, Seventh Cavalry Order Book, LBBNM; Greene, *Indian War Veterans*, 47 (quotation).

57. *Circular No. 44*, Oct. 11, 1882, and *Orders No. 173*, Aug. 8, 1883, Fourth Infantry Order Book, FLNHS; Gustafson, *John Spring's Arizona*, 125.

58. Arthur S. Wallace to Dan, n.d., FLNHS; Smith, *Dose of Frontier Soldiering*, 125 (first quotation); John C. Ford interview, box 1, RC, USAMHI (second quotation); Greene, *Indian War Veterans*, 20 (third quotation).

59. James B. Wilkinson questionnaire, f. 43, box 10, RP, DPL (first quotation); Theodore Goldin to Frederick W. Benteen, Jan. 6, 1896, in Carroll, *Seventh Cavalry Scrapbook*, 25 (second quotation); *ANJ*, May 19, 1883, 957 (third quotation).

60. William Murphy, "Forgotten Battalion," MS, f. 17, box 1, Chapman collection, AHC (first quotation); Walker, "Reluctant Corporal" (pt. 2), 120 (second quotation).

61. Walker, "Reluctant Corporal" (pt. 1), 18.

62. Private Hartford G. Clark diary, May 7, 1891, f. 16, box 1, IWWP, JNEM (first quotation); Grandison Mayo questionnaire, f. 45, box 9, RP, DPL (second quotation).

63. Tetzel memoir, MSHSL (first quotation); Johnson, *Jacob Horner*, 13 (second quotation); Bradley interview, RC, USAMHI (third quotation); Maurer and Maurer, *First Sergeant*, 7.

64. Ben E. Goodin diary, April 18, 1893, f. 67, box 8, RP, DPL (first quotation); *ANJ*, Dec. 1, 1883, 358 (second quotation).

65. Smith, *Dose of Frontier Soldiering*, 19.

66. Ibid., 19 (first quotation); Greene, *Indian War Veterans*, 47 (second quotation).

67. Finley to Mother, Nov. 11, 1879, Walter L. Finley Collection, CHL.

68. Major A. W. Evans to commandeering officer, Co. B, Third Cavalry, Fort Laramie, W.T., April 3, 1879, RG 98, NARA; copy in McDermott File, FLNHS (first quotation); *Omaha Daily Bee*, Jan. 24, 1877 (second quotation).

69. Schubert, *Voices of the Buffalo Soldier*, 189 (first quotation), 65 (second quotation).
70. Godfrey, "Some Reminiscences, Including the Washita Battle" 483; Shirk, "Campaigning with Sheridan," 82 (quotation).
71. *ANJ*, Mar. 20, 1880, 674 (first quotation); Merritt, "Some Defects in Our Cavalry System," 560 (second quotation).
72. A pre–Little Bighorn statistical analyses of Seventh Cavalry personnel is provided in Gray, *Centennial Campaign*, 289–91. Further refined statistics indicate that less than 2 percent of Seventh Cavalrymen present at the Battle of the Little Bighorn had four months, or less, of service in the army and thus could be termed "raw" recruits. Those having up to a year's experience amounted to 17.5 percent. This interpretation is in Hedren, *Great Sioux War Orders of Battle*, 28, relying upon research in MacNeil, "Raw Recruits and Veterans." After the battle, which cost the lives of many veterans, the composition of the regiment changed with the influx of fresh recruits.
73. Samuel L. Meddaugh diary, MS 570, Lisle Brown Papers, ML, UU; "Diary of Matthew Carroll," 238; Eugene Geant journal, f. 67, CC, LBBNM.
74. Richard Flynn diary, Oct. 13, 1876, FLNHS. Arms, equipment, and supplies of all manner were provided by the ordnance and quartermaster depot located adjacent to Fort D. A. Russell. Adams, *Post Near Cheyenne*, 9–10; Greene, "Chasing Sitting Bull," 195; Hedren, "Eben Swift's Army Service," 143–44 (first quotation); King, *Campaigning with Crook*, 160 (second quotation).
75. Goldin, "A Winter Raid," MS, f. 16, Philip G. Cole Collection, Gilcrease Museum.
76. Theodore W. Goldin to Frederick W. Benteen, Jan. 6, 1896, in Carroll, *Seventh Cavalry Scrapbook*, 24 (first quotation); King, *Campaigning with Crook*, 160 (second quotation); *ANJ*, July 3, 1880, 983 (third quotation).
77. Private Adelbert Butler to Mary (sister), June 3, 1877, GTC (first quotation); McAnulty to Lillie Moore, Dec. 19, 1876, McAnulty letters, FLNHS (second quotation).

CHAPTER 5. BRAIN, BONE, AND SINEW

1. McConnell, *Five Years a Cavalryman*, 42.
2. Romeyn, "Desertion: Some Causes and Remedies," 678.
3. Perley S. Eaton to Rickey, Aug. 8, 1954, f. 24, box 9, RP, DPL.
4. The term "battalion" could be applied any subdivision of a regiment consisting of two or more companies. In a formal tactical situation, battalions were formed by an equal division of the regiment's companies: three for cavalry and artillery, each commanded by a major, with the lieutenant colonel acting as the regiment's second-in-command. In infantry regiments, composed of only ten companies, the lieutenant colonel and the major each commanded a battalion of five companies under the overall direction of the colonel. During the Indian Wars in the West, when regiments seldom operated as complete units, battalions often consisted of only two or three companies, even those not always belonging to the same regiment. At those times when not all, or not any, of the field officers were present, captains commanded battalions, according to seniority.
5. James S. Hamilton questionnaire, f. 52, box 9, RP, DPL (first quotation); Comfort, *Trooper Tales*, 82 (second quotation).
6. Greene, *Indian War Veterans*, 43 (first quotation); *ANJ*, Sept. 21, 1867, 74 (second quotation); White, *Custer, Cavalry, and Crows*, 38 (third quotation).
7. An example of a regular enlisted man who gained commissioned rank after the war was Captain Daniel Robinson. Born in Ireland, Robinson served in all ranks from

private to first sergeant, Company C, Seventh Infantry, in addition to ordnance sergeant, from 1849 to 1863. The need for officers during the war caused him to rise to first lieutenant by 1865, when he was summarily dismissed. Starting again at the bottom rung of the ladder, a determined Robinson enlisted as a private in the Sixteenth Infantry then rose to sergeant and regimental quartermaster sergeant before regaining a commission in his old regiment in 1866. He remained a lieutenant in the Seventh Infantry until finally gaining a captaincy in 1888, the year before he retired. Heitman, *Historical Register*, 1:837; First Sergeant Frederick Stortz to Father, Mar. 12, 1877, BHNB (quotation).

8. *Revised United States Army Regulations of 1861*, 9–10.

9. Windolph, *I Fought with Custer*, 5 (first quotation); *Regulations of the Army, 1881*, 309; "Seven Letters," *Titusville (Pa.) Morning Herald*, July 27, 1870, 306 (second quotation); *ANJ*, Sept. 9, 1871: 53 (third quotation).

10. King, *Trials of a Staff Officer*, 12. This is the classic account of the trials and tribulations of an adjutant in the frontier army.

11. Alexander Hatcher questionnaire, f. 58, box 9, RP, DPL.

12. Reinhold R. Geist questionnaire, f. 9, box 9, RP, DPL (first quotation); Maurer and Maurer, *First Sergeant*, 2 (second quotation).

13. Palmer, "Tyranny of an Officer," Edward Palmer Papers, SC, UAL (quotation). A soldier at Camp Grant at that time also recorded that the same officer confined him to the guardhouse for refusing to work during 110-degree heat and that he suspended another soldier by the wrists until he passed out. Dinges, "A New York Private," 63; Schubert, *Voices of the Buffalo Soldier*, 55–62; Potter, "'He . . . Regretted Having to Die That Way,'" 183.

14. Schubert, *Voices of the Buffalo Soldier*, 112; QM Sergeant Maurice H. Wolfe to Cousin Maurice, Jan. 8, 1874, Wolfe letters, FLNHS (quotations).

15. David Lucius Craft Letters, SC, DU, copies at Fort Supply Historic Site, Oklahoma (quotation); Perley S. Eaton to Rickey, Oct. 29, 1954, f. 24, box 9, RP, DPL.

16. McChristian, *Frontier Cavalry Trooper*, 66 (first quotation). This was Second Lieutenant William D. F. Landon. Templeton diary, June 11, 1866, NL; Smith, *Dose of Frontier Soldiering*, 40 (second quotation); McChristian, *Garrison Tangles*, 46–47 (third quotation).

17. Barnard, *Ten Years with Custer*, 97; Jett, "Autobiography," MS, SC, UAL (quotation).

18. McConnell, *Five Years a Cavalryman*, 48, 128 (first quotation); Reneau, *Adventures of Moccasin Joe*, 62; (second quotation); Greene, "Chasing Sitting Bull," 196 (third quotation); Mulford, *Fighting Indians*, 60 (fourth quotation), 64, 102 (eighth quotation); "Memorandum of Edward Williams," MS, LBBNM (fifth quotation); Charles Johnson questionnaire, f. 67, box 9, RP, DPL (sixth quotation); "Memorandum of Edward Williams" MS, LBBNM (seventh quotation).

19. Private Hartford G. Clark diary, Mar. 31, 1891, Fort Niobrara, Neb., IWWP, JNEM (first quotation); Hynes, *Soldiers of the Frontier*, 182–83 (second quotation); George Neihaus questionnaire, f. 93, box 9, RP, DPL (third quotation); James S. Hamilton questionnaire, f. 52, box 9, RP, DPL (fourth quotation); Walter C. Harrington questionnaire, f. 78, box 10, RP, DPL (fifth quotation).

20. Smith, *Dose of Frontier Soldiering*, 40 (first quotation); Private Louis Ebert questionnaire, f. 25, box 9, RP, DPL (second quotation); Armand Unger questionnaire, f. 34, box 10, RP, DPL (third quotation); Reginald Bradley questionnaire, f. 76, box 8, RP, DPL (fourth quotation).

21. Smith, *Sagebrush Soldier*, 91 (first quotation). Bigelow added: "What would a German martinet think of the Commanding Officer of a Camp who would shake hands with an enlisted man, and a colored man at that." Kinevan, *Frontier Cavalryman*, 205 (second quotation).

22. First Lieutenant J. F. Weston to AAG, Dept. of the Gulf, Jan. 11, 1873, Seventh Cavalry Letter Book, Baird collection (first quotation); Innis, "Fort Buford Diary of Pvt. Sanford," 350; Pvt. Hartford Clark diary, Mar. 3, 1891, f. 16, box 1, IWWP, JNEM; William G. Wilkinson questionnaire, f. 44, box 10, RP, DPL (second and third quotations).

23. Theodore E. Guy questionnaire, f. 51, box 9, RP, DPL; McChristian, *Frontier Cavalry Trooper*, 219 (quotation).

24. Theodore E. Guy questionnaire, f. 51, box 9, RP, DPL (first quotation); Mulford, *Fighting Indians*, 111 (second quotation); John O. Stotts reminiscence, Spencer collection (third quotation); Summerhayes, *Vanished Arizona*, 105 (fourth quotation); Hooker, *Child of the Fighting Tenth*, 99–100 (fifth quotation).

25. Before 1862 army officers could simply assign a soldier to act as servant, but Congress enacted legislation in that year prescribing that an officer had to "deduct from his own monthly pay the full amount paid to or expended by the government per month on account of said soldier," an offense being punishable by dismissal. This was quite likely the reason why so many Union officers acquired black "contraband" servants during the Civil War. *Revised United States Army Regulations of 1861*, 536–37.

26. Second Lieutenant Micah J. Jenkins to "Dear Willie" [William E. Jenkins], Nov. 16, 1879, Micah John Jenkins letters, USCL (first quotation); Hooker, *Child of the Fighting Tenth*, 56 (second quotation). I found two other possible origins for the term "striker." A standard definition refers to a blacksmith's assistant, who wields the sledgehammer. The other suggests that the soldier "was not required to give his attention exclusively to official duty": ergo, he was striking, like a worker, against regular duty. Geraldine Hooker only surmised many years later that this second notion might have been the inspiration. In my opinion, neither of these makes a compelling argument for the military application. Both "dog robber" and "striker," defined as a soldier who works for an officer, are found in Reeves, *Manual for Aspirants*, 56, 58.

27. John O. Stotts reminiscence, Spencer collection (first quotation); McChristian, *Frontier Cavalry Trooper*, 12 (second quotation). Second Lieutenant John W. Summerhayes paid a soldier ten dollars a month just to cook. Summerhayes, *Vanished Arizona*, 6–61, 94 (third quotation); Simpson Mann interview, f. 79, box 9, RP, DPL; Upton, *Fort Custer*, 85 (fourth quotation).

28. Officers of like grade were permitted to transfer from one regiment or corps to another by mutual consent and permission of the adjutant general of the army. *Revised United States Army Regulations of 1861*, 12; Reynolds J. Burt Boyhood Data, box 2, RC, USAMHI (quotation).

29. *ANJ*, May 22, 1869, 626; *ANJ*, Mar. 10, 1883, 722. In an example of Clifford's fidelity to his men, he shared the last water in his canteen with an enlisted man during the hard march up the Big Horn River in June 1876. Poitevin, *Captain Walter Clifford*, 73 (quotations).

30. HR Doc. No. 56, "Reorganization of the Army," at 242 (1878).

31. Hynes, *Soldiers of the Frontier*, 93–94; Heitman, *Historical Register*, 1:989; Register of Enlistments, M233, roll 32, NARA; Schubert, *Voices of the Buffalo Soldier*, 154 (first quotation); Hynes, *Soldiers of the Frontier*, 93–94 (second and third quotations).

32. Simpson Mann interview, f. 79, box , 9, RP, DPL; Private Hartford G. Clark diary, April 7, 1891, f. 16, box 1, IWWP, JNEM; Harvey J. Ciscel questionnaire, f. 9, box 9, RP, DPL; Bradley interview, Jan. 10, 1968, f. 76, box 8, RP, DPL (quotation).

33. McChristian, *Frontier Cavalry Trooper*, 123.

34. Greene, *Indian War Veterans*, 17 (quotation); Buecker, "Journals of James S. McClellan," 22.

35. McChristian, *Frontier Cavalry Trooper*, 37–38, 69 (first and second quotations); Greene, *Indian War Veterans*, 43 (third quotation); Jett, "Autobiography," MS, SC, UAL (fourth quotation); Smith, *Dose of Frontier Soldiering*, 95 (fifth quotation).

36. Hayden diary, Dec. 2, 1891, LBBNM (first quotation); Cox, *Five Years in the United States Army*, 14 (second quotation).

37. Smith, *Dose of Frontier Soldiering*, 95.

38. Mazzanovich, *Trailing Geronimo*, 109 (first quotation); Walker, "Reluctant Corporal" (pt. 1), 13; Shirk, "Campaigning with Sheridan," 94 (second quotation).

39. Hebard and Brininstool, *Bozeman Trail*, 2:73 (first quotation); Way, *Sgt. Fred Platten's Ten Years*, 4 (second quotation).

40. First Lieutenant Walter L. Finley to Mother, Nov. 11, 1879, Finley collection, CHL (first quotation); Lauren Aldrich, "Brief Reminiscences," HM65817, HL (second quotation).

41. Barnard, *Ten Years with Custer*, 131.

42. Hynes, *Soldiers of the Frontier*, 149.

43. The rank of first duty sergeant was not recognized officially, but former sergeants Grandison Mayo, Twenty-Fifth Infantry, and George Neihaus, Tenth Infantry, gave their ranks in questionnaires as "first duty sergeant," indicating that this title was used and was important to them even many years later. Reginald Bradley, Fourth Cavalry, also stated: "First sergeant was always in charge of 1st platoon, and First Duty Sergeant in charge of the 2nd platoon." Bradley interview, Jan. 10, 1968, f. 76, box 8, RP, DPL. He also made a second reference: "McGruder was 1st duty sergeant." Bradley interview, Jan. 9, 1968, f. 76, box 8, RP, DPL.

44. Quartermaster Sergeant Maurice H. Wolfe, to Cousin Maurice, July 15, 1870, Wolfe letters, FLNHS.

45. McChristian, *Frontier Cavalry Trooper*, 215, 228, 225 (quotations). Discussion was under way as early as 1870 to abolish the rank of company quartermaster sergeant, as indicated in *ANJ*, Nov. 5, 1870: 182. *GO No. 14*, AGO, Jan. 31, 1873, called for a reduction in the number of sergeants to five per company of infantry (a first sergeant and four duty sergeants). Cavalry companies suffered a similar loss by the elimination of the grade of quartermaster sergeant, leaving them with five duty sergeants. Although incumbent company quartermaster sergeants were permitted to retain the title and wear the distinctive chevrons until discharged at the end of their current enlistment, general orders prohibited any further promotions or appointments to that grade. All were finally eliminated through attrition by the end of the decade. The chevron itself, consisting of three bars topped by a single straight tie, was finally dropped from the table of authorized insignia in 1883. McChristian, *Uniforms, Arms, and Equipment*, 1:179.

46. Reginald Bradley interview, Jan. 10, 1968, f. 76, box 8, RP, DPL (first quotation); Hedren, "Eben Swift's Army Service," 144 (second quotation). Kitchen did make a long career of the army, however, finally retiring as a first sergeant in 1900, with his captain's brief but telling rating of "most excellent." Register of Enlistments, M233, roll 49, NARA; Barnard, *Ten Years with Custer*, 19.

47. Kautz, *Customs of Service*, 131.

48. McConnell, *Five Years a Cavalryman*, 86 (quotation); *GO No. 18*, Fort Bridger, W.T., June 7, 1875, and *GO No. 5*, Fort Sanders, W.T., June 9, 1875, Fourth Infantry Order Book, FLNHS; Schubert, *Voices of the Buffalo Soldier*, 147.

49. Barnard, *Ten Years with Custer*, 115. The role of acting first sergeant naturally fell to Ryan as the senior duty sergeant until such time as a permanent incumbent could be appointed, so he had managed only to keep the same responsibilities and headaches at lower pay.

50. Schubert, "Ten Troopers," 154; Simpson Mann interview, February 1965, f. 79, RP, DPL (quotation). Stance had a long reputation for brutality and as a result was murdered, presumably by men of his troop, near Fort Robinson, Nebraska, in 1887. McChristian, "'Dress on the Colors, Boys,'" 43.

51. Jett, "Autobiography," MS, SC, UAL (first quotation); McChristian, *Frontier Cavalry Trooper*, 321 (second quotation); First Lieutenant Walter L. Finley to Mother, Nov. 30, 1879, Finley letters, CHL.

52. Lauren Aldrich, "Brief Reminiscences," HM65817, HL.

53. McChristian, *Frontier Cavalry Trooper*, 93; Reginald A. Bradley interview, Jan. 10, 1968, f. 76, box 8, RP, DPL (first quotation); Buecker, "Journals of James S. McClellan," 22; *SO No. 8*, Headquarters, Seventh Cavalry Battalion, May 7, 1873, General and Special Orders, 1873–74, Seventh Cavalry, RG 391, NARA; *Order No. 60*, Sept. 29, 1868, Fourth Infantry Order Book, FLNHS (second quotation).

54. Reginald Bradley interview, Jan. 10, 1968, f. 76, box 8, RP, DP; Buecker, "Journals of James S. McClellan," 22. The individuals were Sergeants Mason, Reeves, and Gannon, along with Corporal. Simpson. *SO No. 8*, May 7, 1873, Orders and Circulars, Seventh Cavalry, RG 393, NARA. Gordon later wrote to his old captain to ask if he might reenlist in the company, swearing that he had not touched liquor since being discharged. Utley, *Life in Custer's Cavalry*, 139, 160 (first quotation); McConnell, *Five Years a Cavalryman*, 195 (second quotation).

55. Private Frederick Stossmeister, to AAG, Dept. of Calif., May 28, 1883, f. 42, box 3, IWWP, JNEM.

56. Barnard, *Ten Years with Custer*, 264.

57. Corporal Maurice Wolfe to Cousin Maurice, July 26, 1868, Wolfe letters, FLNHS (first quotation); Schubert, *Voices of the Buffalo Soldier*, 154 (second quotation); Harvey J. Ciscel questionnaire, f. 9, box 9, RP, DPL (third quotation).

58. Rodenbough, *Sabre and Bayonet*, 356.

59. Sergeant Grandison Mayo questionnaire, f. 45, box 9, RP, DPL; Walker, "Reluctant Corporal" (pt. 1), 17 (quotation).

60. Gustafson, *John Spring's Arizona*, 25.

61. Musician James C. Bothwell reminiscence, MS, copy in author's files (first quotation); Barnard, *Ten Years with Custer*, 258 (second quotation); Henry Hubman to Herman (brother), Nov. 19, 1881, Hubman letters, James Mountain files (third quotation).

62. Rodenbough, *Army of the United States*, 282.

63. Hayden diary, Dec. 7, 1891, LBBNM (first quotation); *GO No. 7*, Oct. 31, 1868, Fourth Infantry Order Book, FLNHS (second quotation).

64. McChristian, *Garrison Tangles*, 56 (first quotation); Reynolds J. Burt Boyhood Data, RC, USAMHI (second quotation).

65. *ANJ*, May 23, 1868, 634 (quotation). August V. Kautz served as a private during the Mexican-American War and was afterward appointed to the U.S. Military Academy,

from which he graduated in 1848. He served in both the infantry and cavalry before and during the Civil War, rising to the rank of brigadier general of volunteers in 1864. After filling the post of lieutenant colonel of the Thirty-Fourth Infantry from 1866 to 1869, he was promoted to colonel of the Fifteenth Infantry and subsequently commanded the Eighth Infantry from 1874 until his retirement in 1892. Kautz received several brevets, the highest being major general of volunteers, for his performance during the Civil War. Heitman, *Historical Register*, 1:586. Kautz authored two military manuals, *The Company Clerk: What to Do, and How to Do It* (1863) and *Customs of Service for Non-Commissioned Officers and Soldiers* (1864), which proved to be of great benefit to the enlisted men.

66. Barnard, *Ten Years with Custer*, 257 (quotation). Some examples of company noncoms being detailed as post sergeant major are found in *Post Orders No. 27*, Feb. 8, 1878, Order Book, Co. K, Seventh Cavalry, LBBNM; Eighth Cavalry Returns, May 1872, Returns from Regular Army Cavalry Regiments, M744, NARA.

67. McConnell, *Five Years a Cavalryman*, 56.

68. *ANJ*, June 14, 1884, 943.

69. McChristian, *Uniforms, Arms, and Equipment*, 1:180, 182; Kautz, *Customs of Service*, 130–31 (quotation).

70. These general staff noncoms and their uniforms are discussed more fully in McChristian, *Uniforms, Arms, and Equipment*, 1:240–54; *Regulations for the Army, 1895*, 13 (first quotation); *Regulations of the Army, 1881*, 32 (second quotation). The 1881 regulations did not contemplate the creation of post quartermaster sergeants, so the wording of a later version was altered to be inclusive of them.

71. Register of Enlistments, M233, roll 49, NARA; Register of Post Quartermaster Sergeants, AGO, RG 94, NARA.

72. Register of Enlistments, AGO, RG 94, NARA; Register of Ordnance Sergeants, AGO, RG 94, NARA.

73. Register of Enlistments, M233, roll 38, NARA; Captain J. H. Dorst to AG, USA, May 10, 1891, f. 15, box 1, Forsyth Family Papers, AHS (quotation). For Forsyth's complete story, see McChristian, "Soldier's Best and Noblest Remembrance."

74. *Regulations of the Army, 1881*, 11 (first quotation). The revised procedure for the advancement of noncoms to commissioned rank was formalized in *GO No. 62*, AGO, Aug. 26, 1878. *ANJ*, Nov. 23, 1878, 256 (second quotation).

75. Heitman, *Historical Register*, 1:439–40.

CHAPTER 6. "IT IS JUST DRAGGING OUT A MISERABLE EXISTENCE"

1. The army finally addressed the inconsistency of naming stations in *GO No. 79*, Nov. 8, 1878, which granted to division commanders the authority "to name and style all posts permanently occupied by troops, or the occupation of which is likely to be permanent, 'Forts,' and to style all points occupied temporarily 'Camps.'" Such terms as "cantonment" and "barracks" were to be eliminated, though in practice they continued to be used. An enlightening discussion of this topic is found in Frazer, *Forts of the West*, xix–xxiii; Keim, *Sheridan's Troopers*, 59 (quotation).

2. *ANJ*, Jan. 10, 1885, 465.

3. Musician James C. Bothwell reminiscence, MS, copy in author's files (quotation). A Seventh Cavalryman described a similar arrangement at Fort Rice, Dakota Territory, except that its stockade included blockhouses on two diagonal corners. Barnard, *Ten Years with Custer*, 176.

4. William Murphy, "Forgotten Battalion," MS., f. 17, box 1, Chapman Collection, AHC (quotation). Fort Laramie was never walled, but in the early 1850s prior to its steady expansion a stockade was planned to encompass what is today the parade ground area. McChristian, *Fort Laramie*, 188–90.

5. Robert Greenhalgh to Father and Mother, July 28, 1866, Greenhalgh letters, RP, DPL (first quotation); Utley, *Life in Custer's Cavalry*, 25 (second quotation). The department commander insisted that every post have a blockhouse or some other defensive fortification for protection. Those precautions proved needless, however, and the embrasures became a drafty nuisance that eventually had to be plugged. The blockhouse found alternative use as the post guardhouse. Oliva, *Fort Larned*, 20–21.

6. The structure that Yohn described was termed a *ramada* in Spanish. Ramadas were adopted from the local Hispanic custom of building overhead shades of readily available natural materials to screen the intense rays of the sun from persons engaged in cooking, blacksmithing, marketing, and other outdoor activities in a region where it seldom rained. These cavalrymen, like many soldiers serving in the Southwest, constructed such shelters over their tents to create a marked reduction of the interior heat that would otherwise be intensified by the canvas. Yohn, "Regulars in Arizona," 121–22 (first quotation); Parker, *Personal Experiences*, 42 (second quotation).

7. Hynes, *Soldiers of the Frontier*, 78 (first quotation); Forsyth, *Story of the Soldier*, 110 (second quotation).

8. Fort McKeen, Dakota Territory, was a rare, if not the only, example of a post constructed with physical defenses during the later period. Established on the Missouri River in 1872, this small infantry post was provided with three two-story squared log blockhouses in a triangular arrangement connected by an open-ended stockade to protect the approach from the open plain. A separate cavalry post was later added on the floodplain below, and the whole post was designated Fort Abraham Lincoln. Hart, *Old Forts of the Northwest*, 154–56.

9. Perley S. Eaton questionnaire, f. 24, box 9, RP, DPL.

10. Forsyth, *Story of the Soldier*, 127 (first quotation); Barnard, *Ten Years with Custer*, 178–79 (second quotation).

11. First Sergeant John Ryan, Seventh Cavalry, recorded that at Fort Rice, Dakota Territory, in the mid-1870s he and the company clerk shared a bedroom adjoining the orderly room. Barnard, *Ten Years with Custer*, 178. The standard-pattern 1874 cavalry barracks at Fort Laramie is a surviving example of such an arrangement, wherein the first sergeant had a private bedroom.

12. George Brown, account of service, box 1, UIWV, RC, USAMHI; Gustafson, *John Spring's Arizona*, 25.

13. McChristian, *Frontier Cavalry Trooper*, 272 (first quotation); McConnell, *Five Years a Cavalryman*, 88 (second quotation), 54 (third quotation). Lending credence to McConnell's opinion, Captain Charles King related a humorous story in which his headquarters clerks went on a drunk and burned the regimental returns. King, *Trials of a Staff Officer*, 31.

14. Hooker, *Child of the Fighting Tenth*, 123–24 (quotation). Infantry bugles were keyed higher than cavalry trumpets. Commenting on this distinction, Elizabeth Custer wrote: "When I was first in the army the bugle was used for the infantry and cavalry, but later the trumpet was given to the mounted regiments. In this way it has occurred that the names have been used indiscriminately. The difference between them may be sufficiently indicated by calling the bugle the tenor and the trumpet the barrytone [sic] of military music." Custer, *Following the Guidon*, vi. Drums declined in popularity as field music after

the Civil War because of their fragility, susceptibility to rain, and the impracticality of carrying them for long distances. Bugles proved to be much more useful on the frontier, although I found references to the use of drums in garrison throughout the era. One correspondent called the drum "a barbarous instrument and should be abolished from the service as field music." *ANJ*, Mar. 2, 1872. Another reference indicated that drums were still being used at Columbus Barracks in 1881, probably to acquaint recruits with the signals. Private Henry Hubman to Father, Aug. 17, 1881, Hubman letters, James Mountain files. Both the 1867 and 1874 editions of Upton's *Infantry Tactics* show only a few primary signals to be played on drum and fife, including assembly, reveille, tattoo, and retreat. There were none for routine daily activities. A Seventh Infantry officer recalled that the "long roll," the emergency call to arms, was sounded on drums at his post in 1879. Carroll, *Unpublished Papers of the Order of Indian Wars*, book 2, 7.

15. McConnell, *Five Years a Cavalryman*, 264–65.

16. Smith, *Dose of Frontier Soldiering*, 50 (first quotation); Private Hartford G. Clark diary, July 24, 1891, f. 16, box 1, IWWP, JNEM (second quotation).

17. Smith, *Dose of Frontier Soldiering*, 42 (first quotation); Barnard, *Ten Years with Custer*, 218 (second quotation).

18. Mulford, *Fighting Indians*, 43 (quotations). Former sergeant Samuel Gibson, Twenty-Seventh Infantry, related that at Fort Phil Kearny in 1867: "Our drummer boy, Hines, beat the reveille first call, and fifteen minutes later the company fell in, and answered reveille roll call." Hebard and Brininstool, *Bozeman Trail*, 2:45.

19. Roe, *Army Letters*, 7.

20. Mulford, *Fighting Indians*, 45 (first quotation); McChristian, *Frontier Cavalry Trooper*, 133 (second quotation).

21. Barnard, *Ten Years with Custer*, 179.

22. Smith, *Dose of Frontier Soldiering*, 50; *Circular*, Dec. 21, 1878, Order Book, Company K, Seventh Cavalry, LBBNM (quotation).

23. Mulford, *Fighting Indians*, 6.

24. McChristian, *Frontier Cavalry Trooper*, 78 (first quotation), 320–21; Greene, *Indian War Veterans*, 184–85 (second quotation). Several entries in Private Hartford Clark's diary make it clear that after the creation of a consolidated post mess at Fort Riley, Kansas, privates were detailed for ten days as kitchen police to wait the tables of their respective companies and do the usual chores. Other company members were assigned as waiters for the band, Signal Corps detachment, and NCO staff. Private Hartford G. Clark diary, July 24, 1891, f. 16, box 1, IWWP, JNEM.

25. McConnell, *Five Years a Cavalryman*, 88 (first quotation); McChristian, *Frontier Cavalry Trooper*, 358 (second quotation); Forsyth, *Story of the Soldier*, 118 (third quotation).

26. Second Lieutenant Alexander R. Piper, Eighth Infantry, Dec. 26, 1890, in Carroll, *Unpublished Papers of the Order of Indian Wars*, book 10, 4 (first quotation); Greene, *Indian War Veterans*, 26 (second quotation). By the 1880s a few posts were fortunate enough to have steam pumps for this purpose. Smith, *Dose of Frontier Soldiering*, 73 (third quotation).

27. Private Hartford G. Clark diary, April 18, 1891, f. 16, box 1, IWWP, JNEM.

28. Albin H. Drown, "A Blizzard Campaign," *National Tribune*, Mar. 13, 1913 (first quotation); Christian F. Sommer, "Cantonment North Fork of the Canadian River," MS, 8601-1173, Thoburn Collection, OHS, copy filed at Fort Supply SHS (second quotation); Rolando B. Moffett, "Building Fort Custer, *Winners of the West*, April 30, 1933 (third quotation); Walker, "Reluctant Corporal" (pt. 1), 13 (fourth quotation).

29. Private Hartford G. Clark diary, Sept. 14, 1891, f. 16, box 1, IWWP, JNEM.

30. Mulford, *Fighting Indians*, 45.

31. QM Sergeant Maurice H. Wolfe to Uncle Michael, n.d., Wolfe letters, FLNHS (first quotation); Walker, "Reluctant Corporal" (pt. 1), 13–14 (second quotation); Upton, *Fort Custer*, 79 (third quotation).

32. "No man, unless he be a carpenter, joiner, carriage-maker, blacksmith, saddler, or harness-maker, will be mustered as an 'artificer.'" *Revised United States Army Regulations of 1861*, 19.

33. White, *Custer, Cavalry, and Crows*, 23 (first quotation). Because blacksmiths were so essential, a civilian was often hired in that capacity at infantry posts where none might be available in the ranks. The quartermaster operation always needed the services of a blacksmith to shoe draft animals, to fabricate hardware for buildings, and to repair equipment. Barnard, *Ten Years with Custer*, 261; Hammer, *With Custer in '76*, 140 (second quotation). A civilian veterinary surgeon was authorized for each of the first eight cavalry regiments, and two each for the Ninth and Tenth. Heitman, *Historical Register*, 2:613.

34. Whether or not men on daily and extra duty were to be included in the "for duty" strength of a company was a decision left to post commanders. Although they were occupied with certain assigned tasks, these men were at the post and thus available in the event that they were needed for some emergency. Kautz, *Customs of Service*, 135.

35. The more informal undress guard mounting was permitted in inclement weather. Upton, *Infantry Tactics*, 373–74.

36. Private Hartford G. Clark diary, Mar. 25, 1891, f. 16, box 1, IWWP, JNEM (first quotation); Custer, *Boots and Saddles*, 146–47 (second quotation).

37. Mulford, *Fighting Indians*, 45 (first quotation); Reynolds J. Burt Boyhood Data, box 2, RC, USAMHI (second quotation).

38. Barnard, *Ten Years with Custer*, 114 (first quotation); Reginald A. Bradley interview, Jan. 9, 1968, RC, USAMHI (second quotation). Dadiac was a commercial leather polish available to soldiers, at least by the late 1880s, either at the trader's store or by mail order. Another contemporary preparation noted in the historical record was Frank Miller's Harness Dressing. In the late 1860s and 1870s, however, more primitive methods were used. An officer inspecting troops in the Department of Dakota in 1878 wrote: "I find that it is a general practice to polish leather work with heel ball and ink, and the result is beneficial. I recommend that these articles together with tripoli, which is universally used for cleaning brass work, be supplied upon requisition, as it seems to be unfair to make soldiers pay for these articles. The materials furnished with the cleaning box [per Ordnance Memoranda 19] are not satisfactory." Inspection Report, Seventh Cavalry, April 15, 1878, 2256 Dept. Dakota 1878, RG 393, NARA. Heel ball consisted of a ball or stick of bee's wax, impregnated with lamp black. The name derived from its primary use for polishing the edges of shoe soles and heels. Tripoli is an extremely fine powder of light-colored siliceous material consisting either of weathered chert or limestone. Applied with a lightly oiled (or water-dampened) cloth and wiped clean, tripoli will bring a high shine to brass. Reeves, *Manual for Aspirants*, 56, 58; Reynolds Burt Boyhood Data, box 2, RC, USAMHI (third quotation).

39. Barnard, *Ten Years with Custer*, 113 (quotation). Every post that was not a regimental headquarters had to appoint an "acting" sergeant major, usually selected from the among the duty or first sergeants. Although guard mounting was usually conducted in the morning, in instances the ceremony was rescheduled in the evening. An example is found in Medical History, Fort Laramie, Wyo. Terr., July 1870, RG 94, NARA. Guard

detachments were selected on a rotational basis following the rule "longest off, first on," the number dictated by the number of guard beats established, multiplied by three reliefs, then prorated among the companies present according to their respective strengths. One additional man was included to account for the orderly, who would be removed from the detail after inspection. Regan, *Manual of Guard Duty*, 17, 377. Supernumeraries remained in or near their quarters all day in order to be available as replacements should any member of the guard fall ill or otherwise be unable to complete his tour.

40. Utley, *Life in Custer's Cavalry*, 39.

41. Forsyth, *Story of the Soldier*, 123 (first quotation), 121 (second quotation); Reynolds Burt, Boyhood Data, Box 2, RC, USAMHI (third quotation); Utley, *Life in Custer's Cavalry*, 151 (fourth quotation).

42. Barnard, *Ten Years with Custer*, 113 (first quotation); Private Hartford G. Clark diary, May 5, 1891, f. 16, box 1, IWWP, JNEM (second quotation); Private Eddie Matthews, Eighth Cavalry, in McChristian, *Frontier Cavalry Trooper*, 129 (third quotation); Reynolds Burt, Boyhood Data, box 2, RC, USAMHI (fourth quotation).

43. The officer of the day was either a captain or a lieutenant, depending on the size of the garrison and the number of captains present. He was the equivalent of the chief of police and commanded the guard. He was nominally in charge of the post or camp for a twenty-four-hour period and carried out the standing and special orders of the commander as that officer's primary assistant. He was not required to remain at the guardhouse but was subject to call at all hours and was obligated to visit the guards at their posts during the day and at least once between midnight and reveille. Some large posts also designated a lieutenant to serve as officer of the guard, who did stay at the guardhouse and was in immediate charge of the guard, the prisoners, and fire suppression. Regan, *Manual of Guard Duty*, 61–62, 72.

44. Greene, *Indian War Veterans*, 20 (first quotation); Innis, "Fort Buford Diary of Pvt. Sanford," 353 (second quotation).

45. One might question the need for a sentry to guard haystacks, but forage could be compared with a military gasoline dump of the present day. Hay was fuel for horses and mules, and serious consequences would have resulted if it was accidentally or purposefully destroyed. Post No. 1 was charged with making certain that no prisoners left the guardhouse, being the first to call out the hours of the night, listening for the other sentinels to sound off, turning out the guard for any armed parties and officers coming to the guardhouse, verifying that the weapons of relieved sentinels were unloaded before they entered the guardhouse, and repeating any of alarm calls sounded by other sentries.

46. Reginald A. Bradley notes, f. 76, box 8, RP, DPL.

47. Buecker, "Letters from a Post Surgeon's Wife," 49.

48. Logan, "Fort Laramie—1877," typescript, WSA (quotation). Such conditions at Fort Keogh, Montana Territory, are further described in an article in *ANJ*, Mar. 6, 1880, 621.

49. Bradley notes, f. 76, box 8, RP, DPL (first quotation); Smith *Dose of Frontier Soldiering*, 46 (second quotation).

50. McChristian, *Frontier Cavalry Trooper*, 136.

51. *GCMO No. 45*, April 9, 1877, Fourth Infantry Order Book, FLNHS; Hayden diary, May 1, 1891, LBBNM (quotation); *Orders No. 170*, Oct. 6, 1882, LBBNM.

52. *ANJ*, Feb. 14, 1874, 426 (first quotation); John O. Stotts reminiscence, Spencer collection (second quotation).

53. *ANJ*, June 6, 1868, 665 (first quotation); *ANJ*, Nov. 18, 1871, 219 (second quotation); Mulford, *Fighting Indians*, 37 (third quotation); *ANJ*, Oct. 20, 1883, 227 (fourth

quotation). As deputy judge advocate general of the army, Lieutenant Colonel William Winthrop later authored the official *Military Law* published in 1886.

54. "Notes for Post History—Camp Brown, Wyo.," box 1, acc. 10, Maghee Papers, AHC (first quotation); *ANJ*, June 16, 1883 (second quotation).

55. Barnard, *Ten Years with Custer*, 172. A watering bridle made it easier for a horse to drink. It consisted of a hinged snaffle bit that snapped to the halter and had a one-piece rein that looped over the horse's neck to provide basic control of the animal.

56. Major William B. Royall, Fifth Cavalry, to AG, USA, Papers Relating to the Army Equipment Board, LR, AGO, RG 94, M666, roll 436, NARA (first quotation); House of Representatives, Report No. 56, *Reorganization of the Army*, at 246 (1878); *ANJ*, Dec. 1, 1883, 358 (second quotation).

57. Cozzens, *Eyewitnesses to the Indian Wars*, 1:99–100.

58. Barnard, *Ten Years with Custer*, 19–20 (quotation); *Orders No. 7*, Oct. 31, 1868, Fourth Infantry Order Book, FLNHS. A subsequent directive required attendance for all officers and enlisted men, except those on guard or those who could not be spared from details to the various departments. *Cir. No. 44*, Fort Laramie, W.T., Mar. 22, 1869, Fourth Infantry Order Book, FLNHS; Gustafson, *John Spring's Arizona*, 125.

59. R. Eugene Pelham, "The Passing of the Frontiers," *National Tribune*, Dec. 12, 1918 (first quotation); Smith, *Dose of Frontier Soldiering*, 64 (second quotation).

60. Much of the following discussion derives from McChristian, *Army of Marksmen*.

61. Templeton diary, Aug. 31, 1866, NL; William Murphy, "Forgotten Battalion," MS, f. 17, box 1, Chapman Collection, AHC (quotation).

62. Lauren Aldrich, "Brief Reminiscences," HL (quotation). Company M of the Seventh Cavalry was posted at Fort Larned, Kansas, in the spring of 1867. A member recalled that "we did the usual drilling, target practice mounted, at which we became quite expert, riding at full speed and firing at targets." Barnard, *Ten Years with Custer*, 53.

63. *Co. Orders No. 6*, Sept. 12, 1873, Fourth Infantry Order Book, FLNHS (quotation). See also *GO No. 20*, Fort Bridger, W.T., Sept. 27, 1877, FLNHS. Additional orders for conducting regular practice and the formation of competitive rifle teams at Fort Fetterman, Wyoming Territory, in 1879 suggest that the Fourth Infantry placed more emphasis on marksmanship than did most regiments. *SO No. 76*, July 14, 1879, FLNHS.; *SO No. 6*, April 21, 1874, General and Special Orders, and Circulars Issued, 1873–74, Seventh Cavalry, RG 391, NARA.

64. *ANJ*, Nov. 9, 1872, 202 (first quotation); McChristian, *Frontier Cavalry Trooper*, 46 (second quotation).

65. *ARSW*, 1879, 325, and quoted more fully in McChristian, *Army of Marksmen*, 36–37.

66. Wingate's manual was in use by the Seventh Cavalry, as evidenced in *Circular*, April 28, 1878, Order Book, Co. K, Seventh Cavalry, LBBNM. Because the cost of ammunition had been a factor limiting the amount of practice, Laidley advocated the reloading of cartridges by the troops using round balls and small powder charges for "gallery practice," which could be held indoors during winter. Thus the amount of practice ammunition increased dramatically, and soldiers enjoyed such practice. McChristian, *Army of Marksmen*, 45–46; Upton, *Fort Custer*, 87–89 (quotation).

67. Private Hartford G. Clark diary, May 21, 1891, f. 16, box 1, IWWP, JNEM.

68. Private Charles N. Hayden diary, July 9, 1891, LBBNM; Smith, *Dose of Frontier Soldiering*, 64–65 (quotation).

69. Private Hartford G. Clark diary, May 21, 1891, f. 16, box 1, IWWP, JNEM (quotation); *ANJ*, Sept. 15, 1883, 125.

70. Mulford, *Fighting Indians*, 46.

71. At the discretion of the post commander, the evening parade was sometimes scheduled just prior to supper, which, incidentally, usually was not announced by the orderly trumpeter sounding "Mess Call." During this light meal, often consisting of leftovers, food was placed on the tables and a gong, bell, or triangle sounded at each barracks to summon the men of the respective companies; Smith, *Dose of Frontier Soldiering*, 64 (quotation).

72. Smith, *Dose of Frontier Soldiering*, 73.

73. Rooms in the stables were unheated because of potential fire danger. A separate structure or tent afforded the comfort of a small box or Sibley stove during winter, but even so fire was possible. Former sergeant Charles White, Seventh Cavalry, recorded an instance in 1877 when the "stable guard house" at Fort Rice, Dakota Territory, burned down. Sergeant Charles White diary, Jan. 20, 1877, f. 56, box 1, ECP, DPL. Stable guards fed the horses but were not obligated, in theory, to clean the stalls; that was the province of the assigned stable police. In practice, however, cleaning a stable for 50–60 horses was a big job, and the guards of necessity helped with that work. Regan, *Manual of Guard Duty*, 138–39; Barnard, *Ten Years with Custer*, 178. Other troopers doubled up to groom the mounts belonging to the room orderlies and stable police.

74. *Orders No. 121*, May 29, 1883, Fourth Infantry Order Book, FLNHS (first quotation). The term "Taps" originated during the days when only drums were used to sound calls. A soldier serving during the Mexican War wrote: "About fifteen minutes [after Tattoo] were then allowed to elapse when the drummer beat three distinct taps on the drum, then at this signal every light in tents or quarters had to be extinguished and the most strict silence preserved." Ballentine, *Autobiography of an English Soldier*, 26; Mulford, *Fighting Indians*, 47 (second quotation).

75. McChristian, *Frontier Cavalry Trooper*, 53 (first quotation); *ANJ*, June 8, 1889, 847 (second quotation).

76. Barnard, *Ten Years with Custer*, 179.

77. Private Adelbert Butler to Mary (sister), June 3, 1877, Butler letters, GTC (first quotation); Smith, *Dose of Frontier Soldiering*, 16 (second quotation).

78. *ANJ*, June 8, 1889, 847.

79. McConnell, *Five Years a Cavalryman*, 192.

80. *ANJ*, June 8, 1889, 841 (quotations); *ANJ*, Mar. 30, 1889, 624; Foner, *United States Soldier between Two Wars*, 91. It would seem that in actual practice some officers continued the tradition of conducting weekly inspections on Saturday afternoon or evening. This is reflected in several entries in the Private Hartford G. Clark diary, f. 16, box 1, IWWP, JNEM.

81. *ANJ*, Sept. 27, 1884, 163.

82. R. Eugene Pelham, "The Passing of the Frontiers," *National Tribune*, Dec. 12, 1918 (first quotation); "Frontier" to *Titusville (Pa.) Morning Herald*, July 27, 1870 in "Seven Letters," 305–6 (second quotation).

CHAPTER 7. "THE BED BUGS ARE TOO NUMEROUS FOR ME TO SLEEP"

1. *ANJ*, April 3, 1875, 532 (first quotation); Dinges, "New York Private," 63–64 (second quotation).

2. McChristian, *Frontier Cavalry Trooper*, 53 (first quotation); Ashburn, *History of the Medical Department*, 98 (second quotation). Some frontier posts were considered to be temporary and therefore remained rather primitive for a long time. For example, a veteran recorded that as late as 1878 the barracks at Fort Reno, I.T., were still those of picket construction with dirt floors. Christian F. Sommer, "Cantonment North Fork of Canadian River," MS, Thoburn Collection, OHS (copy filed at Fort Supply SHS).

3. For a reference to this type of construction, see First Sergeant John Ryan's description of the barracks at Fort Rice, Dakota Territory, in Barnard, *Ten Years with Custer*, 178.

4. A rare surviving example of a barracks designed on the standard floor plan can be seen today at Fort Laramie National Historic Site (Wyoming). The walls of the two-story 1874 Cavalry Barracks are constructed of formed lime grout, a primitive type of concrete. *ANJ*, Sept. 21, 1867, 74 (quotation).

5. *ANJ*, Oct. 5, 1867, 106 (first quotation); Billings, *Circular No. 4*, xvi (second quotation); Billings, *Circular No. 8*, xviii (third quotation).

6. Billings, *Circular No. 8*, xviii (first quotation); McChristian, *Frontier Cavalry Trooper*, 53 (second quotation); Smith, *Dose of Frontier Soldiering*, 68 (third quotation). The practice of doubling up is also referenced by First Sergeant John Ryan in Barnard, *Ten Years with Custer*, 178; Simpson Mann interview, f. 79, box 9, RP, DPL; *ARSW*, 1885, 604–5.

7. *ANJ*, Oct. 5, 1867 (first quotation); McChristian, *Frontier Cavalry Trooper*, 45 (second quotation). Standard-pattern lockers were adopted in 1875 but not produced until the following year. *Ordnance Memoranda No. 19*, 59; *ARSW*, 1876, 179.

8. McChristian, *Uniforms, Arms, and Equipment*, 2:220. Photographic evidence suggests that some men acquired an extra footlocker and placed it under the bunk, perhaps as a receptacle for the barracks bag.

9. In a few instances, such as at Fort Grant, Arizona Territory, squad rooms were so narrow that only one row of bunks could be placed in the usual fashion, with additional bunks arranged parallel to the opposite wall. For photos of this and other barracks, see Brown, *The Army Called It Home*, 90.

10. McChristian, *Frontier Cavalry Trooper*, 133 (quotation); Simpson Mann interview, f. 79, box 9, RP, DPL.

11. An example is a Sixth Infantryman's comment: "They are whitewashing the quarters. Color same as before, Blue made out of a mixture of lamp black and whitened flour and salt." Innis, "Fort Buford Diary of Pvt. Sanford," 373.

12. Simpson Mann interview, f. 79, box 9, RP, DPL.

13. Barnard, *Ten Years with Custer*, 179 (quotation); *Order No. 78*, Oct. 20, 1868, Fourth Infantry Order Book, FLNHS; Daily Journal, 1868–76, Fort Fetterman, W.T., RG 393, NARA (Lindmier microfilm, roll no. 803–5). Fire barrels were kept indoors during winter to prevent the water from freezing.

14. Thomas B. Marquis, "Hardin Merchant Tells of Boyhood Incidents," n.d., n.p., Montana Scrapbook, vol. 1, Montana Room, BPL (quotation); Medical History, Fort Sully, Dak. Terr., February 1884, RG 94, NARA.

15. Buecker, "Journals of James S. McClellan," 25 (first quotation); Medical History, Fort Laramie, Wyo. Terr., Dec. 1874, RG 94, NARA (second quotation).

16. Greene, *Indian War Veterans*, 36 (first quotation); George Neihaus questionnaire, f. 93, box 9, RP, DPL; Medical History, Fort Laramie, Wyo. Terr., March 1877, RG 94,

NARA (second quotation); Private Hartford G. Clark diary, Sept. 11, 1891, f.16, box 1, IWWP, JNEM (third quotation).

17. *ANJ*, Feb. 20, 1875, 443 (first quotation); *ANJ*, April 3, 1869, 519 (second quotation); Closson, "Morning Reports," 186 (third quotation).

18. To my knowledge, the earliest official cookbook was Captain James M. Sanderson's *Camp Fires and Camp Cooking; or, Culinary Hints for the Soldier*, published in 1862 as a guide for the thousands of volunteers swelling army ranks. However, for that reason it was primarily concerned with cooking in the field. No further effort was made to develop an army cookbook until a Board on Army Cooking convened in 1877, resulting in the first *Manual for Army Cooks* in 1879. An expanded edition appeared four years later. William Murphy, "Forgotten Battalion," MS, f. 17, box 1, Chapman Collection, AHC (first quotation); McChristian, *Frontier Cavalry Trooper*, 64 (second quotation). Regulations prohibited the hiring of civilian cooks. *Revised United States Army Regulations of 1861*, 255; *Regulations of the Army, 1881*, 240; Billings, *Circular No. 8*, xxxix (third quotation); *ANJ*, Sept. 10, 1870, 56 (fourth quotation). A letter dated Feb. 10, 1882, from the adjutant general officially sanctioned the purchase from the company fund of overalls and aprons for cooks. Such practical acquisitions had probably been made for many years before this. *ANJ*, Feb. 18, 1882, 634.

19. Barnard, *Ten Years with Custer*, 218 (first quotation); Orders No. 5, Aug. 16, 1868, Fourth Infantry Order Book, FLNHS (second quotation).

20. *Revised United States Army Regulations of 1861*, 244, 526.

21. At Fort Stanton, New Mexico Territory, the surplus bread was taken about the garrison in a push cart. Jett, "Autobiography," MS, SC, UAL. Those purchasing bread did so by means of "bread tickets." To avoid cash transactions and accountability at the bakery, customers wishing to buy bread made those purchases through the post treasurer (a designated officer), who provided printed paper tickets. The tickets were then redeemed at the bakery. An original example in my possession is printed on lightweight colored pasteboard measuring 1½ inches by 2⅛ inches. The post treasurer's signature appears on the reverse, presumably to validate the ticket. *ANJ*, Nov. 15, 1873 (quotation). According to earlier regulations, the post fund derived from combining 50 percent of the surplus flour sales with a head-tax on the sutler, up to ten cents, for each officer and soldier in the garrison. At that time, the post fund could be used for maintenance of the band. After the elimination of sutlers in 1866, however, the head-tax disappeared. Along with the fracturing of regiments and the presence of companies from various regiments in a single frontier garrison, this resulted in the respective regimental funds supporting the bands. In those instances when the regimental fund was in excess of the band's needs, it could be distributed equitably to the company funds. *Revised United States Army Regulations of 1861*, 35; *Regulations of the Army, 1881*, 59–60.

22. Murphy, "Forgotten Battalion," MS, f. 17, box 1, Chapman Collection, AHC (first quotation); Sergeant Samuel Gibson, Twenty-Seventh Infantry, quoted in Hebard and Brininstool, *Bozeman Trail*, 2:39–40 (second quotation).

23. Mulford, *Fighting Indians*, 43 (quotation). A Sixth Infantryman at Fort Buford, Dakota Territory, recorded typical meals served to his company during October 1874: "Potatoes and steaks for breakfast, soup for dinner; Dry hash for breakfast and backed [baked] beans for dinner; Stew for breakfast and vegetable soup for dinner; Bacin [sic] for breakfast and potatoes, cabbage, and pork for dinner; Pork and cabbage for dinner; Pork for breakfast and potatoes and cabbage for dinner. Apples [dried] for supper; Pork for breakfast. Potatoes, roast beef, and kraut for dinner. Apples for supper; Pork in the

morning, Beef, mashed potatoes, and plum duff for dinner." He seldom listed the supper menu, which suggests that it either consisted of leftovers or was not worth mentioning, such as bread and coffee. Innis, "Fort Buford Diary of Pvt. Sanford," 340–43.

24. McChristian, *Frontier Cavalry Trooper*, 54 (first quotation). Beef was delivered on the hoof, by either the contractor or soldiers. For example, the post surgeon at Fort Rice, Dakota Territory, recorded that cattle were driven to posts along the Missouri River by relays of soldiers, with each post in turn furnishing a noncom and a few privates as escort. The cattle herd grazed within the military reservation and was watched over by a soldier detailed for the purpose. Mattison, "Diary of Surgeon Washington Matthews," 69 (second quotation). In regions where cattle ranching had begun, the army often contracted locally for beef. For a firsthand description of a butchering operation, see Johnny O'Brian interview, FLNHS. Comments by a soldier detailed as "post cow herder" are found in *ANJ*, Sept. 19, 1885, 148; Reginald Bradley interview, f. 76, box 8, RP, DPL (third quotation).

25. McChristian, *Frontier Cavalry Trooper*, 379 (first quotation); *ANJ*, Oct. 22, 1871, and reprinted in Cozzens, *Eyewitnesses to the Indian Wars*, 1:105; (second quotation). A soldier posted in southeastern Colorado wrote a glowing detailed report of how well his company was faring on a combination of ration items, wild game, garden vegetables, and judicious management of the company fund. *ANJ*, July 24, 1869, 678.

26. Coffee beans were roasted either in a baking pan atop the stove or by means of a patented coffee roaster then ground using a coffee mill. Both were acquired with company funds, because the army did not issue such items. Sanderson, *Camp Fires and Camp Cooking*, 11; Smith, *Dose of Frontier Soldiering*, 18 (quotation).

27. Axel Dahlgren, "Life of Soldiers," *National Tribune*, Oct. 7, 1920 (first quotation); Perley S. Eaton questionnaire, f. 24, box 9, RP, DPL (second quotation).

28. *ANJ*, April 24, 1869: 566 (first quotation); McChristian, *Frontier Cavalry Trooper*, 234 (second quotation); *ANJ*, Sept. 25, 1869, 774 (third quotation); *ANJ*, April 10, 1880, 729. Frederick C. Kurtz, Eighth Cavalry, said that all the men in E Troop "chipped in $2.00 every two months . . . with this we secured Irish potatoes, onions, and a few canned goods." Greene, *Indian War Veterans*, 32.

29. "Rotten stone" is another name for tripoli, which is weathered limestone combined with crystalline silica. Soldiers purchased it for polishing buttons, belt plates, and insignia. Fine emery was employed for burnishing the ironwork on bright-finished rifles and saber scabbards. *ANJ*, May 29, 1869, 646 (quotation).

30. Yohn, "Regulars in Arizona," 123–24 (first quotation); Barnard, *Ten Years with Custer*, 186 (second quotation); R. Eugene Pelham, "The Passing of the Frontiers," *National Tribune*, Dec. 12, 1918 (third quotation).

31. Lieutenant Walter Finley to Mother, Aug. 3, 1881, Finley Collection, CHL; *ANJ*, Nov. 16, 1889.

32. Billings, *Hardtack and Coffee*, 141–42 (first quotation); Ostrander, *Army Boy of the Sixties*, 150 (second quotation). Desiccated vegetables were issued as a substitute for beans, peas, hominy, rice, and fresh potatoes. *Revised United States Army Regulations of 1861*, 244.

33. Steele, *Bleed, Blister, and Purge*, xxii, 83; Anthony Gavin, "Campaigning against the Hostile Sioux," *National Tribune*, April 22, 1926 (quotation).

34. Smith, *Dose of Frontier Soldiering*, 66 (first quotation); Upton, *Fort Custer*, 84 (second quotation).

35. In an earlier attempt to improve the health of the soldiers, the post surgeon introduced the garrison to mescal, a traditional Apache dish made from the bulbous root of

the agave plant. Just how successful that may have been was not recorded. McChristian, *Fort Bowie*, 247–48; *ANJ*, Aug. 14, 1869, 822 (quotation).

36. Byrne, *Frontier Army Surgeon*, 101–2 (first quotation); Zimmer, *Frontier Soldier*, 148 (second quotation); Jett, "Autobiography," MS, SC, UAL (third quotation).

37. A transfer could impose other losses on a company, besides losing its garden, including any livestock it might own, such as pigs or cows. Hardin, "Army Messing," 274.

38. *GO No. 79*, AGO, Sept. 25, 1868.

39. The Subsistence Department purchased baked beans in one-, two-, and three-pound cans. *ANJ*, Oct. 1, 1881, 181; *Army Regulations, 1881*, 241–42. Greene, *Indian War Veterans*, 360 (quotation).

40. McChristian, *Frontier Cavalry Trooper*, 344 (first quotation); White, *Custer, Cavalry, and Crows*, 26 (second quotation). Army tobacco was supplied in half-pound plugs packed in boxes weighing twenty-one pounds net, eight boxes to a case. *ANJ*, July 5, 1873, 748; Simpson Mann interview, f. 79, box 9, RP, DPL (third quotation).

41. Schubert, *Voices of the Buffalo Soldier*, 65 (first quotation); *Regulations of the Army, 1881*, 248; Private Richard F. King to Gabriella King, Jan. 24, 1889, King letters, FUNM (second quotation).

42. This discussion relies heavily on the authoritative treatment of army sutlers presented in Delo, *Peddlers and Post Traders*.

43. *ANJ*, Feb. 19, 1881, 593. The 1867 resolution allowed traders to be retained at posts between 100 degrees west longitude and the eastern border of California. Delo, *Peddlers and Post Traders*, 148, 152 (quotation).

44. Smith, *Dose of Frontier Soldiering*, 36–37.

45. Delo, *Peddlers and Post Traders*, 170.

46. When the Seventh Infantry left Fort Laramie, Wyoming Territory, upon its abandonment in 1890, a number of officers failed to settle up with the post trader, John Hunton, a factor contributing to his financial woes. McChristian, *Fort Laramie*, 397, 397 n. 15; Barnard, *Ten Years with Custer*, 182 (quotation).

47. *GO No. 24*, AGO, May 18, 1878; *ANJ*, Sept. 6, 1879, 75 (quotation).

48. McChristian, *Frontier Cavalry Trooper*, 17 (first quotation); *ANJ*, Sept. 30, 1871, 111 (second quotation); *ANJ*, Dec. 23, 1871, 306. Even though they were in pay status, recruits did not receive any pay until after they reported to their units. At that time, all of the charges that they had incurred both at the depot and the post were placed against the pay due.

49. According one source, a skilled journeyman, such as a carpenter, earned eighteen to twenty dollars a week. Thus comparatively few of them joined the army unless one was "intemperate or has committed some infraction of the civil law." *ANJ*, April 19, 1873, 570; *Regulations of the Army, 1881*, 281, 373.

50. *Revised United States Army Regulations of 1861*, 127 (quotation). The pay rate for privates working as laborers was reduced to twenty cents a day in 1873, and the rate for all other extra-duty men was thirty-five cents. The geographical distinction was eliminated. *Regulations of the Army, 1881*, 374.

51. Private Herman S. Searl to Dear Parents, May 5, 1868, Herman S. Searl letters, WSA (quotation). Fort Boise, Idaho Territory, was another post visited by the paymaster only twice yearly. *ANJ*, Nov. 23, 1867, 217. In contradiction to a persistent belief that army payrolls were made in gold, soldiers were paid in paper money and/or silver coin. If for no other reason, transporting such a heavy load of gold over long distances and often

rough terrain made it impractical. Funds were usually transported in strong boxes or portable safes, though I encountered one instance in which a paymaster carried $7,500 in currency in a valise. Robberies and attempted robberies nevertheless occurred, though the record suggests that such incidents were relatively few and were more common during the 1880s and 1890s than in earlier years, probably because the army had greatly reduced the Indian threat and thereby made banditry a safer occupation. *ANJ*, Mar. 26, 1887, 692.

52. Private Hartford G. Clark diary, Aug. 31, 1891, f. 16, box 1, IWWP, JNEM.

53. Upton, *Fort Custer*, 85–86 (first quotation); Reynolds J. Burt Boyhood Data, box 2, RC, USAMHI (second quotation).

54. Private Charles N. Hayden diary, Aug. 10, 1891, LBBNM.

55. Ibid., Oct. 10, 1891; Reynolds J. Burt Boyhood Data, box 2, RC, USAMHI (quotation).

56. Private Robert Greenhalgh to Father and Mother, May 19, 1866, Greenhalgh letters, RP, DPL (first quotation); McChristian, *Frontier Cavalry Trooper*, 343 (second quotation).

57. For in-depth treatments of army clothing worn during the Indian Wars, see McChristian, *U.S. Army in the West*, and McChristian, *Uniforms, Arms, and Equipment*, vol. 1.

58. Barnard, *Ten Years with Custer*, 183.

59. McChristian, *Garrison Tangles*, 56 (first quotation). Former private Simpson Mann, Ninth Cavalry, said that clothing issues in his troop were made on the seventh day of each month. Simpson Mann interview, f. 79, box 9, RP, DPL; Smith, *Dose of Frontier Soldiering*, 18 (second quotation).

60. *ANJ*, Nov. 27, 1886, 345.

61. Innis, "Fort Buford Diary of Pvt. Sanford, 347.

62. Matthews mentioned that he and most of his comrades wore not only white shirts but also paper or cloth collars. McChristian, *Frontier Cavalry Trooper*, 344 (first quotation); Private Henry Hubman to Herman (brother), Dec. 27, 1881, Hubman letters, James Mountain files (second quotation).

63. McConnell, *Five Years a Cavalryman*, 230 (first quotation); *ANJ*, Oct. 5, 1867, 106 (second quotation).

64. *Regulations of the Army, 1881*, 20; Orders No. 2, July 16, 1878, Fourth Infantry Order Book, FLNHS; *ANJ*, Feb. 12, 1881, 568 (quotation).

65. Sergeant Samuel Gibson, Twenty-Seventh Infantry, quoted in Hebard and Brininstool, *Bozeman Trail*, 2:42–43.

66. Gustafson, *John Spring's Arizona*, 63.

67. Barnard, *Ten Years with Custer*, 28.

68. McChristian, *Frontier Cavalry Trooper*, 86.

69. White, *Custer, Cavalry, and Crows*, 47 (first quotation); Barnard, *Ten Years with Custer*, 257 (second quotation). For in-depth discussions of the development of the Springfield, comparisons with other weapons, and its eventual replacement, see McChristian, *U.S. Army in the West*, 105–16, and McChristian, *Uniforms, Arms, and Equipment*, 2:153–68.

70. Robert C. O. Norman questionnaire, f. 95, box 10, RP, DPL (first quotation); James Hamilton questionnaire, f. 52, box 9, RP, DPL (second quotation); Private John Gibbert questionnaire, f. 42, box 9, RP, DPL (third quotation); John Nixon, "Memories," *Winners of the West*, July 1938.

71. John O. Stotts reminiscence, Spencer collection (first quotation); Barnard, *Ten Years with Custer*, 28 (second quotation). Ryan's memory was correct for the prices that soldiers were charged, but the costs to the government actually were $15.50 for a Springfield carbine and $13.00 for a Model 1873 Colt revolver. *Price List of Ordnance*, 69, 75. Private James Laird was charged $50 for the loss of his Model 1860 revolver. CO to Paymaster General, Oct. 27, 1873, Order Book, Co. L, Seventh Cavalry, Robert Baird collection.

72. Templeton diary, Sept. 4, 1866, NL; Barnard, *Ten Years with Custer*, 300; Lockwood, *Apaches and Longhorns*, 73.

73. *U.S. Army Uniforms*, 283–84 (first quotation); Upton, *Fort Custer*, 89 (second quotation).

74. *ARSW*, 1887, 82.

75. *ARSW*, 1887, 83; Heitman, *Historical Register*, 2:619. The concept and advantages of the consolidated mess are discussed in Hardin, "Army Messing."

76. *ANJ*, Mar. 19, 1881, 675 (first quotation); *ANJ*, Sept. 27, 1884, 163 (second quotation). I recall seeing in the museum collections at Fort Davis National Historic Site cans and slip-on lids embossed "TOPICAN BUTTER," which is probably the product to which the surgeon referred.

77. *ARSW*, 1889, 247–48.

78. McChristian, *Uniforms, Arms, and Equipment*, 2:159.

CHAPTER 8. "OFFENSIVE IN EVERY PARTICULAR"

1. *Regulations of the Army, 1881*, 265; Medical History, Fort Laramie, Wyo. Terr., Sept. 1874, RG 94, NARA (quotation).

2. Ashburn, *History of the Medical Department*, 138.

3. Billings, *Circular No. 4*, xvii.

4. Medical History, Fort Laramie, Wyo. Terr., June 1875, RG 94, NARA.

5. Reginald Bradley interview, "Barracks," f. 76, box 8, RP, DPL (quotation); Medical History, Fort Laramie, Wyo. Terr., June 1886, RG 94, NARA.

6. Billings, *Circular No. 8*, x (first quotation); *ANJ*, Feb. 20, 1875: 443 (second quotation); Hebard and Brininstool, *Bozeman Trail*, 2:40 (third quotation).

7. McChristian, *Frontier Cavalry Trooper*, 120–21 (first quotation); Custer, *Tenting on the Plains*, 322 (second quotation).

8. *Revised United States Army Regulations of 1861*, 481 (first quotation); Private Henry Hubman to Herman (brother), Sept. 12, 1882, James Mountain files (second quotation); Sergeant Samuel Gibson to unknown, Feb. 19, 1924, RC, USAMHI (third quotation). Private George Cranston, Thirty-Second Infantry, indicated that he had worn "Burnsides" (mutton-chops) while in the army but had shaved them off shortly after his discharge in 1870. Dinges, "New York Private," 71. In one instance a post surgeon advised Fourth Infantrymen at Fort Bridger, Wyoming Territory, to allow their beards to grow during the winter as protection against frostbite. QM Sergeant Maurice H. Wolfe to Cousin Maurice, Mar. 29, 1874, Wolfe letters, FLNHS. Private Simpson Mann, Ninth Cavalry, said that the men shaved once a week using washbasins and that even though water could be heated for the purpose most men preferred to shave with cold water. Simpson Mann interview, f. 79, box 9, RP, DPL; Hayden diary, Sept. 5, 1891, LBBNM.

9. Ashburn, *History of the Medical Department*, 135.

10. Mattison, "Diary of Surgeon Washington Matthews," 57.

11. James Tucker, "Served 10 Eventful Years," *National Tribune*, Nov. 24, 1921.

12. The highest rate of scurvy occurred in the Department of Texas, with the Departments of Arizona and Missouri second and third, respectively. Billings, *Circular No. 8*, xxxvii–xxxviii. Dried apples, available by purchase from the Subsistence Department, had a beneficial antiscorbutic effect but were not always stocked. Ibid., xxxii; William Murphy, "Forgotten Battalion," MS, f. 17, box 1, Chapman Collection, AHC (first quotation); Hynes, *Soldiers of the Frontier*, 54 (second quotation).

13. Troops in Arizona and Texas experienced approximately fifteen and thirteen deaths per one thousand soldiers, respectively, while the Departments of Dakota and Columbia had only about three and two, respectively. Black troops also experienced a higher rate of mortality from disease—30 to 50 percent—than did white soldiers, perhaps the effect of more drastic changes in accustomed climate. Statistics concerning disease and mortality are given in Billings, *Circular No. 4*, xxvii–xxviii; Dinges, "New York Private," 66 (first quotation); John Vance Lauderdale journal, f. 110, box 4, Lauderdale Papers, BL, YU (second quotation); QM Sergeant Maurice H. Wolfe to Brother Batt, Dec. 5, 1868, Wolfe letters, FLNHS (third quotation).

14. McConnell, *Five Years a Cavalryman*, 164 (first quotation); Private Herman S. Searl to Dear Parents, Jan. 2, 1868, Herman S. Searl letters, WSA (second quotation); Summerhayes, *Vanished Arizona*, 38 (third quotation).

15. Arthur quoted in Ashburn, *History of the Medical Department*, 116.

16. Steele, *Bleed, Blister, and Purge*, 13–15; Heitman, *Historical Register*, 2:610–13; *Revised United States Army Regulations of 1861*, 315. James M. DeWolf was a case in point. After serving as an enlisted man through the Civil War, he afterward joined the regulars as an infantryman and was later appointed hospital steward. He subsequently studied medicine at Harvard University. Graduating in 1875, he applied to be an assistant surgeon but failed to pass the examination. Undeterred, DeWolf took a contract as an acting assistant surgeon, was attached to the Seventh Cavalry for the Sioux Expedition, and was killed in action at the Battle of the Little Bighorn. Nichols, *Men with Custer*, 85. Dr. Henry Lippincott represented the best of the army medical men. He served as a regimental surgeon with the California Volunteers during the war and was subsequently commissioned in the regular army. In 1868 he accompanied the Seventh Cavalry on the Washita Campaign. Promoted to major and surgeon in 1884, he later rose to lieutenant colonel (deputy surgeon general) and colonel (assistant surgeon general). Heitman, *Historical Register*, 1:634.

17. After local rancher and government contractor John Hunton broke his leg, he was treated in the hospital at Fort Fetterman, Wyoming Territory, for a period of five weeks, for which he was charged $41.00. Flannery, *John Hunton's Diary*, 27–29, 40; Ashburn, *History of the Medical Department*, 116 (quotation). A fee of $1.00 per day for care of civilians seems to have been the usual rate. The money was then deposited in a hospital "boarding" or "slush" fund maintained by the post surgeon and used for replenishing medicines and other supplies.

18. *ANJ*, May 23, 1874, 650.

19. *ANJ*, Aug. 12, 1876, 14.

20. *ANJ*, May 23, 1874, 650 (quotation). The reference is to the table of rank and command found in *Revised United States Army Regulations of 1861*, 9. Hospital stewards were graded in three classes, the first class being attached to a post hospital. Second or third class stewards, usually acting positions, sometimes augmented the medical staff at frontier posts when they could be justified. *ANJ*, April 1, 1882, 783.

21. *ANJ*, May 31, 1873, 670.

22. McChristian, *Frontier Cavalry Trooper*, 136.

23. The dentist was charged a boarding fee of a dollar a day, which the surgeon used to replenish medicines used by the dentist. Medical History, Fort Laramie, W.T., May 1881; Smith, *Dose of Frontier Soldiering*, 68 (quotation).

24. Edgar Hoffner, "Journal of the Sheep Eater Campaign," Brown Papers, UCB.

25. Scott et al., *They Died with Custer*, 294–95 (quotation). Materials used for filling dental cavities in the late nineteenth century included gold, which was preferred, tin because it was economical, and a popular amalgam composed of silver, tin, and mercury. Glenner and Willey, "Dental Filling Materials in the Confederacy," 71–73.

26. McChristian, *Frontier Cavalry Trooper*, 354 (first quotation); Jett, "Autobiography," MS, SC, UAL (second quotation).

27. Wooster, *History of Fort Davis*, 271; John Vance Lauderdale journal, f. 110, box 4, Lauderdale Papers, BL, YU (quotation); Medical History, Fort Laramie, W.T., August 1868, RG 94, NARA.

28. The exigencies of the Civil War caused the army to relax the regulation to permit the hiring of female nurses in "general or permanent hospitals" when authorized by the surgeon general or deemed necessary by the medical officer in charge. *Regulations of the Army, 1881*, 362; *ANJ*, Feb. 22, 1873, 443 (first quotation); Ashburn, *History of the Medical Department*, 100–101 (second quotation); Private George W. McAnulty to Lillie Moore, Dec. 19, 1876, McAnulty letters, FLNHS (third quotation).

29. Private Herman S. Searl to Dear Parents, Oct. 23, 1867, Herman S. Searl letters, WSA (first quotation); Hospital Steward Seymour Kitching to My Own Darling (wife), June 4, 1876, Kitching Papers, DU (second quotation).

30. Reynolds Burt, Boyhood Data, box 2, RC, USAMHI (quotation); Medical History, Fort Laramie, Wyo. Terr., Dec. 1868, RG 94, NARA. "The sick in hospital, not needing full rations . . . only such parts thereof are issued as are actually required for the support of themselves and authorized attendants. The difference between the number of rations due a hospital, at cost price of a complete ration at the station, and the value of the stores issued to it during the same period and at the same prices, constitutes a credit with the Subsistence Department in favor of the hospital. This credit is called 'Hospital Fund.'" *Revised United States Army Regulations of 1861*, 247–48.

31. *Regulations of the Army, 1881*, 243, 371.

32. Bradley Notes, f. 76, box 8, RP, DPL (first quotation). A wide array of ginger-based products, commonly known as essence of Jamaica ginger due to the plant's origin in the tropics, were commercially available during the latter half of the nineteenth century. One study catalogued some thirty-four different brands, many boasting a base of French brandy as a selling point. A survey of medicine bottles recovered at Fort Union, New Mexico, and Fort Laramie, Wyoming, indicated that these patent concoctions were widely used by the resident soldiers, officers, and civilians. Army doctors probably compounded their own, using powdered ginger and hospital brandy. Fike, *Bottle Book*, 128–30; Wilson, *Bottles on the Western Frontier*, 33–35; McChristian, *Frontier Cavalry Trooper*, 328 (second quotation).

33. McConnell, *Five Years a Cavalryman*, 80 (first quotation); Axel Dahlgren, "Life of Soldiers On the Western Frontier," *National Tribune*, Oct. 7, 1920 (second quotation).

34. Ashburn, *History of the Medical Department*, 117–18 (first quotation); Grange, "Treating the Wounded at Fort Robinson," 286 (second quotation).

35. Private Henry Hubman to Herman (brother), Nov. 19, 1881, Hubman letters, James Mountain files (first quotation); James S. Hamilton questionnaire, f. 52, box 9, RP, DPL (second quotation).

36. John F. Farley, "Veteran of the Indian Wars," *National Tribune*, Mar. 19, 1936.

37. *Circular No. 3*, 160, 162.

38. Parker, *Personal Experiences*, 69; *Circular No. 3*, 148–49 (quotation).

39. William Murphy, "Forgotten Battalion," MS, f. 17, box 1, Chapman collection, AHC (quotation); Tenth Cavalry Returns, August 1876, RG 94, NARA.

40. Register of Deaths, vols. 4 and 5, RG 94, NARA, Identification tags or "dog tags" became a required uniform component for army personnel in 1906. Braddock, "Armed Forces Identification Tags," 112; Upton, *Fort Custer*, 92 (quotation).

41. Register of Deaths, vol. 5, RG 94, NARA; Twentieth Infantry Returns, September 1872, RG 94, NARA (quotation). Private William Foster, Twenty-Fourth Infantry, died in a similar accident at Fort Richardson, Texas, in 1869. Register of Deaths, vol. 4, RG 94, NARA.

42. Register of Deaths, vol. 11; Twelfth Infantry Returns, August 1880, RG 94, NARA; Medical History, Fort Laramie, Wyo. Terr., May 1881, RG 94, NARA.

43. *Circular. No. 3*, 23; Oliva, *Fort Larned*, 71; Potter, "'He . . . Regretted Having to Die That Way,'" 182; Register of Deaths, vol. 15, RG 94, NARA.

44. Potter, "'He . . . Regretted Having to Die That Way,'" 178 (quotation). Examining the record for the period 1867 to 1889, I found approximately 325 recorded deaths attributable to firearms accidents, though admittedly the record was not always clear as to the exact cause. Excluding combat deaths, those not defined as "homicide" or "murder" or otherwise indicated as intentional were considered accidental. No completely accurate statistics can be arrived at using this source because nearly all the volumes are lacking pages, sometimes numerous pages. Register of Deaths, RG 94, NARA.

45. McChristian, *Army of Marksmen*, 55.

46. McChristian, *Frontier Cavalry Trooper*, 290 (quotation); details of Van Moll's murder are found in Third Cavalry Returns, December 1877; Medical History, Fort Laramie, Wyo. Terr., December 1877, RG 94, NARA; and Register of Deaths, vols. 8 and 13, RG 94, NARA.

47. Register of Deaths, vol. 15, RG 94, NARA. I compiled a total of 216 suicides occurring from 1867 to 1889, but determining an accurate total is not possible because varying numbers of pages are missing from the volumes of the Register of Deaths.

48. McChristian, *Garrison Tangles*, 22 (quotation). Private Henry C. Beresford, Co. K, Sixteenth Infantry, a native of Warwick, England, enlisted in the U.S. Army at the age of thirty-four on June 25, 1884. He was a chemist by occupation. Register of Enlistments, RG 94, NARA.

49. Mulford, *Fighting Indians*, 36 (quotation). Because the regimental band was not part of the garrison at this post, Mulford correctly relates that the field musicians headed the column and provide the music for this ceremony. The rank of the deceased determined the number of men in the escort—sixteen for staff and line sergeants, twelve for corporals, and eight for privates. According to regulations, the order of march was: (1) music, (2) escort, (3) chaplain and surgeon, (4) the remains and six pallbearers, (5) mourners (if any), followed by the company of the deceased, (6) commissioned officers, according to rank, (7) all others. Upton, *Infantry Tactics*, 377. "In peace, the rule is: The regulations governing the Quartermaster's Department provide that coffins for deceased soldiers

should be made of plain stained pine or walnut, and should, when practicable, be made of material on hand at the post . . . when not practicable . . . plain coffins may be purchased, the cost . . . not to exceed $8." *ANJ*, Oct. 20, 1883, 227.

50. Corporal Emil Bode also provided a useful firsthand account of a funeral. Smith, *Dose of Frontier Soldiering*, 68–69 (quotation).

51. Williams, "Care of the Dead," 14.

52. Private Hartford G. Clark diary, May 28, 1891, f. 16, box 1, IWWP, JNEM.

53. The procedures relating to the disposition of a deceased soldier's effects, consolidated from those in the 1863 edition, are outlined in *Regulations of the Army, 1881*, 27–28. The discussion presented herein is also based on CO to AG, USA, Sept. 3, 1874, and First Lieutenant John F. Watson to AG, Mar. 2, 1874, Letter Book, Co. L, Seventh Cavalry, Baird collection. Several records of post councils of administration are found in Miscellaneous Documents, Fort Fetterman, Wyo. Terr., RG 393, NARA, (Lindmier microfilm roll no. 803–5).

54. Ashburn, *History of the Medical Department*, 135–39.

55. Medical History, Fort Laramie, Wyo. Terr., September 1887, RG 94, NARA.

56. Upton, *Fort Custer*, 80 (first quotation); Ashburn, *History of the Medical Department*, 118 (second quotation).

57. A more detailed discussion of the creation and function of the Hospital Corps, as well as ranks, uniforms, and equipage, is found in McChristian, *Uniforms, Arms, and Equipment*, 1:254–62.

58. Billings, *Circular No. 8*, viii; *ARSW*, 1893, 21. The death rate from disease had been even lower in 1889, only 3.95 per 1,000 men. A revealing compilation of medical statistics is found in *ARSW*, Report of the Surgeon General, 1890.

CHAPTER 9. "IT IS SO LONESOME OUT HERE"

1. Private Maurice Wolfe to Cousin Maurice, Oct. 14, 1867, Maurice Wolfe letters, FLNHS.

2. Forsyth, *Story of the Soldier*, 133–34 (first quotation); Cox, *Five Years in the United States Army*, 85 (second quotation); McChristian, *Frontier Cavalry Trooper*, 334 (third quotation).

3. Regulations held that only single men were to be enlisted in time of peace, but the rule did not apply during wartime, when the army needed to be expanded to meet the emergency. *Revised United States Army Regulations of 1861*, 130. The requirement that first-time enlistees had to be childless was modified in 1878 to apply only to fathers of minor children. *Regulations of the Army, 1881*, 80.

4. Boyd, *Cavalry Life*, 193–94 (first quotation); Upton, *Fort Custer*, 84 (second quotation).

5. Private Charles P. Christian to My Dearest Sister, June 26, 1878, B. William Henry collection (first quotation); Private Adelbert Butler to Mary (sister), April 2, 1878, Butler letters, GTC (second and third quotations).

6. *ANJ*, Mar. 4, 1871, 459.

7. William Brinkman, account of service, Nov. 17, 1920, HM65760, HL; De Trobriand, *Military Life in Dakota*, 317 (quotations).

8. Utley, *Life in Custer's Cavalry*, 164 (first quotation). Sergeant Edward Botzer was killed in action June 25, 1876. A human skull presumed to be Botzer's was discovered on the banks of the Little Bighorn River in 1989. Scott et al., *They Died with Custer*,

174–77. Horner represents an example of a soldier who married after the banning of company laundresses, so his wife was not eligible for appointment. Johnson, "Jacob Horner," 25–26; *ANJ*, Mar. 3, 1877, 483 (second quotation).

9. The Barrett affair is recorded in Acting Assistant Surgeon Thomas B. Maghee to Lt. Col. C. Grover, Dept. of the Platte, Sept. 12,1875, box 1, acc. 10, Maghee Papers, AHC.

10. Hospital Steward Seymour Kitching to My Darling, Jan. 26, 1877, Kitching Papers, Perkins Library, DU.

11. Hawkins, who enlisted as a twenty-seven–year-old native Virginian, may have been a Confederate veteran, a factor that also may have influenced Captain Hobart's decision. McChristian, *Frontier Cavalry Trooper*, 101–2, 101 n. 23.

12. GO No. 72, AGO, June 9, 1868. Examples of ration books listing laundresses show usually two, perhaps three, and rarely four per company. In some instances their husbands' names are also shown. Register of Ration Returns, 1868–71, Fort Laramie, Wyo. Terr., RG 393, NARA; and Memorandum & Account of Rations, 1876–77, Misc. Docs., Fort Fetterman, Wyo. Terr., RG 393, NARA (Lindmier microfilm roll no. 803–5). White's account is among the several mentioning two company laundresses. He additionally revealed that authorized laundresses often were assisted by other soldiers' wives. White, *Custer, Cavalry, and Crows*, 23 (quotation).

13. The unwritten glitch in this system did not allow for a new laundress replacing another within the current rationing period. The former laundress, having already drawn her ration, had no obligation to relinquish the goods, and the new woman occupying the same position was not authorized a ration until the beginning of the next ten-day period. *Revised United States Army Regulations of 1861*, 246.

14. The only indication that laundress quarters were officially sanctioned is a stipulation that laundresses on posts north of thirty-eight degrees latitude were allotted 225 square feet of space and those residing south of that line 256 square feet, making their rooms 15 and 16 feet square, respectively. Actual quarters, however, often did not adhere strictly to those dimensions. *Revised United States Army Regulations of 1861*, 160; McConnell, *Five Years a Cavalryman*, 211 (quotation).

15. The various sobriquets were noted in McChristian, *Frontier Cavalry Trooper*, 133; Forsyth, *Story of the Soldier*, 132–33; Greene, *Indian War Veterans*, 48; Mulford, *Fighting Indians*, 60; and Thomas B. Marquis, "Hardin Merchant Tells of Boyhood Incidents," n.d., n.p., Montana Scrapbook, BPL (first quotation); Medical History, Fort Laramie, Wyo. Terr., November 1868, RG 94, NARA (second quotation). Four years later the laundress quarters were listed as "three sets . . . being each 16 / 20. Slab side and shingle roof, boarded floor and adobe lined." Medical History, Fort Laramie, Wyo. Terr., August 1872, RG 94, NARA. An example of a post order assigning quarters for laundresses is *Orders No. 137*, Fort Union, New Mex. Terr., Oct. 22, 1870, Orders & Special Orders, Fort Union, New Mex., RG 393, NARA; White, "D. J. 'Kid' O'Malley," 62 (third quotation).

16. Lockwood, *Apaches and Longhorns*, 36.

17. McChristian, *Frontier Cavalry Trooper*, 133 (first quotation); Proceedings of Post Council of Administration, June 30, 1868, Misc. Docs., Fort Fetterman, Wyo. Terr., RG 393, NARA (Lindmier microfilm roll no. 803–5). Company laundresses also washed for bachelor officers and for those officers whose servants may not have been able to or desirous of doing the work. The monthly rates at one post were $3.00 for single officers; $6.00 for married officers and their families; and $1.25 per dozen pieces for transient officers. *GO No. 56*, Fort Laramie, Wyo. Terr., July 16, 1868, Fourth Infantry Order Book,

FLNHS; Trumpeter Charles P. Christian to Dear Sister, June 26, 1878, B. William Henry collection (second quotation). Interestingly, an 1879 plat of Fort Laramie indicates that the same set of quarters was being used for both a tailor and a laundress.

18. *ANJ*, Feb. 27, 1875; incident related by Second Lieutenant Richard T. Jacob, Sixth Infantry, in Cozzens, *Eyewitnesses to the Indian Wars*, 5:280–81. Appearing as "Thomas" Boch in the cited source, the soldier's first name has been corrected to "Henry." Adams, *Class and Race*, 99; Dobak and Phillips, *Black Regulars*, 177 (quotation).

19. McConnell, *Five Years a Cavalryman*, 139; Acting Assistant Surgeon Thomas B. Maghee to Post Adjutant, Camp Brown, Wyo. Terr., Sept. 17, 1875, box 1, acc. 10, Maghee Papers, AHC.

20. Mulford, *Fighting Indians*, 60 (first quotation). An example of an unmarried laundress that I noted referred to "Miss Lizzie Henry" being the authorized laundress for Company F, Third Cavalry. Major A. W. Evans to CO, Co. F, Third Cavalry, Nov. 13, 1877, LS, Fort Laramie, Wyo. Terr., RG 393, NARA; *ANJ*, Jan. 23, 1875, 538 (second quotation); *ANJ*, April 3, 1875: 459 (third quotation); McChristian, *Frontier Cavalry Trooper*, 259 (fourth quotation).

21. Forsyth, *Story of the Soldier*, 133 (quotation); Summerhayes, *Vanished Arizona*, 117.

22. John Vance Lauderdale journal, Dec. 18, 1870, Launderdale Papers, f. 136, box 4, BL, YU.

23. Barnard, *Ten Years with Custer*, 102 (quotation). Prior to 1872 the soles of army footwear were attached to the uppers by wood pegs, which often shrank and fell out in dry western climates. Attempting to improve shoes and boots, the Quartermaster Department adopted patented brass cable-screws, which were more durable but were found to conduct frost to the feet in winter. The army finally settled on soles sewn to the uppers with linen thread; thus the soldiers' system of grading of pies, worst to best. McChristian, *U.S. Army in the West*, 21, 74–75, 172–73; R. Eugene Pelham, "The Passing of the Frontiers," *National Tribune*, Dec. 12, 1918; *Circular*, Feb. 7, 1874, Fort Fetterman, W.T., Circulars, 1869–76, Fort Fetterman, Wyo. Terr., RG 393, NARA, (Lindmier microfilm roll no. 803–7).

24. *ANJ*, June 13, 1874, 697.

25. *ANJ*, Feb. 27, 1875, 379 (first quotation); *ANJ*, Aug. 12, 1871, 831 (second quotation); *Orders No. 1*, Jan. 5, 1874, Fourth Infantry Order Book, FLNHS (third quotation); *ANJ*, April 27, 1872, 594 (fourth quotation).

26. Such an instance occurred at Fort Laramie, prompting the commanding officer to restrict the appointment of laundresses to children no younger than age thirteen "and fairly equal to the task." *GO No. 63*, Fort Laramie, Wyo. Terr., Nov. 4, 1874. This woman, whose real name was Charlotte Crampton, even married a member of the company, who deserted to join his bride after arriving in California. Gustafson, *John Spring's Arizona*, 26, 30 (quotations).

27. *ANJ*, Aug. 12, 1871, 831 (first quotation); Annie Hessler to CO, Co. F, Fourth Infantry, May 5, 1874, LR, Fort Fetterman, Wyo. Terr., RG 393, NARA (Lindmier microfilm roll no. 803–13) (second quotation).

28. White, "D. J. 'Kid' O'Malley," 62; *Orders No. 2*, Co. G, May 16, 1868, Fourth Infantry Order Book, FLNHS.

29. By Marcy's calculation, laundresses were costing the army $100,000 per year. *ARSW*, 1875, 175 (first and second quotations). One commander used his authority to restrict each of his laundresses to no more than 155 pounds of baggage during a change

of station, warning: "Any greater amount will be thrown away." *GO No. 56*, Fort Laramie, July 16, 1868, Fourth Infantry Order Book, FLNHS; *ANJ*, Mar. 16, 1878, 507 (third quotation). A plea in favor of post laundries is found in *ANJ*, Feb. 19, 1875, 370.

30. The law was expressed to the army as *GO No. 37*, AGO, June 18, 1878. A case was that of Private Henry Boch and his wife, mentioned earlier. Although Boch had entered his second term of enlistment in 1875 and therefore would not have been eligible for a regular discharge for five years, his wife was known for her frequent associations with drunken enlisted men and was seen in the company of prostitutes in nearby North Platte, Nebraska. Boch himself was apparently a drunkard who had publicly referred to his wife as being a whore. The army found some excuse to give him an early discharge within just a few months after the order abolishing laundresses, thus ridding the service of the undesirable couple. Entry 850, p. 166, roll 38, Register of Enlistments, RG 94, NARA; *ANJ*, June 23, 1883, 1054 (quotation). By the late 1880s it was not unusual for married staff NCOs to be indulged with private quarters. At Fort Laramie, for example, senior noncoms were housed in a separate concrete building containing several apartments. The commanding officer at Fort Davis allowed his post commissary sergeant and post quartermaster sergeant to reside in excess two-story officers' quarters.

31. *ANJ*, Jan. 15, 1876, 454.

32. *Circular No. 1*, AGO, Jan. 3, 1879, published in *ANJ*, Feb. 1, 1879: 452; *ANJ*, April 29, 1882 (first quotation); Phelps, "From Texas to Dakota," 871 (second quotation).

33. *ANJ*, Jan. 8, 1881, 450 (first quotation); Nichols, *Men with Custer*, 73–74; McChristian, *Frontier Cavalry Trooper*, 341 (second quotation).

34. *ANJ*, Aug. 2, 1879, 957 (first quotation); *ANJ*, Sept. 6, 1879, 84 (second quotation); Thomas B. Marquis, "Hardin Merchant Tells of Boyhood Incidents," n.d., n.p., clipping in Montana Scrapbook, BPL; McChristian, *Fort Bowie*, 215–16; Schubert, *Voices of the Buffalo Soldier*, 154. Jacob J. Tomamichel, son of Hospital Steward John Tomamichel, also remembered a Chinese laundry operating in the Old Hospital building at Fort Laramie in the 1880s. Superintendent David L. Heib to park files, Oct. 5, 1950, FLNHS.

35. *ANJ*, Feb. 13, 1886, 583.

36. McConnell, *Five Years a Cavalryman*, 145 (first quotation), 119 (second quotation); Private Maurice H. Wolfe to Cousin Maurice, Oct. 14, 1867, Wolfe letters, FLNHS (third quotation); Thomas P. Downing folder, Seventh Cavalry File, LBBNM (fourth quotation); McChristian, *Frontier Cavalry Trooper*, 152–53 (fifth quotation). The reference is to the great nineteenth-century showman P. T. Barnum. A survey of veteran questionnaires, mostly by men who served in the late 1880s and early 1890s indicates that there was "not much religion among the soldiers." Sergeant Reinhold R. Geist questionnaire, f. 37, box 9, RP, DPL.

37. Jett, "Autobiography," MS, 17, 23, SC, UAL.

38. Stover, *Up from Handymen*, 69 (quotation). Beginning in 1869, the general of the army assigned chaplains to the various geographical divisions and subsequently to posts at the discretion of the division and department commanders, who also were delegated authority to transfer chaplains within their respective commands. *Regulations of the Army, 1881*, 31; *Revised United States Army Regulations of 1861*, 537.

39. Private James B. Wilkinson questionnaire, f. 43, box 10, RP, DPL (first quotation); Sergeant Perley S. Eaton questionnaire, f. 24, box 9, RP, DPL (second quotation).

40. Walker, "Reluctant Corporal" (pt. 1), 22 (first quotation); George Neihaus questionnaire, f. 93, box 9, RP, DPL (second quotation); *Circular*, April 19, 1878, Order Book, Co. K, Seventh Cavalry, LBBNM.

41. McChristian, *Fort Bowie*, 220; John Vance Lauderdale journal, Nov. 13, 1868, Launderdale Papers, f. 112, box 4, BL, YU (first quotation); Acting Assistant Surgeon Andrew T. Fitch to Dear Sister, Mar. 21, 1878, Fitch letters, f. 551, MS S-1638, BL, YU (copy at Fort Supply SHS) (second quotation).

42. A notice that Catholic mass would be held at Fort Whipple appeared in the *Prescott (Ariz.) Daily Miner*, June 22, 1878; QM Sergeant Maurice H. Wolfe to Cousin Maurice, Mar. 29, 1874, Wolfe letters, FLNHS (first quotation); Private Walter C. Harrington questionnaire, f. 78, box 10, RP, DPL (second quotation); Barnard, *Ten Years with Custer*, 258.

43. Green, *Dancing Was Lively*, 77–78 (quotation); Barnard, *Ten Years with Custer*, 258.

44. Schools for enlisted soldiers' children were supported by the post fund. *Revised United States Army Regulations of 1861*, 35. The special emphasis given to basic education in black regiments is elaborated in Fowler, *Black Infantry*, 92–98; *Regulations of the Army, 1881*, 312.

45. Adams, *Class and Race*, 139; Private Herman S. Searls to Dear Parents, Mar. 11, 1868, Herman S. Searls letters, WSA (quotation).

46. Report of Fort Fetterman Post School, 1873–74, Misc. Docs., Fort Fetterman, Wyo. Terr., RG 393, NARA (Lindmier microfilm roll no. 803–5); *ANJ*, Jan. 25, 1873, 373; Green, *Dancing Was Lively*, 82; Private Benjamin F. Brown to Mother, Aug. 1, 1875 (quotation), Find A Grave Memorial No 52568597, findagrave.com.

47. Foner, *United States Soldier*, 26.

48. *GO No. 24*, AGO, May 18, 1879 (quotation). Further discussion of this topic is found in Foner, *United States Soldier*, 26–28; *ANJ*, June 7, 1879, 791.

49. *ANJ*, May 14, 1881, 858 (quotation). Two men who attended the post school at Fort Laramie, Wyoming Territory, as children remembered some of the soldier-teachers treating the children rather roughly. Superintendent David L. Heib to park files, Oct. 5, 1950, FLNHS; *ANJ*, Sept. 23, 1882, *ANJ*, Sept. 23, 1882, 167.

50. Private Arthur McKnight to First Lieutenant George H. Cook, Adjutant, Fort Lyon, Colo., Dec. 9, 1878, f. 107, box 9, RP, DPL (first quotation); Sergeant James S. Hamilton, questionnaire, f. 52, box 9, RP, DPL (second quotation).

51. Green, *Dancing Was Lively*, 83 (first quotation); Samuel Harris questionnaire, f. 57, box 9, RP, DPL; Kinevan, *Frontier Cavalryman*, 144 (second quotation).

52. *ANJ*, Nov. 23, 1889, 235 (first quotation); *ANJ*, Nov. 19, 1881, 339; *ANJ*, Feb. 4, 1882, 597 (second quotation); Lockwood, "Intellectual Improvement," 749 (third quotation). The commanding officer at Fort Laramie reported that "a comfortable room has been fitted up . . . with desks, seats, and all needed appurtenances. Children only are under instruction. No attempt having been made to induce or compel enlisted men to attend." Maj. A. W. Evans to AG, USA, Nov. 30, 1878, LS, Fort Laramie, Wyo. Terr., RG 393, NARA.

53. *ANJ*, June 7, 1879: 791; Foner, *United States Soldier*, 144.

54. *Regulations of the Army, 1881*, 58; *ANJ*, Dec. 17, 1881, 435 (quotation).

55. *ANJ*, Jan. 30, 1886, 537; Reinhold R. Geist questionnaire, f. 37, box 9, RP, DPL (first quotation). The teachers at Fort Custer were Privates Joseph Henry and Frank J. Willis, First Cavalry. Upton, *Fort Custer*, 76 (second quotation); Private Hartford G.

Clark diary, Mar. 23, 1891, f. 16, box 1, IWWP, JNEM (third quotation). King apparently failed to make the grade, for he was discharged as a private. Private Richard F. King to Gabriella King (niece), Jan. 24, 1889, King letters, FUNM (fourth quotation).

56. Walker, "Reluctant Corporal" (pt. 1), 12 (first quotation), 13 (second quotation); Private Richard F. King, to Gabriella King (niece), Jan. 11, 1889, King letters, FUNM (third quotation).

57. *ANJ*, June 8, 1889, 841.

58. Private Howard A. Lyon to Annie, Aug. 21, 1889, Lyon letter, FLNHS.

59. Private Hartford G. Clark diary, June 22 and 26 and Aug. 27, 1891, f. 16, box 1, IWWP, JNEM.

CHAPTER 10. "WE HAVE OUR LITTLE AMUSEMENTS"

1. QM Sergeant Maurice H. Wolfe to Uncle Michael [n.d., late 1869], Wolfe letters, FLNHS.

2. *ANJ*, June 6, 1868, 666 (first quotation); McChristian, *Frontier Cavalry Trooper*, 30 (second quotation).

3. Acting Assistant Surgeon Andrew T. Fitch to Dear Father, Nov. 12, 1866, Fitch letters, BL, YU (copy filed at Fort Supply SHS).

4. Mail was carried on the Bozeman Trail by cavalry detachments. The trip from Fort Laramie to Fort Phil Kearny required four days, plus two more to reach Fort C. F. Smith on Bighorn River in Montana Territory. Templeton diary, Nov. 28, 1866, NL; *ANJ*, Mar. 6, 1880, 621 (first quotation); Greene, *Indian War Veterans*, 20 (second quotation).

5. Dinges, "New York Private," 69 (first quotation); *ANJ*, Nov. 9, 1867, 186 (second quotation).

6. James S. Hamilton questionnaire, f. 52, box 9, RP, DPL; Charles A. Brush questionnaire, f. 3, box 9, RP, DPL (quotation).

7. Browne, *Adventures in Apache Country*, 131–32; reprinted in *ANJ*, Feb. 27, 1869, 442–43 (quotation). In this context mescal was a strong, colorless liquor made by fermenting various varieties of agave plants found in the deserts of the southwestern United States and Mexico. The Apaches also commonly utilized the agave root (baked slowly in a pit oven for three days) as food. It allegedly had a "sweetish taste, not unlike the beet." Cremony, *Life among the Apaches*, 217.

8. Lockwood, *Apaches and Longhorns*, 19 (first quotation); *Winners of the West*, Oct. 30, 1930, 11 (second quotation).

9. Atypical of most commands, the Fort Sanders garrison required enlisted members to wear forage caps, dress coats, and "clean pantaloons" into town. Each man had to stand inspection by his first sergeant before leaving the post. *Orders No. 4*, Fort Sanders, Wyo. Terr., Sept. 11, 1873, Fourth Infantry Order Book, FLNHS.

10. McConnell, *Five Years a Cavalryman*, 163 (first quotation); Brackett, "Trip through the Rocky Mountains," 342 (second quotation); McChristian, *Frontier Cavalry Trooper*, 139 (third quotation).

11. QM Sergeant Maurice H. Wolfe to Cousin Maurice, April 12, 1868, Wolfe letters, FLNHS (quotations); *Circular No. 3*, 8–9.

12. Giddens, "Seven Letters," 306 (first quotation); Simpson Mann interview, f. 79, box 9, RP, DPL (second quotation); McConnell, *Five Years a Cavalryman*, 133 (third quotation); McChristian, *Frontier Cavalry Cavalryman*, 350 (fourth quotation).

13. Reynolds J. Burt Boyhood Data, box 2, RC, USAMHI (first quotation); Perley S. Eaton questionnaire, f. 24, box 9, RP, DPL (second quotation); Samuel Harris questionnaire, f. 57, box 9, RP, DPL; John Gibbert questionnaire, f. 42, box 9, RP, DPL (third quotation).

14. McConnell, *Five Years a Cavalryman*, 24 (first quotation); Utley, *Life in Custer's Cavalry*, 163 (second quotation); Hooker, *Child of the Fighting Tenth*, 198–99 (third quotation).

15. *ANJ*, July 17, 1886, 1048 (first quotation); McChristian, *Frontier Cavalry Trooper*, 357 (second quotation).

16. James Bothwell reminiscence, author's files (first quotation); John Vance Lauderdale journal, Mar. 18, 1869, Launderdale Papers, f. 136, box 4, BL, YU (second quotation); Custer, *Boots and Saddles*, 101 (third quotation); White, *Custer, Cavalry, and Crows*, 30 (fourth quotation).

17. McChristian, *Frontier Cavalry Trooper*, 103 (first quotation); Lauren Aldrich, "Brief Reminiscence," MS, HL (second quotation); John Vance Lauderdale journal, April 2, 1869, Launderdale Papers, f. 136, box 4, BL, YU (third quotation). George N. Christy (aka George Harrington) was a famous stage actor and singer during the 1860s, while Billy Birch was celebrated for his blackface performances during the California gold rush years (www.Wikipedia.com).

18. QM Sergeant Maurice H. Wolfe to Cousin Maurice, June 18, 1869, Wolfe letters, FLNHS (first quotation); Private George McAnulty to Lille Moore, McAnulty letters, FLNHS (second quotation); Private James O. Purvis in *Fort Custer News*, April 9, 1886, reprinted in Upton, *Fort Custer*, 75.

19. Handbill and Lawrence Lea service account, Erik Grant Lea file, f. 42, box 2, IWWP, JNEM; Private Hartford G. Clark diary, f. 16, box 1, IWWP, JNEM (quotations).

20. *Omaha Daily Bee*, Jan. 24, 1877 (first quotation); James S. Hamilton questionnaire, f. 52, box 9, RP, DPL (second quotation); Forsyth, *Story of the Soldier*, 133–34 (third quotation).

21. QM Sergeant Maurice H. Wolfe to Cousin Maurice, Jan. 8, 1873, Wolfe letters, FLNHS (first quotation); Mulford, *Fighting Indians*, 47 (second quotation); Private George McAnulty to Lillie Moore, Dec. 19, 1876, McAnulty letters, FLNHS (third quotation).

22. *ANJ*, April 11, 1874, 348 (quotation). Dress required for such occasions is documented in McChristian, *Frontier Cavalry Trooper*, 297.

23. Private Richard F. King to Gabriella King, Jan. 5, 1890, King letters, FUNM (all odd spellings in the original).

24. McChristian, *Frontier Cavalry Trooper*, 302 (first quotation); John Vance Lauderdale journal, f. 110, box 4, Lauderdale Papers, BL, YU (second quotation).

25. Corporal Maurice H. Wolfe to Cousin Maurice, Feb. 25, 1868, Wolfe letters, FLNHS.

26. McConnell, *Five Years a Cavalryman*, 145 (first quotation); Innis, "Fort Buford Diary of Pvt. Sanford," 365 (second quotation); Zimmer, *Frontier Soldier*, 22 (third quotation); Private Hartford G. Clark diary, Mar. 17, 1891, f. 16, box 1, IWWP, JNEM (fourth quotation); *ANJ*, April 4, 1874, 531 (fifth quotation).

27. *ANJ*, June 6, 1868, 662; quoted from the *Billings Gazette*, June 5, 1886, in Upton, *Fort Custer*, 94–95 (quotation).

28. *Revised United States Army Regulations of 1861*, 43; Dinges, "New York Private," 66 (first quotation); Mattison, "Diary of Surgeon Washington Matthews," 61 (second quotation); Utley, *Life in Custer's Cavalry*, 163 (third quotation).

29. GO No. 26, Fort Laramie, W.T., July 3, 1869, Fourth Infantry Order Book, FLNHS (first quotation). Reference to the gun crew being composed of "men that have been in the Service 'Arilery' [sic] before" is found in McChristian, *Frontier Cavalry Trooper*, 94. De Trobriand refers to Private Charles Rhey, Co. H, Thirty-First Infantry, who as a result of the accident had the lower portion of his right forearm amputated. De Trobriand, *Military Life in Dakota*, 308 (second quotation).

30. *Circular No. 3*, 176. See also ibid., 175–87, for other instances of men being wounded by the accidental discharge of artillery.

31. Smith, *Dose of Frontier Soldiering*, 87 (first quotation); *ANJ*, July 9, 1881, 1023; *ANJ*, July 15, 1882, 1160; *ANJ*, July 17, 1886, 1044 (second quotation).

32. Private Hartford G. Clark diary, June 13 and July 4, 1891, f. 16, box 1, IWWP, JNEM.

33. GO No. 71, Fort Laramie, W.T., Nov. 23, 1870, Fourth Infantry Order Book, FLNHS (first quotation); *ANJ*, Dec. 6, 1884, 363 (second quotation).

34. Zimmer, *Frontier Soldier*, 154 (first quotation); McChristian, *Frontier Cavalry Trooper*, 285 (second quotation).

35. Innis, "Fort Buford Diary of Pvt. Sanford," 348.

36. Wagner, *Old Neutriment*, 111 (first quotation); Private Robert Greenhalgh to Father & Mother, Jan. 2, 1867, Greenhalgh letters, RP, DPL (second quotation); Mattison, "Diary of Surgeon Washington Matthews," 29 (third quotation).

37. Hill and Innis, "Fort Buford Diary of Private Sanford," 32.

38. Private Charles W. Hayden diary, Dec. 25, 1891, LBBNM.

39. Templeton diary, Dec. 25, 1867, NL (first quotation). The vegetables mentioned here were probably of the desiccated kind or perhaps canned goods that had been reserved for the occasion. McChristian, *Frontier Cavalry Trooper*, 124; Roe, *Army Letters*, 26–27 (second quotation).

40. *ANJ*, Jan. 9, 1886, 471 (first quotation); *ANJ*, Jan. 10, 1885, 465 (second quotation).

41. Moore, *Dakota Cowboy Soldier*, 10 (first quotation); Yohn, "Regulars in Arizona," 123 (second quotation); Buecker, "Letters from a Post Surgeon's Wife, 57 (third quotation); Greene, *Indian War Veterans*, 78–79. This and other accounts of Christmas observances, primarily by officers' families, are found in Cox-Paul and Wengert, *Frontier Army Christmas*.

42. Private Charles N. Hayden diary, Dec. 24, 1891, LBBNM; Private Hartford G. Clark diary, Dec. 25, 1891, f. 16, box 1, IWWP, JNEM (quotation).

43. Hooker, *Child of the Fighting Tenth*, 197; *ANR*, April 28, 1883, 3. I found only a few references to football being played by soldiers, and those dated to the 1890s.

44. Reynolds Burt Boyhood Data, box 2, RC, USAMHI.

45. Private James B. Wilkinson questionnaire, f. 43, box 10, RP, DPL (first quotation); Lauren Aldrich, "Brief Reminiscences," HL (second quotation).

46. Grandison Mayo questionnaire, f. 45, box 9, RP, DPL.

47. Cox, *Five Years in the United States Army*, 74 (first quotation); Giddens, "Seven Letters," 311 (second quotation).

48. Barnard, *Ten Years with Custer*, 104 (first quotation); Greene, *Indian War Veterans*, 34 (second quotation).

49. McChristian, *Frontier Cavalry Trooper*, 170 (first quotation); Private Henry Hubman to Father, Sept. 28, 1881, Hubman letters, James Mountain files (second quotation). For Sheridan's views concerning the extermination of the buffalo herds, see Hutton, *Phil Sheridan*, 246, 416 n. 4.

50. McChristian, *Uniforms, Arms, and Equipment*, 2:209.

51. *ANJ*, Jan. 9, 1886, 472; McChristian, *Garrison Tangles*, 43, 78 n. 38 (first quotation); Private Hartford G. Clark diary, April 11, 1891, f. 16, box 1, IWWP, JNEM (second quotation).

52. Martin Andersen questionnaire, f. 59, box 8, RP, DPL (first quotation); Medical History, Fort Laramie, W.T., August 1868, RG 94, NARA (second quotation).

53. *ANJ*, Aug. 1, 1874, 810 (first quotation); McChristian, *Frontier Cavalry Trooper*, 209 (second quotation); Zimmer, *Frontier Soldier*, 157; Smith, *Dose of Frontier Soldiering*, 64 (third quotation).

54. Greene, *Indian War Veterans*, 20 (quotation); Moore, *Dakota Cowboy Soldier*, 15.

55. Private Hartford G. Clark diary, April 5, 1891, f. 16, box 1, IWWP, JNEM.

56. Smith, *Dose of Frontier Soldiering*, 127; McChristian, *Frontier Cavalry Trooper*, 359, 322 (quotation); Reginald Bradley interview, f. 76, box 8, RP, DPL; Private Hartford G. Clark diary, Mar. 16, 1891, f. 16, box 1, IWWP, JNEM.

57. McConnell, *Five Years a Cavalryman*, 60, 173–74. References to these newspapers are found in *ANJ*, Oct. 25, 1873, 164, and June 30, 1883, 1076.

58. McChristian, *Frontier Cavalry Trooper*, 239. Private Wilmot P. Sanford, in addition to practicing photography, was another entrepreneur who bought and sold watches, rings, and razors to his comrades. See various entries in Innis, "Fort Buford Diary of Pvt. Sanford." Private Hartford G. Clark diary, Mar. 1, 1891, f. 16, box 1, IWWP, JNEM (quotation). Following his discharge in 1892, Bloom established a photographic studio in nearby Valentine, Nebraska. Mautz, *Biographies of Western Photographers*, 295.

59. *ANJ*, Dec. 24, 1870, 298 (first and second quotations); *ANJ*, April 8, 1871, 539 (third quotation); White, *Custer, Cavalry, and Crows*, 29; *ANJ*, Sept. 24, 1879, 90 (fourth quotation).

60. This social club and others at the post are listed in an order for candles in Orders for Subsistence Stores, Fort Fetterman, W.T., RG 393, NARA, (Lindmier microfilm roll no. 803–4; Greene, *Indian War Veterans*, 77 (quotation).

61. Mattison, "Diary of Surgeon Washington Matthews," 28 (quotation); Upton, *Fort Custer*, 78.

62. John O. Stotts reminiscence, Spencer collection (first quotation); Barnard, *Ten Years with Custer*, 126 (second quotation); Smith, *Dose of Frontier Soldiering*, 64, 83–84 (third quotation); Hill and Innis, "Fort Buford Diary of Private Sanford," 12–13; White, *Custer, Cavalry, and Crows*, 27 (fourth quotation).

63. McConnell, *Five Years a Cavalryman*, 132 (first quotation); Gustafson, *John Spring's Arizona*, 50 (second quotation).

64. *Winners of the West*, Oct. 30, 1930, 11 (first quotation); Schubert, *Voices of the Buffalo Soldier*, 157; Hill and Innis, "Fort Buford Diary of Private Sanford," 14; Hynes, *Soldiers of the Frontier*, 155–56 (second and third quotations); Private Arthur S. Wallace diary, FLNHS.

65. Barnard, *Ten Years with Custer*, 104 (first quotation); Edgar Hoffner, "Journal of the Sheep Eater Campaign," Aug. 7, 1879, MS, Brown Papers, UCB (second quotation).

66. *ANJ*, Feb. 8, 1873, 403.

67. McConnell, *Five Years a Cavalryman*, 200.

68. *Winners of the West*, Oct. 30, 1930.

69. *Orders No. 19*, Fort Omaha, Nebraska, Nov. 20, 1882, Fourth Infantry Order Book, FLNHS; *ANJ*, Dec. 14, 1872, 278 (quotation); *GO No. 5*, Fort Fetterman, W.T., Jan. 17, 1870, General Orders 1868–82, Fort Fetterman, W.T., RG 393, NARA, (Lindmier microfilm roll no. 803–7); See also *GO No. 51*, Fort Laramie, W.T., June 30, 1868, and *GO No. 52*, Fort Laramie, W.T., July 2, 1868, Fourth Infantry Order Book, FLNHS.

70. Rodenbough, *Sabre and Bayonet*, 360–61; Private Hartford G. Clark diary, Sept. 23, 1891, f. 16, box 1, IWWP, JNEM (first quotation); Hynes, *Soldiers of the Frontier*, 156 (second and third quotations).

71. The rules governing furloughs are set out in *Regulations of the Army, 1881*, 26–27 (first quotation); Alexander Hatcher questionnaire, f. 58, box 9, RP, DPL; James S. Hamilton questionnaire, f. 52, box 9, RP, DPL (second quotation).

72. In 1874 it became possible for a soldier to travel beyond the United States by consent of the secretary of war. In one of these rare instances, Corporal Richard M. Whelan, Co. G, Fourth, Infantry was granted permission to travel "beyond the sea" (probably to his native Ireland), effective May 15, 1881. However, his four-month furlough was granted on the condition that he reenlist upon the expiration of his third enlistment in November 1880. *SO No. 111*, Dept. of the Platte, Nov. 22, 1880, Fourth Infantry Order Book, FLNHS.

73. Private John George Brown service account, UIWV, box 1, RC, USAMHI.

74. McChristian, *Frontier Cavalry Trooper*, 216.

CHAPTER 11. "THE MORAL CONDITION IS VERY POOR"

1. *ANJ*, Oct. 2, 1869, 98. Paydays were to be on the last day of every other month beginning with February. *Revised United States Army Regulations of 1861*, 49; *ANJ*, Oct. 2, 1869, 791 (first quotation); McChristian, *Frontier Cavalry Trooper*, 62 (second quotation).

2. Smith, *Dose of Frontier Soldiering*, 19, 62.

3. Schubert, *Voices of the Buffalo Soldier*, 154 (first quotation). Wagering items of government property could place a soldier in official jeopardy. See McConnell, *Five Years a Cavalryman*, 157–58; Smith, *Dose of Frontier Soldiering*, 62 (second quotation).

4. Reginald A. Bradley interview, Jan. 10, 1968, RC, USAMHI (first quotation); Jett, "Autobiography," MS, SC, UAL (second quotation); White, *Custer, Cavalry, and Crows*, 28 (third quotation).

5. McConnell, *Five Years a Cavalryman*, 157 (first quotation). A Fourth Infantryman's son who had lived at Fort Laramie, Wyoming Territory, in the 1880s attested that "if you went into the saloon you had to stand up, there wasn't no place like there is now to sit down and drink." Johnny O'Brian interview, vertical files, library, FLNHS; Cozzens, *Eyewitnesses to the Indian Wars*, 1:337–38 (second quotation).

6. Giddens, "Seven Letters," 309 (first quotation) Schubert, *Voices of the Buffalo Soldier*, 85 (second quotation).

7. *Omaha Daily Bee*, Jan. 24, 1877.

8. Smith, *Dose of Frontier Soldiering*, 18 (first quotation); Walker, "Reluctant Corporal" (pt. 1), 21 (second quotation); Simpson Mann interview, f. 79, box 9, RP, DPL.

9. McConnell, *Five Years a Cavalryman*, 105; Smith, *Dose of Frontier Soldiering*, 18; *Circular No. 34*, Fort Laramie, Wyo. Terr., Dec. 4, 1870, Fourth Infantry Order Book, FLNHS; *ANJ*, Nov. 9, 1872, 198.

10. For example, the post commander at Fort Fetterman called attention to the "unusual amount of drunkenness" on duty among the men of Co. G, Fourth Infantry. However, he took no action to stop it, beyond threatening future offenders with court martial. *Orders No. 15*, Fort Fetterman, Wyo. Terr., Mar. 11, 1882, Fourth Infantry Order Book, FLNHS; Barnard, *Ten Years with Custer*, 256 (quotation).

11. Utley, *Life in Custer's Cavalry*, 207.

12. Smith, *Dose of Frontier Soldiering*, 133; *Greene, Indian War Veterans*, 180 (quotation).

13. Giddens, "Seven Letters," 306 (first quotation), 309; Private John D. Laird to Nathaniel Laird, Oct. 4, 1867, File 3910-C-AGO 1871, LR, Enlisted Branch, AGO, RG 94, NARA (second quotation).

14. A succinct discussion outlining the development of bottled beer is found in Wilson, *Bottles on the Western Frontier*, 1–2. See also Johnny O'Brian interview, FLNHS.

15. Opiates were in common use for medicinal purposes, as reflected in First Lieutenant John Bigelow's journal comment that another officer's wife was not able to nurse her newborn baby: "The opium, too, that she had been taking to relieve her is bad for the child." McChristian, *Garrison Tangles*, 50; Register of Deaths, AGO, RG 94, NARA; Bradley journal, Nov. 22, 1867, Luther P. Bradley Papers, USAMHI (quotation). My conclusion is based on the virtual absence of drug abuse being mentioned in the approximately 350 personal accounts used for this study.

16. Harvey J. Ciscel questionnaire, f. 9, box 9, RP, DPL (first quotation); Private Henry Hubman to Brother Herman, Oct. 1, 1881, Hubman letters, James Mountain files (second quotation).

17. Hill and Innis, "Fort Buford Diary of Private Sanford," 6. Bradley deserted in September 1876 on the Yellowstone River and made his way, probably aboard a steamer, to Fort Benton, Montana Territory, where he was apprehended a month later. He was tried and discharged the next year. Sixth Infantry Returns, August 1875 and September 1876, RG 94, NARA; Register of Enlistments, RG 94, NARA.

18. Barnard, *Ten Years with Custer*, 102 (quotation). Ryan's account rings true because the Fifth Infantry was stationed in New Mexico Territory from late 1860 until 1866, when it transferred to posts in western Kansas. Elements of the Fifth Infantry and the Seventh Cavalry jointly occupied Fort Hays from late 1869 until 1871. Ryan's company was stationed there for part of that time, which further validates his story. Rodenbough, *Army of the United States*, 472–73; Post Returns, Fort Hays, Kansas, 1869–71, RG 94, NARA. For other versions of the incident, see *Police Gazette*, Feb. 15, 1879; Private John Burkman's account in Wagner, *Old Neutriment*, 112–16, Elizabeth Custer's lengthy but naive recollection in *Boots and Saddles*, 197–202; and Stanislas Roy to Walter M. Camp, April 10, 1912, f. 21, box 1, Camp Papers, BYU. Roy, a former Seventh Cavalryman, seems to have relied more heavily on Mrs. Custer's account than on his own memory of the affair; Mrs. Noonan may have been a hermaphrodite, as discussed in Whitley, "Mysterious Mrs. Nash."

19. *ANJ*, Nov. 9, 1878, 284.

20. The term "homosexual" was not added to the vocabulary until 1895, while "faggot" and "gay" did not appear until the twentieth century. "Sodomy" and "buggery" were the most commonly used terms during the mid-nineteenth century. In attempting to arrive at a number of Civil War soldiers who might have been homosexual, Dr. Lowry used a conservative figure of 1 percent for the rate of homosexuality naturally occurring among the general populace. Applying that to the postwar regular army, there may have

been as many as two thousand or so homosexuals in the service between 1866 and 1891. Lowry, *Story the Soldiers Wouldn't Tell*, 109–14 (quotation).

21. Charles Johnson questionnaire, f. 67, box 9, RP, DPL (first quotation); *Omaha Daily Bee*, May 20, 1881 (second quotation).

22. Robinson, *Diaries of John Gregory Bourke*, 249 (first quotation). "Many prostitutes discovered that the regular use of opiates caused disruption or total cessation of menses, and it is possible that they used these drugs as a form of birth control." Steele, *Bleed, Blister, and Purge*, 93; Greene, *Indian War Veterans*, 47 (second quotation); Thomas E. Gutch questionnaire, f. 50, box 9, DP, RPL (third quotation).

23. Hynes, *Soldiers of the Frontier*, 85.

24. Oliva, *Fort Union*, 346.

25. Captain Gustavus C. Doane to Mary Doane, Jan. 11, 1886 (first quotation), Doane to Mary, July 12, 1886, ibid. (second quotation), Doane Papers, MSU.

26. Captain. Otho E. Michaelis to AG, Dept. of Dakota, April 15, 1878, LR, Dept. of Dakota, RG 393, NARA (first quotation); Forsyth, *Story of the Soldier*, 142 (second quotation).

27. Werner, *On the Western Frontier*, 82–83 (first quotation); McChristian, *Frontier Cavalry Trooper*, 109 (second quotation); Medical History, Fort Laramie, Wyo. Terr., Dec. 1874, Fort Laramie, Wyo. Terr., RG 94, NARA.

28. Green, *The Dancing Was Lively*, 62 (first quotation); Private Arthur S. Wallace diary, July 18, 1881, FLNHS (second quotation).

29. R. Eugene Pelham, "Passing of the Frontiers," *National Tribune*, Dec. 12, 1918 (first quotation); Steele, *Bleed, Blister, and Purge*, 91; Giddens, "Seven Letters," 307–8 (second quotation).

30. Cozzens, *Eyewitnesses to the Indian Wars*, 1:332 (first quotation); Private Walter C. Harrington questionnaire, f. 78, box 10, RP, DPL (second quotation).

31. Green, *The Dancing Was Lively*, 63.

32. Ashburn, *History of the Medical Department*, 112 (quotation). Some 73,382 cases of syphilis and 95,833 cases of gonorrhea were treated during the war. Ibid., 431.

33. In 1885 the highest rate of venereal disease per capita was in the Department of the East, with a ratio of 119 cases per 1,000 men. The Department of the Columbia (Pacific Northwest) had the lowest rate at 47.5 per 1,000. Other western departments reported similar figures: the Departments of Arizona and the Platte tied at 55.6 each, Department of the Missouri 69.4, Department of Dakota 77.7, and Departments of Texas and California 79.4 and 79.6, respectively. The rates for white troops was somewhat lower than those for black troops. *ARSW*, 1885, 721, 738 (tables on 752–57).

34. Examples of such complaints are found in Medical History, Fort Laramie, Wyo. Terr., June 1881 and Feb. 1882, RG 94, NARA. See also the Annual Report of the Surgeon General in *ARSW*, 1888, 693. As late as 1891 the Medical Department reported that the rate of venereal disease at Columbus Barracks, Ohio was 333.88 per 1,000 recruits. *ARSW*, 1888, 152. External therapies for the treatment of syphilis continued to be the only ones available until the introduction of penicillin in the late 1930s. Steele, *Bleed, Blister, and Purge*, 229–30.

35. James B. Wilkinson questionnaire, f. 43, box 10, RP, DPL (first quotation); Barnard, *Ten Years with Custer*, 118–19 (second quotation).

36. Private James B. Wilkinson questionnaire, f. 43, box 10, RP, DPL; Private Hartford G. Clark diary, June 8, 1891, f. 16, box 1, IWWP, JNEM (quotation); Private Eddie

Waller interview, box 1, RC, USAMHI; *GCMO No. 3*, Jan. 15, 1886, RG 153, NARA, in Andrew Davis folder, author's files.

37. *GCMO No. 79*, Dept. of the Platte, Dec. 6, 1883, Fourth Infantry Order Book, FLNHS; *ANJ*, Nov. 8, 1884: 283; Private Herman S. Searl to Dear Parents, June 21, 1868, Herman S. Searl letters, WSA (quotations). It is interesting to note that the entry in the regimental return for Brown's death reads: "Killed—June 14, 1868—En route from Camp near Wyoming, D.T. to Fort Sanders, D.T. by soldiers unknown." Returns, Eighteenth Infantry, June 1868, Returns from Regular Army Infantry Regiments, RG 94, NARA.

38. Private George McAnulty to Lillie Moore, July 26, 1878, McAnulty letters, FLNHS (quotation). Register of Deaths, RG 94, NARA; Entry 20, p. 300, roll 42, Register of Enlistments, RG 94, NARA.

39. Private Hartford G. Clark diary, Oct. 1, 1891, f. 16, box 1, IWWP, JNEM.

40. McChristian, *Fort Laramie*, 297.

41. *ANJ*, Jan. 9, 1886, 472.

42. *Benton Weekly Record*, April 13, 1882 reprinted in *ANJ*, May 6, 1882, 909.

43. Private John G. Brown to Viola Ransom Wood, Oct. 8, 1934, box 1, RC, USAMHI.

44. Schubert, *Voices of the Buffalo Soldier*, 117–18.

45. Ibid., 117–22. Schubert presents full copies of the documents relating to the Fort Concho incident.

46. McChristian, "Shot Like a Dog."

47. Military law made no distinction between misdemeanors and felonies or degrees of offenses. All infractions were considered equally as crimes. Courts-martial were empowered to hear capital cases only in time of declared war; otherwise the appropriate civil courts held jurisdiction. Winthrop, *Military Law*, 1:4, 59, 111, 132, 134. See also Articles 58 and 59, *Regulations of the Army, 1881*, 339.

48. If a particularly harsh sentence called for a soldier to be in solitary confinement or on limited diet for longer than two weeks, he had to be granted an equally long break between those stints, with a maximum of eighty-four days in a one year period. Noncoms of the general staff could not be reduced in rank, only discharged. *Revised United States Army Regulations of 1861*, 126; Dinges, "New York Private," 65 (quotation).

49. *ANJ*, May 9, 1868, 602.

50. *ANJ*, June 26, 1886, 989.

51. John Vance Lauderdale journal, Dec. 10, 1868, Lauderdale Papers, f. 136, box 4, BL, YU (first quotation); Medical History, Fort Laramie, Wyo. Terr., December 1874, RG 94, NARA (second quotation).

52. Oliva, *Fort Union*, 641; McChristian, *Frontier Cavalry Trooper*, 237 (quotation); Walton, *Sentinel of the Plains*, 175. "The guardhouse at some military post may be designated [by the court], the chief of which is situated at Alcatraz island [sic], California, in which are confined most of the deserters from organizations stationed west of the Rocky mountains [sic]." Pope, "Desertion and the Military Prison," 116. The army did not officially designate Alcatraz Island a military prison until 1907 and in 1934 converted it to a civilian high-security prison. Frazer, *Forts of the West*, 19.

53. Congress initially authorized the U.S. Military Prison to be established at Rock Island, Illinois, in 1873, but the act was amended the following year to construct it at Fort Leavenworth, Kansas. S. Doc. No. 44, 45th Cong., 3rd Sess. at 7–8 (1879); McChris-

tian, *Uniforms, Arms, and Equipment*, 1:192–93; Forbes, "United States Army," 130–31 (quotation).

54. Three forms of punishment employed at least as early as the Mexican War were standing on a barrel, bucking-and-gagging, and riding a wooden horse. Ballentine, *Autobiography of an English Soldier*, 332–33; James Foley, "Fourth Cavalry," *National Tribune*, June 5, 1915 (first quotation); Thomas N. Way journal, July 20, 1873, Greene files (second quotation).

55. Barnard, *Ten Years with Custer*, 101.

56. Perley S. Eaton questionnaire, f. 30, box 9, RP, DPL (first quotation). The old term "spread eagle" may have derived from the national coat of arms insignia used by the army on everything from buttons to regimental flags. Murphy, "Forgotten Battalion," MS, f. 17, box 1, Chapman Collection, AHC (second quotation); Private John O. Stotts reminiscence, Spencer collection (third quotation).

57. Jett, "Autobiography," MS, SC, UAL.

58. Brigadier General C. C. Augur, commanding the Department of Texas, was clearly incensed with Wirt's actions. *ANJ*, June 26, 1873, 796 (quotations).

59. SO No. 163, Dept. of the Platte, Aug. 25, 1869, Fourth Infantry Order Book, FLNHS.

60. Private John C. Ford interview, box 1, RC, USAMHI; Private Charles N. Hayden diary, Sept. 3, 1891, LBBNM.

61. *Orders No. 19*, Fort Totten, D.T., April 23, 1881, Order Book, Company K, Seventh Cavalry, LBBNM; McChristian, *Garrison Tangles*, 55.

62. GCMO No. 5, Dept. of the Platte, Jan. 30, 1875, Fourth Infantry Order Book, FLNHS (first quotation); Smith, *Dose of Frontier Soldiering*, 20 (second quotation). In some instances the provost sergeant was a duty sergeant (sometimes a corporal) who had served the previous day as a noncom of the post guard, Usually, however, he was not a member of the guard and was detailed to the job for a specified period, reporting to the post quartermaster, or sometimes to the adjutant, for daily instructions. In either case, he was responsible for general cleanliness of the post. Under the general direction of the officer of the day, he supervised prisoner work details according to the jobs outlined by the quartermaster and, when needed, commanded details of guard on those occasions when law enforcement might be required off-post. Barnard, *Ten Years with Custer*, 116; Werner, *On the Western Frontier*, 83.

63. McChristian, *Frontier Cavalry Trooper*, 136.

64. *Circular*, Fort Laramie, W.T., Oct. 8, 1868, Fourth Infantry Order Book, FLNHS (first quotation); Zimmer, *Frontier Soldier*, 149 (second quotation).

65. GO No. 61, Dept. of the Platte, Oct. 21, 1869, Fourth Infantry Order Book, FLNHS. One soldier claimed that the punishment logs at his post weighed fifty to seventy-five pounds, but that was probably an exaggeration to impress the home folks. Virtually every other account consulted referred to logs weighing about twenty-five pounds. McChristian, *Frontier Cavalry Trooper*, 54; Cox, *Five Years in the United States Army*, 83–84 (quotations).

66. *ANJ*, Aug. 24, 1867: 330 (first quotation); FitzGerald, *Army Doctor's Wife*, 221 (second quotation). An example of such an order is *Circular No. 1*, Fort Laramie, Wyo. Terr., Nov. 1, 1868, Fourth Infantry Order Book, FLNHS.

67. First Sergeant Frederick Stortz to Father, March 12, 1877, Stortz letters, BHNB (first quotation); QM Sergeant Maurice H. Wolfe to Brother Batt, Dec. 5, 1868, Wolfe letters, FLNHS (second quotation); George Neihaus, f. 93, box 9, RP, DPL (third quotation).

68. *ANJ*, April 2, 1881: 721 (first quotation); *ANJ*, Mar. 5, 1881: 637 (second quotation); Forsyth, *Story of the Soldier*, 140–41 (third quotation).
69. *ANJ*, May 19, 1883: 957 (first quotation); Private Richard F. Watson questionnaire, f. 37, box 10, RP, DPL (second quotation).
70. *ANJ*, April 29, 1876, 614.
71. *ANJ*, Feb. 4, 1882, 593.
72. Ibid.; Rodenbough, *Army of the United States*, 678; Foner, *United States Soldier*, 92; *ANJ*, Dec. 12, 1885: 391 (quotation).
73. *ANJ*, Dec. 22, 1888, 321.
74. *ANJ*, Aug. 10, 1889, 1029.
75. *GO No. 75*, AGO, Sept. 27, 1889 (quotations); *ANJ*, Oct. 12, 1889, 121; Delo, *Peddlers and Post Traders*, 201.
76. *ANJ*, May 24, 1890, 737 (quotation). Each post canteen was supervised by a trustworthy commissioned officer who maintained the accounts and regularly apportioned the proceeds among the companies of the garrison. Foner, *United States Soldier*, 93.
77. Major Henry E. Noyes to AAG, Dept. of Arizona, Jan. 6, 1890, LS, Fort Bowie, A.T., RG 393, NARA.
78. *ANJ*, May 17, 1890, 717.
79. *ANJ*, May 24, 1890, 737.
80. Foner, *United States Soldier*, 110.
81. *ANJ*, Nov. 5, 1892, 178.
82. Ibid., 177–78.

CHAPTER 12. "THERE ARE A GREAT MANY
DESERTING FROM OUR REGIMENT"

1. Coffman, *Old Army*, 17–24. The treatment of deserters during the Mexican-American War is discussed in Ballentine, *Autobiography of An English Soldier*, 31. Some 205 deserters were executed during the War of 1812 and a number of were hanged during the Mexican-American War. According to McDermott, hardly a week passed during the dark days of the Civil War, 1863–64, without at least one deserter being executed. McDermott, "Were They Really Rogues?" 165.
2. Gustafson, *John Spring's Arizona*, 58–59 (first quotation); *ANJ*, July 28, 1883, 1164 (second quotation).
3. Major William B. Royall to AG, USA, Papers Relating to the Army Equipment Board, 1878–79, LR, AGO (Main), 1871–80, RG 94, M666, roll no. 436, NARA (first quotation); Romeyn, "Desertion," 675 (second quotation).
4. *ANJ*, Aug. 14, 1871, 871 (first quotation); *ANJ*, Oct. 8, 1870, 122 (second quotation).
5. Louis Ebert questionnaire, f. 25, box 9, RP, DPL (first quotation); Romeyn, "Desertion," 677 (second quotation); *ANJ*, July 26, 1879, 934; *ANJ*, June 21, 1879, 832.
6. Utley, *Life in Custer's Cavalry*, 51, 53 (quotation), 161. Out of an authorized strength of 35,000 men, the army lost nearly 22,000 by desertion during the years 1867–68. Foner, *United States Soldier*, 223; *ANJ*, Nov. 27, 1875, 284.
7. *ARSW*, 1871, 44–45.
8. Templeton diary, Nov. 8, 1866, NL; Godfrey, "Some Reminiscences Including an Account of General Sully's Expedition," 417 (first quotation). A compilation of desertion rates and numbers, compared with aggregate strength of the army, is found in Foner,

United States Soldier, 223; Utley, *Life in Custer's Cavalry*, 44 (second quotation); Windolph, *I Fought with Custer*, 42 (third quotation); *ARSW*, 1874, 96.

9. Closson, "Morning Reports," 189 (first quotation); Barnard, *Ten Years with Custer*, 118 (second quotation); *ANJ*, April 11, 1868, 539 (third quotation).

10. Private Robert Greenhalgh to Father and Mother, July 9, 1865, Greenhalgh letters, RP, DPL (first quotation); *ANJ*, May 1, 1869, 582 (second quotation). McChristian, *Frontier Cavalry Trooper*, 252 (third quotation). Matthews was serving as company clerk and had access to all the returns, so his claim is credible.

11. *ANJ*, April 22, 1871: 570; Private Henry Hubman to Herman (brother), Dec. 27, 1881, Hubman letters, James Mountain files (quotation).

12. Greene, *Indian War Veterans*, 20 (first quotation); "Annual Return of Alterations and Casualties," 1872, Eighth Cavalry Returns, Returns from Regular Army Cavalry Regiments, M744, NARA; *ARSW*, 1871, 110–11 (second quotation).

13. Carter, *On the Border with Mackenzie*, 221.

14. *ANJ*, Aug. 27, 1870, 26.

15. Romeyn, "Desertion," 674; Merritt, "Some Defects," 557 (quotation).

16. *ARSW*, 1874, 95 (quotation). Another authority affirmed that repeaters credited with five to ten fraudulent enlistments were not uncommon and alleged that one man enlisted no less than nineteen times. Pope, "Desertion and the Military Prison," 115. Accordingly, the various published tabulations of desertions may be accurate so far as the numbers of *instances* reported, but the totals are misleading with regard to the numbers of *individuals*, because a great number of repeaters are duplicated. First Lieutenant Frank M. Gibson to CO, Brooklyn Barracks, N.Y., Dec 3, 1873, Seventh Cavalry Letter Book, Baird collection; Entry 31, p. 85, roll 43, Register of Enlistments, RG 94, NARA.

17. De Trobriand, *Military Life in Dakota*, 306 (first quotation); *ANJ*, Sept. 6, 1884, 107 (second quotation).

18. Private James C. Blackwood to Mother, Jan. 18, 1880, copy in author's files (first quotation); Private Henry Hubman to Herman (brother), Mar. 20, 1882, Hubman letters, James Mountain files (second quotation).

19. McChristian, *Frontier Cavalry Trooper*, 140 (quotation); Private Samuel L. Meddaugh diary, June 20, 1876, MS 570, Brown Papers, ML, UU.

20. "Memorandum of Edward Williams," typescript, library, LBBNM.

21. McConnell, *Five Years a Cavalryman*, 55, 205.

22. Mulford, *Fighting Indians*, 56 (quotation); Private Henry Hubman to Father, Mar. 1, 1882, Hubman letters, James Mountain files.

23. Adams, "Journal of Ada A. Vogdes," 10 (first quotation); Zimmer, *Frontier Soldier*, 86–87 (second quotation); Private Henry Hubman to Herman (brother), June 2, 1882, and Dec. 27, 1881, Hubman letters, James Mountain files (third quotation).

24. Dinges, "New York Private," 61–62 (first quotation); *ANJ*, June 26, 1886, 989 (second quotation). Other references to deserters crossing the borders are found in James B. Wilkinson questionnaire, f. 43, box 10 (Canada), and John L. Hubbard questionnaire, f. 62, box 9 (Mexico), both in RP, DPL. Hubman subsequently married an Indian woman and resided in Canada the rest of his life, probably fearing discovery and arrest had he returned to the United States. Author's files.

25. Mulford, *Fighting Indians*, 56; McChristian, *Frontier Cavalry Trooper*, 140 (first quotation); Carter, *On the Border with Mackenzie*, 222–23 (second quotation).

26. White, *Custer, Cavalry, and Crows*, 31 (first quotation); Barnard, *Ten Years with Custer*, 48 (second quotation).

27. De Trobriand, *Military Life in Dakota*, 306 (first quotation); Major Alexander Chambers to AAG, Dept. of the Platte, May 25, 1874, LS, Fort Fetterman, Wyo. Terr., RG 393, NARA (second quotation). Post commanders in the Department of the Platte had been instructed to telegraph notification and descriptions of deserters immediately upon discovery. Similarly, they were to notify all telegraph operators on the east-west routes of escape suspected to have been taken so that deserters might be intercepted. Apparently these measures were not always followed. *ANJ*, Oct. 25, 1873, 164.

28. *Revised United States Army Regulations of 1861*, 29, 515; *ANJ*, July 5, 1873, 750 (quotation); *Regulations of the Army, 1881*, 26.

29. Romeyn, "Desertion," 672–73 (quotation). For a time it was legal for soldiers who were members of a pursuit party to claim the reward when deserters were captured. However, that was rescinded by an 1886 decision of the second comptroller of the U.S. Treasury. *ANJ*, Sept. 15, 1883, 125; *ANJ*, Nov. 20, 1886, 329.

30. Daubenmier, "Empty Saddles," 14 (quotation); Kinevan, *Frontier Cavalryman*, 159; John Bergstrom questionnaire, f. 72, box 8, RP, DPL.

31. Barnard, *Ten Years with Custer*, 101 (first quotation). Ryan's memory of the weight of ball used was probably faulty. A twelve-pound ball hardly would have retarded the movement of a strong man. The most common weighed twenty-four pounds; in fact one order found specified that weight, along with a six-foot chain. GO No. 4, Dept of the Platte, Jan. 25, 1869, Fourth Infantry Order Book, FLNHS. A surviving example of such a ball and chain is in the collections of Fort Phil Kearny State Historic Site, Banner, Wyoming. Semiobsolete twenty-four-pound solid shot provided a ready source of balls through ordnance channels. They measured 5.68 inches in diameter. *Ordnance Manual*, 34; Reynolds J. Burt Boyhood Data, box 2, RC, USAMHI (second quotation).

32. Winthrop, *Military Law*, 1:613–15.

33. Barnard, *Ten Years with Custer*, 47 (first quotation); *ANJ*, April 11, 1868, 539 (second quotation).

34. William Murphy, "The Forgotten Battalion," MS, f. 17, box 1, Chapman Collection, AHC (quotation). Another detailed description of drumming-out in 1869 is found in Mattison, "Diary of Surgeon Washington Matthews," 29.

35. Carriker and Carriker, *Army Wife*, 66–67.

36. McChristian, *Frontier Cavalry Trooper*, 92–93.

37. Winthrop, *Military Law*, 1:622; Article 98, *Army Regulations of the Army, 1881*, 344; McDermott, "Were They Really Rogues?" 166. The adjutant general pointed up the difficulty in properly identifying men applying to enlist: "It is a very easy matter for a soldier to procure affidavits and testimony utterly unreliable, yet bearing the appearance of truth, as to their age, parentage, &c." *ARSW*, 1877, 46.

38. GO No. 102, AGO, Oct. 10, 1873; McChristian, *Frontier Cavalry Trooper*, 286 (quotation).

39. *ANJ*, Nov. 28, 1874, 251.

40. *ANJ*, Dec. 22, 1883, 419 (first quotation); *ANJ*, Dec. 18, 1886n 417; Forbes, "United States Army," 133 (second quotation); Pope, "Desertion and the Military Prison," 114 (third quotation).

41. Pope, "Desertion and the Military Prison," 116; Perley S. Eaton questionnaire, f. 24, box 9, RP, DPL. This was a point of law. Enlistment was a legal contract for the period of five years. A court could not legally sentence a man to serve a period longer than that, even in prison, without first terminating the contract by discharging him. Winthrop, *Military Law*, 1:931.

42. The congressional act of July 24, 1876, authorized cavalry companies to be recruited up to one hundred men, but the army objected on the ground that by not increasing the 25,000-man limit on the overall size of the army the infantry and artillery would be correspondingly reduced to "a number entirely too small for efficient service." Consequently Congress acted quickly to correct the oversight by authorizing the ceiling to be raised by 2,500 men to allow for augmenting the cavalry. *ARSW*, 1876, 25–26, 72–73; King, *Campaigning with Crook*, 163 (quotation).

43. During the first nine months of 1877, 150 underage youths, who had probably contracted "army fever" in the wake of the Battle of the Little Bighorn, were discharged. *ARSW*, 1877, 50 (quotation).

44. *ARSW*, 1881, 39, 79 (quotation); *ARSW*, 1880, 39.

45. Pope, "Desertion and the Military Prison," 113.

46. Winthrop, *Military Law*, 1:930–32.

47. Article 48, *Army Regulations of the Army, 1881*, 337; *ARSW*, 1884, 88–89 (quotations).

48. *ANJ*, Nov. 17, 1883 (quotation); *ARSW*, 1884, 92.

49. *ANJ*, May 19, 1883, 957.

50. Closson, "Morning Reports," 187 (first quotation); Pope, "Desertion and the Military Prison," 112 (second quotation); William G. Wilkinson questionnaire, f. 44, box 10, RP, DPL (third quotation).

51. *ARSW*, 1877, 49; Fowler, *Black Infantry*, 79; *ARSW*, 1891, 3.

52. My conclusions are based on spot-checking reports in *ARSW*, 1879, 34; and *ARSW*, 1882, 52. *ANJ*, Nov. 27, 1880, 330.

53. *ANJ*, Nov. 27, 1886, 345 (first quotation); Holabird, *Some Considerations*, 16 (second quotation). Actual strengths of regiments varied constantly, of course, but for the sake of comparison cavalry regiments averaged 750–800 men and infantry about 350–400. Authorized strengths were 960 and 480, respectively. Heitman, *Historical Register*, 2:612–13.

54. Further discussion is found in Dobak and Phillips, *Black Regulars*, 62–63. The figures presented are compiled from *Roster of Non-Commissioned Officers of the Tenth U.S. Cavalry*, 3–13.

55. Romeyn, "Desertion," 675 (quotation). An earlier measure, enacted in 1872, built into the pay system to discourage desertion, was a regulation withholding longevity allowance for the third, fourth, and fifth years of a man's enlistment until he was honorably discharged, at which time it would be paid in a lump sum on his final statement. *Regulations of the Army, 1881*, p. 320 (Sec. 1281).

56. Civilian appointments were reduced to third priority, and during peacetime only when the applicant was an honorably discharged U.S. Military Academy graduate. Even then the vacancy had to be in excess of the anticipated slots to be filled by the next graduating class. *Regulations of the Army, 1881*, 11–12 (quotation).

57. Private James O. Purvis writing in the *Billings Gazette*, April 12, 1886 (quotation); Upton, *Fort Custer*, 79.

58. *ARSW*, 1884, 85.

59. *ANJ*, Feb. 5, 1887, 548.

60. Ibid.

61. *ARSW*, 1881, 46.

62. *ANJ*, Dec. 12, 1885: 396; *ANJ*, June 23, 1888, 959 (quotation).

63. *ARSW*, 1891, 3 (first quotation); *ANJ*, Nov. 16, 1889, 234 (second quotation).

64. "Will He Enlist?" 1641.
65. Nelson, "Davids Island," 512.
66. GO No. 80, AGO, July 26, 1890.
67. Ibid.
68. Desertion rates were 9.3 percent for 1890, 6.2 percent for 1891, and 5.5 percent for 1892. Tabulated in Foner, *United States Soldier*, 223; *ANJ*, Jan. 28, 1888: 530 (quotation).

CHAPTER 13. "I WILL SEE SOME REAL WILD-WEST LIFE"

1. Private Adelbert Butler to Tom, April 17, 1877, GTC.
2. Corporal Maurice H. Wolfe to Cousin Maurice, Oct. 14, 1867, Wolfe letters, FLNHS (first quotation); McConnell, *Five Years a Cavalryman*, 46 (second quotation).
3. Private Herman S. Searl to Dear Parents, Jan. 2, 1868, Herman S. Searl letters, WSA (first quotation); Giddens, "Seven Letters," 306, 308 (second and third quotations).
4. Private Henry Hubman to Dear Father, Mother, and Brothers, Sept. 10, 1881, Hubman letters, James Mountain files (first quotation); Private Thomas N. Way journal, J. A. Greene files (second quotation).
5. Hynes, *Soldiers of the Frontier*, 15 (first quotation); David W. Luce, "Indian War Campaigning," *National Tribune*, Sept. 18, 1921 (second quotation); John O. Stotts reminiscence, Spencer collection (third quotation).
6. Isaac H. Sembower journal, NPHP (first quotation); Hoffner, "Journal of the Sheep Eater Campaign," June 9, 1879, Sept. 25, 1879, MS, Brown Papers, UCB (second quotation); Corporal Clarence Chrisman diary, Nov. 7, 1885, Chrisman Papers, AHS (third quotation).
7. Albin H. Drown, "A Blizzard Campaign," *National Tribune*, Mar. 13, 1913 (first quotation); Gurnett, "The Old Sergeant"; Private Adelbert Butler to Mary (sister), April 24, 1878, Butler letters, GTC (second quotation).
8. This detachment, sent out in New Mexico during the 1885 Geronimo Campaign, was composed of seven soldiers, a Hispanic packer, and four burros carrying their supplies. Corporal Clarence Chrisman diary, Oct. 23, 1885, Chrisman Papers, AHS (quotation).
9. McChristian, *Frontier Cavalry Trooper*, 267 (first quotation); Gardner, "On the Plains in 1868," *National Tribune*, Feb. 6, 1913 (second quotation). The .50/70-caliber Model 1866 Springfield rifle was commonly known on the frontier as a "needle gun" because of its long firing pin.
10. John O. Stotts reminiscence, Spencer collection (quotation). A newspaper correspondent noted that during a particularly dangerous time on the Smoky Hill Trail in 1868 daily stages were canceled in favor of running two coaches together on alternate days, one carrying passengers and mail, the other heavy cargo with an escort of six Thirty-Eighth Infantrymen. Keim, *Sheridan's Troopers*, 46.
11. For an excellent treatment of the Texas aspect of stage coaching on the Southern Overland Route, see Austerman, *Sharps Rifles and Spanish Mules*.
12. Keim, *Sheridan's Troopers*, 61.
13. Parker, *Personal Experiences*, 56–57 (first quotation). Ryan's reference to "bombproofs" undoubtedly stemmed from his Civil War experience. Barnard, *Ten Years with Custer*, 30 (second quotation). See also Billings, *Hardtack and Coffee*, 48–49. Another person who left a firsthand description of the "monitors" was Dr. William A. Bell, an English physician and adventurer who accompanied the Union Pacific Railroad project

across Kansas in 1867. Bell noted: "The Indians are beginning to understand these covered rifle-pits and the more they know of them the more careful they are to keep at a respectful distance from them." Bell, *New Tracks*, 66.

14. Bob Rea, "Sand Bag Citadels," MS, copy in the author's files.

15. De Trobriand, *Military Life in Dakota*, 162; Summerhayes, *Vanished Arizona*, 103–4 (quotation). For an example, see *SO No. 119*, Fort Laramie, Wyo. Terr., June 19, 1868, Fourth Infantry Order Book, FLNHS.

16. Private Adelbert Butler to Anna (sister), June 26, 1877, Butler letters, GTC (first quotation); Reynolds J. Burt Boyhood Data, box 2, RC, USAMHI. A typical order for a repair party is *SO 218*, Fort Laramie, Wyo. Terr., Nov. 19, 1868, Fourth Infantry Order Book, FLNHS; Smith, *Dose of Frontier Soldiering*, 74–75 (second quotation).

17. Latta, "Winning of the West" (quotation). Perhaps one of the more peculiar details occurred in 1870 when hand-picked regulars, operating in relays from one fort to another, escorted 6 million dollars in currency down the Santa Fe Trail to fund the first national bank in New Mexico Territory. McChristian, *Frontier Cavalry Trooper*, 123, 123 n. 51.

18. William Murphy, "Forgotten Battalion," MS, f. 17, box 1, Chapman Collection, AHC (quotation); McChristian, *Fort Laramie*, 355–58; Private Clarence S. Gould, account of service, f. 76, box 10, RP, DPL.

19. William Gurnett, "The Old Sergeant," 9 (first quotation); Zinser, *Indian War Diary*, 3 (second quotation).

20. Barnard, *Ten Years with Custer*, 26 (first quotation); Mulford, *Fighting Indians*, 59 (second quotation).

21. Mulford, *Fighting Indians*, 59; Forsyth, *Story of the Soldier*, 159.

22. Private Maurice H. Wolfe to Dear Uncle, May 12, 1867, Wolfe letters, FLNHS (first quotation); Godfrey, "Some Reminiscences, Including the Washita Battle," 483; Johnson, "Jacob Horner," 11; Lieutenant J. W. Biddle to Mother, Oct. [?], 1876, Biddle letters, copies in J. A. Greene files (second quotation).

23. Captain Samuel Ovenshine field diary, Ovenshine Family Papers, USAMHI; Hedren, "The Worst Campaign," 4 (quotation).

24. Custer, *Tenting on the Plains*, 302 (first quotation); Finerty, *Warpath and Bivouac*, 249 (second quotation); Joseph A. Gaston, "Cavalry Officer on the Frontier," in Carroll, ed., *Unpublished Papers of the Order of the Indian Wars*, book 5, 7 (third quotation). For further discussion of field clothing, see McChristian, *U.S. Army in the West*, 144–45, 151.

25. Forbes, "United States Army," 144 (first quotation); Bigelow, *On the Bloody Trail*, 197–98 (second quotation).

26. Captain Samuel J. Ovenshine to wife, Aug. 3, 1876, Ovenshine Family Papers, USAMHI (first quotation); Lieutenant Colonel Lewis D. Greene commenting on his unit's preparations for the 1879 Ute Campaign, in Carroll, *Unpublished Papers of the Order of the Indian Wars*, book 2, 8 (second quotation). This discussion also relies on a number of firsthand accounts and field orders. For example, Private George Cranston, Thirty-Second Infantry, recorded that during a scout in Arizona he and two of his comrades elected to allow for contingencies, yet not overload themselves, by sharing equipment. One man carried a blanket, one an overcoat, and the third a rubber blanket. Dinges, "New York Private," 58.

27. Taylor, *With Custer*, 156.

28. The 1870s and 1880s witnessed a great deal of arms experimentation and field trials of various models. Further discussion of the subject is found in McChristian, *U.S.*

Army in the West, 111–21, and *Uniforms, Arms, and Equipment*, 2: 170–79; Bigelow, *On the Bloody Trail*, 198 (quotation).

29. McChristian, "The Best Arms for the Cavalry" (paper presented at the Fort Robinson Conference, Crawford, Nebraska, April 2007) (first two quotations); Greene, *Indian War Veterans*, 38 (third quotation).

30. After the advent of revolvers firing metallic cartridges, cavalrymen carried the ammunition either in a small leather belt pouch or in their trouser pockets. Either method made them difficult to access while mounted horseback. McChristian, *U.S. Army in the West*, 94, 196, and *Uniforms, Arms, and Equipment*, 2:78–79, 185 (quotation).

31. Corporal George C. Brown to Charles E. Rice (friend), April 28, 1876, Seventh Cavalry Personnel Files, LBBNM (first quotation); Sergeant. Charles Scott to Sister, April 23, 1876, LBBNM (second quotation); Mulford, *Fighting Indians*, 58 (third quotation).

32. Saum, "Private John F. Donahue's Reflections," 43 (first quotation); King, *Campaigning with Crook*, 62 (second quotation); Sembower journal, NPHP (third quotation).

33. Carroll and Frost, *Private Theodore Ewert's Diary*, 8–9.

34. Barnard, *Ten Years with Custer*, 287 (first quotation); Windolph, *I Fought With Custer*, 53 (second quotation).

35. Carriker and Carriker, *Army Wife*, 94.

CHAPTER 14. "MORE THAN I EVER THOUGHT I COULD BEAR"

1. First Sergeant John Ryan remembered that each wagon train (with twenty-four wagons) had its own wagon master, assistant, cook, and watchman, in addition to the teamsters, all of whom were armed. Barnard, *Ten Years with Custer*, 22–23; White, *Custer, Cavalry, and Crows*, 55; Daly, "War Path," 16; Godfrey, "Some Reminiscences, Including the Washita Battle," 488; Greene, *Indian War Veterans*, 200 (quotation).

2. Barnard, *Ten Years with Custer*, 35 (quotation); McChristian, *U.S. Army in the West*, 191. That the infantry's commonsense practice of hauling knapsacks and haversacks in wagons whenever possible is also reflected in Third Infantryman John O. Stotts's reminiscence of his service during the late 1860s (Spencer collection).

3. Godfrey, "Some Reminiscences, Including an Account of General Sully's Expedition," 421 (quotation). Transporting physically sound infantrymen in wagons was rarely done, and only when small numbers were involved. Footsore doughboys sometimes were afforded relief by being allowed to ride in wagons not otherwise needed.

4. Greene, *Indian War Veterans*, 100 (quotation). Ryan, who was in a position to know, said that a noncom and three privates from each company served as outlying vedettes. Barnard, *Ten Years with Custer*, 191.

5. Windolph, *I Fought with Custer*, 57 (first two quotations); Barnard, *Ten Years With Custer*, 230–31 (third quotation).

6. Magnussen, *Peter Thompson's Narrative*, 58 (first quotation); Slough journal, June 2, 1875, MHS (second quotation). Because the work could be physically demanding, the men detailed for pioneer duty were rotated daily.

7. Utley, *Frontier Regulars*, 48.

8. Hoffner journal, Aug. 21, 1879, Brown Papers, UCB (quotation). A Sixteenth Infantryman related that his company employed pack mules in New Mexico during the Geronimo Campaign to "haul rations and one blanket per man." Smith, *Dose of Frontier Soldiering*, 151.

9. Way, *Sgt. Fred Platten's Ten Years*, 37 (first quotation); Mears, "Campaigning against Crazy Horse," 68–69 (second quotation).

10. White, *Custer, Cavalry, and Crows*, 23–24 (first quotation). The manner of packing mules was described by Private Dennis Lynch, Seventh Cavalry. Hammer, *With Custer in '76*, 139; Cozzens, *Eyewitnesses to the Indian Wars*, 1:338 (second quotation).

11. Windolph, *I Fought with Custer*, 64.

12. Barnard, *Ten Years with Custer*, 54. Frequent inspections were especially important prior to the advent of brass cartridges during the 1880s because the softer copper alloy cases used previously were prone to swell without contracting. When the ammunition was allowed to become dirty or dented in the men's field belts, fired cases sometimes could not be readily extracted from the chamber, thus rendering the weapon temporarily inoperable. Combat-wise officers and soldiers saw that arms and ammunition were kept clean, while others seemed to be unaware of the causes of jamming. Men of the Second Cavalry and Fifth Infantry, for example, are known to have cleaned their cartridges, while those of the Seventh Cavalry seemed to have been less concerned, at least prior to the Battle of the Little Bighorn. See Reneau, *Adventures of Moccasin Joe*, 69; Miles, *Personal Recollections*, 214–15. A more detailed discussion of the problem is found in McChristian, *U.S. Army in the West*, 114–15. Magnussen, *Peter Thompson's Narrative*, 117 (quotation).

13. Bradley, *March of the Montana Column*, 16 (first quotation); Griffen, "Fred Munn, Veteran of Frontier Experiences," 53 (second quotation).

14. Geant journal, Mar. 17, 1876, Camp Collection, LBBNM (first and second quotations); Greene, *Indian War Veterans*, 361 (third quotation); Hedren, "Worst Campaign," 5 (fourth quotation). The average marching pace, including rest halts, of combined infantry-cavalry commands with trains was about three miles per hour over the plains. Parker, *Personal Experiences*, 23. Captain Simon Snyder's diary agrees with Parker that a day's march overland averaged fifteen to twenty miles, although Snyder's company covered up to twenty-six when necessary. Snyder diaries, LBBNM.

15. Greene, *Indian War Veterans*, 278 (first quotation), 210 (second quotation).

16. Jerome, "Geronimo Campaign," 161 (first quotation); Greene, *Indian War Veterans*, 39 (second quotation).

17. Farrow, *Mountain Scouting*, 135; Dinges, "New York Private," 58 (first quotation); Smith, *Dose of Frontier Soldiering*, 16 (second quotation). Typical infantry daily marches are recorded in Rea, "Red River War Diary of Private John Hechner," 27–28; and Meddaugh diary, May–Sept. 1876, ML, UU. The average day's cavalry march was fifteen to twenty miles, the habitual pace being a walk, with occasional trotting. *Cavalry Tactics*, 477.

18. Way journal, July 10, 1873, copy in J. A. Greene files (first quotation); Zinser, *Indian War Diary*, 5 (second quotation).

19. William Murphy, "Forgotten Battalion," AHC (first quotation); Hedren, "Worst Campaign," 5 (second quotation).

20. "Memorandum of Edward Williams," typescript, LBBNM (first quotation); Schneider, *Freeman Journal*, 45; Private Arthur S. Wallace to Dan, n.d., FLNHS; Way journal, Aug. 10, 1873, J. A. Greene files (second quotation). The horse equipment and wagons were transported on a ferry. McChristian, *Frontier Cavalry Trooper*, 80 (third quotation).

21. Hedren, "Worst Campaign," 6.

22. Greene, *Indian War Veterans*, 122 (first quotation); Magnussen, *Peter Thompson's Narrative*, 56 (second quotation).

23. Edwin M. Brown, "Terror of the Badlands," typescript, MHS (first quotation); Lieutenant Walter L. Finley to Mother, April 14, 1885, CHL (second quotation); Zimmer, *Frontier Soldier*, 16 (third quotation).

24. Hills, "With General George A. Custer," 51 (first quotation); Barnard, *Ten Years with Custer*, 34 (second quotation).

25. Godfrey, "Some Reminiscences, Including the Washita Battle," 488; Anthony Gavin, "Campaigning, " *National Tribune*, April 22, 1926; Arthur Wallace to Dan, n.d., FLNHS; Carter, *On the Border with Mackenzie*, 197 (quotation).

26. Lockwood, *Life and Adventures of a Drummer Boy*, 134 (first quotation); McChristian, *Frontier Cavalry Trooper*, 160 (second quotation); Anthony Gavin, "Campaigning," *National Tribune*, April 22, 1926 (third quotation); James C. Bothwell reminiscence, typescript in author's files (fourth quotation); Private Arthur S. Wallace to Dan, n.d., FLNHS (fifth quotation).

27. Mulford, *Fighting Indians*, 79 (first quotation); Anthony Gavin, "Real Indian Fighter," n.p., n.d., f. 118, ECP, DPL (second quotation).

28. "Memorandum of Edward Williams," typescript, LBBNM (first quotation); McConnell, *Five Years a Cavalryman*, 84 (second quotation); McChristian, *Frontier Cavalry Trooper*, 176 (third quotation); Greene, *Indian War Veterans*, 33 (fourth quotation).

29. This concoction was sometimes known as "skillygalee" during the Civil War, but I have found no references to that term being used by postwar regulars. Billings, *Hardtack and Coffee*, 118. Other references to regulars frying hardtack in this fashion are found in Ostrander, *Army Boy of the Sixties*, 134; Johnson, "Jacob Horner," 9; Schubert, *Voices of the Buffalo Soldier*, 51; Shirk, "Campaigning with Sheridan," 97; Theodore Goldin, "A Winter Raid," f. 16, Philip G. Cole Collection, Gilcrease Museum, 1 (quotation).

30. A contemporary reference to "Cincinnati chicken" is found in Bode, *Dose of Frontier Soldiering*, 25. Mess pork was to be cut in strips from the shoulders and sides of hogs, but wartime contractors were notorious for including portions taken from the necks, bellies, and elsewhere, thus increasing their profits. The brine prescribed for two hundred pounds of pork was to be made of water combined with fifty pounds of coarse salt. An army manual stated that "pork [barrels] should be rolled monthly, and never be exposed to a hot sun" because the pork would spoil. Merely transporting it to the West ensured its exposure to heat, and it is doubtful that barrels were rolled once they were placed in warehouses. Cincinnati, Ohio, was a center for pork processing. Kilburn, *Notes on Preparing Stores*, vii, 15 (first quotation); Johnson, "Jacob Horner," 9 (second quotation). *Circular No. 18*, Department of Arizona, Oct. 21, 1871, directed that "pork shall be issued at least twice a week until the large surplus on hand shall be exhausted." Noted in Post Returns, Camp Apache, Ariz., Nov. 1871. A wartime veteran claimed that salt pork was considered the mainstay of the ration and usually broiled in the field or sometimes even eaten raw in a sandwich of hardtack. Billings, *Hardtack and Coffee*, 137.

31. Some army bacon was packed in wooden boxes, but "where economy of weight is very important, it may be packed in double sacks (inside muslin, outside gunny or strong osnaburg." Kilburn, *Notes on Preparing Stores*, 17; Perley S. Eaton questionnaire, f. 24, box 9, RP, DPL (first quotation); Hoffner journal, July 26, 1879, Brown Papers, UCB (second quotation); Greene, *Indian War Veterans*, 103 (third quotation).

32. Adam Fox, "Fighting the Dog Soldiers," *National Tribune*, Aug. 31, 1911 (first quotation); Reneau, *Adventures of Moccasin Joe*, 72 (second quotation) Zinser, *Indian War Diary*, 26–27 (third quotation); "Memorandum of Edward Williams," Sept. 8, 1877, typescript, LBBNM (fourth quotation).

33. Shirk, "Campaigning with Sheridan," 94 (first quotation); McChristian, *Frontier Cavalry Trooper*, 158–59 (second quotation); Mulford, *Fighting Indians*, 117 (third quotation); "Report of the Medical Department," Dec. 14, 1876, LBBNM (fourth quotation); Hoffner journal, July 8, 1879, Brown Papers, UCB (fifth quotation); *ANJ*, May 6, 1882, 909.

34. Smith, *Sagebrush Soldier*, 54 (first quotation); Geant journal, June 3, 1876, f. 67, Camp Collection, LBBNM (second quotation); First Sergeant Charles N. Jansen, account of service, f. 91, box 10, RP, DPL (third quotation).

35. Hoffner journal, June 4, 1879, Brown Papers, UCB (first quotation); Zimmer, *Frontier Soldier*, 107 (second quotation).

36. Slough journal, Sept. 24, 1875, MHS.

37. Hardin, "Sheep Eater Campaign," 435; Zinser, *Indian War Diary*, 17 (quotation).

38. Hill and Innis, "Fort Buford Diary of Private Sanford," 12 (quotation). Some additional references to soldiers constructing such shades are found in Slough journal, June 16, 1875, MHS; McChristian, *Frontier Cavalry Trooper*, 150; Gustafson, *John Spring's Arizona*, 128; and Bourke, *On the Border with Crook*, 4.

39. Chrisman diary, Nov. 20, 1885, AHS.

40. Slough journal, June 25, 1875, MHS (first quotation); White, *Custer, Cavalry, and Crows*, 24 (second quotation); Zinser, *Indian War Diary*, 16 (third quotation). Plains Indians made these shelters, sometimes known a wickiups or war houses, of two basic designs. Those of the Sioux and Cheyennes were elongated, while those of the Crows were usually circular. Warriors traveling light on raids and hunts employed them as temporary shelters, covering the framework with a blanket. Clark, *Indian Sign Language*, 404; Pearson, *Notes on the Platte-Dakota Campaign*, 14 (fourth quotation).

41. Finerty, *War Path*, 266 (first quotation); Hoffner journal, June 4, 1879, Brown Papers, UCB (second quotation); Smith, *Dose of Frontier Soldiering*, 93 (third quotation).

42. Smith, *Dose of Frontier Soldiering*, 120.

43. Albin H. Drown, "A Blizzard Campaign," *National Tribune*, Mar. 13, 1913 (first quotation); Barnard, *Ten Years with Custer*, 72–73 (second quotation); Rea, "Red River War Diary," 31 (third quotation).

44. A rare earlier instance of the Sibley tent stove being used was during Mackenzie's Powder River Expedition in late fall 1876. Private William E. Smith mentioned that he hated "to leave that little Sibley Stove for it was nice and warm in the tent." However, Smith was detailed as an orderly, so it must be considered that the headquarters staff may have had a few more luxuries than the line companies. Smith, *Sagebrush Soldier*, 39.

45. Carroll and Frost, *Private Theodore Ewert's Diary*, 21–22 (first two quotations); Cozzens, *Eyewitnesses to the Indian Wars*, 5:322 (third quotation). A First Cavalryman noted that in the absence of starch and irons he and his comrades hung their clothes out to dry in the sun, rubbed out the wrinkles by hand as well as possible, then rolled the garments in a flour sack until they were needed. Hoffner journal, July 12, 1879, Brown Papers, UCB (fourth quotation).

46. Smith, *Dose of Frontier Soldiering*, 157.

47. "Memorandum of Edward Williams," typescript, LBBNM (first quotation); Liddic, *I Buried Custer*, 13 (second quotation); Hedren, "Campaigning with the Fifth U.S. Cavalry," 143 (third quotation); Sembower journal, Sept. 6—10, 1877, NPHP; Hynes, *Soldiers of the Frontier*, 149 (fourth quotation); Greene, *Indian War Veterans*, 286 (fifth quotation); Hoffner journal, Brown Papers, UCB (sixth quotation).

48. "Memorandum of Edward Williams," typescript, LBBNM (first quotation); Private Henry Hubman to Herman (brother), Aug. 28, 1882, Hubman letters, James

Mountain files (second quotation). An excellent firsthand account detailing the reliance on civilian scouts for carrying mail and official communications in the field is found in Carriker, "Thomas McFadden's Diary."

49. Perley S. Eaton questionnaire, f. 24, box 9, RP, DPL (first quotation); Zimmer, *Frontier Soldier*, 21 (second quotation). See also numerous entries in the Slough journal, MHS. Corporal Emil A. Bode's quotation relates to Sixteenth Infantrymen in the field in New Mexico Territory during the Geronimo Campaign. Smith, *Dose of Frontier Soldiering*, 157 (third quotation).

50. Windolph, *I Fought with Custer*, 57; Jett, Autobiography, 20, SC, UAL (quotation); Smith, *Sagebrush Soldier*, 36.

51. Magnussen, *Peter Thompson's Narrative*, 98.

52. Way journal, June 29, 1873, J. A. Greene files (first quotation); Private Arthur S. Wallace to Dan, n.d., FLNHS (second quotation); Smith, *Dose of Frontier Soldiering*, 148 (third quotation).

53. Luhn diary, July 27, 1876, AHC.

54. Carroll and Frost, *Private Theodore Ewert's Diary*, 15 (first quotation); Private E. D. Barker journal, July 1, 1877, FLNHS (second quotation). On May 2, 1877 a Second Cavalryman recorded in his diary: "The officers expect to run up Indians very soon. They have got from 10 to 15 Picketposts out, each of 3 men." "Memorandum of Edward Williams," typescript, LBBNM.

55. Mulford, *Fighting Indians*, 94 (quotations); Slough journal, Aug. 9, 1875, MHS.

56. Jett, Autobiography, SC, UAL; Shirk, "Campaigning with Sheridan," 93 (quotation).

57. Barnard, *Ten Years with* Custer, 34, 191.

58. Ibid., 99–100 (first quotation); Smith, *Sagebrush Soldier*, 125 (second quotation). An example of this punishment is found in "Memorandum of Edward Williams," typescript, LBBNM.

59. Zimmer, *Frontier Soldier*, 16 (first quotation); Way journal, July 25, 1873, J. A. Greene files (second quotation).

60. John O. Stotts reminiscence, Spencer collection (first quotation); Reneau, *Adventures of Moccasin Joe*, 75 (second quotation); Greene, *Indian War Veterans*, 195 (third quotation).

61. Hoffner journal, July 7 and 5, 1879, Brown Papers, UCB (first and second quotations); Private George McAnulty to Lille Moore, Aug. 4, 1878, McAnulty letters, FLNHS (third quotation).

62. This incident is recounted in Leckie, *Buffalo Soldiers*, 157–61; Greene, "Chasing Sitting Bull," 195 (first quotation); Zimmer, *Frontier Soldier*, 78 (second quotation); Buecker, "Journals of James S. McClellan," 27 (third quotation).

63. Slough journal, June 28, 1875, MHS (first quotation); Carroll and Frost, *Private Theodore Ewert's Diary*, 33–34 (second quotation).

64. McChristian, *Frontier Cavalry Trooper*, 181 (first quotation); Geant journal, Aug. 17, 1876, f. 67, Camp Collection, LBBNM (second quotation).

65. Cozzens, *Eyewitnesses to the Indian Wars*, 2:24 (quotation); affidavit by Sergeant William Molchert, Pension File, RG15, NARA, copy in author's files.

66. Richard Flynn diary, Aug. 6, 1876, FLNHS.

67. Greene, "Chasing Sitting Bull," 195.

68. Finerty, *War Path*, 256.

69. Ibid., 254.

70. Zinser, *Indian War Diary*, Aug. 13, 1876 (first quotation); Finerty, *War Path*, 263 (second quotation).

71. Ibid., 267 (first quotation); Flynn diary, Aug. 28, 1876, FLNHS (second quotation); Zinser, *Indian War Diary*, 22 (third quotation).

72. Zinser, *Indian War Diary*, 30 (first quotation); Greene, *Indian War Veterans*, 107 (second quotation).

73. Dobak, "Yellow-Leg Journalists," 105 (first quotation). The origin of this verse is presented in King, *Campaigning with Crook*, 158–59 (second quotation). Lieutenant Charles King was a member of the Fifth Cavalry and a participant in the campaign.

74. Greene, *Indian War Veterans*, 115 (first quotation); Anthony Gavin, "Campaigning," *National Tribune*, April 22, 1926 (second quotation).

75. Hedren, "Campaigning with the Fifth U.S. Cavalry," 144 (first quotation); Zinser, *Indian War Diary*, 30 (second quotation), 33 (third quotation).

76. Greene, "Chasing Sitting Bull," 197 (first quotation); Hedren, "Campaigning with the Fifth U.S. Cavalry," 144 (second quotation).

77. Zinser, *Indian War Diary*, 36 (quotation). Arriving at Fort Robinson in late September, forty of Crook's soldiers had to be hospitalized. The expedition was officially terminated in October and the troops returned to their home stations. Buecker, *Fort Robinson*, 87.

78. Werner, *On the Western Frontier*, 32 (first quotation); Cox, *Five Years in the United States Army*, 17 (second quotation).

79. Cozzens, *Eyewitnesses to the Indian Wars*, 1:545 (first quotation); Pagel, "Indians Would Not Pacify," 2 (second quotation); Hoffner journal, Oct. 5, 1879, Brown Papers, UCB (third quotation).

80. Hill and Innis, "Fort Buford Diary of Private Sanford," 23 (first quotation). Zinser, *Indian War Diary*, 38 (second quotation).

81. Zinser, *Indian War Diary*, 36 (first quotation). Private Slough noted that Martha "Calamity Jane" Canary "in womans [sic] dress," in contrast to her usual male garb, joined in the revelry at the hog ranch that night. Slough journal, Oct. 11, 1875, MHS (second quotation); Greene, *Indian War Veterans*, 161 (third and fourth quotations).

82. Forsyth, *Story of the Soldier*, 128.

83. Schubert, *Voices of the Buffalo Soldier*, 188.

84. *ANJ*, Feb. 26, 1887, 611.

85. Rodenbough, *Army of the United States*, 230.

CHAPTER 15. "OUR ORDERS WERE TO GO AFTER THEM"

1. During the period January 1866–January 1891, approximately 1,067 combat engagements are tabulated in *Chronological List of Actions with Indians*; McChristian, *Frontier Cavalry Trooper*, 183 (quotation).

2. McChristian, *Frontier Cavalry Trooper*, 24 (first quotation); Jett, Autobiography, SC, UAL (second quotation).

3. QM Sergeant Maurice H. Wolfe to Cousin Maurice, June 7, 1870, Wolfe letters, FLNHS.

4. Ostrander, *Army Boy of the Sixties*, 114 (first quotation); De Trobriand, *Military Life in Dakota*, 60 (second quotation); Private Henry Hubman to Dear Father, Mother, and Brothers, Sept. 10, 1881, Hubman letters, James Mountain files (third quotation).

5. Carter to Camp, April 3, 1914, f. 127, box 1, ECP, DPL.

6. John O. Stotts reminiscence, Spencer collection.

7. McChristian, *Frontier Cavalry Trooper*, 141.

8. Sergeant James S. Hamilton questionnaire, f. 52, box 9, RP, DPL (quotations); David W. Luce, "Indian War Campaigning," *National Tribune*, Sept. 18, 1921,

9. Greene, *Indian War Veterans*, 119–20 (first quotation) Cozzens, *Eyewitnesses to the Indian Wars*, 5:330 (second quotation).

10. Werner, *On the Western Frontier*, 85–86.

11. B. S. Bivenour to W. M. Camp, Feb. 10, 1921, Camp Collection, BYU (quotation). Lieutenant Charles H. Heyl, Dougherty's company commander and also a participant in what has become known as the "Battle of the Blow Out," cared for the boy after Dougherty's death and had him educated in the East. "An Apache Orphan," *Omaha Daily Bee*, July 29, 1876.

12. Private E. D. Barker journal, FLNHS (first quotation); R. Eugene Pelham, "The Passing of the Frontiers," *National Tribune*, Dec. 12, 1918 (second quotation); Maurer and Maurer, *First Sergeant*, 48–49 (third quotation).

13. Shirk, "Campaigning with Sheridan," 93, 98 (first quotation); Smith, *Dose of Frontier Soldiering*, 135, 29 (second quotation), 53 (third quotation); Giddens, "Seven Letters," 308–9 (fourth quotation).

14. Jett, Autobiography, SC, UAL, 25.

15. Cozzens, *Eyewitnesses to the Indian Wars*, 5:329 (first quotation); White, *Custer, Cavalry, and Crows*, 130 (second quotation).

16. *ANJ*, July 17, 1886, 1048.

17. Clarence C. Gould, "Account of Service," f. 76, box 10, RP, DPL.

18. Carroll, *Unpublished Papers of the Order of the Indian Wars*, book 10, 2 (first quotation); Private Hartford G. Clark diary, Jan. 17, 1891, IWWP, JNEM (second quotation); Private Walter C. Harrington questionnaire, f. 78, box 10, RP, DPL (third quotation).

19. Private Henry Hubman to Herman (brother), Sept. 12 and Oct. 1, 1882, Hubman letters, James Mountain files (first quotation); Smith, *Dose of Frontier Soldiering*, 82 (second quotation) White, *Custer, Cavalry, and Crows*, 144.

20. George Neihaus questionnaire, f. 93, box 9, RP, DPL (first quotation): Smith, *Dose of Frontier Soldiering*, 128 (second quotation); Schubert, *Voices of the Buffalo Soldier*, 158 (third quotation).

21. Talbot, "Indian Question," 143.

22. Private Herman S. Searls to Dear Parents, Jan. 2, 1868, Herman S. Searl letters, WSA (first quotation); QM Sergeant Maurice H. Wolfe to Cousin Maurice, Sept. 11, 1870, Wolfe letters, FLNHS (second quotation); Mulford, *Fighting Indians*, 48 (third quotation).

23. Hoffner, "Journal of the Sheep Eater Campaign," Sept. 20, 1879, MS, Brown Papers, UCB.

24. Second Lieutenant Walter L. Finley to Mother, Nov. 11, 1879, Finley Collection, CHL (first quotation); John Gibbert questionnaire, f. 42, box 9, RP, DPL (second quotation).

25. Hassrick, *Sioux*, 99.

26. McGinnis, *Counting Coup*, 115 (quotation). For an excellent synthesis of the significance of intertribal warfare, see also Ewers, *Plains Indian History*, 166–79.

27. The most memorable exception was the Battle of the Rosebud, wherein Sioux and Northern Cheyenne warriors sought out Crook's strong column and conducted a

surprise attack on the troops at midday. Vaughn, *With Crook at the Rosebud*; Farrow, *Mountain Scouting*, 239 (quotation).

28. De Trobriand, *Military Life in Dakota*, 267 (first quotation), 47 (second quotation).

29. Zimmer, *Frontier Soldier*, 109 (first quotation); Cook, "Art of Indian Fighting," 172 (second quotation).

30. Under some circumstances Apaches could and did assemble in much larger numbers for short periods. Cremony, *Life among the Apaches*, 142. An example was at the Battle of Apache Pass. For a detailed account, see McChristian, *Fort Bowie*, 52–62; Jett, Walker, "Reluctant Corporal" (pt. 1), 12 (first quotation); Second Lieutenant Walter L. Finley to Mother, Nov. 30, 1879, CHL (second quotation); Jerome, "Geronimo Campaign," 161 (third quotation).

31. Barnard, *Ten Years with Custer*, 31.

32. William Miller, "Record of Events," FLNHS (first quotation); Windolph, *I Fought with Custer*, 28 (second quotation).

33. QM Sergeant Maurice H. Wolfe to Cousin Maurice, July 15, 1870, Wolfe letters, FLNHS (first quotation). "The body presented a terrible appearance. Every stitch of clothing was stripped from his person, He had two bullet holes in his breast, six arrow wounds and the most horrible of all, his throat was cut from ear to ear. . . . That is the manner in which the demons mutilate a white person in this region." McChristian, *Frontier Cavalry Trooper*, 59–60 (second quotation).

34. David W. Luce, "Indian War Campaigning," *National Tribune*, Sept. 18, 1921 (first quotation); Sergeant David Kerstetter to Father, Dec. 25, 1866, published in *National Tribune*, n.d., copy in author's files (second quotation).

35. Cozzens, *Eyewitnesses to the Indian Wars*, 2:259–60 (quotation). "The dead that fell across the stream [Battle of the Big Hole] in the Indian camp were not molested as Chief Joseph was a Christian Indian." Private Homer Coon reminiscence, copy at LBBNM.

36. Customs and methods of scalping are discussed authoritatively in Clark, *Indian Sign Language*, 325–28; Buecker, "In Pursuit of Crazy Horse," 29 (first quotation); William Murphy, "Forgotten Battalion," f. 17. Chapman Collection, AHC (second quotation).

37. Vestal, *Warpath*, 95.

38. Ball, *In the Days of Victorio*, 46 (first quotation); Betzinez, *I Fought with Geronimo*, 86 (second quotation); Cremony, *Life among the Apaches*, 257–58, 267.

39. Cozzens, *Eyewitnesses to the Indian Wars*, 1:245 (quotation). First Lieutenant John Bigelow, Tenth Cavalry, saw the body of a white man killed in the Whetstone Mountains of southern Arizona in 1886. He noted that "on the top of his head a raw, white circle about the size of a dollar, which showed him to have been scalped." Bigelow, *On the Bloody Trail*, 207–8.

40. Stands In Timber and Liberty, *Cheyenne Memories*, 61–62 (first quotation); James Tucker, "Served 10 Eventful Years," *National Tribune*, Nov. 24, 1921 (second quotation); Private James B. Wilkinson questionnaire, f. 43, box 10, RP, DPL.

41. Statement attributed to Jean-Baptiste Truteau in Ewers, *Plains Indian History*, 200–202 (first quotation); McGinnis, *Counting Coup*, 58 (second quotation). McGinnis presents a thorough treatment of intertribal warfare on the northern plains, cogently demonstrating how such practices were in place long before the army-Indian conflict of the mid- to late nineteenth century.

42. Clark, *Indian Sign Language*, 326, 328 (first quotation); Private James B. Wilkinson questionnaire, f. 43, box 10, RP, DPL (second quotation). Referring to Apaches,

with whom he had considerable contact during the 1850s and 1860s, John C. Cremony addressed the issue of mutilation: "Whenever the Apache commits an act of atrocity, he does so with design and intention, and not from any ignorance as to whether it is a good or bad deed.... It is done with an object—a purpose.... When an Apache mutilates the dead body of his enemy, he ... judges us from his stand-point, and imagines that sight of the mutilated corpse will produce terror in the beholders." Cremony, *Life among the Apaches*, 269.

43. Dinges, "New York Private," 62 (first quotation); Latta, "Winning of the West" (second quotation).

44. Parker, *Personal Experiences*, 63 (first quotation); Barnard, *Ten Years with Custer*, 58 (second quotation); William Murphy, "Forgotten Battalion," f. 17, Chapman Collection, AHC (third quotation). The coin toss being unsuccessful, the soldiers next offered the youth a free meal if he could hit a cap thrown in the air. "The cap was thrown up and we all thought he had lost, but a hole was found through the middle, to the great sorrow of the owner." Smith, *Dose of Frontier Soldiering*, 127 (fourth quotation).

45. Latta, "Winning of the West" (quotation); Mason, *North American Bows*, 18; Taylor, *Native American Weapons*, 69. Captain Albert Barnitz pointed up this limitation, stating: "They cannot shoot their arrows with much accuracy except when the air is comparatively still." Utley, *Life in Custer's Cavalry*, 201–2.

46. Utley, *Life in Custer's Cavalry*, 63.

47. Carriker, "Thompson McFadden's Diary," 204 (first quotation); McConnell, *Five Years a Cavalryman*, 94 (second quotation); Dinges, "New York Private," 62 (third quotation). The lances used by the Southern Cheyennes were described as having "a blade about two feet long and about two inches wide, sharpened on both edges. There is a wooden staff attached to it about five feet long and one inch in diameter ... [with] a hole bored through and a piece of rawhide attached to it, which the Indian can fasten to his wrist." Barnard, *Ten Years with Custer*, 28.

48. Latta, "Winning of the West."

49. Cremony, *Life among the Apaches*, 194 (first quotation); McChristian, *Frontier Cavalry Trooper*, 213 (second quotation).

50. Extract from *Bridgeport (Conn.) Post*, July 27, 1933, f. 60, box 8, RP, DPL (first quotation); Giddens, "Seven Letters," 310 (second quotation); Gibbon, "Arms to Fight Indians," 244 (third quotation).

51. Scott et al., *Archaeological Perspectives*, 117–21; James S. Hamilton questionnaire, f. 52, box 9, RP, DPL (first quotation); Zimmer, *Frontier Soldier*, 69 (second quotation).

52. *ARSW*, 1879, 324.

53. Gibbon, "Arms to Fight Indians," 239.

54. Cremony, *Life among the Apaches*, 194 (first quotation); Gibbon, "Arms to Fight Indians," 239 (second and fourth quotations); Schubert, *Voices of the Buffalo Soldier*, 14 (third quotation)). Gibbon suffered the loss of two officers, twenty-one enlisted men, and six citizens killed, plus forty more wounded, two of whom later died. Nine noncommissioned officers were among the dead, proof that the Nez Perce warriors not only were excellent marksmen but also understood the significance of military shoulder straps and chevrons. The standard account of the entire Nez Perce War is Greene, *Nez Perce Summer 1877*.

55. De Trobriand, *Military Life in Dakota*, 64.

56. Finerty, *War Path and Bivouac*, 236.

57. "Summary Reports Relative to the Non-Effectiveness of Cavalry," M666, roll 41, NARA.
58. Gray, *Centennial Campaign*, 291; "Summary Reports," NARA (quotation).
59. McConnell, *Five Years a Cavalryman*, 216 (first quotation); *ANJ*, June 6, 1874, 682 (second quotation).
60. *ANJ*, Oct. 14, 1876, 154.
61. House of Representatives, Report No. 56, *Reorganization of the Army*, at 242 (1878).
62. Greene, *Lakota and Cheyenne*, 37 (first quotation); *Cheyenne Daily Leader*, Aug. 5, 1876 (second quotation).
63. A detailed account of this episode is presented in Greene, *Yellowstone Command*, 147–82.
64. Lauren W. Aldrich, "Brief Reminiscences," MS, HL (quotation). That portion of the Fourth Infantry posted at Fort Laramie also maintained a twelve-man mounted detachment under the command of a lieutenant. *SO No. 224*, Fort Laramie, Wyo. Terr., Nov. 23, 1869, Fourth Infantry Order Book, FLNHS.
65. Private George Cranston, Thirty-Second Infantry, informed his parents that he had been detailed to serve in a mounted detachment of twenty men on a forty-day scout from Tubac, Arizona. Dinges, "New York Private," 66. According to Private Samuel Gilpin, Company A, Thirteenth Infantry, was mounted during the Geronimo Campaign. Greene, *Indian War Veterans*, 361; De Barthe, *Life and Adventures of Frank Grouard*, 221–22 (quotation).
66. *ANJ*, Aug. 2, 1879, 958.
67. Zimmer, *Frontier Soldier*, 59 (first quotation). Some mounted infantrymen were subjected to an imitation of the "bull ring," used to train cavalry recruits at Jefferson Barracks. During the Milk River Campaign an observer noted that the first sergeants drilled the men on a "sort of impromptu track where the neophyte is put on his horse bareback and made to walk, trot, and gallop around." *ANJ*, Aug. 2, 1879, 958; Mulford, *Fighting Indians*, 95 (reference to the "Eleventh Cavalry"); Woodruff, "We Have Joseph," 32 (second quotation).
68. Greene, *Indian War Veterans*, 215 (quotation); Second Lieutenant Alexander Piper, Eighth Infantry in Carroll, *Unpublished Papers of the Order of the Indian Wars*, book 10, 13. In addition to those mentioned herein, other infantry regiments known to have mounted some of their companies for scouting or campaigning include the Second, Seventh, Nineteenth, Twenty-First, and Twenty-Third.
69. McConnell, *Five Years a Cavalryman*, 216 (first quotation); Christian Madsen, "Five Years War," MS, BBHC (second quotation). The authoritative account of this episode is Hedren, *First Scalp*, 60, 67; Maurer and Maurer, *First Sergeant*, 31.
70. Private Homer Coon reminiscence, copy at LBBNM (first quotation); McConnell, *Five Years a Cavalryman*, 82 (second quotation).

CHAPTER 16. "THE GOVERNMENT PAYS YOU TO GET SHOT AT"

1. George Neihaus questionnaire, f. 93, box 9, RP, DPL.
2. Cook, "Art of Indian Fighting," 176.
3. *ANJ*, Feb. 4, 1871, 391.
4. *Omaha Daily Bee*, March 27, 1876.

5. Magnussen, *Peter Thompson's Narrative*, 46 (first quotation); Private William Lossee to Father and Mother, April 20, 1876, f. 280, nonaccession file, LBBNM (second quotation); Private Marion Horn to Dear Sister, Mar. 21, 1876, Seventh Cavalry Personnel File, LBBNM (third quotation).

6. Sergeant William B. Cashan to Mary (cousin), May 6, 1876, Seventh Cavalry Personnel File, LBBNM (all odd spellings in the original).

7. Way journal, Aug. 4, 1873, J. A. Greene files (first quotation); Frederick Stortz to Father, Mar. 12, 1877, BHNB (second quotation); Windolph, *I Fought with Custer*, 68 (third quotation).

8. Anthony Gavin, "Campaigning," *National Tribune*, April 22, 1926 (first quotation); Hoffner journal, July 31, 1879, Brown Papers, UCB (second quotation); Lockwood, *Apaches and Longhorns*, 53 (third quotation).

9. Gavin, "Campaigning," *National* Tribune, April 22, 1926 (first quotation); McChristian, *Frontier Cavalry Trooper*, 169 (second quotation); Jesse G. Harris questionnaire, f. 56, box 9, RP, DPL (third quotation).

10. Magnussen, *Peter Thompson's Narrative*, 74 (first quotation); Hedren, "Worst Campaign," 7 (second quotation); account by Sergeant Hugh McGrath, Slough Papers, MHS (third quotation); White, *Custer, Cavalry, and Crows*, 50 (fourth quotation); Geant journal, f. 67, Camp Collection, LBBNM (fifth quotation).

11. Bradley, *March of the Montana Column*, 30, 131 (first quotation); "Diary of Matthew Carroll," 229–30 (second quotation). The incident is also mentioned in Geant journal, f. 67, Camp Collection, LBBNM.

12. William Miller, "Record of Events," FLNHS (first quotation); McChristian, *Frontier Cavalry Trooper*, 166–67 (second quotation); First Sergeant Thomas H. Wilson, to Friend Wallace, July 9, 1875, author's files (third quotation).

13. Sembower journal, Aug. 20, 1877, NPHP.

14. Barker journal, July 23, 1877, FLNHS.

15. Saddler John H. Niehause was a forty-five-year-old German in his sixth enlistment. Walker, "Reluctant Corporal" (pt. 1), 34–35.

16. McChristian, *Frontier Cavalry Trooper*, 163–64.

17. Gibbon, "Arms to Fight Indians," 240 (quotation). Skirmish practice for marksmen was restricted to only ten rounds of ammunition per man per year. Laidley, *Course of Instruction in Rifle Firing*, 162–65.

18. Lauren W. Aldrich, "Brief Reminiscences," HL (quotation); Magnussen, *Peter Thompson's Narrative*, 136–37.

19. Dinges, "New York Private," 60 (first quotation); Lockwood, *Apaches and Longhorns*, 31 (second quotation).

20. Mazzanovich, *Trailing Geronimo*, 160–63 (quotation). The man killed in action was Sergeant Albert Burford, Co. F, Sixth Cavalry. Sixth Cavalry Returns, October 1881, Returns from Regular Army Cavalry Regiments, M744, NARA.

21. Greene, *Indian War Veterans*, 17.

22. Sergeant Hugh K. McGrath in Slough Papers, MHS (first quotation); Maurer and Maurer, *First Sergeant*, 26 (second quotation).

23. Private Homer Coon reminiscence, LBBNM.

24. Smith, *Sagebrush Soldier*, 66 (first quotation); Windolph, *I Fought with Custer*, 76 (second quotation).

25. William G. Wilkinson, "Death of Sitting Bull," MS, f. 45, box 10, RP, DPL (quotation). In at least two instances, the Battle of the Washita and the Reynolds Fight

on Powder River, some of the troops removed their overcoats for ease of movement in combat and piled them some distance from the targeted villages. Meanwhile Indians discovered the coats and absconded with them, leaving the soldiers exposed in bitterly cold conditions. Barnard, *Ten Years with Custer*, 78; Hedren, *Powder River*, 138.

26. Zinser, *Indian War Diary*, 32 (first quotation); Greene, *Indian War Veterans*, 271 (second quotation); Private Homer Coon reminiscence, LBBNM (third quotation).

27. Private Richard Flynn diary, Sept. 9, 1876, FLNHS.

28. Keim, *Sheridan's Troopers*, 116 (first quotation); Barnard, *Ten Years with Custer*, 79 (second quotation). For additional evidence regarding this incident, see Greene, *Washita*, 185.

29. Private Homer Coon reminiscence, LBBNM (first quotation); *Wooden Leg*, 168 (second quotation).

30. George Whittaker questionnaire, f. 42, box 10, RP, DPL (first quotation); Smith, *Sagebrush Soldier*, 81 (second quotation).

31. Hebard and Brininstool, *Bozeman Trail*, 2:52 (first quotation); Cozzens, *Eyewitnesses to the Indian Wars*, 2:129 (second quotation); Greene, *Indian War Veterans*, 92 (third quotation).

32. Taylor, *With Custer*, 37 (first quotation); Brininstool, *Troopers with Custer*, 48 (second quotation).

33. Hills, "With General George A. Custer," 54 (first quotation); Smith, *Sagebrush Soldier*, 76 (second quotation).

34. Smith, *Sagebrush Soldier*, 77 (first quotation); Way, *Sgt. Fred Platten's Ten Years on the Trail*, 34–35 (second quotation).

35. Hammer, *With Custer in '76*, 106 (first quotation); Brininstool, *Troopers with Custer*, 56 (second quotation); Nichols, *Men with Custer*, 293 (third quotation).

36. Zinser, *Indian War Diary*, 13 (first quotation); Vaughn, *With Crook*, 122 (second quotation); Private Thomas Lloyd to Cousin Peter, Jan. 20, 1877, Minnesota Historical Society, St. Paul (third quotation); Finerty, *Warpath and Bivouac*, 136 (fourth quotation).

37. Buecker, "Journals of James S. McClellan," 29.

38. This was the encounter at Spring Creek, Montana Territory, on Oct. 11, 1876. Greene, *Battles and Skirmishes*, 122; Buecker, "In Pursuit of Crazy Horse," 28 (first quotation); Finerty, *War Path and Bivouac*, 93 (second quotation).

39. Taylor, *With Custer*, 58 (first quotation); Windolph, *I Fought with Custer*, 103 (second quotation), 101 (fourth quotation); Barnard, *Ten Years with Custer*, 298 (third quotation).

40. Fred W. Mixer, "An Indian Skirmish," *National Tribune*, Aug. 11, 1904.

41. Cozzens, *Eyewitnesses to the Indian Wars*, 2:449, 358.

42. Private Homer Coon reminiscence, LBBNM (first quotation); Greene, *Indian War Veterans*, 273 (second quotation).

43. Greene, *Indian War Veterans*, 284.

44. John M. Hoover to W. M. Camp, Mar. 4, 1916, ECP, DPL; Hebard and Brininstool, *Bozeman Trail*, 2:57 (quotation).

45. John R. P. Foster, "Fight at Sierra Diablo," *National Tribune*, Sept. 30, 1920.

46. Carroll, *Benteen-Goldin Letters*, 43–44.

47. Greene, *Indian War Veterans*, 272.

48. Cruse, *Apache Days and After*, 166–67.

49. Cozzens, *Eyewitnesses to the Indian Wars*, 4:98.

50. Brady, *Indian Fights*, 207.

51. When the Certificate of Merit was revived, it was made retroactive for combat actions occurring after June 22, 1874. Scott, *Custer's Heroes*, 48–55; *Revised United States Army Regulations of 1861*, 353; GO No. 19, AGO, Feb. 9, 1891. Those medals and certificates awarded while the men were in service occasioned a special parade. An example is described in *ANJ*, Mar. 6, 1880, when seven men of the Fifth Cavalry were honored with certificates for distinguishing themselves in action with Ute Indians at Milk River, Colorado.

52. The First World War witnessed the addition of the Distinguished Service Cross and the Distinguished Service Medal, both authorized in 1918. Many of the deeds earning the Medal of Honor prior to that date likely would have been recognized with one of those lesser awards or the Silver Star or Bronze Star, introduced even later. Because some felt that the prestige of the Medal of Honor had been diminished, the criteria were changed in 1897 to stipulate that only officers could make nominations for the award. Going even further, a board convened during 1916–17 reviewed the evidence for previous awards and purged over one-third of the recipients from the Medal of Honor rolls. An authoritative synthesis of the topic is found in Scott, *Custer's Heroes*, 58–60.

53. Captain J. H. Dorst to AG, USA, May 10, 1891, Forsyth Papers, AHS (first quotation); McChristian, "Soldier's Best and Noblest Remembrance," 30–31 (second quotation).

54. The four L Troop men were Sergeant John Rowalt, Corporal George Foos, and Privates A. P. Davis and John C. Wilson. McChristian, *Frontier Cavalry Trooper*, 173 n. 27, 203 (quotations)–204, 204 n. 11; Eighth Cavalry Returns, February 1873, Returns from Regular Army Cavalry Regiments, M744, NARA.

55. The deeds for which medals were awarded for the Battle of the Little Bighorn are detailed in Scott, *Custer's Heroes*, 13–32.

56. Hammer, *With Custer in '76*, 127 (quotation); Scott, *Custer's Heroes*, 75; Nichols, *Men with Custer*, 137–38. Some sources state that Hanley began his fifth enlistment in 1873, which is in error. He first enlisted in the Third Cavalry in 1863, serving in the South and, after the war, in New Mexico Territory. Soon after his discharge in 1868, he enlisted again and served in Company L, Second Cavalry, a component of the so-called Montana Battalion. Register of Enlistments; Soldiers and Sailors System; Rodenbough, *Army of the United States*, 202–4.

57. A narrative of this fight is found in Amos, "Above and Beyond," 22–27 (quotations); *Record of Engagements*, 100; Ninth Cavalry Returns, August 1881, Returns from Regular Army Cavalry Regiments, M744, NARA.

58. McConnell, *Five Years a Cavalryman*, 99 (quotations). Private Robert Fawls, age thirty-six, after deserting twice in 1870, eventually surrendered himself in 1875 and was dishonorably discharged the following year. Register of Enlistments, RG94, NARA; De Trobriand, *Military Life in Dakota*, 134–35.

59. Zimmer, *Frontier Soldier*, 23 (first quotation); Carroll, *Papers of the Order of Indian Wars*, 15 (second quotation); "John Burkman Notes," *Billings Gazette*, June 21, 1931; Hoffner journal, Aug. 20, 1879, Brown Papers, UCB (third quotation).

60. Private John Lanahan to Ed (brother), July 3, 1876, published in *Illinois State Register* (Springfield), July 12, 1876, reprinted in *Big Horn-Yellowstone Journal*, Autumn 1993.

61. This man was Private Richard Bennett, L Troop, Third Cavalry. Brady, *Indian Fights*, 208; Vaughn, *With Crook*, 127 (first quotation); White, *Custer, Cavalry, and Crows*, 78–79 (second quotation).

62. Liddic, *I Buried Custer*, 20 (first quotation); Private Frank O'Toole to *Pittsburgh Leader*, July 28, 1876 reprinted in *That Fatal Day*, 12–13 (second quotation). A notable

exception was recorded by a Fifth Infantry soldier during the Battle of the Bear's Paw Mountains in 1877. After some of his comrades had fallen between their lines and those of the Nez Perces, "instead of being tomahawked and scalped, the Indians helped them to a safe place where they would not be run over by charging horses or ponies." Such leniency was almost never shown by Indians but may have resulted in this instance because the surrounded Nez Perces realized that there was no escape from their position and that such an act might garner them favorable treatment. Greene, *Indian War Veterans*, 283.

63. Zinser, *Indian War Diary*, 18.
64. Barnard, *Ten Years with Custer*, 77–78.
65. Private Charles Lester to Dear Sister, June 16, 1869, Lester letters, FLNHS (first quotation); Greene, *Indian War Veterans*, 247 (second quotation); Hedren, "Worst Campaign," 8 (third quotation); Cozzens, *Eyewitnesses to the Indian Wars*, 2:129–30 (fourth quotation).
66. Way, *Sgt. Fred Platten's Ten Years on the Trail*, 12; White, *Custer, Cavalry, and Crows*, 74 (first quotation); Private Hartford G. Clark diary, Jan. 10 and 12, 1891, IWWP, JNEM (second and third quotations).
67. White, *Custer, Cavalry, and Crows*, 82 (first quotation); Taylor, *With Custer*, 117 (second quotation); [Arthur S.?] Wallace, "Episode of the Fifth Cavalry," 2.
68. Hedren, "Worst Campaign," 9 (quotation); Gerhard Luke Luhn, "Autobiography," AHC; Barnard, *Ten Years with Custer*, 197, 202.
69. Hedren, *Powder River*, 195; Cozzens, *Eyewitnesses to the Indian Wars*, 2:358 (quotation).
70. Brininstool, *Troopers with Custer*, 61 (first quotation); Barnard, *Ten Years with Custer*, 303 (second quotation). The story of the burials and reburials on the Little Bighorn Battlefield is chronicled in Greene, *Stricken Field*, 19–36.
71. Samuel L. Meddaugh diary, July 4 and Aug. 2, 1876, Lisle Brown Papers, ML, UU.
72. William Murphy, "Forgotten Battalion," MS, f. 17, Chapman Collection, AHC (first quotation); Cozzens, *Eyewitnesses to the Indian Wars*, 2:549 (second quotation).
73. Greene, *Indian War Veterans*, 109 (first quotation); Private Louis Ebert, account of service, f. 25, box 9, RP, DPL (second quotation).
74. Report of the Medical Department, LBBNM (quotation); Luce, "Diary and Letters," 75.
75. Finerty, *War Path and Bivouac*, 145 (first quotation); Sergeant John A. Kirkwood to W. M. Camp, Oct. 9, 1919, ECP, DPL (second quotation).
76. Buecker, "Journals of James S. McClellan," 30 (quotation); McClellan, "A Day with the 'Fighting Cheyennes,'" 22; Register of Enlistments, RG 94, NARA.
77. Lockwood, *Apaches and Longhorns* (first quotation) 64; Maurer and Maurer, *First Sergeant*, 63 (second quotation).
78. Finerty, *War Path and Bivouac*, 85;
79. White, *Custer, Cavalry, and Crows*, 84.
80. Billings, *Circular No. 9*, 17; Mulford, *Fighting Indians*, 125 (first quotation); account by Sergeant Hugh K. McGrath, Slough Papers, MHS (second quotation).
81. Hedren, "Worst Campaign," 9–10 (first quotation); Geant journal, June 28, 29, 1876, f. 67, Camp Collection, LBBNM (second quotation).
82. Greene, *Indian War Veterans*, 287.
83. Taylor, *With Custer*, 118.

704 NOTES TO PAGES 570–78

84. Reneau, *Adventures of Moccasin Joe*, 65 (first quotation); King, *Campaigning with Crook*, 95 (second quotation). Post-traumatic stress disorder and other health issues among members of the Seventh Cavalry are examined in Scott and Willey, *Health of the Seventh Cavalry*.

85. Hoffner journal, Sept. 4, 1879, UCB (first quotation); Edwin M. Brown, "Terror of the Badlands," MS, 36, MHS (second quotation).

86. Greene, *Frontier Cavalry Soldier*, 147 (first quotation); Reneau, *Adventures of Moccasin Joe*, 83 (second quotation).

87. Brown, "Terror of the Badlands," MS, MHS.

88. Private Thomas Lloyd to Cousin Peter, Jan. 20, 1877, Minnesota Historical Society, St. Paul.

CHAPTER 17. "THANK GOD I AM DONE SOLDIERING"

1. George McAnulty to Lillie Moore, Dec. 19, 1876, FLNHS (first quotation); James Tucker, "Served 10 Eventful Years," *National* Tribune, Nov. 24, 1921 (second quotation); Private Charles Lester to Dear Sister, Sept. 6, 1869, FLNHS (third quotation); Zinser, *Indian War Diary*, 23 (fourth quotation).

2. Waler "Reluctant Corporal" (pt. 1), 7 (first quotation); John O. Stotts reminiscence, Spencer collection (second quotation).

3. Private Jesse G. Harris questionnaire, f. 56, box 9, RP, DPL (first quotation); Dinges, "New York Private," 68 (second quotation); R. Eugene Pelham, "Passing of the Frontiers," *National Tribune*, Dec. 12, 1918 (third quotation).

4. Robert Greenhalgh to Father and Mother, May 19, 1866, Greenhalgh letters, RP, DPL (first quotation); McChristian, *Frontier Cavalry Trooper*, 332 (second quotation); Greene, *Indian War Veterans*, 41 (third quotation).

5. *ANJ*, Dec. 16, 1882: 437 (first quotation); James G. Morrison, questionnaire, f. 90, box 9, RP, DPL (second quotation); Grandison Mayo questionnaire, f. 45, box 9, RP, DPL (third quotation); Windolph, *I Fought with Custer*, 2 (fourth quotation); Joseph Kuhn questionnaire, f. 71, box 9, RP, DPL (fifth quotation).

6. John O. Stotts reminiscence, Spencer collection; Nichols, *Men with Custer*, 179; Private John G. Kimm to C. E. Rice, Nov. 1, 1876, Seventh Cavalry personnel files, LBBNM (quotation).

7. Trumpeter Charles P. Christian to My Dearest Sister, June 26, 1878, B. William Henry collection (first quotation); 1880 U.S. Census, Pima Co., Arizona Territory; Johnson, "Jacob Horner," 5 (second quotation).

8. Sergeant James S. Hamilton questionnaire, f. 52, box 9, RP, DPL (first quotation); Washington McCardle questionnaire, f. 82, box 9, RP, DPL (second quotation).

9. Private Richard F. King to Gabriella King, Jan. 24, 1889, FUNM (first quotation); Simpson Mann interview, f. 79, box 9, RP, DPL (second quotation); George Whittaker questionnaire, f. 42, box 10, RP, DPL (third quotation); Perley S. Eaton questionnaire, f. 24, box 9, RP, DPL (fourth quotation).

10. Ostrander, *Army Boy of the Sixties*, 174 (first quotation); White, *Custer, Cavalry, and Crows*, 123 (second quotation); McChristian, *Frontier Cavalry Soldier*, 380.

11. As an example, a soldier who had enlisted on the tenth day of the month was to be discharged on the ninth day of that month, five years later. *Regulations, 1881*, 30.

12. Captain Thomas H. French correctly dated Ryan's discharge certificate as required but permitted him to leave two days early in order for him to meet the train. Barnard, *Ten Years with Custer*, 314 (quotation).

13. A common practice was to leave short-timers behind at their posts, usually as guards over company property, when the command expected to be in the field beyond their termination dates. They would be attached to another company in the garrison for purposes of rationing and messing.

14. Walker, "Reluctant Corporal" (pt. 1), 43–44.

15. David Kerstetter, article fragment, n. p., n.d., John D. McDermott files.

16. Yohn, "Regulars in Arizona," 124.

17. John O. Stotts reminiscence, Spencer collection (quotation). A discharged soldier was not compelled to return to his place of enlistment. He was at liberty to go elsewhere, but travel pay was based on the mileage from his last station to the city or post where he had enlisted. Barnard, *Ten Years with Custer*, 183–84.

18. *ANJ*, Nov. 23, 1867, 217.

19. De Trobriand, *Military Life in Dakota*, 366 (first quotation), 364 (second quotation). Several other references to the use of mackinaw boats by discharged men from Missouri River posts are found in Mattison, "Diary of Surgeon Washington Matthews": 21, 22, 41, 44, 45 50.

20. Walker, "Reluctant Corporal" (pt. 2), 112–13.

21. QM Sergeant Maurice H. Wolfe to Dear Michael, n.d. [late 1869], FLNHS (quotation). Armand Unger also confirmed that "most of the noncoms were old timers." Unger interview, f. 34, box 10, RP, DPL; *ANJ*, April 21, 1883: 865. The provisions relating to reenlistment and longevity pay are found in *Regulations of the Army, 1881*, 320–21.

22. Liddic and Harbaugh, *Camp on Custer*, 31–32.

23. Way, *Sgt. Fred Platten's Ten Years on the Trail*, 24 (quotations). At the end of his second enlistment in 1882, Platten was discharged as first sergeant of H Troop. Register of Enlistments, AGO, RG 94, NARA.

24. Charles N. Jansen, account of service, f. 91, box 10, RP, DPL.

25. *ARSW, 1884*, 53; Forsyth, *Story of the Soldier*, 132 (quotation).

26. Thomas Ross folder, author's files.

27. Another of Michael McLennon's four daughters married Sergeant Mildon H. Wilson, Co. I, Seventh Infantry. Wilson also was awarded the Medal of Honor for his actions during the Battle of the Big Hole. Mark J. Nelson, "Brief Biographies," Rogan-McLennon file, FLNHS.

28. Fegan's full story is found in Rodenbough, *Sabre and Bayonet*, 350–59 (quotations on 355); Register of Enlistments, RG 94, NARA.

29. *Regulations of the Army, 1881*, paragraphs 836–37.

30. Mulford, *Fighting Indians*, 151 (first and second quotations); File WC-323–678, Pension Application Files, RG 15, NARA (third and fourth quotations).

31. *GO No. 18*, AGO, Feb. 27, 1885. In addition to their monthly pay, minus the standard deduction for support of the Soldiers' Home, retirees also received twenty-two and a half cents per day for subsistence, plus a clothing allowance of 75 percent of the amount that they were receiving at the time of discharge. *Regulations of the Army, 1895*, paragraphs 135–38.

32. Nelson, "Davids Island," 512; *ARSW*, 1891, 83; *Regulations of the Army, 1895*, paragraph 823.

33. Schubert, *Voices of the Buffalo Soldier*, 149; Nichols, *Men with Custer*, 235-36, 254, 289; George Neihaus questionnaire, f. 93, box 9, RP, DPL; McChristian, *Frontier Cavalry Trooper*, 393-99.

34. Cady, *Arizona's Yesterday*, 44, 75-76, 81, 83; John Gibbert questionnaire, f. 42, box 9, RP, DPL; Martin Andersen questionnaire f. 59, box 8, RP, DPL; Joseph Kuhn questionnaire, f.71, box 9, RP, DPL.

35. John L. Hubbard questionnaire, f. 62, box 9, RP, DPL; Nichols, *Men with Custer*, 361.

36. Mazzanovich, *Trailing Geronimo*, 337-38; Way, *Sgt. Fred Platten's Ten Years on the Trail*, 37 (quotation); Christian Madsen affidavit, Aug. 28, 1929, BBHC; Martin Welsh, service record, UIWV, f. 24, box 11, RP, DPL.

37. Charles N. Jansen, account of service, f. 91, box 10, RP, DPL; William G. Bowen, account of service, f. 2, box 9, RP, DPL (quotation).

38. Dinges, "New York Private," 55; Lockwood, *Apaches and Longhorns*, 118; Walker, "Reluctant Corporal" (pt. 2): 139-41.

39. "Bunkies in Indian Service," Montana Scrapbook, BPL (quotation); Rasmus Pilgard questionnaire, f. 106, box 9, RP, DPL.

40. Bigelow, *On the Bloody Trail*, 94 (quotation); John Bergstrom questionnaire, f. 72, box 8, RP, DPL.

41. Ostrander, *Army Boy of the Sixties*, 121; McAnulty folder, FLNHS.

42. *Proceedings of the American Numismatic and Archeological Society*, 49; Greene, *Indian War Veterans*, xv-xvi.

43. In 1899 the union modified its constitution and name to include former volunteers. *Proceedings of the American Numismatic and Archeological Society*, 57.

44. This discussion borrows heavily from a thorough treatment of the subject in Greene, *Indian War Veterans*, xvii-xlii.

45. *Winners of the West* (Oct. 1925).

46. Ostrander, *Army Boy*, 121.

47. William Murphy, "The Forgotten Battalion," f. 17, box 1, Chapman Collection, AHC.

48. R. Eugene Pelham, "The Passing of the Frontiers," *National Tribune*, Dec. 12, 1918 (first quotation); Walker, "Reluctant Corporal" (pt. 1), 13 (second quotation).

49. Gurnett, "Attention Co. K, 8th U.S. Infantry, 1871-76."

Bibliography

MANUSCRIPT SOURCES

American Heritage Center, University of Wyoming, Laramie
    M. A. Chapman Collection
    Gerhard Luke Luhn Papers
    Thomas G. Maghee Papers
Arizona Historical Society Library, Tucson
    Biographical Files
    Clarence Chrisman Diary
    Newspaper Clip File
    John A. Spring Papers
Big Hole National Battlefield, Wisdom, Montana
    Frederick Stortz Letters
Chavez History Library, Museum of New Mexico, Santa Fe
    Walter L. Finley Letters
Coe Library, Western Americana Collections, Yale University, New Haven, Connecticut
    Homer Coon Papers (copy in library, Little Bighorn Battlefield National Monument, Crow Agency, Montana)
Denver Public Library, Western History Collection, Denver, Colorado
    Robert S. Ellison, Walter M. Camp Papers
    Don Rickey Papers
Fort Laramie National Historic Site library, Fort Laramie, Wyoming
    E. D. Barker journal
    Reynolds J. Burt Boyhood Data
    Richard Flynn diary
    Edward Lautenschlaeger letters
    Charles Lester letters
    Howard A. Lyon letters
    George W. McAnulty letters

708 BIBLIOGRAPHY

    McDermott File
    George W. McIver file
    Johnny O'Brian interview
    Order Book, Co. G, Fourth U.S. Infantry
    Maurice H. Wolfe letters
Fort Supply Historic Site, Fort Supply, Oklahoma
    David L. Craft letters
    Andrew T. Fitch letters
    O. C. McNary letters
    Christian F. Sommer file
Fort Union National Monument Archives, Watrous, New Mexico
    Richard F. King letters
    William E. Matthews letters
Gilcrease Museum, Tulsa, Oklahoma
    Philip G. Cole Collection
Jerome A. Greene files, Arvada, Colorado
    Jonathan W. Biddle letters (copies)
    H. B. Boyer reminiscence. Interviews with Signal Sergeants (copy)
    Isaac M. Cline reminiscence. Interviews with Signal Sergeants (copy)
    Thomas N. Way journal (copy)
Gerald H. Groenewald-Connie Triplett Collection, Grand Forks, North Dakota
    Adelbert Butler letters
    Walter Mason Camp Papers
B. William Henry Collection, Eugene, Oregon
    Charles P. Christian Letters
Holland Library, Manuscripts, Archives and Special Collections, Washington State University, Pullman
    Lucullus V. McWhorter Papers
Huntington Library, San Marino, California
    Aldrich, Lauren. "Brief Reminiscences of the Soldier's Life on the Plains and in the Mountains during the Early Days of 1867–68–69 and 1870"
    E. R. Strumpf diary
    Fred H. Toby diary
Jefferson National Expansion Memorial Archives, St. Louis, Missouri
    Indian Wars Widows Project Records
Harold B. Lee Library, Special Collections, Brigham Young University, Provo, Utah
Little Bighorn Battlefield National Monument, Crow Agency, Montana
    Gibson-Fougera Collection
    Kenneth M. Hammer Collection
    Charles N. Hayden diary
    "Memorandum of Edward Williams, Company H, Second Cavalry, Fort Ellis, M.T., 1876 and 1877"
    Order Book, Co. K, Seventh U.S. Cavalry, Jan. 1878-Dec. 1881
    Seventh Cavalry Personnel Files
    Simon Snyder diaries
    Vertical files, nonaccessioned material from National Archives
    Report of the Medical Department of the Big Horn and Yellowstone Expedition of 1876

Marriott Library, University of Utah, Salt Lake City
> Lisle Brown Papers

McCracken Research Library, Buffalo Bill Historical Center, Cody, Wyoming
> Madsen, Christian. "Five Years War on the Prairies of West-America," Typescript, translated by Kirsten Fearn. Originally published as "Fem Aars Felttog paa Deftamerikas Praerier," *Danebrog* 36 (June 4, 1881): 577–84.

John D. McDermott Files, Rapid City, South Dakota
> *National Tribune* articles (copies)

Minnesota Historical Society, Manuscript Collections, St. Paul
> Thomas Lloyd letter

Missouri State Historical Society Library. St. Louis
> Army Collection
> Herman T. Hesse Papers
> Jefferson Barracks Papers
> Memoir of an unidentified trumpeter (Tetzel)

Montana Historical Society, Helena
> John P. Slough Papers

Montana Room, Parmly Billings Library, Billings, Montana
> Billings Scrapbook, vol. 3
> Montana Scrapbook, vol. 1
> Vertical Files

Montana State University, Merrill G. Burlingame Special Collections, Bozeman
> Gustavus C. Doane Papers

James Mountain Files, Ashburnham, Massachusetts
> Henry Hubman Letters

National Archives and Records Administration, Washington, D.C.
> Record Group 15, Records of the Department of Veterans Affairs
> Pension Application Files, Indian Wars
> Record Group 94, Records of the Office of the Adjutant General
> General Orders
> Letters Received, Enlisted Branch
> Letters Received (Main Series)
> Papers Relating to the Army Equipment Board, 1878–79
> Medical History, Fort Laramie
> Post Returns
> Carlisle Barracks, Pennsylvania.
> Columbus Barracks, Ohio
> Fort Hays, Kansas
> Fort Leavenworth, Kansas
> Jefferson Barracks, Missouri
> Newport Barracks, Kentucky
> Register of Deaths, Regular Army, 1860–89
> Registers of Enlistment in the United States Army, 1798–1914 (M233)
> Returns from Regular Army Cavalry Regiments, 1833–1916 (M744)
> Returns from Regular Army Infantry Regiments, 1821–1916 (M665)
> Record Group 98, Record of United States Army Commands, 1784–1821
> Fort Laramie, Wyoming
> Record Group 153, Records of the Office of the Judge Advocate General

BIBLIOGRAPHY

Record Group 391, Records of U. S. Regular Army Mobile Units
Cavalry, Seventh Cavalry, 1866–1917, General and Special Orders Issued, 1873–74
Record Group 393, Records of United States Army Continental Commands, 1821–1920
Department of Dakota, Letters Received
Fort Fetterman, Wyo. Terr., General Orders 1868–82
Fort Fetterman, Wyo. Terr., Proceedings of Post Councils of Administration
Fort Fetterman, Wyo. Terr., Report Book of Post School, 1873–74
Fort Fetterman, Wyo. Terr., Telegrams Sent, 1868–82
Fort Laramie, Wyo. Terr., Register of Ration Returns, 1868–71
Fort Union, New Mex. Terr., Orders and Special Orders, 1858–81
Newberry Library, Chicago, Illinois
George M. Templeton diary, 1866–68
Nez Perce National Historical Park library, Spaulding, Idaho
Isaac H. Sembower journal
Oklahoma Historical Society, Oklahoma City
Thoburn Collection
Parmly Billings Library, Billings, Montana
Billings Scrapbook
Biography File
Montana Scrapbook
Pamphlet File
South Caroliniana Library, University of South Carolina, Columbia
Micah Jenkins Papers
Jack Spencer Files, Maria, California
John O. Stotts Reminiscence
University of Arizona Library, Special Collections. Tucson
George Cranston Letters
Autobiography of William Bladen Jett
Edward Palmer Papers
U.S. Army Military History Institute Archives, U.S. Army Heritage and Education Center, Carlisle, Pennsylvania
Luther P. Bradley Papers
Daughters of the U.S. Army Collection
Order of the Indian Wars Collection
Samuel J. Ovenshine Family Papers
Don Rickey Jr. Collection
Western Historical Collections, Norlin Library, University of Colorado, Boulder
William Carey Brown Papers
Edgar Hoffner Journal of the Sheepeater Campaign
Wyoming State Archives, Cheyenne
Logan, Earnest A., "Fort Laramie—1877"
Stephen R. Richey diary (microfilm)
Herman S. Searl Letters

BIBLIOGRAPHY 711

BOOKS

Adams, Gerald M. *The Post Near Cheyenne: A History of Fort D. A. Russell, 1867–1930.* Boulder, Colo.: Pruett Publishing, 1989.
Adams, Kevin. *Class and Race in the Frontier Army: Military Life in the West, 1870–1890.* Norman: University of Oklahoma Press, 2009.
Alexander, Eveline M. *Cavalry Wife: The Diary of Eveline M. Alexander, 1866–1867.* Edited by Sandra L. Myres. College Station: Texas A&M University Press, 1977.
Amos, Preston E. *Above and Beyond in the West: Black Medal of Honor Winners, 1870–1890.* Arlington, Va.: Potomac Corral of the Westerners, 1974.
Annual Reports of the Secretary of War. Washington, D.C.: Government Printing Office, 1865—94.
Ashburn, P. M. *A History of the Medical Department of the United States Army.* Cambridge, Mass.: Houghton Mifflin Co., 1929.
Athearn, Robert G. *William Tecumseh Sherman and the Settlement of the West.* Norman: University of Oklahoma Press, 1995.
Austerman, Wayne R. *Sharps Rifles and Spanish Mules: The San Antonio-El Paso Mail, 1851–1881.* College Station: Texas A&M Press, 1985.
Bailey, Lynn R., ed. *A Tenderfoot in Tombstone: The Private Journal of George Whitwell Parsons—The Turbulent Years, 1880–82.* Tucson, Ariz.: Westernlore Press, 1996.
Ball, Durwood. *Army Regulars on the Western Frontier, 1848–1861.* Norman: University of Oklahoma Press, 2001.
Ball, Eve. *In the Days of Victorio: Recollections of a Warm Springs Apache.* Tucson: University of Arizona Press, 1970.
Ballentine, George. *Autobiography of an English Soldier in the United States Army.* Chicago: R. R. Donnelley and Sons Co., 1986.
Barnard, Sandy, ed. *Ten Years with Custer: A Seventh Cavalryman's Memoirs.* Terre Haute, Ind.: AST Press, 2001.
The Battle of Beecher Island Fought September 17, 18, 1868 (n.d.). Reprint. Wray, Colo.: Beecher Island Memorial Association, 1960.
Bell, William A. *New Tracks in North America: A Journal of Travel and Adventure Whilst Engaged in the Survey for a Southern Railroad to the Pacific Ocean during 1867—8.* Albuquerque, N.Mex.: Horn and Wallace, 1965.
Betzinez, Jason, with Wilber S. Nye. *I Fought with Geronimo.* Lincoln: University of Nebraska Press, 1959.
Bigelow, John. *On the Bloody Trail of Geronimo.* Los Angeles: Westernlore Press, 1958.
Billings, John D. *Hardtack and Coffee, or, The Unwritten Story of Army Life.* Boston: G. M. Smith and Co., 1887. Reprint. Chicago: R. R. Donnelly, 1960.
Billings, John S. *Circular No. 4, Report on Barracks and Hospitals with Descriptions of Military Posts and Chapter on "Arrow Wounds" from Circular No. 3, Arrow Wounds, Report of Surgical Cases Treated in the Army of the United States* (1870 and 1871). Reprint, with introduction by Herbert M. Hart. New York: Sol Lewis, 1974.
———. *Circular No. 8, Report on Hygiene of the United States Army with Descriptions of Military Posts and Circular No. 9, Report to the Surgeon General on the Transport of Sick and Wounded by Pack Animals* (1875 and 1877). Reprint. New York: Sol Lewis, 1974.
Billington, Monroe Lee. *New Mexico's Buffalo Soldiers, 1866–1900.* Niwot: University Press of Colorado, 1991.

Bourke, John G. *Mackenzie's Last Fight with the Cheyennes* (1890). Reprint. Bellevue, Nebr.: Old Army Press, 1970.

———. *On the Border with Crook* (1891). Reprint. Lincoln: University of Nebraska Press, 1971.

Boyd, Frances Anne Mullen. *Cavalry Life in Tent and Field* (1894). Reprint, with an introduction by Darlis A. Miller. Lincoln: University of Nebraska Press, 1982.

Bradley, James H. *March of the Montana Column: A Prelude to the Custer Disaster.* Edited by Edgar I. Stewart. Norman: University of Oklahoma Press, 1961.

Brady, Cyrus Townsend. *Indian Fights and Fighters.* Lincoln: University of Nebraska Press, 1971.

Brininstool, E. A. *Troopers with Custer: Historic Incidents of the Battle of the Little Big Horn.* Harrisburg, Pa.: Stackpole Co., 1952.

Brooks, Clinton E., and Frank D. Reeve, eds. *Forts and Forays, James A. Bennett: A Dragoon in New Mexico 1850—1856.* Albuquerque: University of New Mexico Press, 1948.

Brown, William Carey. *The Sheepeater Campaign 1879.* Boise: Idaho Historical Society, 1926.

Brown, William L., III, *The Army Called It Home: Military Interiors of the 19th Century.* Gettysburg, Pa.: Thomas Publications, 1992.

Browne, John Ross. *Adventures in Apache Country: A Tour through Arizona and Sonora, with Notes on the Silver Regions of Nevada* (1871). Reprint. New York: Promontory Press, 1974.

Buecker, Thomas R. *Fort Robinson and the American West, 1874–1899.* Lincoln: University of Nebraska Press, 1999.

Butler, Anne M. *Daughters of Joy, Sisters of Misery: Prostitutes in the American West, 1865–90.* Urbana: University of Illinois Press, 1987.

Byrne, Bernard James. *A Frontier Army Surgeon: Life in Colorado in the Eighties.* New York: Exposition Press, 1962.

Cady, John. *Arizona's Yesterday* (1915). Reprint, with a foreword by L. Boyd Finch. Tucson, Ariz.: Adobe Corral, Westerners International, 1995.

Carriker, Robert C., and Eleanor R. Carriker, eds. *An Army Wife on the Frontier: The Memoirs of Alice Blackwood Baldwin 1867–1877.* Salt Lake City: University of Utah Library, 1975.

Carrington, Frances C. *My Army Life and the Fort Phil Kearney Massacre.* Philadelphia: J. B. Lippincott Co., 1910.

Carroll, John M., ed. *The Benteen-Goldin Letters on Custer and His Last Battle.* Lincoln: University of Nebraska Press, 1974.

———, ed. *The Black Military Experience in the American West.* New York: Liveright Publishing, 1971.

———, ed. *The Papers of the Order of Indian Wars.* Fort Collins, Colo.: Old Army Press, 1975.

———, ed. *A Seventh Cavalry Scrapbook.* Bryan, Tex.: John M. Carroll, 1978.

———, ed. *The Unpublished Papers of the Order of the Indian Wars, Book 1.* N.p., New Brunswick, N.J.: n.d.

———, ed. *The Unpublished Papers of the Order of the Indian Wars, Book 2.* N.p., New Brunswick, N.J.: n.d.

———, ed. *The Unpublished Papers of the Order of the Indian Wars, Book 5.* N.p., New Brunswick, N.J.: 1977.

———, ed. *The Unpublished Papers of the Order of the Indian Wars, Book 8.* N.p., New Brunswick, N.J.: 1977.

———, ed. *The Unpublished Papers of the Order of the Indian Wars, Book 9.* N.p., New Brunswick, N.J.: 1977.
———, ed. *The Unpublished Papers of the Order of the Indian Wars, Book 10.* N.p., New Brunswick, N.J.: 1977.
Carroll, John M., and Lawrence Frost, eds. *Private Theodore Ewert's Diary of the Black Hills Expedition of 1874.* Piscataway, N.J.: Consultant Resources, 1976.
Carter, R. G. *The Old Sergeant's Story.* New York: Frederick H. Hitchcock, 1926.
———. *On the Border with Mackenzie.* Foreword by Charles M. Robinson. Austin: Texas State Historical Association, 2007.
Cashin, Herschel V. *Under Fire with the Tenth Cavalry.* New York: Bellwether Publishing Co., 1970.
Cavalry Tactics. New York: D. Appleton and Co., 1878.
Chronological List of Actions & c. with Indians from January 15, 1837 to January, 1891: Adjutant General's Office. Introduction by Dale E. Floyd. Fort Collins, Colo.: Old Army Press, 1979.
Circular No. 3: A Report of Surgical Cases Treated in the Army of the United States from 1865 to 1871. Washington, D.C.: Government Printing Office, 1871.
Clark, William Philo. *The Indian Sign Language.* Facsimile of the first edition. Philadelphia: L. R. Hamersly and Co., 1885.
Coffman, Edward M. *The Old Army: A Portrait of the American Army in Peacetime, 1784–1898.* New York: Oxford University Press, 1986.
Collins, John S. *Across the Plains in '64.* Omaha, Neb.: National Printing Co., 1911.
Comfort, William Levington. *Trooper Tales: A Series of Sketches of the Real American Private Soldier.* New York: Street and Smith, 1899.
Compilation of General Orders, Circulars, and Bulletins of the War Department Issued between February 15, 1881, and December 31, 1915. Washington, D.C.: Government Printing Office, 1916.
Cooke, Philip St. George. *Cavalry Tactics.* Philadelphia: J. B. Lippincott and Co., 1862.
Cox, John E. *Five Years in the United States Army* (1892). Facsimile of the first edition, with an introduction by Don Russell. New York: Sol Lewis, 1973.
Cox-Paul, Lori, and James W. Wengert. *A Frontier Army Christmas.* Lincoln: Nebraska Historical Society, 1996.
Cozzens, Peter, ed. *Eyewitnesses to the Indian Wars 1865–1890.* Vol. 1, *The Struggle for Apacheria.* Mechanicsburg, Pa.: Stackpole Books, 2001.
———, ed. *Eyewitnesses to the Indian Wars 1865–1890.* Vol. 2, *The Wars for the Pacific Northwest.* Mechanicsburg, Pa., Stackpole Books, 2002.
———, ed. *Eyewitnesses to the Indian Wars 1865–1890.* Vol. 3, *Conquering the Southern Plains.* Mechanicsburg, Pa., Stackpole Books, 2003.
———, ed. *Eyewitnesses to the Indian Wars 1865–1890.* Vol. 4, *The Long War for the Northern Plains.* Mechanicsburg, Pa.: Stackpole Books, 2004.
———, ed. *Eyewitnesses to the Indian Wars 1865–1890.* Vol. 5, *The Army and the Indian.* Mechanicsburg, Pa.: Stackpole Books, 2005.
Crawford, Lewis F. *The Exploits of Ben Arnold Indian Fighter, Gold Miner, Cowboy, Hunter, and Army Scout* (1926). Reprint, with an introduction by Paul L. Hedren. Norman: University of Oklahoma Press, 1999.
Cremony, John C. *Life among the Apaches* (1868). Facsimile reprint. Tucson: Arizona Silhouettes, 1954.
Crook, George. *General George Crook, His Autobiography.* Edited and annotated by Martin F. Schmitt. Norman: University of Oklahoma Press, 1960.

Cruse, Thomas. *Apache Days and After* (1941). Reprint, edited with an introduction by Eugene Cunningham. Lincoln: University of Nebraska Press, 1987.

Custer, Elizabeth B. *Boots and Saddles, or Life in Dakota with General Custer.* New York: Harper and Brothers, 1885.

———. *Following the Guidon.* New York: Harper and Brothers, 1890.

———. *Tenting on the Plains, or General Custer in Kansas and Texas* (1895). Reprint. Williamstown, Mass.: Corner House Publishers, 1973.

De Barthe, Joe. *The Life and Adventures of Frank Grouard, Chief of Scouts, U.S.A.* (1894). Reprint. New York: Skyhorse Publishing, 2014.

Delo, David Michael. *Peddlers and Post Traders: The Army Sutler on the Frontier.* Salt Lake City: University of Utah Press, 1992.

De Trobriand, Philippe Régis. *Military Life in Dakota: The Journal of Philippe Régis de Trobriand.* Translated and edited by Lucile M. Kane. St. Paul, Minn.: Alvord Memorial Commission, 1951.

Dobak, William A., and Thomas D. Phillips. *The Black Regulars, 1866–1898.* Norman: University of Oklahoma Press, 2001.

Eales, Anne Bruner. *Army Wives on the American Frontier.* Boulder, Colo.: Johnson Books, 1996.

Ewers, John C. *Plains Indian History and Culture: Essays on Continuity and Change.* Norman: University of Oklahoma Press, 1997.

Farrow, Edward S. *Farrow's Military Encyclopedia.* New York: Military-Naval Publishing Company, 1895.

———. *Mountain Scouting: A Handbook for Officers and Soldiers on the Frontiers* (1881). Facsimile reprint with a foreword by Jerome A. Greene. Norman: University of Oklahoma Press, 2000.

Fike, Richard E. *The Bottle Book: A Comprehensive Guide to Historic, Embossed Medicine Bottles.* Salt Lake City: Gibbs M. Smith, 1987.

Finerty, John F. *War Path and Bivouac: The Big Horn and Yellowstone Expedition.* Chicago: R. R. Donnelly and Sons Co., 1955.

FitzGerald, Emily McCorkle. *An Army Doctor's Wife on the Frontier.* Edited by Abe Laufe. Lincoln: University of Nebraska Press, 1986.

Flannery, L. G., ed. *John Hunton's Diary, 1878–79.* Vol. 3. Lingle, Wyo.: Guide-Review, 1960.

Foner, Jack D. *The United States Soldier between Two Wars: Army Life and Reforms, 1865–1898.* New York: Humanities Press, 1970.

Forsyth, George A. *The Story of the Soldier.* New York: D. Appleton and Co., 1900.

———. *Thrilling Days in Army Life* (1900). Reprint, with an introduction by David Dixon. Lincoln: University of Nebraska Press, 1994.

Fowler, Arlen L. *The Black Infantry in the West 1869–1891.* Westport, Conn.: Greenwood Publishing, 1971.

Frazer, Robert W. *Forts of the West: Military Forts and Presidios, and Posts Commonly Called Forts, West of the Mississippi River to 1898.* Norman: University of Oklahoma Press, 1972.

Furness, William Eliot. "The Negro As a Soldier." In *Military Essays and Recollections*, 457–87. Chicago: A. C. McClurg and Co., 1894.

Ganoe, William Addleman. *The History of the United States Army.* Ashton, Md.: Eric Lundberg, 1964.

Gatewood, Charles B. *Lt. Charles B. Gatewood & His Apache Wars Narrative.* Edited by Louis Kraft. Lincoln: University of Nebraska Press, 2005.

Gillett, Mary C. *The Army Medical Department 1865–1917.* Army Historical Series. Washington, D.C.: Center of Military History, U.S. Army, 1995.
Glasrud, Bruce A., and Michael N. Searles, eds. *Buffalo Soldiers in the West: A Black Soldiers Anthology.* College Station: Texas A&M University Press, 2007.
Gray, John S. *Centennial Campaign: The Sioux War of 1876.* Fort Collins, Colo.: Old Army Press, 1976.
Green, Bill. *The Dancing Was Lively, Fort Concho, Texas: A Social History, 1867–1882.* San Angelo, Tex.: Fort Concho Sketches Publishing Co., 1974.
Greene, Jerome A., ed. *Battles and Skirmishes of the Great Sioux War, 1876–1877: The Military View.* Norman: University of Oklahoma Press, 1993.
———, ed. *Indian War Veterans: Memories of Army Life and Campaigns in the West, 1864–1898.* New York: Savas Beatie, 2007.
———, ed. *Lakota and Cheyenne: Indian Views of the Great Sioux War, 1876–1877.* Norman: University of Oklahoma Press, 1994.
———. *Nez Perce Summer 1877: The U.S. Army and the Nee-Me-Poo Crisis.* Helena: Montana Historical Society Press, 2000.
———. *Stricken Field: The Little Bighorn since 1876.* Norman: University of Oklahoma Press, 2008.
———. *Washita: The U.S. Army and the Southern Cheyennes, 1867–1869.* Norman: University of Oklahoma Press, 2004.
———. *Yellowstone Command: Colonel Nelson A. Miles and the Great Sioux War, 1876–1877.* Lincoln: University of Nebraska Press, 1991.
Gruber, Robert, Maizie Johnson, et al., comps. *Preliminary Inventory of the Records of United States Army Continental Commands, 1821–1920.* Washington, D.C.: National Archives and Records Administration, 1999.
Gustafson, A. M., ed. *John Spring's Arizona.* Tucson: University of Arizona Press, 1966.
Guthrie, James M. *Camp Fires of the Afro-Americans.* Philadelphia: Afro-American Publishing Co., 1899.
Hammer, Kenneth, ed. *With Custer in '76: Walter Camp's Notes on the Custer Fight.* Provo, Utah: Brigham Young University Press, 1976.
Hardorff, Richard G., comp. *Camp, Custer, and the Little Bighorn: A Collection of Walter Mason Camp's Research Papers on General George A. Custer's Last Fight.* El Segundo, Calif.: Upton and Sons, 1997.
Hart, Herbert M. *Old Forts of the Northwest.* New York: Bonanza Books, 1968.
Hassrick, Royal B. *The Sioux.* Norman: University of Oklahoma Press, 1989.
Hebard, Grace Raymond, and E. A. Brininstool. *The Bozeman Trail: Historical Accounts of the Blazing of the Overland Routes into the Northwest, and the Fight with Red Cloud's Warriors* (1922). Reprint, 2 vols. in 1. Glendale, Calif.: Arthur H. Clark Co., 1960.
Hedren, Paul L. *First Scalp for Custer: The Skirmish at Warbonnet Creek, Nebraska, July 17, 1876.* Glendale, Calif.: Arthur H. Clark Co., 1980.
———. *Great Sioux War Orders of Battle: How the United States Army Waged War on the Northern Plains, 1876–1877.* Norman, Okla.: Arthur H. Clark Co., 2011.
———. *Powder River: Disastrous Opening of the Great Sioux War.* Norman: University of Oklahoma Press, 2016.
———. *We Trailed the Sioux: Enlisted Men Speak on Custer, Crook, and the Great Sioux War.* Mechanicsburg, Pa.: Stackpole Books, 2003.
———. *With Crook in the Black Hills: Stanley J. Morrow's 1876 Photographic Legacy.* Boulder, Colo.: Pruett Publishing Co., 1985.

Hein, O. L. *Memories of Long Ago.* New York: G. P. Putnam's Sons, 1925.
Heitman, Francis B. *Historical Register and Dictionary of the United States Army , from Its Organization, September 29, 1789, to March 2, 1903.* 2 vols. Washington, D.C.: Government Printing Office, 1903.
Henry, Guy V. *Army Catechism, or Simple Questions and Answers for Non-Commissioned Officers and Soldiers.* Salt Lake City, Utah: Star Printing Co., 1881.
———. *Target Practice—Information for Soldiers.* Ordnance Notes No. 340. Washington, D.C.: Government Printing Office, 1884.
Hershler, N. *The Soldier's Handbook for the Use of the Enlisted Men of the Army.* Washington, D.C.: Government Printing Office, 1884.
Holabird, Samuel B. *Some Considerations Respecting Desertion in the Army.* Ordnance Notes No. 232. Washington, D.C.: Government Printing Office, 1882.
Hooker, Forrestine C. *Child of the Fighting Tenth: On the Frontier with the Buffalo Soldiers.* Edited by Steve Wilson. New York: Oxford University Press, 2003.
House of Representatives. Report No. 56. *Reorganization of the Army.* Forty-Fifth Congress, Second Session (1878). Washington, D.C.: Government Printing Office.
———. Report No. 384. *Reorganization of the Army.* Washington, D.C.: Government Printing Office, 1874.
———. Report No. 1061. Fifty-First Congress, First Session. Washington, D.C.: Government Printing Office, 1891.
Hutton, Paul A. *Phil Sheridan and His Army.* Lincoln: University of Nebraska Press, 1985.
Hynes, William F. *Soldiers of the Frontier.* N.p.: W. F. Hynes, 1943.
Jamieson, Perry D. *Crossing the Deadly Ground: United States Army Tactics, 1865–1899.* Tuscaloosa: University of Alabama Press, 1994.
Jensen, Richard E., ed. *The Indian Interviews of Eli S. Ricker, 1903–1919.* Vol. 1, *Voices of the American West.* Lincoln: University of Nebraska Press, 2005.
———, ed. *The Settler and Soldier Interviews of Eli S. Ricker, 1903–1919.* Vol. 2, *Voices of the American West.* Lincoln: University of Nebraska Press, 2005.
Jocelyn, Stephen Perry. *Mostly Alkali.* Caldwell, Idaho: Caxton Printers, 1953.
Kautz, August V. *Customs of Service for Non-Commissioned Officers and Soldiers as Derived from Law and Regulations and Practised in the Army of the United States.* Philadelphia: J. B. Lippincott and Co., 1864.
Keim, De B. Randolph. *Sheridan's Troopers on the Borders: A Winter Campaign on the Plains* (1870). Facsimile of the first edition, with an introduction by John Greenway. Glorietta, N.Mex.: Rio Grande Press, 1977.
Kilburn, G. I. *Notes on Preparing Stores for the United States Army; and on the Care of the Same, Etc., with a Few Rules for Detecting Adulterations.* Cincinnati: W. A. Webb, 1862.
Kinevan, Marcos E. *Frontier Cavalryman: Lieutenant John Bigelow with the Buffalo Soldiers in Texas.* El Paso: Texas Western Press, 1998.
King, Charles. *Campaigning with Crook and Stories of Army Life.* New York: Harper and Brothers, 1890.
———. *Trials of a Staff Officer.* Philadelphia: J. B. Lippincott Co., 1895.
King, C. Richard, ed. *Marion T. Brown: Letters from Fort Sill.* Austin, Tex.: Encino Press, 1970.
Knight, Oliver. *Life and Manners in the Frontier Army.* Norman: University of Oklahoma Press, 1978.
Koury, Michael J. *Diaries of the Little Big Horn.* N.p.: Old Army Press, 1970.

Laidley, T. T. S. *A Course of Instruction in Rifle Firing*. Philadelphia: J. B. Lippincott Co., 1880.

Lane, Lydia Spencer. *I Married a Soldier or Old Days in the Old Army* (1893). Reprint, with an introduction by Mrs. Dwight D. Eisenhower. Albuquerque: Horn and Wallace Publishers, 1964.

Langellier, John P. *The Drums Would Roll: A Pictorial History of U.S. Army Bands on the American Frontier, 1866–1900*. Poole, England: Arms and Armour Press, 1987.

Leckie, William H. *The Buffalo Soldiers: A Narrative of the Negro Cavalry in the West*. Norman: University of Oklahoma Press, 1967.

Liddic, Bruce R., ed. *I Buried Custer: The Diary of Thomas W. Coleman*. College Station, Tex.: Creative Publishing Co., 1979.

Liddic, Bruce R., and Paul Harbaugh, eds. *Camp on Custer: Transcribing the Custer Myth*. Spokane, Wash.: Arthur H. Clark Co., 1995.

Lockwood, Frank C., ed. *Apaches and Longhorns: The Reminiscences of Will C. Barnes*. Los Angeles: Ward Ritchie Press, 1941.

Lockwood, James D. *Life and Adventures of a Drummer Boy or, Seven Years a Soldier*. Albany, N.Y.: John Skinner, 1893.

Lowe, Percival G. *Five Years a Dragoon ('49 to '54) and Other Adventures on the Great Plains* (1906). Reprint, with an introduction by Don Russell. Norman: University of Oklahoma Press, 1965.

Lowry, Thomas P. *The Story the Soldiers Wouldn't Tell: Sex in the Civil War*. Mechanicsburg, Pa.: Stackpole Books, 1994.

Magnussen, Daniel O., ed. *Peter Thompson's Narrative of the Little Bighorn Campaign, 1876*. Glendale, N.Y.: Arthur H. Clark Co., 1974.

Marshall, J. T. *The Miles Expedition of 1874–75: An Eyewitness Account of the Red River War*. Vol. 1 of *Narratives of the American West*. Edited by Lonnie J. White. Austin, Tex.: Encino Press, 1971.

Mason, Otis Tufton. *North American Bows, Arrows, and Quivers* (1893). Facsimile of the first edition, with an introduction by Ernest Berke. Bryan, Tex.: J. M. Carroll and Co., 1972.

Mattes, Merrill J. *Indians, Infants, and Infantry: Andrew and Elizabeth Burt on the Frontier*. Denver, Colo.: Old West Publishing Co., 1960.

Maurer, Charles, and Richard D. Maurer. *The First Sergeant: The Military Career of Charles Maurer*. Davis, Calif.: Maurer Options, 1986.

Mautz, Carl. *Biographies of Western Photographers: A Reference Guide to Photographers Working in the 19th Century American West*. Nevada City, Calif.: Carl Mautz Publishing, 1997.

Mazzanovich, Anton. *Trailing Geronimo*. Los Angeles: Gem Publishing Co., 1926.

McChristian, Douglas C. *An Army of Marksmen: The Development of United States Army Marksmanship in the 19th Century*. Fort Collins, Colo.: Old Army Press, 1981.

———. *Fort Bowie: Combat Post of the Southwest, 1858–1894*. Norman: University of Oklahoma Press, 2005.

———. *Fort Laramie: Military Bastion of the High Plains*. Norman: Arthur H. Clark Co., 2008.

———, ed. *Frontier Cavalry Trooper: The Letters of Private Eddie Matthews, 1869–1874*. Albuquerque: University of New Mexico Press, 2013.

———, ed. *Garrison Tangles in the Friendless Tenth: The Journal of First Lieutenant John Bigelow, Jr., Fort Davis, Texas*. Mattituck, N.Y.: J. M. Carroll and Co., 1985.

———. "A Soldier's Best and Noblest Remembrance: First Sergeant Thomas Hall Forsyth in the Dull Knife Fight November 25, 1876." In *The Dull Knife Symposium*, 27–31. Sheridan, Wyo.: Fort Phil Kearny/Bozeman Trail Association, 1989.

———. *Uniforms, Arms, and Equipment: The U.S. Army on the Western Frontier, 1880–1892.* 2 vols. Norman: University of Oklahoma Press, 2007.

———. *The U.S. Army in the West, 1870–1880: Uniforms, Weapons, and Equipment.* Norman: University of Oklahoma Press, 1995.

McConnell, H. H. *Five Years a Cavalryman: Sketches of Regular Army Life on the Texas Frontier Twenty Odd Years Ago* (1888). Facsimile reprint of the first edition. Freeport, N.Y.: Books for Libraries Press, 1970.

McDermott, John D. *A Guide to the Indian Wars of the West.* Lincoln: University of Nebraska Press, 1998.

McGinnis, Anthony. *Counting Coup and Cutting Horses: Intertribal Warfare on the Northern Plains 1783–1889.* Evergreen, Colo.: Cordillera Press, 1990.

Merington, Marguerite, ed. *The Custer Story: The Life and Intimate Letters of General George A. Custer and His Wife Elizabeth.* Lincoln: University of Nebraska Press, 1987.

Meyers, Augustus. *Ten Years in the Ranks, U.S. Army* (1914). Reprint. New York: Arno Press, 1979.

Miles, Nelson A. *Personal Recollections and Observations of General Nelson A. Miles* (1896). Reprint, with an introduction by Robert Wooster. 2 vols. Lincoln: University of Nebraska Press, 1992.

Moore, Rex, ed. *Dakota Cowboy Soldier: A Collection of Documented Letters by Michael Vetter, U.S. Army—7th Cavalry Regiment, Dakota Territory and Little Big Horn, Montana.* Fort Totten, N.Dak.: Devils Lake Sioux Manufacturing Corp., n.d.

Mulford, Ami Frank. *Fighting Indians in the 7th United States Cavalry* (1878). Facsimile reprint of the second edition, with an introduction by Michael J. Koury. Bellevue, Nebr.: Old Army Press, 1970.

Myers, Sandra L., ed. *Cavalry Wife: The Diary of Eveline M. Alexander, 1866–1867.* College Station: Texas A&M University Press, 1977.

Nankivell, John H., comp. *History of the Twenty-Fifth Regiment, United States Infantry, 1869–1926.* Denver: Smith-Brooks Printing company, 1927.

Neihardt, John G. *Black Elk Speaks: Being the Life Story of a Holy Man of the Oglala Sioux.* New York: Washington Square Press, 1972.

Nichols, Ronald H., ed. *Men with Custer: Biographies of the 7th Cavalry.* Hardin, Mont.: Custer Battlefield Historical and Museum Association, 2000.

Notson, William M. *Fort Concho Medical History 1869 to 1872.* San Angelo, Tex.: Fort Concho Preservation and Museum, 1974.

Oliva, Leo E. *Fort Larned.* Topeka: Kansas State Historical Society, 1982.

———. *Fort Union and the Frontier Army in the Southwest.* Santa Fe: Division of History, National Park Service, 1993.

Ordnance Manual for the Use of the Officers of the United States Army. Philadelphia, Pa: J. B. Lippincott and Co., 1861.

Ordnance Memoranda No. 19: Proceedings of the Board of Officers Convened under Special Orders No. 120, A.G.O., 1874, on Infantry Equipments, and Materials and Supplies Necessary for Efficient Outfit of Infantry Troops in Field and Garrison. Washington, D.C.: Government Printing Office, 1875.

Ostrander, Alson B. *An Army Boy of the Sixties.* New York: World Book Co., 1924.

Parker, W. Thornton. *Personal Experiences among Our North American Indians from 1867 to 1885* (1913). Reprint. Whitefish, Mont.: Kessinger Publishing, n.d.

Paul, R. Eli, ed. *The Nebraska Indian Wars Reader, 1865–1877.* Lincoln: University of Nebraska Press, 1998.

Pearson, Daniel C. *Notes on the Platte-Dakota Campaign of 1876.* New York: Republic Press, 1896.
Poitevin, Norman, comp. *Captain Walter Clifford: A 7th Infantry Army Officer's Career in the Indian Wars.* Santa Cruz, Calif.: n.p., 2002.
Price List of Ordnance and Ordnance Stores. Washington, D.C.: Government Printing Office, 1877.
Proceedings of the American Numismatic and Archeological Society of New York City. New York: n.p., 1901.
Prucha, Francis Paul. *A Guide to the Military Posts of the United States, 1789–1895.* Madison: State Historical Society of Wisconsin, 1964.
Record of Engagements with Hostile Indians within the Military Division of the Missouri from 1868 to 1882 (1882). Facsimile reprint. Fort Collins, Colo.: Old Army Press, 1972.
Reese, Timothy J. *Sykes' Regular Infantry Division, 1861–1864: A History of Regular United States Infantry Operations in the Civil War's Eastern Theater.* Jefferson, N.C.: McFarland and Co., 1990.
Reeves, Ira L. *A Manual for Aspirants for Commissions in the United States Army.* Kansas City, Mo.: Hudson-Kimberly Publishing Co., 1901.
Regan, James. *Manual of Guard Duty and Kindred Subjects for the Regular Army, Volunteers and Militia of the United States.* New York: Harper and Brothers, 1883.
Regulations for the Army of the United States, 1895. Washington, D.C.: Government Printing Office, 1900.
Regulations of the Army of the United States and General Orders in Force on the 17th of February, 1881. Washington, D.C.: Government Printing Office, 1881.
Reneau, Susan C. *The Adventures of Moccasin Joe: The True Life Story of Sgt. George S. Howard.* Missoula, Mont.: Blue Mountain Publishing, 1994.
Revised United States Army Regulations of 1861. Washington, D.C.: Government Printing Office, 1863.
Richardson, Heather Cox. *West from Appomattox: The Reconstruction of America after the Civil War.* New Haven: Yale University Press, 2007.
Rickey, Don, Jr. *Forty Miles a Day on Beans and Hay: The Enlisted Soldier Fighting the Indian Wars.* Norman: University of Oklahoma Press, 1963.
Robinson, Charles M., ed. *The Diaries of John Gregory Bourke.* Vol. 2, *July 29, 1876–April 7, 1878.* Denton: University of North Texas Press, 2005.
Rodenbough, Theophilus F., ed. *The Army of the United States: Historical Sketches of Staff and Line with Portraits of Generals-in-Chief* (1896). Reprint. New York: Argonaut Press, 1966.
———. *From Everglade to Canyon with the Second United States Cavalry: An Authentic Account of Service in Florida, Mexico, Virginia, and the Indian Country, 1836–1875* (1875). Facsimile reprint of the first edition, with a foreword by Edward G. Longacre. Norman: University of Oklahoma Press, 2000.
———, ed. *Sabre and Bayonet: Stories of Heroism and Military Adventure.* New York: G. W. Dillingham Co., 1897.
Roe, Frances M. A. *Army Letters from an Officer's Wife, 1871–1888* (1909). Reprint, with an introduction by Sandra L. Myers. Lincoln: University of Nebraska Press, 1981.
Roster of Non-Commissioned Officers of the Tenth U.S. Cavalry with Some Reminiscences, Appendixes, Etc., Connected with the Early History of the Regiment (1897). Reprint, with an introduction by Douglas C. McChristian. Bryan, Tex.: J. M. Carroll and Co., 1983.

Sanderson, Captain James M. *Camp Fires and Camp Cooking; or, Culinary Hints for the Soldier.* Washington, D.C.: Government Printing Office, 1862.

Schneider, George A., ed. *The Freeman Journal: The Infantry in the Sioux Campaign of 1876.* Introduction by John M. Carroll. San Rafael, Calif.: Presidio Press, 1977.

Schubert, Frank N. *Voices of the Buffalo Soldier: Records, Reports, and Recollections of Military Life and Service in the West.* Albuquerque: University of New Mexico Press, 2003.

Scott, Douglas D. *Custer's Heroes: The Little Bighorn Medals of Honor.* Wake Forest, N.C.: AST Press, 2007.

Scott, Douglas D., Richard A. Fox Jr., Melissa A. Connor, and Dick Harmon. *Archaeological Perspectives on the Battle of the Little Bighorn.* Norman: University of Oklahoma Press, 1989.

Scott, Douglas D., and P. Willey, eds. *Health of the Seventh Cavalry: A Medical History.* Norman: University of Oklahoma Press, 2015.

Scott, Douglas D., P. Willey, and Melissa A. Connor. *They Died with Custer: Soldiers' Bones from the Battle of the Little Bighorn.* Norman: University of Oklahoma Press, 1998.

Simpson, G. W. *Manual for U.S. Army Chaplains.* Fort Yates, S.Dak.: n.p., 1893.

Smith, Sherry L., ed. *Sagebrush Soldier: Private William Earl Smith's View of the Sioux War of 1876.* Norman: University of Oklahoma Press, 1989.

———. *The View from Officers' Row: Army Perceptions of Western Indians.* Tucson: University of Arizona Press, 1990.

Smith, Thomas T., ed. *A Dose of Frontier Soldiering: The Memoirs of Corporal E. A. Bode, Frontier Regular Infantry, 1877–1882.* Lincoln: University of Nebraska Press, 1994.

———. *The U.S. Army and the Texas Frontier Economy, 1845–1900.* College Station: Texas A&M University Press, 1999.

Stallard, Patricia Y. *Glittering Misery: Dependents of the Indian-Fighting Army.* Norman: University of Oklahoma Press, 1992.

Stands In Timber, John, and Margot Liberty. *Cheyenne Memories.* Lincoln: University of Nebraska Press, 1972.

Steele, Volney. *Bleed, Blister, and Purge: A History of Medicine on the American Frontier.* Missoula, Mont.: Mountain Press Publishing Co., 2005.

Stover, Earl F. *Up from Handymen: The United States Army Chaplaincy, 1865–1920.* Vol. 3. Washington, D.C.: Office of the Chief of Chaplains, Department of the Army, 1977.

Summerhayes, Martha. *Vanished Arizona: Recollections of My Army Life.* Edited with an introduction by Milo Milton Quaife. Chicago: Lakeside Press, 1939.

Sweeney, Edwin R., ed. *Making Peace with Cochise: The 1872 Journal of Captain Joseph Alton Sladen.* Norman: University of Oklahoma Press, 1997.

Tate, Michael L. *The Frontier Army in the Settlement of the West.* Norman: University of Oklahoma Press, 1999.

Taylor, Colin F. *Native American Weapons.* Norman: University of Oklahoma Press, 2001.

Taylor, Morris F. *First Mail West: Stagecoach Lines on the Santa Fe Trail.* Albuquerque: University of New Mexico Press, 1971.

Taylor, Quintard. *In Search of the Racial Frontier: African Americans in the American West, 1528–1990.* New York: W. W. Norton and Co., 1998.

Taylor, William O. *With Custer at the Little Bighorn: The First and Only Eyewitness Account Ever Written.* New York: Penguin Books, 1997.

That Fatal Day, Eight More with Custer: First-Hand Accounts of the Battle of the Little Big Horn. Howell, Minn.: Powder River Press, 1992.
Toole, K. Ross; John Alexander Carroll, Robert M. Utley, and A. R. Mortensen, eds. *Probing the American West: Papers from the Santa Fe Conference.* Introduction by Ray A. Billington. Santa Fe: Museum of New Mexico Press, 1962.
Upton, Emory. *Infantry Tactics, Single and Double Rank.* New York: D. Appleton and Co., 1874.
Upton, Richard, comp. *Fort Custer on the Bighorn, 1877–1898: Its History and Personalities as Told and Pictured by Its Contemporaries.* Glendale, Calif.: Arthur H. Clark Co., 1973.
Urwin, Gregory J. W. *The United States Cavalry: An Illustrated History, 1776–1944.* Norman: University of Oklahoma Press, 2003.
U.S. Army Uniforms and Equipment, 1889: Specifications for Clothing, Camp and Garrison Equipage, and Clothing and Equipage Materials (1889). Reprint. Foreword by Jerome A. Greene. Lincoln: University of Nebraska Press, 1986.
Utley, Robert M. *Frontier Regulars: The United States Army and the Indian, 1866–1891.* New York: Macmillan, 1973.
———. *Frontiersmen in Blue: The United States Army and the Indian, 1848–1865.* New York: Macmillan Co., 1967.
———, ed. *Life in Custer's Cavalry: Diaries and Letters of Albert and Jennie Barnitz, 1867–1868.* New Haven, Conn.: Yale University Press, 1977.
Vaughn, J. W. *With Crook at the Rosebud.* Lincoln: University of Nebraska Press, 1956.
Vestal, Stanley. *Warpath: The True Story of the Fighting Sioux Told in a Biography of Chief White Bull.* Lincoln: University of Nebraska Press, 1984.
Viola, Herman J., ed. *The Memoirs of Charles Henry Veil: A Soldier's Recollections of the Civil War and the Arizona Territory.* New York: Orion Books, 1993.
Von Ostermann, Georg F. *The Last Sioux Indian War.* San Antonio, Tex.: Palm Tree Press, 1942.
Wagner, Arthur L. *The Service of Security and Information.* Kansas City, Mo.: Hudson-Kimberly Publishing Co., 1892.
Wagner, Glendolin Damon. *Old Neutriment.* New York: Sol Lewis, 1973.
Walton, George. *Sentinel of the Plains: Fort Leavenworth and the American West.* Englewood Cliffs, N.J.: Prentice-Hall, 1973.
Way, Thomas E., ed. *Sgt. Fred Platten's Ten Years on the Trail of the Redskins.* Williams, Ariz.: Williams News Press, 1959.
Weigley, Russell F. *History of the United States Army.* New York: Macmillan, 1977.
Werner, Herman. *On the Western Frontier with the United States Cavalry Fifty Years Ago.* N.p., 1934.
White, William. *Custer, Cavalry, and Crows.* Fort Collins, Colo.: Old Army Press, 1975.
Wilhelm, Thomas. *A Military Dictionary and Gazetteer.* Philadelphia: L. R. Hamersly and Co., 1881.
Willert, James, ed. *Letters from the Field: Wallace at the Little Big Horn.* Orange, Calif.: Paragon Agency Publishers, 1997.
Wilson, Rex L. *Bottles on the Western Frontier.* Tucson: University of Arizona Press, 1981.
Windolph, Charles. *I Fought with Custer: The Story of Sergeant Windolph, Last Survivor of the Battle of the Little Big Horn, as Told to Frazier and Robert Hunt.* New York: Scribner's Sons, 1947.
Winthrop, William. *Military Law.* 2 vols. Washington, D.C.: W. H. Morrison, 1886.

Wooden Leg: A Warrior Who Fought Custer. Interpreted by Thomas B. Marquis. Lincoln: University of Nebraska Press, 1931.
Wooster, Robert. *History of Fort Davis, Texas.* Santa Fe, N.Mex.: National Park Service, 1990.
———. *The Military and United States Indian Policy, 1865–1903.* Lincoln: University of Nebraska Press, 1995.
———. *Soldiers, Sutlers, and Settlers: Garrison Life on the Texas Frontier.* College Station: Texas A&M Press, 1987.
Zimmer, William F. *Frontier Soldier: An Enlisted Man's Journal of the Sioux and Nez Perce Campaigns, 1877.* Edited by Jerome A. Greene. Helena: Montana Historical Society, 1998.
Zinser, Louis. *Indian War Diary: Expedition of 1876.* Vienna, W.Va.: Old West Shop, n.d.
Zogbaum, Rufus Fairchild. *Horse, Foot, and Dragoons: Sketches of Army Life at Home and Abroad.* New York: Harper and Brothers, 1888.

ARTICLES

Adams, Donald K., ed. "The Journal of Ada A. Vogdes, 1868–71." *Montana The Magazine of Western History* 13 (July 1963): 2–18.
Anderson, Harry H. "The Benteen Base Ball Club: Sports Enthusiasts of the Seventh Cavalry." *Montana The Magazine of Western History* 20 (July 1970): 82–85.
Ball, Larry D. "The United States Army and the Big Springs, Nebraska Train Robbery of 1877." *Journal of the West* 34 (January 1995): 34–45.
Brackett, Albert G. "Our Cavalry: Its Duties, Hardships, and Necessities, at Our Frontier Posts." *Journal of the Military Service Institution* 4 (1883): 383–407.
———. "A Trip through the Rocky Mountains." *Contributions to the Historical Society of Montana* 8 (1917): 329–44.
Braddock, Paul F. "Armed Forces Identification Tags." *Military Collector & Historian* 24 (Winter 1972): 112–14.
Buecker, Thomas R., ed. "In Pursuit of Crazy Horse: A Letter from the 1876 Powder River Expedition." *Annals of Wyoming* 82 (Spring 2010): 26–30.
———, ed. "The Journals of James S. McClellan, 1st Sgt., Company H, 3rd Cavalry." *Annals of Wyoming* 57 (Spring 1985): 21–34.
———, ed. "Letters from a Post Surgeon's Wife." *Annals of Wyoming* 53 (Fall 1981): 44–63.
———. "One Soldier's Service: Caleb Benson in the Ninth and Tenth Cavalry, 1875–1908." *Nebraska History* 74 (Summer 1993): 54–62.
Bush, Virginia Balance. "Garrison Life in Colorado." *Colorado Magazine* 1 (April 1893): 4–13.
Carriker, Robert C., ed. "Thompson McFadden's Diary of an Indian Campaign, 1874." *Southwestern Historical Quarterly* 75 (October 1971): 198–232.
Chappell, Gordon Stelling. "Surgeon at Fort Sidney: Captain Walter Reed's Experiences at a Nebraska Military Post, 1883–1884." *Nebraska History* 54 (Summer 1973): 419–44.
Clark, Gerald R. "Sergeant Glover: The Making of a Medal 1876–1881." *Hoofprints* 18 (Fall–Winter 1988): 11–16.
Clary, David A. "The Role of the Army Surgeon in the West: Daniel Weisel at Fort Davis, Texas, 1868–1872." *Western Historical Quarterly* 3 (January 1972): 54–66.

Closson, Henry W. "Morning Reports and Afternoon Speculations." *Journal of the Military Service Institution* 6 (1885): 184–98.
Cook, James A. "The Art of Indian Fighting." *American Mercury* 23 (June 1931): 170–79.
"Custer: One of His Discharged Soldiers Takes a Hand in the Discussion." *Big Horn-Yellowstone Journal* 1 (Winter 1992): 18–20.
"Custer's Death Trap." *Big Horn-Yellowstone Journal* 3 (Spring 1994): 18–21.
Daly, Henry W. "The War Path." *American Legion Monthly* (April 1927): 16–19, 54.
Dapray, John A. "A Subaltern's View of the Army." *United Service* 5 (December 1881): 707–12.
Daubenmier, Judy. "Empty Saddles: Desertion from the Dashing U.S. Cavalry." *Montana The Magazine of Western History* 54 (Autumn 2004): 2–17.
Dean, Alexander T. "A Hero in the Ranks." *Recreation* 3 (July 1895): 77–80.
DeWolf, James M. "The Diary and Letters of James M. DeWolf, Acting Assistant Surgeon, U.S. Army; His Record of the Sioux Expedition of 1876 as Kept until His Death." *North Dakota History* 25 (April-July 1958): 59–67.
"Diary of Matthew Carroll." *Contributions to the Historical Society of Montana* 2 (n.d.): 229–40.
Dickson, Ephriam III. "Soldier with a Camera: Private Charles Howard's Photographic Journey through Eastern Wyoming, 1877." *Annals of Wyoming* 77 (Autumn 2005): 22–32.
———. "With General Crook's Campaign: A Soldier's Letter Home, 1876." *Little Bighorn Associates Newsletter* 60 (June 2006): 4–5.
Dinges, Bruce J., ed. "A New York Private in Arizona Territory: The Letters of George H. Cranston, 1867–1870." *Journal of Arizona History* 26 (Spring 1985): 53–76.
———. "The San Angelo Riot of 1881: The Army, Race Relations, and Settlement on the Texas Frontier." *Journal of the West* 41 (Summer 2002): 35–45.
Dobak, William A. "Licit Amusements of Enlisted Men in the Post-Civil War Army." *Montana The Magazine of Western History* 45 (Spring 1995): 34–45.
———. "Yellow-Leg Journalists: Enlisted Men as Newspaper Reporters in the Sioux Campaign, 1876." *Journal of the West* 8 (January 1974): 86–112.
Dugan, Lawrence. "Real Service." *Winners of the West* (November 1938): 6.
Ellis, Horace. "A Survivor's Story of the Custer Massacre." *Big Horn-Yellowstone Journal* 2 (Spring 1993): 5–11.
Faust, David T., and Kenneth A. Randall. "Life at Post: Fort Lowell, Arizona Territory 1873–1891." *Smoke Signal* 74 (Spring 2002): 62–96.
"Fighting the Redskins." *Big Horn-Yellowstone Journal* 1 (Spring 1992): 7–8.
Fite, Gilbert C. "The United States Army and Relief to Pioneer Settlers." *Journal of the West* 6 (January 1967): 99–107.
Fitzgerald, Maurice. "Sixteen Young Men." *Winners of the West* (January 30, 1931): 12.
Forbes, Archibald. "The United States Army." *North American Review* 135 (July 1882): 127–45.
"From the Sioux Country." *Big Horn-Yellowstone Journal* 2 (Autumn 1993): 21–22.
"From the Yellowstone." *Big Horn-Yellowstone Journal* 1 (Winter 1992): 8–9.
"Garrison Life at Governor's Island." *Scribner's Monthly* 21 (February 1881): 593–602.
Gibbon, John. "Arms to Fight Indians." *United Service* 1 (April 1879): 237–44.
Giddens, Paul H., ed. "Seven Letters from Wyoming Territory." *Annals of Wyoming* 50 (Fall 1978): 303–18.
Glenner, Richard A., and P. Willey. "Dental Filling Materials in the Confederacy." *Journal of the History of Dentistry* 46 (July 1998): 71–75.

Godfrey, Edward S. "Cavalry Fire Discipline." *Journal of the Military Service Institution of the United States*, (September 1896): 252–59.

———. "Some Reminiscences, Including an Account of General Sully's Expedition against the Southern Plains Indians." *Cavalry Journal* 36 (July 1927): 417–25.

———. "Some Reminiscences, Including the Washita Battle, November 27, 1868." *Cavalry Journal* 37 (October 1928): 481–500.

Grange, Roger T., Jr. "Treating the Wounded at Fort Robinson." *Nebraska History* 45 (Summer 1964): 273–94.

Greene, Jerome A. "Chasing Sitting Bull and Crazy Horse: Two Fourteenth U.S. Infantry Diaries of the Great Sioux War." *Nebraska History* 78 (Winter 1997): 187–201.

———. "Sutlers, Post Traders, and the Fort Laramie Experience, 1850s-1860s." *Journal of the West* 41 (Summer 2002): 17–25.

Griffen, Robert A., ed. "Fred Munn, Veteran of Frontier Experiences, Remembered the Days He Rode with Miles, Howard, and Terry." *Montana The Magazine of Western History* 16 (Spring 1966): 50–64.

Gurnett, William. "Attention Co. K, 8th U.S. Infantry, 1871–76." *Winners of the West* (June 1924): 3.

———. "The Old Sergeant Relates Some Incidents of Pioneer Life in the West during the Indian Uprisings." *Winners of the West* (October 30, 1936): 8–9.

Hamersly, L. R., ed. "The Indian as a Soldier." *United Service* 3 (March 1890): 229–38.

Hardin, E. E. "Army Messing." *Journal of the Military Service Institution* 6 (1885): 274–75.

Hardin, M. D. "The Sheep Eater Campaign." *Recreation* 6 (June 1897): 435–41.

Hedren, Paul L., ed. "Campaigning with the Fifth U.S. Cavalry: Private James B. Frew's Diary and Letters from the Great Sioux War of 1876." In *The Nebraska Indian Wars Reader, 1865–1877*, edited by R. Eli Paul, 131–56. Lincoln: University of Nebraska Press, 1998.

———, ed. "Eben Swift's Army Service on the Plains, 1876–1879." *Annals of Wyoming* 50 (Spring 1978): 141–55.

———. "An Infantry Company in the Sioux Campaign." *Montana The Magazine of Western History* 33 (Winter 1983): 31–39.

———. "The Sioux War Adventures of Dr. Charles V. Petteys, Acting Assistant Surgeon." *Journal of the West* 32 (April 1993): 29–37.

———. "Three Cool, Determined Men: The Sioux War Heroism of Privates Evans, Stewart, and Bell." *Montana The Magazine of Western History* 41 (Winter 1991): 14–27.

———, ed. "The Worst Campaign I Ever Experienced: Sergeant John Zimmerman's Memoir of the Great Sioux War." *Annals of Wyoming* 76 (Winter 2004): 2–14.

Hennessy, Francis, and Patrick D. O'Flaherty. "The Memories of a Regular." *Military Collector & Historian* 17 (Winter 1965): 125–28.

Hill, Michael D., and Ben Innis, eds. "The Fort Buford Diary of Private Sanford, 1876–1877." *North Dakota History* 52 (Summer 1985): 2–40.

Hills, Louis E. "With General George A. Custer on the Northern Pacific Surveying Expedition in 1873." *By Valor and Arms* 1 (October 1974): 49–55.

Hynes, W. F. "A Reminiscence of Fort Casper." *Sons of Colorado* 1 (November 1906): 3–11.

Innis, Ben, ed. "The Fort Buford Diary of Pvt. Sanford." *North Dakota History* 33 (Fall 1966): 335–78.

Jerome, Lawrence R. "The Geronimo Campaign As Told by a Trooper of 'B' Troop of the 4th U.S. Cavalry." *Journal of the West* 11 (January 1972): 157–69.
Johnson, Roy P. "Jacob Horner of the Seventh Cavalry." *North Dakota History* 16 (April 1949): 3–28.
Kanipe, Daniel A. "A New Story of Custer's Last Battle." *Contributions to the Historical Society of Montana* 4 (1903): 277–83.
Kenner, Charles. "Guardians in Blue: The United States Cavalry and the Growth of the Texas Range Cattle Industry." *Journal of the West* 34 (January 1995): 46–54.
King, Charles. "The Leavenworth School." *Harper's New Monthly Magazine* 76 (1886): 778–92.
King, James T. "The Military Frontier—What Was It?" *Westerners Brand Book* 21 (1965): 89–96.
Kolarik, Charles. "Comrade Kolarik Talks." *Winners of the West* (January 1940): 3.
Koster, John, ed. "The Forty Day Scout: A Trooper's Firsthand Account of an Adventure with the Indian-Fighting Army in the American Southwest." *American Heritage* 31 (June–July 1980): 99–107.
Kurtz, Henry I. "A Soldier's Life." *American History Illustrated* 7 (August 1972): 25–34.
Latta, Emmet G. "Winning of the West." *National Tribune*, December 22, 1921.
Lee, Robert. "Warriors in the Ranks: American Indian Units in the Regular Army, 1891–1897." *South Dakota History* 21 (Fall 1991): 263–316.
Lockwood, John A. "The Intellectual Improvement of the Enlisted Man." *United Service* 5 (December 1881): 747–50.
Lowell, Frank. "Indian Fighter Recalls Eventful Days on Frontier." *Winners of the West* (August 1939): 4.
Luce, Edward S. "Diaries and Letters of Dr. James DeWolf." *North Dakota History* 25 (April–July 1958): 33–81.
Lynch, Dennis. "Oral History c. 1909: Recollections of Dennis Lynch, a Trooper of the 7th Cavalry, 1866–1881." *Military Collector & Historian* 25 (Summer 1973): 69–71.
MacNeil, Rod. "Raw Recruits and Veterans." *Little Big Horn Associates Newsletter* 21 (October 1987): 7–8.
Mattison, Ray H., ed. "Diary of Surgeon Washington Matthews, Fort Rice, D. T." *North Dakota History* 21 (January–April 1954): 5–74.
McChristian, Douglas C. "Apaches and Soldiers in West Texas." *Periodical: Journal of the Council on America's Military Past* 13 (August 1985): 3–17.
———. "Custer's Avengers." *Greasy Grass* 8 (May 1992): 2–10.
———. "'Dress on the Colors, Boys': Black Noncommissioned Officers in the Regular Army, 1866–1898." *Colorado Heritage* (Spring 1996): 38–44.
———. "Shot Like a Dog: Soldier Justice at Fort Walla Walla." *Wild West* (February 2010): 54–61.
McClellan, James S. "A Day with the 'Fighting Cheyennes.'" *Motor Travel* (January 1931): 20–22.
McDermott, John D. "Crime and Punishment in the United States Army: A Phase of Fort Laramie History." *Journal of the West* 7 (April 1968): 246–55.
———. "Were They Really Rogues?: Desertion in the Nineteenth-Century U.S. Army." *Nebraska History* 78 (Winter 1997): 165–74.
Mears, David T. "Campaigning against Crazy Horse." *Nebraska Proceedings and Collections* 10 (1904): 68–77.

Merritt, Wesley. "The Army of the United States." *Harper's New Monthly Magazine* 80 (March 1890): 493–509.

———. "Some Defects in Our Cavalry System." *United Service* 1 (October 1879): 557–61.

———. "Three Indian Campaigns." *Harper's New Monthly Magazine* 80 (December 1889–May 1890): 720–37.

Moyne, Ernest J., ed. "Fred Snow's Account of the Custer Expedition of 1874." *North Dakota History* 27 (Summer and Fall 1960): 145–51.

Munn, Fred M. "Fred Munn, Veteran of Frontier Experiences, Remembered the Days He Rode with Miles, Howard, and Terry." *Montana The Magazine of Western History* 16 (Spring 1966): 50–64.

Nelson, Henry Loomis. "Davids Island: The Enlisted Man of the Army." *Harper's Weekly* 34 (June 28, 1890): 509–12.

Nixon, John. "Memories." *Winners of the West* (July 1938).

"Offenses, Punishments, and Morals of Enlisted Men: Their Causes of Complaint, and Measures of Correction." *United Service* 9 (July 1883): 42–50.

Olch, Peter D. "Medicine in the Indian-Fighting Army, 1866–1890." *Journal of the West* 21 (July 1982): 32–41.

Pagel, E. W. "Indians Would Not Pacify." *Winners of the West* (May 30, 1926): 2.

Peck, Robert Morris. "Recollections of Early Times in Kansas Territory." *Transactions of the Kansas State Historical Society* 8 (1904): 484–507.

Phelps, Frederick E. "From Texas to Dakota: The Eighth Cavalry's Long March." *Journal of the U.S. Cavalry Association* 15 (April 1905): 858–71.

Pope, J. Worden. "Desertion and the Military Prison." *Cosmopolitan* 10 (November 1890): 111–20.

Potter, James E. "The Great Source of Amusement." *Montana The Magazine of Western History* 55 (Autumn 2005): 34–47.

———. "'He . . . Regretted Having to Die That Way': Firearms Accidents in the Frontier Army, 1806–1891." *Nebraska History* 78 (Winter 1997): 175–86.

Price, Byron. "The Utopian Experiment: The Army and the Indian, 1890–97." *By Valor and Arms* 3 (Fall 1977): 15–35.

Rea, Bob, ed. "The Red River War Diary of Private John Hechner." *Panhandle-Plains Historical Review* 71 (1998): 24–38.

Rickey, Don. "An Indian Wars Combat Record." *By Valor and Arms* 2 (Fall 1975): 4–11.

Robinson, Charles M., III, ed. "Brigadier General George Crook's Horse Meat March and the Fight at Slim Buttes: A Letter by Walter Scribner Schuyler." *Montana The Magazine of Western History* 56 (Spring 2006): 42–49.

Romeyn, Henry. "Army Clothing and Equipage." *United Service* 9 (May 1893): 447–53.

———. "Desertion: Some Causes and Remedies." *United Service* 12 (June 1885): 671–80.

Russell, Don. "The Army of the Frontier: 1865–1891, Organisation, Tactics, and Defence Policies of the Period of the Indian Wars." *English Westerner's Brand Book* 2 (January 1960): 2–7.

Saum, Lewis O. "Private John F. Donohue's Reflections on the Little Bighorn." *Montana The Magazine of Western History* 50 (Winter 2000): 40–53.

Schubert, Frank N. "Ten Troopers: Buffalo Soldier Medal of Honor Men Who Served at Fort Robinson." *Nebraska History* 78 (Winter 1997): 151–57.

Sellars, Mrs. Thomas Crighton, ed. "Oral History c. 1909: Recollections of Dennis Lynch, A Trooper of the 7th Cavalry, 1866–1881." *Military Collector & Historian* 25 (Summer 1973): 69–70.

Shirk, George H. "Campaigning with Sheridan: A Farrier's Diary." *Chronicles of Oklahoma* 37 (Spring 1959): 68–105.

———. "Military Duty on the Western Frontier." *Chronicles of Oklahoma* 47 (Summer 1969): 118–25.

Smith, Duane A. "A Strike Did Not Always Mean Gold." *Montana The Magazine of Western History* 20 (July 1970): 76–81.

Stewart, Edgar I., ed. "Letters from the Big Hole." *Montana The Magazine of Western History* 2 (January 1952): 53–56.

Talbot, James Joseph. "The Indian Question." *United Service* 1 (January 1879): 141–52.

Tate, Michael L. "Soldiers of the Line: Apache Companies in the U.S. Army 1891–1897." *Arizona and the West* 16 (Winter 1974): 343–64.

Thompson, Erwin N. "The Negro Soldiers on the Frontier: A Fort Davis Case Study." *Journal of the West* 7 (April 1968): 217–36.

Twitchell, Phillip G., ed. "Camp Robinson Letters of Angeline Johnson, 1876–1879." *Nebraska History* 77 (Summer 1996): 89–95.

Walker, Henry P., ed. "The Reluctant Corporal: The Autobiography of William Bladen Jett" (pt. 1). *Journal of Arizona History* 12 (Spring 1971): 1–50.

———. "The Reluctant Corporal: The Autobiography of William Bladen Jett" (pt. 2). *Journal of Arizona History* 12 (Summer 1971): 112–44.

Wallace, [Arthur S?]. "Episode of the Fifth Cavalry." *Winners of the West* (September 30, 1933): 2.

Welty, Raymond L. "The Daily Life of the Frontier Soldier." *Cavalry Journal* (October 1927): 584–94.

White, John I. "D. J. 'Kid' O'Malley: Montana's Cowboy Poet." *Montana The Magazine of Western History* 17 (Summer 1967): 60–73.

Willey, P., Richard A. Glenner, and Douglas D. Scott. "Oral Health of Seventh Cavalry Troopers: Dentitions from the Custer National Cemetery." *Journal of the History of Dentistry* 44 (March 1966): 3–14.

"Will He Enlist?" *Harper's Weekly* 32 (May 20, 1888): 1641.

Williams, Mary L. "Care of the Dead at 19th Century Posts." *Periodical: Journal of the Council on America's Military Past* 13 (May 1984): 14–30.

Wood, Cynthia A. "Army Laundresses and Civilization on the Western Frontier." *Journal of the West* 41 (Summer 2002): 26–34.

Woodhull, Alfred A. "The Enlisted Soldier." *Journal of the Military Service Institution of the United States* 8 (March 1887): 18–65.

Woodruff, Thomas Mayhew. "We Have Joseph and All His People: A Soldier Writes Home about the Final Battle." *Montana The Magazine of Western History* 27 (Autumn 1977): 30–33.

Yohn, Henry I. "The Regulars in Arizona in 1866: Interviews with Henry I. Yohn." Comment by Constance Wynn Alshuler. *Journal of Arizona History* 16 (Spring 1975): 119–26.

NEWSPAPERS

Army & Navy Journal
Army & Navy Register
Billings (Mont.) Gazette
Bridgeport (Conn.) Post

Cheyenne (Wyo.) Daily Leader
Harper's Weekly
National Police Gazette
National Tribune
Omaha (Nebr.) Daily Bee
Omaha (Nebr.) Daily Republican
Providence (R.I.) Journal
(Pueblo) Colorado Chieftain
Winners of the West

UNPUBLISHED MATERIAL

Coughlan, T. M. "Varnum: The Last of Custer's Lieutenants." Edited by John M. Carroll. N.p., n.d. Copy in author's files.

Nelson, Mark J. "Brief Biographies." Rogan-McLennon file. Library, Fort Laramie National Historic Site.

Rea, Bob. "Sand Bag Citadels on the Plains: Redoubts on the Fort Dodge—Camp Supply Trail." Typescript copy in author's files.

Seventh Cavalry Letter Book. Private collection of Robert Baird.

John O. Stotts reminiscence. Private collection of Jack Spencer.

Thomas N. Way Journal. Copy in Jerome A. Greene files.

Whitley, Nora L. "The Mysterious Mrs. Nash." Paper presented at the Annual Meeting of the Custer Battlefield Historical & Museum Association, Hardin, Montana, June 2000. Copy in author's files.

ELECTRONIC RESOURCES

Ancestry.com. U.S. Federal Census Collection, 1850–1940.

H. B. Boyer reminiscence. Interviews with Signal Sergeants: http://www.history.noaa.gov/stories_tales/signal_boyer.html.

Benjamin F. Brown, Find A Grave Memorial No. 52568597: http://www.findagrave.com.

Civil War Soldiers and Sailors System: http://nps.gov/civilwar/search-soldiers-detail.htm.

Isaac M. Cline reminiscence. Interviews with Signal Sergeants: http://www.history.noaa.gov/stories_tales/signal_cline.html.

Index

Aber, F. Z., 242
accidents, 269–71, 331, 669n44; artillery, 337–38
adjutant, 135–36, 187, 205
affidavit man, 409
Alcatraz Island, Calif., 383; prisoners confined at, 417, 682n52; survey of prisoners at, 402
alcohol: beer, 366; consumption of, 334, 341, 362; effects of, 389–90; flavoring extracts containing, 363; price of, 231, 325–26, 366; restrictions on sale of, 391–92, 395; whiskey, 362–63, 364–65; whiskey orders, 364–65
Aldrich, Lauren W.: on bullying, 118; on fist-fighting, 152, 345; on journey to join regiment, 86; on mounted infantry, 525–26; on target practice, 201; on veterans in 30th Inf., 111
Allen, Clarence, on mounted drill, 66
Allen, Peter, 72; on being wounded, 565; on route taken to join regiment, 91
Allen, William W., 549
ambulance. *See* medical care
American Fur Company, 514
Andersen, Martin, 348, 588

Anderson, Thomas M., 317
Angel Island, Calif., 583; as recruiting depot, 94
Apache Indians, 9, 267, 268, 323, 434, 458, 504, 509; Chiricahua, 490, 512, 537–38, 554, 697n30; Jicarilla, 496; Lipan, 9; Mescalero 9, 490, 512, 553; mutilation by, 513; Plains, 9, 499; procurement of arms by, 517; scalping by, 512–13; tactics employed by, 508; Tonto, 498; torture by, 513; Warm Springs, 490; weapons used by, 515; women, 499
App, George, 517
Appleby, John C., 349
Arapaho Indians, 9
arms, 444; accountability for, 245–46, 646n24, 666n71; cavalry, 108, 120, 244, 440, 445–46, 522–23, 524, 628n6, 640n74, 690n30; Indian, 515–20; infantry, 120, 242–45, 444–45, 523–24, 553, 628n6, 688n9; Krag-Jorgensen rifle, 250; mounted infantry, 526; prices of, 666n71; privately purchased, 246; problem with jamming, 691n12; for recruits,

arms (*continued*)
85–86, 91, 93–94, 640n74, 642n14, 642n19, 643nn25–26, 648n54; for replacements, 107; shotguns, 347; of Signal Corps, 638n47; Springfield compared with Winchester repeater, 249; theft of, 364, 408–9. *See also* Indian weapons

army life, 160, 180, 185, 323, 572–74

Army & Navy Journal: on abolishment of Sunday inspection, 210; on adjustment to company life, 122, 124; on amnesty for deserters, 416; on army bands, 102; on army's dilemma in fighting Indians, 521–22; on band leaders, 166; on benefits of post canteens, 396, 397; on black soldiers, 423–24; on camps of instruction, 491; on cavalry, 523; on Christmas dinner, 342; on chronic deserters, 117; on civilians' opinions of soldiers, 71; on comparison of civilian and army pay, 23; on cooking, 219; on creation of depot detachments, 75; on dances, 333, 335; on dental care, 260; on desertion, 407, 412; on drill, 197; on drinking, 390, 391; on enlisting inebriates, 32–33; on enlisting substandard men, 34–35; on examination for commission, 170; on extra duty men, 108; on fragmentation of regiments, 98; on gardens, 227; on garrison courts, 382; on hazing of recruits, 111–12; on illegal sale of clothing, 240; on improved quality of recruits, 129; on laundresses, 306; on mail service, 324; on married soldiers, 298, 322; on nurses, 262; on recruits' behavior, 81; on recruit training, 73; on reenlistments, 429, 574; on Saturday policing, 207; on segregated schools, 320; on sergeant major, 164; on Sherman's adoption of "troop," 100; on shooting prisoners, 195–96; on target practice, 202; on tattooing deserters, 414–15

Army Regulations, 320

Arthur, William H., 257, 277

Articles of War, 55, 387, 420

artificer, 186

artillery, 5, 100, 635n2, 677n29. *See also* salute gun

Ashdown, Charles, desire to see the West, 25

Assiniboine Indians, 497, 514

athletic activities, 344–45, 677n43. *See also* sports

Atwood, George K. (alias George Torrens), 407

Augur, Christopher C., 196, 387

Ault, Garner O., 158

Bahr, Conrad, 155

Baker, Henry, funeral of, 273

bakery, 221

bands, 101–3, 571, 645n12

Bannock Indians, 490, 627n1

barber, 74

Barker, Edward D., 478; on picket duty, 537; on trading with Indians, 498

Barker, Luther: on conditioning of men, 457; on Indian marksmanship, 552; on return from campaign, 490; on tobacco shortage, 474

Barnes, Will C.: describes Tucson, 326; on first combat experience, 540; on laundress quarters, 301; on travel to join post, 94; post-army career of, 590; purchases rifle, 246

Barnitz, Albert, 159; describes Fort Larned, 173–74; describes Independence Day celebration, 337; on desertion, 402, 403; on field music at Fort Hays, 189–90; on inspection for guard mounting, 190; on whiskey orders, 364–65

barracks: arrangement of squad room in, 180–81, 661n9; color of, 216,

661n11; condition for inspection, 208; described, 176–77, 655n11, 661n2; furnishings of, 214–17, 426, 661nn7–8; how cleaned, 180, 207–8, 217–18; kitchen, 218; mess hall, 218, 220; room orderly for, 181; stripping of, 441; types of, 213–14, 661n2; wives excluded from, 295
Barrett, Bridget, wish to marry soldier, 298
Barrett, Thomas, 298
Bartlett, Charles G., 137
bathing, 253
battalion, defined, 649n4
battery, as term, 100
battles: Allen Creek (Mont. Terr.), 547, 563; Bear's Paw Mountain (Mont. Terr.), 474, 527, 552, 569, 702n62; Beecher's Island (Colo. Terr.), 490; Big Dry Wash (Ariz. Terr.), 141, 547, 554; Big Hole (Mont. Terr.), 520, 543, 544, 551–52, 553, 585, 698n54; Camas Meadows (Idaho Terr.), 551; Cedar Springs (Ariz. Terr.), 540–41; Cibicu Creek (Ariz. Terr.), 513, 567; Cuchillo Negro Creek (N.Mex. Terr.), 558; Dull Knife Fight (Wyo. Terr.), 142, 168, 547, 549, 556, 566; Fetterman Fight (Dak. Terr.) 507, 511; Guadaloupe Canyon (Sonora, Mex.), 537–38, 591; Horseshoe Canyon (N.Mex. Terr.), 567; Lava Beds (Ore.), 546; Little Bighorn (Mont. Terr.), 72, 91, 99 72, 114, 127, 129, 199, 203, 249, 262, 297, 314, 418, 441, 518, 543, 546, 548, 550, 553, 557, 559, 562, 564, 568, 569; Lyry Creek (Ariz. Terr.), 556; Powder River, 542–43, 545, 563, 565, 571; Rosebud (Mont. Terr.), 109, 127, 483, 522, 548, 554–55, 559, 566, 571; Sappa Creek (Kans.), 562; Slim Buttes (Dak. Terr.), 544, 571; Wagon Box Fight (Dak. Terr.), 546, 552, 554; War Bonnet Creek (Neb.), 528; Washita (Ind. Terr.), 112, 126, 499, 561; White Bird Canyon (Idaho Terr.), 522, 564; Wolf Mountains (Mont. Terr.), 525, 571; Wounded Knee (S.Dak.), 357, 374, 501, 562
Beatrice, Neb., 365
bed check, 326
beef. *See* cattle
beer. *See* alcohol
Belger, Edward A., 144
Belknap, William W., 232
Bell, William W., 377
Benicia Barracks, Calif., 168, 634n2
Benicia, Calif., recruiting station at, 30
Bennett, Richard, 702n61
Benteen, Frederick W., 557; courage of, 553; loss of horses by, 39; on soldier's plight, 543
Bentley, Samuel H., 546
Benzine Board, 6, 139–40
Beresford, Henry C., 669n48
Bergstrom, John, 592
Berry, George C., 461, 497
Biddle, Jonathan W., 442
Bigelow, John: excuses informality by soldier, 142; on clothing issue, 239; punishes soldier, 387; rewards noncoms, 163; on soldier deaths, 272
Big Horn and Yellowstone Expedition, 329, 454, 471, 485, 566
Billings, John S.: on bathing facilities, 253; on bunks, 214; on recruiting depot food, 57
Bingham, Wallace, motivation for enlisting, 26
Birch, Billy, 676n17
Bivenour, Bernard S.: fraudulent enlistment by, 35; on troop's adoption of Indian boy, 498
Bivens, Horace, reason for enlisting, 26
bivouacs, 461–62
Black Hills (Dak. Terr.), 128, 154, 410, 418, 486, 537; paleontological expedition to, 439

732   INDEX

Black Hills Expedition (1874), 473; (1875), 469
Black, Peter Y., on camp songs, 329
Blackfoot Indians (Piegan), 514
blacks: areas of recruitment, 20–21, 632n41, 632n43; discrimination against, 327, 628n6; drafts of, 78; influence of Civil War on, 21–22; motivation for enlisting, 20–22, 26, 27; schools for, 317–18, 319; treatment of at recruiting depots, 52–53
blacksmith, 186, 440, 657n33
Black Wolf (Cheyenne), 498
Blackwood, James C., contemplates desertion, 408
Bloom, Oscar, 351
Boch, Henry, 672n18, 673n30
Boch, Mrs. Henry, scandalous behavior of, 303
Bode, Emil A., 181; on alcoholics, 363; on army coffee, 223; on construction of telegraph line, 438–39; on enlistment, 40; on field shelter, 471; on guard duty, 124; on hazing of recruits, 112; on Independence Day celebration, 338; on Indian women, 499; on library, 348; on Lt. Col. John W. Davidson, 138; on marching in field, 458; on noncoms drilling recruits, 122; on payday, 360; on physical examination, 41; promotion of, 148; on soldiers' opinion of Indians, 502; on Sunday inspection, 208; on theft of clothing, 239; on tooth extraction, 261
Boise Barracks, 355, 504, 570–71
Bothwell, James C.: describes Camp Cooke, 173; on buffalo chips as fuel, 464; on minstrel troupe, 329; on noncoms, 161; on veterans in regulars, 111
Botzer, Edward, marries laundress's daughter, 297, 670n8
bounty jumpers, 646n35

Bowen, William G.: later career of, 590; reason for enlisting, 27
Bowie Station, Ariz. Terr., 371
Boyer, Harry B., 64, 65
Bozeman Trail, 8, 14, 168, 173, 324, 373, 495
Brackett, Albert G., 132
Bradley, Elmore, 367
Bradley, Luther P., 367
Bradley, Reginald: as a price recruit, 124; on food, 223; on medical care, 265; on noncoms, 147; on officers, 142; reasons for enlisting, 26
branding: of deserters, 414–15, 416–17; of deserters abolished, 415–16
bread, 221, 662n21
bread tickets, 662n21
brevet rank: modification of rules governing, 135; officers to be addressed by, 134–35; origin of, 134
Brill, J. H., 48
Brinkman, William, 297
Brisbin, James S., 141
Brocard, Francis, 645n12
Brown, Benjamin F., 317
Brown, Edwin M.: describes return to post after campaign, 571; on winter campaigning, 461
Brown, George C., 177, 447
Brown, James, 377, 682n37
Brown, John G., 78; on furloughs, 358
Browning, George L., 551
buffalo (bison), 432
Buffalo City, Wyo. Terr., 373
Buffalo Soldiers, 628n6
Buford Station, Wyo. Terr., 439
bugle, 655n14
bugle calls. See service calls
bugler. See musicians
bullring, 66, 699n67
bunks: arrangement of in barracks, 215; bedding for, 214–15, 218, 247; how made up, 180–81; of iron construction,

123, 636n17; of wood construction, 214–15
bunkies, 122–23
Burford, Albert, 700n20
burials, 255; in the field, 562–65
Burke, William J., 387
Burkman, John, 340
Burnett, George R., 558
Burt, Andrew S., 146, 235
Burt, Reynolds J.: describes payday, 235; on fraternization among soldiers, 104; on guard mounting, 190; on camp songs, 328
Busch, Adolphus, 366
business ventures, 351
Butler, Adelbert: corresponds with woman, 296; on army life, 129–30; on Sunday inspection, 208; on being in the West, 431
Byers, Joe, 28
Byrne, Bernard J., on company gardens, 228

Cady, John H., 588; as camp follower during Civil War, 20
California Volunteers, 513
campaigns: Cheyenne (1868), 126; Geronimo, 110, 443, 473; Modoc, 488; Nez Perce, 474, 478; Red River, 472; Sheepeater, 474, 559; Sioux (1876), 118, 127, 310, 338, 408, 440, 441, 446, 470, 490, 518, 559; Sioux (1890), 468, 472, 583; Tonto Apache, 498
Camp Brown, Wyo. Terr., 115, 196; black laundress at, 303, 503; domestic strike at, 298
Camp Buffalo Springs, Texas, 363
Camp Cooke, Mont. Terr.: entertainment at, 329; soldier's description of, 173
Camp Crittenden, Ariz. Terr., 111, 325
Camp, Frederick E., 137
Camp Grant. *See* Fort (Camp) Grant, Ariz. Terr.
Camp of Instruction, 491–92

Camp Pena Colorado, Texas, 319
Camp Poplar River, Mont. Terr., 346
Camp Stambaugh, Wyo. Terr.: Sunday inspection at, 208; telegraph at, 438; winter at, 212
Canary, Martha "Calamity Jane," 695n81
Canby, Edward R. S., 562
Cantonment on Tongue River, Mont. Terr., 199; desertion from, 410; laundress quarters at, 301; troops return to after campaign, 571. *See also* Fort Keogh, Mont. Terr.
Carlisle Barracks, Pa., 52, 67, 70, 71, 76, 77, 80, 634nn1–2; abandonment of depot at, 45, 642n19; description of, 46; departure of recruits from, 80; food at, 58; mounted recruiting depot at, 44; training at, 87, 120
Carpenter, Louis H., 446
Carr, Camillo C. C., 143
Carroll (steamboat), 104
Carter, Albert, 495
Carter, John R., 377
Carter, Robert G., 411
Casey, John F., 155
Cashan, William B., 532–33
casualties, 627n2, 647n39
Catalina Mountains (Ariz. Terr.), 174
Cathey, William, 636n21
cattle, 663n24
cavalry: ineffectiveness of, 521–24; typical role of, 433
Cavalry Depot. *See* Jefferson Barracks
Cavalry Tactics: Cooke's, 100, 120; 1874 edition, 100, 120
cemeteries, 274–75
Certificate of Disability, 586
Certificate of Merit, 555–56, 593, 702n51. *See also* combat
chain guard. *See* guard duty
Chambers, Alexander, 140; commands infantry battalion during Starvation

Chambers, Alexander (*continued*) March, 484–85; on intercepting deserters, 412
chaplain: post, 227, 311–14, 328, 673n38; regimental, 315–16
charge of quarters, 149, 151; duties of, 180–81
Cherokee Indians, 499
Cheyenne, Wyo. Terr., 128, 322, 326, 327, 334, 431, 438, 439; soldier's description of, 373
Cheyenne Agency, Dak. Terr., 125, 332; drinking at, 363
Cheyenne and Black Hills Stage Co., 438
Cheyenne-Arapahoe Agency, Ind. Terr., 498, 542
Cheyenne Daily Leader, compares carbine with infantry rifle, 524
Cheyenne Indians, 9, 86, 202, 490, 501, 513, 524; at Dull Knife Fight, 543; firearms used by, 518; incendiary arrows used by, 516; at Little Bighorn battle, 557; mutilation of dead by, 560–61; participation in Fetterman Fight, 507; at Rosebud battle, 548; skirmish with troops near Fort Hays, 520; at Wagon Box Fight, 546; at Warbonnet Creek, 528; women, 501–2
Chickasaw Indians, 499
Chinese: abuse of, 83; as laundrymen, 310–11
Chrisman, Clarence, 470; describes appearance of soldiers returning from field, 489
Christian, Charles P.: corresponds with woman, 296; on his wife as a laundress, 302; on taking his discharge, 575
Christy, George N., 676n17
Cimarron, N.Mex. Terr., 496
Ciscel, Harvey J., 160
civilians: attitudes toward soldiers, 71, 327, 334; killing of by Indians, 510; sympathy with deserters, 413

Civil War: effect on enlistments, 13, 19; effect on medical field, 254; regiments remaining in West during, 627n3; veterans of, 110–11, 123, 131, 133, 136, 202, 403
Clark, George, 144
Clark, Hartford G., 118; on hunting party, 347; on Independence Day celebration, 339; on Indian women, 501; on kitchen police, 179; on longevity of noncoms, 147; on muster inspection, 235; on post cemetery, 274; on punishment for theft, 376; on raising money for injured soldier, 331; on recoil of carbine, 203; on school, 320; on selection of orderlies, 190–91; on soldier's wedding, 322; on souvenirs, 562
Clark, William Philo: on purpose of scalping, 511, 514
Claus, Frederick, 18
Clifford, Walter, 146, 651n29
Closson, Henry W., 422
clothing, 236–41; allowance, 238–40, 665n59; campaign, 442–43; civilian, 665n62; clothes bag, 215; footwear, 672n23; improvements in, 248–49; initial issue at recruiting station, 37–38, 639n64; issued to black regiments, 628n6; issued to replacements, 107; sale of civilian, 38; uniform issued at posts, 107
Cody, William F. "Buffalo Bill," 25
Collins, James, 137
Columbus Barracks, Ohio, 92; general recruiting depot at, 45; parade at, 69; school at, 317; venereal disease at, 375; winter roll call at, 6
Comanche Indians, 211, 338, 481, 490, 499, 517; lance used by, 516; range of, 9
Comancheros, 517
combat: attitudes about, 533–34; courage demonstrated in, 552–58; experiences in, 546–51; preparation for, 543–44; 700n25

company (troop): adjusting to life in, 122–23; conditioning of new men in, 125–27; numbering of members, 119; official use of terms, 100; rivalries among, 118–19; soldier's principal identity with, 118; strength of, 105, 645n18, 647n39, 657n34; uses of surnames in, 119. See also troop
company clerk: corporal as, 150, 177; duties of 108, 177, 182, 187, 197, 576; quarters for, 655n11
company fund. See fund
Confederates, former in regular army, 116–17, 630n7
Conn, Daniel, wounded in action, 554
Convers, Edward, 210
convicts: confinement of, 382–84; escorts for, 417–18
cook: company, 178–79, 181, 218–19, 247; hospital, 264; recruiting depot, 58–59
cookbook, 247, 662n18
Cook, Charles H., 314
Cooke's Springs, N.Mex. Terr., 174
cooking: as cause for desertion 404–5, 426; in field, 463–64, 467–68, 692n29
Cook, James H., 531
cook's police. See kitchen police
Coon, Homer, 528; on attacking Indian village, 544, 552; on preparation for combat, 543 Cooper, James Fenimore, 494
Cornwell, Oscar R., 570
corporal of the guard, 150, 195
Costigan, James, 367
council of administration, 232, 275
counting coup, 505. See also Indian culture
Courts-martial: garrison, 382, 397; general, 381–82, 397; jurisdiction of, 381, 682n47; regimental, 382; summary, 398
cowardice, 558–59
Cox, John E.: becomes minister, 588; courts girl, 294; enlistment experience of, 32, 631n29; expresses joy on returning from field, 488–89; describes depot routine, 55; on his promotion, 149; on hunting, 347; on leaving depot, 76; on travel as motivation for enlistment, 24; on working prisoners, 389
Craft, David L., 138
Cranston, George H.: later life of, 590; on celebrating Independence Day, 337; on combat, 540; on desert environment, 88, 212; on desertion, 410; on health of troops, 256; on Indian weapons, 515, 516; on marching in desert, 458; on motivation for enlisting, 28; on personal growth, 573; on reading, 325
Cree Indian Reservation, 375
Cree Indians, 410
Cremony, John C., on practice of scalping among Apache Indians, 513
Crimean War, 147
Crocker, Marshall, 67
Crook, George, 127, 459, 521; commands Starvation March, 104, 483–88; institutes camps of instruction, 491–92; nickname of, 140; on Indian warfare, 11; soldiers' opinion of, 329, 486–87; use of Indian scouts by, 509; use of mounted infantry by, 526; use of pack trains by, 454, 526
Crow Agency, Mont. Terr., 497
Crow Indian Reservation, 296, 375
Crow Indians, soldiers' opinions of women among, 497, 500, 502
Curtiss, Kate, 310
Curtiss, William A., 310
Custer, Elizabeth: on campaign outfits, 442–43; on enlistees evading the law, 28; on winter guard mounting, 188
Custer, George A., 11, 132, 314, 447, 473; abuse of soldiers by, 402; defeat, effect of on army, 127–28; forms pack train, 455; indulges garrison, 330; punishes

Custer, George A. (*continued*)
  bandsmen, 103; training emphasized by, 199; use of Indian scouts by, 509
Custer, Thomas, 156
Custer Avengers, 72, 128–29, 419, 441

Dadiac (leather polish), 657n38
Dahlgren, Axel, 223, 265
dances. *See* recreation
Darnel, William, 116
Davids Island, N.Y., 53, 82, 229; cooks trained at, 59; general recruiting depot on, 45
Davis, Andrew, 376
Davis, A. P., 702n54
Davis, Martin, 3
Davis, Ransom, 116
deadbeats (beats), 117
dead house, 258
Decker, Theodore, 137
De Hanne, Jean V., 374
Delany, William, 168
Denny, George, 161
dental care, 260–62, 668nn23–24
Denver, Colo., recruiting station at, 31
depot detachment, 74–75, 635n9, 640n76. *See also* permanent party (depot)
descriptive list, 108, 635n13
deserters: amnesty for, 416; arrest of, 410–13, 427; ball-and-chain for, 686n31; bounty-hunting for, 413; character of, 422; civilian sympathy for, 413, 420; pursuit of, 410–12, 686n27; reward for, 412–13, 420, 686n29
desertion: across international borders, 410; causes of, 400–402, 404–6; chronic, 117, 404, 407; civilian views on, 413, 420; gold fever as cause for, 403; punishments for, 399–400, 414–16, 417, 686n41; rates of, 418, 422–23, 427, 684n6; reasons cited for, 421–22; by "repeaters," 407, 685n16; theft in connection with, 408–9

De Trobriand, Philippe Régis, 112; on cavalry, 521; on Indian tactics, 506–7
Devine, Samuel, 271
DeWolfe, James M., 667n16
Diffley, Edward, killed by lightning, 270
discharge, 576–79, 704n11; in the field, 578, 705n13; purchase of, 429
discipline: as cause for desertion, 402; of ex-volunteers, 111; in field, 478; at recruiting depots, 54–55, 59; of volunteers contrasted, 131
disease, 638n36; cholera, 255; death rate from, 278, 667n13, 670n58; dysentery, 255; scurvy, 255–56
District of New Mexico, 383
Doane, Gustavus C.: on prostitutes, 371; soldier's opinion of, 133
doctor. *See* surgeon
Dodge, Richard I., 469
dog robber. *See* striker
dogs. *See* pets
Dorst, Joseph H., 168
doughboy: origins of term, 101. *See also* walk-a-heaps
Dougherty, Timothy, 498
Downing, Thomas P. 28, 312
drill, 197–200; bayonet, 198, 203; dismounted cavalry, 148, 442, 643n28; infantry recruit, 68, 94, 95, 119, 121–22; mounted cavalry, 659n62; mounted recruit, 65–68, 87, 120–21, 639n57; prior to campaign, 532
Drown, Albin H., 184; on preparation for winter field service, 434
drowning. *See* accidents
drug abuse, 366, 367, 689n15, 681n22
drum, 655n14
Drum, Richard C., 74, 426, 587
Drum Barracks, Calif., 88
Dugan, Lawrence, 116
Dull Knife Outbreak, 528
Dunbar, George W., 316
Dunn, William, 268

Dunne, Edward W., 591
duty men, 187, 198

Eagle Pass, Texas, shooting at, 137
Eagle Spring Station, Texas, defenses at, 436
Eaton, Perley S.: on army service, 576; on bacon, 466; on deserters, 417; enlistment experience of, 32; on field service, 475; on food, 224; on nicknames, 119; on officers, 132; on punishment, 385; on religion, 313; on singing, 328
Ebert, Louis: on being wounded, 565; on discipline, 402; on officers, 142
Ecoffey, Jules, 378
Edgerly, Winfield S., 548
education, 315–21, 425; breakdown of system, 319; self, 348. *See also* school
Egan, Harry, 3, 627n1
Eighteenth U.S. Infantry, 14, 81, 92, 102, 149, 246, 316, 405, 495, 515; desertion from, 407, 410; difficulty crossing river by, 269, 459; murders in, 377; rations issued to, 219, 222; replacements for 85; scurvy in, 256; soldier of spread-eagled, 385; soldier's impression of the Great Plains, 431; veterans pay tribute to Sherman, 111
Eighth U.S. Cavalry, 99, 115, 122, 136, 147, 158, 167, 177, 191, 196, 213, 215, 218, 261, 295, 302, 304, 372, 422, 443, 459, 534, 536; attitudes toward Southerners, 116; Christmas celebrated by, 341; civilian treatment of, 327; cooks in, 219; desertion from, 405, 408; encounter with Indians, 496; fresh beef acquired by, 224; hardship of married men in, 309; hosts ball, 340; hunting by, 346; longevity of noncoms, 147, 160; nicknames of officers in, 141, 143; route taken to Ariz. Terr. 88; route taken to N.Mex. Terr., 90; skirmish near Fort Bascom,

556–57; special enlistment in, 299; target practice by, 202; tobacco use in, 229
Eighth U.S. Infantry, 272; engages in fight with cavalrymen, 104–5; member of accidentally shot, 204; officer's wife comments on soldiers of, 144
"Eleventh California Dragoons," 527
"Eleventh Infantry," 527
Eleventh U.S. Infantry, 168, 184; drinking by, 363; sponsors dance, 332
engagements, number of with Indians, 493
enlisted men, commissioning of, 169–70, 649n7
enlistees, former occupations of, 23–24
enlistment: of blacks, 20–22; of ex-Confederates, 15–16; fraudulent, 35–36, 39, 633n57, 686n37; to gain free transportation to West, 39; of married men, 670n3; motivation for, 14–17, 24–29; oath of, 37; physical examination for, 34, 36–37, 41; physical standards for, 33–34; regrets about, 70–71, 640n69; regulations governing, 33; terms of, 13–14, 406; in unit, 41–42
entertainment. *See* recreation
equipment: accountability for, 107, 646n24; cavalry, 107–8, 444–45, 482; infantry, 243, 444; issued at recruiting depots, 42, 77, 85, 641n83; issued to black regiments, 628n6; preparation of for field service, 440; used for light marching order, 444, 689n26, 690n2
escorts. *See* field Service
Evans, Sam, 27
Ewert, Theodore: describes departure of Black Hills Expedition, 448; on doctors, 482; on laundry in field, 473
expeditions: organization of, 451–52
extra duty, 657n34; use of skilled tradesmen for, 108

INDEX

Fahlbush, Gustave W., 167
Farley, John F.: on journey to join regiment, 90; wounded, 267
farrier, 186, 440
Farrow, Edward S., 506
Far West (steamer), 485
fatigue duty: complaints about, 185–86, 400–401, 427–28; general, 183–86
Fawls, Robert, 702n58
Fechet, Edmond G., 543
Fegan, James, 160, 585
Fetterman, William J., 507
field service: bathing during, 473; bivouacs, 461–62, 469–70; condition of men for, 456; cooking, 463–64, 467–68; decline of, 490–91; departure for, 448–49; drill during, 473; escorts, 439–40, 689n17; guard duty during, 475–78, 694n54; inspection prior to, 447–48; laundry during, 473, 693n45; light marching order for, 444, 689n26; mail delivery during, 474–75; marching distances during, 457–58, 691n14, 691n17; preparation for, 447; sanitation, 462; scouting, 433, 434; shelters fabricated during, 469–71, 693n40; sources of fuel during, 463–64; winter, 434, 461, 471–72, 483
Fifteenth U.S. Infantry, 90; arming of recruits bound for, 643n26; hosts ball, 340
Fifth U.S. Cavalry, 26, 113, 127, 132, 154, 344, 354, 373, 459, 474, 477; arrives on northern plains, 128; desertion rate of, 423; Irishmen in, 115; lack of drill in, 197; member of smitten by Indian woman, 500; participation in Starvation March, 488; quality of recruits, 419; singing in, 329; at Warbonnet Creek, 528
Fifth U.S. Infantry, 109, 126, 146, 368, 442, 461, 472, 553, 569; band, 102, 338, 571; in Civil War, 627n3; departure for Sioux Campaign, 449;

desertion from, 410; extra drill in, 199; field equipment of, 444; lack of drill in, 197; as mail guards, 435; scout by, 440; skirmish involving, 542
Fighting Indians in the 7th United States Cavalry (Mulford), 586
final statement: for deceased soldier, 275; for discharged soldier, 576, 577, 581
Finerty, John: describes field hospital, 566; on Indian marksmanship, 550; on infantry, 484; on soldier humor, 485
First Colorado Volunteer Cavalry, 461
First U.S. Cavalry, 87, 99, 110, 118, 125, 145, 159, 186, 235, 247, 253, 271, 277, 326, 401, 474, 500, 533; band, 339; at Camp Lowell, 174, 225; defeated at White Bird Canyon, 563–64; dogs with, 355; in Idaho Terr., 433; ill-prepared for combat, 521–22; member of, drowned, 269; prevention of cowardice in, 559; returns to Fort Klamath, 570–71; soldier commissioned, 425; target practice by, 203
First U.S. Infantry, 89, 116, 132, 294, 318, 325, 332, 488, 497; mounted, 527
First U.S. Volunteer Cavalry, 590
fishing, 469
Fitzgerald, Maurice, 546, 562
Fitzgerald, Michael, 115
Fitzgerald, William W. 120
Flint, Franklin F., emphasizes training, 199
floaters, 24
Flynn, Andrew M., 182
Flynn, Richard: on crossing rivers, 484; on enduring hail, 485; on Slim Buttes battle, 544
Foley, James W.: on character of Fourth Cavalrymen, 111; life after discharge, 589; as post commissary sergeant, 168; on whipping, 384
food, 220–29; canned, 228–29, 256, 425–26, 468; as cause for desertion,

404–5; coffee, 466, 663n26; field ration, 93, 457–58; locally procured, 224–25; packing of, 692nn30–31; quality of, 219, 222–24; at recruiting depots, 56–59, 637n35; shortages of in field, 468–69; table of standard ration, 220–21; travel ration, 92–94; typical mess hall, 662n23; vegetables, 226–28, 663n32, 663n35, 677n39. *See also* garden

Foos, George, 702n54

Ford, John C., 387; refuses to drill recruits, 122

Forsyth, George A., 490, 645n15; on hog ranches, 391

Forsyth, Thomas H., 168; awarded Medal of Honor, 556

fort(s): campaign preparation at, 532; characteristics of frontier, 105–6, 171–76, 213–14, 654nn3–5, 654n8; consolidation of, 210; distinguished from camps, 654n1; field fortifications at, 173, 175, 370; fire protection at, 216–17, 654n1, 661n13; garrisons of, 98, 433; sanitary conditions at, 175; strategic considerations for, 175–76

Fort Abraham Lincoln, Dak. Terr., 91, 95, 114, 486, 564, 578; bartering for sex at, 371; campaign departure from, 448–49; canteen organized at, 392; Christmas dinner at, 342; homosexual incident at, 368; recruits at, 128; target practice at, 201; theater at, 330; vista near, 432; wedding at, 297

Fort (Camp) Apache, Ariz. Terr., 246, 270, 304, 326, 534, 567; laundress quarters at, 301; mail service to, 438

Fort Arbuckle, Indian Terr., 302

Fort Assiniboine, Mont. Terr., 92, 241, 254, 379, 407; desertion from, 410; entertainment at, 331; hog ranch near, 372; recruit walks away from, 109–10; venereal disease at, 375

Fort Bascom, N.Mex. Terr., 224, 329, 348, 517; skirmish near, 556–57

Fort Bayard, N.Mex. Terr., 157

Fort Benton, Mont. Terr., 89, 266; sham fight at, 379

Fort Bidwell, Calif., 252; gambling at, 361

Fort Bliss, Texas, 248, 327

Fort Bowie, Ariz. Terr., 26, 97, 124, 192, 349, 354, 583; garden at, 227; itinerant preacher at, 314; lack of canteen at, 396–97; laundry at, 311; skirmish near, 267

Fort Brady, Mich., 356

Fort Bridger, Wyo. Terr., 22, 195; altercation at, 137–38; officer memorialized at, 146; religion at, 315; scarcity of women at, 332

Fort Buford, Dak. Terr., 191, 240; bayonet exercise at, 198; food at, 225; laundress sells pies at, 305; officer describes his routine at, 138; peaceful Sioux at, 498; photographic studio at, 351; return of command after campaign, 489; St. Patrick's Day at, 335

Fort Canby, Wash. Terr., 271

Fort Caspar, Dak. Terr., 256

Fort C. F. Smith, Mont. Terr., 173, 246, 495; Christmas at, 341; desertion from, 403; opium abuse at, 367; target practice at, 200

Fort Clark, Texas, 135; artillery accident at, 338; hunting at, 346

Fort Cobb, Indian Terr., 467

Fort Columbus, N.Y., 45, 46, 63, 584, 634n1, 642n19. *See also* Governors Island

Fort Concho, Texas, 372, 591; school at, 316, 319; soldiers murdered near, 379

Fort Craig, N.Mex. Terr., 379; skirmish near, 558

Fort Cummings, N.Mex. Terr., 26; described, 174–75

Fort Custer, Mont. Terr., 52, 247; construction of, 184; Decoration

Fort Custer, Mont. Terr. (*continued*)
Day at, 336; drowning at, 269; fire brigade at, 217; fraternal and social organizations at, 352; garden at, 227; hospital at, 277; laundress quarters at, 300; laundry at, 311; school at, 320; scouting at, 434; single women at, 296; venereal disease at, 375

Fort D. A. Russell, Wyo. Terr., 41, 96, 103, 128, 158, 373, 457, 572, 582, 589; campaign preparation at, 442; cleaning of barracks at, 217; holiday celebrations at, 334, 338; ordnance depot at, 649n74; violence at, 327

Fort Davis, Texas, 163, 262, 272, 347, 382; accidental shooting at, 271; chapel at, 315; desertion from, 410; fraternization at, 139; murder at, 118; newspaper published at, 350; Tenth Cavalry assembled at, 98–99; venereal disease at, 375

Fort Dodge, Kans., 126, 441; field fortification near, 437; troops from intercept Indians, 528

Fort (Camp) Douglas, Utah, 277; marriage at, 296; school at, 320

Fort Elliott, Texas, 319

Fort Ellis, Mont. Terr., 91, 92, 107, 128, 577; Crow Indians at, 502; described, 106; entertainment at, 330; gardens at, 228; Indians at, 497; library at, 348; pet bear at, 353; return of troops to, 571; shakedown march from, 456; Templars lodge at, 352; Thanksgiving at, 340

Fort Ellsworth, Kans., 106, 173, 324

Fort Fetterman, Wyo. Terr., 457, 480, 485; desertion from, 51, 401, 412; dog problems at, 356; drowning at, 269; education at, 316; hospital described, 257; lack of pay at, 234; laundress problems at, 307; laundry prices at, 302; mail service to, 438; mounted infantry at, 526; social club at, 352

Fort Fletcher, Kans., 173, 324

Fort Fred Steele, Wyo. Terr., 146, 256; entertainment at, 330; mounted infantry at, 525–26; skirmish near, 561; temperance movement at, 390

Fort Garland, Colo., 91, 157; military ball at, 335

Fort Gibson, Indian Terr., 365

Fort (Camp) Grant, Ariz. Terr., 92, 112, 515, 575, 589; abusive commander at, 137; desertion from, 410; hog ranch near, 370; payday at, 362; skirmish near, 540–42; soldier's comment about, 212; soldiers confined at, 381

Fort Griffin, Texas, civilians killed near, 510

Fort Halleck, Nev. Terr., 272

Fort Harker, Kans., 93

Fort Hartsuff, Neb., 332; preservation of, 592

Fort Hays, Kans., 90, 337, 373, 436, 479; cavalry training at, 120; desertion from, 403; dog problems at, 356; field music, at, 189–90; Mrs. Nash at, 368; punishment at, 402; recruits arrival at, 106; schools at, 316; skirmish near, 520; troops from break up riot, 152

Fort Huachuca, Ariz. Terr., 168, 313, 357, 537, 579; baseball played at, 344

Fortieth U.S. Infantry, 6

Fort Kearny, Neb., 85; hazing of recruits at, 113; target practice at, 201; tribute paid to Sherman at, 111

Fort Keogh, Mont. Terr., 307, 373; canteen established at, 392; Independence Day at, 338; Indian arms turned in at, 518; mail service to, 324; march from, 457; preparation for scout from, 440

Fort Klamath, Ore., 447, 498; described, 488

Fort (Camp) Lapwai, Idaho, 94, 390

Fort Laramie, Wyo. Terr., 93, 105–6, 515; accidental death near, 372; accidental shooting at, 125, 271; Christmas at, 340; condition of barracks at, 218; consolidated sink at, 253; drill for noncoms at, 163; effect of changes to brevet rank at, 135; entertainment at, 328, 332; field fortification at, 173; fire protection at, 217; foot racing at, 344–45; friendly Brule Sioux at, 499; guardhouse conditions at, 383; hog ranch near, 369; hospital animals at, 264; hunting and fishing at, 345; Independence Day at, 337; lack of training at, 120; laundress quarters at, 300; library at, 348; mail service to, 438, 526; medicinal alcohol at, 263; moral conditions at, 365; mounted infantry at, 699n64; policing at, 388; quality of recruits received at, 51, 106, 128; restrictions on drinking at, 365; sanitary conditions at, 276; sawmill at, 185; soldier killed by lightning at, 270; soldier's assessment of life at, 211; soldier's impression of countryside near, 431; suicide at, 272; theft of arms at, 364; trader's store closed for holiday, 339; troops return to after campaign, 489; whiskey ranch near, 378; winter guard duty at, 193

Fort Laramie Treaty, 517

Fort Larned, Kans.: accidental shooting near, 271; country in vicinity described, 432; described, 173–74

Fort Leavenworth, Kans., 40, 41, 72, 93, 94, 111, 138, 154, 356; closure of depot at, 45; as disembarkation point, 85, 449, 642n19; mounted recruiting depot at, 44, 87, 168; prison at, 384, 417; as supply depot, 87, 642n19; troops dispatched from, 442

Fort Lewis, Colo., 339

Fort (Camp) Lowell, Ariz. Terr., 88, 103, 325, 374, 400, 580; Christmas at, 343; described, 174

Fort Lyon, Colo., 308–9; Christmas at, 341; pet buffalo at, 353; school at, 318; soldiers punished at, 386; transportation from, 580

Fort Maginnis, Mont. Terr., 342; soldier's description of, 172

Fort McDermitt, Nev. Terr., 204

Fort McKavett, Texas, 386

Fort McKenzie (Dak. Terr.), 514

Fort McKinney, Wyo. Terr., 373, 376; poem written at, 500

Fort McPherson, Neb., 96, 303

Fort McRae, N.Mex. Terr., 269

Fort Meade, Dak. Terr., 318, 395

Fort Mojave, Ariz. Terr., 88, 270

Fort Myer, Va., 70, 93; Signal School at, 46; recruit reception at, 64; recruit training at, 61, 64–65

Fort Niobrara, Neb., 99, 118, 185, 322, 457; accidental shooting at, 271; bed bugs at, 218; benefit performance at, 331; Christmas at, 343; hog ranches near, 369, 374; hunting party from, 347; Independence Day at, 339; library at, 349; murder at, 377–78; muster inspection at, 235; photography studio at, 351; soldier wed at, 322; St. Patrick's Day at, 335

Fort Omaha, Neb.: dogs at, 356; hard labor punishment at, 377; prisoners drunk at, 195; recruit training at, 121; soldiers out of quarters after tattoo, 206–7

Fort Phil Kearny, Dak. Terr., 122–23, 512, 552; ambush near, 507; band at, 102; bathing at, 253; construction of, 173; desertion from, 403, 415; discharged soldiers walk from, 579; food at, 222; mounted infantry at, 525; new rifles at, 243; scurvy at, 256; target practice at, 200

Fort Randall, Dak. Terr., 89, 294, 347, 488, 588; chapel at, 315; temperance society at, 351

Fort Reno, Dak. Terr., 173, 222; soldier spread-eagled at, 385
Fort Reno, Indian Terr., 184, 438
Fort Reynolds, Colo. Terr., 406
Fort Rice, Dak. Terr.: control of drinking at, 364; fire protection at, 217; funeral at, 273; Independence Day at, 337
Fort Richardson, Texas, 303, 327; desertion from, 411; guardhouse dog at, 355; newspaper published at, 350
Fort Riley, Kans., 86, 642n19; Christmas at, 341, 342; consolidated mess at, 182
Fort Ringgold, Texas, 330
Fort Robinson, Neb., 210, 480, 488; canteen at, 394; Christmas at, 343; laundry at, 311; soldier fight at, 104
Fort Sanders, Wyo. Terr., 91, 92; described, 175, insubordinate laundress at, 305–6; passes issued at, 326; restrictions on drinking at, 365; shootings near, 377; tailor's prices at, 242; target practice at, 201; temperance at, 351; transfer of troops from, 307
Fort Sedgwick, Colo. Terr., 431; absence of women at, 294; lack of religion at, 312; rescue of wood cutters near, 472; winter pursuit from, 434
Fort Selden, N.Mex. Terr., 90
Fort Shaw, Mont. Terr., 319, 457, 585; winter march to, 483
Fort Sidney (Sidney Barracks), Neb., 26; canteen established at, 393; preparation for field service at, 440; quality of recruits received at, 106
Fort Sill, Indian Terr., 91, 96, 107, 126, 183, 194, 349, 365, 471, 502; Catholic sisters visit, 314; firing evening gun at, 205–6; gambling at, 361; Independence Day at, 338; library at, 348; tame deer at, 353; telegraph line to, 438
Fort Snelling, Minn., 95
Fort Stanton, N.Mex. Terr., 157; dairy at, 225; mail service to, 324; scarcity of women at, 321

Fort Stevenson, Dakota Terr., 112, 224, 558; artillery accident at, 337–38; Indians at, 494; mail service to, 438; transportation available at, 581; wedding at, 297
Fort Stockton, Texas, 211
Fort Sully, Dak. Terr., 398; dances at, 332; fire at, 217
Fort (Camp) Supply, Indian Terr.: barracks at, 213, field fortification near, 437; hospital steward's quarters at, 299; trader at, 231
Fort (Camp) Thomas, Ariz. Terr., 372
Fort Totten, Dak. Terr., 121, 181, 270, 297, 312; Christmas at, 343; mail service to, 438
Fort Union, N.Mex. Terr., 87, 90, 115, 157, 181, 194, 230, 299; description of squad room at, 216; deserters surrender at, 416; desertion from, 411; entertainment at, 330; holiday celebrations at, 334; homicide near, 271; hospital at, 257; illicit dive at, 370; laundress quarters at, 301; lecture at, 350; mail escorts from, 435; music club at, 328; newspaper published at, 350; prison at, 383; quartermaster depot at, 258, 370; shortage of single women at, 295; soldiers' ball at, 340; sordid village near, 372; star fort at, 370
Fort Vancouver, Wash. Terr., 94, 306; canteen established at, 392–93
Fort (Camp) Verde, Ariz. Terr., 296, 302, 575, 589; Chinese laundrymen at, 310–11; desertion from, 417
Fort Wallace, Kans., 171; construction of, 184; mail escorts from, 435
Fort Walla Walla, Wash. Terr., 270; guardhouse dog at, 356; soldiers riot at, 381
Fort Washakie, Wyo. Terr., 92, 193; Christmas at, 343; hospital described, 257

INDEX   743

Fort Whipple, Ariz. Terr., 88, 109; barracks at, 213; bedding used at, 214; food at, 222; mail service to, 324; officers at, 138; religious services at, 315; soldier wounded near, 268; target practice at, 202

Fort Wingate, N.Mex. Terr., 331, 358, 360; deserters drummed out of, 415; return of soldiers to after campaign, 489

Fort Yates, Dak. Terr., 272, 347; shooting affray near, 378

Forty-First U.S. Infantry, 6

Fort Yuma, Calif., 88, 262, 383; death of laundress at, 304; entertainment at, 330; holiday celebrations at, 334

Foster, John R. P., 553

Foster, William, 669n41

Fourteenth U.S. Infantry, 114, 128, 140, 161, 481, 561; drill by, 121, 459; dogs kept by, 354; field service training in, 456; laundress in, 306; member of, wounded, 268; mounted company in, 526; mule litters used by, 568–69; participation in Starvation March, 484; picket duty by, 535; recruits assigned to, 106, 442; route taken to Arizona, 88

Fourth New York Heavy Artillery, 110

Fourth U.S. Cavalry, 26, 78, 85, 91, 99, 160, 185, 264, 321, 391, 498, 499, 508, 528, 536, 543; alcoholic in, 363; arms and equipment of, 107, 189; band, 353; character of men, 111; clerks in, 177; desertion from, 406, 411; discipline in, 479; drunken officer of, 139; at Dull Knife Fight, 168, 543; field appearance of, 443; food served in, 223; at Horseshoe Canyon fight, 567; noncoms, 147, 163; soldiers riot, 381; use of prostitutes by, 371

Fourth U.S. Infantry, 116, 121, 125, 155, 220, 270, 315, 316, 326, 377, 387, 484, 494, 572; homicides in, 377; participation in Starvation March, 484, 485; skirmish with Indians, 561

Fox, Adam, 466

Franco-Prussian War, 115

Franklin, Texas, 327

Frank Miller's Harness Dressing, 657n38

fraternal organizations: Ancient Order of Hibernians, 352; Independent Order of Good Templars, 351–52, 390, 577; Independent Order of Odd Fellows, 352; Masons, 352

fraternization, among soldiers, 103–4

Freedmen's Bureau, 316

French, Thomas H., 144; punishes soldier, 479

Frew, James B., 38, 72, 474

Frierson, Eugene, 126, 491

Frith, Henry, 591

frostbite. *See* medical care

Fuller, Alvarado M., 170

fund: company, 224–25, 405; hospital, 668n28; post, 221; regimental, 221

funeral, formal military, described, 273, 669n49

furloughs, 357–58, 429

Galisteo, N.Mex. Terr., 327

gambling. *See* recreation

garden, 226–28, 256

Gardner, Samuel, on mail station guards and escorts, 435

Gavin, Anthony, 534

Geant, Eugene: on illness in the field, 483; on marches, 457

Geist, Reinhold R., 136, 320

General Service Cavalry, 635n7

General Service Infantry, 584, 635n7

George, William, 564

Germans. *See* immigrants

Geronimo, 504, 540, 567

Ghost Dance, 457, 534

Gibbert, John, 505, 588

Gibbon, John, 127–28, 456, 459, 460; at Big Hole battle, 551–52, 553; on army

744 INDEX

Gibbon, John (*continued*)
　marksmanship, 539; on Indian arms, 518; on Indian marksmanship, 520
Gibson, Samuel: on bathing, 253; on Wagon Box Fight, 546, 554
Gilpin, Samuel D., 456; on canned beans, 93, 229
ginger, 668n32
Girard, Alfred C., 276
Godfrey, Edward S., 126; on expedition's order of march, 452
Golden, Patrick, 122
Goldin, Theodore W.: on adjusting to army life, 122; on cooking in field, 465; on reaction of veterans to new recruits, 129; on use of surnames, 119
Goll, John, 95
Gomez, Victor, 590
Goodin, Ben, 124
Gordon, David, 271
Gordon, Francis S., 159
Gould, Clarence, 77
government property, misappropriation of, 58, 84
Governors Island, N.Y., 634n1, 635n4; barracks described, 49; departure from, 76; descriptions of, 45, 46; general recruiting depot at, 44–45; musicians' training at, 63; old noncoms at, 60–61; quality of food at, 56; recruit draft sent from, 80–81, 84
Grady, John, 554
Grand Army of the Republic, 336, 592
Grant, "Shorty," plays prank on sergeant, 500–501
Grant, Ulysses S.: amnesty for deserters granted by, 416; appointment of Indian agents by, 503; on army's role in West, 8
Gray, Thomas, 489–90
Great Plains, described, 431–32
Green, Henry, 156
Greenhalgh, Robert: on Christmas, 340; on desertion, 404; on discharge, 573; on discipline, 15; impression of Fort Laramie, 105–6; on payday, 236
Grey, George, 338
Grierson, Benjamin H., 380
grooming, 666n8
Grouard, Frank, 526
guard duty, 124–25, 191–96; in field, 475–78, 534–36, 694n54; how organized, 658n39, 658n45; old guard, 191, 326
guardhouse: described, 193; furnishings of, 193–94
guard mounting: depot, 61–62, 70; detachment, 192–93; post, 187–91; undress, 657n35
Gurnett, William, 440, 596
Gutch, Thomas E., 370
Guy, Theodore E., 118

Haddo, John, 552
Haley, Daniel, 38
Hallauer, John, 272
Halleck, Henry W., 9
Hamilton, James S.: on arms, 245, 518; on army life, 576; on card playing, 325; on furloughs, 357; on Indians, 497; motivation for enlisting, 23; on officers, 132, 141; on school, 318; on Southerners in ranks, 116
Hammond, Charles L.: on Indian marksmanship, 550; on scalping, 512
Hanley, Richard P., awarded Medal of Honor, 557, 702n56
Harbers, Herman: on army doctors, 267; on barracks at Camp Supply, 213; on journey to join unit, 90; on nurses, 263
Harmont, P. W., 511
Harrigan & Hart, ballad by, 486
Harrington, Walter C.: encounter with Indian woman, 501; on hog ranch, 374; on religion, 315
Harris, Jesse G., 573
Harris, Samuel, 319; on singing, 328
Harvey, Lawrence J., desire to be a soldier, 26

INDEX 745

Harvey, Winfield S., 126; on baking bread in field, 467; on discipline in the field, 479; on Indian women, 499; on intentional demotion, 150
Hatcher, Alexander: desire to be a soldier, 27; on furloughs, 357; on officers' relationship with soldiers, 136
Hauser, Charles R., 593
Hawkins, John L., special enlistment of, 299
Hawkins, John P., 248
Hayden, Charles N.: on Christmas, 343; on costs of promotion, 149; on guard being drunk, 195; on payday, 236
Hayes, Rutherford B.: describes combat experience, 542; issues order prohibiting liquor at army posts, 391
Hayman, Perry A., 126; promoted, 148; on tobacco, 229
Hays City, Kans., 346; civil riot at, 152; first impression of, 95; soldier's description of, 373
Hechner, John, 472
heel-ball, 643n36, 657n38
Hemstreet, Charles, 204
Henke, Charles, 60, 638n45
Henley, John, 582
Henry, Guy V.: on beans, 223; on drill, 198
Henry, Lawrence J., desire to be a soldier, 26
herd guard, 158, 204
Hessler, Annie, 307
Heth, Henry, 200
Hettinger, August: on his assignment as wagoner, 451; on marching, 457
Heyl, Charles H., 696n11
Hills, Louis E.: describes picket line, 462; first combat experience, 547; fraudulent enlistment in Seventh Cavalry, 40
Hobart, Charles, enlists married man, 299
Hoffner, Edgar, 471; on anticipation of combat, 533; on company dog, 355; on cowardice, 559; describes Idaho, 433; extracts own tooth, 261–62; on false alarms of Indian depredations, 504; on field cooking, 467; on mules, 454; on return from field, 489
hog ranch, 369–70, 391, 489
Holabird, Samuel B., 246, 423
Holden, Henry, 567
holidays: Christmas, 340–43; Decoration Day, 335–36; Independence Day, 336–39; New Year's, 334; St. Patrick's Day, 335; suspension of duty on, 333; Thanksgiving, 339–40; Washington's Birthday, 334
Holmes, James, 271
homicide, 271–72, 327, 377–78
homosexuality, 367–68, 680n20
Hooker, Forrestine, 329
Hoover, John M., 552
Horner, Jacob: on acceptance in company, 124; on army life, 576; on lack of training, 441; on salt pork, 465; secretly wed, 297–98
horse holders, 523
Horse Meat March. *See* Starvation March
horses, theft of, 408–9
hospital, 257–58, 277; field, 566; treatment of civilians at, 259
Hospital Corps, 277–78, 320, 334, 492, 670n57
hospital matron, 264, 299
hospital steward, 259–60, 262–63, 298–99, 667n20; drug abuse by, 367
Howard, George S., 570; on captured Indian foodstuffs, 487; on coffee in field, 466; criticizes General Crook, 140; on snakebite treatment, 480
Howard, Oliver O., 390
Hubbard, John L., 589
Hubman, Henry: befriends fellow recruit, 50; carries mail, 475; on civilian clothing, 241; contemplates desertion, 408; debauchery as reason for enlisting, 28; on depot food, 56;

Hubman, Henry (*continued*)
on depot noncoms, 60; develops relationship with Indian woman, 501, 685n24; on first sergeant, 162; on hunting, 346; on journey to join regiment, 92; on lice, 254; on pay, 405; on reconsidering enlistment, 70–71; on sex, 367; startled by Indian, 495; on target practice, 75–76, 641n79
Humfreville, Jacob Lee, 137
Hunteole, William, 23
Hunter, Moses, 270
hunting, 345–47, 469
Hunton, John, 667n17
Hynes, William F. (alias William Jones): on field ration, 93; on journey to join regiment, 86; life after discharge, 589; on mounted training, 120; opinion of company commander, 141; on vegetables, 256

identification tags, 669n40
illness: feigning, 265–66; in the field, 482–83. *See also* disease; medical care
immigrants: character of 114–16; enlistment as means of acculturation, 17–18; Germans as singers, 329; as percentages of enlistees, 16; relative qualities of nationalities, 115–16
Indian agents, 503–4
Indian Bureau, 504, 517
Indian culture: stealing horses in, 505–6; warfare in, 505–7
Indian depredations: false alarms of, 504; killing of civilians during, 510
Indian marksmanship, 519–20, 550–52
Indians: opinions of cavalry and infantry, 524; soldiers' views on, 502, 505, 510, 528
Indian policy 502–3, 505
Indian scouts, 509
Indian warfare: Indian women as combatants in, 544–45; killing of noncombatants, 545; mutilation practiced in, 510–14, 560–62, 697n33, 697n42; nature of, 507–9, 510, 520, 529–31, 546; strategy employed in, 530; tactics employed in, 508–9, 523–28, 531, 536–38; treatment of casualties, 538, 703n62
Indian weapons: bow, 515–16, 698nn44–45; firearms, 515–20; how procured, 517–18; lance, 516, 698n47
infantry: advantages of, 524; mounted, 525–27, 699nn64–65, 699nn67–68; typical role of, 433, 523–24; wagon-borne, 528, 690n3
Infantry Tactics (Upton), 163, 637n33
inspection: payday muster, 234–35; at recruiting depot, 69, 70; of stables, 209–10; Sunday, 207–10, 428; weekly, 660n80
Inspector General's Department, 139
Irish Brigade, 584
Irishmen. *See* immigrants

Jackson, James, 447
Jacob, Richard T., 437
James, John F., 366
Jansen, Charles N.: on canned food, 468; later life, 590; reenlists, 583
Jefferson Barracks, Mo., 52, 53, 56, 66, 71, 72, 84, 634n1; bawdy houses near, 70; drill sergeants at, 66–68; mounted recruiting depot at, 45, 87; mounted training at, 65–68, 120; musicians' training at, 62–63; quality of recruits sent from, 106–7; retention of recruits at, 72–73, 91, 126
Jenkins, John W., 16
Jenkins, Micah J., 144
Jerome, Lawrence R., on pursuing Apaches, 458
Jerome, Lovell H. (alias Laurence Vinton), 140; on pursuing Apaches, 508
Jett, William B.: enlistment experience, 33; on alcoholic soldier, 363; on army service, 573; arrested, 160; on black

sergeant of the guard, 62; on bullying, 117; defended by bunkie, 123; on depot food, 57; on depot officers, 60; describes combat experience, 537–38; on fatigue duty, 185–86; on fellow recruits, 38; on garden, 228; on guard duty, 476; on Indians, 494; on leaving depot, 77; post-army career of, 591; on punishment, 386; on religion, 312, 313; refuses promotion, 149; refuses to salute officer, 579; travels to join unit, 91
Jewell, Brady, 387
Jewitt, William, killed at sawmill, 270
Johnson, Andrew, amnesty policy of, 7
Johnson, Charles, 141, 369
Johnson, Stanislaus, 386–87
John Stands In Timber, 513
"Jonahs," 117
Jordan, William W., 481, 484; on profiteers, 488
Joseph (Nez Perce), 551
Julesburg, Colo. Terr., 269, 459

Kane, William (Cavalry Depot noncom), 46–47, 635n9
Kane, William (Fourth Cavalry), 591
Kansas State Penitentiary, 377
Kautz, August V., 653n65
Kearney, James, 269
Keim, DeBenneville Randolph, on Indian women as combatants, 545
Kelley, Bernard, 266
Kelton, J. C., 587
Kennedy, John M., 272
Kenney, Francis Johnson, fraudulent enlistment by, 35
Kerr, John B., 103
Kerstetter, David, 511, 579
Kimball, James P., 106–7
Kimball, John, 327
Kimm, John G., 575
Kincaid, James B., on effects of fraudulent enlistment, 36

King, Charles: on duties of adjutant, 135–36; on formal ball, 334; on headquarters clerks, 655; on recruits, 128–29, 418; on veterans, 96
King, Richard F., on education, 320–21; on reenlistment pay, 576
Kiowa Indians, 9, 338, 490, 499, 517, 556
Kirkwood, John A., 566
Kitchen, George K., 154, 652n46
kitchen police: in companies, 178–79, 181; deliver food to prisoners, 388; at depots, 59
Kitching, Seymour: on nurses, 264; marriage of, 299
knapsack, 215
Kolarik, Charles: as a recruit, 49; on depot food, 58
Kuhn, Joseph, 574
Kurtz, Frederick: on bed sacks, 218; on hardtack, 465; on hunting, 346; on saber, 446; on surviving an enlistment, 574

labor. *See* fatigue duty
Laidley, Theodore T. S., 203
Laird, John D., 365
Lambert, Leonard, 158
Landon, William D. F., 650n16
Lang, John, 565
Laramie City, Wyo. Terr., 326
Last of the Mohicans, 494
Las Vegas, N.Mex. Terr., 295, 324
latrine. *See* sink
Latta, Emmet G., 515
Lauderdale, John Vance: on entertainment, 329–30; on guardhouse conditions, 383; on health of troops, 256; on hospital stewards, 262–63
laundresses, 294, 299–311, 332, 343; for bands, 300; black in white units, 303, 363; character of, 302–4; elimination of, 308–11, 321, 672n29; married, 308; minor children as, 672n26; for noncommissioned staff, 300; numbers

laundresses (*continued*)
  allowed, 299; problems with, 302–3, 305–7, 363; quarters for, 300–301, 671nn14–15, 671n17; rates charged by, 302, 671n17; ration for, 300; repair clothing, 304; sell pies to soldiers, 304–5; soldier's tribute to, 310; unmarried, 672n20
laundries, Chinese, 310–11, 673n34
Lea, Lawrence, 73; benefit performance for, 331
Lehman, Joseph, 41
Lemly, H. R., 559
Lester, Charles, 561, 572
Lewis, Granville, 370
Lewis and Clark expedition, 568
library, 347–49
Lincoln, Abraham, 339
Lipowitz, Max, 161
Lippincott, Henry, 667n16
liquor. *See* alcohol
Lister, Joseph, 276
Littman, Max, 18; on his promotion, 151
Lloyd, Thomas, 549: on campaigning, 571
locker (foot), 215, 661nn7–8
Lockwood, James D.: on anonymity of ex-volunteer soldiers, 110; on buffalo chips as fuel, 463; on journey to join regiment, 85; on reason for enlisting, 14
Loma Parda, N.Mex. Terr., 158, 372
Lowell, Frank: upon assignment to unit, 76; on march to join regiment, 88
Loynes, Charles N.: describes charge on Indian position, 554; on attacking Indian village, 544
Luce, David W. (alias Charles Newton): describes death of comrades, 510–11; on mounted training, 87
Luff, Edmund, 143
Luhn, Gerhard L., 477
Lynch, David, 186
Lyon, Annie, 322
Lyon, Howard, 322

Macfeely, Robert, 426
Mackenzie, Ranald S., 11, 411, 463, 468, 480, 556; nickname of, 142; soldiers' opinion of, 142; use of scouts by, 509
Madsen, Christian, 18, 590; on Warbonnet Creek skirmish, 528
Maghee, Thomas G., 196
mail: delivery in field, 474–75; delivery on Bozeman Trail, 675n4; importance of, 323–24; station guards, 435–36. *See also* U.S. Mail; stage stations
Mangas (Apache), 156
Mann, Frank, 550
Mann, Simpson, 215; on army life, 576; on Indians, 502; on relationships between cavalry and infantry, 104–5; on serving as striker, 145; on troop dog, 354; on whiskey, 363
Manning, James, 196
Marcy, Randolph B.: on desertion, 404, 407; on laundresses, 307
Maricopa Well, Ariz. Terr., 325
marksmanship, 539. *See also* target practice
marriage, 295–99, 322
Marshall, David, 554–55
Marshall, Moses, 118
Mason, Edwin C., 421
Matthews, Washington, 254–55; on Christmas celebration, 340–41
Matthews, William E.: anticipates combat, 534; on bathing, 253; as company clerk, 177; on company comrades, 109; demotion of, 154; on dental care, 262; on depot food, 56; describes final formation at depot, 77; describes homicide, 271; experiences homesickness, 49; on fellow recruits, 84–85; on Franco-Prussian War, 115; on furloughs, 358; on hardtack, 465; on Indians, 494; on Indian traders, 517; on journey west, 80; on lack of tents, 482; on library, 348; on laundresses, 304; on maintaining neat appearance,

241; on motivation for enlisting, 22; on officers, 85; on personal expenses, 236; promotion of, 148; on pursuit of deserters, 411; on recruit guard mounting, 62; on recruit training, 61–62; reenlists, 588; on religion, 312; on routine duty, 180; on strikers, 145; on term of enlistment, 36; on theft by deserters, 408; on treatment by civilians, 327

Maurer, Charles, 37; on prelude to attacking village, 543; on relationship with Indians, 498; on transportation of the wounded, 567

Mayo, Grandison: on army service, 574; on athletics, 345; motivation for enlisting, 25; on noncoms, 160; on relationship with company members, 123

Mazzanovich, Anton, 362, 589; describes skirmish with Apaches, 540–41; on packing mules, 455; on payday drinking, 362

McAnulty, George, 572; on army life, 130; on dances, 332; on mosquitoes, 481; on nursing, 263; post-army life of, 592

McCardle, Washington, 23, 576

McClellan, George B., 147

McClellan, James S., 567; on cleaning barracks, 217, 482; on Dull Knife Fight, 549; promotion of, 148

McConnell, Henry H., 76; appointed first sergeant, 155; appointed lance sergeant, 81; on character of men in his company, 110; on depot experience, 55; on desertion, 82, 409; on dogs, 353; on drill sergeant, 66; on drinking, 362; on enlistment of former volunteers, 14–15; on food provided recruits, 85; on foreign-born soldiers, 16; on Great Plains, 431; on Indian preference for fighting cavalry, 522; on inspection, 209; on Kiowa lances, 516;

on laundress quarters, 300; on officers' nicknames, 140; on sick book, 182; on singing, 328–29; on St. Patrick's Day, 335; on tailor, 241; on trumpeters, 178

McCook, Alexander McD., 396

McDonald, Bryan, 23–24

McDougal, Barney, involved in shooting affray, 303

McGregor, Thomas, on poorly trained recruits, 521–22

McKay, Barney, fraudulent enlistment by, 35

McLennon, John, 585

McLennon, Margaret, 584

McLennon, Michael, 584, 705n27

McReynolds, Willis, 113

Medal of Honor, 141, 555–58, 585, 593, 702n52

medical care: anesthesia, 267; for arrow wounds, 267–68; for frostbite, 266–67; at recruiting depots, 57; for snakebite, 480; surgery, 266; transportation of the wounded, 567–69; treatment of in the field, 566–67, 569

Medical Department, 258, 277–78

medicine, as field, 254–57, 264–65

Medicine Bow, Wyo. Terr., 412

Medicine Lodge Treaty, 497

medicines, 265

Meigs, Montgomery C., 237, 426

Melus, Walter L., 377

Mercer, John, 305

Merriam, Henry C., 276

Merritt, Wesley, 103; on enlisted life, 406; on quality of recruits, 127

Mescal, 663n35, 675n7

Mesilla-Tucson Road, 174

mess: company, 181–82; consolidated, 58–59, 247, 656n24; ironstone dishes for, 248

Mexican-American War, 133

Michaelis, Otho E., 202

Middleton, Passmore, 268

750   INDEX

Miles, Nelson A., 11; advocates winter campaigning, 525; emphasizes training, 199; indulges troops, 490; institutes field training, 491; on married soldiers, 309; use of mounted infantry, 526–27
Miles City, Mont. Terr., 373
military departments: Arizona, 491; Columbia, 94, 309; Dakota, 256, 357; Missouri, 87, 358, 492; Platte, 224, 387, 421
military divisions: decision by, regarding shooting of prisoners, 196; Missouri, 9, 347, 391; Pacific, 9, 383; recruitment in, 30; transportation to, 87–88
Military Order of the Loyal Legion, 592
military reservation, 325
Miller, Emil, 99
Miller, William, 510, 536
minstrels. *See* recreation
Mixer, Fred W., on Indian marksmanship, 451
Modoc Indians, 504, 511, 546, 562
Moffett, Rolando B., 184
Monnette, Joseph, 527
Monroe Doctrine, 102
Montana Battalion. *See* Second U.S. Cavalry
Monument Station, Kans., 270
Moore, Charles E., 638n45
Moore, Dennis, 115
Moore, Francis, 461
Moore, Michael, 60–61, 638n45
morality, 365, 369–73
Morgan, Charles, 194
Moriarty, Patrick, 303
Morris, William E., 161, 588
Morrison, James G., 574
Morrow, Henry A., pioneers canteen movement, 393
Mowry Mine, Ariz. Terr., 591
Mulford, Ami F.: on check roll call, 409; on company commander, 144; describes funeral, 273; describes mess hall, 181; describes physical training, 53; disability of, 586–87; on discipline in field, 478; enlistment in unit, 41; on fatigue, 185; on pranks by recruits, 93; on reception by company, 109; on recruit experience, 94–95; on reveille, 179; on stag dances, 332; on training, 120–21; on travois, 568
Mullins, George G.: on attitudes of black soldiers, 22; on whiskey, 362–63
Munger, Daniel E., 110, 646n32
Munn, Fred, 41: on campaign shakedown march, 456; describes first uniform, 49; describes reception by his unit, 107; motivation for enlisting, 25
murder. *See* homicide
Murphy, Lawrence, 143
Murphy, William A.: on bunkies, 122–23; on condition of bacon, 222; on construction of fort, 173; on crossing river, 269, 459; on drumming out deserters, 415; on medical care in field, 565; on railroad protection, 439; reflections on army service, 595; on scalping, 512
Murray, Patrick, 386
music, 328–29. *See also* band; songs
musicians: band leader (drum major), 166; chief trumpeter, 165–66; Custer punishes, 103; enlistment of, 102; field, 178; how armed, 64, 445; orderly trumpeter, 178; principal musician, 166; rules for enlistment, 33–34; training for, 51–52, 63–64, 70; trumpeter of the guard, 178, 179, 181
mutilation. *See* Indian warfare

Nana (Apache), 558
narcotics, 366, 680n15
National Armory, 347
National Indian Wars Veterans Association, 593–95
Navajo Indians, 9, 589
Neifert, William W., 97

Neihaus, George, 27, 588; on bed sacks, 218; on drinking, 390; on Indians, 502; opinion of company commander, 141; on religion, 314

Neihause, John H., 123, 700n15; killed in action, 537–38

Newport Barracks, Ky., 83, 634n1, 642n19; closure of depot at, 45; description of, 46; quality of food at, 56; recruiting depot at, 44

newspapers, 348–49, 350

New York National Guard, 202

Nez Perce Campaign, 310, 432, 466, 528, 533, 563, 569, 571; dawn raid during, 536; effect on recruit training, 73; use of mounted infantry during, 527

Nez Perce Indians, 202, 490, 511, 520, 543; noted for marksmanship, 551–52

nicknames: officers', 140–41; soldiers', 119

Nineteenth U.S. Infantry, 318; transported in wagon, 528

Ninth U.S. Cavalry, 77, 118, 157, 160, 170, 216, 338, 363, 502, 536, 628n6; accidental shooting in, 271; associations with Cheyenne women, 501; conflict with citizens, 379; crosses frozen river, 461; desertion rate of, 423; engages in fight with infantrymen, 104–5; gambling in, 361; musicians in, 328; recruit inspection in, 125; skirmish with Apaches, 558; theft in, 376–77; troop dog with, 354

Ninth U.S. Infantry, 128, 303, 484, 627n3

Nixon, John R., on kitchen police, 59

noncommissioned officers: in black regiments, 156, 162, 163; as bone and sinew, 146; character of 152, 157; chief trumpeter, 165–66; color sergeant, 166; commissioning of, 169–70; company quartermaster, 153–54, 157, 177, 182, 440, 652n45; corporal, 148, 149–50, 195, 582; at depots, 60–61, 109; as drill masters, 122; duty sergeant, 150–52, 153, 180, 182, 195, 216, 234, 582, 652n43; first sergeant, 154–55, 177, 180, 182, 187, 402, 409, 440, 441, 576; hospital steward, 259–60; how addressed, 119; as kitchen supervisors, 179; lance (acting), 81, 84, 94, 148, 642n5; longevity of, 147; married, 298, 309–10; men's confidence in, 552; numbers of company, 146–47; ordnance sergeant, 167–68, 185, 259; police sergeant, 183, 191; post commissary sergeant, 165, 167–69; post quartermaster sergeant, 152, 654n70; principal musician, 166; provost sergeant, 683n62; punishment of, 158–59; quarters for, 673n30; reduction of, 156–57, 159–60, 653n49; reenlistment of, 582, 635n11, 637n23; regimental commissary sergeant, 165; regimental quartermaster sergeant, 164–65, 234, 260; relationship with company members, 160; saddler sergeant, 165–66; school for, 318; selection of, 148; separate mess tables for, 181; training of, 162; sergeant major, 164, 260, 654n66, 657n39; Tenth Cavalry, 424; treatment by, 402, 422; treatment of recruits by, 60–61, 66–67, 76–77, 80; Signal Corps, 65; soldiers' opinions of company, 108–9; special recognition of, 163; warrant for, 149

Noonan, John, 368, 680n18

Norman, Robert C. O., 18

Northern Boundary Survey, 355

North Platte City, Neb., 579

Norvell, Steven T., 542

Nugent, William D., on order of march, 452

nurses, 263–64, 668n28

Oakes, James, 106

O'Brien, John D., 316

O'Brien, Joseph: kicked by horse, 270

officer of the day, 180, 295, 658n43

officers: abuse by, 137; appointed from among noncommissioned officers, 169–70; civilian appointments of, 687n55; club room for, 207; company, 136; field grade, 132–33; former volunteer, 136–37, 141; indulgences of soldiers by, 143; informality of, 142; inspection of kitchens by, 79; leniency shown by, 142, 143; men's confidence in, 552; poor conduct of, 137–39; promotion of, 145; nicknames for, 140–41; relationship with enlisted men, 132, 136, 143–44, 422; servants for, 144–45, 294–95, 332, 630n8, 651nn25–27; "shavetail" defined, 136; soldiers' opinions of, 80, 108–9; transfers by, 651n28; wives of, 299
O'Halloran, Jack, 152
old guard fatigue, 191, 388
old soldiers, 583: definition of, 646n34; opinions of former volunteers, 110–11; recruits receive guidance from, 122
O'Leary, Maurice J., 326, 354
Olwill, Edward, 377
Omaha Daily Bee, 363
O'Neill, Thomas F., 548, 588
orderly, 188–91
orderly bucker, 188–89, 190–91
orderly room, 176–77. *See also* barracks
orderly trumpeter. *See* musicians
Order of Indian Wars, 593
Ordnance Department, 590; experiments with infantry equipment, 243
Oregon Trail, 8, 86, 87
O'Reilly, Robert M., 106
Ostrander, Alson B.: on courage, 495; describes desiccated vegetables, 226; on depot noncoms, 60–61; on discharge, 577; ignores officer, 54; reflects on army service, 595
Otis, Elmer, 140, 314, 478
Otis, Elwell S., 645n16
O'Toole, Francis, 560
Ovenshine, Samuel J., 444

pack mules, 454–56, 541, 688n8, 690n8
Pagel, E. W., 489
Paiute Indians, 490, 504
Panama, 88
Panic of 1873, 418
parade: muster day, 234–35; retreat, 204–5, 660n71; Sunday, 68
Parker, W. Thornton, 437
Parnell, William R., on mounted drill, 87
Parsons, George W., 628n6
passes: day, 326, mounted, 326; weekend, 70
Pasteur, Louis, 275, 365–66
pastimes. *See* recreation
pay, 232–34; extra duty, 233–34, 664n50, 263; recruit, 69–70; reenlistment, 581; retained, 233, 428–29, 687n54; travel, 579–80, 705n17
payday, 234–36, 360–62, 398, 679n1; effect on desertion, 405–6, 407, 424; upon discharge, 577
paymaster, 234, 314, 360, 577, 664n51
Pelham, R. Eugene, 305: on army life, 211, 573; on arrival at Hays, Kans., 95; visits site of Fort Buford, 596
Penrose, W. H., 342
permanent party (depot), 51–52, 642n3; abolished, 74, 635n9; described, 46–47, 640n76; duties of, 47; reorganization of, 74–75. *See also* recruiting depot; depot detachment
pets, 353–57
physical examination, of recruits: at depots, 51; at posts, 106–7, 642n8; upon enlistment, 34, 36–37, 428
Pickering, Abner, 491–92
pickets. *See* guard duty
Pilgard, Rasmus, 591
Pinder, Hiram E.: murdered, 379
Pine Ridge Reservation, Dak. Terr., 365, 457, 501, 527, 534
pioneers, 452–53
Pittsburgh Leader, 560

Platten, Fred: on activities after discharge, 583; collects war bonnet, 562; describes combat experience, 547; life after discharge, 589; on mounted training, 87; on pack trains, 454; on promotion, 151; reenlists, 583
policing: general, 183–84, 388; at recruiting depot, 69
Pollock, Oliver, 486
Pond Creek Station, Kans., 86, 184
Pope, James W., 518
Poplar Creek Agency, Mont. Terr., 495
post canteen, 392–98, 684n76
post exchange, 398. *See also* post canteen
post trader, 230–32, 393–98, 664n43. *See also* sutler
Powder River Expedition, 468
Powell, James, 552
Powell, William H., 201; dismisses laundress, 305
Powers, John, 486
prairie monitor. *See* stage stations
Prescott, Frank G., on disorderly conduct by recruits, 84
Price, George F., on nationalities of enlistees, 17. *See also* U.S. Army
prisoners: fired on, 195–96; how confined, 194; how fed, 194, 388; made to attend religious services, 313–14; where confined, 382–83, 479; work details, 192. *See also* punishment; recruiting depot
prostitution, 137, 369–73, 396–97, 681n22, 681nn32–34
punishment: company, 209, 376; for deserters, 402, 414–16; forms of, 384–89, 683n54, 683n56, 683n65; in field, 478–80
Purvis, James O.: on Decoration Day, 336; on fatigue duty, 186; on garden at Fort Custer, 227; on German soldiers, 19; on paymaster, 235; on target practice, 203
Pyne, Michael, 318

Quartermaster Department, 242; barracks study by, 213; fatigue duty with, 184; improves clothing, 249; purchases tableware, 248; responsible for cemeteries, 274; sells obsolete clothing, 240–41, 443
Quinette, William H., 231

Rae, Thomas, 304
Raper, George S.: on arms for recruits, 643n25; on drill sergeant, 122; on mail service, 324; on old guard fatigue, 191; on sale of citizens' clothing, 38
railroads, 79; in Ariz. Terr., 89; Atchison, Topeka & Santa Fe, 89, 90, 91, 434; Denver & Rio Grande, 91; effect on mail delivery, 434; effect on military operations, 342, 442, 449; facilitates desertion, 412; Kansas Pacific, 89, 90, 434; Missouri, Kansas & Texas, 91; Northern Pacific, 89, 91, 92, 432, 452, 510; Southern Pacific, 90; Union Pacific, 8, 85–86, 89, 296, 326, 412, 434, 439, 579
ramadas, 470, 655n6
rations: field, 457–58, 464–68; travel, 579. *See* food
rattlesnakes, 480–81
Rawn, Charles C., 553
recreation, 325, 678n58; cards 325; dances, 332–33, 343; entertainment by professional troupes, 331; in field, 475–78; formal balls, 333–34, 343; gambling, 326, 374; lyceums, 350; minstrels, 329–31; scholarly activities, 349; singing, 328–29, 335; varieties, 330–31. *See also* holidays
recruiting depot, 634n1; abolished, 641n78; at Angel Island, 94; barracks at, 48–49; companies of instruction, 51; cooks at, 58–59; at Denver, 632n46; detachments at, 640n76; discipline at, 54–55; disease at, 637n36; desertion from, 55, 76; drill

recruiting depot (*continued*)
sergeants at, 66–68; food at, 56–59, 637n35; gardens at, 56, 57; graft at 58; guard mounting at, 61–63; locations of, 44–45, 94; medical care at, 57; noncommissioned officers at, 46, 48, 54, 60–61, 74; opinions of depot experience, 77–78; permanent party at, 46–47, 51–52, 53, 74, 635n9, 640n76; physical examination at, 51; prisoners, 63; reception of recruits at, 47–48; reorganization at, 74–75; retention of recruits at, 71–74, 91, 126; routine duty at, 69; staff at, 46; theft at, 59–60, 61; training at, 54, 55, 63–64, 65–68, 74–76; 1; transfer to, 42–43

Recruiting Service (general and mounted), 169; effort by to improve quality of recruits, 418; replacements provided by, 105; segregation of stations, 29; size of permanent parties, 640n76. *See also* depot detachment

recruiting stations, 634n1; description of typical, 31–32; desertion from, 54–55; 38; distribution of, 30–31, 632n41, 632n43, 632n46, 633n68; issue of clothing at, 37–38; at military posts, 39; oath of enlistment given at, 37; physical examination at, 34, 36–37; regimental, 641n78; staff at, 31; training at, 38

recruits: adjustment to life in company, 122–23; appearance of, 48, 49, 96; arms for, 85–86, 91, 93–94, 640n74, 642n14, 642n19, 643nn25–26, 648n54; arrival at headquarters or station, 96, 97, 643n40; assignment to permanent units, 71–72, 96; clothing issued to, 37–38; 636n17, 639n64; company organization of, 51; conditioning of in companies, 125–127; desertion by, 55, 76, 82, 95, 641n84; disorderly conduct by, 83–84; disposable, 52, 75; drafts of, 77–78; equipment issued to, 77, 641n83; first combat experience of, 547; food provided to en route to regiments, 85, 92–93; hazing of in company, 111–14; impressions of new comrades, 50; influence of popular literature on, 494; means of transportation to regiments, 79, 85–92, 97; nationalities of, 17, 629n8–9; necessities purchased by, 50; opinions of depot officers and noncoms, 79; percentage of in companies, 105; physical examinations of 34, 36–37, 51, 106–7, 428; physical standards for, 33–34, 428, 633n54; poorly trained, 521–22, 640n74; pranks by, 82–84, 93; quality of, 38–39, 51, 636n21; quality of after training, 125–27, 129, 418–20, 521–22, 640nn74–75; reception at permanent units, 107–9; requisitions for, 76, 126–27, 641n80; retention of at depots, 426; segregation of black, 52; select, 52–53; for Seventh Cavalry, 128–29; training of, 52–54, 61, 63–68, 72, 75, 120–22, 124–26, 426, 639n57, 640nn73–75, 643n28; unassigned, 53

Red Horse (Lakota), respect of for infantry, 524

Red River War, 141, 168

reenlistment, 581; of noncommissioned officers, 582, 635n11, 637n23; statistics concerning, 583

regiment: black, 5–6, 422–424; composition of, 99, 649n4; desertion rates of compared, 422–23; dispersal of, 98–99, 644n2; field staff of, 132–33; recruiting by, 641n78; relationships among, 104–5, 645n17; strength of, 687n52. *See also* U.S. Army

Regiment of Mounted Riflemen, 525, 627n3

Regular Army Division, 4, 551

religion, 311–15, 674n42

Reno, Marcus A., 548, 557

retirement, 587

retreat, 204–5
Rhey, Charles, 677n29
Rice, Edmund, 126; on lack of drill, 197
Richey, Stephen R., 64
river crossings, 458–61
Robertson, David, 635n7
Robertson, Frank, 546
Robinson, Daniel, 649n7
Robinson, Richard, 118
Rodgers, Alexander, 139
Roe, Fayette W., 341
Roe, Frances, 341
Rogan, Patrick, 584–85
Rogers, B. H., 261
roll call: check, 326, 409, 428; retreat, 204; reveille, 180; tattoo, 206, 428
Romeyn, Henry, 131; on army pay, 401; on desertion, 424
room orderly, 181
Roque, Emanuel, on recruit experience at Angel Island, 94
Rosebud Agency, Dak. Terr., 501
Ross, Thomas, 584, 632n47
Rough Riders, 590
Rovinsky, John, 594
Rowalt, John F., awarded Medal of Honor, 556–57
Royall, William B., 123; on desertion, 400; on lack of drill, 197
Rushville, Neb., 473
Russell, Elwood, 272
Ryan, John: on acting post sergeant major, 164; on branding deserters, 414; on bucking and gagging, 385; on campaign preparation, 440; on cavalry arms and equipment, 244; on cleaning barracks, 207–8; on departure for campaign, 448; on discharge, 578; field sanitation, 462; on fortified stage stations, 437; on homosexuality, 368; on hunting, 347; on Indian marksmanship, 551; on inspection for guard mounting, 189; on killing of an Indian woman, 545; on laundresses, 304; on loss of arms, 246; on mess hall tableware, 220; on nicknames, 119; on noncoms inspecting kitchens, 179; on orderly buckers, 188; on pioneer troops, 453; as police officer after discharge, 588; on punishment of bandsmen, 103; on punishment for theft, 376; purchases Sharps rifle, 246; reason for enlisting, 15; on reduction of noncoms, 159; requests demotion, 156, 653n49; on rifle ammunition, 245; on room orderly, 181; on taking a scalp, 561; on theft, 404; on wagons, 451

Sacket, D. B.: on sentences for desertion, 420–21; on recruit training, 640n73
saddler, 186
Salt Lake City, Utah, soldiers marry women at, 296–97
salute gun: evening, 205–6; morning, 179; on holidays, 337–38
San Angelo, Texas, 372–73, 379–81
San Antonio, Texas, recruiting station at, 30
San Carlos Agency, 438
Sanders, Charles, 549
Sanford, Wilmot P.: on Christmas celebration, 341; modifies uniform coat, 240; on old guard fatigue, 191; on self-education, 348; treated kindly by officer, 143
San Francisco, Calif., recruiting station at, 30
sanitation, 252, 278, 462
San Marcial, N.Mex. Terr., 379
Santa Fe Trail, 8, 87, 173, 340, 406, 580; buffalo along, 432; resupply of mail stations along, 435
sawmill, 185
scalping, 511–14, 561–62, 697n39. *See also* Indian warfare
Schall, Lafayette, 52, 74, 637n23
Schell, Henry S., 264

Schofield, John M., advocates abolition of Sunday inspection, 210
school: attendance at, 319–20; influence on literacy, 349; noncommissioned officers', 318; post, 162, 317–21, 425, 674n44, 674n49, 674n52, 674n55; segregated, 320; teachers for, 317–18. *See also* education
Schorr, John P., 551, 564
Schreiber, Phillip, 74; on officers and noncoms, 133
Scott, Charles, 447
scouting. *See* field service
scurvy, 226, 256, 667n12
Searl, Herman S.: describes hospital, 257; on Indian agents, 503
Second U.S. Cavalry, 80, 82, 91, 105, 107, 110, 116, 122, 124, 128, 140, 173, 296, 303, 389, 468, 473, 474, 481, 500, 514, 560, 565; bad water consumed by, 482; benefit performance for member of, 331; black laundress in, 303; carbine used by, 244; character of men in, 114; company dog killed in action, 357; condition of after campaign, 571; desertion from, 403, 404; in Dull Knife Fight, 546; laundress problem in, 307; noncoms in, 147; pack mules with, 455; passes through western Kansas, 432; pet bear kept by, 353; in Powder River fight, 542–43; returns to post after campaign, 489; soldier kicked by horse, 270; in Starvation March, 487; St. Patrick's Day celebrated by, 335; treatment by civilians, 327; troop rivalries in, 118; winter scout by, 434
Second U.S. Dragoons, 141
Second U.S. Infantry, 94, 491
Selander, Ernest: reason for enlisting, 25–26; on fatigue, 183
Sembower, Isaac H., 447; describes Indian raid, 536; describes Yellowstone Park, 433; on selling tobacco, 474

sergeant of the guard, 151, 195
servants. *See* officers
service calls (bugle and drum), 534; assembly, 204; boots and saddles, 434; fatigue call, 183; first call, 179, 656n18; first sergeants call, 197; the general, 456; learned by recruits, 56; mess call, 181, 197; recall, 204; reveille, 179; scheduling of, 178; sick (surgeon's) call, 182–83, 456; stable call, 180, 204, 206; taps, 207, 428, 660n74; tattoo, 206, 428; water call, 180, 196, 204
Settle, Green, trains recruits, 52
Seventeenth U.S. Infantry, 272, 322; Christmas dinner, 342; hunting by, 347
Seventh U.S. Cavalry, 42, 95, 96, 98, 99, 114, 118, 119, 181, 182, 188, 297, 317, 340, 349, 432, 453, 460, 497, 504, 508, 515, 524, 539; accidental shooting in, 161, 271; at Allen Creek fight, 547; band, 102–3; bathing by, 473; at Battle of the Little Bighorn, 543, 550, 553; cowardice in, 559; discipline in, 479; dogs, with, 354; drinking in, 364–65; ex-Confederates in 116; field appearance of, 442–43; at Fort Larned, 173; holiday celebrations by, 337, 340, 341, 342; homosexuality in, 368; infantryman's opinion of, 105; instructed to spare noncombatants, 545; laundresses in, 303, 310; musicians in, 329; nicknames in, 119; noncoms desert from, 158; oral health of, 262; receives recruits during Sioux Campaign, 128; receives recruits on eve of Washita Campaign, 126, 441; Second Cavalryman's opinion of, 99; soldiers pay officer's fine, 139; statistical analysis of, 649n72; target practice by, 202, 203; training, 121; veterans in ranks of, 111
Seventh U.S. Infantry, 235, 461, 528, 559; honors officer's memory, 146; marriage

in, 296–97; on Sioux Campaign, 128; on sparing noncombatants, 545; transports wounded men, 569; winter march by, 483
Shafter, William R., 527
shavetail. *See* officers
Sheepeater Campaign, 261, 433
Sheepeater Indians, 490, 504, 533
Sheridan, Philip H., 645n15; on laundresses, 311; requests clarification of temperance order, 391
Sherman, William T.: commands Division of the Missouri, 9; on cost of maintaining laundresses, 307; on post traders (sutlers), 230; on quality of recruits, 419; on religion, 313; supports target practice, 203; on teachers, 318
Shoshone Indians, 494, 627n1
Sibley stove, 472, 693n44
Sidney, Neb., 439
Signal Corps, 96, 246, 492; arms of, 61, 93–94, 638n47; enlistment for, 45; examination, 65; organization of, 639n53; telegraph lines operated by, 438–39; training, 61, 64–65
Signal School. *See* Fort Myer
Silver City, N.Mex., 228
singing. *See* recreation
sink (latrine), 252; consolidated, 252–53
Sioux (Lakota) Indians, 9, 202, 495, 498, 527, 531, 558; at Fetterman Fight, 507; firearms of, 518; at Little Bighorn battle, 557; method of scalping, 512; mutilation of dead, 560–61; at Rosebud battle, 548; shooting skill of, 515; at Wagon Box Fight, 546; women, 499
Sitting Bull (Lakota), 483, 504, 518, 549, 551
Sixteenth U.S. Infantry, 40, 112, 138, 181, 211, 239, 261, 349, 363, 388, 471, 515; soldier murdered by citizens, 379; training in field, 473

Sixth U.S. Cavalry, 87, 142, 150, 185, 296, 311, 363, 455, 528, 558, 565; band, 103; black laundress in, 303; bunkies in, 123; character of men in, 110; dogs with, 355; drug abuse in, 366; immigrants in, 116; laundress, 302; marriage of soldier in, 322; murder in, 377–78; newspaper published by, 350; officers' nicknames, 140; opinion of trumpeters in, 178; skirmishes with Apaches, 540–41; training of, 120; troop rivalries in, 118
Sixth U.S. Infantry, 95; bayonet drill in, 198; company dog in, 354; constructs field fortification, 437; desertion from, 408; drill in, 198, 199; eggs procured by, 225; establishes canteen, 392; homosexuality in, 367; movement to Powder River country, 128; recovers dog, 357; recruits 106; returns to Fort Buford following campaign, 489; Southerners in, 116; St. Patrick's Day celebrated by, 335; Thanksgiving celebration by, 340
Slaper, William C.: on benefit of veterans in combat, 548; on depot training, 65–66; enlistment experience, 32; first combat experience, 546; on field burials, 564; on physical examination, 34; on recruits bartering government property, 84
Slaughter, William J., 365
Slough, John P., on tents, 470
Smith, Andrew J., 132
Smith, Jacob Clay, 587
Smith, James, 271
Smith, Oskaloosa M., 550
Smith, William Earl: on Col. Mackenzie, 142; on first combat experience, 547; on old guard duty in field, 476
Smoky Hill Trail, 8, 86, 184, 324, 403, 516; combining stage runs on for protection, 688n10; fortified mail stations along, 436–37

Society of Veterans of Indian Wars, 593
soldiers: attitudes about civilians 327, 334; attitudes about Indians, 494–502, 528; career, 583–84; commissioning of, 169–70, 406, 425; correspondence with women, 130, 263, 296; effects of deceased, 275; embarrassed by enlistment, 71; esprit de corps among, 103–4; fighting among, 104, 115, 118–19, 345; impressions of the West, 79, 88–89, 430–33; loyalty to officers, 143–44; married, 295–300, 309–10; mutilation of dead by, 560–62; nationalities of, 17, 629nn8–9; nicknames among, 119; numbering of, 119, 648n53; reflections on their service, 572–74; use of surnames, 119; views on Indian policy, 505
Soldiers Home, 233, 585–87, 705n31
Sommer, Christian F., 184
songs, 78, 103, 112, 329. *See also* bands; music
Southern Overland Route, 436
souvenirs, collected by soldiers, 562
Spanish-American War, 170, 247, 250, 590, 593
sports: baseball, 339, 344, 345; football, 677n43; teams at recruiting depots, 70. *See also* athletic activities
Spring, John (Hans): as company clerk, 177; barters for beer, 161; on desertion, 400; on dogs, 353; on drill, 199; on journey to Arizona, 88; languages spoken by, 114; on laundress scam, 306; on motivation for enlisting, 19; on noncoms, 161
squadron, 644n6
stable duty, 180
stable guard, 206, 660n73; in field, 476
stage stations, 435–36; defenses at, 436–37
Staked Plains (Texas), 346, 463, 481, 516, 534, 538
Stallard, Thomas, 378–79
Stance, Emanuel, 156, 653n50

Standing Rock Agency, Dak. Terr., 504
Stanley, David S., 459
Stanton, Edwin M., 20
Stark's Ranch, Dak. Terr., 158
Starvation March, 483–88, 571
Stevenson, John D., 146
Stimson, Charles, 271
Stokes, John T., 112, 370
Stortz, Frederick: abstains form alcohol, 390; anticipates combat, 533; aspires to commissioned rank, 134; death of, 552
Stossmeister, Frederick, 159
Stotts, John O.: encounter with friendly Indians, 496; enlistment, 40; loses rifle, 245; motivation for enlisting, 20; on pet buffalo, 353; on rattlesnakes, 480; on resupply of mail station guards, 435; on strikers, 145; on returning home, 580; reflections on service, 573
strikers, 144–45, 630n8, 651n26. *See also* officers
Sturgis, Samuel D., 132
Subsistence Department, 225; canned goods provided by, 228–29, 256, 425–26; duty with, 184–85; objects to post canteens, 394; purchases margarine, 248; ration issued by, 220–21; stocks can openers, 247; tobacco issued by, 230
suicide, 272, 669n47
Sullivan, James W., 269
Sullivan, Thomas, 152; writes epitaph for dog, 357
Sully, Alfred, 452
surgeon, 251 258, 265, 267, 566; acting assistant, 258; assistant, 258; qualifications for, 258–59
Surgeon General's Office, 375
surgery. *See* medical care
sutler, 197, 230–32; checks issued by, 231–32, 636n18; restrictions on, 365; soldiers' bar, 362, 679n5; tax on, 662n21. *See also* post trader

Suttles, John J., 96
Swift, Eben, 103, 128; on his first sergeant, 154
Sykes, George, 4

tactics: skirmish line, 540; used against Indian villages, 542–43, 544
tailor, 241–42
target practice, 200–4, 425, 446, 659nn62–63, 659n66; accidents during, 204, 271; in preparation for field service, 441; by recruits, 75, 641n79; skirmish, 203, 441, 700n17
Taylor, Arthur W., 276
Taylor, William O.: describes field equipment, 444; first combat experience, 546; on field burials, 563
telegraph, 438–39
temperance movement, 351–52, 390–92
Templeton, George M., 80–81
Tenth U.S. Cavalry, 26, 77, 139, 155, 255, 269, 413, 572, 628n6; conditioning of recruits in, 126, 491; desertion rate of, 423; education in, 319; field appearance of, 443; fragmentation of, 98–99; loyalty of soldiers in, 144; noncommissioned officers in, 424; scalping rejected by, 561; scout across Staked Plains, 481; singing in, 329; soldier murdered by citizens, 379; tobacco use in, 229; treatment of recruits in 113
Tenth U.S. Infantry, 218, 314, 502
tents, 451, 470–71, 472
Terry, Alfred H., 127, 483, 500
Tetzel, Karl, 63: on acceptance by company, 123
Texas Rangers, 380
theft, 376–77; in connection with desertion, 408–9, 411
Third U.S. Cavalry, 118, 132, 138, 176, 266, 372, 440, 550, 560, 563, 572, 590; adopts Indian boy, 498; appearance of after campaign, 488; beans served in, 223; in Civil War, 627n3; desertion from, 417, 423; at Dull Knife Fight, 549; en route to N.Mex., 87; fishing in field, 469; member murdered, 327; pokes fun at mounted infantry, 527; singing in, 328
Third U.S. Infantry, 144, 174, 213, 496; Christmas celebrated by, 341; desertion from, 408; parades in St. Louis, 40; preparation by for campaign, 441; prisoner shot, 195; soldiers punished, 386; strikers in, 145
Thirteenth U.S. Infantry, 78, 102, 177, 189; marriage in, 296–97; in N.Mex. Terr., 433, 489; shooting by sergeant in, 376
Thirtieth U.S. Infantry, 327, 358, 390; mounted detachment in, 525; presents watch to commanding officer, 146; quality of food served in, 223–24; target practice by, 201; veterans in, 111
Thirty-Eighth U.S. Infantry, 6, 245, 270
Thirty-Fifth U.S. Infantry, 327
Thirty-Ninth U.S. Infantry, 6
Thirty-Second U.S. Infantry, 337
Thompson, Peter: on campaign preparation, 532; on crossing rivers, 461; first combat experience of, 539; on graft at recruiting depots, 58; on pioneer duty, 453
Thornton, Edmund, 388
Titus, Joseph H., 269
tobacco, 229–30, 473–74, 664n40
Toby, Fred H., 497; associates with Crow woman, 500
Tomamichel, John, 673n34
Towar, George W., 251
Towne, Phineas, 555; on mutilation of soldiers, 560
Townsend, Edward D.: frustration with fraudulent enlistments, 35; on desire to retain recruits at depots, 72–73; on recruiting, 419
Townsend, Thomas G., 143

tradesmen, army's use of skilled, 184
training, 52–54, 61, 63–68, 72, 75, 119–22, 124–26, 426, 532, 639n57, 640nn73–75. *See also* drill
transportation: for discharged soldiers, 579–81; frontier development of, 79, 85–92, 434, 442; mackinaw boats, 705n19; stagecoach, 97, 434–35, 688n10; steamboat, 92, 128, 412, 442, 454, 459, 568, 580; wagon, 92, 128, 568; of wounded, 567–69. *See also* railroad
travel ration. *See* food
travois. *See* medical care
Trinidad, Colo. Terr., 327
tripoli, as brass polish, 657n38, 663n29
troop: use of term, 100–1, 644n7; strength of, 105. *See also* company
trumpet, 655n14
trumpeter of the guard. *See* musicians
Tubac, Ariz. Terr., 256, 336
Tucker, James, 255, 513, 572
Tucson, Ariz. Terr., 161, 325, 354, 374; described, 326
Tuttle, John, 547
Twelfth U.S. Infantry, 94, 270
Twentieth U.S. Infantry, 95, 270, 355
Twenty-Fifth U.S. Infantry, 6, 118, 123, 160; desertion rate of, 423; drunkenness in, 362–63; education in, 319; singing in, 328; sports played by, 343
Twenty-First U.S. Infantry, 119, 315, 374
Twenty-Fourth U.S. Infantry, 6, 137, 303, 357, 536; desertion rate of, 423
Twenty-Ninth U.S. Infantry, 168
Twenty-Second U.S. Infantry, 104, 487, 533, 550; adopts Indian orphan, 498; temperance society formed in, 351; use of vinegar in, 226
Twenty-Seventh U.S. Infantry, 115, 253, 439, 495; at Wagon Box Fight, 546, 552

Twenty-Third U.S. Infantry, 184; mascot with, 356
Tyrrel, William, 378

Unger, Armand: on acceptance of recruits in troop, 113; on athletic activities, 344; desire to see the West, 25
uniform. *See* clothing
Upton, Emory, 120, 637n33
U.S. Army: casualties, 3, 627n2; composition of by nationality, 17, 630n9; consolidation of, 10–11, 33, 105, 139–40, 210; distribution of troops in West, 98–99; frontier mission of, 7–8; immigrants in, 16; organization of, 4–6; purging officers from, 139–40; role of in Reconstruction, 7, 629n9; strength of, 5–6, 629n15; 687n42
U.S. Colored Troops, 5; given priority for transfer to regulars, 20
U.S. Dragoons, 627n3
U.S. Mail: delivery of, 434, 437, 438; military escorts for, 435–36, 688n10. *See also* mail
U.S. Marine Corps, 407, 587, 590
U.S. Military Academy, 133, 141; placement of graduates from, 134, 425
U.S. Military Prison, 682n53; comments on convicts' life at, 384; inmate life at, 421; inmates at, 417; survey of prisoners at, 29
U.S. Military Telegraph, 438
U.S. Navy, 407, 587
U.S. Post Office Department, 434, 438
U.S. Supreme Court, 427
U.S. Treasury, 275
Ute Indians, 9

Valentine, John, 407
Valentine, Neb., 374
Van Moll, John, 272, 669n46
Van Vliet, Robert C., 141
venereal disease, 374–75, 681nn32–34
Veteran Reserve Corps, 6, 584

veterans: of regular army service, 575
veterans organizations: Grand Army of the Republic, 352; Military Order of the Loyal Legion, 592; National Indian Wars Veterans Association, 593–95; Order of Indian Wars, 593; Regular and Volunteer Army and Navy Union, 353, 593; Society of Veterans of Indian Wars, 593, United Indian Wars Veterans, 595
veterinary surgeon, 657n33
Vetter, Michael, 49; on Christmas, 342; requests German newspaper, 349
Victorio (Apache), 512
Virginia City, Mont. Terr., 327
Von Hammerstein, Herbert, 147

wagoner, 186
wagon train: composition of, 451, 690n1; use of, 453
Walla Walla, Wash., 99
Walborn, Frank R., 297
walk-a-heaps, 101. *See also* doughboy
Wallace, Arthur S.: on crossing river, 459; on depot noncoms, 54; on dogs, 354; on mounted drill, 67
Waller, Reuben, 21; on scalping, 561
Walley, Augustus, awarded Medal of Honor, 558
Walsh, Robert, 66
War of 1812, 134
water: distribution at posts, 183, 656n26; in the field, 481–82
Watkins, William, 379
Watson, Richard F., 392
Way, Thomas N.: describes vista at Fort Lincoln, 432; on discipline, 480; on picket duty, 477; on river crossings, 459
weapons. *See* arms
Webb, George W., 594–95
Well, Elijah R., 141
Welsh, John, 327
Welsh, Martin, 590

Werner, Herman, 497
West, Frank, 141
Whelan, Richard M., 679n72
whiskey. *See* alcohol
whiskey orders, 364–65
whiskey ranch, 370
White, Charles, 50
White, Henry, 425
White, Thomas, 347
White, William H.: on abuse of Chinese, 83; on blacksmith, 186; blanket stolen, 59; on Crow Indian women, 500, 502; on depot officers, 80; embarrassment for enlisting, 640n69; on entertainment, 330; on pet bear, 353; on pursuit of deserters, 411; on mutilation of soldiers, 560; on tents, 470; on transporting wounded, 568; travels to join regiment, 91
White Bull, 512
Whittaker, George, 116, 546; career after discharge, 590; on remaining in the army, 576
Wilkinson, James B., 345, 514, 587–88
Wilkinson, William G.: on character of deserters, 422; desire to be a soldier, 27; on preparation for combat, 543; on religion, 313; on Southerners in ranks, 116
Williams, Edward: on crossing Yellowstone River, 459; on desertion, 409; on hardtack, 464; on tobacco, 473
Williams, Moses, awarded Medal of Honor, 558
Wilson, George E., 558
Wilson, John C., 702n54
Wilson, Mildon H., 705n27
Wilson, Thomas H., 536
Windolph, Charles: on band music, 102–3; on brevet rank, 135; on combat, 533, 551; on his army service, 574; on gold fever, 404; on Indian marksmanship, 550; life after discharge, 589; motivation for

Windolph, Charles (*continued*)
enlistment, 18; on murder of civilians, 510; on tobacco, 229; on unit pride, 448–49; on veterans in ranks, 111
Wingate, George W., 202
Winners of the West (periodical), 594
Winslow, Hal, 113
Wint, Theodore J., 386
Wolfe, Maurice H.: on abstinence from alcohol, 390; on army life, 160, 185; on campaign preparation, 441; on Fenians, 19; on Franco-Prussian War, 115; on Indian agents, 503–4; on reenlistment, 582; on religion, 312; on serving as company quartermaster sergeant, 153; on the West, 431
women: demand for 294–95, 332; Indian as combatants, 544–45; officers' servants, 207, 295; relationships with Indian, 499–502; scarcity of at western posts, 294–95, 321, 332, 343
Wooden Leg (Cheyenne), 545
Woods, Charles O., 55
Woodward, Frank E., 635n12
wounded: care of, 464–69; transportation of, 567–69
wounds. *See* medical care
Wyllyams, Frederick, 28

Yellowstone Expedition (1873), 432, 452, 459, 479, 480, 510
Yellowstone National Park, 433, 590
Yohn, Henry, I.: describes Camp Lowell, 174; on locally procured food, 225; on minstrel show, 343; on travel after discharge, 580

Zimmer, William F.: on condition of company after campaign, 571; on cowardice, 559; on crossing rivers, 461; on deserter, 410; on discipline, 480; on gardens, 228; on Indian arms, 518; on Indian warfare, 507; on mounted infantry, 527
Zimmerman, John: describes mule litters, 568–69; on difficulty crossing rivers, 460; on field burials, 563; on picket guard duty, 535
Zinser, Louis: on attacking Indian village, 544; on being a prisoner, 389; on coffee in field, 466; on crossing river, 459; on preparing for field service, 440; reaction to Custer's defeat, 561; on Rosebud battle, 548; on soldiers' appearance after campaign, 488; on soldiers fighting, 118

www.ingramcontent.com/pod-product-compliance
Lightning Source LLC
Chambersburg PA
CBHW020216240426
43672CB00006B/330